The
QUEEN CHARLOTTE
ISLANDS
Volume 2
PLACES AND NAMES

Kathleen E. Dalzell

HARBOUR PUBLISHING

Published by
HARBOUR PUBLISHING
PO Box 219, Madeira Park, BC Canada V0N 2H0

Printed & bound in Canada

Cover photograph: Lindsay Eberts
Book design by E.W. Harrison
Cover design by Christopher J. Miller

Canadian Cataloguing in Publication Data

Dalzell, Kathleen E., 1919–
    The Queen Charlotte Islands

    Includes indexes.
    Vol. 2. first published: Cove Press, 1973.
    Partial contents:
            v. 2. Places and names
    ISBN 1-55017-011-2 (v. 2)

    1. Names, Geographical—British Columbia—
Queen Charlotte Islands.   2. Queen Charlotte
Islands (B.C.)—History.   3. Queen Charlotte
Islands (B.C.)—Description and travel.
I. Title.
FC3845.Q3D34 1989   971.1'31   C89-091334-X
F1089.Q3D34 1989

ACKNOWLEDGEMENTS

My sincere thanks again to all those who assisted in the compilation of Volume 1 of the history of the Charlottes, *The Queen Charlotte Islands - 1774 to 1966.* Much of the data given to me for that first book has been utilized in background information for this second book.

I am indebted to the Hydrographic and Geographic Departments in Victoria for valuable help with material from their files, and also to Mr. Williard Ireland and his staff at the Provincial Archives. Without their willing and competent assistance no project of this type would ever be possible.

My gratitude to the British Columbia Historical Association for once again sponsoring me for a most useful Leon and Thea Koerner Foundation grant.

To G. Gray Hill, who supplied many of the photographs of the more inaccessible places - and who went out of his way to obtain most of the shots. His interest is greatly appreciated.

My thanks to Mrs. J.W. Gibbs of Sidney who assisted in the editing of the first book and who unhesitatingly took over the same task for this book. Her advice has been invaluable.

A very special bouquet to my husband, Albert, who prodded in just the right places to keep things going when the project appeared to falter from time to time and who was a veritable dragon during final editing.

Kathleen E. "Betty" Dalzell

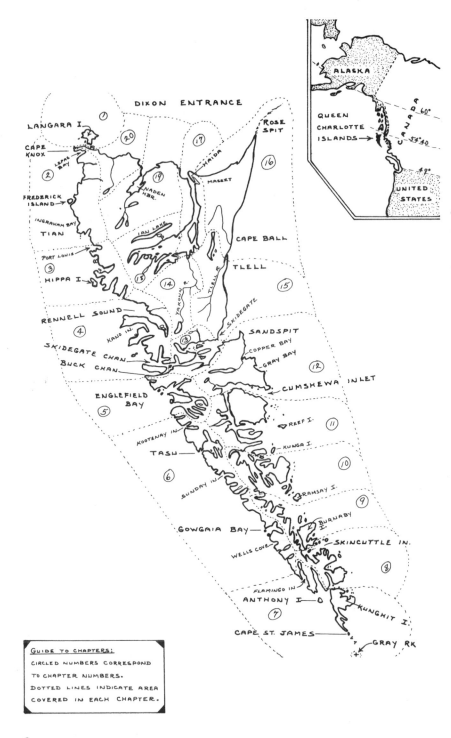

DIXON ENTRANCE

LANGARA I.

① ②⓪ ⑰

CAPE KNOX

LEPAS BAY

② FREDERICK ISLAND

INGRAHAM BAY

TIAN

PORT LOUIS

③ HIPPA I.

RENNELL SOUND

④ KANO IN.

SKIDEGATE CHAN

BUCK CHAN

ENGLEFIELD BAY

⑤

KOOTENAY IN.

TASU

⑥ SUNDAY IN

GOWGAIA BAY

WELLS COVE

⑱ ⑲ NADEN HBR.

IAN LAKE

⑭ ⑬

YAKOUN

HAIDA

MASSET

ROSE SPIT

⑯

CAPE BALL

TLELL

TLELL

⑮

SKIDEGATE

SANDSPIT

COPPER BAY

GRAY BAY

⑫ CUMSHEWA INLET

REEF I.

KUNGA I.

⑪ ⑩ RAMSAY I.

⑨

BURNABY I.

SKINCUTTLE IN.

⑧

FLAMINGO IN

ANTHONY I. ⑦

CAPE ST. JAMES

KUNGHIT I.

GRAY RK

ALASKA

QUEEN CHARLOTTE ISLANDS →

60°

55°40'

49°

UNITED STATES

GUIDE TO CHAPTERS:
CIRCLED NUMBERS CORRESPOND
TO CHAPTER NUMBERS.
DOTTED LINES INDICATE AREA
COVERED IN EACH CHAPTER.

6

TABLE OF CONTENTS

TABLE OF CONTENTS (continued)

FOREWORD

Few areas possess the profusion of names which have been lavished on features and waters of the Queen Charlotte Islands. In fact some places have been named and renamed so often that, in any discussion about a given point, the first thing to be decided is exactly which physical part of the Islands is being referred to.

A map is unfolded and a finger indicates - "There. . . "

"Oh?" will be the response, "We always call that so-and-so. Never heard of *your* name for it." And if there are others taking part in the conversation, both those names will probably be challenged and still another put forth as the presumed designation.

Even the place names on official maps from government departments such as the Hydrographic, Geographic and Geological offices were at variance with one another. The free-lance names on numerous blueprints issued during the many surveys furthered the growing confusion.

In the 1940s the Geographic Branch and, more especially, the Hydrographic Service made a study of the situation. They were deeply concerned that confusion over a location by a vessel answering a distress call could result in tragedy. Maps and names had to be standardized.

Today there are approximately 1134 officially gazetted Queen Charlotte Islands place names, and these are the only ones used on all up-to-date Government maps and charts. This has been a help.

But many of the old names are still in use. Islanders know their bays and inlets so well they rarely bother with maps, and are truly unaware of a newer official name. However some of the confusion also arises because of the fierce possessiveness felt by residents - and ex-residents - for this unique group of islands. They deeply resent anything being changed about the Charlottes.

It can be a point of pride to deliberately use the old familiar names.

In this book it is proposed to list all the currently gazetted names, as well as those by which a feature may formerly have been known, and where possible a brief history connected with the bestowing of the name. Where it is thought that the reader might like to have fuller information about an item which is also covered in some detail in the first book of this series, *The Queen Charlotte Islands - 1774 to 1966,* a footnote will indicate - See Vol. 1. This will avoid unnecessary duplication in the two books. In any instance where a discrepancy exists in data given in both books, the material in this, the second volume, consists of the more recent information.

Included are more than 500 names for features which are unidentified on today's maps. Many of these names are in current local use and others were well enough known at one time to be recorded here.

Haida history is bound firmly to the Islands' nomenclature. The work of several dedicated researchers, among them Dr. C.F. Newcombe, have made the recording of Indian names possible. In the changing times this history was in grave danger of being forgotten. Patiently and painstakingly the old people's stories were recorded while memories were still fresh. One researcher utilized notes from another in the project.

During Dr. Newcombe's many visits to the Charlottes he came to know Charles A. Smith. Mr. Smith arrived in the Masset area in 1909 and became tremendously intrigued by all that Dr. Newcombe told him of his absorbing work in collecting Haida history. Charlie Smith knew the north end of the Charlottes from Rose Spit to Langara Island intimately. The idea of making a map showing the Haida names of the places along this stretch fascinated him.

When he obtained a job as watchman at the Naden Harbour Whaling Station during Depression years Mr. Smith found his ideal opportunity to add to Dr. Newcombe's basic information. His neighbours were Haidas who were keenly concerned about preserving the old names. They joined in the project of the map with delight. The work took years of careful checking and rechecking with parents, grandparents, uncles and aunts.

Shortly before he died many years later, he became concerned that the information so diligently gathered might never be utilized and gave his maps and notes to the writer to be included in this book. Some of the placements may seem to be at variance with maps made by Dr. Newcombe who inspired him to begin his studies, but it must be remembered that Mr. Smith made his map after Dr. Newcombe and had the advantage of being able to check accordingly.

In the Haida language there are many words which sound so similar their meaning can only be ascertained by the context in which they are used. Pronunciation is almost always a corruption by tongues other than Haida, and the transforming of the word from unwritten Haida into printed English brings more changes. Then too, older Haidas say their language has changed through the years. Some words in ancient use have no place in modern Haida, consequently the meaning of earlier interpretations may be puzzling today. And so the reader must ever use his own judgment.

All names supplied by Mr. Smith are indicated in the text of this book by (C. Smith) and on the maps by an Ⓢ Many names still remain to be entered for Charlie Smith did not presume his work to be complete.

I am deeply honoured to be entrusted with the relaying to you of this precious information about the old place names.

K.E.D.

THE QUEEN CHARLOTTE ARCHIPELAGO

THE QUEEN CHARLOTTE ISLANDS have been known by many names -from the old Haida reference of *Islands-of-the-People* to the modern day MISTY ISLES often affectionately bestowed on them.

The first European name given to them as a group was probably that of James Hanna's NOVA HIBERNIA in 1786. Hanna had sailed from Macoa that year in the *Sea Otter*, a brig of barely 60 tons, and traded briefly around the southern shores of the Charlottes. Twelve years previously, in 1774, Juan Perez had named two features, Cape Santa Margarita and the San Christoval Mountains but, since he believed the Islands were part of the mainland continent, he did not give the archipelago a separate designation.

On August 3, 1787, Captain George Dixon reported, "This is not one continued land, but rather a group of islands." In true seafaring tradition he named them for his ship, *Queen Charlotte*, a British snow of some 200 tons. She was one of two ships sent by The King George Sound Company of Britain to trade in the New World. The other, *King George*, a larger vessel commanded by Nathaniel Portlock, had accompanied the *Queen Charlotte* to the west coast of the Islands the autumn before. Finding no signs of life during the first visit they left to winter in the Hawaiian Islands. When they returned to the northwest coast the following summer the two ships separated in Prince William Sound, with Dixon sailing his vessel again to the Charlottes and subsequently naming them.

Entrepreneur John Meares of Nootka, an ex-British Navy man, heard of the fur bonanza Dixon discovered on the Charlottes, but unaware, or uncaring, that Dixon had given the Islands a name, Meares called them THE GREAT ISLAND. He despatched one of his ships, *Iphigenia* under Captain Douglas, to trade along the shores of The Great Island in August 1788.

13

The following year the Islands received another name when, in June 1789, Captain Robert Gray of the American sloop *Lady Washington* called them WASHINGTON'S ISLE. And about this time a map drawn under the direction of Esteban Jose Martinez showed still another name, ISLA INFANTE DON FERNANDO, a name corrupted to "Elefante" by the man who drew the map.

As an omen of the future, perhaps, it was Dixon's British name QUEEN CHARLOTTE'S ISLANDS which became the accepted name.

Lying about 50 miles from the nearest mainland point off northwest Canada and less than 30 miles from the southern tip of Alaska, the climate on the Charlottes is mild and temperate - kept so by the warm Japanese Current sweeping along the coast.

It is estimated that there are about 150 islands and islets in the group which stretch approximately 175 miles from Langara Island at the northwest tip to the Kerouard Islands, strung sentinel-fashion, off the extreme south end.

How long they have been occupied by people is still a matter of conjecture. Recent archaeological evidence scooped out of the shore-lines near Masset and Lawn Hill indicated that there may have been continuous residence on some parts of the Islands for possibly 10,000 years. But who the earliest people were, where they came from or how long they stayed is still under assessment.

By the time Europeans discovered the Charlottes Haida Indians were the sole inhabitants and had developed a culture so advanced they were considered to be the elite of all coastal tribes. The culture grew from human adaptation to an environment. European contact brought new adjustments and a situation was set up which eventually destroyed life as the Haida had known it. One of the few good points resulting from the years of fearful change was the freeing of all slaves.

Today a new Queen Charlotte Islands' culture is evolving and may prove to be as satisfactory as any previous one. Creed, colour or sex are unimportant - so is wealth of a monetary type. The prime bond is a desire to guard and retain all the unique physical factors of these Islands. To use and fully enjoy the environment in the manner the Creator surely intended. For although human values change, the Islands themselves remain constant and create, in those who achieve rapport, a sense of personal involvement infinitely fulfilling. The Charlottes do not morally *belong* to anyone, be it a nation - a government - or profit-hungry corporations. They are the *Islands-of-the-People* . . . all people . . . and are in trust.

Come, look more closely. Perhaps you, too, will feel their magic - be it for the first time, or to repeat and savour the enchantment you have always felt.

This book will identify many of the features and guide you on your trip.

LEARMONTH BANK

DIXON ENTRANCE

JUNE 3, 1963 —
101 PEOPLE DIE
CRASH OF DC-7

55 MILES OFF
LANGARA ISLAND

LANGARA PT.
YA-SIT-KUN RESERVE
"END-OF-ISLAND-TOWN"
"POINT-WITH-ISLAND" GWAES KWOON Ⓢ

"HIGH CLIFFS" ("CHIQ-WA") Ⓢ
"LIGHTHOUSE SLOUGH" ("JUL-TIGANS) Ⓢ
"SAND-BAY-BEACH-VILLAGE" ("CHSI-SUN") Ⓢ
ST. MARGARET POINT
"EAST-AND-WEST-SEA-LION-ROCKS" ("KAI-CUDLAY) Ⓢ
"BAY-ABREAST-ROCKS-VILLAGE" ("KUNG-CHA) Ⓢ
"VILLAGE-AROUND-POINT" ("AH-DONGA) Ⓢ

LANGARA ROCKS

McPHERSON PT.
"MUSSEL-VILLAGE" ("TÄ) Ⓢ
EXPLORER BAY
("AH-GAN-SLUNG) Ⓢ
AH-GANS ROCK Ⓢ
ANDREWS PT.
("YA-KWOON) Ⓢ
YASL'N VILLAGE
DIBRELL BAY
("YA-SLUNG) Ⓢ
COHOE PT.
"JAH'AS KWOON" Ⓢ
YESTA-SOOS VILLAGE Ⓢ
JAH-AS VILLAGE Ⓢ
EGERIA BAY
JAH-SLUNG Ⓢ
JAH Ⓢ

THRUMB ISLET

LANGARA
(OR NORTH ISLAND)
(OR KUSGWAI)

LANGARA LAKE
GEODETIC
GUDT SKUN RESERVE
HART PT.
HAZARDOUS COVE

KUDGEONANTS Ⓢ
"HEAD-SHAKE-VILLAGE"

LORD BIGHT

Ⓢ "WEST POINT"
GWAICE KWOON NONGI
LACY ISLAND Ⓢ
Ⓢ DAH-JAH "ROCK ISLAND"

FURY BAY
RHODES PT.
SUNDAY REEF
HARVEY ROCK
CLOAK BAY
COX I.
SWANTON BANK
OCEAN SHOAL
Ⓢ RED-NOSE-BIRD CLIFF
KUSGWAI
IPHIGENIA PT.
TESTLATLINTS

ANTHER-OF-THE-FLEET PASSAGE
HENSLUNG COVE
BEAL COVE
VILLAGE PT.

DADENS VILLAGE
HOLLAND PT.
SOLIDE PASSAGE
ALERT RK.
LUCY ISLAND

PARRY PASSAGE

YAKU VILLAGE

KIUSTA VILLAGE

PARRY PASSAGE

SPANISH CROSS 1792

LEPAS BAY

GRAHAM ISLAND

All names supplied by Mr. Charles A. Smith are shown on this map by Ⓢ

16

CHAPTER ONE

*LANGARA ISLAND— forms the northwest tip of the Queen Charlotte group. The early Haidas called it KUSGWAI or KATTSSEQUEYE. British Captain George Dixon named it NORTH ISLAND. Spanish Lieutenant Jacinto Caamano proclaimed it ISLA DE LANGARA. Mariners frequenting its wild shores have occasionally used more unprintable names - accompanied by even saltier adjectives.

By turns fog-shrouded and storm-wracked, only the abundant harvest from its surrounding seas draws them, inexorably, to try their luck. And, as so frequently happens when men must pit their very natures against forces awesome to the beginner and fatal to the careless, a comradeship exists of a special nature. There emerges an affection, though it might never be admitted, for this rugged hunk of rock off whose shores they wrest their living.

In the heyday of the Haida a succession of villages and encampments were established more or less along its entire shoreline. The adaptable canoe could be pulled high and dry and did not require an anchorage like today's vessels. Skilled in seamanship and wise in local knowledge the Haida could live in relative comfort almost anywhere.

For generations these early residents of the Charlotte group had been attracted northward to the chunky island at the extreme tip of the islands. Haidas from all sections of the Charlottes came, few at a time, until the region became over-populated. The shore of Alaska, seen clearly on fine days, grew irresistible. The first families to move across Dixon Entrance to southern Alaska did so following a dispute with neighbours. It took only an incident to set the trend in motion. Gradually more people left until the exodus became a migration *en masse*. These hereditary Haidas of the Charlottes now became the Kaigani, Haidas-of-Alaska.

The only human voices left to break the silence of Langara were those of the seal and otter hunters or in the seasonal fishing camps. A keening cry of the Peregrine falcon announced the return of the isolated island to nature's wildlife.

During this time according to legend, Raven, one of the supernatural creatures in Haida mythology, tried to repopulate old Kusgwai. (Langara) Choosing a nesting spot among the softly rolling hills in the centre of the island he created some special People-eggs. His eggs seemed to take an unconscionable time to hatch. As the storms raged about Kusgwai and mists hung heavily, he grew discouraged. Finally he could stand it no longer and left. To this day it is said you can still see the depression where he nested - now a lake. The People-eggs, long abandoned, have turned to stone. They, too, may be seen beside the lake.

When Europeans discovered the Charlottes and began to make a written record, there were still several occupied villages on Kusgwai. The greater portion were used only seasonally. Of the first Europeans to arrive, five men contributed to the pattern of names for this little island prior to the advent of territorial charting by the British Admiralty in 1853. These five men were - Don Juan Perez, George Dixon, William Douglas, Joseph Ingraham and Jacinto Caamano.

Perez and Caamano, acting under the direction of the Spanish representatives in Mexico, were primarily interested in taking possession of land for Spain. Perez, in 1774, had been told to go as far as the 60th parallel, but the constant foul weather coupled with incessant sea-sickness and scurvy in the crew, made the voyage pure misery. By the time his ship *Santiago* stood off what is now Dixon Entrance Perez had endured enough. When a vague headland appeared out of the mist, he decided this was as far as he would carry Spain's colours.

In anticipation of his reception by the Spanish authorities when they learned of his abortive trip, he crossed himself and, influenced by the two Franciscan priests aboard, fervently invoked the blessing of Santa Margarita. Then he named for her the only point of land seen clearly on the entire cursed trip. Rough seas prevented him from going ashore to erect a prepared marker. Only a Spanish name lay claim to wild Kusgwai's shores.

The next visitor, George Dixon, was not seeking land. He was a trader. But to log a voyage a mariner must have names for identification of features. He named Kusgwai NORTH ISLAND after Lord North and Cloak Bay for the wealth of otter cloaks and furs he acquired during the bartering there.

William Douglas, another British trader, felt the magic of the Islands themselves far beyond the thrill of lucrative trading. Although he sailed to Parry Passage in 1788 on the *Iphigenia,* the lateness of the season prevented more than a brief visit. When he returned to trade in June of the following year his mission was accomplished at the beginning of a spell of superb weather. Douglas taking full advantage of this became probably the Charlottes' first tourist - nosing into every bay and cove along the channel now known as Parry Passage. It was he who left the name of Cox for this region - applying it to the passage after John Henry Cox, one of the owners of the *Iphigenia*. Later this name was deleted and reapplied to an island in Cloak Bay.

The first description of elaborately carved totem poles at old Tartanee (now

Dadens) is credited to William Douglas, who added that he had found a patch of cultivated land near this village into which he planted a few bean seeds of his own and ". . . hoped the people would enjoy the benefits."

The fourth man to leave an early name for Langara's region was Joseph Ingraham of the American trading brig *Hope*. The name THRUMB is from one of his maps. In his direction for entering Parry Passage, which he called Cunneyah's Straits, he appears to have placed the name Thrumb Cap on a headland near the present Iphigenia Point.

Like Douglas, Ingraham was greatly fascinated by the Islands. He spent so much time ashore collecting flora and writing notes in his journals that the burden of the real reason for the trip, trading, fell almost entirely on the shoulders of his supercargo.

The fifth man to leave a name was Jacinto Caamano in the ponderously slow Spanish frigate *Aranzazu* and he also succeeded in doing what his countryman Perez could not. Caamano planted a marker cross for Spain. On July 22, 1792, he conducted a brief ceremony and planted a suitably inscribed marker on the north shore of the present Graham Island. Preparing a map of the area, Caamano showed the island north of the cross as ISLA DE NAVARRO. Then he named the larger island nearby ISLA DE LANGARA after Admiral Langara of the Spanish Admiralty.

Perhaps the name of a sixth man should be added to the early history of Langara Island's name pattern - Captain George Vancouver. In September 1793 he sailed along the west coast of the Charlottes in the course of his survey and apparently felt the Spanish name suitable. He adopted LANGARA ISLAND to his own chart. But the picturesque name CAPE SANTA MARGARITA was deleted and an unimaginative NORTH POINT applied to that historic headland.

In 1853 the British Admiralty sent warships to the Charlottes to take soundings and be much in evidence at strategic places. They hoped this action would establish ownership and discourage all other countries from contemplating taking possession of these far-off islands. The Hudson's Bay Company, almost synonymous with British Columbia's Government at that time, were anxious to avoid inroads into their trading regions.

Langara Island was included in the survey made by Commander James Prevost and Master Surveyor George Inskip on the *Virago* in 1853. Both Caamano's names were struck. Isla de Navarro became LUCY ISLAND and Langara Island was renamed NORTH ISLAND. Later this was to be changed again.

In 1907 another Admiralty survey was made, this time by the *Egeria* under Captain F.C. Learmonth, and most of the names as we know them today were applied during that period. Learmonth's survey covered from Rose Spit to Frederick Island.

These hydrographic surveys made sailing of the waters somewhat less hazardous, but the main navigational aid was the installation of the big light-station on the northwest tip of the Charlotte group. By the time the first light-keeper took charge in May 1913 the old name for the island on which it stood, North Island, had been dropped. The more distinctive LANGARA ISLAND was officially adopted, as there would be less likelihood of an incorrect identification of this important light under the Spanish name.

And so, in a way, the Spanish history came full circle. For now the most important marker on the Charlottes wore a Spanish name and it was located on almost the same site as poor worried Don Perez had expected to erect his cross in 1774.

*LANGARA ISLAND is its official name, but locally it is still usually called NORTH ISLAND.

Beginning our tour around Langara, or North Island, at the western entrance of Parry Passage and continuing in a counter-clockwise direction, the following are names which have been applied to Langara's features, nearby islets and waters. *GAZETTED NAMES HAVE AN ASTERISK.*

*PARRY PASSAGE— separates Langara Island from the northwestern end of Graham Island. Tidal streams in this waterway attain a rate of about 2 knots at the eastern and western approaches, but in the narrowest section, near the west end of Lucy Island, the velocity increases to 5 knots on the flood tide.

During the first British Admiralty survey of the region in 1853 Commander James Prevost of the *Virago* named the passage after his close friend, Sir William Edward Parry, the noted Arctic explorer.

Previous to this the waterway had been known by several other names. William Douglas called it COX'S CHANNEL after one of the outfitters of the *Iphigenia*, commanded by Douglas in 1788 and 1789. Joseph Ingraham of the America brig *Hope* prepared a sketch map during 1791 and 1792 showing the passage as CUNNEYAH'S STREIGHTS (sic) after the chief of nearby Kiusta village.

Jacinto Caamano in 1792 named it PUERTO DE FLORIDABLANCA after Conde de Floridablanca. His ship anchored off the south side of Lucy Island for a few days. During this time, to take possession of the area for Spain, Caamano had a 28-foot-high marker cross erected on Graham Island on the west shore of the cove called Ahkwans by the Haidas.

The first accurate charts of the waterway were prepared in 1791 when Captain Etienne Marchand, master of the 300-ton French ship *La Solide*, anchored in Cloak Bay. Marchand's officers spent a week in Parry Passage making a detailed survey and prepared a chart.

*IPHIGENIA POINT — is on the southwest tip of Langara Island and has a navigational light. A steep bluff behind the point rises to 400 feet. Outward, to the west, curious rock pillars 100 to 120 feet high hug the shoreline. Named by the Hydrographic Service after the snow *Iphigenia Nubiana*, owned by the Associated Merchants Trading to the Northwest Coast of America who were John Meares, John H. Cox, Richard C. Etches, John W. Etches, William Fitzhugh, Henry Land and Daniel Beale.

RED-NOSE-BIRD-CLIFF *Si-ainchung* — the point north and west of Iphigenia Point. (C. Smith)

MOTHER-OF-THE-FLEET-ROCK — on the west shoreline of Henslung Cove near the entrance. Named by Fisheries Protection Officer Howard Fairbairn of Queen Charlotte City. Mr. Fairbairn, observing the rock's silhouette, felt it kept a watchful eye on the trollers anchored in the cove.

Mother-of-the-Fleet Rock on the west shoreline of Henslung Cove.

Photo--Mary Viereck.

*HENSLUNG COVE — is the larger and more westerly of two coves off the south end of Langara Island. Shown on early maps variously as COVE DOUGLAS, BABBINGTON BAY and HENSLUNG BAY.

Ingraham's 1791 map showed it as Cove Douglas after William Douglas master of the *Iphigenia*. Henslung is a corruption of the Haida name for the cove - *slung* means the bottom end of a bay.

In November 1907 when Norman Broadhurst came to the Charlottes to look for caribou for the Provincial Museum, Captain Hume Babbington, his brother-in-law, asked him to stake two lots for him at the head of Henslung. For several years the cove was known as Babbington Bay. In 1919 Babbington, in partnership with Captain Eugene Simpson, built a rough one-line cannery there to can the superb spring salmon which abound in nearby waters. The project was not a financial success and the next year the two men moved their operation to Naden Harbour.

The best known resident of Henslung was Al Peevey who built a neat cabin on the east shore where he lived for the next 25 to 30 years. The isolation did not bother him. He was too busy trapping, doing a bit of fishing and acting as lineman on the emergency telephone line which ran from Henslung to the light-station. A garden supplied his fresh vegetables and the seas and forests yielded fish and meat.

He managed to gain the trust of marten enough for some of them to take food from his hand. This gave him the idea of applying for a homestead on nearby Lucy Island to establish a marten farm. He caught and set out several pairs. But Mr. Marten is an aggressive animal with his own ideas about territory. The plan did not succeed.

Henslung Cove has long served as headquarters for fish camps during the summer months. These camps bought fish, sold gas, oil and groceries, handled mail and so on. During fishing season Peevey often had more visitors than he knew what to do with as trollers fled from the wild seas outside to take refuge for a few days and "grub up." It was on the beach outside his cabin that the first meeting of the old North Island Trollers Co-operative took place on June 15, 1935.

Al Peevey of Henslung Cove. Photo taken in 1939 by Ed Crawford, one of the fishermen who visited Peevey frequently.

Only the hardy fishermen plying Langara's waters would call Henslung an anchorage, for it offers poor shelter from most winds and is plagued by swirling tides and ocean swell. Nevertheless it is the main anchorage for Langara Island.

*TESTLATLINTS — a large rock on the shoreline between Henslung Cove and Beal Cove. Known locally also as FLOWER POT ROCK, PLUM PUDDING and PRINCESS ROCK. This last name is from the legend telling of a Haida princess being laid there following her premature death from grief when her lover was lost at sea.

Archaeologists say the grave on Testlatlints contained a shaman.

Testlatlints is a modification of the Haida name which meant Round-topped-rock. High on a hillside above Testlatlints are the old burial caves said to have been associated with ancient Tartanee. (Dadens)

*BEAL COVE — the smaller and more easterly of the two coves off the south end of Langara Island. Also shown on early charts as BEALE'S HARBOUR, the name given it by William Douglas in June 1789. Daniel Beale was one of the partners in the company which owned the *Iphigenia*.[1]

Douglas is said to have taken his first stroll ashore on the Charlottes when he landed at this cove and is credited with being the second white man known to have actually set foot on the soil of the Queen Charlotte Islands. (The first was Robert Haswell, mate on the *Columbia* who went ashore at Anthony Island, June 11th, 1789, 12 days earlier.)

[1]See Iphigenia Point.

22

TESTLATLINTS between Henslung Cove and Beal Cove.
Also known as Flower Pot Rock, Plum Pudding Rock and Princess Rock.

Photo - G. Gray Hill.

Beal Cove about 1935. Bobolink *in centre of photo serving as a fish camp.*
The Iphigenia *anchored here in June of 1789.*
Photo - Howard Phillips.

23

*VILLAGE POINT — the rocky point forming the south portion of Beal Cove. Named for its proximity to the village of Dadens, it has a 20-foot-high, semi-detached islet off its tip.

*DADENS — on the southeast tip of Langara Island, facing Lucy Island. Shown earlier also as TADENTS and TADENSE. In 1789 the village Douglas called TARTANEE stood on this site. Small, but seemingly prosperous, Tartanee contained several large lodges, totem poles and a cultivated garden patch. Following Douglas's visit Tartanee was swept by fire. The residents unwilling to rebuild joined the migration to Alaska. Other Haidas took over and for years it remained a seasonal and favourite campsite. It is part of the 16-acre Tatense Reserve and belongs to the Masset Band.

Dadens in the 1880s. Near camera in left foreground is Roderick Dodd, Hudson's Bay Factor at Masset. Beside him, holding her son, Stephen, is Chief Weah's first wife, Sarah.

Photo - Mrs. Godfrey Kelly.

*LUCY ISLAND — a densely wooded island lying off the southeast tip of Langara Island. Shown on early maps as NAICE, HIPPA, MIDDLE ISLAND and ISLA DE NAVARRO.

Naice is a modification of its Haida name. Hippa was the designation given it by Ingraham on his sketch map in 1791. The following year he showed it as Middle Island. That same year, 1791, Jacinto Caamano arrived in Parry Passage. His officers were directed to prepare a survey and plan of the waterway. The completed plan shows the southern part of Langara Island, Parry Passage and the north shore of Graham Island in the vicinity of Kiusta and Gunia Point. Lucy Island appears on that map as Isla de Navarro.

Captain Etienne Marchand's notes made during *La Solide's* visit in 1791 indicate that at least one Haida house stood on the west end of Lucy at that time.

During the 1853 British Admiralty survey by Commander James Prevost and Captain George Inskip the name of Lucy was applied to the island.

A navigational light stands on the east end of the rock-fringed shores of Lucy Island.

*SOLIDE PASSAGE — separates Lucy Island from Langara Island. Named after the French ship *La Solide* by Captain F.C. Learmonth during his 1907 hydrographic survey.

In August 1791 Captain Etienne Marchand, a French navigator, arrived at Cloak Bay in *La Solide,* a vessel built by the wealthy house of Baux, Marseilles, expressly for a cruise to the northwest coast and around the world. She was 300 tons and fitted in the most complete manner for a scientific as well as commercial voyage. Her total complement consisted of 50 persons. Officers from this ship made the first accurate charts of Parry Passage.

Both sides of Solide Passage are bordered by rocky ledges, but navigation is considered easy for small vessels.

*ALERT ROCK — lies nearly awash off Lucy Island near the southeast entrance of Solide Passage.

In 1860 *H.M.S.Alert* visited Virago Sound and Houston Stewart Channel making some additions to previous sketch-charts of these waters. She also, under Commander William Pearse and Captain A.F. Boxer, made a line of soundings off the east coast of the Charlottes, from Cape Fife to Cumshewa Inlet.

Some years later, in 1875, the *Alert* made Canadian history by wintering at Cape Sheridan in the Arctic, the farthest north any ship had ever wintered. *Alert* eventually ended her days as a lightship in the St. Lawrence River.

*HOLLAND POINT — at the southeast corner of Langara Island is fringed by foul ground. A thick kelp bed extends north to Cohoe Point, 3 miles to the north.

The Haidas called Holland Point KWA'KED-JOAS. (C. Smith)

JAH — a descriptive Haida name for the rocky point about 1¼ miles north of Holland Point. (C. Smith)

*EGERIA BAY — a large indentation of the east coast of Langara. Names in 1907 after *H.M.S. Egeria* which, under the command of Captain Frederick C. Learmonth, was engaged that year in a hydrographic survey from Rose Spit to Frederick Island. The *Egeria,* a 940-ton steam screw sloop built at Pembroke in 1874, was fitted out for surveying duties.

The Haidas called Egeria Bay, JAH'SLUNG, The-bay-of-Jah. (C. Smith)

JAH'AS VILLAGE — lay at the head of Egeria Bay. (C. Smith)
In 1916 there were still several houses at this site, used seasonally by the Haidas.

YESTA-SOOS, Old-North-Village — stood adjacent to Jah'as, but was on the north side of the stream entering the head of Egeria Bay. (C. Smith) A 25-acre reserve at the head of Egeria Bay includes the sites of both villages and belongs to the Masset Band. It is interesting to note that at the time of granting on February 7, 1916, the condition was that ". . . all mineral and oil rights will be retained by the Government."

*COHOE POINT — the north entrance point to Egeria Bay. A Government

Reserve covers most of this point.

The Haida name for Cohoe Point was JAH'AS KWOON, The-point-of-Jah'as-village. (C. Smith)

*DIBRELL BAY — between Cohoe Point and Andrews Point. Named by Captain F.C. Learmonth in 1970 for the captain of the U.S. surveying ship *Explorer* which was engaged in charting the southern Alaskan waters at that time.

YA'SLUNG, East-Middle-Bay, was its Haida name. (C. Smith)

YASL'N VILLAGE, Town-straight-back-in — the name of the Raven Crest village at the head of Dibrell Bay. An old story tells of the chief of Yasl'n losing his daughter in a raid. She was taken to Port Simpson on the mainland to be a slave, but was so beautiful the chief's son would not allow it, and married her. Later her children returned to her former home bringing with them new crests for the family, obtained as a result of the marriage.

The 25-acre Cohoe Point Indian Reserve includes this village site, which had several houses used seasonally by the Haidas in 1916 when the reserve was granted.

*ANDREWS POINT — separates Explorer and Dibrell Bays, and has a rock ledge extending off its tip for about 1,000 feet.

The Haidas called Andrews Point YA-KWOON, Straight-Middle-Point-on-the-east. (C. Smith)

AH-GANS, The-big-rock — close to shore in Explorer Bay is about 14 feet high. (C. Smith)

*EXPLORER BAY — north of Andrews Point. Named in 1907 by Captain F.C. Learmonth of the *Egeria*, giving a courtesy nod to Captain Dibrell of the *Explorer* engaged in a similar survey of southern Alaskan waters at that same time. A trail leads in from the rocky shores of Explorer Bay to the site of a geodetic point which surveyors have established near one of the inland lakes.

AH-GAN-SLUNG, Bay-of-the-big-rock, — was the Haida name for Explorer Bay, (C. Smith)

*McPHERSON POINT — the northeast corner of Langara Island was named by Captain Learmonth in 1907 after the carpenter on the *Egeria*, who excelled as an axeman. Rocky and precipitous, fully exposed to the prevailing ocean swell, nevertheless, there were two small Haida village sites on either side of McPherson Point.

The Haidas called the point TA-KWOON, Mussel-Point. (C. Smith)

TA VILLAGE, Mussel-Town — nestled in a bight on the south side of Mc-Pherson Point. A stream draining a small lake flowed by the village.

VILLAGE-AROUND-POINT *Ah-Dongas* — was in a small cove on the north side of McPherson Point. (C. Smith)

*LANGARA ROCKS — off the north end of the island were named in association with Langara Island by the Hydrographic Service. Consisting of two bare conspicuous rocks 26 and 30 feet high, they have rocky ledges in and about them.

Known to the Haidas as EAST and WEST SEA LION ROCKS, *Kai-cudlay*. (C. Smith)

McPherson Point on northeast side of Langara Island. Called Ta-Kwoon by the Haidas, two villages nestled on either side of the small peninsula. Ta Village lay on the south and Ah-Dongas in the bight on the north shore.

Photo - Mr. R.B. Young, Hydrographic Service.

BAY-ABREAST-ROCKS-VILLAGE *Kung-cha* — snuggled in a bay to the south of Langara Rocks. (C. Smith.

*ST. MARGARET POINT — south and west of Langara Rocks is part of the headland which received the first European name in British Columbia, CAPE SANTA MARGARITA.[1] It is thought also to be the CAPE COOLIDGE mentioned by Robert Haswell in his log April 1792 aboard the *Adventure*. R.D. Coolidge captained the schooner *Grace*, a position he had to assume when William Douglas, her master and owner, died aboard in the autumn of 1791.[2] Captain Vancouver applied NORTH POINT to the headland.

When the Langara Lighthouse was established, the Hydrographic Service chose two names for the headland. The outer westerly point became LANGARA POINT. The inner one was given Juan Perez's historic Cape Santa Margarita. Put into English it became ST. MARGARET POINT.

[1]Queen Charlotte Islands - 1774 to 1966, Chapter 1.
[2]See also Douglas Rock.

Langara Lighthouse. Photo taken in 1952 by Otto Lindstrom. This rocky headland was the Gwai-es-kwoon of the Haida.

SAND-BAY-BEACH-VILLAGE *Chisi-sun* — lay in the bight on the west side of St. Margaret Point. (C. Smith)

JUL-TIGAN, Lighthouse-Slough — the Haida name for the site used to land supplies for the light-station from the lighthouse tenders. (C. Smith)

HIGH-CLIFF *Chig-wa* — on the north side of Langara Point. (C. Smith)

*****LANGARA POINT** — the *Gwai-es-kwoon* of the Haida, **End-of-Island-Point**, is the northwest extremity of Langara Island and of the Queen Charlotte Group.

Langara Point received its name in association with the island when the lighthouse was built on this point. One of two lighthouses on the Charlottes (the other is at Cape St. James) Langara Light-station went into operation in May 1913 and is today equipped with completely up-to-date navigational aids, including a great booming fog-horn.

During World War II a radar station built west and south of the lighthouse proved to be a rugged project and several lives were lost during attempts to land supplies. This radar station with a complement of 65 men operated from April 1943 to August 1945. When it became abandoned at the close of hostilities the residents of the lighthouse fell heir to many comforts unheard of in those days of government direction of "the keepers of the light."

Landing supplies for the Langara station has ever been dependent on weather and it is commonplace for vessels servicing the light to lay offshore for weeks waiting for a break in the weather. The building of a helicopter pad has helped immensely and in particular means help can be obtained more easily in emergencies.

LANGARA LAKE — the name pilots of fixed wing aircraft have given to a small lake with an islet, about 2 miles south of the light-station. So far only Beaver aircraft have been used and it takes a skilled pilot to achieve both the landing and tricky take-off. "And we never try it with more than a half-load," said a North Coast Air Services pilot in Prince Rupert who made four such landings in 1970, the first year this was attempted.

The greatest tragedy ever to occur off Langara's shores was an aircraft disaster. On the morning of June 3, 1963, a chartered Northwest Airlines DC-7 with 101 people on board disappeared an estimated 55 miles off Langara under circumstances which suggested sudden disaster. There were no survivors.

The 4-engined plane, on a routine flight carrying military personnel and dependents, was under the command of veteran pilot Albert Olson. It had left McChord Air Force Base in Washington bound for Elmendorf Air Force Base near Anchorage, Alaska. At 11 a.m. the pilot radioed the Sandspit Air Station for a change of altitude. This was the last ever heard from the plane. When an effort to raise a reply from the DC-7 proved unsuccessful a search began immediately. There were several fishing boats in the presumed region as well as a Japanese freighter. All were requested to assist. When the planes flew over the waters they spotted extensive debris - but nothing else.

*****DIXON ENTRANCE** — which separates the Charlottes from southern

Alaska had been known by numerous names - ENTRADA DE JUAN PEREZ, ENTRADA DE FONT, GRANITZA SOUND, DOUGLAS CHANNEL, HANCOCK'S STRAITS, ADDAM'S STRAIT and KYGANNIE STRAIT - before the British Admiralty settled the matter by adopting the name Sir Joseph Banks gave the waterway following George Dixon's return to England in 1788.

"When I laid my manuscript chart before Sir Joseph for his approbation," wrote Captain Dixon, "I asked him to fill in the names of some of the places and he did me the honour of putting my name to this waterway." The statement was in reply to some hotly worded accusations from John Meares that Dixon had himself applied the name "for his own glorification." Meares believed the channel should have been named after William Douglas "who had boldly pushed through it, whereas Dixon only passed across the entrance in the offing."

George Dixon was an experienced mariner. Among the ships he served on was the *Discovery* on the last voyage of James Cook. At that time he held the position of armourer - a skilled mechanic with the rating of first-class petty officer whose duties consisted of assisting the gunner to keep the arms in order.

He was in command of the *Queen Charlotte* from 1785 to 1788 during which time he twice voyaged to the Charlottes, the first late in the summer of 1786 when he and Portlock, master of the *King George*, made a brief trip to the west coast and finding it deserted left immediately to winter in the Hawaiian Islands. Returning the following year to Prince William's Sound, the two vessels separated. Dixon brought the *Queen Charlotte* southward and traded along the shores of an unknown land to which on August 3, 1787, he gave the name of his ship in bestowing QUEEN CHARLOTTE'S ISLANDS, when he realized he was cruising the shores of a group of islands.[1]

Historians know little of Dixon's life after this historic voyage, but he is believed to have taught navigation at Gosport and may have been the George Dixon who wrote *The Navigator's Assistant* in 1791. He died about 1800.

[1]Q.C. Islands, Vol. 1, Chapter 2.

*LEARMONTH BANK — lies in the western entrance of Dixon Entrance and extends from 8 to 18 miles northward from Langara Island. The charts warn of heavy tide rips and overfalls off the south side of the bank. Named after Captain Frederick C. Learmonth who, in the *Egeria*, made a survey in 1907 for the British Admiralty which covered the area from Rose Spit to Frederick Island.

END-OF-ISLAND-POINT-VILLAGE *Gwai-es-kwoon* — lay in the rocky bay to the south and west of the present Langara Point. Owned by the Eagle Crest tribe of the Stustas it is now part of the 50-acre Haida Reserve known as the Ya-sit-kun Reserve.

*THRUMB ISLET — about 65 feet high and connected to Langara Island by a drying rocky ledge. It is south and west of Langara Point. This exposed islet actually manages to support some stunted bushes - perhaps because its offshore rocks deflect the ocean swell to some extent. Lacy Island to the south with the same height and exposure, but with no outer rocks, is completely bare.

The name THRUMB honours a designation from Joseph Ingraham's old 1791-92 charts when he applied the name of Thrumb Cap to a headland near Iphigenia Point.

POINT-WITH-ISLET-ON-IT *Gwaice-kwoon* — the Haida name for the rocky point off which lies Thrumb Islet. (C. Smith)

Looking southward from Langara Point.
The old Gwai-es-kwoon village lay in this rock-fringed bay.
Photo - Mr. R.B. Young, Hydrographic Service.

*LORD BIGHT — a rock-encumbered bay lying between Lacy and Thrumb Islets. Named after a seaman on one of the *Egeria's* sounding boats during the 1907 survey by Captain F.C. Learmonth.

HEAD-SHAKE-VILLAGE *Kudgeonanants* — was located on a rocky point in Lord Bight about 4 miles south of the lighthouse. (C. Smith)

*LACY ISLAND — at the south end of Lord Bight off the west coast of Langara Island. The name has been on the charts since 1853. Sixty-five feet high and bare, it takes some terrific seas.

During the 1960s the Surveys and Mapping Branch of Victoria ran some survey checks on the Charlottes. Art Sutherland of Victoria was with the party and has vivid memories of the hazardous experience of landing his crew on Lacy Island. "We had to set up a check point there," he says. "The seas were huge . . . surging in and around the island. Took us two solid hours. The breakers swamped the boat several times and during one of the swampings one of the men was nearly drowned." They were all soaked to the skin by the time they did finally manage to scramble ashore. "Then we had to repeat the whole perilous operation to get off again." says Mr. Sutherland.

Lacy Island was the DAH-JA, Rock-island, of the Haidas. (C. Smith)

WEST-POINT *Gwaice-kwoon-nongi* — the Haida name for the point of Langara Island inshore from Lacy Island. It also had a second name DAH-JA-KWOON, Rock-island-point. (C. Smith)

*FURY BAY — to the east of Lacy Island is well and truly named. Wild and violent are its waters in a storm. Fully exposed to the ocean swell, the seas break for a considerable distance offshore then sweep inward to smash against the rocks. Although the name does fit descriptively it was actually named in association with Parry Passage. *Fury* was the name of one of Sir William Edward Parry's ships on his second Arctic expedition.

GUOY-SKUN-VILLAGE — lay at the head of Fury Bay and is believed to be the village which provided the lush otter pelts which caused George Dixon's heart to leap in amazement when he traded there in 1787. This old village site is now part of the 51-acre Guoy-skun Haida Reserve.

*RHODES POINT — in the Guoy-skun Reserve, is the south point of Fury Bay. Rising sharply to 220 feet, this rock-fringed point was named in 1907 by Captain F.C. Learmonth after a stoker on the *Egeria* who also served as a crew member on a sounding boat during the survey of this area.

*CLOAK BAY — off the southwest bight of Langara Island. Named July 3, 1787, by Captain George Dixon for the bonanza in beautiful sea otter cloaks obtained in trade from the Haidas there at the beginning of his voyage around the Charlottes.

Two years later another trader, the American Captain Robert Gray, had reason also to remember this bay. It was with these uninitiated villagers he obtained the best bargain any trader ever accomplished. A bargain that was to have far-reaching repercussions for others.

Whereas Dixon had taken special care to see that furs were traded for equitably, Gray adopted a "let the buyer beware" attitude. He secured 300 prime otter skins for a mere one chisel each. The "chisels" were crude bits of flat iron drawn to a cutting edge.

When the Haidas learned of the poor value they had unknowingly accepted from Gray there was deep resentment. It wouldn't happen again they told themselves. When other traders heard of Gray's bargain they tried similar tactics with the Haidas, but found conditions greatly altered. The price of furs began to soar with each trip as the Haidas became hard bargainers - almost to the point of pricing themselves out of a market at the north end of the Charlottes.

It was Gray's incident at Cloak Bay which contributed to the disastrous brawl in Houston Stewart Channel between Captain John Kendrick and Chief Koyah.[1] Kendrick, Gray's senior, having heard Gray brag repeatedly of his coup at Langara Island, tried to bully the Houston Stewart Haidas into giving him a similar deal.

---

(1) Incident covered more fully in the introduction to Chapter 7; also in *Q.C. Islands*, Volume 1, Chapter 4.

*SWANTON BANK — occupies a large portion of Cloak Bay. With depths of from 12 to 16 feet it lies a little to the west of centre of the bay, and is indicated by frequent heavy undulation. With a strong southwest sea the swell will break almost constantly - the rollers reaching almost to Hazardous Cove. Named after Dr. J. R. Swanton whose contribution to the recording of Haida history has been of inestimable value. His report published in 1905 is considered to be basic material for any serious student of this subject.

The Haidas called Swanton Bank TH'CAREWAY, kelp-bed-and-breakers. (C. Smith)

*HARVEY ROCK — on Swanton Bank, is south of Rhodes Point and has a depth of less than 6 feet over it. The sea usually breaks on this rock. Named after Lieutenant J.R. Harvey who assisted in the 1907 hydrographic survey conducted by Captain Learmonth on the *Egeria*.

*SUNDAY REEF — in the northeast corner of Cloak Bay. The reason for the naming of this rocky ledge which dries at 12 feet has led to several interesting suggestions, but the real reason so far has not been ascertained.

*HART POINT — northeast of Sunday Reef and approximately the west entrance point of Hazardous Cove. George Hart was quartermaster of *H.M.S.Discovery* under Captain Vancouver in 1791 and it has been mooted that the point was named after him. In 1915 the lot covering the end of Hart Point was Crown Granted according to the records of the Court House in Prince Rupert, but the name of the grantee is not on file.

*HAZARDOUS COVE — an appropriate name for the entrance to this cove which lies off the northeast side of Cloak Bay. However, once inside the cove there is a pleasant beach on its north side, with a stream entering the bay.

*COX ISLAND — in Cloak Bay and to the south of Hazardous Cove. Wooded in the main and about 375 feet high, Cox Island is precipitous on the west and south sides with sheer cliffs. Close off these cliffs stand conglomerate pillars 100 to 135 feet high. Named after the same John Henry Cox for whom William Douglas first named what is now Parry Passage.(1)

(1) Parry Passage - page 20; Iphigenia Point - page 20.

*KUSGWAI PASSAGE — separating Cox Island from Langara Island. Formerly called BOAT PASSAGE, but renamed by the Hydrographic Service owing to the number of duplications of that name on the coast. KUSGWAI was the old Haida name for Langara Island.

Kusgwai Passage is narrow and shallow with ledges on either side and considerable kelp.

*OCEAN SHOAL — lying at the west entrance to Parry Passage frequently has heavy undulation. The shallowest depth is about 54 feet. Named by the Hydrographic Service for its outward position.

INTRODUCTION TO GRAHAM ISLAND AND
PLACES AND NAMES ALONG ITS WEST COAST
FROM CAPE KNOX TO FORTIER HILL.

CHAPTER TWO

*GRAHAM ISLAND — the largest island in the Queen Charlotte group, has its northwest tip adjacent to Langara Island - the two being separated by Parry Passage. Named in 1853 by Commander James Prevost of the *Virago* during his hydrographic survey of Charlotte waters for the British Admiralty. Sir James Robert Graham, for whom it is named, held the post of First Lord of the British Admiralty from 1852 to 1855.

Like the legendary admiral of *H.M.S.Pinafore* who ". . . never, never went to sea," Sir James did not have a naval career. He became a brilliant orator in the British House of Commons and had a keen sense of timing when delivering his speeches, which usually had a memorable punch line. Born in 1792 Graham, always an impressive personality, was considered to be one of the advanced reformers of his day. In addition he was a very capable administrator.

The wedge-shaped island to which Prevost applied his name is about 75 miles long and 60 miles across at its widest, the north end. Its terrain is one of interesting contrasts. Mountains rise from the ocean floor along the west coast; rugged and with heavily forested slopes in the southwest they gradually taper off towards the northwest. Those in the Seal Inlet region have rolling grassland near their tops.

East of the coastal range are river valleys lush with some of the finest timber in the world, and where Sitka spruce trunks can measure over 17 feet in *diameter*.

Lakes, creeks and flats abound with fish and waterfowl. Acres of muskeg - a miniature fairyland with its dwarf pines - contains countless species of mosses, lichens, berries. Parts of this huge muskeg came into existence following a tremendous fire which swept from Masset to the headwaters of the Tlell River. Thought to have occurred about 1840,[1] legends say it was started by a wax

[1] For more about this fire see TLELL RIVER.

match tossed carelessly aside. The summer had been exceptionally dry - this excessive dryness was explained wryly by one old Haida, "Oh, it was always good weather over here until the white man came."

Probably the feature attraction of Graham Island for most visitors is the great stretch of unbroken sand beach which fringes much of the north end of Graham and extends all along the east coast - a beachcomber's delight. The large tidal lake almost in the centre of the island, which is connected by a slim 20-mile inlet to the ocean, adds more variety with its numerous islets dotting a jewel-like setting.

Most of the Queen Charlotte Islands settlements are on Graham Island and today they are all connected by roads. A ferry provides access to Moresby Island for motor vehicles and passengers.

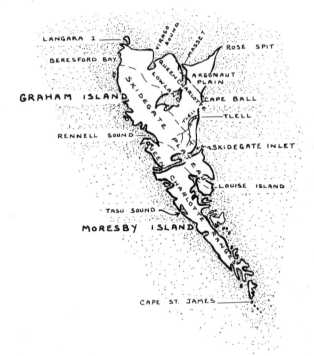

*QUEEN CHARLOTTE MOUNTAINS — consist of two units, the Queen Charlotte Ranges, which form the mountainous backbone of the Islands and lie mostly along their western side, and the Skidegate Plateau, an elongated belt of plateau-like country flanking them on the east.

*QUEEN CHARLOTTE RANGES — stretch from Rennell Sound, on southwest Graham Island, to Cape St. James at the south end of Moresby. Despite the fact that their peaks only rise to about 3,700 feet at the highest, these mountains are extremely rugged, their serrated peaks having been sculptured by glaciers thousands of years ago.

34

*SKIDEGATE PLATEAU — extending from the vicinity of Pivot Mountain on the northwest side of Graham Island to Louise Island off the east side of Moresby Island is approximately 10 miles wide and 100 miles long and varies in height from 2,600 feet to a little over 1,500. The northern section of the plateau has flat uplands with muskegs and alpine meadows for the most part, but the remainder contains some of the most heavily timbered regions on the Charlottes.

QUEEN CHARLOTTE LOWLAND — the geological name for the land lying east of the Skidegate Plateau, and which extends from Virago Sound to Tlell.

*ARGONAUT PLAIN — covers the northeast portion of Graham Island from the Masset area to north of Cape Ball and includes the region out to Rose Spit. It is a gazetted name as well as a commonly used geological description.

The west coast of Graham Island, like that of Moresby, has an unbelievable grandeur. Mountains and hills appear to be piled on one another, their tops frequently lost in misty overcast. Sand beaches appear in every possible nook and give emphasis to the rocks, crags and perpendicular cliffs. Breakers roll in furiously and seas can be tremendous.

"Even on a nice day when it hasn't been blowing for some time, there will be an 8-foot swell," say men who fish these waters regularly. "In storms it can be wicked. Huge waves all around. You can be on top of a comber before you know it and a mountain of water heaped up in front of you. With tides against the winds it's treacherous. The surge from the big swells can toss a boat just like a matchstick."

There are numerous caves and the water ". . . rushes in and out of them. You'd think it would wash the very Islands away sometimes," said one man. "There seems to be a continual roar on."

Larger vessels which travel the west coast keep well clear of the ledges and reefs which lie offshore. But for those who would explore this area intimately they must, like the Haida of earlier years, have small easily handled craft which can be landed, then quickly hauled up before the next breaker rolls in. People who frequent this coast become adept quickly. They need to. Even so, it is not uncommon to be dumped and have to swim when the size and speed of a following breaker is miscalculated.

Two brothers, Don and Bill McNaughton of Pender Harbour, hunted seals[1] on this wild coast for six years. "We would go out for seven or eight months at a time some years," says Don. "It was a fabulous life . . . constantly interesting and always challenging. We would anchor our launch in a safe harbour for base camp, then with the 13-foot fibreglass skiff manoeuvre pretty well anywhere we wanted." They grew to know every cove, rocky crag and islet "like the back of our hands."

But even these two intrepid hunters did not fight the weather. No one does when gales roar along the west coast. As Don McNaughton says, "The secret of successful travel out there is enough time. Time so that you are not tempted

---

[1] This seal hunting required a high-powered rifle and telescopic sight. The seal never knew what hit it - in contrast to the brutal blood bath associated with the operation on the Atlantic coast.

to take dangerous chances."

Shank's mare accounted for some of the travel along the northwest part of Graham Island, especially in earlier years. Men would leave their boats at Kiusta, on Parry Passage - pulled well up out of the tide's reach. Then, crossing the narrow isthmus to Lepas Bay, would strike out, some going as far as Tian Bay. There were several claims staked out between Frederick Island and Tian, presumably for coal and oil, but mostly for resale to the gullible.

Crossing the larger creeks needed ingenuity to stay dry. Some didn't. "But the worst problem was the bear traps built by the Indians," recalled Norman Broadhurst when telling of the hike he and Bill Haylmor took in November 1907. "The tides were so high we found we really couldn't use the beaches at all, so followed the bear trails along the top. And those blamed traps! Took a sharp eye to spot them. I hate to think what would happen if you didn't . . . so they were a constant worry."

Mr. Broadhurst was looking for signs of the caribou, now extinct, which were peculiar to the Charlottes. He had been commissioned by the Provincial Museum to secure some speciments.[1] Mr. Haylmor, later Gold Commissioner at Lillooet, made the trip to investigate reports by the Haidas of a curious blue and white rock near Frederick Island.

The places and names of Graham Island's west coast are described in this and the two succeeding chapters. The list is probably far from complete for, as has been the case with much of Queen Charlotte Islands history, we have waited too long to make the written record. Verbal records, unfortunately, prove fragile - especially where a region has become abandoned.

[1]Q.C. Islands, Volume 1, page 307

*CAPE KNOX — the extreme northwest tip of Graham Island is rocky and constantly wave-swept. Lying at the end of a narrow 2½ mile peninsula which extends off Graham Island, the cape was named in 1853 by Commander James Prevost of the *Virago* after Sub-Lieutenant Henry Needham Knox, who gave valuable assistance during the survey of these waters that year.

The Haida name was GWAINTAS KWOON. (C. Smith)

*LEPAS BAY — lies inside and to the southeast of Cape Knox. Named in 1878 by Dr. G.M. Dawson, and might better have been called False Pass according to navigators of earlier years because it was easy to mistake the bay for the entrance to Parry Passage. Instructions to mariners all cautioned, "Be positive that you have passed Cape Knox before altering course to the east."

An eddy sets into Lepas Bay at certain stages of the tide and all manner of beachcombing treasures are drawn on to the broad expanse of beach at the head of the bay. Among the flotsam a few years ago came an unwelcome object, a World War II mine. When it was subsequently detonated by the navy, the smoke from the blast was visible for miles and the huge crater left in the beach gave dramatic evidence of its potency.

The Haidas called Lepas Bay, DEDALLUN SLUNG, Long-beach-near-Dedallun-Rock. (C. Smith)

KATE-AH ISLAND — the Haida name for the 100-foot-high islet close offshore in Lepas Bay. (C. Smith)

*CAREW ROCK — rises to 14 feet above sea level, 1½ to 2 miles southwest of Cape Knox. Named by Captain F.C. Learmonth during the 1907 hydrographic survey. John Ewen Carew served as first mate aboard the *Queen Charlotte* when Captain George Dixon passed along here in 1787.

The Haidas have a legend describing the ocean spirit who dwelt under this rock, Spirit-of-the-round-reef-rising-to-a-point.

*TURNER REEF — only 5 feet high, is a little to the east of Carew Rock and there is a deep passage between the two. Captain F.C. Learmonth named the reef after James Turner, the second mate aboard the *Queen Charlotte* under Dixon.

SLUNG-SOAS — camp sites used by Haida sea otter hunters. One camp by this name lay in the first small indentation along the rocky shore south and west of Lepas Bay. A second Slung-soas camp nestled precariously in a bight immediately north of Sadler Point. The rock ledges offshore a short distance at the second site gave scant protection. (C. Smith)

*NEWCOMBE HILL — about 4 miles south of Lepas Bay, is 540 feet high. There are conflicting opinions as to which Newcombe the hill is named for and both are equally esteemed travellers of this part of the coast. One is Dr. C.F. Newcombe, the well-known anthropologist, and the other is Captain Holmes Newcombe, the Fisheries Protection Officer who knew the west coast well prior to his retirement in 1926.

The Haidas called the hill KATE-AH, the same name they gave to the islet in Lepas Bay. (C. Smith)

SHICALSLUNG — the bay at the base of Newcombe Hill. (C. Smith)

DEDALL KWOON — the Haida name for the rocky point forming the southwest edge of Shicalslung, and which extends from the base of Newcombe Hill. *Kwoon* means point. (C. Smith)

DEDALLUN ROCK — the 10-foot-high rock on the point of Dedall Kwoon. (C. Smith)

*LAUDER POINT — southwest of Newcombe Hill. Named in 1907 by Captain F.C. Learmonth after Dr. William Lauder, surgeon aboard the *Queen Charlotte* in 1787.

*GATENBY ROCK — awash and with a sea usually breaking over it, lies about 1½ miles to the west of Lauder Point. Named in 1907 by Captain Learmonth of the *Egeria* after Bo'son Gatenby of Dixon's *Queen Charlotte*.

*SADLER POINT — about 1¼ miles south along the rocky shore from Lauder Point. Named in 1907 by Captain F.C. Learmonth after John Sadler, the carpenter aboard the *Queen Charlotte* in 1787.

Called SHLICKALKWOON, Seal-Bank-Point, by the Haidas. (C. Smith)

James G. Swan, in his 1883 report of the trip he made along this west coast, wrote of being caught off here in a sudden storm and his Haida guides took him ashore. "We had to scramble over a reef of rocks extending along the shore for miles," he said. "It was dangerous for anyone but the Haidas who are accustomed to this hazardous landing. Once ashore we had to stay for 3 days waiting for a break in the weather."

*BERESFORD BAY — a large bight extending from Sadler Point on the north to White Point on the south. Named in 1907 by Captain F.C. Learmonth after William Beresford, supercargo and assistant trader aboard Dixon's *Queen Charlotte* in 1787.

Surf on beach at Beresford Bay.
Photo - Art Sutherland.

*SIALUN BAY — lies in the northeast portion of Beresford Bay. This picturesque bay with a fine sand beach at its head is one of the sites chosen recently by some young people in the ever-growing movement to seek comparative isolation and live in a natural environment.

When asked about the perils of choosing such an inaccessible homesite young Ken Peerless, who went with his wife to live at Sialun Bay, said, "Every place demands dues. We find the benefits of what we have out there are well worth the inconveniences." The birth of their baby son Tao, in the fall of 1971, kept Mrs. Peerless away only briefly. Her return to Sialun brought home to the couple just how isolated they really were, when the launch taking her back was wrecked in the bay and most of the precious food supplies were lost. Later Ken had to walk the shoreline to the Naden Harbour logging camp to summon help when the baby's milk supply grew low. A rugged mid-winter hike which took him 8 days - and spoke highly of his physical condition from the life at Sialun Bay.

The Haidas called the bay SEE-ALUN-SLUNG and also DARL-SLUNG. (C. Smith)

SEE-ALUN-HILL — the Haida name for the hill behind Sialun Bay. (C. Smith)

*SIALUN CREEK — flows onto the beach at Sialun Bay and has its headwaters some 8 to 10 miles inland.

DJAH-AL — the Haida name for a 20-foot-high rock on the rocky point at the south end of Sialun Bay. (C. Smith)

DJAH-AL-SLUNG — the bay immediately south of Sialun Bay. WAYGANS was another name applied to this bay. (C. Smith)

AH-SETS — a former sea otter camp used by Haida hunters. It lay in the bight between Djah-al-slung and Fleurieu Point. (C. Smith)

Geologists found a fossil site at the old Ah-sets camp site.

*FLEURIEU POINT — a rocky projection into Beresford Bay. Named in 1907 by Captain F.C. Learmonth of the survey ship *Egeria*, after Comte de Fleurieu. As mentioned under Solide Passage, Captain Etienne Marchand spent considerable time in 1791 exploring the northwest part of the Charlottes and carefully recorded his observations at some length in a journal. He died suddenly the following year. Before his work could be put into print all his papers were somehow lost. Comte de Fleurieu, a famous scientist and geographer of that day, undertook the compilation of the saga of Marchand's voyage, using the log of the *Solide* and a diary kept by Captain Prosper Chanal, second-in-command.

KEENQOT, long-sand-beach-river — flows from the east into the bay south of Fleurieu Point. (C. Smith)

KESA VILLAGE — located near the Keenqot River belonged to the Raven Crest Sand-Town-People whose ancestors had originated from House Island on the east side of Moresby Island. The Ravens of Kesa were among those who later migrated to Alaska. At the south end of the bay, where Kesa formerly lay, is a fossil site.

*CASWELL POINT — south of both Fleurieu Point and the Keenqot River, has a reef close offshore. The point was named by the Hydrographic Service after Joshua Caswell, second mate on the second voyage of the American vessel

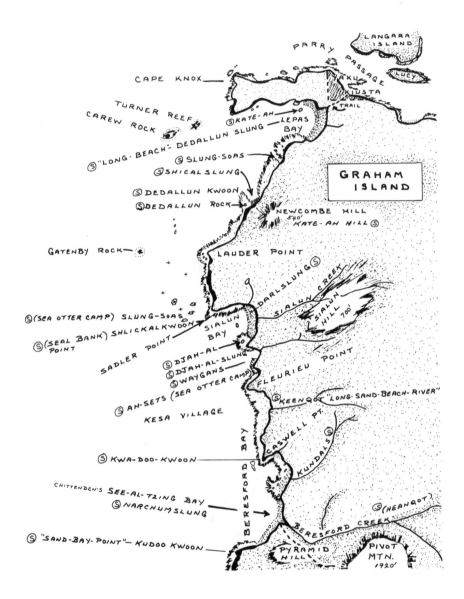

All names supplied by Mr. Charles A. Smith are shown on this map by Ⓢ

Columbia. Caswell, very popular, loved to hunt and fish and never missed a chance to go ashore to try his luck. It was his fondness for fishing which may have cost him his life in 1791. During the cruise in what is now Alaskan waters, the *Columbia* dropped anchor off a point midway up the east side of Prince of Wales Island. Captain Gray, anxious to get away in a rising breeze, was nevertheless persuaded by the amiable Caswell to let him go to a nearby cove for an hour's fishing whilst the ship made ready for sailing.

Taking a jolly boat and two other ardent fishermen, Bo'son's Mate John Folger and Seaman Joseph Barnes, Caswell was soon out of sight around a point about a quarter of a mile away. It was 9 a.m. At 11.30 the *Columbia* signalled them to return. When by noon there was still no sign of them, Captain Gray became alarmed and sent out a heavily armed pinnace. A bloody sight met the eyes of the searchers. On the beach lay Joseph Barnes; naked and stabbed to death. The jolly boat swung at anchor near the shore. As the pinnace approached cautiously Caswell's body, terribly mutilated, could be seen lying in the bottom of the small boat. He, too, had been stripped naked. There was no sign of Folger.

Fearing an ambush the rescuers did not dare to venture ashore. Barnes's body was left on the beach, a line attached to the jolly boat then the pinnace fled from the awful place. Upon rejoining the *Columbia* the body of 26-year-old Joshua Caswell was prepared for burial. The following morning, less than 24 hours after he had set out with his shipmates for the fishing trip, the mate was buried "somewhere near Cape Chacon."[1]

Caswell Point is the KWA-DOO-KWOON of the Haidas. (C. Smith)

[1]The information concerning this episode is at variance with that given on page 32, Volume 1, *Q.C. Islands*, in which it was stated that Caswell was killed and buried in Cumshewa Inlet. Since the material in Volume 2 has been obtained from the journals of both Hoskins and Haswell, who were present at the time of the murder, it should be considered more accurate than that given in the earlier volume.

There were two instances of 3 men being killed in Cumshewa Inlet, i.e. Captain Stephen Hill, his purser and steward, of the *Sea Otter*, were killed there in 1796 and, in 1798, Captain Asa Dodge of the *Alexander* lost 3 men in a fight with the Cumshewas. But, according to the log of the *Columbia*, the deaths of Caswell, Folger and Barnes took place in what is now Alaska.

KUNDALS — the river flowing into the bight immediately south of Caswell Point. The first part of the name means point. (C. Smith)

*BERESFORD CREEK — named in conjunction with Beresford Bay, into which it flows about 1½ miles south of Caswell Point. This creek has branches which drain a muskeg 8 to 10 miles inland. A fine stretch of sand beach fringes the shoreline at the mouth of Beresford Creek and the Pivot Mountain trail leads in from the south side of the mouth of the creek.

The Haida name for the creek was HEANQOT. (C. Smith)

NARCHUM-SLUNG — the Haida name for the bight into which Beresford Creek flows. (C. Smith) In 1884 Newton Chittenden applied the name EZRA BAY to the basin saying, however, that his guides called it *See-al-tzing*. These names are not in use today.

*PIVOT MOUNTAIN — inland from the mouth of Beresford Creek, rises to 1,920 feet. Being somewhat detached from other coastal heights it is easily identified from the sea. The name was applied before 1914 and is believed to have been from a land survey made in connection with oil and coal claims.

The Haida name for it was SQAT-TELAGANS. (C. Smith)

*PYRAMID HILL — named about the same time, is west of Pivot Mountain.

KUDOO-KWOON, sand-bay-point — the Haida name for the rocky point below Pyramid Hill. (C. Smith)

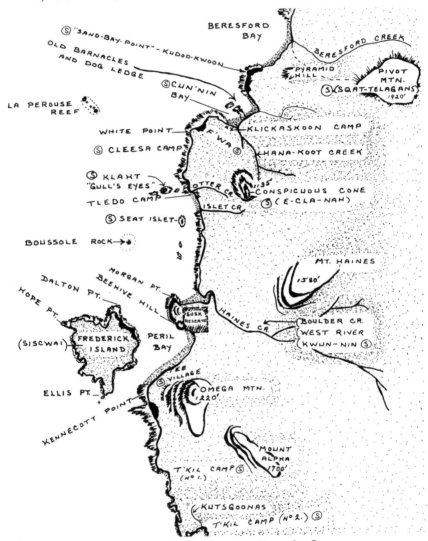

All names supplied by Mr. Charles A. Smith are shown on this map by Ⓢ

*HANA KOOT CREEK — flows into the cove at the south end of Beresford Bay. *Koot* means eagle. On the Hydrographic chart issued about 1914 it was shown as Mana Koot and Mr. C. Smith also shows it on his map as Mana Koot. Gazetted as Hana Koot Creek.

CUN'NIN — a descriptive Haida name for the sandy-beached bay into which the Hana Koot Creek runs. (C. Smith)

KLICKASKOON — a well-known Haida campsite on the west side of the mouth of the Hana Koot Creek. (The Li'kas kun of Newcombe and Swanton.)

OLD BARNACLES — a reef lying in front of Klickaskoon. (Swanton)

DOG LEDGE — also at Klickaskoon. (Swanton)

F'WA, Hill-with-white-cliffs — the Haida name for the headland at the south end of Beresford Bay where there are conspicuous white cliffs. (C. Smith)

*WHITE POINT — the western extremity of the headland of F'Wa. Given its name in 1907 by Captain F.C. Learmonth, who named it after George White, Third Mate on Dixon's *Queen Charlotte* in 1787.
Mr. G. Gray Hill of Duncan, B.C., who sails to the Charlottes each summer, found a large petrified tree stump near White Point.

CLEESA — by the mouth of a stream a little south of White Point. One of the numerous camps of the Haida hunters. (C. Smith)

*LA PEROUSE REEF — which dries at 8 or 9 feet, is about 2 miles west of White Point. Named in 1946 by the Hydrographic Service after Jean Francois de Galaup, Comte de Laperouse, who, with Captain de Langle, was commissioned by the French Government in 1785 to find the Northwest Passage. He was also to complete a scientific journey across the Pacific Ocean, charting islands and studying natives, as well as flora and fauna, with a special eye to commercial possibilities.
The King of France, Louis XVI, had decided to challenge England's supremacy on the high seas. Two ships were outfitted and manned with a total complement of 223 men. Laperouse, 44 years old, a skilled and resourceful commander of the French Navy, was placed in charge of the flagship of the expedition, *La Boussole.* Vicomte de Langle captained the second ship, *L'Astrolabe.*
Laperouse sailed southward along the west coast of the Charlottes in 1786 and named several features.[1] He is credited with being the first to suspect that the Charlottes were not part of the mainland.
But the voyage around the world was never to be accomplished. In December of 1787 Captain de Langle and 11 of his crew were murdered by the natives in the Samoan Islands. The following year Laperouse and all hands were lost at sea. In 1825 a Captain Dillon found the mute evidence - wreckage of the two ships washed up on a reef north of New Hebrides.

[1]Q.C. Island, Volume 1, page 20.

*BOUSSOLE ROCK — about 2 miles southwest of White Point, has a depth of about 18 feet over it. The seas break heavily here in a moderate swell. Named in 1907 by Captain F.C. Learmonth of the *Egeria* during a survey of these waters. It is after *La Boussole*, the vessel commanded by Laperouse.[1]

*CONSPICUOUS CONE — is not particularly conspicuous according to fishermen who ply these waters. It is 1,135 feet high and lies southeast of White Point.
    The Haidas called it E-CLA-NAH. (C. Smith)

TLEDO — one of the more important and frequently used camps of the Haida sea otter hunters. It had a totem pole - highly unusual in seasonally occupied sites. The village was located at the north end of the sandy beach which lies to the west of Conspicuous Cone. When James Deans visited there in the 1880s he found 8 houses at the site. Today a distinctive greenness marks the region of the old campsite.
    During Newton Chittenden's visit in 1884 there was an abnormally low tide which exposed the petrified trunks " . . . of a great number of trees varying from 1 to 6 feet in diameter," he wrote and added that he wondered if this had occurred as a result of the sinking of the land. Large pieces of lignite coal were sighted along this stretch of beach.

KLAHT ISLET, Gull's-eyes — a 6-foot-high islet which lies to the west of Tledo and slightly north. (C. Smith)

SEAT ISLET — southwest of Tledo, is 80 feet high. (C. Smith)

OTTER CREEK — the name given by Chittenden to the stream at the north side of Tledo and seems to be the only recorded name for the creek. Like most of Chittenden's names, it was never adopted. James Deans mentioned this creek in his report and said he felt the mouth had at one time been 1 mile further to the southeast.

ISLET CREEK — the name given by Chittenden in 1884 to the stream flowing onto the beach south of Tledo, the mouth of the creek being opposite the 80-foot Seat Islet. There are fossils south of this creek.

*HAINES CREEK — east of Morgan Point has had several names. The Haidas called it KWUN-IN. (C. Smith) Chittenden in 1884 referred to it as BOULDER CREEK. E.J. Tingley at the invitation of the Hydrographic Service in 1910 suggested WEST RIVER, which it was called for years, and still is locally. To avoid possible confusion owing to duplications of that name, the Hydrographic Service applied Haines River. In 1961 this was changed to Haines CREEK, under which it is now gazetted.
    In the bay created by the shifting shoreline at the mouth of the Haines, the seal-hunting McNaughtons made their home base. "We would take the

[1]See La Perouse Reef.

launch through the neck on a surge," says Don, "then once inside the boat was perfectly safe to leave unattended as we hunted seals along the outer coast with the skiff and outboard. (McNaughton - page 35.)

It was also a former Haida camping site. Norman Broadhurst recalled finding an old canoe on the south shore of the Haines River in 1907. "Pretty tough shape, but we patched it up and went across to Frederick Island in it," he said.

MOUNT HAINES — lies about 2½ miles east of the mouth of Haines creek, which flows on the south side of the mountain. It rises to 1580 feet. The name is from Mr. Charles Smith's map, which showed an extensive "caribou range" between this and Jalun Lake.

*MORGAN POINT — west of Haines Creek, rises steeply to a summit of 440 feet. Named in 1907 by Captain Learmonth after a seaman of the *Egeria* who became painfully injured in a fall down a cliff when assisting with the survey in this region.

The Haida name for the point was K'WA KWOON. (C. Smith)

*Beehive Hill, north entrance of Peril Bay
on the west coast of Graham Island.*

Photo - G. Gray Hill

*BEEHIVE HILL — named for its distinctive shape, is a little south of Morgan Point. Near Beehive Hill in 1967 the McNaughtons found a wrecked junk. "It had 3-inch rough teak planks," says Don, "and almost certainly had smashed against Frederick Island, then broke up to drift ashore by the Beehive." G. Gray Hill, of Duncan, found the remains still there a year later. It had company by then - an enormous whalebone which had rolled in on the waves.

*PERIL BAY — separates Frederick Island from Graham Island and has a fine sand beach on its east side. This beach is frequently referred to as THE BEEHIVE BEACH by local people. It was here that surveyor Art Sutherland of Victoria found one of the rare blue agates "and so many Japanese glass floats I couldn't begin to carry them home." News of the interesting treasures which collect on the Beehive Beach attracted a party of ardent beachcombers in October 1971. They came in a small wheeled aircraft. "We made a good landing," said pilot Alec Pidherny of Masset, "but when we were taxiing off one wheel hit a soft spot. The plane nosed over and damaged the prop." An alert pilot from the seaplane base in Masset discovered their plight and, courtesy of the U.S. Coastguard helicopter, all were soon rescued. The plane was later repaired and flown out.

Peril Bay was known to the Haidas as TEE-UNDLAY, *undlay* meant the water of a place. It took its name from the nearby village of Tee. (C. Smith)

TEE VILLAGE — near the south end of the Beehive Beach at Peril Bay is shown on one of Mr. C. Smith's maps as DEE VILLAGE. White people called this village SUSK. The Haidas referred to nearby Frederick Island as Siscwai, and it is presumed that traders adopted a modification of that name in referring to Tee Village. It was a Raven Crest village belonging to the Sand-Town-People whose ancestors came from the old House Island village off the east side of Moresby Island. People from Tee traded with George Dixon on the *Queen Charlotte* on July 5th and 6th, 1787. A few years later they abandoned the village to join the migration to Alaska.

The Susk Indian Reserve containing 155 acres lies north of the old village and is mainly east of Beehive Hill. It was granted in 1916. Prior to 1913 the entire region was blanketed by coal and petroleum licences.

*OMEGA MOUNTAIN — named prior to 1914 is about 2 miles south of Beehive Hill. A conspicuous summit 1,220 feet high, it has an extensive valley off its northern slope which runs southeastward from the head of Peril Bay.

The Haidas called Omega Mountain THE-MOUNTAIN-OF-TEE. (C. Smith)

MOUNT ALPHA — is the name shown on Mr. Charles Smith's chart for a 1700-foot mountain lying about 2½ to 3 miles southeast of Omega Mountain.

*KENNECOTT POINT — at the south end of Peril Bay. First named POINT EDWARD in 1884 by Newton Chittenden and one of the few of his place-names to be recorded on Admiralty charts.

When the vessel *Kennecott* slammed onto the rocks near Hunter Point in 1923, the first distress message sent out gave her location incorrectly as being near Frederick Island. Retired members of the Hydrographic Service think that the name Kennecott was applied to Edward Point later, in the mistaken belief that this was where the vessel had been wrecked. Edward Point appeared on maps up to 1927. The newer name of Kennecott Point became officially confirmed on July 3, 1946.

The Haidas called this point by two names; TEE-KWOON in association with the old village, and SOUTH-END-OF-CHANNEL-POINT. (C. Smith)

*FREDERICK ISLAND — the rock-fringed island lying off Peril Bay. Named after Frederick Ingraham, nephew of Joseph Ingraham of the Boston-owned brig *Hope*. Ingraham, never too sharp with geographic details, really named Hippa Island after his nephew. When Captain Vancouver noted that Dixon had already named Hippa, he transferred "Young Frederick's" name to the island lying north of Hippa Island. Ingraham had put the name Hippa on Lucy Island, in Parry Passage, on one of his charts.

During the early years of coal and oil interest, Frederick Island became a regular point of call with prospectors looking for "signs." Many were the narrow escapes from treacherous seas. In September 1907 Bill Hayes and J.W. Holland of Vancouver had their boat swamped when making a landing on Frederick and lost all their supplies and clothing.

By some miracle a jar into which they had put a few matches floated ashore and the two prospectors were able to get a fire going. The *Egeria* was engaged in surveying Langara waters at that time. When one of her officers reported smoke on Frederick Island, Captain Learmonth, knowing the island was uninhabited, cruised down that way after a few days. A small boat was sent ashore and the starving men rescued.

Eli Tingley and John Coates, well-known Graham Island pioneers, anchored their launch *Little Johnny* off Frederick Island in 1910 to go ashore in the dingy. Hardly had they pulled away from the launch when they were caught by a big wave and both thrown into the sea. Rapidly separated from both boats they had a long hard swim to shore and became so exhausted they barely made it. The subsequent trip back to the launch on a makeshift raft was almost as perilous.

Bert Roberts, veteran fisherman from Queen Charlotte City, has a happier memory of these wild waters off Frederick when late in August 1931 they suddenly stilled to a flat calm and in one day he pulled over 100 prime spring salmon aboard his small troller.

Frederick Island was the SISCWAI of the Haidas.

*DALTON POINT — northeast extremity of Frederick Island. Named by Captain F.C. Learmonth after the artificer engineer on the *Egeria* in 1907. Numerous rocks extend from it, the outermost of which is 25 feet high. Considerable kelp lies about the point.

*ELLIS POINT — at the south tip of Frederick Island is also rocky. Named in 1907 by Captain Learmonth after a popular coxswain on one of the sounding boats. Ellis is said to have handled his duties with particular competency during the hydrographic survey. There is a fossil site on the unnamed point to the northeast of Ellis Point.

*HOPE POINT — the northwest point of Frederick Island has a rock ledge extending about 1,000 feet westward with an islet on it. During World War II a small radar station was established at this point similar to the station at Marble Island farther south.

The *Hope*, for which Captain Learmonth named the point in 1907, was a 70-ton brigantine owned by Thomas H. Perkins and James Magee of Boston.

Joseph Ingraham, who had been first mate[1] on the 1787-1790 voyage of the *Columbia* to the northwest Pacific coast, was asked to assume command of the *Hope* for a similar trip. Leaving Boston on September 17, 1790, "We arrived on the North West Coast of America, June 29, 1791," reported Ingraham. Trading principally in the vicinity of the Charlottes gave them a successful season before leaving to sell the furs in China that autumn.

On April 26, 1792, in company with two other ships, *Grace* and *Hancock*, the *Hope* left China for another season of trading. Arriving off the north end of the Charlottes, July 2nd, Ingraham this time fell captive to the enchantment of the Islands to such a degree that instead of tending to his trading he spent most of his time exploring.

The voyage lost over $40,000 for the owners of the *Hope*.

T'KIL — there were, apparently, two camps by this name used by Haida hunters. One lay in a small bight slightly less than 2 miles south of Kennecott Point, and almost due west of Mount Alpha. The other is said to have been located at the mouth of the Kutsgoonas Creek about 1½ miles south and east of the first T'Kil camp. This second camp was also called the Kutsgoonas, in association with the creek. (C. Smith)

KUTSGOONAS — a small creek which flows from the north to empty on the sand beach in the first bay north of Cave Creek. (C. Smith)

*CAVE CREEK — about 1 mile north of Ingraham Bay, takes its name from the numerous caves along this section of shoreline - particularly to the north. The Haidas knew it as OYEAN river. (C. Smith)

KUTCHEMS — the more northerly of the two Haida sites at the head of Ingraham Bay. (C. Smith)

KWAI-KANS — the Haida site at the head of Ingraham Bay. It lay to the south of Kutchems.

*INGRAHAM BAY — about 5 miles south of Kennecott Point, was originally named CAVE BAY by Newton Chittenden in 1884 because of a deep cave in the high rock bluff near the north entrance to the bay. "Cave Bay has a fine sand beach," he wrote. "Three streams flow onto it and it is a good canoe landing in pleasant weather. But in storms the seas break all round. We barely escaped losing everything in effecting a landing at the quietest place we could find."

Joseph Ingraham had named the present Nesto Inlet, PORT INGRAHAM, during his 1791 and 1792 trips along this coast. In sorting out the maze of duplications the Hydrographic Service applied Ingraham's name to Chittenden's Cave Bay. The newer name of INGRAHAM BAY was officially confirmed in 1946.

[1]When the *Columbia* left Boston Ingraham had been taken on as second mate. But at the Cape Verde Islands Simon Woodruff, who was first mate, left the ship. Ingraham was promoted to Woodruff's job.

48

MOUNT INGRAHAM — a local name applied to the mountain about 2½ miles inland and a little southeast of the head of Ingraham Bay. It rises to a height of 2,055 feet.

*JOSEPH CREEK — flows into the head of Ingraham Bay. Named in this association by the Hydrographic Service. Joseph Ingraham knew the shorelines of the Charlottes well during his two seasons as master of the brig *Hope*, 1791 and 1792.

POINT PATIENCE — the name given to a point between Joseph Rocks and Tian Head by Chittenden in 1884. It appears to be the same point that Dr. C.F. Newcombe called DJITKUN.

The cave near the north entrance to Ingraham Bay on the west coast of Graham Island which caused Newton Chittenden to name this bay Cave Bay in 1884.

Photo - G. Gray Hill

*JOSEPH ROCKS — composed of columnar basalt lie off the south entrance to Ingraham Bay. Named by the Hydrographic Service in association with Ingraham Bay. They are called SEA LION ROCKS locally, a name first given them by Chittenden in 1884. His name did not go on any map. In 1911 Eli Tingley, too, suggested Sea Lion Rocks when invited by the Hydrographic Service to supply names for some of the features of this region. Eli's name was not adopted either because of duplications along the coast. The name of Joseph Rocks was applied instead.[1]

"These rocks are a favorite haunt of sea lions . . . always seem to be covered with them," says Bert Roberts of Queen Charlotte City, who fished these waters for most of his life. "You could smell them a mile away. Sea lions smell worse than a whaling station."

But smell or no, during the check survey by the Surveys and Mapping Branch of Victoria in the 1960s it was necessary to put a marker on these rocks. "They seemed literally alive with the great beasts," says surveyor Art Sutherland.

[1]Q.C. Islands, Volume 1, Page 329 says that Tian Rocks were formerly called Sea Lion Rocks. This is an error. Up-dated information discloses that this should have read Joseph Rocks, *not* Tian Rocks.

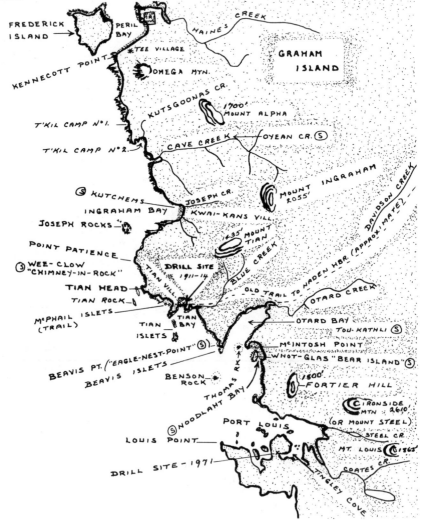

All names supplied by Mr. Charles A. Smith are shown on this map by ⓢ

"Curiously the noise of the helicopter which landed us didn't seem to cause any alarm." Seal hunters Don and Bill McNaughton also commented about their indifference to noise. "We could go right up to the rocks using the skiff and outboard and they hardly gave us a glance. But when we sailed up . . . panic broke loose!"

WEE-CLOW, Chimney-in-rock — the Haida name for a rock formation located a little north of Tian Head. (C. Smith)

*TIAN HEAD — is a prominent point. A conspicuous wooded summit 500 feet high lies about ¾ of a mile to the northeast of it. On older maps it is shown as Tian Point and is about 3 miles south of the Joseph Rocks. The name comes from the old village of Ti-ahn which formerly lay in a bay to the south and east of the head.

*TIAN ROCK — about 25 feet high, lies off Tian Head and was named in this association by the Hydrographic Service.

McPHAIL ISLETS — are a group of rocky islets lying about 2 miles east of Tian Head and were well-known in earlier years. Jagged in appearance they are joined to Graham Island at low tide. A trail from the old drill site at Tian village came out across the peninsula to emerge near the McPhail Islets. From midden signs along this trail it obviously pre-dated the oil discovery by a good many years.

A.A. McPhail and Allan Stewart[1] staked oil claims in the vicinity of Tian in the early years of this century. They organized a company to drill for oil and set up an office in Vancouver from which they sold shares to obtain the money for drilling. They did fairly well until war broke out in 1914 when, with no money in sight, they had to abandon the project. (see also Tian Village)

[1]Stewart Bay, Masset Inlet named after Allan Stewart.

*TIAN ISLETS — lie off the tip of an unnamed peninsula at the west side of Tian Bay and take their name from the bay.

*TIAN BAY — which has two coves at its north end was named in association with the old Haida village which lay in the more westerly of the two coves.

TIAN VILLAGE — also written as Teaen and Ti-ahn was a much beloved town of the sea otter hunters. Its name meant good-hunting. There were several totem poles at Ti-ahn as well as comfortable lodges. In 1836-1841 Hudson's Bay Company Trader John Work noted that Tian had 10 houses and 196 people. By 1913 when the first application was registered to have it declared a Haida Reserve, only one old house remained plus the ghostly tree graves of its ancient occupation. One hundred acres was requested for the reserve, but because of a coal and petroleum licence covering most of the area the application was denied. In 1928 the matter was reconsidered and a total of 5.8 acres granted - making it the smallest of all Haida reserves.

51

Petroleum possibilities at Tian were first seriously considered shortly after the turn of this century when, in 1905, a Ketchikan syndicate chartered the *Eurus* with Captain Thompson to take prospectors Victor Virgalias and L.T. "Lucky" Watson to the isolated region. Ten claims were staked by the men for the syndicate. Shortly afterwards several other claims were staked by a Victoria company covering the coastline from Tian to Frederick Island. One by one the licences were subsequently dropped.

A.A. McPhail and Allan Stewart picked up 22 of the claims and in 1911 organized the British Columbia Oilfields Company. They chose a location on the east side of the small stream which flows through the centre of the Tian Reserve to put down their drill hole.

C.D. Emmons, veteran prospector of the Charlottes who had done most of the ground work for the company, found additional property nearby which attracted the interest of some Prince Rupert men. In August 1911 they announced the formation of the Graham Island Oil Company and sold shares in the new venture for 25 cents each. Dr. Kergin was president, George Tite, vice-president, Police Chief Billy Vickers, secretary-treasurer, with J. Lorne McLaren, Austin Brown and Indian Agent Thomas Deasy of Masset, as directors. Selling shares was about all they did accomplish.

By September of 1911 the first company was hard at work drilling. "Blue shales have been passed, also the black . . . containing many marine fossils. We are now in limestone," said Mr. McPhail and, like all good promotors should, he added, "We are meeting with considerable oil and indications are that the main source will soon be encountered."

Victor Virgalias had blazed a rough trail from the drill site to the Naden Harbour Whaling Station, 25 to 30 miles away. Mail could be brought along it and men could get out when weather forbade travel along the west coast. Transporting supplies to the drillers was always a hazard. Several boats were lost, but luckily no lives.

By the summer of 1912 the drill had reached 1,000 feet. In December an important piece of the drill broke " . . . just two weeks away from striking oil," moaned Mr. Slater, the driller-in-charge. The season was too late to have another part sent out by boat so the operation shut down for the winter. When they renewed activities in the spring of 1913 bad luck plagued them; a cave-in at the drill site, continual supply difficulties, poor morale amongst the men which meant constant changeover in crew and, even worse, the oil body seemed more elusive with each passing week.

The drill had barely reached 1200 feet when war broke out in 1914 to write the final chapter to the project. There was no more money. Old Ti-ahn was left to its memories.

Today a mixture of water and oil bubbles merrily out of the old drill hole - an object of interest to all visitors, as are the unusual agates in this area, some of which contain globules of oil. "And those agates contain all the oil we need to find on these islands," say lovers of this place.

MOUNT TIAN — the local name for the 1,435-foot mountain overlooking Tian Bay. It stands about 1½ miles north of the mouth of Blue Creek.

*BLUE CREEK — runs into the northeast portion of Tian Bay, in the cove to the east of the old Tian drill site. Named by Eli Tingley at the invitation to Captain P.C. Musgrave of the survey ship *Lillooet* in 1912. "He named it for a type of blue rock found along it," says Eli's brother Bert, now of Victoria. A trail came from the Tian drill site to Blue Creek, which it followed for a short distance before cutting across to Otard Creek and thence eventually to the Naden Harbour Whaling Station.

*BEAVIS ISLETS — at the west entrance to Otard Bay, consist of 2 islets, 45 and 15 feet high. They are connected to Beavis Point by a drying ledge and were named after L.R.W. Beavis, an officer on the survey ship *Lillooet* during part of the survey of this region 1912 to 1915.

*BEAVIS POINT — off which the Beavis Islets lie at the west entrance to Otard Bay. Named in association with the islets.

The Haida name for the point was KOOT-TELLGAS-KWOON, Eagle-nest-point. (C. Smith)

*OTARD BAY — the indentation to the east of Tian Bay. From his description, "The old abandoned village of Tiahn is situated facing south with a sandy beach fronting the second indentation north of Stowe Harbour," it is believed that Otard Bay is the STOWE HARBOUR of Newton Chittenden's 1884 report. He refers to Port Louis as Kiokathli Inlet.

Otard Bay was the TOU-KATHLI of the Haida. *Tou* means the place-of-food or mussels, and *kathli* is an open bay or slough. (C. Smith)

*OTARD CREEK — named August 28, 1791, by Captain Prosper Chanal, second-in-command on board the French vessel *La Solide*. Captain Chanal named it after a close friend. In his description it would seem that he may in fact have been naming what is now Otard Bay. "The creek is about 2,500 feet wide at its entrance, bottom of fine sand, with a depth of water from 12 to 20 fathoms. It is terminated by two sandy beaches and a rivulet discharges on the south shore where our longboat landed."

The stream gazetted as Otard Creek today enters the northeast side of Otard Bay. The old trail to Naden Harbour went inland near the mouth of this creek and followed its valley for part of the way.[1]

[1]See also Davidson Creek.

*THOMAS ROCK — at the east entrance to Otard Bay dries at 10 feet. There is a great deal of kelp around this region.

*McINTOSH POINT — a rocky peninsula east of Thomas rock, which hooks around the top of the northwest side of a drying unnamed bay. Believed to be named after the ex-Chief of Police from New Westminster who, from the time he first bought Charles Harrison's land at Masset in a tax sale, was active in almost every promotional plan that came along in pioneering days. Harrison was able to redeem his land in time, but the loss of the anticipated ranch did not deter McIntosh. He became one of the area's most avid boosters. Speculative coal drilling at Skonun Point and elaborate land settlement schemes for the west side of Masset Sound were two projects which brought him chiefly into the news. But the prospective sale of "oil lands" in and about Tian were equally irresistible to Mr. McIntosh.[1]

[1]Mr. McIntosh's activities are covered in more detail in Volume 1 of the Q.C. Islands.

WHOT GLAS, Bear-Island — the name given by the Haidas to the island which lies near the central edge of the drying bay southeast of McIntosh Point. The island rises to 190 feet at its summit. (C. Smith)

NOODLAHT — was the name given by the Haidas to the drying bay back of Whot-glas or Bear Island. (C. Smith)

***BENSON ROCK** — lies about 1 mile southwest of Beavis Point. It has a depth of less than 6 feet over it and there are several shallow patches close by.

***FORTIER HILL** — about 1,800 feet high, lies between Otard Bay and Port Louis - being a little nearer Port Louis. It is named after Mr. R.L. Fortier of the survey vessel *Lillooet*. Fortier assisted L.R. Davies in the 1912 portion of the Port Louis - Otard Bay survey. Under the direction of Captain P.C. Musgrave surveying was mainly handled by Davies for the first two years. Fortier assisted him in 1912 and O.R. Parker assisted in 1913. Mr. Parker then took over and completed the survey in 1914 - 1915.

CONTINUING WEST COAST OF GRAHAM ISLAND;
CHANAL POINT TO THE ENTRANCE OF
RENNELL SOUND.

CHAPTER THREE

The section of coastline along the Charlottes north of Chanal Point offers little in the way of harbours. Southward, however, the situation changes and several places provide excellent havens from the wild fury of Pacific gales.

Evidences of old Haida camping sites and villages are frequently found, although they did not necessarily seek the sanctuary of an enclosed harbour to locate. And it is also not uncommon to find the remains of old prospectors' cabins - mute testimony to dreams of earlier years. There were several in the Port Louis region where this chapter begins.

*CHANAL POINT — a rocky bluff extending from the north shoreline at the approach to Port Louis. Named after Captain Prosper Chanal, second-in-command on the vessel *La Solide* under Captain Etienne Marchand. They were circumnavigating the world and dropped anchor off Cloak Bay in August of 1791. Captain Chanal was sent south along the coast to chart the shoreline from Parry Passage to Hippa Island. Chanal applied several names, some of which are still in use today.[1]

[1]See Otard Creek; Port Louis; Port Chanal.

WHITE-VILLAGE — one of the numerous Haida sites in this region, White Village lay in the bay east of Chanal Point. (C. Smith)

*NEWINGTON ROCK — southeast of Chanal Point dries at 4 feet. Named after the well-remembered lighthouse tender *Newington* which was purchased in 1909 by the Canadian Government to assist the overworked *Quadra*.

*BARNES SHOAL — southeast of Newington Rock. Named in 1946 by the Hydrographic Service after Captain Charles Barnes. Barnes, who had been second officer on the *Quadra*, became the first skipper for the newly acquired *Newington* in 1909. When the *Estevan* was built in 1913 Barnes became her first captain.

*TURNER POINT — on the north shore of the entrance to Port Louis. It is a rocky point with two islands leading off to the west in such a way as to form a lagoon inside the curve of the point. Named during the 1912 to 1915 hydrographic survey of this region.

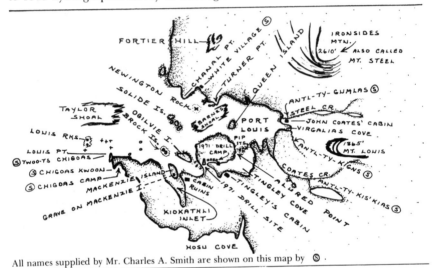

All names supplied by Mr. Charles A. Smith are shown on this map by Ⓢ .

*PORT LOUIS — one of the most protected harbours on the west coast. It received its name on August 29, 1791, from Captain Prosper Chanal who named it for Louis Marchand, brother of the captain of *La Solide*. Louis accompanied Chanal on his survey of the shoreline from Parry Passage to Hippa Island.

The Haidas called Port Louis KIO-KATHLI.[1]

[1]See also Chanal Point and Port Chanal.

*IRONSIDE MOUNTAIN —rising to 2,610 feet, overlooks Port Louis from the northeast. Bert and Eli Tingley prospected in that region and in 1911 staked a claim on this mountain. Captain Musgrave of the survey ship *Lillooet* invited Eli to supply some names for features of this area. Eli submitted IRON MOUNTAIN for this peak because it had a large iron-coloured patch on a bluff. The name was adopted with a variation to Ironside Mountain. (Also shown on some early maps as MOUNT STEEL.)

It had earlier been named MOUNT RICHARD by Newton Chittenden when he visited Port Louis in 1884. But like almost all the names Chittenden supplied few were adopted - despite the fact that he was on a trip commissioned by the British Columbia Government.

*STEEL CREEK — flows into Port Louis north of Virgalias Cove. "We had our log cabin at Tingley Cove," says Bert Tingley as he recalled the early years of 1910 and 1911, "but we also lived for some time in a tent at Steel Creek doing development work on our Iron Mountain claim and location oil claims . . . or hoping to. Eli named Steel Creek because of numerous showings of iron in it. Musgrave liked the name and put it on his charts." Steel Creek drains two small lakes 2 and 4 miles inland.

The Haidas called the creek ANTL-TY-GUMLAS. (C. Smith)

*VIRGALIAS COVE — at the head of Port Louis and south of Steel Creek. Named by Eli Tingley after Victor Virgalias, the man who blazed the first trail from Otard Bay to Naden Harbour. Virgalias had much variety in early-day spellings.

Virgalias, the little Scandinavian prospector had, among other things, operated a flourishing dance hall in Alaska before coming to the Charlottes in 1905. But it was his nose for minerals which got him the job with the Ketchikan syndicate when he was sent with L.T. "Lucky" Watson and Captain Thompson in the *Eurus* to stake oil lands around Tian Point. That mission completed, Virgalias stayed to have a better look at the Islands. "I think he literally walked every inch of the northern part of Graham Island," says Bert Tingley " . . . usually in search of minerals."

It was Virgalias who, with Charlie Spence, recovered the first gold in paying amounts from the black sands off Cape Fife. They obtained upwards of $300 in 1908, but when they returned from celebrating their bonanza they found big tides had obliterated every trace of the gold-bearing sand. The well-known poem of early days *The Tale of the Moveable Mine* was written around this episode.

John Coates, another well-known prospector of early years, built a cabin on the north shore of Virgalias Cove in connection with his activities there in 1911 with Bert and Eli Tingley.

The creek flowing into the south side of Virgalias Cove was called by the Haidas ANTL-TY-KIG'NS. (C. Smith)

*COATES CREEK — enters Port Louis to the southwest of Virgalias Cove. One of the names submitted by Eli Tingley to Captain Musgrave in 1911 and subsequently adopted.

John A. Coates first came to the Charlottes in 1896. By the time he met the Tingleys in Victoria in 1910 he had trapped and prospected every accessible part of Graham Island. "He was very enthusiastic about the iron showings on Iron Mountain," recalls Bert Tingley, "and I guess we caught some of the fever too.

The three men bought a 26-foot boat on Vancouver Island which they named *Little Johnnie* for Coates, and the trip from there to Port Louis was a series of hair-breadth escapes. At Port Louis the men set up their base camps and prepared to do some serious prospecting. "Coates left the Charlottes for good about 1913," says Bert, "and settled on a farm near Duncan on Vancouver Island.

First shown as Coates River, this designation was amended to Coates Creek in 1961 by the Hydrographic Service. The creek drains 3 lakes, one of which is about 1½ miles long. Some of its tributaries run inland almost to Ian Lake.

It was called ANTL-KISKIAS by the Haidas and they reported falls not too far upstream. (C. Smith)

MOUNT LOUIS — a little over a mile inland, rises to a summit of 1,865 feet. Standing east of the head of Port Louis with Steel Creek flowing along its north sides and Coates Creek on the south.

*****TINGLEY COVE** — off the south side of Port Louis is where Bert and Eli Tingley built their snug cabin. During the survey of Port Louis the Hydrographic crew used it frequently. Big windows, tables to lay out charts and comfortable camping conditions made a grateful crew name the bay in honour of their hosts. "The cabin stood by a stream which made things pretty convenient," says Bert. "Eli, Johnny Coates and I spent some happy days there. Eli's townsite proposition at Port Clements seemed hopelessly blocked by the timber claims on it, so he put the turn of events to good use prospecting out on the west coast."

Cabin built by Bert and Eli Tingley in 1911 in Tingley Cove.
Ironside Mtn. on left.

Photo - Bert Tingley

In 1971 the small bay once more became the site of prospecting when the Commonwealth Rig No. 22 prepared to drill for Union Oil of Calgary. They set up camp on a point on the west side of Tingley Cove, then laid out the drill site close to the shoreline on the isthmus of the peninsula which forms the northwest side of Tingley Cove. With a crew of about 25 men operations continued from April to the end of August when, at just over 5000 feet, the drilling was abandoned.

Only a small capped pipe remains today. "And if you didn't know where to look, you would never notice it," says Bob Anderson, pilot for North Coast Air Services of Prince Rupert, who flew the aircraft which serviced the base.

"Those fellows really deserve credit for the immaculate condition they left the area in. Not a scrap of debris anywhere."

The early Haidas knew this cove well and called it SKAO DU-LCE. (C. Smith)

*PIP ISLETS — at the entrance to Tingley Cove. A group of rocky islets from 1 to 10 feet high, their name dates back to the 1911 hydrographic survey but the origin of the name not known.

*ALURED POINT — on the west side of the entrance to Tingley Cove. The rocky point of Alured extends into the channel facing Pip Islets - making a very narrow passageway.

Bert Tingley standing with his brother, Eli, and sister, Laura, sitting.

Photo - Mrs. Eli Tingley.

*QUEEN ISLAND — rises to 210 feet and is at the entrance to Port Louis, a little to the east of Barnes Shoal. First named CHANAL ISLAND by James G. Swan in 1883, but this name was never adopted. When Captain Musgrave invited Eli Tingley to name it in 1911, Eli chose the name of his first boat on the Charlottes, the *Queen*. She was a 30-foot Columbia River model with a tall mast, big mainsail and small jib. Eli brought her to Masset Inlet in 1908 on the steamer *Amur*. Later the *Queen* crossed Hecate Strait many times under her own sail. After a few years Eli installed a 3½ H.P. Palmer engine and added a cabin. Charlie Adam, Eli's townsiting rival in Masset Inlet, ran the boat for awhile taking supplies to Tian for the drilling crew and subsequently bought it from Eli.

The *Queen* spoiled Charles Harrison's attempt to discourage settlers who proposed going up into Masset Inlet to pre-empt. He told them that Inlet waters were not navigable "blocked by a huge bar." Then he would talk them into taking up land adjacent to Masset so as to bolster his various enterprizes. One day the *Queen* capsized. With Eli clinging to her bottom and the 30-foot mast hanging straight down, she was caught in the strong Inlet current and swept southward to the inland expanse of Masset Inlet, thus giving the lie to any bar blocking passage.

*SOLIDE ISLANDS — four islands ranging up to 180 feet in height which form a chain in the middle of the approach to Port Louis. They are named after the French ship *La Solide* which sailed along the west coast of the Charlottes in 1791 during the course of a voyage around the world. Her captain, Etienne Marchand, had been directed to pay especial attention to commercial possibilities which might be developed on "the northwest coast of America."[1]

[1]See Solide Passage.

*OGILVIE ISLAND — south of the Solide Islands is about 250 feet high and has a drying spit which connects it to Graham Island. Named during, or shortly after, the geological survey made by J.D. Mackenzie in 1913 and 1914 of Graham Island. William Ogilvie was a well-known geological surveyor who carried out several surveys in the Yukon. He worked with Dr. George Dawson in 1887 during a survey which took in the Pelly River. In later years Mr. Ogilvie became Commissioner in the Yukon for the Federal Government.

Commonwealth Rig No. 22 drilling for oil in 1971 at Tingley Cove.

Photo - Bob Anderson.

*MACKENZIE ISLAND — southwest of Ogilvie Island is also connected to Graham Island by a drying bank. An old grave has been found on the southwest part of Mackenzie Island at one end of the drying bank. At the other end of the bank, on Graham Island, are the remains of an old cabin. The island is named after James D. MacKenzie who conducted the 1913-14 geological survey of Graham Island.[1]

[1]See also Mackenzie Cove; MacKenzie Bay, MacKenzie Passage. (Mackenzie Cove and Island spelled with small "k". Others follow MacKenzie's own spelling of his name using the capital "K".)

*BROCK ISLANDS — lie outward between Ogilvie and Mackenzie Island. A compact group with rocky shores and connected by ledges. The largest island rises to 250 feet. Named during, or shortly after, the MacKenzie survey 1913-14. Reginald Walter Brock was Director of the Geological Survey and Deputy Minister of the Department of Mines in 1914, when MacKenzie was undertaking the geological survey of Graham Island.[1]

[1]See also Brock Bay and Brock Point.

*KIOKATHLI INLET — runs off the south side west of the entrance to Port Louis, and also west of Brock and Mackenzie Island. It is a modification of the Haida name for Port Louis. Some maps have shown it as KYOKATHLI and others as KAI QA-TI. *Kathli* means open bay or slough.

*TAYLOR SHOAL — west of the Solide Islands is a bank with two shallow areas which break with a westerly swell. The northern bank has a depth of about 11 feet and on the south bank depths vary from 13 to 21 feet.

*LOUIS ROCKS — consisting of two heads, 1 and 6 feet high, lie on a drying reef at the outside edge of a rock-strewn section off Louis Point. Named in association with Louis Point by the Hydrographic Service.

*LOUIS POINT — is the northern extremity of an islet 79 feet high connected by a drying ledge to Graham Island, and is the southwest entrance point to Port Louis. Named by the Hydrographic Service in association with Port Louis. All this rocky region from Kiokathli Inlet and west proved to be the best for finding Japanese glass floats when the drillers were camped at Tingley Cove in 1971. "The good beaches had been picked clean, we found," said one of them, "but we collected more than we could carry from the less attractive looking places."

Between Louis Rocks and Louis Point are several rocky heads which dry.

"Louis Point is a particular terror to those of us who go along there," says Gray Hill, a veteran mariner of over 30 years sailing British Columbia and Alaska coasts. "A chain of black spouting rocks lie a bit off. There is a deep way inside them, but two breakers bar the way. Yet it is just passable when one is unwilling to go 2 miles out and around. The rocks of this coast are very black and menacing. The great surf descends back and down . . . like waterfalls of quicksilver. And from here we can see the cloud-capped hills of old Hippa," is his descriptive version.

Louis Point is the north end of a T-shaped rock formation. The Haidas called this north end TWOO-TS CHIGOAS. (C. Smith)

CHIGOAS KWOON — the Haida name for the south end of the peninsula mentioned above. (C. Smith) On the east side of Chigoas Kwoon lies a small cove, this is the site of a former Haida camp.

Neil and Betty Carey, an American couple who came to visit the Charlottes some years ago then fell in love with a wild Canadian shoreline so much they returned to make their permanent home on the Islands, have travelled the west coast numerous times. To the south of Chigoas Kwoon campsite used anciently by Haidas the Careys found a curious boat 10 feet long, with an unentered logbook, 4-inch compass, unused flares and portions of a 1945 Portland, Oregon, newspaper. To add to the mystery it was found 50 feet above the highwater mark. This last might be explained by a tidal wave, but despite intense research by Mr. and Mrs. Carey, the origin of the boat is still a mystery.

BLUFF BAY — "Opening to the south, at the north entrance to Athlow Inlet, with a small island opposite," is the way Newton Chittenden described the cove in his report of 1884. The name was not gazetted.

*ATHLOW BAY — the large outer bay extending from Bluff Bay to Selveson Point and which takes in both Hosu Cove and Port Chanal. It is from the old Haida name for the present Port Chanal. Captain Absolom Freeman is thought to have applied the name first to the outer bay (rather than to Port Chanal) when he drafted his west coast charts in 1912.

*HOSU COVE — in the northeast part of Athlow Bay. Shown on old maps as NORTH COVE. Since this name was duplicated frequently along the coast the Hydrographic Service adopted a modification of the old Haida name for the bay and renamed it Hosu Cove. Numerous islets and rocks dot this interesting bay, and a stream enters the northeast corner. Those who know it say competent local knowledge is required to enter the uncharted waters with any degree of safety.

CLOO-WHOCK — a former Haida camp in Hosu Cove. (C. Smith)

*GILLAN POINT — is the southwest extremity of a peculiarly shaped peninsula which forms the southern part of Hosu Cove. The peninsula is really two islands which dry to form part of Graham Island. Mr. W.H. Gillen was second mate on the *Celestial Empire* under Captain Absolom Freeman. He drafted charts of Athlow Bay and Port Chanal in 1912 which were adopted by both Captain Freeman, who then was skipper on the *Flamingo*, and Captain B. Barry, who took over as master of the *Celestial Empire*. Freeman named the point after Mr. Gillen, but over the years a typographical error changed the spelling from Gillen to Gillan.
Dr. C.F. Newcombe calls this point TA'NWILKUN on his map.
There are several interesting caves in this area. A stalactite cave is near Gillan Point and the south side of the inner island has a large red cavern.
The unnamed bay south of Gillan Point contained several Haida cabins in earlier years.

*FLAMINGO ROCK — about 1½ miles southwest of Gillan Point. Seas break over it in heavy weather. Named by Captain Freeman after the Canadian Fishing Company's steam trawler *Flamingo* which carried a crew of 23 men. Several well-known skippers operated this vessel, including pioneer Walter Dass who began his career on the Charlottes as a prospector in the Jedway area in 1906.

*BARRY ISLAND — on the north side of the entrance to Port Chanal. Named after Captain B. Barry, mate under Captain Absolom Freeman on the *Flamingo*; later became captain of the *Celestial Empire*.

Dr. C.F. Newcombe shows Barry Island as LUOKGWAI on his map.

On the shoreline of Graham Island, east of Barry Island, is a large cave, the entrance of which is estimated to be about 100 feet high with a second entrance about 40 feet high. "A nice beach extends well into the cave," says Gray Hill, "and also in this cave is a bridge of cormorant nests. Huge waves have taken driftwood logs an incredible distance inside . . . probably by one of the earthquake-generated tidal waves."

*CELESTIAL BLUFF — on the north side of the entrance to Port Chanal. The old name for this was BLUFF POINT, a name duplicated many times for coastal features. The name Celestial Bluff was suggested by the Hydrographic Service and confirmed by the Permanent Names Committee in 1946. It is after the 121-foot iron steam trawler *Celestial Empire* owned by the Canadian Fishing Company. Originally a North Sea trawler which had been built at Hull, she was brought to British Columbia by the Canadian Fishing Company for their halibut banks operation. Later owned by Captain B.L. "Barney" Jones and called the *Cape Scott*, she was eventually sold to Pacific Coyle Navigation.

*CAMERON RANGE — lies along the north side of Port Chanal. A conspicuous range of mountains with a height of about 2,595 feet on the bare western part and decreasing to 2,000 feet as it runs to the east. It was the east section which Chittenden in 1884 named GREEN MOUNTAIN, a name never used other than in his report.

*PORT CHANAL — the AT-LOO INLET of the Haidas, was given the name it now bears, Port Chanal, by Captain Etienne Marchand, master of the French ship, *La Solide*. He named it in 1791 after his second-in-command, Captain Prosper Chanal. Captain Chanal was a retired French naval officer who had also been a hydrographic surveyor when he signed on for the round-the-world voyage of *La Solide*. It was Chanal who, accompanied by Louis Marchand, brother of the *Solide's* captain, made a survey along the west coast of Graham Island from Parry Passage to Hippa Island and produced the first accurate charts of these waters.

Like the rest of the west coast, the seas off this region can be fierce, making Port Chanal a welcome harbour for vessels caught in a gale. It can also be hazardous to enter these narrow-necked inlets in huge seas, the giant rollers crashing shoreward, sheeting off rocks, spuming and shooting out in all directions.

In the fall of 1884 Newton Chittenden was in the perilous position of having to press onward to meet a deadline, an extremely dangerous situation on the west coast. September gales were beginning, his rations getting low, yet his task of exploring the Charlottes for the Government had not been completed. Having lain at Frederick Island for several hours waiting for the seas to run down, an impatient Chittenden decided he could wait no longer.

The little canoe was launched and as it rounded the first point immediately wallowed in the midst of gigantic rollers. "Turn back," he was implored by the rest of the party. "Turn back! My God! Look at the distance we must go. We can't possibly make it!" Chittenden refused. They would go to Port Chanal he told them. Perhaps it was stormy, but their craft was designed for this. The others were appalled. One man, Ben Melin, who had sailed both the Pacific and Atlantic Oceans for 13 years, said such a small boat couldn't possibly outlive such seas, now rolling in like mountains. Bill, a young Skidegate Haida who had seen his fair share of wild weather, agreed. They would all be drowned.

Seas swept the small canoe from stem to stern but, like her master, she kept doggedly on. Nearing Port Chanal the whole shoreline seemed to be a foaming

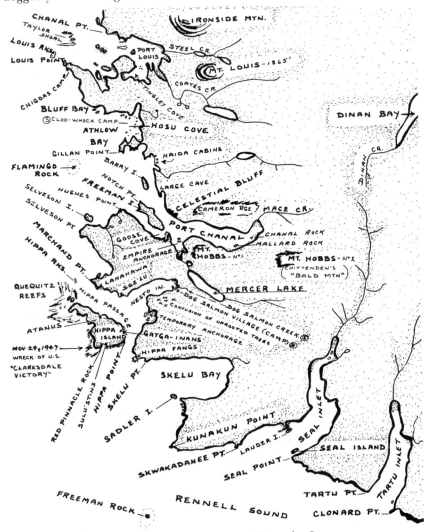

All names supplied by Mr. Charles A. Smith are shown on this map by ⑤ .

line of breakers. A northwest wind howled around them. Suddenly Bill motioned to Chittenden. There! Between two huge rocks a relatively quiet place appeared, quiet long enough, perhaps, for them to get through. "Bill stripped off his clothes and I, hanging on to the tiller, managed to get some of mine off," said Chittenden later. Then with more good luck than skill they sailed through on the crest of a big breaker, hit the opening square on and were through. "Just when we thought we were in safe waters," said Chittenden, "an unobserved cross-breaker hit us broadside, dashing us violently onto a rock. The naked Bill dove over and I followed him." By a superhuman effort, born of stark necessity, the two somehow squeezed between the rock and canoe and pushed it off, saving it from certain destruction as two succeeding breakers dashed in heavily and surged them towards land. Throwing gear ashore to lighten the craft it was "all hands to pull her high on the rocks."

"To our amazement the only injury she had sustained," wrote Chittenden, "was a 3-foot split above the waterline." But disaster had come too close - even for Chittenden. There would be no more travelling that day.

They noticed a large cave nearby so, instead of putting up a tent, the exhausted men decided to use the natural rock shelter. Wearily they lit a fire, dried their blankets and turned in. Someone did say he wondered if the storm might drive the tide high enough to enter - but this idea was pooh-poohed. A few hours later every man jack of them was rudely jolted from a dead sleep by the sound of waves washing against the mouth of the cave. Knocking their skulls against rocky walls and roof they fled in desperate haste grabbing supplies and belongings and clambered over rocks at the base of a high precipice. No beach to walk on. Pitch dark and a howling wind driving the rain like demons, the dog-tired party would long remember the day they arrived in At-loo. (Port Chanal) They had taken refuge in a rockbound bay on the south shore of Port Chanal but soon moved to a more comfortable camp from which Chittenden fully explored the inlet and named many features. None of the names were subsequently adopted.

*MACE CREEK — flows into the head of Port Chanal. When Chittenden visited it, the Haidas with him called the river AT-LOO, whereupon Chittenden anglicized this to ATHLOW RIVER. It is not known when or why it was named Mace Creek.

*CHANAL ROCK — named in association with Port Chanal is about ¾ of a mile from the head of the inlet. About 4 feet high, it has other drying rocks nearby.

*MALLARD ROCK — lying to the west of Chanal Rock. On Captain Musgrave's 1914 chart this 6-foot-high rock was shown as MALLARD ISLAND.

*MOUNT HOBBS — on the south side of Port Chanal, is a name which has apparently been applied to two separate peaks. Some maps show it near Empire Anchorage with heights given varyingly from 800 to 1100 feet. Other maps show it farther to the east, roughly south of the head of Port Chanal and give heights for it from 2,350 to 2,850 feet. In this latter position it is described as having a bare summit and, as such, is the mountain which Chittenden in 1884 named BALD MOUNTAIN.

*MERCER LAKE — about 2 miles long, drains into Empire Anchorage. Named after Dr. George Mercer Dawson during the hydrographic survey about 1914. This was the lake Chittenden called SOOK LAKE after a word the Haidas used for it.

*EMPIRE ANCHORAGE — on the south shore of Port Chanal. Formerly called EMPIRE HARBOUR by Captain Absolom Freeman who named it in 1912 after the *Celestial Empire*, one of the Canadian Fishing Company trawlers. (See Celestial Bluff)

*GOOSE COVE — to the west of Empire Anchorage, from which it is separated by a fingerlike rocky point. The name dates back to the 1920s.

*FREEMAN ISLAND — lies at the entrance to Port Chanal. In 1884 Chittenden said of it, "this island so thoroughly protects the inner waters of the inlet from westerly storms, that I have called it PROTECTION ISLAND," In later years it was named after Captain Absolom Freeman.

Absolom Freeman was born at Champneys, Newfoundland, in 1867 - the son of Sprague and Mary Freeman. He was only 11 years old when he went to sea, first off the coast of Labrador then later on the Grand Banks. In 1890 the 23-year-old man, then a veteran fisherman, came to British Columbia. Freeman organized the original Canadian Fishing Company, first called the New England Fishing Company, and during his years with this organization he captained the *New England, Flamingo* and *Celestial Empire*. He is credited with the introduction of otter-trawling in B.C. His carefully prepared notes and collection of navigational data concerning the little-known west coast of the Charlottes were made into reports so accurate that they were recognized and utilized by the Marine Department in Ottawa.

Captain Freeman died in March 1930 in his 63rd year after an illness of two years.

*NOTCH POINT — at the north end of Freeman Island was named by the Hydrographic Service for the shape of the feature. There are shoals and a drying rock off this point.

*HUGHES POINT — to the southwest of Notch Point, is on Graham Island. Captain Harry S. Hughes was the third captain to take command of the lighthouse vessel *Estevan*. It is not known who applied the name to this point, but it dates back to at least 1916, when it was shown on Captain Freeman's charts. Abrupt and precipitous, Hughes Point has a cluster of small lakes inland from it and two drying rocks lie close off its base.

*SELVESON POINT — is the southwest entrance point to Athlow Bay. The name appeared on Captain Freeman's charts of 1912 to 1916.

*SELVESON ISLAND — lies a short distance to the northeast of Selveson Point and was named in this association by the Hydrographic Service in 1946. It is a small wooded island with a rock which dries at 13 feet to the northwest; a great deal of kelp surrounds this rock.

*MARCHAND POINT — at the east side of the north entrance to Hippa Passage. Chittenden's Haida guides in 1884 called the point SKOOT-KOON. Dr. C.F. Newcombe a few years later showed it similarly as SKU'TKUN on his map. The Hydrographic Service named the point after Captain Etienne Marchand, master of the French ship *La Solide* which visited the Charlottes in 1791 in the course of a round-the-world voyage. This name was confirmed by the Permanent Names Committee in 1946.[1]

[1]See also Solide Passage; Port Chanal.

LANAHAWA, Swampy-Village — lay in the cove to the southeast of Marchand Point and was also known by two other names; LANAHEGUNS, Town-where-there-is-a-noise-of-drums and LANAHLTUNGUA, Town-where-there-are-plenty-of-feathers. A Raven Crest site, it was occupied by people from Chaatl and another tribe which had originally come from the old Rose Spit village. The two tribes lived harmoniously for several years. Eventually a decision to move was made, some of the group migrated northward and later joined the Kaigani. The rest moved by stages southward to live again in Chaatl from where they finally joined other west coast people in a move to Skidegate Inlet.

SQE'LU VILLAGE — lay near the northwest entrance of the present Nesto Inlet. It, too, was a Raven Crest site, probably only a camp, but it was from this village that Nesto Inlet took its first name, SKA-LOO - a name later transferred to the next inlet to the south.

DOG-SALMON-VILLAGE — a Haida fishing camp at the head of the present Nesto Inlet. (C. Smith)

DOG-SALMON-CREEK — the name given by the Haidas to the creek at the head of Nesto Inlet; the Dog-Salmon-Village lay beside the creek and took its name in this association. (C. Smith) In 1884 Chittenden reported finding coal in this area.

A rock formation at one end of the beach provides a natural breakwater and trollers anchored there during bad weather. During the 1920s two enterprising ladies from Queen Charlotte City, Mrs. Sybil de Bucy and her friend Mary Sinclair, operated THE BAKERY. "The first owner was supposed to have made a fortune out there," said Mrs. De Bucy, "so when he offered to sell out for just fifteen dollars it sounded pretty good to us."

The two young women were a welcome addition to the isolated anchorage and the fishermen did all they could to make them welcome. "The fresh baked goodies went over well, but either our prices were too low, or we didn't have enough volume . . . at any rate we only just broke even," recalls Mrs. de Bucy, "then too, we did learn later that the former baker had sold some potent liquid goods as well as his baking. Perhaps that was what had made his fortune.

But it was a lot of fun. Always something going on and the days went quickly, if not profitably."

Mary Sinclair later married Bert Roberts, one of the young fishermen who had found this a good place to anchor.

*NESTO INLET — which opens to the east off Hippa Passage. Called SKALOO INLET for years, after the Haida name for the bay. Both James G. Swan and Chittenden used this name in their writings of 1883 and 1884. Years earlier in 1791 and 1792 Joseph Ingraham, in preparing his map to show Young Frederick's Island,[1] added the note, "My officers have done me the honour of naming the harbour behind the island PORT INGRAHAM after me." He also wrote that Port Ingraham was divided in two by Young Frederick's Island.

The name NESTO INLET was applied later in connection with the Haida name for Hippa Island, Nasto.

The small unnamed bay southwest of the entrance to Nesto Inlet is occasionally used by boats as a temporary anchorage. Inland from this bay is a curious confusion of uprooted and demolished trees. "Very extensive," says Gray Hill, "even the rocks are split asunder . . . the result of an earthquake perhaps. Whatever it was, it appears to have been stupendous." Geologists say this was the region of an earthquake epicentre on February 27, 1948, which measured 6½ on the Richter scale. The estimated epicentre was placed offshore from Hippa Island.

[1]See Frederick Island. Ingraham named Hippa Island after his nephew, Frederick. Captain Vancouver changed this, moving Frederick's name to the island north of Hippa.

*HIPPA PASSAGE — separates Hippa Island from Graham Island. Named in association with Hippa Island by the Hydrographic Service. The first white man known to have sailed through part of this channel was Captain Prosper Chanal, who hoped to make a close examination in August 1791. But a combination of strong tide and wind drove his longboat violently back to the southward. The sight of the *Solide* standing offshore to pick him up ended his plans to try again.

*HIPPA ROCKS — lie in the middle of the north entrance to Hippa Passage and consist of 2 rocks, one 31 feet high and the other about 20 feet. They are surrounded by reefs and sunken rocks and take their name from Hippa Island.

*QUEQUITZ REEFS — which lie off the northwest and western extremities of Hippa Island, take their name from the old Haida reference which meant they were sea-otter-reefs. Dr. J.R. Swanton in his book *The Haida* spells this name Qogi'ts.

*HIPPA ISLAND — lying off Nesto Inlet takes its name from the original HIPPAH applied to the island by Captain George Dixon, July 1787. The Haida name for the island was Nesto or NESTOW. It meant impregnable. Dixon's choice of name came from the strong resemblance of Haida habitations he saw from offshore to the hippah's of the New Zealanders.

The ham-shaped island is steeped in Haida legends. Every rock and reef held an ocean spirit. One particular reef at the outer end of Hippa, which has a small tree upon it, would return a small variety of whale to the supplicants when offerings were made.

As Europeans began to visit the Charlottes, Hippa received its share of naming and renaming. In 1791-92 Joseph Ingraham called it YOUNG FREDERICK'S ISLAND after his nephew. Shortly afterwards Captain Vancouver, in 1793, changed the name back to Hippa and put young Frederick's name on the island to the north. In 1794 Lieutenant Henry Roberts prepared a coastal map and is said to have called Hippa Island MARSHALL ISLAND.

During World War II there was a small radar station on the northwest corner of Hippa similar in size to the one at Frederick Island.

On November 24, 1947, its close association with the sea brought Hippa Island into tragic headlines when the United States transport *Clarksdale Victory* slammed onto the rocks off its southwest corner.

Remains of the Clarksdale Victory, wrecked on the southwest shore of Hippa Island, November 24, 1947.

Photo - G. Gray Hill

The vessel, some 500 feet long, was south-bound after having discharged cargo in Alaska. Her course was set at about 25 miles offshore. In the blackness of night it was not realized that a strong current drift inshore, coupled with heavy winds, had drastically altered her position. Captain Gerald Laugesen going on deck to peer into the inky night, suddenly sensed the alarming proximity of land - too close. "Change course! Immediately!" came his urgent command. But it was too late. Seconds after with a great shuddering crash his ship drove hard aground - bow on. Her stern, however, still floated free. "Full astern!" came the desperate order. The engines went into a mighty reverse which violently shook the whole vessel. It was no good. She was too firmly wedged on whatever she had struck.

69

The seas were mountainous now as they tore over the stricken ship.

An SOS flashed out, but the nearest ship to answer was a full 13 hours away. The dreadful seas, the darkness, the possibility of unknown hazards between ship and the invisible shoreline made abandonment of the vessel at that stage too dangerous. The entire ship's complement of 53 men mustered on deck to wait for daylight.

Third Mate Bill Rasmussen, 21 years old at the time, had been on duty when the ship drove ashore and remembers the awful vigil of grimly hanging on. The wild ocean washed over the boat crashing against the funnels and super-structure with fury. Then, taking all manner of debris and oil, swept seaward again, surging over the men. "You hung onto anything you could, and you hung onto the guy beside you when he lost his grip. Next time he probably grabbed you . . . most of the time you didn't even know who was beside you." There was no panic he recalls, but - as it is in most times of extreme human peril - there was unbelievable heroism as each man struggled to help the other.

The ship took a mortal pounding and some time through that terrible night broke in two. The men were swept into the sea. Many of the crew by then were badly injured from the battering during the long wait. All were numb with cold and strain. Out of a total of 53 men only 5 made it safely to shore; three mates - Henry Wolfe, Claire Driscoll and Bill Rasmussen, and two seamen - Carlos Sanabria and Peter Roman. Owing to the size of the waves it was 3 days before the survivors could be rescued by the Coast Guard vessel from Alaska. During the 3-day wait Peter Roman died.

On their trips along the west coast of the Charlottes Neil and Betty Carey, of Sandspit, went to look at the remaining portion of the *Clarksdale Victory* on Hippa. Betty, deeply moved by the tragedy, found that little information was available and began a patient research into the story. In the course of her study she learned of Bill Rasmussen. Through her correspondence with him Mr. Rasmussen was drawn, perhaps by an inexplicable need to settle old ghosts, to the idea of revisiting the scene of the old wreck. In August 1971, with his wife Annette, Bill Rasmussen made his pilgrimage.

As Betty Carey accompanied them to isolated Hippa memories of the tragedy flooded the conversation. "I think the most unexpected things emerged," said Betty, "such as because Bill, having been on duty when the ship struck, was fully clothed. Realizing that Henry Wolfe had come ashore clad only in pyjamas and robe, Bill gave the older man his jacket. How the men with numbed fingers struggled to get the frozen legs of Wolfe into the arms of Bill's jacket then, somehow, zip up the front . . . and the sleet coming in around the waist . . ."

"The wreck is much bigger than it appears from seaward," says Gray Hill who took the photos shown herein. "It rests on a shelf which has caused it to roll over, with port side inshore. It is hard to believe but until recently the boatswain's locker was still intact, saved from souvenir hunters because of its isolated position." And so the *Clarksdale Victory* rests forever, perhaps, a grave-marker for the 49 men who lost their lives on a strange and lonely shore.

To take the photos Gray Hill anchored his own vessel off the red pinnacle rock near the west end of the south shore of Hippa Island and was surprised to find that the indentations to the west were lined with a growth of sponges.

There are known to have been three Haida villages or encampments on this island. All were Eagle Crest sites.

SULUSTINS — reported to have been close to the pinnacle rock described above. Another name for it was SKAO NANS.

GATGA-INANS — lay on the east shore of Hippa. Chief He-is-the-greatest was the head man. There is some speculation that Gatga-inans may also have been the former site of Sulustins.

ATANUS, Bilge-water-town — stood on the northeast shore, about mid-way along.

The big earthquake centered close to Hippa Island in February of 1948, caused many changes in the shoreline from the time the Haidas knew it. Mr. Rasmussen commented that he had seen it in November 1947 prior to the upheaval, and in 1971 found the region greatly contorted from what it had been previously.

*HIPPA POINT — the southeast extremity of Hippa Island. Named by the Hydrographic Service in association with the island.

HIPPA FANGS — a local name for the pinnacle rocks which lie immediately north of Skelu Point. They were given the name by Fisheries Officer Howard Fairbairn, of Queen Charlotte City, who thought they were much too distinctive to be noted on the chart merely as "conspicuous rock pinnacle."

*SKELU BAY — the large indentation southeast of Hippa Island. It has been written variously as SKALU INLET and SKALOO BAY. The old Haida name for the present Nesto Inlet, to the north, was Ska-loo. When that inlet was renamed for its association with Nesto (Hippa) Island, the name of Skelu was used to designate this larger bay to the south. It is still completely uncharted. The old Haida name for the bay was HL'KIEU.

*SKELU POINT — the northwest entrance point to Skelu Bay. Named in association with the bay by the Hydrographic Service in 1946.

*SADLER ISLAND — at the south entrance to Skelu Bay. Named for John Sadler, the carpenter on George Dixon's *Queen Charlotte* in 1787. The wave-eroded rocks of Sadler Island testify graphically to the raging storms which beat in during the winter.

*KUNAKUN POINT — south of Sadler Island, is the northwest entrance to Rennell Sound. It is a modification of the Haida name for this point. Haida legends tell of a great ocean spirit which dwelt under Kunakun Point - similar to a powerful one which lived under Nesto (Hippa) Island. They often held rival potlatches, and thunderous was the noise which resulted.

*FREEMAN ROCK — about 2¼ miles southwest of Kunakun Point, has seas breaking over it occasionally. Named after Captain Absolom Freeman, founder of the Canadian Fishing Company, and who charted much of the west coast from 1912 to 1916.[1]

[1]See also Freeman Island.

*SKWAKADANEE POINT — the north entrance point to Seal Inlet is a modification of a Haida name meaning point-of-heavy-seas; an appropriate name for most of these exposed west coast points.

*LAUDER ISLAND — off the north shore near the mouth of Seal Inlet. Named after Dr. William Lauder, surgeon aboard George Dixon's *Queen Charlotte* in 1787. Lauder Island is 180 feet high and is connected to a peninsula off Graham Island by a series of islets and rocks. These form a natural breakwater for the sand beaches on either side of the peninsula, and has proved to be a lucrative spot for beachcombing treasures. There are rocks straggling off Lauder Island for about 2,000 feet to the southwest.

Wave erosion on Sadler Island, off west coast of Graham Island.

Photo - G. Gray Hill.

*SEAL INLET — opens off the north side at the entrance to Rennell Sound. Named by Newton Chittenden in 1884 and is perhaps remarkable for being the only one of the numerous names Chittenden applied to the Charlottes to have been adopted by the government. Chittenden named the inlet after seeing hundreds of hair seals on an island off the south shore near the entrance. He reported that the Haidas with him called the inlet KUNG-WA.

The creek draining into the head of Seal Inlet has branches which run inland almost to the headwaters of Dinan Creek, which drains into Dinan Bay, Masset Inlet. In ancient years a trail led from Seal Inlet to Dinan Bay, along the valleys of these creeks. During the 1913-14 geological survey conducted by J.D. Mackenzie, Mr. Dolmage, a member of the party made a reconnaissance traverse over the trail from Dinan Bay to Seal Inlet and estimated the distance to be about 10 miles. Hikers attempting to use the trail in recent years report that it has become badly overgrown.

SEAL ISLAND — off the south shore of Seal Inlet, near the entrance. It had numerous seals on it when Newton Chittenden visited in 1884. He named it Seal Island. Mariners say the seals still favour this island.

*SEAL POINT — the south entrance point to Seal Inlet and named by the Hydrographic Service in association with the inlet. Dr. C.F. Newcombe called it T'US on his Haida names map.

*TARTU POINT — northwest entrance point of Tartu Inlet and named in this association by the Hydrographic Service. The rock formation at Tartu Point has a face-like silhouette when viewed from one angle - causing it to receive the local name CHIEF OF TARTU.

*TARTU INLET — opening off the north side of the entrance of Rennell Sound is about 4 miles long and has two good salmon streams at its upper end. One flows on to the beach about 3 miles from the entrance on the east side, and the other runs into the head of the inlet. The name Tartu is a modification of the original Haida name, and was shown on earlier maps as Tartoo and also Tattoo. A small low island in this inlet is a favourite place for hair seals to congregate, much as they do on Seal Island.

*CLONARD POINT — near the south entrance point of Tartu Inlet. The name applied by the Hydrographic Service in 1946 in association with the former name for Rennell Sound - *Baie de Clonard*, applied by Laperouse in 1786. Clonard was one of Laperouse's officers.

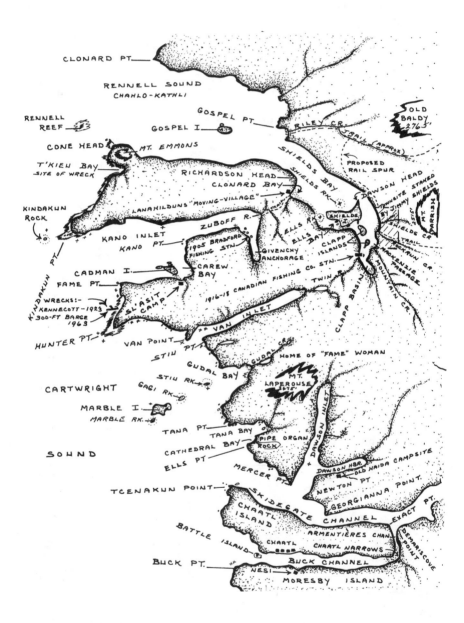

CLONARD PT.

RENNELL SOUND
CHAHLO-KATHLI

GOSPEL PT.
RILEY CR.

OLD
BALDY,
2765,

RENNELL
REEF

GOSPEL I.

TRAIL (APPROX)

PROPOSED
RAIL SPUR

CONE HEAD
MT. EMMONS

SHIELDS BAY

T'KIEU BAY
SITE OF WRECK

RICHARDSON HEAD

SHIELDS RK.

DAWSON HEAD

TOWNSITE STAKED
BY JIMMY SHIELDS

CLONARD BAY

KINDAKUN
ROCK

LANAHILDUNS "MOVING-VILLAGE"

SHIELDS CR.

SHIELDS.

ELLS R.

MT. CARRICK

KANO INLET

ZUBOFF R.

KANO PT.

1905 BRADFORD
FISHING STN.

ELLS
BAY

CLAPP
ISLANDS

SHIELDS CR.

OCHUN CR.

CADMAN I.

CAREW
BAY

GIVENCHY
ANCHORAGE

MACKENZIE
PASSAGE

KINDAKUN PT.

FAME PT.

1916-18 CANADIAN FISHING CO. STN.

TWIN

MOUNTAIN CR.

KINDAKUN WRECKS:-
KENNECOTT - 1923
300-FT BARGE
1963

SL'ASIT
CAMP.

VAN INLET

CLAPP BASIN

HUNTER PT.

VAN POINT

STIU PT.

GUDAL CR.

HOME OF "FAME" WOMAN

STIU PT.

GUDAL BAY

CARTWRIGHT

STIU RK.

GAGI RK.

MT.
LAPEROUSE

DAWSON INLET

MARBLE I.

MARBLE RK.

SOUND

TANA PT.

TANA BAY

CATHEDRAL BAY

PIPE ORGAN
ROCK

ELLS PT.

MERCER PT.

DAWSON HBR.

OLD HAIDA CAMPSITE

NEWTON PT.

GEORGIANNA POINT.

TCENAKUN POINT

SKIDEGATE CHANNEL

EXACT PT.

CHAATL
ISLAND

ARMENTIÈRES CHAN.

DEMARISCOVE
POINT

BATTLE ISLAND

CHAATL

CHAATL NARROWS

BUCK PT.

NESI

BUCK CHANNEL

MORESBY ISLAND

74

SOUTHWEST COAST OF GRAHAM ISLAND;
FROM RENNELL SOUND TO BUCK CHANNEL.

CHAPTER FOUR

*RENNELL SOUND — the largest inlet on the west coast of Graham Island. From Kunakun Point on the north to Kindakun Point on the south, the entrance waters of Rennell Sound are about 10¼ miles across, and it runs inland for 18 to 20 miles. The physical features of its approach render it more easily identified than most of the other sounds and inlets along this coast.

On August 14, 1786, Laperouse gave the sound its first European name, *Baie de Clonard*, after one of the officers on his ship. In July of the following year George Dixon on the *Queen Charlotte* renamed it Rennell's Sound after John Rennell, a geographer and naval man. Dixon's naming was adopted by Captain Vancouver in 1793. The Haidas called it CHALO-KATHLI.

"I think it was the variety of drift on the beaches of Rennell Sound which astounded me most of all," says Mr. C.G. Dunham, now of West Vancouver. "I went up in 1923 to cruise timber. I remember finding a collection of small dried up sea horses, and a short distance from this, a palm tree. Further along . . . cocoanuts. And almost every kind of driftwood you could name. It struck me as so curious I've never forgotten it."

There were no government charts available for Mr. Dunham's purpose, "only Captain Freeman's sketch map. Not really very true as to scale, but all the rocks, coves and points were there . . . and unmistakable," he says.

Under the direction of Mr. H.D. Parizeau an excellent hydrographic chart was prepared in 1935-36 showing in detail the entire region of Rennell Sound from its entrance to Clapp Basin at its head.

The wooded shores of the big inlet are backed by mountains rising to high peaks. Several natural stone bridges and caves have been discovered on its north edges, testifying to the fierce pounding of seas during a strong westerly all along this vicinity.

*RENNELL REEF — at the entrance to Rennell Sound. First shown as ENTRANCE REEF on the sketch map prepared by Captain Holmes Newcombe when he sailed the west coast in the 1920s in the course of his duties as Fisheries Protection Officer. Renamed by the Hydrographic Service owing to duplications of that name. Rennell Reef consists of a rock which dries at 5 feet and 3 submerged rocks close by.

*GOSPEL ISLAND — lying in the middle of Rennell Sound, is a wooded island rising to 180 feet with a straggle of rocks off its north side. First shown under this name on a chart prepared by Captain Absolom Freeman 1912-16 and officially confirmed by the Permanent Names Committee in 1946.

Mr. Henri D. Parizeau, hydrographic surveyor

Photo - Agnes Mathers.

Mr. C.D. Emmons, the beloved geologist of the Charlottes. Emmons, with beard, and his crew improvise transportation to cross Yakoun Lake.

Photo - Dorothy Richardson.

*GOSPEL POINT — on the north shore of Rennell Sound, is 2 miles east of Gospel Island and was named in this association by the Hydrographic Service in 1946. On the north side of the point, which is steepto, lies an unnamed bight containing two sandy coves with fair-sized creeks running into the head of each. Midway between the two coves is the *Gospel Mineral Claim* with showings of iron and antimony.

On the south side of Gospel Point is another unnamed bay. Riley Creek enters the head of this bay. All this shoreline takes a terrific pounding from heavy seas during westerly gales.

*RILEY CREEK — empties into an unnamed bay close southward of Gospel Point. Named after the engineer who surveyed the proposed railway route to the west coast of Graham Island. The main line was to run from Skidegate Inlet to Masset Inlet through the coal-fields, with a spur line out through Yakoun Pass to Rennell Sound.

"Riley was a short, chunky man and a going concern," says Charlie Hartie of Queen Charlotte City. "Unfortunately he came to the Charlottes rather late in the season and all the best men had already found jobs. He was left with no choice but the raggedty-tags. He daren't take his eyes off them or they would be resting and at the drop of a hat would leave - heading for town (Queen Charlotte City) to spend the few dollars earned. Riley would let most of them go. No loss. But the better ones . . . he would have to come in and round them all up and once again begin his survey. Luckily he did have a couple of good men or the situation would have been impossible."

A trail ran in along Riley Creek, crossed over to Phantom Creek and joined the network of trails in the Yakoun Valley. During World War I an antimony find was made on Riley Creek, but little done about it. In 1942 Mr. V. Courte staked 18 claims in the region - which are now known as the *Courte Antimony Claim*.

YAKOUN PASS — the name given locally to the proposed route of the railway spur to Rennell Sound. Expected to carry coal from the Wilson Creek mine, the railway would have left the main Yakoun Valley line at Ghost Creek, whose valley it would follow to its headwaters in a small muskeg - also the headwaters of Riley Creek. From this point it would follow Riley Creek to within about 4 miles of the mouth, at which point it would turn southwestward to emerge in Shields Bay near Shields Island. Mr. Hartie recalls walking the old route over 50 years ago. "I went in to see C.D. Emmons," he says. "Emmons had quite a crew in there one summer clearing trails and building a cabin when he was staking out oil shale in that region."

*OLD BALDY — a 2,765-foot mountain which overlooks Riley Creek and the old Yakoun Pass region. This mountain was named by the Hydrographic Service in 1945 after Lieutenant C.M. Flowerdew, V.C., who won his award March 30, 1918, near Bois de Moreuil.

*SHIELDS BAY — near the head of Rennell Sound and

*SHIELDS ISLAND — in Shields Bay, were named in 1885 by William Robertson for Jimmy Shields, the little ex-sealer, who had accompanied him from Victoria that year to prospect for coal on the Charlottes. Shields staked out a proposed townsite on the present Lots 30 and 31 in connection with their coal mining dream. The lots fronted on water well-protected by Shields Island - a fine harbour for the ships to anchor while loading coal.

Unknown to both Shields and Robertson another traveller, Newton Chittenden, the previous year, 1884, had called Shields Island EDWARD ISLAND. In the mid-1920s Captain Holmes Newcombe of the Fisheries Protection Branch named Shields Island CROSS ISLAND. Neither of the other names was used, apparently.

Shields Island is connected to Graham Island by a drying reef. It is also connected in the same manner to the most northerly of the Clapp Islands, resulting in the formation of a shallow lagoon off its south end.

*SHIELDS ROCK — which dries at 14 feet is off the north side of Shields Island and was named in this association by the Hydrographic Service.

*SHIELDS CREEK — enters Shields Bay through a portion of Jimmy's townsite plan. First shown as WILSON CREEK on early day maps, this was changed after a short time to avoid confusion with the other Wilson Creek - site of the coal discovery in the Yakoun Valley. This was not the only townsite venture Jimmy Shields was connected with for in 1889 he and James R. McKenzie bought a goodly part of what is now the eastern portion of Queen Charlotte City. They were Crown Granted Lots 15 and 15A, a total of 353 acres - for which they paid one dollar per acre. At that time Skidegate Landing was the metropolis and any expansion of the place would logically take place on these lots.

*DAWSON HEAD — on the northeast corner of Shields Island. Named after Dr. George M. Dawson who wrote a meticulous and comprehensive report following his visit to the Charlottes in 1878.[1]

[1]See also Dawson Harbour, Inlet, Islands, Point and Bay.

*ROCKRUN CREEK — enters Shields Bay south of Shields Creek. At one time shown as Rockrun River. In early years a well-used trail went in along this creek to take hikers to Yakoun Lake.

*MOUNT PARRISH — overlooks both Shields and Rockrun Creeks and is about 2,515 feet high. Named after Mr. H.E. Parrish, the civil and mining engineer who opened up the Camp Robertson coal vein for its discoverer, W.A. Robertson. Mr. Parrish also worked on the Camp Anthracite and Camp Wilson coal seams doing assessments.

*MACKENZIE PASSAGE — separates the southern Clapp Island from Graham Island. Named by the Hydrographic Service in 1948 after James D. MacKenzie who conducted a geological survey of Graham Island in 1913 and 1914 and wrote a book about it, *Geology of Graham Island*. Mr. MacKenzie was held in very high esteem by all those who worked for him. He named many of the creeks and lakes in the Yakoun Valley.[1]

[1]See also Mackenzie Cove, Island and Bay.

*MOUNTAIN CREEK — flows into the south end of MacKenzie Passage and was formerly called Mountain River.

*CLAPP BASIN — the extreme head of Rennell Sound. Shown as RENNELL HARBOUR by Captain Absolom Freeman, who called the outer part of the big inlet only, Rennell Sound. In 1948 the name of Clapp Basin was confirmed by the Permanent Names Committee. It is after Dr. C.H. Clapp who made a short geological reconnaissance of part of Graham Island in 1912. His report of this trip made evident the necessity for further and more detailed study, thus James D. MacKenzie was detailed in 1913 to undertake the project.

*CLAPP ISLANDS — named in association with Clapp Basin, extend from the south end of Shields Island and consist of four main islands. The largest of the Clapp Islands was called CYPRESS ISLAND by Newton Chittenden in 1884, " . . . from having seen a considerable amount of yellow cedar growing thereon," he wrote on page 40 of his report.

*TWIN RIVER — enters Clapp Basin from the west. The mouth of the river is opposite a small island near the head of Clapp Basin. In 1916-17 the Canadian Fishing Company built a fishing station on the north side of the mouth of Twin River. A wharf 90 feet long was erected with a roof over most of its length, and was intended as a collection point. Fish caught by small boats were to be kept on ice there until the large packers could transport it to the mainland. The station was only used for two seasons then abandoned.

Part of the old shed still stood there when Mr. C.G. Dunham of West Vancouver paid a visit in 1923 during a timber cruising trip. "On one of the doors left intact," he said, "was a coat-of-arms with a double eagle painted in black. Under this was the name of a German under-officer and beneath that, in German, the equivalent of 'died for the Fatherland.' No one I talked to knew anything about it."

*ELLS BAY — separating Shields Island from Graham Island, off the west side of Shields Island, and

*ELLS ROCK — at the entrance to Ells Bay were both named after Dr. R.W. Ells who, in 1905, made a geological survey of part of Graham Island. "We used a Columbia River fishing boat, 25 feet long, with a 7-foot beam," he wrote. "It had a centreboard, mainsail, jib and 4 oars. We were unable to obtain a pilot familiar with the west coast waters we planned to sail through, so considerable anxiety was felt on the trip. Safe shelter had to be sought each night, making progress exasperatingly slow." Nevertheless they did safely navigate Skidegate Channel to the west coast, from which point they travelled to the north end of Graham Island and east as far as Masset.

At Masset the party divided, some went overland along the Yakoun Valley to return to Skidegate. The rest sailed out along the north beach, then south along the east coast. Storms forced them to take refuge for 10 days at Tow Hill. When they finally left they had a hair-raising trip around Rose Spit. "The most dangerous place navigationally, on the whole island," said Ells afterwards, despite his hazardous trip along the west coast a short time earlier.

*CLONARD BAY — northwest of Shields Island. Formerly called INDIAN COVE by Captain Absolom Freeman who noted several Haida cabins at the head of the bay in 1912. Clonard Bay was suggested by the Hydrographic

Service in 1948, in remembrance of the fact that Rennell Sound had been called *Baie de Clonard* by Laperouse in 1786.

MOVING-VILLAGE, Lanahilduns — which was also called CHALO and sometimes RENNELL-TOWN, stood at the head of Clonard Bay. The Raven Crest people of this village had come from Swampy-Village near Hippa Island. Even in 1920 one of the houses still remained and was used frequently by trappers. The others had fallen down but were easily distinguishable. A trail led from Moving-Village to the northeast corner of Kano Inlet. Haidas from this village subsequently went to Chaatl, then later all families moved to Skidegate inlet.

*RICHARDSON HEAD — north of Clonard Bay is named for another geologist. (Rennell Sound holds the names of five - Clapp, Dawson, Ells, MacKenzie, Richardson and, at the mouth, a sixth, Emmons.) Richardson Head is named after James Richardson, the geologist who made a report on the coal possibilities at the Cowgitz Mine in 1874.
Named by the Hydrographic Service in 1948.

See also Richardson Inlet, Passage, Point and Bay.

*MOUNT EMMONS — overlooks Cone Head at the south entrance point to the main part of Rennell Sound. It is 1,755 feet high and has a pyramidal peak which appears symmetrical from all sides except northward. Named in 1946 by the Hydrographic Service after Mr. C.D. Emmons, probably one of the best known pioneers in all aspects of Queen Charlotte Islands prospecting.

Born in Lapeer, Michigan in 1864, he graduated from the American Institute of Mining and Metallurgical Engineering. At 19 he served in the Oregon National Guards and at 25, in 1889, went to Alaska where he became Deputy Collector of Customs for the Bering Sea area. A job he held for 5 years. Stationed at Unalaska, Emmons had little patience with mere desk work and at any excuse would take a field trip. He was the first white man to reach the Tenanah River and go onto the Glacier. Leaving Dawson, Yukon Territory, on New Year's Eve, 1897, he reached the glacier's headwaters, Tenanah River, and was back again in Dawson exactly 6 months later. Then in 1899 Mr. Emmons made a trip over the ice from Skagway to Fort Selkirk, via Dawson, and on to the headwaters of the White River and the Tenanah.

When he left Alaska in 1904 his interest was drawn to the Charlottes. For some forty years he prospected, surveyed and "geologized" from one end to the other, concentrating mainly on Graham Island. In later years his wife came to live on the Charlottes to be near him. Small and slight, like her husband, she also had another similar trait, she dearly loved to talk. When the Emmons's were visiting, there were often two conversations going at once, both of interest, and listeners would find it hard to choose between them.

*CONE HEAD — below Mount Emmons at the south entrance point to Rennell Sound proper. Named by Captain A. Freeman 1912-16 and officially adopted by the Permanent Names Committee in 1933.

80

T'KIEW BAY — the small cove south of Cone Head and Mount Emmons. A well-known name in early years and shown variously as T'Kiew, Kiu and Keyw Bay. All are modifications of the original Haida name. Two creeks flow into this rocky bight which is exposed to the full sweep of the Pacific Ocean and which has an old clearing at the head of the bay on the south side. A clearing which appears to have been man-made.

The bleached timbers of a ship, believed to have been wrecked about 1903 could be seen by mariners for years, but the inhospitable shore did not invite closer inspection even by the intrepid fishermen. Her wreckage is said to have been first sighted by a Skidegate Haida. He promptly claimed her for his own, and prepared to strip her of anything salvagable.

His claim was hotly disputed by another Skidegate Haida who said the beach belonged to him and therefore anything on it was rightfully his. So fiercely did they argue that the owner of the beach, in a fit of pique, burned the wreckage beyond any hope of reclamation - including a fine figurehead. Those who remember the incident say the name of the vessel included the word "Flora".

The fate of her survivors, if any, is still unknown at this time.

*KINDAKUN POINT — a low featureless point southwest of T'Kiew Bay, is the north entrance point to Kano Inlet. A rock ledge holding several bare and wave-swept islets projects for more than 1/3 of a mile off the point. Kelp lies all around the region warning mariners of the inherent dangers. Strong cross-currents can make the rounding of the point even more tricky. "The Haidas had a particular dread of rounding Ki'ndakun," said Dr. C.F. Newcombe who gave the point its name in 1897.

During World War II the Candian Government established a coast watcher station on the bluff above the point. Behind the log cabin used for living quarters was the "watching tree' complete with bars for the men to climb the trunk and peer out into the expanse of ocean.

When Neil and Betty Carey visited the lonely place in 1972 they found that the watching tree had fallen across the roof of the cabin, almost dead centre. "Such a low cabin," says Neil Carey, "that its occupants must have had to stoop nearly double if they were of average height." A story is told that the cabin was occupied by a very tall man who grew so unbalanced by his quarters he built a canoe and set off into the Pacific to escape the wretched place and was never seen agains. A story which varies with storytellers.

*KINDAKUN ROCK — about 2 feet high, lies 1¼ miles off the point and was named in association with the point.

*KANO INLET — a hook-shaped inlet lying to the south of Rennell Sound, takes its name from the old Haida word for the inlet. In earlier years it was also frequently called Cartwright Sound by mariners, although Cartwright Sound is the name properly given to waters farther south - off Marble Island.

Near the bend of Kano Inlet, where it takes a sharp turn to the south, a Captain Bradford established a fishing station for collecting halibut in 1905. As far as is known it was used actively for only one season. Captain Bradford owned the *Nellie G. Thurston* described under Thurston Harbour.

ZUBOFF RIVER — enters the northeast corner of Kano Inlet. Named by Chittenden in 1884 but never adopted. Chittenden and his party camped on the sandy beach near the mouth of this fair-sized stream. "We found a scene of much activity," he wrote. "Large schools of dog salmon were rushing in and out at the time of our arrival ... hundreds jumping their full length out of the water."

The trail from Clonard Bay came out near the mouth of this stream.

*GIVENCHY ANCHORAGE — at the head of Kano Inlet. Named in 1935 after the *H.M.C.S. Givenchy*, in appreciation by the Hydrographic Service of the assistance given by the officers and crew of the *Givenchy* during the surveying of inlets on the west coast of Graham Island at that time.

During World War I, the *Givenchy* served on the Atlantic as a minesweeper. In August of 1919 she began work with the Fisheries Protection Branch on the British Columbia coast and there were few bays and inlets along the coastline that were not visited at one time or another by this well-remembered ship. Her last skipper, Captain A.M. Henderson, as equally well-known as his vessel during his 30 years of service, was an invaluable man who used common sense in the dispatch of his duties without worrying unduly about the book of rules or the red tape of officialdom.

Newton Chittenden, in 1884, had named the present Givenchy Anchorage ISLET INLET, "from its having four islets near its entrance," he wrote.

*KANO POINT — is on the south shore of Kano Inlet where the inlet begins to narrow from its wide mouth. Named in association with the inlet by the Hydrographic Service. Two rocks lie off the point.

*CAREW BAY — south of Kano Point, in the wider section of Kano Inlet. Cadman Island forms the western shoreline of this bay which is named after John Ewen Carew, first mate on the *Queen Charlotte* in 1787.

SL'ASIT — a former Haida camp at the head of Carew Bay. There is a sandy beach with a fair-sized stream at the head of the bay. Several cabins have been built there over the years by Haida trappers and hunters. During the winters the tremendous winds and seas which sweep this section of the coast were so fierce the cabins blew to pieces. Waves crash over everything during the gales, say old timers who spent a night or two in misery there. The surge comes through the narrow neck of land separating Cadman Island from Graham Island with a force that is almost unbelievable.

*CADMAN ISLAND — on the west side of Carew Bay, near the entrance of Kano Inlet. Named after Richard Cadman Etches who, with other British traders under the title of The King George's Sound Company sent two ships in May 1786 to trade along the northwest Pacific coast, the *King George* commanded by Nathaniel Portlock and the *Queen Charlotte* under Captain George Dixon. It was the following year that Dixon made his historic trip along the shores of the Charlottes. The *Princess Royal* commanded by Charles Duncan, and the *Prince of Wales* under James Colnett were also associated with the same company.

Cadman Island, 380 feet high, has small islets to the north and west, and is joined at low water to Graham Island by a drying spit.

*FAME POINT — to the west of Cadman Island, is the south entrance point to Kano Inlet. Named by the Hydrographic Service in 1946. Captain George Vancouver who, in 1793, named Hunter Point, to the southwest of Fame Point, served as a lieutenant aboard the *HMS Fame* when he was stationed in the West Indies. During this time he met, and became a firm friend of, Dr. John Hunter, superintendent of military hospitals in Jamaica.

*HUNTER POINT — named after Dr. John Hunter by Captain Vancouver in 1793. It is about 2 miles south and west of Fame Point. With drying ledges and rocks, kelp-strewn shores and cross-currents, made savage when wind meets tides, it was a terror for canoes to pass in bad weather. The Haidas with Newton Chittenden in 1884 called it TSET-LA-KOON.

The rocky stretch of shoreline between Hunter Point and Fame Point was the site of two American marine losses but unlike the more tragic ones farther north - *Clarksdale Victory* and the DC-7 disaster off Langara Island - these did not take lives.

The 469-foot *Kennecott* built in Tacoma in 1919-20 did a comfortable 11 knots and carried a crew of 30. On October 9, 1923, under charter to the Alaska Steamship Company, she was under the command of Captain John A. Johnson. The ship was carrying 6,000 tons of copper and 40,000 cases of salmon from Cordova, Alaska, to Tacoma. The third officer had come on duty to find the ship surrounded by heavy fog but with his course laid out at 25 miles offshore there appeared little cause for alarm. There had been some grumbling among the ship's officers because Captain Johnson kept the charts locked in his desk, "Oh well," mused the Third," the Old Man has been on ships for over 20 years all the way from Nome to Cape Horn. He *should* know what he's doing . . ." Then, unbelievably, the vessel drove hard aground.

Not sure of exactly where they were, the first SOS sent out gave the position erroneously as being off Frederick Island. Later it was realized they were much further south, near Hunter Point. In the grounding the *Kennecott* had suffered serious damage and as swells swept over her the pounding was merciless. Fearing she might break up Captain Johnson ordered a breeches buoy rigged and all her crew reached shore safely.

Johnson felt confident that his ship could be salvaged if the tug *Algernine* could reach the site in time - the only salvage vessel that could do the job. When the *Algernine*, in rushing to the rescue, struck a rock herself and became seriously damaged it put an end to that dream. He became unnaturally despondent. An earlier loss of a ship in the Finlayson Channel region loomed as an accusation which coupled with this wreck of the *Kennecott* became factors which made him question his own worth.

He had taken command of the combination passenger and freight vessel *Ohio* for that fatal trip in August 1909 when she struck a rock near Sarah Island when bound from Seattle to Alaskan ports. Johnson had attempted to sail the stricken ship to Carter Bay and beach her, but she foundered in less than 40 minutes in 5 fathoms of water. Five passengers were drowned. His handling of the accident had been greatly praised, but he brooded over the event for some time.

The loss of the *Kennecott* brought it all back. During the trip back to Victoria on the rescue ship the 60-year-old captain ended his life by leaping into the sea. The place he is believed to have chosen was near the site of the first ship wrecked under his command.

In her exposed position *Kennecott* shifted several times as gales drove her further inshore, then she broke in two, and over the years disintegrated. Her copper cargo became a prime target for salvage hunters in the next few years and several operations were moderately successful before she finally went to the bottom. Even today the shores in the area have a strong rusty stain - now becoming green. Divers who have been down to size up salvage prospects in recent years say that the cargo is scattered all over the bottom of the sea. Too risky to recover.

Forty years later, almost to the day, on October 16, 1963, the tug *Winquattwas* towing a 300-foot barge from Alaska to the Columbia River, ran into a storm producing waves of 35 feet or more. The $1,600,000 barge, considered at that time to be one of the largest in the world, was partially loaded with construction equipment valued at $200,000. Winds were gusting to an estimated 80 miles an hour when the barge broke loose from the tug and, swept shoreward, crashed onto the rocks at almost the same place as the *Kennecott* had come to grief. For a week or more four tugs, which had been sent to attempt a salvage, stood by in Kano Inlet as the storm raged. At last it was realized that nothing could be done and they were recalled. The *Winquattwas* reached port safely with all hands.

This rocky bay which claimed two U.S. cargoes is a catch-all for other wave-flung objects. It was here that the two seal-hunters, Don and Bill McNaughton of Pender Harbour, found a large Japanese wartime mine on the beach in the mid 1960s.

*CARTWRIGHT SOUND — includes the waters between Hunter Point and the northwestern point of Chaatl Island according to the B.C. Pilot. The sound received its name on September 25, 1793 from Captain George Vancouver, who named it after John Cartwright. Cartwright served in the British Navy under Admiral Howe and later became a noted political reformer in England.

*VAN INLET — which runs straight inland for about 5 miles appeared on Captain Absolom Freeman's charts of 1912-16 as VAN HARBOUR. The Haida name for it was KI-OW according to Newton Chittenden in 1884. Dr. C.F. Newcombe thought it sounded more like XI'AO. The origin of the name Van is not known, but several suggestions include that of an abbreviation for Vancouver.

Although the entrance to the inlet is strewn with rocks and shallows, navigational instructions advise that small vessels can obtain anchorage off a flat at the head of Van Inlet . "But with the wind in the right direction," say mariners, "Van Inlet becomes a horror. It draws down the full length, with high land on either side to assist it to funnel. Well, there you are and *there* you stay, cursing the idea of ever coming in."

There is a stream running into the head of this inlet which drains a series of three small lakes. Other streams with cataracts tumble down the steep mountainous terrain fringing the shoreline of the inlet.

The *Northwester Mineral Claim* is at the head of Van Inlet. An iron-copper deposit, it was first discovered in 1928 by George McRae and Archie Duval, Queen Charlotte City pioneers. Through the years the showings have been held intermittently by variously located claims. In 1962 Mastodon-Highland Bell Mines held 11 claims and carried out a series of tests to explore the possibilities of the area.

*VAN POINT — the north entrance point of Van Inlet. Named by the Hydrographic Service in 1946 in association with the Inlet. It was at this time the name Van Harbour was changed to Van Inlet.

*STIU POINT — the south entrance point of Van Inlet. Named in 1946 by the Hydrographic Service.

*STIU ROCK — about 2 miles south of Stiu Point, is a 68-foot-high islet. The name was applied on Dr. C.F. Newcombe's sketch maps of 1897 and is a modification of the Haida name. Officially adopted to the charts in 1946.

*GUDAL BAY — due east of Stiu Rock, is another Haida name which has been adopted to the chart. Always a favorite camping site, in 1884 when Chittenden visited he reported, "It has a beach of finest sand and several racks for drying fish were set up."

*GUDAL CREEK — enters Gudal Bay and drains two lakes, one of which has a legend. An important Creek-woman dwelt in this lake, Supernatural-woman - ruling - with - the - fair - weather - clouds - upon - the - mountains-whose-fame-goes-around. She was the wife of an ocean spirit, The-One-in-the-Sea, and they had ten children, all of whom became important spirits. But Fame did not exactly stay home tending fires. She had a roving eye, which might explain the last part of her name, "whose-fame-goes-around." One-in-the-Sea began to suspect that his wife might be playing the field a little, so he sent a hair seal up to the lake to keep an eye on her. Fame spotted the amateurish act in a moment and plied the seal with all sorts of treats. When he settled down to sleep after his gorgings she went off with her current lover. Time after time the ruse was successful and the old One-in-the-Sea none the wiser.

Most of the ten children went to live with their father, for Fame soon found her style cramped with such a brood under foot. However, one daughter took up her abode on a reef near the mouth of her mother's river, her name was Supernatural-Woman-into-whose-house-whales-flow.

*GAGI ROCK — is 41 feet high and bare and lies 1¼ miles southwest of Stiu Rock. The name Gagi is an adaption of the Haida word Ga'gi gen, taken from Dr. C.F. Newcombe's sketch maps of 1897.

*MARBLE ISLAND — about one quarter mile from Gagi Rock in Cartwright Sound, is a 475-foot-high wooded island which is only about 1 mile across. During World War II there was a small radar station on this island, similar to the Frederick and Hippa stations. When it was abandoned campers built a cabin of material left behind. Being infrequently visited, it did not suffer the ravages of vandalism for the first few years, but inevitably progress caught up. Little remains of the structure today.

The name Marble Island appeared on Captain Freeman's 1912-16 chart. Dr. C.F. Newcombe showed it on his map as GWA'IGITS in 1897.

*MARBLE ROCK — lies about a quarter of a mile southwest of Marble Island. A bare white rock with an elevation of 20 feet, it received its name in association with the island.

*TANA POINT — the north entrance point of Tana Bay is southeast of Marble Island. Several islets and rocks lie adjacent to the point, to which they are connected by a drying bank. Named by the Hydrographic Service in association with Tana Bay.

*TANA BAY — lies between Gudal Bay and the western entrance to Skidegate Channel. Two small streams flow into the head of this rock-encumbered bight. First shown on Dr. C.F. Newcombe's maps of 1897 as Ta'na and this modification of the Haida name subsequently adopted by the Hydrographic Service.

PIPE ORGAN ROCK — a magnificent basalt formation so much resembling a great organ that Fisheries Officer Howard Fairbairn of Queen Charlotte City gave it the name by which it has been known locally for years. The formation is on the south shore of Tana Bay, near Ells Point.

CATHEDRAL BAY — the local name given to the small indentation in which Pipe Organ Rock is located. This is another of the picturesque names for west coast rock features which originated with Mr. Fairbairn during his many years cruising these waters.

*ELLS POINT — the south entrance point of Tana Bay. Named after Dr. R.W. Ells the geologist who sailed this part of the coast in 1905 during his inspection trip. The name was confirmed in 1946.[1]

[1]See also Ells Bay and Ells Rock.

*SKIDEGATE CHANNEL — the western entrance and central section of the waterway separating Graham Island from Moresby Island. The eastern part is called Skidegate Inlet. Both take their name from the Haida village on the southeast coast of Graham Island.

Described as a geological accident, it has often been called the Panama Canal of the Charlottes by mariners who wanted to save the long voyage around Cape St. James.

Joseph Ingraham in 1792 called the western portion THE GREAT SOUND.

The Haidas, who had several favorite camping places along the north shore, called it the equivalent of LONG BAY.

Skidegate Channel and Skidegate Inlet covered more fully in Chapter 13.

***MERCER POINT** — the west entrance point of Dawson Inlet. Named in 1945 by the Hydrographic Service in association with Dawson Inlet — both are after Dr. George Mercer Dawson, the geologist who conducted a survey of the east and north coasts of the Charlottes in 1878.

See Dawson Harbour for full account.

***MOUNT LA PEROUSE** — a bare conspicuous mountain, 3,675 feet high, standing between Gudal Bay and the head of Dawson Inlet. The name was suggested in 1946 by the Chief Geographer in Victoria after Jean Francois de Galup, Comte de Laperouse, who sailed along the west coast of the Charlottes in 1786.[1]

[1]See La Perouse Reef.

***DAWSON INLET** — runs in a northerly direction off Skidegate Channel and

***DAWSON HARBOUR** — which branches off Dawson Inlet to run to the east, were both named after Dr. George Mercer Dawson by Dr. C.F. Newcombe in 1897.

On some earlier maps this waterway was shown as SWAN INLET after Judge J.G. Swan who made a reconnaissance along these shores in 1883 for the United

Dr. George Mercer Dawson, small figure in centre.
"He was tiny and his back was curved, but he ranged far,"
wrote Courtenay Bond of this remarkable man.

Photo - Provincial Archives, Victoria.

States Government. Later maps referred to the present Dawson Harbour as EAST ARM with the term Dawson Harbour being applied to what is now Dawson Inlet.

Chittenden, in 1884, mentioned finding "three cabins in a sheltered cove" in the present Dawson Harbour, and noted that the cabins were in frequent use by Haida seal hunters and fishermen.

Dr. George M. Dawson was born August 1, 1849 in Pictou, Nova Scotia. Slender, delicate, with such a curvature of the spine from a childhood illness, that he barely reached four-foot-eight - George Dawson left an indelible mark in Canadian history.

Educated at McGill and the Royal School of Mines, London, he was, at 24 years of age, appointed geologist and naturalist to the North American Boundary Commission in 1873. From his careful notes he wrote the *Geology and Resources of the 49th Parallel*, which was published in 1875, a book greatly valued in this field. That same year he received an appointment to the Geological Survey of Canada. For many years he was engaged in the active exploration and survey of both the Northwest Territories and British Columbia. It was in this connection that during June, July and August of 1878 he personally directed the survey and mapping of the east and north coasts of the Queen Charlottes.

Using the 20-ton schooner, *Wanderer*, Dr. Dawson was accompanied only by his assistant, Rankine Dawson, and a crew of three men. Occasionally this was supplemented by the engaging of one or two Haidas with particular local knowledge - charts being almost non-existent.

The report he wrote of this exploration and survey was meticulous and his descriptions so accurate that one can make no error in understanding exactly what is meant. Numerous features were named and they remain on the maps today unchanged.

The following year, 1879, Dr. Dawson travelled with a group of surveyors along the Skeena River and overland to Stuart Lake, thence to the Parsnip River. Thus he undertook at all times a schedule which would tax the most robust physique - let alone one with his handicaps. In 1895 he was made Director of the Geological Survey of Canada, a post he held until his premature death on March 1, 1901, shortly before his 52nd birthday. "He was tiny and his back was curved, but he ranged far," wrote Courtenay Bond of this remarkable man in his book, *Surveyors of Canada*.

*NEWTON POINT — opposite Mercer Point, at the entrance to Dawson Inlet and Dawson Harbour. This name, confirmed in 1946, is after Newton H. Chittenden, who was employed by the British Columbia Government to make an extensive exploration of the Charlottes in 1884. Mr. R. Maynard accompanied him for much of the trip to take photographs.

Chittenden wrote an interesting report following the trip and, although his judgement of distance is at odds with reality, his descriptions of the features are so clear one can easily follow his narrative. Each bay and cove is quickly identified despite his discrepancy in mileage. He made his exploration with the same thoroughness as Dawson, but not with Dawson's particular knowledge. He reached into every bay and inlet, hiked to the head of every river of any size, climbed to the top of several mountains and spent time living in some of the villages with the Haidas.

His conveyance was a small canoe with reinforced ribs and partial decking. He mentions only incidentally the injuring of his right hand so badly at the onset of the trip that it was practically useless, which makes one realize how courageous he was for he did not let it interfere with his plans, despite the ruggedness of the undertaking.

Like Dr. Dawson, Chittenden applied numerous place names, but unlike Dawson's, only one, Seal Inlet, survived to reach the maps of today.

Newton H. Chittenden who made an extensive exploration of the Queen Charlotte Islands in 1884 at the request of the British Columbia Government.
This photo taken at Camp Maynard, but the location of the camp is not known.

Photo - Provincial Archives, Victoria.

*GEORGIANNA POINT — which lies to the southeast of Newton Point,

*EXACT POINT — on the northeast corner of Chaatl Island and

*DEMARISCOVE POINT — due east of Exact Point, were all names confirmed in 1946 and are reminders of the days of the Queen Charlotte Islands' gold rush in 1851.

It began in July 1851 when the Hudson's Bay Company representatives took the company vessel *Una* from Port Simpson to what is now Mitchell Inlet to have a closer look at some gold-bearing quartz which had been found there.

A few samples were obtained from Haidas encamped at the site. They made it quite clear that the white men would have to barter for anything taken and, when they saw how interested the whites were, the barter price rose grossly

89

with each transaction. Knowing the company would not sanction exhorbitant payment, Captain Mitchell of the *Una* abandoned the trading. He took the few lumps of quartz they had managed to get to Victoria for assay and to secure company guidance for future action.

Everyone connected with the venture was sworn to secrecy, but gold news spreads like wildfire. It soon created a sensation in the bars of Puget Sound ports. In late October and early November three American ships left for the new find. The *Exact* under Captain Folger raced northward. He found 160 profit-minded Haidas now camping on the site. "They wanted in barter more than twice the value of the gold," he reported. Whites were not used to bartering for unmined gold. They generally took it. But those 160 Haidas determined to protect their rights were too formidable. Although it was now winter, Folger decided to stay and look for gold elsewhere.

From November to March, *Exact* cruised Island waters. "We have seen more of Queen Charlotte Islands than white men ever before," Folger told a newspaper reporter when they returned. "We have been in many harbours and on numerous high mountains, have seen several beautiful waterfalls from inland lakes . . . for we were often bound for weeks in different harbours . . . but except for Gold Harbour we did not again see any Haidas. Nor did we find any gold."

The other two ships, *Georgianna* under Captain Rowland and *Demaris Cove* under Captain Balch, left Puget Sound shortly after the *Exact*. *Georgianna* sailed first, her captain agreeing to meet with *Demaris Cove* at the gold site - a rendezvous that would never be kept.

Securing the services of John, a highly recommended Haida pilot, she pulled in to anchor in Skidegate Inlet at dusk on November 19, 1851. John pointed out a good anchorage. Captain Rowland imperiously disagreed and fetched up in water only 2½ fathoms deep. There were 5 crewmen and 22 passengers on board the *Georgianna* one of whom, Captain George Moore, became alarmed at Rowland's actions. "I pleaded with him to seek a better anchorage, especially as a wind was even then getting up," he reported later. It was useless. Captain Rowland remained adamant."

By midnight a gale was on them. The ship broke adrift - striking heavily on the shore with seas breaking right over her. As daylight came it was obvious she was doomed. And just as disconcertingly obvious was the sight of over 100 Haidas watching menacingly from the shore.

When it became finally necessary to abandon the vessel everyone scrambled ashore any way he could. "The Indians taking advantage of our exhausted condition after coming through the icy surf, plundered us of our weapons, caps and such clothing as they could pull off us," said Captain Moore. "Since there were now about 150 of them...brandishing knives and acting very hostile...no resistance was possible on our part. Indeed the situation looked very ugly."

At this point John, the pilot, offered to take them to his home across the bay. With some misgivings, but very little choice, the offer was accepted.

The gale raged for two weeks and it was not until December 6 that a canoe could be sent to Port Simpson to get help. By that time the addition of 27 strangers to an already overcrowded Haida house began to produce hostility. The Haidas were openly contemptuous of them, for their helpless condition

90

was tantamount to slave status - yet the whites would not work. "Oh well, there would be ransom money," mused the old ones. "There had better be," warned some of the young bucks.

The pilot John did what he could to intervene, but Captain Rowland's arrogant manner made the situation difficult for everyone.

The canoe which had been sent with some of *Georgianna's* crew to Port Simpson for help had a perilous trip across the still stormy waters of Hecate Strait. Their plea to the Hudson's Bay Company trader, W.H. McNeill, did not produce the expected action. Instead, McNeill showed intense displeasure at the Yankee invasion of what was considered to be H.B.C. preserves. And the fact that these interlopers had got themselves into a sticky situation with the Haidas was something he wanted no part of. Still - they were whites. He really *couldn't* refuse. So he stalled.

Four weeks passed and knowing their countrymen on the Charlottes would be suffering by then from scanty diet, most of their clothing stolen and the cold of winter, the worried Americans decided they would have to do something - in spite of McNeill. But what?

Then to their amazement, on January 10, an American ship, bristling with armaments, hove-to off Port Simpson. It was the *Demaris Cove* under Captain Lafayette Balch. Captain Balch told them that when the *Georgianna* failed to rendezvous with him at Gold Harbour he had become alarmed and made inquiries of the Haidas at the gold site. They were none too friendly and told him, rather gloatingly, that the *Georgianna* had been wrecked, all her crew enslaved and hinted that even worse might happen.

This photograph taken in 1884 by Mr. R. Maynard, who accompanied Newton Chittenden to the Charlottes, is an interesting combination of old and new. In an unidentified village he found grandpa sitting in the sun warming old bones and kept snug and cosy in new trading blankets. Grandma smiles shyly, her labret and cedar basin (bottom of photo) part of her own culture, but she utilizes white man's basins and clothes where practical.

Photo - Provincial Museum, Victoria.

Balch sailed immediately for home to report the incident, whereupon the U.S. Government outfitted the *Demaris Cove* as an armed cutter to go to the rescue. *En route,* Balch decided to put in at Port Simpson to buy more guns.

McNeill was alarmed. "My God, man! You'll bring blood on all our heads if you start shooting it out with Haidas. You'll probably cause the death of your own fellows into the bargain. Look...I know that bunch. They'll do almost anything for trade. You try bartering before you do anything like shooting."

The advice was sound. The crew were ransomed with ease for five blankets apiece. Ransom? Board money? It depends on your point of view.

*ARMENTIÈRES CHANNEL— separates Chaatl from Moresby Island on the east side of Chaatl Island. Named on October 20, 1936, after *H.M.C.S. Armèntieres,* a minesweeper employed in the spring of 1935 in hydrographic surveying operations with *C.G.S. Stewart.* The *Armèntieres* under the command of Lieutenant-Commander H.W.S. Soulsby, anchored in this channel while Mr. L.R. Davies conducted a survey of Skidegate Channel.

*CHAATL NARROWS — off the southeast end of Chaatl Island, separating Armentières Channel and Buck Channel. Formerly called CANOE PASS, a term which included Armentières Channel as well. Chaatl Narrows dry for over 1 mile, but are navigable for small craft at about half-tide.

*CHAATL ISLAND — at the west entrance to Skidegate Channel, is about 9 miles long and 2 miles across. Like so many west coast places it is steep, rocky and with hills rising to nearly 2,400 feet. The name of Chaatl is a modification of the Haida word for both this island and the village which lay on its south shore, Chaatl Village.

*TCENAKUN POINT — the northwestern tip of Chaatl Island. Also called SKIDEGATE POINT, it has a navigational light. The name Tcenakun is an adaption from Dr. C.F. Newcombe's 1897 map, and is a modification of Haida words meaning Salmon Point.

BATTLE ISLAND — lies off the southwest corner of Chaatl Island at the entrance to Buck Channel. A name from ancient years of Haida intertribal warfare.

*CHAATL VILLAGE — fronted a cove on the south side of Chaatl Island, towards the west end of Buck Channel. Originally settled by an Eagle tribe, the Sea Lions of Scotsgay Baeach near Skidegate, Chaatl did not develop into a village of any size until the Raven tribe living opposite, in Nesi, took it over, purchasing the site from the Eagles. In 1836 to 1841, John Work, the H.B.C. trader from Port Simpson estimated that there were 35 houses and about 561 people living in Chaatl. Some time afterward a fire swept the village destroying a large part of it, so that when Dr. J.R. Swanton made his survey in 1905 he could only list 21 houses.

It is interesting to note that the name of Gold Harbour has been applied to this place in some early stories - one of four places on the Charlottes to have had this name. When the Sea Lion tribe sold Chaatl to the Ravens, they moved to Kaisun - also called Gold Harbour. And so Chaatl was sometimes called the-village-where-the-people-of-Gold-Harbour-used-to-live, which became shortened to Gold Harbour.

Kaisun was called Gold Harbour because of its proximity to Mitchell Inlet, the site of the original gold find, and the true Gold Harbour of early days. When all the Haidas from Chaatl and Kaisun moved to Maude Island in Skidegate Inlet, about 1870, the village they established on Maude Island also became known as Gold Harbour, with the pre-fix of New sometimes applied.

However, even after the move to Skidegate Inlet, the old village of Chaatl was occupied regularly during fishing season for many years.

It was from either the village of Chaatl or Kaisun that George Dixon is said to have obtained the first labret - a lip decoration of much curiosity to traders. It was an ornament inserted into the lower lip of Haida women, who had their flesh specially pierced for it.

Dr. C.F. Newcombe took this photo of abandoned Chaatl in 1903.

Photo - Provincial Museum, Victoria.

NESI — the village on the south shore of Buck Channel which lay across the water from Chaatl. The Pebble-Stone-People and the Sqoaladas, Raven Crest tribes, formerly at Skidegate Inlet had lived harmoniously until one day an Eagle woman from Skidegate was mysteriously killed.

It appeared that someone from one of these two Raven Tribes was responsible. Not able to obtain a satisfactory explanation, the Skidegate Eagles declared war and fought so fiercely the Ravens had to flee for their lives.

In panic they headed for the west coast, and chose a small cove near the entrance of Buck Channel. They named the village Nesi, but the site was too exposed to be satisfactory. The Eagle tribe who owned Chaatl were happy to sell it to the newcomers, for they were anxious to move to Kaisun to join relatives.

Nesi was joyfully abandoned and in the village of Chaatl the Pebble-Stones and Sqoaladas began a new life. After a time the Sqoaladas became restless and began a migration which took them as far as Hippa Passage where they established a village called Swampy-Village. They were joined at this place by Ravens from the north end of the Charlottes. After some years Swampy-Village, too, was abandoned, some of the villagers going to join the Kaigani migration to Alaska, and others eventually going south, first to Rennell Sound, then back to old Chaatl, from whence all moved to Skidegate Inlet about 1870.

*BUCK CHANNEL — off the south shore of Chaatl Island. Shown as CANOE PASS, CANOE PASSAGE and DOUGLAS INLET on various early maps. Named Buck Channel in association with Buck Point, which is south and west at the entrance to the Channel. It appeared under the name of Buck Channel on the 1912-16 map of Captain Absolom Freeman.

NORTHWEST COAST OF MORESBY ISLAND;
FROM BUCK POINT TO ANTIQUARY BAY.
(INCLUDES GOLD HARBOUR.)

CHAPTER FIVE

*MORESBY ISLAND — south of Graham Island, is the second largest of
the Queen Charlotte group. Named in 1853 by Commander James Prevost
after his father-in-law, Rear Admiral Fairfax Moresby, who held the post of
Commander-in-Chief of the Pacific Station from 1850 to 1853.

Moresby Island is a long slender island of fiords and mountains. The west
coast has the same exposure to the full sweep of the Pacific as Graham Island,
but is, perhaps, more stark and wild. Its rockbound shores are not fringed
with great stretches of sand beaches and the 100-fathom line extending off
from 1 to 3 miles, suddenly loses bottom as the ocean floor falls off to great
depths.

In this chapter, and for seven successive ones, it is proposed to explore fully
this island and the off-shore islands which lie adjacent - sometimes only separated
by a mere thread of a channel.

*BUCK POINT — the northwest tip of Moresby Island, is also the south
entrance point of Buck Channel. It received its name on September 25, 1793,
from Captain George Vancouver as he journeyed along the west coast of the
Charlottes on his way to the Hawaiian Islands for the winter after his season's
examination of the northwest coast. He is believed to have named the point
in honour of the Buck family of Norwich.

High and bold, with off-lying rocks and reefs some of which dry - Buck
Point was the STA'NLENGESALSKUN of Dr. C.F. Newcombe.

*KITGORO INLET — the first large inlet south of Buck Point, has a narrow
channel leading into the inlet with considerable kelp along the shores. Two
streams run into the head of the inlet with a drying flat off the mouth of

the streams. There was a former Haida settlement on the north shore at the head of the bay. Frequently called FRENCH HARBOUR by fishermen in early years.

Dr. C.F. Newcombe shows it as QA'ITGAOGAO on his map of 1897.

*KITGORO POINT — named in association with the inlet, is south of it.

*ENGLEFIELD BAY — the largest bay on the west coast of Moresby Island, is south of Kitgoro Point and lies between Annesley Point and Cape Henry. Named on September 25, 1793, by Captain George Vancouver after his close friend Sir Henry Charles Englefield who, at forty-one, had already become a well-known archaeologist and writer. His particular interest was English cathedrals and churches.

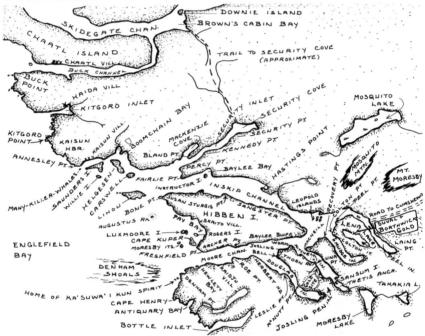

Englefield Bay had been the recipient of two other names before Vancouver's. On August 18, 1786, seven years previously, Laperouse had named the bay *Baie de la Touche* in honour of the famous French naval commander, La Touche-Treville. A few years later in 1791 or 1792, Joseph Ingraham of the American brig *Hope* showed it on his maps as PORT YORK. But this whole region came to be known generally as Gold Harbour after the gold find in 1851.

GOLD HARBOUR — a name never shown on official maps, nor gazetted, but widely known. Sometimes used in connection with three other sites:- Chaatl, Kaisun and Haina. Originally applied to the present Mitchell Inlet and later expanded to include the entire Englefield Bay area and bays and inlets leading off it.

Archie Duval, centre, and Jack Borthwick, right, discoverers of Lena Lake,
together with poet George Winkler, wearing bowler hat.
One of Mr. Winkler's best known poems was The Tale of the Movable Mine,
mentioned under Virgalias Cove.

Photo - Bert Roberts

H.M.S. Thetis *used during the survey of Englefield Bay and Kuper Inlet in 1852. Augustus Leopold Kuper, who captained the* Thetis *when the survey was made, contributed many of the names for this region.*

Photos - Provincial Archives, Victoria.

The actual gold site was a small area of hilly shoreline, part way along the west side of Mitchell Inlet. It came into the news in 1851 when the Hudson's Bay Company took a serious interest in some specimens brought earlier to Port Simpson. There was a wild scramble in southern ports - especially those in Puget Sound. The rush of American vessels to the Charlottes alarmed the Hudson's Bay Company officials and they immediately pressured for protection.

Her Majesty's Government became sufficiently stirred by the plea to order Governor James Douglas in Victoria to issue a proclamation. Thus, by a mere flip of a pen five hundred miles away, the Queen Charlotte Islands became "possessed" by representatives of Her Majesty's Government. "But, it must be understood," Douglas was warned, "that, although Her Majesty's Government is interested in securing the Islands' resources, there is no intention of placing any establishment on Queen Charlotte's Islands."

It was agreed, however, that a naval ship could be sent to stand off in Charlotte waters. Her officers would survey and chart waters in strategic places to give weight to the Proclamation of Possession.

Had the Americans been more determined, or had the gold in Mitchell Inlet proved to be more than a pocket - it is hard to say what the outcome might have been. At least it did result in hazardous waters being surveyed and those surveys supplied a great many names for the Islands - some of which honour brave men who did a difficult job.

And from the days of the gold find onwards the Charlottes had a new owner. Little would transpire when money was involved without the sanction of an officialdom 500 miles away and, occasionally, even more distant - across a continent in Ottawa.

The place names of Englefield Bay and vicinity are, for the most part, connected with the survey made in 1852 by the frigate *Thetis*, Hudson's Bay Company and men connected with the days of the Queen Charlotte Islands gold rush.

*ANNESLEY POINT — the north entrance point of Englefield Bay. Hoping to deter Americans from entering Hudson's Bay Company's trading region, the British Government sent the 1,450-ton armed frigate *Thetis* to cruise conspicuously in this waterway and make a detailed survey in 1852. The ship was commanded by Captain A.L. Kuper and the survey made under the direction of George Moore.

Annesley Turner Denham, a midshipman on the *Thetis*, was in charge of one of the cutters and assisted George Moore in part of the survey. Annesley Point named by Mr. Moore in 1852.

A Naval Intelligence map dated 1921 shows this point as CULTUS POINT, but that name apparently never came into common usage.

*KAISUN VILLAGE — lay east of Annesley Point and fronted along the shore of a bay behind what is now Saunders Island. It is a very old village site used in ancient years by the Raven tribe called Pitch-Town-People. When the Skidegate Inlet Eagles moved to occupy it, the original Raven owners had died, except for one man of gigantic stature. All the Pitch-Towns were said to be unusually big and enormously strong. Other Haida tribes regarded them as not too intelligent, some of their fears and superstitions were foolish to the point of being ridiculous.

It is as an Eagle village that Kaisun is best remembered, and because of its proximity to the Mitchell Inlet gold find was frequently called Gold-Harbour-Village.

Like all winter-occupied villages of any size, Kaisun had people of both Raven and Eagle tribes living there. In 1840 John Work estimated that there were 329 people in the village and in 1905 Dr. J.S. Swanton listed 20 houses at Kaisun. Two of the Raven lodges had the intriguing names of "Shout-loud-house" and "House-where-people-are-always-filled."

*KAISUN HARBOUR — fronts along the site of the old Kaisun village.

MANY-KILLER-WHALES-ISLAND — lies at the western entrance to Kaisun Harbour, and is the outermost island. Legends say that long ago a bad killer-whale with two dorsal fins lived under the island, and it destroyed great numbers of the Kaisun people by upsetting their canoes. A relative of one of the victims, using great cunning and magic potions, killed the whale. Not long afterwards he, too, was upset at sea and drowned, but from that time on no killer-whale ever lived under the island.

ALWAYS-WET-REEF — lay near Kaisun and was so named because the seas broke heavily over it. One of the good ocean spirits dwelt there and Haidas fishing for halibut offered supplications to it, saying; "Give us food, oh Great One. Let our hands indeed be covered with fish slime."

*SAUNDERS ISLAND — forms the outer shore of Kaisun Harbour. The name was adopted from Mr. A.E. Wright's survey and blueprint of 1924.

On the north shore of Saunders Island stood the old Raven Crest village of the Pitch-Town-People, the Town-the-sun-does-not-shine-on.

*WILLIE ISLAND — south of Saunders Island has an islet lying off it to the northwest. Willie Island is named after Captain William Mitchell, skipper of the H.B.C. vessel *Una,* which took the first gold out of Mitchell Inlet.

*HELGESEN ISLAND — lies to the east of Saunders Island. The name was adopted from Mr. A.E. Wright's 1924 survey and blueprint.

*BOOMCHAIN BAY — north of Helgeson Island, a local name which was submitted by Mr. A.E. Wright. Officially confirmed in 1946.

*CARSWELL ISLAND — lies off the southeast end of Helgeson Island. It was also known as CLIFF ISLAND. Named after James Carswell, a partner in Hibben & Company, which sold charts in Victoria, B.C. It is said that Mr. Carswell was known as Cliff Carswell. The name CARSWELL ISLAND was confirmed by the Permanent Names Committee in 1946. (Bone Point on Hibben Island was named for another partner of Hibben & Co.)

*LIHOU ISLAND — lies south of Carswell Island. Name adopted from A.E.

Wright's blueprint and survey of 1924. Norman Lihou was a member of Wright's survey party.

The Pitch-Town-People's village, Throwing-Grease-Around, stood on Lihou Island. The name meant that the villagers were so well-supplied with food they could afford to be careless.

Legend says that the people of this place were attacked by the Pitch-Towns of Kaisun. All but four were killed. The survivors fled across the island to a salt-water pond where kelp grows and were changed into rocks. These knocked loudly against one another whenever a storm was brewing.

*AUGUSTUS ROCK — southeast of Lihou Island in Englefield Bay. About 19 feet high, Augustus Rock has a reef off its south side. Named after Captain Augustus L. Kuper, captain of the *Thetis* during the 1852 survey.

*MORESBY ISLETS — lie off the southwest part of Hibben Island close to Cape Kuper. The group of islets and rocks was named Moresby ISLANDS by Captain A.L. Kuper, after John Moresby, a gunnery lieutenant on the *Thetis* in 1852. During his naval career John Moresby rose steadily in rank until he became a full admiral. His father was Admiral Sir Fairfax Moresby for whom Moresby Island is named.

*LUXMOORE ISLAND — north and slightly east of Moresby Islets. It was named by Captain A.L. Kuper during the 1852 survey, after Benjamin Lux-moore, a clerk and paymaster on the *Thetis*. Luxmoore Island has a cleft through it with a natural stone bridge. The cleft angles through, but from one position daylight can be seen shining from the opposite side.

Called HOLE ISLAND by the Kaisun people, who regarded the spirit dwelling there to be the strongest of all Ocean-People in this district. Petitions to it might even result in the gift of a whale.

A man from Kaisun, named Standing-Shining-in-the-Ocean, discovered an even more miraculous power of this magic place. Miserable and despondent with the knowledge that he had contracted syphilis - he jumped into the sea and swam through the cleft. On the way he could feel barnacles scraping his body and blood flowing out. Upon reaching the other side he found himself cleansed and completely healed.

*ROGERS ISLAND — east of Luxmoore Island. Named by Captain A.L. Kuper after William Rogers, assistant paymaster on the *Thetis* during the 1852 survey. Rocks straggle off the northeast and southeast parts of Rogers Island and with the island form the west portion of Pay Bay.

*PAY BAY — a bight on the west side of Hibben Island. During the 1852 survey it was named ROCKY BAY. Renamed by the Hydrographic Service in later years owing to duplications of that name. PAY BAY is in association with clerk paymasters Luxmoore and Rogers for whom nearby islands were named.

*KUPER INLET — refers to the waters east of Englefield Bay, and takes in Inskip and Moore Channels. Named after Captain A.L. Kuper of the *Thetis*. The PORT KUPER of the 1852 survey referred to the main portion of the present Moore Channel. The Moore Channel of that day only referred to the western entrance. The name PORT KUPER no longer in use.

*CAPE KUPER — a semi-detached island off the southwest side of Hibben Island. Named in 1852 after Captain Augustus Leopold Kuper who commanded the *Thetis* during the survey. Name applied by George Moore who conducted the survey.

Born in 1809, the son of a clergyman, Kuper joined the British Navy when only 14 years old and was a first lieutenant before he became 21. By the time he commanded the *Thetis* for the 1852 survey of Gold Harbour, Kuper already had a distinguished career behind him, and had married the daughter of another naval man, Captain Sir James Bremer, stationed in the Far East. Captain Kuper attained the rank of full admiral in 1872 and died in October 1885.

*HIBBEN ISLAND — the largest island in the Gold Harbour area. Originally named KUPER ISLAND by the British Hydrographic Office, after Captain A.L. Kuper, the name was changed to Hibben Island in 1905. The change was ordered by the Geographic Board because of possible confusion with another Kuper Island, off the east coast of Vancouver Island.

Thomas Napier Hibben, after whom the island is named came from Charleston, Carolina. Lured to San Francisco during the gold rush days of 1849 he had come as a young man of 30 to Victoria in 1858. There, in partnership with James Carswell, he had purchased a book and stationery shop. A few years later Hibben bought Carswell out and took over the business for himself. He became very well-known to mariners when his store was appointed agent for Admiralty charts.

The Haida name for Hibben Island was GŪL and like most places it, too, had a legend. Gūl Island was a favorite hunting place for a special species of bird which men from Kaisun village hunted at night - using torches. The young son of the Town Chief at Kaisun had begged for a long time to be allowed to accompany the hunters but he was always turned down and his pleadings brushed aside. He persisted and one night, with much reluctance, it was agreed he could go.

After the hunt, when it was time to return home, the boy refused to leave - darting away and vanished into the darkness. The hunters were forced to return without him. Weeks later they saw his smoke and it was said he had grown wings. Food was ample for the boy - he speared birds at will or caught them easily with a snare.

But one day whilst crossing a log he let out wind, as though carrying a heavy burden. Next day not a single bird remained on the island. In a short while the boy almost starved. Why had the birds all left so suddenly? he wondered. Then he remembered what had happened when he crossed that log. Retracing his steps carefully to the exact place, he found a small black hole in the ground. Cutting it out with his knife, he threw it far into the sea. That night all the birds came back to Gūl, and once again food was plentiful.

From that time on, no one who went to the island was ever allowed to break wind.

It was said that no mice could exist on Gūl. When the wife of a Skidegate chief lay dying, she begged that when she passed on, she would be placed where there were no mice. So her family placed her body in a cave on Gūl, and some of them stayed to settle nearby. The chief had a garden on the west end of the island and, curious about the legend that no mice *could* exist, captured two mice elsewhere, put them in a tobacco can, then released them in his garden. They immediately ran to a cliff and jumped into the sea.

*FRESHFIELD POINT** — the bold southwest point of Hibben Island. Named in 1852 by Captain A. L. Kuper after William Freshfield, Master's Assistant on the *Thetis*. As one of the navigating staff, Mr. Freshfield took an active part in the survey of the Gold Harbour region.

*ARCHER POINT** — east of Freshfield Point, on the south side of Hibben Island. Named by Captain A.L. Kuper in 1852 for another member of the *Thetis*, Archibald Leslie Archer, the assistant surgeon on the ship. There is a small cove on the west side of Archer Point into which a stream flows.

*BAYLEE BLUFF** — on the south side of Hibben Island, opposite the entrance to Mitchell Inlet. Named in 1852 by Captain A. L. Kuper after Reverend William Cecil Percy Baylee, the popular chaplain and instructor aboard the *Thetis* during the survey.

See also Baylee Bay, Percy Point and Instructor Island.

*SANGSTER POINT** — the southeast tip of Hibben Island. This bold bluff was named also by Captain Kuper during the 1852 survey and is after Lieutenant James Sangster, one of the officers on the *Thetis*.

*SUSAN STURGIS POINT** — on the north shore of Hibben Island. Named by the Hydrographic Service after an American schooner of that name. In April or May of 1852, with five other vessels, this Boston-owned ship arrived at Gold Harbour to look for the much talked about gold. Her visit was brief and unfruitful. In the fall she returned for a more extended search. Once again the search in the Mitchell Inlet area was unrewarding, so the skipper, Matthew Rooney, took his vessel to the east coast, via Cape St. James. Trading, prospecting and exploring, he sailed north as far as Skidegate where he met Chief Edenshaw. Learning that he might find some profitable trading in Edenshaw's territory near North Island (Langara Island), Rooney asked Edenshaw to come aboard and pilot the ship.

When they were off Masset, the *Susan Sturgis* was hi-jacked by the Massets. During the fierce skirmish which followed, the whites would have been murdered but for Edenshaw's intervention. Reminding the Massets of the ransom paid for Americans off the *Georgianna*[1] he persuaded them to consider similar action - probably the only way he could have made any effective appeal. The ship

[1]See Georgianna Point.

herself was pillaged and burned.

The *Susan Sturgis* under Captain Rooney figured in two other incidents which are related to the history of the Charlottes. She was the vessel which came to the rescue of the shipwrecked *Una* at Neah Bay in December 1851 when that vessel ran into a storm *en route* to Victoria with gold from Mitchell Inlet. She was also one of the platforms in James Douglas's campaigns to persuade the British Government to give "protection" to the far-off islands when he wrote the home office to say,

> Fort Victoria, 26th August, 1852.
> I have just received information to the effect that the master of the American brig *Susan Sturgis* lately cut, and carried off a cargo of spars from Queen Charlotte's Islands, a liberty that no British vessel would be permitted to take on the American coasts.

*BONE POINT — the western extremity of a semi-detached island off the northwest tip of Hibben Island. Named after Mr. Bone, the partner in Hibben & Bone Company of Victoria.

*SECURITY INLET — the entrance to this long slim inlet which opens off the north side of Inskip Channel is north of Bone Point. In earlier years it was sometimes called SECURITY BAY or SECURITY COVE - the one name for the whole waterway. The word "cove" now only refers to the bay at the head of the inlet and the main channel is gazetted as Security Inlet.

*SECURITY COVE — at the head of Security Inlet has two creeks flowing into it, both of which are fronted by extensive mud flats.

In 1908-09 a trail was cut out along the valley of the creek which flows in from the north. This trail, about 8 miles long, went overland to emerge in a bay between Demariscove Point and Downie Island, on the south shore of Skidegate Channel. The government put it through when the mine at Mitchell Inlet was in operation, to enable people from the area to get out when weather along the west coast was stormy.

*SECURITY POINT — is the south entrance point to the cove at the head of Security Inlet.

*KENNEDY POINT — on the south shore of Security Inlet, about halfway along. Named after Dr. John F. Kennedy, Chief Trader at the Hudson's Bay post in Port Simpson in 1852. Dr. Kennedy had been to Skidegate in 1852 with Captain Mitchell and Captain Stuart, assessing trading conditions in those troubled days. Name confirmed in 1946.

*BLAND POINT — on the north shore of Security Inlet, is at the end of a peninsula at the entrance to Mackenzie Cove. Named after Nathaniel Bland Herbert, second master on the *Thetis* in 1852. Bland Point confirmed by the Permanent Names Committee in 1946.

104

*MACKENZIE COVE — on the north shore of Security Inlet near the entrance. Named after James D. MacKenzie, the geologist who made a survey of Graham Island in 1913 and 1914. The old name for this cove was OPEN BAY. The current name Mackenzie Cove was confirmed in 1961. (J.D. MacKenzie spelled his name with the capital K; MacKenzie Bay and MacKenzie Passage follow that form. Mackenzie Cove and Mackenzie Island have been gazetted with the small *k* spelling.)

A stream of some length runs into the head of Mackenzie Cove and there is a broad flat fronting the mouth of the stream.

*PERCY POINT — the south entrance point to Security Inlet. Named after William Cecil Percy Baylee, chaplain on the *Thetis* in 1852.

See also Baylee Bay, Baylee Bluff and Instructor Island.

*FAIRLIE POINT — south of Percy Point is on the north shore of Inskip Channel. Named by the Hydrographic Service in association with Inskip Channel. *Fairlie* was one of the fine old frigate ships engaged in the East Indian and Australian trades. George Inskip began his naval career on her in 1839, when she was under the command of Edward Garrett. *Fairlie* is also believed to have been the first ship Captain George Vancouver served on.

*INSKIP CHANNEL — runs along the north shore of Hibben Island. Named after Captain George Hastings Inskip of the *Virago* who surveyed the channel in 1853, the same year he also conducted a survey of Virago Sound and Houston Stewart Channel.

Inskip joined the merchant service in 1839 and 4 years later entered the Royal Navy as a master's assistant for the survey of the North Sea. Three years later he helped in the survey of Australian waters, then in 1851 received an appointment as master to the *Virago* when she came to the Pacific coast under Commander Houston Stewart. (The following year Captain J.C. Prevost relieved Houston Stewart.) George Inskip's naval career was chiefly in the Hydrographic surveying field and he became involved in some hair-raising incidents.

The *Virago* had only left the Straits of Magellan *en route* to the Pacific coast, when she was ordered back. Some Chilean revolutionists had hi-jacked two ships, one British and another American. The Britisher was recovered at the western entrance of the Straits - full of troops and about 60 tons of silver ore. The American vessel, finally located at San Carlos required a daring manoeuvre for her recovery. The *Virago* entered the harbour in a dense fog to capture her, and found a special prize aboard the second ship, the leader of the revolution, plus $150,000. All were returned to the Chilean Government for it to mete out justice.

Another exciting trip on the *Virago* took place in 1854 during the Russian war when Inskip was aboard during the attack on Petropaulovski.

*INSTRUCTOR ISLAND — east of Fairlie Point and off the north shore of Inskip Channel, it lies at the entrance to Baylee Bay.

*BAYLEE BAY — about 1¼ miles east from Fairlie Point. Both Instructor

Island and Baylee Bay were named for William C. Percy Baylee, the popular chaplain and instructor on the *Thetis* during the 1852 survey. The names were confirmed by the Permanent Names Committee in 1946.

*HASTINGS POINT — on the north shore of Inskip Channel, is south and east of Baylee Bay, and extends hook-like into Inskip Channel. Named after George Hastings Inskip, who conducted a survey of Inskip Channel in 1853 aboard the *Virago*. The name was confirmed in 1946.

A small cove lies on the south side of Hastings Point with a creek running into it which drains a lake high in the hills behind.

*LEOPOLD ISLANDS — a group of wooded islets with drying and submerged rocks which extend off the shore at the south end of Inskip Channel near the entrance to Peel Inlet. They were named after Captain Augustus Leopold Kuper, master of the *Thetis* during the 1852 survey.

*PEEL INLET — the most easterly of the four arms off the south side of Moore Channel. Named after Lieutenant Francis Peel, a third lieutenant on the *Thetis* during the 1852 survey. Peel Inlet is about 3½ miles long and contains several islands and islets, ranging from 80 to 120 feet high. A rough road comes into Peel Inlet from Cumshewa Inlet which was formerly used by a logging camp working in Peel Inlet. The road is extremely steep in parts and requires suitably equipped vehicles to successfully negotiate the distance.

The old Haida name for the Peel Inlet area was NAAWE.

*LAING POINT — on the east side of Peel Inlet. Named after Robert Laing who was on the schooner *Susan Sturgis* when she was captured by the Masset Haidas.[1] Laing born in Fifeshire, Scotland, in 1816, learned the shipwright trade in his native land. Following the *Susan Sturgis* incident, when the men were finally released by the Massets and taken to Port Simpson, the H.B.C.'s vessel *Beaver* took them to Victoria. As the *Beaver* crossed Millbank Sound she encountered a heavy gale and her rudder was put out of commission in the violent waters. Laing's skill and marine knowledge enabled him to make the vital repairs and he was credited with having saved the ship from certain loss in the severe seas.

Upon his arrival in Victoria the Hudson's Bay Company, recognizing the value of his skill, immediately offered him a job. He worked for them for several years. Laing is said to have operated the first shipyard in Victoria and hauled the first vessel ever taken from the waters in the colony.

[1] Susan Sturgis Point.

*PEEL POINT — outside, but near the entrance to Peel Inlet. Named in 1852 by George Moore after Francis Peel, third lieutenant on the *Thetis*. There is a reef of rocks off Peel Point which projects about 1000 feet.

*COLTON POINT — the east entrance point of Mudge Inlet,

*COLTON ISLET — at the entrance to Mudge Inlet, and

*MUDGE INLET — which lies to the west of Peel Inlet, were all named after Henry Colton Mudge, a lieutenant on the *Thetis* in 1852. Mudge Inlet was originally called MUDGE HARBOUR. Lieutenant Mudge was the grandson of Admiral Zachary Mudge for whom Cape Mudge on Vancouver Island is named.

Several streams run into Mudge Inlet, a boot-shaped fiord which the Haidas called HOWT-TELM.

LENA LAKE — lies between Peel and Mudge Inlets at about 400 feet elevation. It was discovered and named by Jack Borthwick and Archie Duval of Queen Charlotte City in the spring of 1909.

"The overflow from the lake comes down into Mudge Inlet in a series of waterfalls, so there are no trout or fish of any kind in the lake," says Charlie Hartie of Queen Charlotte City, who knew both men well. "I remember Archie Duval telling me of their mining experiences at Lena Lake. They had found some showings of gold in a small vein on the north shore of the lake. Like most prospectors they had very little capital. So by the time they had bought powder for blasting, some drills and so on . . . it took pretty well all their money. Just enough left for a sack of flour, some mush, a fishing line and a few shotgun shells and they figured they could live off fish and game until they came in with their first poke of gold .

"They drove a tunnel in for about 20 feet then the last showing of gold disappeared. Geologist say the surface of the rock is worn away by heat or erosion and the gold, being heavier and having a lower melting point, sinks into the small veins on the surface. A common situation in the case of all the gold strikes on the Charlottes."

*RECOVERY POINT — the west entrance point of Mudge Inlet. Named after the Hudson's Bay Company schooner *Recovery* which went to the Mitchell Inlet gold site in March of 1852.

See story Una Point.

*MACNEILL POINT — the east entrance point of Mitchell Inlet. Although spelled slightly differently, the point is generally believed to be named after Trader W.H. McNeill, the Hudson's Bay Company official who went on the *Una's* second trip to the Mitchell Inlet gold site in October 1851. (McNeill is also mentioned under Georgianna Point)

*MITCHELL INLET — lies between Mudge and Douglas Inlets, and opens off the south shore of Moore Channel. Named in 1852 by Captain A.L. Kuper, as MITCHELL HARBOUR, it became much better known as GOLD HARBOUR.

Captain William Mitchell, born in Abderdeen in 1802, came to the Pacific coast in 1837. A popular H.B.C. employee affectionately known as "Wullie" Mitchell, he was a kind-hearted sailor who utterly despised anything small or mean.

Mitchell commanded several H.B.C. vessels, *Cadboro, Una, Recovery* and *Beaver,* and, like many skippers, acted as both sailor and trader for the company when occasion demanded. But he was too kind-hearted to make a successful trader when the bargaining got tough. It was Mitchell who brought the *Recovery* to Mitchell Inlet following the wreck of *Una*.[1]

[1]Story under Una Point.

*SANSUM ISLAND — at the entrance to Thetis Anchorage, head of Mitchell Inlet. Arthur Sansum served as first lieutenant on the *Thetis* during the 1852 survey. In April of 1853 he died suddenly aboard the ship at Guarmas, Gulf of California.

Sansum Island was a favorite camping place with the Haidas and in 1870 ruins of a number of houses could still be seen.

*THETIS ANCHORAGE — at the head of Mitchell Inlet. Named THETIS COVE by Captain A.L. Kuper during the 1852 survey of the region. In recent years the term *cove* was change to *anchorage*. Named after the 1,450-ton frigate *Thetis* employed in the Gold Harbour survey of 1852. She had been built about 5 years before at Devonport. In 1854 *Thetis* was given by the British Government to Prussia in exchange for two small paddle steamers, and the Prussian Government used her as a training ship for seamen.

There is a sandy beach at the head of Thetis Anchorage with a good stream running into it. The stream, unnamed, drains a network of lakes, the two largest of which are Moresby Lake and Takakia Lake.

*MORESBY LAKE — at the 300-foot level is about 2 miles long. Named by Captain A.L. Kuper after Lieutenant John Moresby - for whom Moresby Islets were also named - a gunnery lieutenant on the *Thetis*. During the survey Lieutenant Moresby, accompanied by Nowell Salmon, one of the midshipmen, climbed the hillside behind Thetis Anchorage and explored this lake and region. According to Captain John Walbran's *British Columbia Coast Names*, the whole cluster of lakes was called Moresby Lakes. Today only the largest in the group bears Lieutenant John Moresby's name.

*TAKAKIA LAKE — lies to the east of Moresby Lake and is smaller. It drains into Moresby Lake and was named in 1964 after a genus of plant called Takakia, a member of the Bryophta moss family. This lake has also been shown as ALPINE LAKE.

*NIVEN POINT — on the west side of Mitchell Inlet, a little to the north of Sansum Island. Named during the 1852 survey by George Moore.

*UNA POINT — on the west shore of Mitchell Inlet, is slightly north of the gold site on the Charlottes which made history in 1851 and 1852. Immediately south of the point is a stream and the initial gold find was on the south side of this stream. The Indian encampment was also on the south side of the stream during the early stages of the gold interest.

By the spring of 1851 the Hudson's Bay Company in Port Simpson had seen enough evidence to convince them that there possibly might be gold on the Charlottes. In July they delegated Captain Wullie Mitchell to take the brig *Una* and go with John Work to have a closer look at the location in the present Mitchell Inlet.

There were a number of Haidas at the site when the *Una* arrived and the Indians had laboriously dug out some of the gold-bearing quartz. "This is fine," thought Mitchell. "It will be easier to barter for the stuff than try to dig it ourselves." Trading began moderately, but as soon as the Haidas sensed the keen interest of the whites they put up the price out of all reason.

Mitchell knew the company would not sanction extravagance - even for gold. Taking a few samples he sailed to Victoria for an assay. "Let the company decide," he thought.

The assay proved good, but there was no question of bartering for the prices the Haidas were asking. The company decided to quarry the ore themselves. In October of 1851 Governor James Douglas sent the *Una* again under Captain Mitchell to the gold site. This time, in addition to her crew, the vessel carried Trader W.H. McNeill and a party of miners who had agreed to do the quarrying for shares.

The Haidas, still camping near the site, watched with interest as the miners went about locating the main gold pocket and became more curious as the whites began drilling and blasting. That method was an improvement over the back-breaking digging they had been doing. But when the whites began loading the ore on board the *Una* without the expected bargaining, the Indians became alarmed.

They reacted swiftly. As soon as a blast was set off, they rushed forward, scrambling with the whites for the ore. Tempers quickly flared and there were angry clashes. Fearing an outbreak of real ugliness Trader McNeill made the decision to withdraw, taking the $75,000 worth of gold they had managed to collect. Badly as they wanted the gold it was not the policy of the Hudson's Bay Company to create undue hostility in their trading areas.

The miners were furious at being so close to a potential fortune and then being made to leave it to "them savages." Irate, they wanted no part of McNeill's offer to divide the gold at Port Simpson. They were disgusted with McNeill and insisted that the settling be done in Victoria under Governor Douglas's supervision.

The little *Una* had a rough but uneventful trip south until she entered the Strait of Juan de Fuca and ran headlong into a heavy gale. The tide set them onto the American side. Neah Bay hove in sight. Changing course Captain Mitchell steered for it, planning to anchor and wait out the storm. They were scudding towards the harbour when with a grinding crash the *Una* fetched up on an uncharted reef and heeled over sharply. When Neah Bay Indians came out to pillage the stricken vessel a fierce fight broke out between Indians, sailors and miners - the Indians quickly getting the upper hand. At that moment the American schooner *Susan Sturgis*, under Captain Matthew Rooney, happened by and arrived in the nick of time to save the whites. As the *Susan Sturgis* left the scene the *Una* was set afire by the Indians, burned to the waterline, then slipped off the reef taking her golden cargo with her to the bottom of the bay. It was December 24, 1851.

The H.B.C. began outfitting the *Recovery* to take over the gold operation. This time they sent a strongly armed party to repel any hostile attacks by the Haidas. The *Recovery* arrived at the gold site in 1852, but this time the men were able to establish a good working agreement with the Haidas. The miners began blasting and discovered that the gold was only a pocket.

The arrival in April and May of several American gold-seeking ships alarmed the H.B.C. who feared invasion by any ships - particularly American competitors so close to H.B.C. posts. Governor James Douglas was galvanised into action and petitioned the British Government. "Not only are these foreigners after gold, but in addition they are taking the most proprietory actions. The American schooner *Susan Sturgis* actually cut and took away a cargo of spars from Queen Charlotte's Islands. In no time they may even establish a settlement. Measures *must* be taken to guard against this at once or we may find it impossible to maintain our northern outposts against this foreign invasion of our territory," he complained.

This plea resulted in the *Thetis* being sent to cruise the waters at the gold site - under the guise of making a survey, but with her 32 guns very much in evidence.

Although the gold at Una Point did not prove to be a strike, it kindled interest intermittently for many years. John McLellan, a former B.C. assayer, is the man best remembered for making it profitable in a small way. He put in a stamp mill about 1907 and operated until about 1933. The last known production of gold from Gold Harbour took place in 1939 when Mr. D.F. Kidd obtained about 150 ounces of gold from 15 tons of ore.

By that time the centre portion of the peninsula contained 16 claims which extended for some distance beyond the original find - an open cut not far from the high-tide mark.

*THORN ROCK — north of Una Point. Named by Captain Kuper in 1852. It has a depth of less than 6 feet over it and is believed to be named after Charles Thorn, an engineer on the H.B.C. ships connected with the gold excitement in 1852.

*WORK POINT — near the west entrance of Mitchell Inlet. Named in 1852 after John Work (sometimes spelled Wark), the H.B.C. trader, who came from Port Simpson by canoe in May of 1851 to locate the exact site from which Haidas had brought ore samples. He was guided to the place by Haidas and the trip made with utmost secrecy. Following his report the company sent the *Una* with Mitchell in command, to enable Work to make a closer examination, as mentioned under Una Point.

John Work was the man who, about 1840, made the first population count of Haidas on the Charlottes and noted the number of houses and totem poles.

*JOSLING PENINSULA — lying between Mitchell and Douglas Inlet, and

*JOSLING POINT — on the north end of the peninsula, were both named by Captain Kuper after John James Stephen Josling, a second lieutenant on the *Thetis* in 1852.

On some maps this name is shown as Jopling, while on others one spelling is given for the point and the other for the peninsula. This may be a typographical error according to the Hydrographic Office who confirm that Josling is the correct name.

Lieutenant Josling served on several ships, gradually advancing in rank until 1862 when he served as flag captain to Kuper, who by then was a Rear Admiral. The following year Captain Josling lost his life in a battle off Japan. The round shot killed both Josling and the commander of the flag ship, Edward Wilmot, who was standing close to him on the bridge of the frigate.

SKAITO — a Haida town reportedly occupied during the gold rush days. Dr. C.F. Newcombe's map shows this town to have been in a cove on the north end of the Josling Peninsula. However, Dr. G.M. Dawson's map showed it to be on the west end of Hibben Island, north of Pay Bay.

*BELL POINT — at the eastern entrance of Douglas Inlet. Named after John Bell, paymaster on the *Thetis* in 1852, and who that year was serving his 31st year as paymaster. He retired 3 years later.

*DOUGLAS INLET — the foot-shaped inlet which opens off the south side of Moore Channel, west of Mitchell Inlet. It was not named after Governor James Douglas as has been commonly supposed. Captain Kuper named it after Dr. John Douglas, the surgeon aboard the *Thetis* at the time of the 1852 survey. Kuper called the inlet DOUGLAS HARBOUR.

The old Haida name for the inlet was SKEN-TAI.

*McNUTT POINT — midway along the eastern shore of Douglas Inlet. Named after the second officer on the Hudson's Bay Company vessel *Una,* and the name confirmed in 1946.

*LESLIE POINT — is the name given to an irregularly shaped peninsula projecting into Douglas Inlet from the west shore. It is after Dr. Archibald Leslie Archer, assistant surgeon on the *Thetis* in 1852.

*HERBERT HEAD — the west entrance point of Douglas Inlet. Named in 1852 after Nathaniel Bland Herbert, second master on the *Thetis*. He assisted George Moore in the surveying of the waters of this region.

*ROE POINT — west of Herbert Head on the south shore of Moore Channel. The name was applied during the 1852 survey.

*HEWLETT BAY — on the south shore, almost at the mouth of Moore Channel, has a rocky island off its west side. Named by Captain Kuper in 1852 after William Hewlett who, like William Freshfield, (see Freshfield Point on opposite shore) was a master's assistant and assisted George Moore with the survey of 1852. The two young men were transferred the next year to the brig *Cockatrice*, but young Freshfield became ill and died shortly after the transfer. Hewlett eventually rose to the rank of Staff Commander in 1869.

KAIDJU, Songs-of-Victory-Town — a Raven Crest village of the Pitch-Town-People in the area somewhere between Hewlett Bay and Roe Point.

*****DENHAM POINT** — the south entrance point of Moore Channel. Named in 1852 after Annesley Turner Denham, midshipman aboard the *Thetis* during the survey of Gold Harbour. Denham took charge of one of the cutters used in the survey. Admiral Sir Henry M. Denham the noted surveying officer was Annesley Denham's father.

KA'SUWA'I KUN — the largest of the group of islets lying off Denham Point. It harboured an ocean spirit, Supernatural-being-of-the-point-towards-the-south, who belonged to the Eagle Crest. The supplicants prayed,"Give me food, Greatest One," as opposed to asking for a specific type of food. type of food.

*****DENHAM SHOALS** — lie about 2¾ miles west from Denham Point and Cape Henry, and are an area of irregular bottom. Shallow patches, several shoal heads and two rocks, one of which has a depth of less than 6 feet, occupy part of Denham Shoals. Named in association with the point.

*****CAPE HENRY** — to the southwest of Denham Point is a hook-nosed point with some rocks and islets off it. Named in 1793 by Captain George Vancouver for his friend Sir Henry Englefield, and named in association with Englefield Bay to the north of the point.

*****ANTIQUARY BAY** — about ¾ of a mile to the southeast of Cape Henry. The old name for this cove was LITTLE INLET. Renamed Antiquary Bay in association with Cape Henry and Englefield Bay. Sir Henry Englefield was an antiquary, or archaeologist, of much note.

There are two lakes close in behind Antiquary Bay, at the 300-foot level. These lakes are almost joined together, the larger and more easterly lake is over 2 miles long. Both lakes are drained by a creek which runs into a small unnamed bay less than half a mile south of Antiquary Bay. As yet the lakes are also unnamed.

WEST COAST OF MORESBY ISLAND,
BOTTLE INLET TO McLEAN FRASER POINT.
(INCLUDES TASU AND GOWGAIA)

CHAPTER SIX

*BOTTLE INLET — south of Cape Henry and Antiquary Bay. Known to early fishing captains as BOTTLENECK HARBOUR, it has thick patches of kelp extending for some 60 feet from either side of the narrow entrance, leaving a navigable passage of about 150 feet at the mouth. Once inside the inlet gradually widens. The land is high and somewhat bare near the entrance, but becomes low with some timber near the head.

The Haidas called the inlet KA'IGAOS.

*BOTTLE POINT — named in association with the inlet, is outside and to the south of Bottle Inlet.

*KOOTENAY INLET — to the south of Bottle Point, is entered from an unnamed bight which contains small islets, reefs and submerged rocks. "You need to know what you are doing to enter old Kootenay," say mariners, "and even then, you don't try it in a heavy sea."

There are two arms opening off the bight mentioned above - one runs off to the northeast and the other to the southeast. In early years they were called NORTH and SOUTH ARMS (of Kootenay). Today, however, the term Kootenay Inlet refers only to the south arm. The name is a modification of the old Haida name for the inlet.

A Haida settlement had been established years ago at the head of Kootenay Inlet (or South Arm), which was still in seasonal use in pioneering years. Bert Roberts, pioneer of Tlell and Queen Charlotte City, recalls his first trip to the

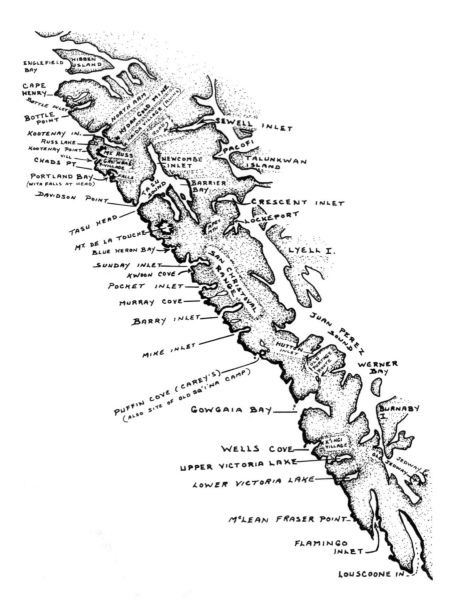

ENGLEFIELD BAY
HIBBEN ISLAND
CAPE HENRY
BOTTLE INLET
BOTTLE POINT
KOOTENAY IN.
RUSS LAKE
KOOTENAY POINT VILL
CHADS PT
PORTLAND BAY (WITH FALLS AT HEAD)
DAVIDSON POINT
TASU HEAD
MT DE LA TOUCHE
BLUE HERON BAY
SUNDAY INLET
KWOON COVE
POCKET INLET
MURRAY COVE
BARRY INLET
MIKE INLET
PUFFIN COVE (CAREY'S) (ALSO SITE OF OLD SQI'NA CAMP)
GOWGAIA BAY
WELLS COVE
UPPER VICTORIA LAKE
LOWER VICTORIA LAKE
McLEAN FRASER POINT
FLAMINGO INLET
LOUSCOONE IN.

NORTH ARM
HYDN CHRO MINE
MT RUSS
CLATHEDAL VILLAGE
FALLS
TASU SOUND
NEWCOMBE INLET
BARRIER BAY
SAN CHRISTOVAL RANGE
HUTTON INLET
SEWELL INLET
PACOFI
TALUNKWAN ISLAND
CRESCENT INLET
LOCKEPORT
LYELL I.
JUAN PEREZ SOUND
HOT HOUSE
WERNER BAY
BURNABY I.
K'INGI VILLAGE
JEDWAY

114

west coast when he and Joe Molitor rowed their small leaky boat out to look for a good trapping area. "The seas were mountainous. We seemed to row for endless hours looking for Kootenay one day," he said. "Thought we were all alone on that wild sea. Then were amazed to see a boat right behind us. Several Haidas and their wives were also on their way to Kootenay to trap. We felt like intruders, so when they invited us to join forces with them it was pretty good news." All winter the two young men joined in the trapping of bear and marten - sharing the pelts. "We learned to live off the land as they did," said Bert, "...eating seal meat among other things. And when you got as hungry as we did it tasted just fine!"

A trail ran from the Haida camp to the head of Newcombe Inlet in the Tasu region, which was in regular use in the early days of prospecting. About ¾ of a mile along the north shore of the inlet from the Haida camp is the old Hydah Gold Mine, which George Chapman first owned in 1913. Over the years it has been called *Kootenay, Rupert* and *Blue Mule,* but seems best known by the original name given it by Chapman, *Hydah Gold Mine.* The claims have been worked spasmodically over the years, but the gold proved to be mostly surface ore.[1]

[1]Q.C. Islands, Volume 1, page 305 to 306.

*MOUNT RUSS — a little over 3000 feet high, lies southwest of Kootenay Inlet. Known to early Haidas as SUNSHINE-UPON-HIS-BREAST, it harboured a spirit not directly connected with the Haidas, but who was very influential with other spirits.

The name of Russ by which the mountain is now known is after Amos Russ of Skidegate, one of the most courageous of all Haidas.

*RUSS LAKE — a small lake northwest of the mountain, also named after Amos Russ. Both names confirmed by the Permanent Names Committee in 1964.

The bravery of Amost Russ was equalled only by his monumental love and concern for his people. Born in 1849, he was still in his teens when he became acutely aware of the desperate need to stem increasing Haida corruption which was leading that great nation into oblivion. Russ had been chosen with care by an equally worried grandfather, a powerful Raven Crest chief of Skidegate, to be the one who would lead the Haida people back to the greatness which was their heritage, and was trained and educated for this role under the chief's personal supervision.

The young Russ became even more troubled, for he could not believe that the old ways held the solution. It was at this time he came under the influence of a Methodist missionary, and was converted to a way of thinking which he believed *might* hold the answer. It seemed to work for white people.

In the zeal of conversion Russ cast off traditions which, from the point of view of hindsight, may appear to have been unnecessary. But those were terrible times. The gangrene of corruption had set in. As the heroic young man set out to save his people, he defied his ancestral customs and put up with scorn which would have broken a less dedicated man.

There were others who had also wondered about the old ways in this growing emergency. But it was Amos Russ who took the lead. And it was Amos Russ who had to take the full brunt of censure. After he broke trail, the way was easier.

Destined to be a Raven chief of Skidegate, he came from one of the most influential families in the village. This made it more difficult initially; the fall is always hardest from the highest peak. But once the turn had been made, his influential position was an incalculable help in leading others. From a point where outsiders felt that the Skidegates were beyond help, their gradual recovery to proper balance has put them in the position where they are again the elite of all coastal tribes. No small part of this can be attributed to the bravery of Amos Russ.[1]

[1]Q.C. Islands, Volume 1, Chapter 18, contains the Amos Russ story.

*KOOTENAY POINT** — named in association with Kootenay Inlet, lies south of the entrance to Kootenay Inlet.

GASI'NDAS, Gambling-Village — stood at the head of a small unnamed inlet about 1¾ miles south of Kootenay Point. Even today the ruins of three of the old lodges may be found. "To see these old remains where they belong . . . in the rocks and dark forest . . . with the wind and driving rains. This is the real essence," says Gray Hill, who supplied many photos for this book. For visitors such as he, a violation or souvenir theft from these old sites is unthinkable. Observe, not touch, is their creed and thanks to them we learn about places inaccessible to most.

*CHADS POINT** — south of the unnamed bay mentioned above. Named after Captain H. Chads of *H.M.S. Portland*, flagship of Admiral Fairfax Moresby, for whom Moresby Island was named. Moresby was Commander-in-Chief of the Pacific Station from 1850 to 1853.

*PORTLAND BAY** — south of Chads Point, and named after *H.M.S. Portland*, is a bay wide open to the full sea. At its eastern end there is a waterfall and above the waterfall a small lake. All about this region the mountains rise to bare summits which attain heights of over 3000 feet.

TASU SOUND REGION

The entrance to Tasu Sound from the ocean is difficult to detect and the best landmark for it is the soaring

*MOUNT DE LA TOUCHE** — about 3¼ miles southeast of the entrance. Bare and conspicuous its 3,685-foot summit stands out boldly on a clear day to make an excellent guide.

Laperouse named this mountain in 1786 as he sailed along the west coast of the Charlottes. As he passed the present Englefield Bay he applied the name of *Baie de la Touche*, also for the same man. It is generally believed that Laperouse was honouring La Touche-Treville, the famous French naval commander, when

116

Mount de la Touche,
south of the entrance to Tasu Sound.

Photo - G. Gray Hill

he applied the names. But some authorities feel that Laperouse's first lieutenant was the De La Touche for whom both the *Baie* and the mountain were named.

*DAVIDSON POINT — is the north entrance point of Tasu Narrows. Named after Mr. Davidson of the National Defence, who was employed on a topographical survey with the *William J. Stewart* in 1935.

*TASU HEAD — is the south entrance point of Tasu Narrows. On a 1908 Department of Mines map, both this point and Davidson Point, opposite, were called TASSOO HEAD.

*TASU NARROWS — is entered from the Pacific Ocean by passing Davidson Point and Tasu Head. The deep channel of the Narrows is about 1 mile long and, at its narrowest, about 1/3 of a mile wide. There is nearly always an ocean swell near the entrance and sometimes this is quite heavy, but by the time the inside of the Narrows is reached the surge is almost spent. Three navigational lights direct ships safely from the ocean into Tasu Narrows and thence into Tasu Sound.

*TASU SOUND — which in early years was shown as TASSOO HARBOUR, is the main portion of the large basin which opens from Tasu Narrows. The name is from a Haida word meaning Lake-of-Plenty. It was the PORT MONTGOMERY of American traders in the years 1791-92 and was so named by Robert Haswell for General Richard Montgomery, who fell in the attack on Quebec in 1775.

The three main points of interest regarding the history of the Tasu area are; first - its ancient Haida history; second - the mining and prospecting; and third - it was donated to the Russian fishermen to be used as a free harbour, the only place in Canada to have this distinction.

There were numerous Haida villages and encampments around the shores of Tasu, some of which dated to the long-extinct Pitch-Town-People. One large village, Singa (Winter-Village), lay on the shore of Lomgon Bay. Burial caves associated with that village are on the point at the east end of the bay and, until a few years ago, contained burial boxes and skeletons. Souvenir hunters removed them. Now, little remains.

At the head of Newcombe Inlet a regularly used Haida camp lay at one end of a trail, which led from this point east to Sewell Inlet, and was occasionally used as a portage route, Thlcaggans Cass. Today a gravel road connects the two inlets, and is believed to follow the general route of the old Thlcaggans Cass. Another old trail from the head of Newcombe Inlet ran towards the west to the head of Kootenay Inlet.

The first prospecting to be done at Tasu was reported in 1907. By the next year the Department of Mines issued a map showing claims located in several sections. That year the Government authorized three trails to facilitate access to the east coast of Moresby. One trail was swamped out along the old Thlcaggans Cass and in 1909 it was corduroyed and a couple of cabins were built at either end to shelter freight whilst portions of the load were being portaged across the route.

A second trail was put in along what is now called Flat Creek, this trail came out near the head of Crescent Inlet, from this point it joined a third trail which went from the head of Crescent Inlet to Lockeport. There was another trail which led from Lockeport up to Anna Lake and thence, by way of Apex Mountain, to the head of Botany Inlet, the southeast arm of Tasu. This latter trail was really a series of blazes after it left Apex Mine, and was not a government trail.

It is mining and prospecting which still dominates the region, for this is the site of the big Westfrob mine - located at the north end of Fairfax Inlet. Its modern townsite nearby on Gowing Island is unexpected in that land of wilderness.

In 1970 when Russian fishing boats interfered with fishermen off the west coast of Vancouver Island, the Canadian Government - under pressure - offered harbour privileges at Tasu Harbour to the Russians, as well as complete and free fishing inside the territorial boundary waters off Tasu, if the Russian fishermen would keep out of the Vancouver Island grounds. This was agreed to. The harbour has been much in use by the Russians since - as many as 17 boats at anchor at the same time during the height of summer. The crews of these ships are not allowed ashore nor may they receive any visitors, other than officials.

On September 4, 1971, a disillusioned radio operator, 20-year-old Sergei Kourdakov, took advantage of midnight darkness combined with a raging storm to jump ship at Tasu. After a harrowing swim in icy waters he finally hauled ashore on rocks near Tasu townsite and through an interpreter pleaded for asylum. When investigations showed that the burly blonde sailor had been named the number one Communist youth in Eastern Russia, Canadian officials were chary of his sincerity and young Kourdakov spent the first few weeks in his newly-adopted land being shifted from one jail to another while his fate was being decided. Eventually he was granted sanctuary.

After his defection he joined an evangelistic movement based in California. On the last day of 1972 in a cabin he had rented for the New Year's weekend in the San Bernadino Mountains, Kourdakov apparently showed his girl friend how to safely play Russian roulette with a .38-calibre pistol, but misjudged and died of the resulting shot to his head.

The history of Tasu is reflected to some extent by its place names, but a number of the names applied to points in recent years by the Hydrographic Service are those of sealing ships based in Victoria in the 1880s.

*LOMGON BAY — on the north side of Tasu Sound. Formerly called ANCHOR BAY and also LOMCORN BAY. The name of Lomgon was finally adopted from the 1924 blueprints of Mr. A.E. Wright's 1924 survey.

WINTER-VILLAGE, *Singa* — lay near the stream which runs into the head of Lomgon Bay. It is said that the first Haida tattooing was done there during a potlatch feast celebrating the wedding of an important Eagle Crest woman from Cumshewa to the young Raven Chief of Winter Village. The potlatch celebrated both the wedding and the erection of the chief's new house. From this feast, tattooing became a common part of Haida rituals.

*LOMGON ISLETS — in Lomgon Bay, were named in 1946 by the Hydrographic Service in association with the name of the bay.

*SHEARER POINT — the west entrance point of Newcombe Inlet. Named after Squadron Leader Shearer, who was engaged on a mission for the Department of National Defence on the Charlottes in 1935. South and west of Shearer Point are the burial caves of old Winter Village.

*SHEARER ROCK — marked by kelp, is off Shearer Point, and has about 18 feet of water over it. Named in 1962 by the Hydrographic Service in association with the point.

*NEWCOMBE INLET — the north arm off Tasu Sound. Formerly called NORTH ARM, but renamed in 1936 because of the numerous duplications of that name. Changed to Newcombe Inlet, honouring Dr. C.F. Newcombe, anthropologist and leading authority on aboriginal British Columbia tribes. He made his first trip to the Charlottes in 1895, and a second more extended trip in his own boat *Pelican* in 1897. During the second trip Dr. Newcombe made a sketch survey of Tasu Sound, entering Haida names for features, as they were told to him at that time. (See also Newcombe Peak)

*WINNIFRED ROCKS — a compact group of drying rocks which lie off the southeast shore of the entrance to Newcombe Inlet. Named in 1962 by

the Hydrographic Service after the sealing vessel *Winnifred* which sailed out of Victoria in the 1880s. She was one of the boats seized by the Americans in the Bering Sea in 1892 during the Canadian-American sealing dispute, and towed into Unalaska where charges were laid.

*ARIEL ROCK — northwest of the Winnifred Rocks, is in the centre of the channel, and is 7 feet high. Named by the Hydrographic Service after the sealing schooner *Ariel*, based at Victoria in the 1880s. Captain Bucknam, formerly in charge of the *Sardonyx*, went east to buy the *Ariel* and brought her to the Pacific coast via the Horn. He made one trip to the Bering Sea before being ordered out during the sealing dispute. At one time James C. Prevost, son of Admiral Prevost, of the *Virago*, owned the *Ariel*.

*McALMOND POINT — on the west shore of Newcombe Inlet has a group of rocks off it. Named after Captain E.H. McAlmond by the Hydrographic Service in 1962. Born in Belfast in 1828 Captain McAlmond came to the Pacific coast shortly after his 22nd birthday. He sailed out of San Francisco as master of the schooner *Ino* and subsequently commanded a succession of ships, one of which was the schooner *Rebecca*, which brought Francis Poole to the Skincuttle Inlet region to look for copper, August 1862.

Between McAlmond Point and the head of Newcombe Inlet there were several mining claims staked as early as 1908 and the old trail out to Kootenay Inlet had been brushed out and was in use - although reportedly quite rough to traverse.

*TASU CREEK — flows into the eastern and larger of the two bays at the head of Newcombe Inlet. Early maps spelled it as TASSOO CREEK. It is off this eastern bay that the road to Sewell Inlet begins.

Geologists say that in ancient years the valley between the head of Sewell Inlet and the head of Newcombe Inlet was a saltwater channel.

*BLUNT POINT — on the eastern shore of Newcombe Inlet is opposite McAlmond Point. Blunt Point was named for the shape of the feature by the Hydrographic Service in 1962.

*CRAZY CREEK — on the east side of Newcombe Inlet, enters the inlet south of Blunt Point. One of the Pitch-Town-People's camping sites lay near the mouth of this creek. The name Crazy Creek dates back to at least 1912, but the reason for its name is not known.

*TWO MOUNTAIN BAY — a cove on the northeast side of Tasu Sound, acquired its name about 1911 when the Queen Charlotte Fishing Company, with headquarters in Vancouver, built a small fishing station and boat-building plant. A steam-powered mill was set up and enough yellow cedar lumber cut to build two boats, each about 50 feet long. "Yellow cedar. Fine above the water," say boatbuilders, "but below . . . how the teredos love it! Pure cake to them." The boats were built, but not yet outfitted when they were siezed and sold in a sheriff's sale, January 1913. One boat, *Dorothy Kalon* was used by the T.A. Kelley Company as a tug, with Walter Dass, well-known Islands skipper, as her first captain. Under another captain later on she was wrecked on Cumshewa Rocks and Jimmy Clark, the engineer, was drowned. The second boat, *Rennell*, became a halibutter out of Prince Rupert and she, too, met an untimely end, sinking in Wright Sound.

*EDWARDS CREEK — flows into Two Mountain Bay, a little to the north of where the old wharf stood. This creek, which has a waterfall about a mile upstream, is believed to owe its name to a mining claim staked there in late 1907 or early 1908. Hjawkins "Frank" Edwards, a prospector, miner and former ore sampler from the Nelson district did some staking in the Tasu area and sold his claim, before registration, to James E. Corlett, Mr. Corlett registered the claim in May of 1908, calling it the *Edwards Mineral Claim*. It was still registered to him some years later. "Frank" Edwards, meanwhile, returned to the Tasu region in the summer of 1908 with a partner, Harry Crouse of Slocan, for another prospecting trip. The two men were caught in a series of gales and had such a narrow escape they decided they were finished with the wild coast off Tasu.

Edwards, however, liked living on Graham Island and applied for a pre-emption near Miller Creek. He built a cabin on Lot 494 and eventually received his Crown Grant for the land.

When the fishing station came into operation at Two Mountain Bay in 1911, water rights were applied for on Edwards Creek - called EDWARDS RIVER then, and it appeared under the latter name on Captain Freeman's chart published shortly afterwards.

*FLYAWAY ISLET — is 195 feet high, and joined by a drying ledge to the narrow peninsula fronting Two Mountain Bay. There are rocks and a reef off the east tip of Flyaway Islet also. Named after the 7-ton sloop, *Flyaway*, commanded by Captain Daniel McLean, a native of Cape Breton. Captain McLean came to the Pacific coast in 1880 and sailed more than 3,000 miles along the shores of British Columbia and Alaska prospecting for minerals. Later he went into sealing. Flyaway Islet named by the Hydrographic Service in 1962.

*BARRIER BAY — a name from the prospecting era of 1907. This is the bay south and east of Two Mountain Bay.

*FLAT CREEK — empties into a bight on the east side of Barrier Bay. In the years 1908 to 1912 this creek was known as DUCK CREEK. The Government trail to the head of Crescent Inlet followed its valley for much of the way. The creek runs diagonally along a lush timber valley and drains a small lake which is a fisherman's paradise. The distinctive Red Top Mountain overlooks Flat Creek valley.

*AMETHYST ROCK — at the entrance to Wilson Bay was named in 1962 by the Hydrographic Service after the sealing vessel *Amethyst* of the 1880s. In the summer of 1876 when Lord Dufferin, Governor-General of Canada, paid a visit to North coastal places, he was on the steamer *Sir James Douglas*, accompanied by the *Amethyst*. They were in Skidegate Inlet on September 4, and during the short visit interpreter Mr. Blenkinsop was sent ashore to see if a totem pole could be purchased. The quest was unsuccessful.

When the party visited William Duncan at Metlakatla they learned that the little jail held a man serving 2 months for distilling spirits on the Charlottes. The prisoner, highly indignant at being so held, told Lord Dufferin, "The Haidas were showing me how to make booze and I was the one who got jugged."

*WILSON BAY — south of Barrier Bay. This name was taken from Mr. A.E. Wright's blueprint and survey of 1924. A creek runs into the head of Wilson Bay and some of the old maps show a trail following this creek part way, before cutting over to the head of Crescent Inlet, where it intersected a trail to Lockeport.

*WILSON ISLET — on the west side of Wilson Bay about 500 feet off the shore of Botany Island. Wooded and about 180 feet high, it was named in association with Wilson Bay by the Hydrographic Service in 1962.

*BOTANY INLET — a name from the 1907-08 days of prospecting, although at that time it was called BOTANY BAY. Its Haida name was GAO'D'JAN. A slim inlet about 3 miles long, it is the southeast arm of Tasu waters.

A Mr. H.B. Cannon had some mining claims at the head of Botany Inlet in 1909-10 and used the route via Sewell Inlet to Newcombe Inlet to get in and out to them - finding it extremely inconvenient. "He was talking to Dad, wishing he could find a shorter way," recalled Harry Morgan, pioneer prospector of Lockeport. "So Dad took him in from Lockeport by way of Anna Lake where we had our claims. Cannon had two boys with him from California who had never seen snow. They had 2 miles of the stuff to cross at that time of year, in back of Anna Lake. They really were worried . . . thought for sure their feet would freeze off before they got across. Cannon left about 1910."

*BOTANY ISLAND — lies at the entrance to Botany Inlet. In 1908 it was called BELL ISLAND after Ross Bell, one of the first prospectors in Lockeport and Tasu areas, having arrived about 1907. Bell was one of the original owners of the Apex Mine on the ridge between Botany Inlet and Anna Lake. It is believed by old timers that he also had a claim on Botany Island. The island renamed from Bell to Botany Island following Mr. A.E. Wright's 1924 survey.

*WESTER POINT — the north tip of Botany Island. Named in 1962 by the Hydrographic Service after Captain George Wester. An extremely handsome man according to his photograph, George Wester was born in Norway and came to San Francisco in 1880 before his 21st birthday. He sailed on many ships out of that port, and in later years came to Victoria in command of the sealer *City of San Francisco*.

CORLETT PENINSULA — not gazetted nor on maps, but well-enough known in early prospecting days so that the 1909 mining report used the name to identify the *Ajax Mining Claim*. It is the peninsula separating Fairfax Inlet from Botany Inlet. Named after James Emery Corlett, the managing-director of the Moresby Lumber Company mill at Queen Charlotte City. Corlett had such a capable mill manager in Emmanuel Girard, he had little to do and could indulge in his growing interest of speculative mining from 1908 to 1915. Tasu attracted him. He owned several claims, beginning with his 1908 purchase of the *Edwards* claim. By 1910 he had become part owner in the *Warwick Group* on the north slope of Mount Moody - the site of the Westfrob mine today.

The *Ajax* property on the northwest end of Corlett Peninsula belonged originally to George Chapman, Robert Kitson and Dick Husband, well-known pioneers of the Queen Charlotte City area. These three young men had put in a 70-foot adit in 1908. In 1965 Moresby Mines Limited owned this property and the claims were under a new name, *Garnet*.

*REID POINT — the northeast tip of the Corlett Peninsula. Named after Commander H.E. Reid who, in the spring of 1935, made an inspection trip of harbours and anchorages on the west coast of the Charlottes for the Department of National Defence.

*FAIRFAX INLET — has been known by several names, SOUTH WEST ARM, SOUTH ARM, TASSOO HARBOUR and WRIGHT INLET. Named Wright Inlet after Mr. A.E. Wright, B.C.L.S., who made an extensive triangulation over the mountain ranges between Skidegate Channel and Tasu Sound, and a complete triangulation of all the inlets and channels between Skidegate Channel and Botany Bay. Wright Inlet was confirmed in 1946, but because of duplications in other B.C. waters, the name was changed in 1951 to Fairfax Inlet after Rear Admiral Fairfax Moresby, for whom Moresby Island was named. In 1908 mining claims almost solidly ringed the entire shore of this inlet. Rand McDonald, pioneer of Lockeport, owned part of the *Sullivan* group on this inlet and by 1908 had built a cabin, several trails and made other improvements on the claims.

WRIGHT LAKE — at the head of Fairfax Inlet, source of the water supply for the present Tasu townsite. The mining company have dammed the lake and put in a powerhouse to enable them to pump water to the townsite.

*HUNGER HARBOUR — on the west side of Fairfax Inlet. Named about 1908. "I don't think it would be hard to see why it got its name," said one old-timer. "A prospector likely got weather-bound there and ran out of grub." At the south end of Hunger Harbour a stream comes out near the site of an ancient Haida encampment. This was also the proposed location of the first townsite in Tasu when mining began to show definite promise in 1908 to 1912.

OLIVER MOUNTAIN — shown on all early maps, lay almost due south of the old proposed Tasu townsite. Rising to a little over 3,000 feet mining claims had been staked on its slopes extensively by 1908. Named after William Oliver, well-known Methodist missionary and pioneer of Sandspit.

MOODY MOUNTAIN — north of Oliver Mountain, towers above the present townsite of Tasu and the Westfrob mine operation in process along its slopes. It, too, was named about 1908 and is after Henry Moody of Skidegate who is reported to have made the first significant ore discovery in Tasu. He subsequently sold his holdings to the Elliott Mining Company early in 1909 - a company which had acquired other claims as well in the Tasu region. Mining reports now refer to Moody Mountain as MOUNT TASU. It is between 3300 and 3399 feet high.

*GOWING ISLAND — at the entrance to Hunger Harbour, and lying at the approach to Fairfax Inlet. Named about 1908 after Arthur Gowing who came to Tasu from Trout Lake and Revelstoke. Gowing was very active in

Tasu Mine on the side of Moody Mountain (now called Tasu Mountain) in 1966.
The townsite lies on Gowing Island, the buildings seen through the trees left of centre.

Photo - G. Gray Hill

Tasu townsite - 1971.
School in centre of picture.
It was 92° in the shade when
this photo was taken in July,
1971.

Photo - K.E. Dalzell

staking mining claims in Tasu in 1908 and played a leading part in bringing the Elliott Mining Company into being. The claim they subsequently mined later became part of Westfrob Mines Limited. Mr. Elliott, consistently beset by financial problems, tried hard to sell the mine almost from the beginning.

"I remember working for him for awhile," said Harry Morgan, formerly of Lockeport, "and he wanted to show his place to some eastern company, hoping to sell it. The tunnel was about 300 feet long, and they wanted a sample the full length. So we put a hole, 1 foot deep, every 18 inches and set it so they would blow - one after another. One man started at the face with what we called a spitter, a piece of fuse about 4 feet long, notched about 1 inch apart. When that burned out, another man took over until they had all the shots going. Caused such a commotion some Indians working across the bay came hi-tailing it over to see what the heck was going on. Elliott closed down just after that."

Gowing Island is best known today as the site of the present townsite of Tasu and, strictly speaking, it is not an island now, for a causeway connects it with Moresby Island.

TASU TOWNSITE — straddling Gowing Island, is where the employees of the Westfrob open-pit mining operation have their living quarters. The townsite contains a small co-operative store, modern apartments, row houses, excellent gymnasium and indoor swimming pool among other amenities. There are two approaches to living at Tasu. One, you grin and bear it until you can get out. But there are other views. Such as that held by the young, handsome Dr. Peter Mylechreest. "For most of my life in England I avidly read stories about Canada, and longed to go there," he recalls. "Finally a chance came, but working in the hospitals in large Canadian cities was disillusioning. Then came one of those fluke opportunities. I heard about isolated Tasu. At last I felt I was really in the Canada I had always pictured. The abundance of wildlife, rugged terrain, huge mountains, trees right down to the water's edge. I found it a fascinating place to explore."

Visitors, as well as residents, soon found how much he valued Tasu. Woe betide anyone who abused hunting or fishing privileges. They quickly felt the scalpel edge of this outspoken doctor's tongue. As for those unspeakables - the souvenir hunters of old Indian burial caves in the region - his denunciation was withering.

Early predictions of a town containing upwards of 1000 people have not materialized. "Probably between 400 and 500 would be closer, and part of those are always on the move, one crew coming, one going. Isolation and rain, and a longing for the bright lights of the cities exert a pull too great to resist," said a former resident as he left on his way "outside."

*MAGNESON POINT** — west of Gowing Island. Named after Captain Louis Magneson of the Victoria sealing schooner, *Walter A. Earle*, which was lost with all hands on April 14, 1895. With the schooners *Favorite* and *Libbie*, she had been following seals up the coast, and on the 13th all vessels were 30 miles off Pappalonas, a small submerged reef to the south of Cape St. Elias. Weather was fine in the morning, but at noon the barometer dropped quickly and all small boats were signalled to return to the schooners. By night a gale raged. The *Libbie* and *Favorite* managed to ride out the storm, but both had narrow escapes - to the point where hope had almost been abandoned. When morning dawned the two vessels could see no sign of the *Walter A. Earle*, until a stunned lookout pointed to a slowly heaving object. She rode bottom up, rudder missing - a lethal loss in a gale such as they had encountered.

*HORN ISLAND — a name from the days of 1908. About 160 feet high and wooded, this island is connected to Moresby Island by a drying and above-water reef. There is a light on the north end of Horn Island and some privately owned floats in the small bay between the island and Magneson Point.

*HORN ROCK — is the bare 8-foot-high rock lying at the north part of the group of rocks which were formerly called, as a group, SEAL ROCKS. The name was changed because of numerous duplications in coastal waters and the newer name of Horn confirmed in 1946. It lies east and north of Horn Island and was named in association.

This marks the end of the Tasu region names. From this point it is proposed to leave Tasu Sound and continue southward along the west coast of Moresby Island.

Pinnacle rocks near entrance to Pocket Inlet,
west coast of Moresby Island, south of Tasu Sound.

Photo - G. Gray Hill

SAOLANGAI VILLAGE — as shown on Dr. C.F. Newcombe's map, appears to have been in one of the three indentations which lie between Tasu Head and Sunday Inlet. It belonged to the Pitch-Town-People and had a stream entering its head which drained a small lake.

BLUE HERON BAY — the largest and most southerly of the three indentations between Tasu Head and Sunday Inlet. Named by Neil and Betty Carey of Sandspit for identification purposes during Texas Gulf Sulphur mineral explorations in 1971, the name is now used locally with much frequency. A stream leads into the head of Blue Heron Bay from a lake at the 385-foot level.

*SUNDAY INLET — formerly called SUNDAY HARBOUR by Captain A. Freeman on his sketch map of 1912. The creek flowing into the north side of Sunday Inlet, near the head, drains a veritable network of small lakes, some of which are little larger than pools, and are very near another network of lakes which drain the opposite way - into Bigsby Inlet on the east side of Moresby Island. Two of the lakes which drain into Sunday Inlet are the Summit Lakes, which lie south of the west end of Anna Lake.

*SAN CHRISTOVAL RANGE — lies a short distance inland and extends between Sunday Inlet and Mike Inlet. Bare and rugged, it rises to elevations just over 3,000 feet - the highest peak, a little to the north of Barry Inlet, is slightly over 3,500 feet. These mountains received their name from the first white man known to have visited the Queen Charlottes - Juan Perez, captain of the Spanish ship *Santiago,* who sailed to waters off the north end of the Charlottes in 1774. Stormy waters prevented them from landing, but Perez did leave behind the first two recorded names to be applied in British Columbia, Cape Santa Margarita to the northwest extremity, and the name applied to this mountain range on Moresby Island, SIERRA DE SAN CHRISTOVAL, which Perez named after the beloved St. Christopher, known especially for his great height and his protection of travellers.

*KWOON COVE — is the bight immediately south of the entrance to Sunday Inlet. The name was confirmed in 1964 and is a modification of the Haida word for whalebone.

*POCKET INLET — south of Sunday Inlet and Kwoon Cove, has a summit with a conspicuous white scar to mark the north side of its entrance. The first European name given to this inlet was in 1884 when Newton Chittenden called it GRAND VIEW INLET. "It is one of the securest retreats for small boats ever seen. When opposite the entrance, the rocky shore seemed to offer no landing place unless the storm should abate," he wrote. "Then unexpectedly my Indian guides turned directly towards land and ran through a narrow rock-bound passage into a little basin, surrounded by mountains rising very precipitously. Ten cataracts plunged down their sides. The smallest canoe could lie in safety here at all times. And the scenery is magnificent."
Fishermen who used this harbour in early years called it GOD'S POCKET. The northwest entrance point is high and, extending well southward, partly

overlaps the entrance - similar to a pocket-flap. The name was shortened by Captain Freeman on his 1912 map to Pocket Harbour and this in turn was changed to Pocket Inlet. A 1921 Naval Intelligence Return called it THOMSON HARBOUR, but the name apparently never in use other than on that particular map.

MURRAY COVE — lies between Pocket Inlet and Barry Inlet. There are three indentations along this portion of the coast. Murray Cove is the middle bay. Open to the sea, it has a high pinnacle rock lying off its southeastern entrance. There is a boulder beach at the head of Murray Cove, onto which an unnamed stream flows draining a lake at the 200-foot level, which is about 1½ miles long.
Murray Cove named by Captain A. Freeman about 1912.

BARRY INLET — about 2½ miles south of Murray Cove. Named in 1912 by Captain A. Freeman after Captain B. Barry who, after serving as mate for Freeman, was afterward in command of the trawler *Celestial Emprie* for the Canadian Fishing Company. Barry Inlet, about 3 miles long, has a sandy beach at its head. Close inside the entrance on the south side is a high, bare granite bluff.

MIKE INLET — south of Barry Inlet was also named by Captain Freeman after one of the skippers on boats belonging to his company. Captain Mike Scott ran the halibutter *New England* for some time.

PUFFIN COVE — a little over 3 miles south of Mike Inlet. This is the name Neil and Betty Carey have bestowed on the bay which fronts their beloved west coast homesite - however it is usually called CAREY'S by their friends and visitors.
Neil and Betty Carey are Americans who came to visit the Charlottes some years ago and were so captivated by the west coast, they became permanent Island residents. Their "official" home is at Sandspit, where they have established an extremely interesting collection of beachcombed treasures from all sections of Queen Charlotte Islands beaches - but the home of their hearts is the little cabin at Puffin Cove.
Although it does not have a gazetted name, the bay is described with a fair amount of detail in the B.C. Pilot, which particularly notes the 490-foot islet off the northwest entrance to the bay. A creek with branches draining several lakes runs into the head of the cove.

SQ'I'NA — the Haida encampment of early years at the head of Puffin Cove.

GOWGAIA BAY — lies about 33 to 35 miles south of Tasu Narrows and has had several names over the years. The first European name given it was MAGEE'S SOUND, applied by Joseph Ingraham on June 1, 1791, after one of the owners of his vessel *Hope*. The passage between the two Nangwai Islands at the mouth of Gowgaia he named PORT PERKINS after Thomas Hanasyd

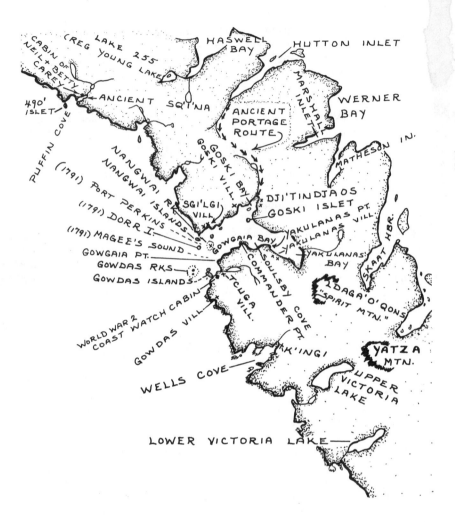

Perkins of the Boston importing firm of Perkins and Company who specialized in trade with China. Later the south Nangwai Island was named by Ingraham, DORR ISLAND, after Ebenezer Dorr, supercargo on the *Hope*.

It was in 1792 on his second trip to the Charlottes as master of the *Hope* that Ingraham, already greatly fascinated with the place, decided to try an experiment. Noting that there were no wolves or similar predators on the Islands, he put ashore at Gowgaia Bay two sows and a boar, hoping ". . . they will thrive and increase." Nothing was heard of the pigs again.

In 1884 Newton Chittenden called Gowgaia Bay ROBSON INLET.

Fishermen about the turn of the present century called Gowgaia Bay BIG BAY. This name became officially adopted by the Permanent Names Committee in 1933. Later because of numerous duplications of that name the Hydrographic Service suggested a modification of the old Haida name for the bay and in

1947 it was officially renamed GOWGAIA BAY.

There are five known former Haida village sites in Gowgaia Bay with a sixth close by, to the south of the entrance.

*NANGWAI ISLANDS — are the two wooded islands at the north part of the entrance to Gowgaia Bay and were named in 1949 after the Haida name for these islands. As mentioned earlier, the south Nangwai Island was called DORR ISLAND by Joseph Ingraham in 1792 and the passage between north and south Nangwai, PORT PERKINS.

*NANGWAI ROCK — lying east of the south Nangwai Island, dries at 8 feet. Named in 1962 by the Hydrographic Service in association with the islands.

SGI'LGI, Duck-Town — lay on the north shore of Gowgaia Bay near the entrance. Owned by an Eagle tribe formerly of Louscoone Inlet, the chief of this village bore the name Ninstints, and his wife was a shaman. They called their lodge Thunder-rolls-upon it. The fifth successor to Ninstints became the famous chief of Anthony Island whose ten potlatches brought him such fame that not only Anthony Island, but the whole region was known as Ninstints Territory.

*GOSKI BAY — takes in the northeast part of Gowgaia Bay and is a modifica-tion of the Haida name for the village which lay on the west shore of this bay. The larger village of Dj'tindjaos stood on the east, near the mouth of the stream coming into the head of the bay.

In 1884 when Newton Chittenden made an exploratory trip to the Charlottes for the British Columbia Government, he walked along the old trail which led south from the head of Hutton Inlet, on the east coast of Moresby, and following the valley emerged at Goski Bay. The route followed the Hutton Inlet creek then crossed over to go along the valley of a creek emptying into the head of Goski Bay. "In making the crossing I found hundreds of acres of pasture land surrounding a beautiful lake," he reported. His Haida guides told him that this old trail was a portage route used by their forebears.

*GOSKI ISLET — which was named in association with the bay in 1962, is a grey sparsely wooded islet on the east side of the entrance to Goski Bay.

GOSKI VILLAGE — on the west side at the entrance to Goski Bay.

DJI'TINDJAOS VILLAGE — larger than Goski village, was on the east side of the mouth of the stream entering the head of Goski Bay.

*YAKULANAS BAY — an arm running from the southeast part of Gowgaia Bay. Named for the old village which years ago lay on its west shore. Two creeks come into Yakulanas Bay, one at the head and another on its east side. Both have drying flats off their mouths, and the latter creek drains a lake at the 250-foot level.

LDAGA'O'QONS, Spirit-Mountain — the mountain overlooking the head of Yakulanas Bay which harbours a protective spirit who guards the creeks in this area.

YAKULANAS VILLAGE — lay in a cove on the west shore of Yakulanas Bay, near the entrance.

*YAKULANAS POINT — the west entrance point of Yakulanas Bay, and it also marks the east extremity of Soulsby Cove.

*SOULSBY COVE — on the south shore of Gowgaia Bay and west of Yakulanas Bay, is fringed by rock ledges interspersed with sandy beaches. Named in 1936 after Lieutenant Commander H.W.S. Soulsby who anchored in the cove with the *H.M.C.S. Armentières* in the spring of 1935 when on a special mission for the Department of National Defence. *Armentières* was a mine sweeper engaged in surveying operations with the *C.G.S. Stewart*.

*COMMANDER POINT — the west entrance point of Soulsby Cove, was also named after Commander Soulsby.

*GOWGAIA POINT — a rocky point on the southwest shore of Gowgaia Bay, near the entrance. Named by the Hydrographic Service in association with the bay.

TCUGA, Mouth-of-the-tide-village — stood on the east shore of the unnamed inlet near the south entrance of Gowgaia Bay. A tidal lagoon lay close to this village; the narrow entrance to the lagoon became a miniature rapids at certain stages of the tide as the water rushed in and then out. The village took its name from this. Sea otters often came into the inlet to sleep and, because the inlet belonged to the chief's wife, he had the option of killing them. His name had the curious translation of "one-without-entrails."

During World War II the R.C.A.F. occupied a small outpost in the inlet west and south of the old Haida site. One of the former guards who spent time on watch said that they were required to report on all Japanese warships entering the bay. "We spent the whole wartime there. Never saw a thing to report. Had a fine camping holiday . . . with pay." Visitors say the well-built cabin is still in fair condition. Several ricks of firewood await a burner, but moss and lichen cover them. In one corner of the cabin lies a stack of wartime magazines, the men whose names headline them are all dead now. The old cabin remains in the lonely woods watching the vast rolling ocean.

*GOWDAS ISLANDS — at the south entrance of Gowgaia Bay. Two in number and both wooded, the north island has numerous rocks close by. The south, and larger of the Gowdas Islands, is joined by a drying ledge to Moresby Island. Named by the Hydrographic Service after the old Haida village which lay 1¼ miles to the south.

*GOWDAS ROCKS — west of the Gowdas Islands. Formerly called BLACK

ROCKS, but owing to duplications of that name the rocks were renamed in association with the Gowdas Islands by the Hydrographic Service. The largest of the Gowdas Rocks is 19 feet high.

GOWDAS VILLAGE — lay in a rock-fringed cove 1¼ miles south of the Gowdas Islands.

*WELLS COVE — the first large indentation south of Gowgaia Bay. Named by Captain A. Freeman after one of the mates on the *Celestial Empire*. Islets and rocks are scattered haphazardly in the entrance to this bay.

K'INGI VILLAGE — lay at the head of the present Wells Cove, near the stream at the head of the bay.

*UPPER VICTORIA LAKE — drains into the unnamed bay south of Wells Cove. In ancient years there lived in this area a tribe of Indians which other Haidas called the Fresh-Water-Haidas. Nothing seems to be known of these people. Caves have been located in and around the approach to the lake, which may be burial caves or even former habitations. There are skeletons in some of the caves - still unmolested. Woe to the visitor who disturbs their slumber.

Upper Victoria Lake is at the 140-foot level and extends eastward for nearly 4 miles. It drains into a smaller lake and thence by a creek into the ocean - the mouth of the creek having a protected entrance.

*YATZA MOUNTAIN — overlooking the east end of Upper Victoria Lake, is about 2,400 feet high. The name, applied in 1964, is a modification of the Haida word for knife. Yatza's sharp silhouette is visible from the east side of Moresby Island as well as from the west, as it straddles the backbone of the mountain range running down the spine of Moresby Island.

*LOWER VICTORIA LAKE — south of its counterpart, Upper Victoria, lies at the 130-foot level and is slightly smaller. It drains into an unamed bay with a hook-shaped peninsula off its north entrance point, which Dr. C.F. Newcombe called GWA-IXILA in 1897.

HADJILTA — an ancient Haida village or camping site lay along the rugged coast between Lower Victoria and McLean Fraser Point, and was indicated by Dr. C.F. Newcombe on his sketch map of Haida sites.

*MCLEAN FRASER POINT — is approximately 5 miles south of Lower Victoria Lake and some 3 miles north of Nagas Point. Named after Dr. C. McLean Fraser, head of the Department of Zoology at the University of British Columbia at one time and for 12 years held the position of Director of the Pacific Coast Biological Station at Departure Bay. Dr. Fraser spent 2 months on board the *C.G.S. Stewart* in the summer of 1935, making shore animal collections. His work began at this point.

The rocky spires off McLean Fraser Point are spectacular, and the vicious tide rips off this part of the coast can be equally spectacular under certain conditions.

CHAPTER SEVEN

When the first white men arrived in this region Koyah was the undisputed chief of all Raven Crest villages and encampments in the area. He headed a proud, vigorous and extremely aggressive tribe. Warring at the slightest excuse, the fighting prowess of this branch of the Haidas caused panic and fear in mainland tribes whenever the name of *Haida* was heard. For Koya's people ranged far - and they ranged at will - usually leaving a bloody swath.

During the early years of fur trading Koyah always led the bartering for the people of the Houston Stewart region. A diminutive man with an exceedingly savage countenance, he was instantly recognized by the vessel captains who came in to do business, and the entire region was called, simply, KOYAH'S.

In 1789 two American ships came to trade along the Northwest coast. The 212-ton *Columbia Rediva* and the 90-ton sloop *Lady Washington* had left Boston in the fall of 1787 with 47-year-old Captain John Kendrick on the larger ship and in charge of the expedition. Robert Gray, 15 years his junior, commanded the consort sloop. If the roles had been reversed perhaps history might have taken a significantly different turn.

Kendrick, a dawdler and dreamer, was no leader of men. Being in command of such a pioneer trading trip proved utterly beyond him. The contrast of Captain Gray's courage and initiative, which sometimes bordered on rashness, did nothing to ease Kendrick's situation. Proud and dictatorial, John Kendrick overcompensated for his shortcomings by taking an unreasonable attitude to those of his crew and officers who suspected their captain's inaptitude.

By the time the *Columbia* arrived at the Cape Verde Islands, the conditions on the ship had become so bad the first mate, Simon Woodruff, quit the vessel and stayed at the Cape Verdes.[1] Dr. Roberts, the ship's surgeon, equally disgusted with Kendrick by that time also, resigned-giving ill-health as his reason. Kendrick furiously refused to let him go. When the doctor went ashore in spite of him, Kendrick went after him with a sword. However, the police on the Cape Verdes intervened and Dr. Roberts did not rejoin the *Columbia*.

When the ships reached the Falkland Islands, Second Mate Robert Haswell, promoted from 3rd mate when Woodruff left, asked to be transferred to the sloop *Washington*. Surprisingly, Kendrick complied - but his self-confidence grew even less because of the low morale aboard the *Columbia*. He dawdled about decisions to such an extent the vessels did not reach Nootka until September 1788, a full year after leaving Boston.

Captain Gray, impatient to begin trading as soon as they arrived, was promptly forbidden to do so - presumably as an exercise in authority by the senior commander, Kendrick. Not until March would Kendrick give consent. Gray immediately left for northern waters in the *Washington*. The *Columbia* swung at anchor awaiting his return.

Gray sailed northward, possibly as far as Bucarelli Bay, Alaska, and the *Washington* is believed to have been one of the first vessels to pass the full length of Hecate Strait. Returning southward the *Washington* sailed along the west coast of the Charlottes.

When they anchored in Cloak Bay, off Langara Island, 20 to 30 canoes came out to trade from nearby Haida villages. "June 1st, 1789:-" wrote Second Mate Haswell in the ship's log, "In a few minutes we had purchased 200 prime skins for only one chizzle each." It was the bargain of the century. Gray bragged about it for some time to come. But as the Haidas grew more experienced they realized how they had been victimized and - for future traders - this region would prove to be one of the most expensive places to trade for furs.

The next stop for the *Washington* was in the present Houston Stewart Channel, which at that time Gray named Barrell's Sound after one of the owners of his ship. Haidas from Anthony Island came off to trade and good relations were established. Chief Koyah very much to the fore. The Americans noticed some petty pilfering on the part of these Haidas, but with lucrative trading under way, it was thought advisable to pay no special attention to the "shoplifting."

The small cove to the south of the large Haida village on Anthony Island where the *Washington* dropped anchor on June 11, 1789, became Gray's Cove. The Charlottes as a whole were named WASHINGTON'S ISLE, by Captain Gray who believed they were one continuous island. It was at this time 2nd Mate Robert Haswell decided to go ashore to stretch his legs and became the first white man known to have actually set foot on the Charlottes.

When Gray rejoined the *Columbia* at Nootka he found Captain Kendrick preparing to sail north. For some reason the two men exchanged ships. Gray took over the *Columbia,* but instead of going north for more trading he was sent with what furs he had, to Boston, via China. Kendrick moved on board the little *Washington* and at long last began to undertake the mission of trading.

He was no more adept as a trader than he had been as leader of the expedition.

[1]Story under Woodruff Bay.

Having heard repeatedly about Gray's wonders and especially his bargain at Cloak Bay, Kendrick was in an irritable mood the day they drew in to Koyah's. When Koyah and his chiefs proved to be formidable bargainers, Kendrick's mounting frustration reached breaking point. He noticed the Haidas pilfering whenever they thought they were unobserved. This did not help. When he caught them helping themselves to his own personal laundry, that finished things. Calling for head chief Koyah to be seized and bound, along with one of the lesser chiefs, Kendrick also ordered his sailors to cut off the chiefs' hair and their faces to be insultingly splashed with paint.

The watching Haidas backed off in alarm. This was incredible. No one had ever laid a hand on Koyah before - or would have dared. Worse was to come. Kendrick had the cannons dismounted and the legs of the two hapless chiefs placed in the barrels. It was made clear that they would be blown to bits unless all trading proceeded according to his dictates. Stunned, Koyah's people complied. If such treatment could be meted out to their bravest chief - what might be done to them if they refused?

Their complete obedience to his command afforded Kendrick a measure of satisfaction. "Damn thieving savages! Who did they think they were?" And in the eyes of his crew he must now appear in a more favorable light. Perhaps he wouldn't hear so much about that cursed Gray after this. He weighed anchor and left - sailing to China shortly afterwards.

Better by far for Kenrick to have killed Koyah outright than to have released him. The small humiliations Kendrick had suffered as he strove to maintain a semblance of leadership in the face of odious comparison with Gray, was nothing to the humiliation he had caused Koyah.

For Koyah to have been made a helpless prisoner and so grossly insulted was an insufferable offense. In the eyes of his tribe he had been reduced to slave status. The great Koyah had lost face. His disgrace could only be overcome by returning the same treatment to someone else, in even stronger fashion.

Koyah planned and schemed for two years. Slowly a plan took shape as to how the revenge might be accomplished. Not only would he kill a white man, but he would also capture an entire ship. But Haida knives are small defence against cannons - no matter how brave a warrior might be. By great irony it was Kendrick himself, who provided Koyah's opportunity.

In June 1791, returning to the northwest coast from China, Kendrick took the *Washington* into Koyah's waters. Befuddled by too many sips from his ever-present bottle these days, John Kendrick had grown careless. Too many Haidas allowed on board. White men's weapons unguarded in the heat of bargaining. Koyah's moment had come. The ship was overpowered, but in his moment of elation Koyah, too, became careless and the Americans were able to turn the tables.

Guns were retrained full blast on every Haida in sight. This carnage should have been enough. The ship was free. But Kendrick's self-confidence had been so badly shaken by the encounter - which he knew was caused by his own inattention - he viciously ordered his men into the small boats to pursue the few Haidas who did escape into the woods. "Kill them all! The treacherous devils!" he screamed.

The slaughter became incredible. Unfortunately, once again, Koyah lived.

His hatred and his now abysmal disgrace became his demon. To kill and kill and kill - this was all that could possibly assuage the dreadful degradation.

He began by making war on other Haidas - the Skidegates and the Kloos. Their weapons were the same as his. A few successes. He became enboldened to try more - the foreigners. How many ships and crews fell victim to his onslaught will never be known, but this fanaticism led to his being referred to as Old Scorch-Eye.

When 19-year-old Captain John Boit sailed his vessel *Union* into Koyah's in 1895, plans were laid to make her a victim. But young Boit managed to out-manoeuvre the raiding party and saved both his ship and crew. To do so he was compelled to open fire on the Haidas who swarmed aboard. Mercifully Koyah was among those killed. The terrible days of Koyah's revenge were over. But the actions of Koyah and Kendrick left a legacy of distrust and bitterness. More lives were lost, both white and Haida, before peace finally came to the people of these lovely islands.

Towards the middle of the 1800s an Eagle Crest chief, Ninstints, began to rise in prestige, not for battle honours, but because of wealth. Astute trading with white men brought Ninstints a fortune which enabled him to give potlatches so lavish and with such frequency he became compared with the richest, most powerful chief at that time - the great Edenso of the north end of the Charlottes. Ninstints became a name of status. The region formerly called "Koyah's" was now known for this new and even more powerful chief, Ninstints, He-who-is-equal-to-two. The island with his head village, the surrounding waters, the land and even the people became Ninstints.

But human glory is ever fleeting. The very things which bring it into being can often deliver the backlash into oblivion. Battle made Koyah the man of importance. Fighting drove him to his ultimate disgrace. Trading with the whites brought Ninstints his wealth. But it also brought the ravages of civilization. When the decline of the Haida set in, one of the first of the large villages to be wiped out was the head village of Ninstints on Anthony Island. Today few Haidas can trace even a remote connection with the fabulously wealthy Chief Ninstints.

In the nomenclature of the region covered by this chapter, some of the old Haida history will be recognized - rubbing shoulders with the lusty crews of fur trading ships and their owners. Here, too, are names from the British Navy, who played a significant part in the early surveys of these waters. The days of the whalers provide names of more recent history. All leave reminders of events those of us who come after should ponder.

NAGAS POINT — the southwest entrance point of Flamingo Inlet. In 1921 a Naval Intelligence map showed this point as POST POINT, but the name never in general use. The Hydrographic Service suggested the modification, NAGAS, after the Haida name for Town-inhabited-village, a Raven Crest site which lay close inside the point. Chief Ga'i'ins headed the tribe in this village who were known as Slave-People, a name they acquired as a result of a derisive remark by a chief's wife.

Low in importance to begin with, they later grew powerful and some of their chiefs were considered the bravest of the region.

In a neighbouring village an alert shaman found a large piece of iron from which these villagers made spear-points. People came to trade for the points from all over the Islands. One day 10 canoe-loads of Massets arrived to trade and began to gamble. While they were gambling others in the town fell upon the visitors, killing all the men and enslaving the women and children.

Word of the treachery reached Masset and retribution planned. The village of Nagas was selected as the victim to satisfy avengement. In Nagas the Slave-People had begun ceremonies connected with erecting a gravepost. The Massets landed at the back of the village, descended swiftly and killed every man in sight, then carried away the best of the Nagas women and children to be slaves.

*NAGAS ROCKS — to the southeast of Nagas Point. Named in association with the point. The name of NAGAS ISLET was first applied to the 52-foot islet in the group, however, in 1963 the term of NAGAS ROCKS was substituted to include the other rocks close by. In addition to the 52-foot islet there is a 7-foot rock close southward with 2 drying rocks, one to the east and another to the north.

*FLAMINGO INLET — the 5½ mile inlet off the southwest corner of Moresby Island named by Captain A. Freeman about 1912 after the Canadian Fishing Company's steam trawler, *Flamingo*. Freeman called the fiord FLAMINGO HARBOUR. In 1933 the Hydrographic Service changed the designation to FLAMINGO INLET. A 1921 Naval Intelligence Return showed the inlet as GORDON HARBOUR. The old Haida name for it was STA'KI.

*STAKI BAY — is that portion of Flamingo Inlet, north of Staki Point, where the waters widen slightly to form a basin. It is well-charted today - the numerous shoals and rocks, both drying and submerged, clearly shown. There are several streams running into Staki Bay and on the east side a cabin has been built for the Fisheries Protection Officer, stationed at Staki Bay during the salmon run.
Staki Bay named in 1946 by the Hydrographic Service after the old Haida name for Flamingo Inlet.

*STAKI POINT — on the east side of Flamingo Inlet at the entrance to Staki Bay. Named in 1963 by the Hydrographic Service.

*SPERM BAY — on the east side of Flamingo Inlet, south of Staki Point. The skippers of whalers operating out of Rose Harbour Whaling Station applied the name which was officially adopted in 1946. It is considered a good anchorage for small boats - the recommended place being off the bluff in the northwest part of the bay.

*SHORT INLET — about 1 mile south of Sperm Bay. A descriptive name applied by the Hydrographic Service in 1963.

*SARGISON REEF — west and to the north of the mouth of Short Inlet, the reef consists of 2 drying rocks and 2 submerged. Named by the Hydrographic Service in 1963 after Captain G. Sargison, skipper of the whaler *Green* in 1929, during the time she frequently based at the Rose Harbour Whaling Station.

*ANVIL ROCK — south of Sargison Reef and lying towards the middle of Flamingo Inlet, this bare 10-foot-high rock has kelp patches and a drying rock off its southeast tip. Named in 1962 by the Hydrographic Service in association with Anvil Cove.

*ANVIL COVE — east of the rock of this name, the cove was named in 1962 by the Hydrographic Service for the shape of the feature which resembles an anvil when delineated on the chart. On the 1921 Naval Intelligence Return map this cove was shown as ROCKY BAY, but the name never in general use. A chain of rocks extends across the entrance to the cove from its southeast side and a large island, with drying banks connecting it with Moresby Island, fills the northwest part of the cove.

STLINDAGWAI, Village-deep-in-the-inlet — lay at the mouth of a stream entering Anvil Cove. Owned by the Raven Crest Striped-Town-People, the head man was Chief Hawk-Feathers. Ancestors of this tribe belonged to the old Bolkus Island village in Skincuttle Inlet.

*SNUB POINT — south of Anvil Cove and directly east of Nagas Point. Named for the shape of the feature in 1963 by the Hydrographic Service. Several bare islands and drying rocks lie close-off it.

SNUB BAY — is southeast of Snub Point. The large island extending southward from Snub Point, with a string of islets hanging off it, to the south again, forms a miniature bay.

*HENDERSON ROCKS — lie about 1¼ miles southeast of Nagas Point. Formerly called HENDERSON ISLETS, one is 28 feet high and the other 5 feet. Off the smaller islet lie several drying and submerged rocks. Named in 1962 by the Hydrographic Service after Captain A.M. Henderson, well-known skipper of the *Givenchy*. During his years aboard her in service with the Department of Fisheries, Captain Henderson cruised extensively along the inlets and shores of the west coast of the Charlottes. He was one of the rare government officials who didn't consult his book of rules or worry about what Ottawa would say, but used good common horse sense. Many a mercy trip and call for help was answered without hesitation - patrol duties could wait!

*BILLINGTON ROCKS — lie about 1¼ miles northwest of Cape Freeman. The group consists of one rock about a foot high and another which dries at 2 feet, as well as several which are awash and some submerged. Named in 1963 by the Hydrographic Service after Captain Billington, skipper of the whaler *Grey* when she operated out of Rose Harbour Whaling Station in 1922.

*CAPE FREEMAN — lies at the end of a hook-nosed peninsula, south of Snub Point. The peninsula extends about ¾ mile out from the coast of Moresby and is low, wooded and greatly indented - with numerous islets and rocks off its south side. Named by the Hydrographic Service in 1963 after Captain Absolom Freeman, organizer of the original Canadian Fishing Company. See also Freeman Island.

KAIDJUDAL — a Raven Crest village which lay in a cove on the north side of the Cape Freeman peninsula. The people of this place were of the same tribe as the Nagas, Slave-People, and the chief called He-who-is-prepared.

The wife of one of the villagers of Kaidjudal became a shaman with special powers from the moon. She could keep the waters calm for fishermen and, so it was said, should a wind spring up, she could command it to cease, and it would, until the fishing was completed. But one day she took a lover and from that time on her power left her.

HLGADUN VILLAGE — when one strains to get ahead of others, the Haidas would say "Hlgadun. They will pay." (with overwork) The tribe owning this site were the Eagle Crest Powerless-Town-People, headed by Chief Ga'oskit, Loud-Noise. Hlgadun village lay south of Cape Freeman.

CHUGA VILLAGE — south of both Cape Freeman and Hlgadun village, it lay near a semi-detached islet. Raven and Eagle Crests both used this site. The name meant "to-go-for-cedar-planks," and the Eagle tribe were under Chief Thunder, whilst the Raven head man was Chief Whale-Grease.

*LOUSCOONE POINT — the west entrance point of Louscoone Inlet, at the south end of Moresby Island. Named in 1962 by the Hydrographic Service in association with Louscoone Inlet.
Dr. C.F. Newcombe called this point LGADJUKUN in 1897.

*LOUSCOONE INLET — 8 miles long, opens off the south end of Moresby Island. First applied to the charts in 1853 by the British Admiralty surveyors, undoubtedly a modification of the Haida name. In 1935 a detailed survey was made of the inlet by Mr. H.D. Parizeau, assisted by Mr. L.R. Davies, whose name appears on so many Queen Charlotte Islands charts.

XIL VILLAGE — lay between Louscoone Point and Tuga Point, and was an Eagle Crest village of some importance historically, being the ancestral village of Chief Ninstints's forebears. A smaller Haida camp also in use, lay nearer to Louscoone Point.

*TUGA POINT — on the west shore of Louscoone Inlet, 1½ miles from Louscoone Point. Named in 1962 by the Hydrographic Service who used a modified version of the name of the old Haida village which stood to the southwest of the point on the outer coast, Chuga Village. (Tc'uga)

CH'H'NLA VILLAGE — also on the west side of Louscoone Inlet, lay on the shoreline at the north end of Louscoone Inlet near Head Rock.

*HEAD ROCK — named by the Hydrographic Service in 1962 because of its position near the head of Louscoone Inlet. North of Head Rock the inlet gradually narrows to an apex; several rocks, most of which dry, and beaches of sand and stones fringe the shoreline on each side. Fossils may be found in this area.
The Fisheries Department maintain a cabin for their Protection Officer during the salmon run in Louscoone, and built it on the shore near Head Rock. The tidal wave created by the big Alaska earthquake of 1964 hit Louscoone with tremendous force - huge logs and driftwood were hurled far up into the timber and many trees torn out by the roots. Among the debris found 30 feet or more above the high tide mark was a huge boulder which came to rest high up in a tree. The backwash of the wave took out the little Fisheries cabin. So next year the guardian had a new cabin.

*SKINDASKUN ISLAND — is on the east side of Louscoone and is south of Head Rock. Named in 1962 by the Hydrographic Service after a former Haida village near here. Skindaskun Island is low and wooded, and connected to Moresby Island by a drying bank.

XO'TGILDA VILLAGE — is shown on Dr. C.F. Newcombe's map as slightly south of Skindaskun and is probably in the vicinity of Cadman Point.

*CADMAN POINT — on the east side of Louscoone Inlet, south of Skindaskun Island. Richard Cadman Etches was one of the partners in the King George Sound Company which sent the two ships, *King George* under Captain Nathaniel Portlock and the *Queen Charlotte* under Captain George Dixon, to trade on the northwest coast of America. The vessels arrived off the west coast of the Charlottes in the fall of 1786, but finding it deserted left almost immediately. In the summer of 1787 they returned, this time separating, and Dixon made his historic trip along most of the coastline of the Charlottes and gave the Islands their present name.

TA'DJNL VILLAGE — stood between Etches and Cadman Point.

*ETCHES POINT — south of Cadman Point on the east shore of Louscoone Inlet. Named also after Richard Cadman Etches. Between Cadman and Etches Point is a bight with two low wooded islands, several islets and drying rocks. The southernmost islet is off the mouth of a creek and is connected to Moresby by a drying bank.

*CROOKED POINT — south of Etches Point, was named in 1962 by the Hydrographic Service for the shape of the feature. It is on the outer part of a peninsula which forms the western shore of Small Cove.

*SMALL COVE — lies inside and east of Crooked Point on the eastern shore of Louscoone Inlet. Named in 1962 by the Hydrographic Service for the size and shape of the bay. It has a number of rocks at the entrance and one near its head.

*NINSTINTS POINT — south of Crooked Point. Named in 1962 by the Hydrographic Service after the old village on Anthony Island, which in turn received its name from the powerful Eagle chief who reached his zenith between 1866 and the 1880s. He acquired wealth to such an inordinate degree that he was able to host ten successive potlatches of great lavishness. Only one other Haida chief until then had achieved this, the great Edenso of Kung, Naden Harbour. A chief of Skedans is said to have also given this number of potlatches, but it is generally conceded that they were not on the scale of the Ninstints and Edenso celebrations.

*CAPE FANNY — the southern extremity of Moresby Island, lies east of the entrance to Louscoone Inlet, and has an unnamed 16-foot bare rock about 600 feet off it. The cape received its name during the 1853 survey of Houston

Stewart Channel by the British Admiralty hydrographers. It has been rumoured that in the vicinity of Cape Fanny an old cannon was cached during the Houston Stewart battle of Koyah's Revenge,[1] and is still in its original hiding place - although seen by several people over the years.

[1]Koyah's battles described in introduction section of Chapter Seven.

*ADAM ROCKS — lie off Louscoone Point near the west entrance to Louscoone Inlet. Named during the 1853 survey of Houston Stewart Channel by officers on the *Virago*. The largest of the rocks is a scrub-covered islet, but the others are bare - some being below water.

This is supposed to be the site of the reef Ki'l, connected by legend to the origin of the Haida nation. One story says that when all the world was water, only this reef was showing. The supernatural beings who were to control Haida destinies lay upon the reef waiting for the waters to subside.

Another story follows this telling of the waters diminishing, but the only living creature was Raven. Desperate with loneliness he searched around the emerging islands looking for a companion. On a beach he found a cockle-shell from which voices seemed to come. Examining it more closely he found several male infants struggling to get out. When he released them they grew rapidly to manhood and joined Raven in a common search for mates.

As he winged his way through the air, Raven flew over Ki'l, then sped swiftly back with the news, "There are women clinging to the reef!" Whereupon the cockle-shell braves raced to the rescue, married the maidens and peopled the land.

*ANTHONY ISLAND — south of Adam Rocks and Louscoone Point. Called SKANG'WAI or RED COD ISLAND by the Haidas. In 1853 George Inskip, in charge of the survey of Houston Stewart Channel, with the *Virago*, named it after an Irish Archdeacon, father of Midshipman Edward Denny of the *Virago*. Thus it was Venerable Anthony Denny's name was applied to a Haida island in waters he would never see.

QADADJANS, Mad-talking-village — an ancient Raven Crest site on the east side of a secluded cove on the north end of Anthony Island. Numerous rocks, islets and islands form a natural barrier to protect it completely from the wild seas which pound the outer shorelines. Some of the depressions of the old house sites may still be seen, with moss-covered hewn timbers lying close by. Chief New-Grass headed this village.

On the west side of the cove fronting Qadadjans is an even older site. Only an ancient midden marks its location. North and west of this midden is a cave, 30 feet above the present shoreline and about 300 feet in, along a wooded canyon. It is believed by archaeologists this was first used as a camping site then later as a burial cave.

SKANG'WAI VILLAGE, Red-cod-island-village — better known as NINSTINTS VILLAGE, stood on the east side of Anthony Island in a bay partially protected by the island which fronts it. Traditionally an Eagle Crest location, families of both Ravens and Eagles lived there, as was common in all the larger villages.

Descendants of both Koyah and the town chief of old Qadadjans owned houses there, and both brought the house names for their lodges from villages lived in previously. The descendants of the Qadadjans chief called theirs *People-*

wish-to-be-there and built the house on a terrace almost in the centre of the community. Koyah's people called theirs, appropriately, *Raven-house*. The name for the great Ninstints's own house, *Thunder-rolls-upon-it,* had also been brought from another village, his forbears had used it when they lived at Gowgaia Bay.

In 1840 there were over 300 people living in Ninstints village. Forty years later, in 1884, only 30 people remained. Newton Chittenden visited them that year and was invited to share in a feast. The men of the village had returned earlier in the day with a fine haul of halibut caught off the west coast of Kunghit Island. Shortly after Chittenden's visit the people abandoned the village and moved to Skidegate.

Abandoned physically, perhaps, but phantoms always hauntingly present in old Haida villages are particularly evident in Ninstints. A visitor is conscious of an atmosphere of past - so pronounced it becomes reality.

The awareness is created for the most part by the few remaining totem poles silently keeping watch along the shoreline of the small cove. Grey, weathered, some tilted, others fallen - all have immense dignity. A visitor's hand put out to stroke a curve or to finger an intricate design, does so with respect - for one is compellingly aware that Ninstints is not a dead village. It is alive with memories of other years and another culture.

That rotten post; this depression; a house stood here; a great lodge filled with people; laughing children. There was the fire-pit, possessions of every

Totems at the old Ninstints village, Skang-wai,
on the east shore of Anthony Island.

Photo taken in 1970 by G. Gray Hill.

144

sort would be strewn about - food, woven mats, chests and tools - each would have borne some form of decoration. Birth, death and the rituals of all aspects of life took place here. Walls of great hewn timbers would have surrounded this space and huge beams provided support. Now buried in the moss and spruce needles of the encroaching forest.

Like all the big winter villages of the Haida, Ninstints has a picturesque setting. A sloping shingle beach ringed with driftwood, lush wild grass snugged carpetlike around the base of the old totems, and the vigorous second-growth spruce, so green and perfectly formed. It is a tranquil place in sunshine. In wind and rain the ghosts come too disconcertingly close and melancholy is hard to shake off.

In 1957, to give this site legal protection, Anthony Island was declared a Provincial Park, Class A.

GRAY'S COVE — mentioned in an early fur trading ship's log, is believed to be the small cove to the south of the big Ninstints village, on the east side of Anthony Island, where Captain Robert Gray anchored the *Lady Washington* on his first visit to this region, June 11, 1789. It may have been the place that young Robert Haswell, Gray's second mate took a short excursion ashore to stretch his legs - and became the first white man known to have set foot on any part of the Queen Charlotte Islands.

*MACLEOD SHOAL — lies northeast of Anthony Island, marked by kelp and is about 1200 feet long with a depth of 30 feet of water over it. Named in 1962 by the Hydrographic Service after William MacLeod, first mate on the *King George*.

The 320-ton *King George* under Captain Nathaniel Portlock, accompanied the smaller *Queen Charlotte* to the Northwest coast of America 1786 and 1787. In addition to Captain Portlock and Mate MacLeod, there were Mates Samuel Hayward and John Christleman; Dr. James Hogan, surgeon; traders Robert Hill and William Wilbye; boatswain Archibald Brown; carpenter Robert Horn and 50 seamen - some of whom were mere boys.

MacLeod Shoal is the only place on the Charlottes named in connection with the *King George* which made a brief trip with the *Queen Charlotte* to the west coast of the Charlottes in 1786. Neither vessel stayed at that time. The following year Dixon returned for his historic trip.

*IBBERTSON BANKS — south of MacLeod Shoal, lie midway between Anthony Island and the Gordon Islands. The banks have about 50 to 60 feet of water over them and were named in 1962 by the Hydrographic Service in remembrance of the first European name given to nearby Houston Stewart Channel when, in 1787, Captain George Dixon called that waterway Ibbertson's Sound.

*FLATROCK ISLAND — is at the west entrance to Houston Stewart Channel. Named in 1948 by the Hydrographic Service, it is a descriptive name for this 69-foot-high island which is bare and has a flat summit. There is a navigational light on the highest point of Flatrock Island.

In June 1789, after trading at Ninstints village, Captain Robert Gray prepared to leave the area. Strong winds and a heavy ocean swell forced the *Lady Washington* back and she obtained "some shelter in the lee of a large rock at the entrance (to Houston Stewart Channel) for several hours."

*GORDON ISLANDS — a compact group, south of Flatrock Island, off the west entrance to Houston Stewart Channel. Named Gordon ISLES in 1853 by G.H. Inskip after William Elrington Gordon, who assisted Inskip in the survey of Houston Stewart Channel. In 1946 the name was changed to Gordon ISLANDS. The islands are generally wooded and fringed with kelp and mainly connected to each other by drying reefs. Several rocks lie offshore, some submerged, but one of the above-water rocks is 28 feet high.

*KUNGHIT ISLAND — lies off the south end of Moresby Island, from which it is separated by the Houston Stewart Channel. It is an adaption of the old Haida name for the island, meaning to-the-south. About 15 miles long and perhaps 8 miles across at its widest, it was selected in 1853 to bear the name of Commander James Prevost, master of the *Virago* during the survey of the Houston Stewart Channel by G.H. Inskip. When the Geographic Board realized that Prevost's name had also been applied to an island off the east coast of Vancouver Island, they reinstated the old Haida name to the island off the south end of the Charlottes, and in 1904 it became KUNGHIT ISLAND for all successive maps.

One of Ingraham's 1791-92 charts showed the island as KINGSETT, but this is generally believed to be a variation of Kunghit.

The place names of Kunghit Island include many of the crew of the *Columbia Rediva* as well as those of whalers.

*ARNOLD POINT — on the west side of Kunghit Island, opposite the Gordon Islands. Named in 1948 by the Hydrographic Service after Nathan Arnold, bosun's mate on the first trip of the *Columbia*. Arnold joined the ship in Boston, August 1787, under the command of John Kendrick and remained on her for 3 years, during which time an exchange of captains tooks place, so that he served under Robert Gray for the latter half of his time. He received the same pay as the bosun, John Annis (Annis Point), two pounds, five shillings per month.

SI'NIT VILLAGE — located in the rock-fringed bay to the south of Arnold Point. According to Dr. C.F. Newcombe's map it lay about due east of the south end of Gordon Islands.

*BOWLES POINT — at the south end of the unnamed bay, south of Arnold Point, there is an unnamed bay with an islet off its north end and another off its south end. Bowles Point is the western extremity of the southernmost of the two semi-detached islets off the south end of the peninsula.

William Bowles, for whom the point was named by the Hydrographic Service in 1948, was a member of the crew of the *Columbia* when she left Boston for her first voyage in 1787, and saw much of the Charlottes in succeeding years.

After leaving the *Columbia* he became mate on the *Sea Otter.* In 1796 when that vessel put in to trade at Cumshewa a fight broke out in which Captain Stephen Hill, and the purser and steward, Elliott and Daggett, were killed. William Bowles assumed command of the ship, finished the trading season and sailed for China. His Boston employers were so satisfied with his capabilities that the following year, they gave him full command of another of their ships, *Alert,* for several voyages. All his trips took him to the rich fur-trading grounds of the Charlottes for at least part of his journeys.

TA'DASL VILLAGE — lay in a cove near the mouth of the creek to the east of Bowles Point.

SKE'LDAWA VILLAGE — stood slightly south of Ta'dasl village, with a rocky shoreline in front of it.

QAI'DJU, Sons-of-victory-village — lay midway between Bowles Point and Gilbert Bay. A Raven Crest site, it was one of the many villages of this name owned by a group of Haidas of the Sand-Town-People, whose ancestors had originally come from House Island. Kan'nskina was the Town Chief of most of these villages, but fierce little Koyah ruled overall - the Family Chief.

*GILBERT BAY — between Bowles Point and Barber Point on the west side of Kunghit Island, has sand dunes lying along part of it. Named in 1948 by the Hydrographic Service for another member of the crew of the *Columbia,* Jonathan Gilbert, who signed on in Boston in 1787.

SAO'KUN — the north entrance point of Gilbert Bay.

SAO VILLAGE — lay east of Sao'kun, close to the mouth of the stream which enters the north portion of the bay.

SWA'NA'I VILLAGE — also in Gilbert Bay, lay south of Sao Village. Both of these villages may have only been in seasonal use - as opposed to the big winter villages generally regarded as headquarters for the tribes.

*BARBER POINT — the south end of Gilbert Bay. Named by the Hydrographic Service in 1948 after John Barber, a shipmate of Jonathan Gilbert's on the first voyage of the *Columbia.*

KUNDI VILLAGE — about 1¼ miles southeast of Barber Point an unnamed creek emerges close by a rocky promontory which extends into the ocean for ½ a mile. Kundi village lay on the south side of the creek.

*ST JAMES ISLAND — a saddle-shaped island off the south tip of Kunghit Island. Bare and grassy, the southern extremity is a vertical cliff about 100 feet high. It was called HUMMOCK ISLAND for a time, but the name St. James Island was confirmed in 1949. The lighthouse is on the south end of the island and has an automatic radio beacon in continuous operation.

St. James Island with lightstation on its summit.
Photo taken in 1970 by G. Gray Hill facing west.
Supplies delivered by boat are landed at the foot of the slope.

Tender landing supplies for Cape St. James lightstation.

Photo - Major George Nicholson.

Mr. and Mrs. Charles Smith, keepers of Cape St. James Lightstation during the years of World War 2.

Christmas dinner, 1943, in the R.C.A.F. mess at Cape St. James. Mrs. Smith sits by the window at right.

Photo - Mr. Charles Smith.

*CAPE ST JAMES — is the southern extremity of St. James Island, and has been known by several other names - CAPE HECTOR, PUNTO DE SANTIAGO and CAPE HASWELL.

On August 19, 1786, Laperouse named it Cape Hector after the Commandant of Marine at Brest. The following year on July 25, 1787, Captain George Dixon

149

in the *Queen Charlotte* rounded the point on St. James Day and named it *CAPE ST JAMES*. A Spanish chart of 1791-92 showed the point as Punto de Santiago, and an American chart of that era showed it as Cape Haswell, after young Robert Haswell, mate on the *Columbia*. However, another American, Joseph Ingraham, showed the headland as Cape St. James on his 1792 map, and it is by this name it has been known ever since.

The light-station at Cape St. James is one of the important meteorological stations of the British Columbia coast, and weather reports from "the Cape" have an impact on all forecasts. Built in 1913, the big Cape St. James light flashes every 6 seconds and can be seen for 24 miles.

From August 1943 to August 1945 the R.C.A.F. manned a radar station at the Cape comparable to the one in operation at Langara at that time. Sixty-five men were stationed at this isolated outpost.

Charlie Smith, who supplied the list of northcoast Haida place names for this book, was lightkeeper at Cape St. James during the war years. "We had some high-jinx with those young lads," he recalled, "and my wife and I joined in. When we took the job, we were told we could pretty well take anything with us we wanted except two things - a piano and a goat. The piano would be too heavy to get up to the place and the goat would smell too bad."

A section of the Kerouard Islands which extend
off the south tip of the Charlottes.

Photo - G. Gray Hill.

*KEROUARD ISLANDS — consist of two groups of islets and rocks; some bare and white, some pillarlike. Extending in a chain for about 2½ miles off Cape St. James they have served for centuries as a favorite breeding place for sea-lions and colonies of sea-birds. The Kerouard Islands have the largest breeding population of Stellar's Sea-Lion in B.C. "The din of their constant barking

150

is deafening," say visitors whose noses permit them to approach. "It sounds like a hundred people retching, and the whole rookery stinks to high heaven." The bulls are massive, weighing about 2,000 pounds and each has from 10 to 50 smaller females in his harem - depending on battle prowess during mating season.

In 1775 the three small islands lying immediately south of Cape St. James were named ISLAS DE AVES by Bodega. Later they were designated as the LADRONES, and some early Admiralty charts called these three the PROCTOR ISLANDS. They owe their present name to Laperouse who, on August 19, 1786, called the entire group ISLES KEROUART, since modified to KEROUARD ISLANDS.

*GRAY ROCK — the extreme southerly part of the Queen Charlotte Islands, it lies 6 miles from Cape St. James and 3½ miles southeast of the last of the Kerouards. A solitary peak in the deep waters which surround it, Gray Rock is covered with about 6 feet of water. Seas break on it in a moderate swell and there are heavy tide rips at times.

It was first discovered late in June, 1792, by Captain Robert Gray of the *Columbia* - the hard way. "Fresh winds, all sail out with a smooth sea," wrote 16-year-old John Boit, fifth mate. "At 2 p.m. the ship struck a rock which lay about 7 feet under water and did not break. Hove all back and she came off clear. Tried the pump and found she leaked 1000 smart strokes per hour. Sounded all around the rock and found no ground at 70 fathom." When the vessel was later beached they found she had split her keel and the lower part of the stem was entirely gone. Three planks were stove-in next to the garboard, as well as damage to the sheathing.

Robert Gray, for whom the rock is named, was born May 10, 1755, at Tiverton, Rhode Island, and died in the summer of 1806 of yellow fever. A courageous, self-reliant man, sometimes criticized for overdoing things to the point of being foolhardy. When the *Columbia* and the *Washington* left Boston in 1787, 32-year-old Gray took charge of the smaller *Washington*. John Kendrick, captain of the *Columbia* and in command of the expedition, became a continual frustration to the go-getting Gray. It was an infinite relief when the exchange of ships took place and from that moment Gray could be his own man.

The *Columbia* left for her second voyage to the northwest coast in 1791 with Robert Gray not only her skipper, but also part owner.

In view of her first unprofitable trip, the other owners insisted that young John Hoskins go along as clerk on the second voyage to keep a careful note of all proceedings. Deeply resentful, Captain Gray, not above turning a few sharp trading policies himself whenever he could, felt Hoskins looking over his shoulder would not make for good relations - especially when Gray knew that, unlike most of the other men, Hoskins greatly admired John Kendrick, the former captain of the *Columbia*.

*HECATE STRAIT — which separates the Charlottes from the mainland off its east side, is commonly called "The Pond" by some of the tugboat skippers, but never taken lightly by any of them. Considered to be one of the trickiest stretches of water on the coast, the strait is shallow and unpredictable. It can

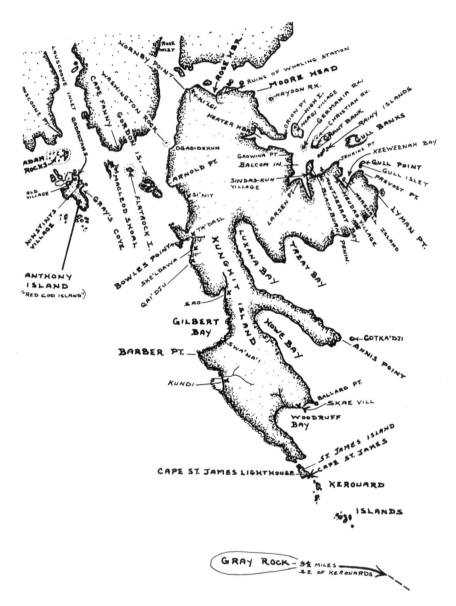

be mirror smooth then, within hours, a violent rage. "Aye . . . she's a black-hearted bitch," said one veteran fisherman, "sometimes I think she just wants to keep the Charlottes for herself."

Named after the surveying vessel, *H.M.S. Hecate,* a paddle-wheel sloop of 860 tons, rigged as a brigantine, and which arrived on the Pacific coast in 1860. In 1862 she visited Skincuttle Inlet during Poole's mining activities with her five guns prominently displayed to deter possible hostilities to the miners by some of the Haidas. Following this she ran a line of soundings from Skincuttle to Bonilla Island.

The straits were named in 1861 or 1862 by Captain Richards, her skipper at that time. Daniel Pender was senior surveying officer.

*WOODRUFF BAY — the most southeasterly bay on Kunghit Island. Named for a man who never saw the Charlottes, although he had been on the Pacific coast. Simon Woodruff was gunner's mate on Captain Cook's last voyage. A well-known navigator and experienced seaman, he commanded ships out of London before he signed on as first mate under John Kendrick for the initial voyage of the *Columbia*.

Woodruff had little difficulty in seeing through Kenrick's excuses and did not disguise his contempt. The situation had become so intolerable by the time the *Columbia* reached the Cape Verdes, Kendrick reduced Woodruff to ship's cook - if he wished to continue the journey. The elderly Woodruff asked to be transferred to the smaller *Washington* to which Kendrick at first agreed. Then, brooding over his decision, Kendrick drew up a form for Woodruff to sign which was so derogatory Woodruff refused. Kendrick then ordered Captain Gray to return the man to the *Columbia* and, despite the bad weather, made the old sailor spend the night on deck with no blankets - unless he signed the form. By morning Woodruff had endured enough. Obviously he could not win. He signed and quit the expedition completely.

Woodruff Bay named by the Hydrographic Service in 1948.

Newton Chittenden visited the bay in 1884. "The whole bay was alive with seals," he wrote, "so we called this place SEAL COVE." The name was never adopted.

SKAE VILLAGE — in Woodruff Bay near Ballard Point. A Raven Crest village said to have received its name because these villagers skinned and processed the sea-lions they caught on the Kerouards. The chief had the hospitable name, Master-of-the-fire.

*BALLARD POINT — at the north entrance to Woodruff Bay. Named after Bartholomew Ballard, the busy tailor who joined the *Columbia* for her first voyage in 1787 and stayed for the full three years. He collected two pounds, five shillings per month for the trip.

There is a semi-detached islet off Ballard Point, and off this islet kelp hugs several submerged rocks. Ballard Point named in 1948 by the Hydrographic Service.

*HOWE BAY — is the indentation north of Ballard Point. It has a wide stretch of beach at its head, pounded well by a surf usually present in this bay. Named in 1948 by the Hydrographic Service after Lieutenant Richard S. Howe, who was captain's clerk and supercargo on the first voyage of the *Columbia*, 1787 to 1790. Lieutenant Howe managed to get along with both Gray and Kendrick, apparently keeping strictly to his own business and remaining neutral.

*ANNIS POINT — at the end of the peninsula between Howe Bay and

Luxana Bay, has a 38-foot islet off it called GOTKA'DJI by the Haidas. In 1948 the Hydrographic Service named the point after John Annis, the boatswain on the first voyage of the *Columbia.*

*LUXANA BAY — Captain Charles Duncan of the *Princess Royal,* a sloop of 50 tons belonging to the same company as the *Queen Charlotte,* traded in this region in 1787 and 1788. It is believed Duncan first applied the name of LUXAENA to this bay on May 14, 1788.

A Spanish chart of about 1791 showed the bay as PUERTO DE BUENAS MURGERES. By 1795 it was regularly shown as Luxaena, later modified to the Luxana of today. A large stream enters this bay at its head and there is a good beach. Like Howe and Woodruff to the south, Luxana also is subject to heavy swells.

There are fossils at the head of Luxana.

*TREAT BAY — east of Luxana Bay, is a boulder-strewn cove. Named in 1948 by the Hydrographic Service after John B. Treat, furrier on the first voyage of the *Columbia.* He served amicably under Captain Kendrick then, when the exchange of captains took place, finished the voyage under Robert Gray.

*LYMAN POINT — the most easterly point of Kunghit Island. First named EAST POINT by Dr. G.M. Dawson in 1878 in recognition of its geographic location. The two rocks on a reef off this point form the most easterly above-water feature of the entire Queen Charlotte group. (Gray Rock is more easterly, but is underwater.)

Because of numerous duplications of the name, this point was renamed LYMAN POINT by the Hydrographic Service in July 1945 and is after Sir Lyman Poore Duff, a Chief Justice of Canada, called to the Bar in February, 1895.

*PREVOST POINT — north and west of Lyman Point. Named by the Hydrographic Service in 1962 in honour of Commander James Prevost, who in company with G.H. Inskip, conducted a survey of Houston Stewart Channel area in 1853 on the *Virago.* At one time the entire island bore Prevost's name.

*GULL POINT — on the northeast extremity of Gull Islet. Named by Dr. G.M. Dawson in 1878.

*GULL ISLET — northeast of Prevost Point, named in association with the Gull Point given to this islet's extremity by Dr. Dawson. Gull Islet is connected to Kunghit Island by a drying rock ledge.

*GULL BANKS — about 1½ miles northwest of Gull Islet, were named in this association by the Hydrographic Service in 1962.

*MARSHALL ISLAND — in the centre of Keeweenah Bay, west of Prevost Point. Named by the Hydrographic Service in 1962 in association with Prevost Point. Commander Edward Marshall relieved Prevost during the survey in 1853 of the Houston Stewart Channel.

HEUDAO VILLAGE, Village-that-fishes-towards-the-south — stood near the mouth of a creek which runs into Keeweenah Bay. A Raven Crest site it belonged to Koyah's tribe.

*KEEWEENAH BAY,

*JENKINS POINT,

*MONTSERRAT BAY, and

*BLACKBURN PENINSULA — all in a row to the east of Prevost Point were named in 1962 by the Hydrographic Service. The *Keeweenah* under Captain William Jenkins, and the *Montserrat* under Captain David Blackburn, were lost in a terrific gale off the entrance to the Straits of Juan de Fuca in December 1894. Many other ships were lost in that storm and wreckage strewn all along the coast. Parts of the wreckage from these two ships were found in what is now Rose Inlet by a member of the *Maude S.* in May 1895.

David Blackburn was a Nova Scotian who started as a Columbia River fisherman and ended as a ship-owner and captain. Known in all west coast ports as "Lucky" Blackburn, he skippered many a famous ship without the misfortunes usually accompanying captains of those early years.

But he took terrible risks - with many hairbreadth escapes. His ship, always overloaded, put out in weather when no other captain would consider leaving harbour. He had an inordinate faith in his last command, the *Montserrat,* and would grin through his huge mustache at the sceptics and boom, "Och, never mind. Why this ship could climb a tree."

Perhaps he was pushing his famous luck once again when he tried to help the less sturdy *Keeweenah* in a wild December gale. No one will ever know. All hands went missing on both ships.

SINDAS-KUN VILLAGE, Village-on-a-point-always-smelling — another Raven Crest site, it formerly stood on the west shore of Blackburn Peninsula, across from Larsen Point.

*RAINY ISLANDS — are a chain of islands curving out from Blackburn Peninsula to form an arc over the north portion of Montserrat Bay. Named in 1878 by Dr. G.M. Dawson, they consist of four main islands, some of which are wooded. Several above-water and submerged rocks lie close by.

*GRANT BANK — about 300 feet northwest of the Rainy Islands. Named in 1962 by the Hydrographic Service after Captain William Grant, one of the founders of the Victoria Whaling Company in 1905. Grant had been one of the officials of the Victoria Sealing Company in earlier years, and Grant's Wharf was home base for the sealers. Across the road from the dock Captain Grant built his home, complete with tower, where he went to watch for his vessels returning.

When red began to appear in the books of the sealing company, Grant joined the Balcom brothers and went into whaling. The *William Grant* was one of the whalers operating out of Rose Harbour in 1912.

*CHRISTIAN ROCK — is on the north side of Grant Bank and has a depth of about 9 feet over it. Named by the Hydrographic Service in 1962 after Captain Lars Christian, master of the whaler *Germania* which plied waters off the Charlottes.

*GERMANIA ROCK— at the west end of Grant Bank, is a large bare rock, 18 feet high. Named for the whaler *Germania.*

*LARSEN POINT — divides the two arms of Balcom Inlet and was named in 1962 by the Hydrographic Service after Captain Louis Larsen, who skippered the whaler *James Carruthers* in 1948, a vessel with many years of service behind her at that time. The *Carruthers* served in the whaling operation until 1956 when she was converted to a barge and renamed *NSP No 14.* Two years later she sank while under tow.

*BALCOM INLET — which lies to the west of Blackburn Peninsula, extends about 1¼ miles in a southerly direction, with two arms at its head. Captains Ruben and Sprott Balcom, for whom it was named, formed a partnership with Captain William Grant (Grant Bank) and in 1905 established the Victoria Whaling Company.

Ruben Balcom was born in 1855 in Sheet Harbour, Nova Scotia, and in his time sailed the Seven Seas. About 1894 he arrived in Victoria to engage in sealing. Sprott Balcom joined his brother in the venture, which took them from Cape Horn to the Bering Sea chasing seals.

Intrigued by possibilities in whaling, Sprott Balcom did some careful investigation which captured the interest of his brother and Captain Grant, both of whom felt the days of profitable sealing were at an end. Ruben Balcom went to Norway to buy two steam whalers, the *Orion* and *St. Lawrence,* and the Victoria Whaling Company became operative.

Balcom Inlet named in 1962 by the Hydrographic Service.

*GAOWINA POINT — is the south entrance point of Heater Harbour. Named in 1962 by the Hydrographic Service and is a modification of the Haida name of an ancient site which lay to the northwest of Orion Point according to Dr. C.F. Newcombe's map.

*HEATER HARBOUR — entered between Gaowina Point and Orion Point, extends 1¾ miles to the northwest, with two small arms at its head, into which streams flow. A large flat lies off the mouths of the creeks. In earlier years the harbour was known as SLEEPY HARBOUR and also as HIGH HARBOUR. The name HEATER HARBOUR was confirmed in July 1946 and is after Captain William Heater, brother of the somewhat more flamboyant George Heater.

The Heaters were from Newfoundland, attracted to the Pacific coast by sealing opportunities. William acted as mate for his brother on sealing schooners, then as whaling replaced the sealing industry, he became a skipper on the whalers. He often put in to Rose Harbour in command of whalers operating out of there in early years.

*ORION POINT — north entrance point of Heater Harbour and named in 1962 after the 95-foot steam whaler, *Orion,* a steel vessel built in Norway 1904 to 1905, one of two such ships purchased by the Victoria Whaling Company - the other being the *St. Lawrence.*

The successful use of these vessels prompted the Consolidated Whaling Corporation to bring out from England a fleet of 102-ton steel boats. Registered at Liverpool, England, they were designated *Black, White, Blue, Green* and *Brown.* The story behind the choice of names is worthy of Solomon. A German scientist retained by the company insisted that the boats be named for rivers of his German homeland.

His demands were being acceded to until Vancouver shareholder Lieutenant Colonel J.M. MacMillan heard about it. Enraged, he said bluntly that the ships must bear the names of rivers of *his* country Scotland. In a desperate bid to keep the controversy from getting out of hand the directors suggested the compromise of "colour" names. Even the mother ship, the former *Petriana,* was renamed and became *Gray* when purchased late in 1910.

*HIGH ISLAND — named by Dr. G.M. Dawson in 1878. Fairly conspicuous from the northeast and about 580 feet high, it is separated from Orion Point by a passage some 1200 feet across. With considerable kelp lying off High Island, the channel is constricted to 600 feet in places. In addition to it having been selected in ancient years as a Haida village site (see next item) it also attracted a Japanese prospector. In 1913 Mr. J. Uniaka recorded the *Copper Coin* claim. Located on the east side of High Island it had a showing of copper.

HLAGI VILLAGE — a Raven Crest site which lay in a bight midway along the east side of High Island.

*HAYDON ROCK — this 21-foot-high rock lying northwest of High Island was named during the 1853 survey of Houston Stewart Channel, when Commander James Prevost named it for Charles Haydon, the acting second master on the *Virago.*

*MOORE HEAD — the southeast entrance point of Houston Stewart Channel. Named in 1853 by Commander Prevost after Lewis James Moore, 2nd Lieutenant on the *Virago.* Mr. J. Uniaka recorded the *Sakai* mineral claim in 1913 at Moore Head, and made an open cut about 50 feet long near the shoreline at the south end of his claim, but apparently abandoned it shortly afterwards.

*ROSE HARBOUR — lies midway along the north shore of Kunghit Island. There has been confusion as to the location of this place. All early maps except one show the name of Rose Harbour in the arm of the present Rose Inlet. The one exception is an 1824 Arrowsmith map which put the name in its present position.

Steam whaler Green.

Photo - Albert Dalzell

Rose Harbour Whaling Station in 1936.

Photo - Dorothy Barge.

Whale ready for processing at Rose Harbour.

Photo - Provincial Archives, Victoria.

The original name of ROSE HARBOUR was applied in 1787 by James Johnstone to what is now Rose INLET. He named it for George Rose, a political writer and statesman, who had taken especial interest in the voyage of the *King George* and *Queen Charlotte* to the Pacific coast. Mr. Johnstone sailed aboard the *Prince of Wales* under Captain Colnett when, following Dixon's trip to the Charlottes earlier, Colnett anchored his ship in what is now Rose Inlet, and at which time Johnstone applied the name.

The rocky bay which *today* bears the name of Rose Harbour, was first called PORT HUFF in 1910 after G.A. Huff of Alberni, sent by a syndicate of Victoria and Vancouver businessmen to choose a site for a whaling station. He selected this bay on the north end of Kunghit Island. Charts issued up to 1927 still showed the bay as PORT HUFF, but the whaling station built on the east side of a stream running into the head of Port Huff was called *The Rose Harbour Whaling Station*. Confusion arose. Shortly afterwards the former Rose Harbour was renamed Rose Inlet and Port Huff became the official ROSE HARBOUR.

The whaling station built in 1910 by the Queen Charlotte Whaling Company began operation that summer with from 100 to 150 men. In recent years the beachcombing Carey family of Sandspit reported they had found so many old saki bottles at the whaling site they wondered whether the employees had worked harder at processing whales or consuming saki. During construction there were fights breaking out frequently due to someone drinking too much saki. And in July 1910 Rose Harbour experienced its first murder when one Japanese drank too much and took the law into his own hands concerning a fellow countryman.

But whale processing prospered and Captain R. Balcom noted that by September the plant had put through 80 large whales in the first six week of operation.

In 1918 the Consolidated Whaling Incorporation of Toronto bought both the Rose Harbour and Naden Harbour Whaling Stations, operating them until 1943. This company went bankrupt in 1946 and the following year Western Whaling bought the properties from the trustees. B.C. Packers, one of the partners in Western Whaling, later bought out the other shareholders. In 1948 all machinery and equipment not obsolete was moved to Coal Harbour, on Vancouver Island, and the stations on the Charlottes were abandoned.

In 1913 a Fisheries report recorded, "A crude abalone factory erected at the mouth of Rose Harbour by the Japanese, and a number of sample cases put up. The building is merely a rough shack, the boiler is an oil-barrel. Everything is apparently temporary. At the time of inspection all seemed abandoned, as they had no licence, but there are few sites better suited for such a factory."

Geologists report that there are fossils at the head of Rose Harbour.

*HORNBY POINT — the northwest tip of Kunghit Island. Named during the 1853 survey by Commander James Prevost after William St. John Sumner Hornby, a midshipman on the *Virago*. Hornby had recently joined the vessel, prior to this he had been a naval cadet on Admiral Fairfax Moresby's flagship, *Portland*.[1]

[1]See Portland Bay.

KI'LGI VILLAGE — lay on the east side of the stream coming into the bay to the east of Hornby Point. Shown on the Admiralty charts of 1853 and presumably occupied at that time.

OGADIDSKUN — the name given by Dr. C.F. Newcombe to the point on the west side of Kunghit Island about 3 miles south of Hornby Point. There is a fossil site in the small bight north of Ogadidskun and another similar site north of this, between Hornby Point and Ogadidskun.

ISLANDS OF HOUSTON STEWART CHANNEL,
NORTH SHORES AND NORTH TO SKINCUTTLE
INLET AND THE COPPER ISLANDS.

CHAPTER EIGHT

*HOUSTON STEWART CHANNEL — the waterway separating Moresby
Island from Kunghit Island. In 1787 George Dixon named it IBBERTSON'S
SOUND. Two years later Robert Gray named it BARRELL'S SOUND after
Joseph Barrell, one of the principal owners of the *Washington* and the *Columbia*.

When Joseph Barrell read the account of Captain Cook's third voyage, he
realized the furs from the northwest Pacific coast could offer an opportunity
for fabulous wealth in trading with China. Barrell interested five other men
- Samuel Brown, prosperous Boston merchant; Charlies Bullfinch, also of Boston;
Crowell Hatch, a sea captain of Cambridge; John Derby, a wealthy Salem shipow-
ner; and John M. Pintard, a New York merchant. In 1787 the six adventurers
purchased and outfitted the two vessels, *Columbia Rediva* and *Lady Washington*,
at a cost of $50,000. The *Columbia* was 212 tons with a length of 83½ feet
and beam of just over 24 feet. Her consort, the sloop *Washington*, was about
90 tons.

As explained in the introduction to Chapter seven, they engaged John Kenrick
to command the *Columbia* and lead the expedition with Robert Gray in charge
of the *Washington*. Kendrick, totally unsuited for his role, proved to be a handicap
and the ships took a full year to reach Nootka from Boston. In July of 1788
the two men exchanged ships, Kendrick taking over the *Washington*. His
employers never again saw this ship, for he apparently appropriated it for his
own use.

His efforts were financially dismal and, when he was killed in 1794 by a
stray bullet during a salute from another ship, he left an awesome pile of debts.

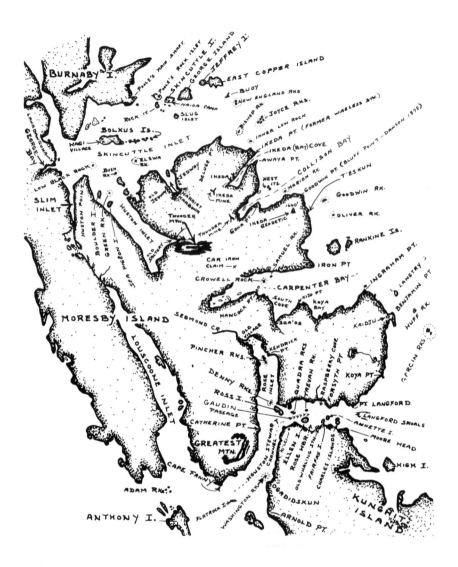

Gray returned to Boston with the *Columbia,* and subsequently left for a second expedition for the company in 1790.

Despite its name of Barrell's Sound on the American charts, the common name for this channel in fur trading days was KOYAH'S STRAIT, after the leading chief of the region.

During the 1853 hydrographic survey by the British Admiralty, Commander James Prevost named it for the first commander of the *Virago* during the survey, William Houston Stewart, whom Prevost relieved.

*WASHINGTON ROCK — is at the south entrance of Houston Stewart Channel and lies off Kunghit Island about 1¼ miles north of Arnold Point and in the vicinity of Dr. C.F. Newcombe's Ogadidskun (Point). Three feet high and bare, Washington Rock has a sunken rock close off its northwest side with only 6 feet of water over it.

Named by the Hydrographic Service in 1962 for the American ship *Lady Washington* which was unsuccessfully attacked by Chief Koyah and his tribe in Houston Stewart Channel, June, 1791.[1]

[1]Page 136.

*CATHERINE POINT — is on the west shore of Houston Stewart Channel at the point where it divides into two arms - one of which becomes Rose Inlet. Named during the 1853 survey of Houston Stewart Channel.

GREATEST MOUNTAIN — in the vicinity of Catherine Point. According to Haida legend an Eagle Crest ancestress, Djila'qons, who had been placed in the creek at the head of Cumshewa Inlet, bore several children. One of these went to live on the south end of Moresby Island where she became known as Greatest-Mountain, and from her all the Eagles of Ninstints are said to have been descended.

*ROSE INLET — an arm running to the north off Houston Stewart Channel. This was the ROSE HARBOUR of early years[1] and it was so named by James Johnstone in 1787 when he accompanied Captain Colnett on the *Prince of Wales* to this area. Named after George Rose, well-known political writer and statesman of that day. Born in 1744 near Brechin, Scotland, Mr. Rose entered the navy at an early age, serving until he was 18, when he left to work in the Records Office at Westminster. He rose rapidly and one of his first duties consisted of supervising a publication of the Domesday Book. He became an M.P. in 1784 and was an intimate friend of William Pitt.

Rose Inlet is about 3½ miles long and separated from Carpenter Bay on its north by a narrow neck of land, one mile across, which creates a funnel for winds sweeping through. The land on the west side of Rose Inlet rises boldly, whilst on the east it is lower.

[1]Rose Harbour - page 159.

*DENNY ROCKS — at the entrance to Rose Inlet, lie on the east side of the main centre channel and consist of several drying and submerged rocks. Named by Commander Prevost in 1853 after Edward Denny, midshipman on the *Virago* during the survey. Denny was the eldest son of Anthony Denny for whom Anthony Island was named.

BOLD ROCKS — the name given to some "small islands" just outside what is now Rose Inlet by James Johnstone in 1787 at the same time as he named the inlet. Identification today could only be tentative.

*PINCHER ROCKS — near the head of Rose Inlet were named during the 1853 survey of Houston Stewart Channel. The Pinchers are actually a group of rocky ledges. From this point to the head of the inlet there are several such ledges.

*KENDRICK POINT — lies northeast of Pincher Rocks and was named in 1962 by the Hydrographic Service after the dilatory, acid-tempered Captain John Kendrick, who nearly lost his ship to revenge-seeking Chief Koyah in the battle in Houston Stewart Channel in 1791.

*SEDMOND CREEK — enters the head of Rose Inlet on the west side. Named in 1853 during the survey of Houston Stewart Channel by the *Virago*. The chart prepared by Inskip, Gordon and Knox pertaining to this survey showed a Haida village located on the north bank of the stream at its mouth. Many years previously on July 10, 1791, John Hoskins, clerk on the *Columbia* wrote of going to the head of Rose Inlet, then unnamed, in a pinnace with Captain Robert Gray. He mentioned a fine meadow with numerous grasses and wild celery, but makes no note of any village. Either they didn't see it or there wasn't one at that time.

The large mud flat off Sedmond Creek is a haven for ducks and geese during the season. And for those interested in fossils, samples may be found on the point south of the Sedmond Creek mouth.

*ROSS ISLAND — kidney-shaped and with a rocky shoreline, it lies at the east entrance to Rose Inlet. Connected to Moresby Island by a drying flat the island rises to a height of over 210 feet. Named during the 1853 survey of Houston Stewart Channel after Dr. William Ross, assistant surgeon aboard the *Virago*. There are fossils on the northeast end of Ross Island, as well as the point of land on Moresby to the northeast of Ross.

*QUADRA ROCKS — east of Ross Island, consist of two rocks about 300 feet apart. The north rock is awash and the south one has a depth of less than 6 feet over it. They were discovered abruptly in May 1892 when the *C.G.S. Quadra* struck hard.

She was under the command of Captain James Gaudin at the time *en route* to the Bering Sea in the interests of the sealing industry. Captain Gaudin beached his ship and proceeded to make temporary repairs, while his second engineer, W.J. Cullim, took a crew in one of the ship's small boats to Port Simpson to send a message to the Department.

The *Quadra* had been built in Scotland the year before and came out via the Straits of Magellan under the command of Captain John Walbran. Built of steel the single screw ship was 175 feet long and her quadruple engines gave her a speed of 11 knots.

*GAUDIN PASSAGE — is that portion of Houston Stewart Channel which flows between Quadra and Trevan Rock and Ellen Island. Captain James Gaudin replaced Walbran, her regular skipper, on the *Quadra* for a few months in 1892. Born on the Isle of Jersey in 1839, James Gaudin served his naval apprenticeship on English merchantmen. He worked on ships in the East Indian and Australian trade most of the time until 1865 when he began sailing between London and Victoria. In 1881 he settled in British Columbia and two years later engaged in piloting until 1888 when he took command of *Sir James Douglas* in lighthouse service. In 1892 he became Marine Agent at the Victoria Customs.

*TREVAN ROCK — east of Quadra Rocks, dries at 10 feet. "Low water slack is the best time to pass through Gaudin Passage," advises the B.C. Pilot, "as Trevan Rock will then be visible and provide a good lead to clear Quadra Rocks." Trevan Rock was named in 1853 after Dr. Henry Trevan, surgeon aboard the *Virago* during the survey made under Commander James Prevost.

It seems surprising that soundings were made all around this region according to the old charts of that 1853 survey, yet Quadra Rocks were not detected, even though kelp surrounding them is plainly visible at slack water. When the tidal stream is running there are tide rips and overfalls in the immediate area of Quadra Rocks. Trevan was charted in 1853, but despite trained and competent men making a fairly close examination of these waters, neighbouring Quadra remained to be found the age-old way of most rocks.

*ELLEN ISLAND — on the south side of Gaudin Passage, is off what is now Rose Harbour. Named in 1853 by Commander James Prevost after his wife, the former Ellen Moresby. Many years earlier, in 1787, it had been called ROUND ISLAND by James Johnstone for its shape. Johnstone was aboard the *Prince of Wales* with Captain Colnett.

The bay between Ellen Island and the old whaling station site in Rose Harbour is much encumbered with rocks and ledges.

*FAIRFAX ISLAND — east of Ellen Island and Rose Harbour, is a small island with a height of 125 feet. Named in 1853 by Commander James Prevost after his brother-in-law, Lieutenant Fairfax Moresby, son of Rear Admiral Moresby, for whom Moresby Island is named.

*ANNETTE ISLAND — north and a little east of Fairfax Island. Named in 1853 by Commander Prevost for one of his daughters.

*CHARLES ISLANDS — the Siamese twins, first shown on the 1853 chart as a single island, were named after Commander James Charles Prevost during the 1853 survey of Houston Stewart Channel and were shown as the singular CHARLES ISLAND. Later this was amended to Charles Islands.

*RASPBERRY COVE — is on the north shore of Houston Stewart Channel, directly across from Rose Harbour. The stream running into the head of Raspberry Cove was considered a good watering place for the *Virago*. Her crew found lush salmonberries when they went ashore. (Visiting ships of early years commonly called these wild berries, raspberries.) Named in 1853 by the men of the *Virago*, and on their chart the rocks off the mouth of the stream are carefully indicated.

During the mining boom following the turn of the present century, a copper claim at Raspberry Cove with showings of copper and some zinc drew temporary interest.

*FORSYTH POINT — a rocky point east of Raspberry Cove. Named in 1853 by Commander James Prevost after William Codrington Forsyth, first lieutenant on the *Virago* during the survey of the Houston Stewart Channel.

*POINT LANGFORD — the north entrance point of Houston Stewart Channel. Named during the 1853 survey. In the bay to the northeast of the point are two fossil sites which interested Dr. Dawson greatly in 1878 - especially the ammonitoid shell impressions which were different from those of the Houston Stewart region in general.

*LANGFORD SHOALS — south of Point Langford and named in association with the point by the Hydrographic Service in 1962. Tidal streams in this part of the channel can attain a rate of 5 knots at times, and when strong southeasterly winds are in opposition to the tide, heavy overfalls occur over Langford Shoals.

*KOYA POINT — about 1½ miles northeast of Point Langford, has been on the charts since around 1927, but date of naming not established. Chief Koyah, the Raven, the undisputed leader of the Kunghit Island area in his day, was the Family Chief for all Raven Crest villages in the region belonging to members of his tribe.

There is a 16-foot-high rock off Koya Point which is connected to the point by a drying reef. North of the point a stream flows from the west draining five small lakes, the largest of which has two islets in its.

*BENJAMIN POINT — is 2 miles north of Koya Point. Formerly known as BENJAMIN ISLAND and shown on a 1927 map as ISLET POINT. Confirmed as Benjamin Point in 1946, it takes the name in association with Carpenter Bay which was named after William Benjamin Carpenter. There are coves on both sides of the neck of this peninsula-like point. Kaidju village lay on the north side.

KAIDJU, Songs-of-victory-village — nestled along the shoreline of the cove on the north side of Benjamin Point. This was Koyah's favorite village, although he was not the Town Chief. That honour belonged to Chief Kan'nskina. Koyah being a Family Chief was head of the numerous branches of his tribe, but not necessarily Town Chief in any of their settlements. Dr. C.F. Newcombe reported that when he visited this Kaidju village in 1903 there were still some of the old lodges standing and remains of totem poles.

*GARCIN ROCKS — about 1¼ miles southeast of Benjamin Point, consist of three large conspicuous rocks, from 42 to 48 feet high, in a compact group with several other submerged and drying rocks close by. A navigational light has been installed in the middle of the three large rocks. Old charts show the group as DANGER ROCKS, but because of numerous duplications of that name in coastal waters the Hydrographic Service requested a new designation. In 1948 they were renamed GARCIN ROCKS after Alfus Garcin, general manager of the Consolidated Whaling Corporation which, in 1918, purchased and operated both the Rose Harbour and Naden Harbour Whaling stations. Garcin, a Newfoundlander, hand-picked his captains and crew and was commonly known as "The Chief" of the Consolidated Whaling Corporation.

The B.C. Pilot warns especially of tide rips, eddies and overfalls occuring at certain stages of tide and wind in the region between Garcin Rocks and

Langtry Island to the north.

*HUFF ROCK — is 10 feet high. Bare and surrounded by foul ground, it lies about ¾ mile northwest of Garcin Rocks. Named by the Hydrographic Service in 1962 after Captain G.A. Huff, one of the pioneers of whaling at Rose Harbour. As early as 1908 he came to the south end of the Charlottes looking for the best site for a station and, in 1910, announced purchase of land at what is now Rose Harbour. He represented the Queen Charlotte Whaling Company.

*LANGTRY ISLAND — a sparsely wooded island, about 160 feet high, which lies 2 miles northwest of Garcin Rocks. Name appeared on the 1927 maps but origin of name has not been confirmed. Called SKA'TSGIDAWA-I by Dr. C.F. Newcombe on his map of Haida place names made in 1897.

G'DAWA-I VILLAGE — according to Dr. Newcombe's map this village lay west of Langtry Island on the rocky shoreline near Ingraham Point.

*INGRAHAM POINT — is the south entrance point of Carpenter Bay. Called ISLET POINT by Dr. Dawson in 1878, he notes it as being about 2 miles from IRON POINT, thereby ruling out the possibility that he meant the present Benjamin Point, which is 4 miles from Iron Point. A bare islet lies at the north end of a drying rocky ledge extending about 600 feet north from Ingraham Point with a bare rock, some 9 feet high, off the islet. This may have been the reason for Dawson having chosen the name ISLET POINT. Renamed in 1962 by the Hydrographic Service after Joseph Ingraham, skipper of the brig *Hope*.[1]

[1]See Hope Point.

*CARPENTER BAY — extends in a westerly direction for about 5 miles. Formerly called PORT STURGIS by Captain Joseph Ingraham in 1792. Mr. R. Sturgis was part of a group owning the *Margaret* and is thought to have had an interest in the *Hope* which Ingraham commanded.

In 1878 Dr. G.M. Dawson named this bay after a noted English naturalist of that time, Dr. William Benjamin Carpenter. Dr. Carpenter's keen interest in the puzzling question of ocean circulations led to his appointment as chief naturalist for the British Government's deep-sea exploration of the North Atlantic. He took an active part in the expeditions from 1868 to 1876 and his theories played a significant role in subsequent conclusions in scientific circles. A valued member of the Royal Geographical Society, Dr. Carpenter became president of the British Association for Advancement of Science.

*KOYA BAY — on the south shore of Carpenter Bay, is west of Ingraham Point and has a stream entering at its head. Rocky ledges fringe much of its shoreline. Named in 1962 by the Hydrographic Service for the Haida chief of the Houston Stewart Channel area in the late 1700s.

*KIJU POINT — separates Koya Bay from South Cove. Name applied to the point in 1962 by the Hydrographic Service and is a modification of the old village KAIDJU at Benjamin Point.

*SOUTH COVE — west of Kiju Point. Named in 1878 by Dr. G.M. Dawson when he visited on June 17th. "There were many seals here when we came in," he wrote, "playing in the water and lying on the rocks. Some mothers carried their young on their backs . . . the two heads coming up together in a most amusing manner."

There are fossils on the west side of South Cove, and this west shore forms the edge of a fault running through to Rose Inlet. Less than a mile of land separates the cove from Rose Inlet, and down this valley pour winds during southerly gales which can cause havoc to boats anchored in Carpenter Bay.

SQA-OS VILLAGE — lay at the mouth of the stream entering the head of South Cove.

*HANCOCK POINT — on the south shore of Carpenter Bay, is northwest of South Cove. Named in 1962 by the Hydrographic Service after the American brigantine *Hancock*, owned by Messrs. Crowell and Creighton of Boston. The 157-ton *Hancock* left Boston in November 1790 with Samuel Crowell as master. She arrived on the northwest Pacific coast in July the following year and traded for a good portion of the season in the Queen Charlotte Islands area. The first European boat to be built on the Charlottes, a tender for the *Hancock*, was built on Maast Island off Masset in July 1791. The *Hancock* is known to have made three journeys to waters of the Charlottes. After sailing to China in the fall of 1791 to sell her cargo of furs, she returned to the Islands in 1792 and 1793.

Two wooded islets front Hancock Point and beyond this the head of Carpenter Bay contains several other islets.

*CROWELL ROCK — which dries at 14 feet, is almost mid-channel and is northeast of Hancock Point. Named in 1962 by the Hydrographic Service in association with Hancock Point.

*SAMUEL ROCK — connected to the north shore of Carpenter Bay by a drying ridge, is 12 feet high, and is north of Crowell Rock. Formerly called SAMUEL ISLET, it received its name in 1962 from the Hydrographic Service who named it after Samuel Crowell, master of the *Hancock*.

West of Samuel Rock and inland on the rise of land, lay the *Car* mineral claim of early mining years. It was an iron showing in contrast to most of the Moresby claims of that era, which were usually for copper.

*IRON POINT — the north entrance point of Carpenter Bay. Named by Dr. Dawson in 1878, who noted additionally the presence of fossils in the region of the point.

*RANKINE ISLANDS — northeast of the entrance to Carpenter Bay, consist of two wooded islands, one 255 feet high and the other, more easterly, is 125 feet. A straggling line of rocks, both above-water and submerged, stretch from the largest Rankine Island north to Oliver Rock.

"I have named these islands for my assistant, Mr. Rankine Dawson," wrote G.M. Dawson in 1878.

*OLIVER ROCK — only 4 feet high, is ¾ of a mile north of the largest Rankine Island. Named in 1962 by the Hydrographic Service after William Oliver, the Scottish carpenter who built the *Glad Tidings* and contributed to the early missionary work of the Methodist Church on the Charlottes. More than a missionary in the accepted sense, William Oliver became a true pioneer of the Islands and lived for most of his life on the Charlottes in Sandspit.
See also Oliver Islet, Point, and Mountain.

IKEDA GEODETIC — an important geodetic point located on Moresby Island west of Oliver Rock and about 1,660 feet above sea level. The rocky point below this site Dr. C.F. Newcombe called T'ESKUN.

*GOODWIN POINT — south side of the entrance to Collison Bay. Named BLUFF POINT in 1878 by Dr. Dawson. By 1945 there were at least ten other Bluff Points on the coast and the Hydrographic Service suggested the name of Goodwin, after the maiden name of Archdeacon Collison's wife. For a time Goodwin Point was known also as GOODWIN BLUFF.

*GOODWIN ROCK — is about ¾ of a mile east of Goodwin Point and named in association with the point in 1945. It is a bare rock, 13 feet high.

*MARION ROCK — west of Goodwin Point. Named in 1962 by the Hydrographic Service after Mrs. Marion Goodwin Collison, wife of Archdeacon Collison, the first white woman to live on the Charlottes. Marion Rock is 10 feet high and bare.

*COLLISON BAY — extends about 2 miles in a southwesterly direction and lies between Ikeda Cove and Carpenter Bay. Named in 1878 by Dr. G.M. Dawson after William Henry Collison, a native of Ireland and graduate of the Church Missionary College, Islington, London. He became the first resident missionary on the Charlottes. Sent to Metlakatla, on the mainland, in 1873, when Metlakatla missionary William Duncan planned to go to Rupert's Land and Collison expected to take over the Metlakatla mission. Mrs. Collison, the first white woman to live at Metlakatla, came with her husband as a bride.

When Duncan changed his mind about leaving Metlakatla, Collison, greatly intrigued by the Haidas he had met, asked to be allowed to go to the Charlottes to open a mission. An experimental visit was made in June 1876 at the request of the dying Chief Seegay of Masset and feelers were put out by Collison to the head chief of the village, Weah. The old chief gave his consent, but only on a trial basis.

In November of that same year, Marion and William Collison and their baby son, Will, the first white child born in Metlakatla, were taken to the land of the Haida by the Hudson's Bay Company vessel *Otter* and put ashore at Masset

1907 tunnel at "Meal Ticket" about a 1/2 mile from the head of Collison Bay.

Photo - Provincial Archives, Victoria.

C.P.R. steamer Tees *unloading supplies at Collison Bay.*

Photo - Provincial Archives, Victoria.

by an absolutely horrified captain. "You'll be murdered in your beds before the week is out," he predicted.

The Collisons were in Masset for 3 years - years of extremely cautious behavior, for they were always very much aware that they were "breaking trail." Those who came after would reap the benefits, or otherwise, of their actions.

"The worst thing of all," Mrs. Collison said afterwards, "was the fact that there was always a face at the window, or peering in through the top part of our divided door, watching with much curiosity what we did. We could never relax our best behavior . . . not for one inadvertent moment. A baby daughter, Emily, arrived in August 1877, the first white child to be born on the Charlottes.

In 1879 Collison was asked to return to Metlakatla to assist Duncan for a time, Duncan being very ill. The Queen Charlotte Islands were put into the care of other missionaries, all of whom paid tribute to the tremendous challenge the Collisons had met - to say nothing of real personal danger had they made an improper move.

During the 1906 to 1913 mining interest there were a number of claims staked around Collison Bay and one young prospector wrote home enthusiastically, "Not only is there a chance of riches from the ground, but as I write this (in September) there are hundreds of ducks and geese at the head of this bay, and the creeks are so filled with salmon trying to climb them, they have formed dams in a number of places. It truly is God's Country!"

In 1908 Mr. M.W. Young opened a small store among the cluster of cabins nestled near the head of the bay and built a good float. In 1909 the C.P.R. listed Collison Bay as a regular port of call. A branch telephone line connected Collison Bay to the Jedway - Ikeda Bay line. And Joe Tritheway put in an "eating house."

One of the best known early-day names was that of the Daykin brothers who, in 1906, had staked, among others, the *Oceanic* and *Wireless* claims on the shore at the head of the bay, so near the tide line they could only be worked at low water. *Meal Ticket* and *Maple Leaf* claims about a ½ mile south of the head of the bay were also staked in 1906. These were later developed by the Collison Bay Mining Company. The *Thunder* property on the ridge between Ikeda and Collison was located in 1907 by the Daykins and another equally well-known pioneer, Ike Thompson, and a 300-foot adit later put in. Claims changed hands for fairly substantial prices and the Bellingham Copper Company which bought some of them put out an alluring brochure about the advantages of Collison Bay for young men, and especially its mining future.

*GONA POINT — on the south shore of Collison Bay. Named by the Hydrographic Service for a former Haida village located in Collison Bay, the name taken from Dr. C.F. Newcombe's Haida map.

*NEST ISLETS — two in number, are at the entrance to Collison Bay. First shown as NEST ROCKS on Dr. G.M. Dawson's 1878 map, the name at that time was applied to the outer and smaller of the islets.

*AWAYA POINT — the south entrance point of Ikeda Cove. Named in 1948 by the Hydrographic Service for a member of the firm, Awaya and Ikeda Company. Arichika Ikeda fished for this company prior to discovering ore in the hills behind Ikeda Cove.

*IKEDA COVE — formerly known as IKEDA BAY and changed to *cove* in 1951. Named after Arichika Ikeda, the Japanese fisherman who staked the first copper claim from which a profitable mine came into being on the Charlottes. Ore was being shipped from here in 1906. The initial methods were appallingly crude and backbreaking, but they produced good results as long

Ore bunkers at Ikeda Cove in 1913 on north shoreline near the head of the bay.

Photo - Provincial Archives, Victoria.

Sternwheeler Dawson *serving as a bunkhouse at Ikeda Mines in 1907.*

Photo - Provincial Archives, Victoria

as the ore was relatively easily available. Improvements were made steadily and by 1908 there were 118 Japanese and two white men working. Over $60,000 was spent in putting in a good wharf, bunkers, tramway and buildings.

The old sternwheeler *Dawson* was purchased, pushed against the shoreline and converted into a confortable bunkhouse. Horses were used to haul the tram cars of ore. Considerable prejudice existed against Orientals at that time, but friendly Archie Ikeda with his considerate helpfulness for anyone in the region became one of its most popular residents.

In 1910 the Ikeda Bay Mines were sold to a Vancouver firm, Mr. Ikeda remained as one of the directors, however. About 1920 the mine closed and the fine venture ended.

Today the skeletal remains of the old *Dawson* lie drowsily on the beach, one of her lifeboats in the forest nearby. The old tramline to the mine is easily followed - although windfalls along the way make for heavy walking in places. As one nears the mine, it is rather a surprise to climb a hill from the forest floor and there find a broad gravel highway intersecting the ancient tram tracks. This highway results from the Jedway open-pit mine operation of the 1960s.

Extensive midden signs show that a Haida village of some size lay near the mouth of the creek at the head of Ikeda Cove.

LILY CREEK — flows into the head of Ikeda Cove and the tramline followed near the creek, crossing it at one point. *Lily* was the name of Ikeda's first ore claim and the site of his first tunnel and stopes.

CARNATION CREEK — a tributary of Lily Creek, has its headwaters on the *Carnation Mineral Claim* of the Ikeda Mines Property and is south of Lily Creek. Both Carnation and Lily Creeks are shown on the map of Ikeda Mines Limited.

IKEDA CREEK — is the name given to the joint mouth of Lily and Carnation Creeks, where the streams enter Ikeda Bay. Not gazetted, but so identified in several mining reports and a brochure prepared by Dr. C. Nogero in 1909.

*IKEDA POINT — the north entrance point of Ikeda Cove and the site of the first wireless station on the Charlottes. Built in 1909 it had the tallest mast on the coast, a huge 228-foot spar. The first telephone lines were put in there when a line ran from the wireless station to Ikeda Mine, then over the ridge to the old townsite of Jedway - with a branch line south to Collison Bay. Mr. Harry Davies went north on the *Quadra* in October 1909 to become the first wireless operator at Ikeda station. In September 1920, eleven years later, it was closed.

*INNER LOW ROCK — bare and 16 feet high, lies 5 cables north of Ikeda Point. Named by Dr. G.M. Dawson in 1878. The present Joyce Rocks Dawson called LOW ROCKS, and then designated this as INNER LOW ROCK.

*BISHOP ROCK — northwest of Inner Low Rock. This 3-foot-high rock was named by the Hydrograpic Service after Charles Bishop, captain of the

Ruby. Owned by Sidenham Teast, the 101-ton vessel left Bristol in October 1794 carrying a crew of 17 men, including a surgeon, and arrived on the Pacific coast in May of the following year.

They spent most of that season trading around the Charlottes, during which time the *Ruby* struck and grounded on a rocky ledge. For a time they feared she might be lost. Worried that his ship had sustained grave damage, Captain Bishop decided to sail directly for the Columbia River instead of continuing his trading along the east coast of the Charlottes.

He afterwards learned that had he kept to his original trading plan his ship was scheduled for an attack by Koyah, who had enlisted the help of the Cumshewas for the proposed capture of Bishop's ship.

After spending the winter at the Columbia River, Bishop set sail for China to sell his furs, but the vessel grounded heavily as it passed over the Columbia River Bar and was then so badly damaged it was decided to sell her in China.

*JOYCE ROCKS — at the east entrance to Skincuttle Inlet, are a compact group of 5 bare rocks, from 12 to 27 feet high. Lying northeast of Bishop Rock, they were the LOW ROCKS of Dawson's 1878 map. During the days of the whalers they were called the GULL ROCKS - a name duplicated all too often on coastal charts. Renamed in 1945 by the Hydrographic Service after Captain Joyce, skipper of the vessel *New England,* when she struck rocks to the northwest of Joyce Rocks - and which were subsequently named after that vessel.

*NEW ENGLAND ROCKS — are 2 close-lying rocks which dry at 2 and 3 feet and are 6½ cables northwest of Joyce Rocks. In 1899 the New England Fishing Company's steamer, *New England,* employed in halibut fishing in Hecate Strait under command of Captain Joyce, entered Skincuttle Inlet and struck hard on these hitherto unknown rocks. Today a black spar buoy with white reflectors is moored 4 cables northwest of these rocks to warn mariners.

The *New England* was built at Camden, New Jersy in 1897 especially for the Boston-based fishing company's use on the Pacific coast. She left Boston in December of that year and, despite a mid-winter voyage, took only 80 days to arrive in Vancouver.

*DELUGE POINT — 1½ miles northwest of Ikeda Point, and named in 1878 by Dr. G.M. Dawson. This is the south entrance point of Skincuttle Inlet and on the southwest side of the point is an interesting fossil site.

*SKINCUTTLE INLET — first called PORT UCAH by Ingraham in 1791-92, after the chief of that region who had his head village in the present Jedway Bay - west of Harriet Harbour. Chief Ucah or Ugah, as it was also written, is mentioned several times in the log of the *Columbia.* He visited that ship when it anchored off Rose Inlet in July 1791 and again when the *Columbia* lay off what is now Skincuttle Inlet. Ingraham mentions him in his journal and he was considered to be the important chief of Skincuttle at that time.

In 1862 when Francis Poole came to establish a copper mine on Burnaby Island, he noted that the Haidas called the inlet SOCKALEE HARBOUR, and

174

one of the small islands off Burnaby Island was called by the Indians Skincuttle. Dr. Dawson in 1878 applied the name of SKINCUTTLE to the entire inlet and the old Poole name of Sockalee Harbour was deleted.

At one time 10 Haida villages stood along the shorelines of Skincuttle Inlet - all belonging to Raven Crest tribes known as the Middle-Towns.

*STANDARD CREEK — is west of Deluge Point and flows north into Skincuttle Inlet. The name was applied in 1961 when Silver Standard Mines applied for water rights to divert the stream a short way in from its mouth so that it would flow, not in its natural northerly direction, but to the west to the mining claim owned by Silver Standard on the east shore of Harriet Harbour (later purchased by Jedway Iron Ore Limited.)

*FUNTER POINT — on the east side at the entrance to Harriet Harbour. During the mining activity at Jedway in the 1960s, Funter Point was the site of the dock - a 360-foot concrete pontoon. Secured parallel to the shore at the end of a rock-fill causeway, to which it was connected by a ramp, the pontoon could accommodate ships up to 26,000 tons dead weight. There were 6 mooring buoys close by for securing lines from the ships and a helicopter pad near the wharf.

Named in 1962 by the Hydrographic Service after Captain Robert Funter, master of the *North West America,* the first ship to be built on the Pacific coast by Europeans. She was constructed at Nootka in 1788 by John Meares and traded along the coast of the Charlottes under Captain Funter.

Fossils are located to the northeast of Funter Point.

*HARRIET HARBOUR and

*HARRIET ISLAND — at the entrance to Harriet Harbour on the south shore of Skincuttle Inlet, were both named by Francis Poole in 1862, after the British schooner *Harriet*, which brought men and supplies to Poole during his mining venture on Skincuttle and Burnaby Islands.

Poole had looked at the harbour from the outside only in 1862, saying then that "it appears to be a magnificent bay." In 1864 he made a more thorough examination and wrote, "Nothing had prepared me for such a scene of beauty. At the mouth of the bay is an islet, some 2 acres in extent, which acts as a breakwater, and a more charming and useful harbour of this magnitude does not exist to my knowledge in the North Pacific."

However, the thing that most people remember about this harbour are the sudden and violent squalls. It was this factor which caused the Haidas to call it GIGAWAI - a trap for the unwary.

*HARRIET CREEK — runs into the head of Harriet Harbour and was named in 1962. Called SALMON RIVER by Francis Poole.

*JEDWAY (TOWNSITES) — both took their name from the Haida term of *gigawai* used in speaking of the harbour. The first Jedway settlement grew, squatter style, along the west side of Harriet Harbour, near its head. Two wharves,

175

Old Jedway in 1909 on the west side of Harriet Harbour. Sivart's store to left of sail.
Record Office on hill (above stern of ship.) Dolmage and Sivart homes in group to right of Record
Office.
Large building was the Jedway Hotel. Saw mill lay on right of photo (out of picture).
Tramline to Copper Queen up side of mountain.
Information from Mrs. J. McGregor.

Photo - Provincial Museum, Victoria.

Residents and visitors
at Jedway in 1907.
Jennie (Dolmage) McGregor
who lived in Jedway in 1908
says she remembers this carved stump
very well. Recent visitors to the place
have found the stump still standing,
now shrouded in trees.

Mr. A. Sivart, storekeeper at Jedway sits
at left in front row; beside him in
dark clothes is Arichika Ikeda, owner
of Ikeda Mine.
Man in white shirt is Abe Heino,
who first came to the region in 1889 and
was still there in the late 1920s.

Photo - Provincial Archives,
Victoria.

*The second Jedway townsite as it looked in 1966. By 1971 only
gravel roads and a few piles of debris marked the site.*

Photo - G.Gray Hill

sawmill, hotel, store and numerous cabin homes appeared as if by magic when
the lure of possible wealth from the hills drew men from all parts of the world.
In November of 1908 the Government sent surveyors to lay out a proper townsite.

And true to form the townsite was laid out - not where it was wanted, but
where government officials thought it should go - across the bay, inaccessible
by road or trail, and ignoring the fact that wharves, dwellings and so on were
already built and in use on the opposite side. They never sold a lot. But the
Mining Recorder's Office, previously located conveniently beside Sivart's General
Store, was changed. A fine new building was erected for the commissioner's
use, the solitary dwelling in the new townsite. "Someone is going to live
there, b'gawd," said the officials in Victoria.

When the Jedway Iron Ore Company began its open-pit mining operation
in 1961, they did establish their townsite on the east side, so the old government
site finally came into the use for which it was planned. However the newer
Jedway townsite, intended only as a 5-year venture, always had the atmosphere
more of a camp than a town. It was a neat little place and served well the
purpose intended, before it, too, became abandoned. By 1971 only gravel roads
and a few piles of debris marked the site - all the buildings have been demolished
or removed.

Harriet Harbour on a warm sunny day is as beautiful now as it was when
Poole first fell in love with it over a hundred years ago.

GAEDI VILLAGE — on the east side of Harriet Harbour near its head,
belonged to the Raven Crest tribe whose town chief was Kan'nskina. These

177

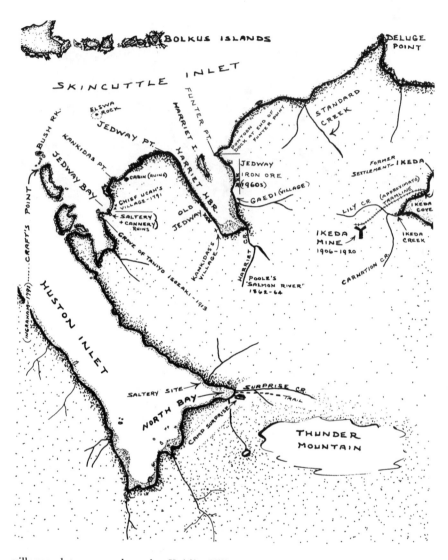

villagers later moved to the Kaidju Village at Benjamin Point. They named their village, Gaedi, in Harriet Harbour, after a small fish.

KANKIDAS VILLAGE — on the west side of Harriet Harbour near the head.

JEDWAY POINT — named in 1962 by the Hydrographic Service in association with the Jedway settlements, is at the west entrance to Harriet Harbour.

ELSWA ROCK — lies northwest of Jedway point about a mile away, and is almost in the middle of the channel between the Bolkus Islands and the

Jedway region. It dries at 8 feet.

Named in 1962 by the Hydrographic Service after Johnny Kit Elswa, the Haida interpreter for Judge J.G. Swan on his 1883 expedition to the Charlottes.

> "I secured the services of an assistant and interpreter, Johnny Kit Elswa of Klue in Cumshewa," wrote the Judge. "I had personally known this young Haida for some time, one of the most reliable of natives I've ever met. Not only is he intelligent and faithful, but he is also an excellent cook and speaks most fluent English. In addition he is a working jeweller, skilled in making silver bracelets, ear-rings, charms and a good carver in stone and wood. He is also an artist and has drawn for me a series of mythological sketches of the folk-lore of his tribe."

Although not named until 1962, Elswa Rock appeared on charts from 1791. Ingraham indicated it on his sketch map of Port Ucah, dated September 1791 and it is also shown on G.M. Dawson's 1878 map, again not named, but with "awash at H.W." beside it.

*KANKIDAS POINT — the east entrance to Jedway Bay (which is *west* of Harriet Harbour and not to be confused with the site of Jedway townsite.) Named in 1962 by the Hydrographic Service for the former village at the head of Harriet Harbour. The ruins of an old prospector's cabin lie in the unnamed cove to the east of Kankidas Point, and fossils may also be found in that cove.

*JEDWAY BAY — is west of Harriet Harbour and received its name from shipping men making regular calls at the former saltery and cannery located there in the 1920s. But its history goes back much further than that. For this was the head village of Chief Ucah in 1791, the most important chief in Skincuttle Inlet at that time according to Hoskins of the *Columbia* and Ingraham of the *Hope*. Jedway Bay has also been called LIZZIE COVE and SALTERY BAY in earlier years.

Between 1910 and 1913 abalones were canned there by the Japanese and it was known as Lizzie Cove at that time. Not too much has been reported about the operation, as Canadian laws forbade Japanese to obtain licences and, since this product was for their own use, it proved difficult to obtain a white sponsor. (The white person procured the licence and held it for a Japanese, as with all salteries.)

On the small peninsula extending into Jedway Bay is the grave of Mrs. Taniyo Isozaki, who died March 21, 1913, age 30 years. The cleared portion where her grave lies seems parklike and peaceful - a fitting memorial for this gentle lady from so far away.

A saltery operated in this same bay; known to have been running in 1917, is believed to have been established several years earlier. At that period the bay became known as SALTERY BAY. Operated off and on, sometimes as a saltery and occasionally as a cannery, it closed for good in the early 1930s by the then owners, B.C. Packers.

Saltery-cannery at Jedway Bay, 1920s

Photo - Mrs. Louise Dover

Grave of Mrs. Taniyo Isozaki who died March 21, 1913, age 30. At Jedway Bay.

Photo taken in 1970 by G. Gray Hill.

180

UCAH'S VILLAGE — on the east side of Jedway Bay, the head village of the Skincuttle Inlet chief in 1791. (See Jedway Bay and Skincuttle Inlet.)

*BUSH ROCK — with some sparse scrub on its 15-foot summit, lies at the north end of a string of islands which form the west side of Jedway Bay. Named in 1878 by Dr. G.M. Dawson. It was shown, but not named, on Ingraham's chart of 1791.

CRAFT'S POINT — the north point of the large islet immediately south of Bush Rock. Named by Joseph Ingraham in 1791 after his first mate on the *Hope,* John Craft. Mr. Craft died shortly afterwards, when the ship was *en route* to Hawaii after trading around the Charlottes. The point is unnamed today.

*HUSTON INLET — west of Jedway Bay, first shown on a map drawn by Ingraham in 1791, but he left it unnamed. Francis Poole in 1862 applied the first European name, designating it as HUSTON BAY. Dr. Dawson changed this to Huston Inlet and so it has remained from that time on.

During the mining interest at the turn of the present century, the whole of the peninsula - using a line drawn from the head of Carpenter Bay to the head of Huston Inlet - literally swarmed with young prospectors. The lure of staking proved irresistible as the captain of a sealer discovered. When the *Markland* put in to Jedway in June 1908, on her way to the Bering Sea, three of her crew took advantage of the stop to steal one of the sealer's boats and disappeared into one of the numerous inlets to try their luck. The furious skipper was forced to send to Victoria for three crewmen to replace the deserters before he could proceed.

THUNDER MOUNTAIN — on the ridge at the head of Huston Inlet had several claims on its slopes. The peak of this mountain is seen clearly from the head of Skincuttle Inlet.

NORTH BAY — the southeast corner of Huston Inlet, a small cove with two streams running into it. Frequently referred to in early mining reports.

SURPRISE CREEK, entered North Bay on the north side, and

CAMP SURPRISE — the supply base at the mouth of Surprise Creek. There was a cabin built there and used by all the prospectors. The stream took its name from the mining claim staked near the creek in 1907 by Frank Watson. It lay about ¾ of a mile from the inlet and had the tongue-in-cheek name of *Surprise.*

With so much activity in the region, the Mining Recorder, E.M. Sandilands, hired a crew of men in the fall of 1908 to cut a trail through from the head of Huston Inlet to Collison Bay. It went in from Camp Surprise.

In the 1920s and 1930s a saltery operated in this vicinity and, for a time also, a small abalone cannery. It was the abalones sampled from this operation which caused one official to say, "They were pure rubber - absolutely nothing you could do with them. Would have made good shoe material is the best you could say for them." At any rate the abalone plant operated only briefly, probably due to the difficulty of obtaining a licence and, perhaps, the quality of the product.

*SEA PIGEON ISLAND — near the mouth of Huston Inlet was first shown on Joseph Ingraham's 1791 map, with soundings and submerged rocks indicated nearby, but he did not apply a name. Poole's 1862 map also showed the island. Not until Dr. G.M. Dawson arrived to sketch the Skincuttle area, however, did the little island become SEA PIGEON ISLAND.

*BOULDER ISLAND — north and west of Sea Pigeon Island. Named by Dr. Dawson in 1878. It was indicated, but not named on Ingraham's 1791 map. Ingraham seemed more interested in the large kelp patch around it, and the foul ground northward, than in the island itself.

*GREEN ROCK — an 11-foot-high rock with a grass-covered summit lying east of Boulder Island, almost in the middle of Huston Inlet, near its entrance. Named in 1878 by Dr. G.M. Dawson.

*HUSTON POINT — is the west entrance point of Huston Inlet, and was named in 1962 by the Hydrographic Service in association with the inlet.

*LOW BLACK ROCK — a 2-foot-high rock lying northeast of Huston Point. Named in 1878 by Dr. G.M. Dawson.

*SLIM INLET — west of Huston Inlet. Named for the shape of the feature by the Hydrographic Service in 1962. Three streams, draining several small lakes, run into the head of Slim Inlet. Geographical maps indicate a fault line running from Slim Inlet to the head of Louscoone. Had the valley floor been only slightly lower, Moresby Island would have had another offshore island with a waterway to Louscoone Inlet.

*GEORGE BAY — is the name which today is applied to a bight northwest of Slim Inlet. A sizeable stream running into its head has a mud flat off the mouth which dries to fill the bay completely.

This is not the George Bay of Francis Poole and G.M. Dawson, however. Their maps showed the waters off the entrance to Slim Inlet as George Bay. Poole named it in 1862. The Haidas used to call Poole, King-George-Tyhee-Poole, meaning a Britisher of importance. (Britishers were frequently referred to as King-George-Men.) Poole named the waters GEORGE HARBOUR, Dawson changed it to GEORGE BAY.

LANADANGUNA VILLAGE, Bad-talking-village — According to James White, F.R.G.S. in his book *Indians of Canada*, this village lay between George Bay and Tangle Cove to the north. Francis Poole in 1862 indicated a Haida site at this place, but did not name it. Dr. C.F. Newcombe on his map in 1897 placed the village in the bay at the south end of Dolomite Narrows. It belonged to an Eagle Crest tribe who were reported to say unkind things about the people of the Bolkus Island village.

*BOLKUS ISLANDS — lie almost in the centre of Skincuttle Inlet and consist of one large island, which has a chain of smaller ones extending east from it. They were called NEEDHAM'S ISLES by Ingraham in 1791, and BALKUS by Poole in 1862. Dawson modified Poole's naming to the BOLKUS which is on the maps of today.

These are the legendary islands which according to some Haida legends were the first to rise from waters following the Flood.

It is said that when the Flood subsided a reef near the Bolkus came to the surface. On this reef sat Foam-Woman, who became the ancestress of all the Middle-Town-Raven Crest people. As the families grew and multiplied, migrations began to other parts of the Charlottes. The Haidas who remained had their head village on the largest Bolkus island and became known as the Striped-Town-People, taking their name from a rock on the island.

HAGI VILLAGE — lay along the west side of the largest Bolkus Island, and was a village of some size. The house pits in rows paralleling the beach may still be clearly seen. The cove on the northwest corner of the island is obviously the main approach to the village. These Raven Crest villagers were the Striped-Town-People under Chief Wada.

*COPPER ISLANDS — extend along the northeast side of Skincuttle Inlet and were, in the main, all named by Francis Poole in 1862. As one leaves the head of Skincuttle Inlet and travels east by boat, these islands stretch across the horizon in the morning sun and give a Hawaiian appearance to the inlet.

*EAST COPPER ISLAND — is at the outer east end of the Copper group and joined to its neighbour, Jeffrey Island, by a ledge. Both Dawson and Poole considered it to be one island with Jeffrey. But when prospecting interest resulted in filing of claims, EAST COPPER ISLAND was applied to the outermost of the group. From the time Francis Poole did exploration work on the south side, the island has interested prospectors. Abe Heino made it his particular point of activity for years.

Abe had prospected on the Charlottes since 1889, locating several claims - among them the original workings on this island of Poole's. He did quite a bit of work in 1902 then let the claim lapse. Whereupon it was restaked by another Abe, Abe Johnson, and named *Red Raven*. Mr. Heino took it over a few years later. By 1914 he had made several shipments of ore and employed a crew of 10 men.

As late as 1917 he was still making small shipments of ore. A well-known figure to steamers servicing the Charlottes, he came out in his small boat to meet them to take his supplies from "over the side." Shafts, open cuts and tunnels criss-crossed the island - testimony to his industry.

"Abe always had a dog," recalls Charlie Hartie of Queen Charlotte City, "but as fast as he would break them in, they would suddenly die. Lord knows how many he had . . . they ate exactly the same food as Heino and he thrived

The **Red Raven** *mineral claim on the south side of East Copper Island.*
Worked by Francis Poole briefly in 1862-63. Relocated years later,
it was best known as Heino's mine. He made several shipments of copper
from his claim on this island. Photo taken in 1907.

Provincial Archives photo.

on the fare."

"He would go over to Jedway to yarn with Ike and Sadie Thompson. They had been in the Yukon and Sadie could tell some hair-raising stories of her life there. But Abe was no pal of Sadie's, and she never made any bones about it.

"He was a tough old sea dog and his *Awaska* was his pride and joy. She had once won a sailing race for him and he loved her dearly . . . even when she got so old and leaky he could hardly keep her afloat."

*JEFFREY ISLAND — connected to the west side of East Copper Island, received its name from Francis Poole, in 1862. A house, garden and well, long-abandoned, remain on the south coast of Jeffrey Island.

*GEORGE ISLAND — the largest of the Copper group is also the centre of the chain. From 1910 to 1912 Mr. W. Campbell worked a claim on this island and made a shipment of copper ore which the Mining Records rated as high grade. George Island was named by Poole in 1862.

*SKINCUTTLE ISLAND — west of George Island. It was here, late in the afternoon of August 11, 1862, that the *Rebecca* dropped anchor and put Poole and his party ashore to begin explorations. They sunk a shaft to a depth of 15 feet and made several open cuts before deciding later to move to a more likely-looking site on Burnaby Island.

Skincuttle Island was also the site of the first terrible smallpox outbreak among the Haidas. In describing this, Poole wrote that although he moved his headquarters to Burnaby Island, he kept a small work party on Skincuttle - paddling them across each day. "But the shaft did not repay the trouble and expense," he went on, "and I had gradually been determining to abandon it when an outbreak of smallpox among the Indians brought things to a head. Several died, one of whom was Indian George, a very handy fellow, and another a pretty Haida girl. Seeing these two were dying, the other Haidas strangled them and immediately left the camp on Skincuttle . . . fleeing in a panic and leaving us to bury their dead. Which we did to prevent further spread of the disease. My foreman and I then set fire to the Indian huts and to the bushwood.

"A fierce gale of wind began to blow at that time and the whole of Skincuttle was soon one sheet of flame. Not a stick would have been left on any part of it, if a sudden cloudburst had not descended and poured down such a rain as I never beheld before in my lifetime.

"The rain lasted without any let-up for thirty-four hours . . . almost to the minute. Thus by the action of two powerful elements did poor Skincuttle receive its purification. I ordered total evacuation of the islet then."

Poole named the island SKINCUTTLE, as it was the nearest he could come to the Haida name.

*ROCK ISLET — the most easterly of the Copper group, is not the Rock Islet of Poole, for he said, "It was a mere ledge of rocks and wholly destitute of vegetation. I named this ledge ROCK ISLAND." His map showed that it lay north of what is Rock Island today. The Rock Island of present maps is 140 feet high and wooded.

*SLUG ISLET — dangling off the southeast part of the Copper group was first named in 1878 by Dr. G.M. Dawson, who called it SLUG ROCK.

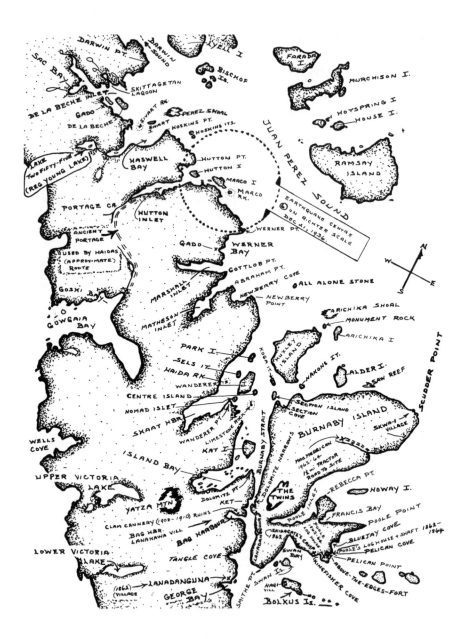

EAST SIDE OF MORESBY ISLAND; FROM
BURNABY ISLAND TO DARWIN POINT.

CHAPTER NINE

*BURNABY ISLAND — on the northwest side of Skincuttle Inlet has drawn
men's interest over the years for its three basic potentials: wealth from the
ground; forested slopes; and fertile beaches. Of these, the latter probably yielded
most lucratively. The ancient Haida established his villages and camps in strategic
places for the gathering of shellfish, fish, seals and otter. The white man looked
for mineral and timber, but was not rewarded to the same extent. Of these
commodities, it was the search for minerals which brought Burnaby into the
news first and last.

The first shaft on Burnaby Island was sunk in 1862 when a young mining
engineer, Francis Poole, representing the Queen Charlotte Mining Company
of Victoria, came to Skincuttle Inlet to look for copper. After satisfying himself
that the most promising mineral site in the area lay on the southeast part of
Burnaby, Poole had his men build log shelters and establish their main shaft
at what is now Pelican Point. For nearly two years the explorations continued.
The results were unrewarding and the project abandoned in 1864.

One hundred years later, Burnaby again appeared in the news when two
companies, Burnaby Iron Mines Limited and Merrican International Mines Limited, put out a great deal of hoopla about their "finds." Burnaby Iron Mines
had 47 claims which spread over much of southeast Burnaby Island, including the old Poole workings, and extended out to Skincuttle Island. The interest was iron.

Merrican International Mines claims covered most of northeastern Burnaby,
with their main activities centered 3 miles southwest of Scudder Point. A rough

supply road was built from the east coast to the site which lay 1½ miles inland. Their interest was also iron.

There have been other mining claims on Burnaby. It received its share of eager prospectors during the 1906-1912 boom and, from time to time, through later years interest has been shown in one or two locations for brief periods. So far nothing of financial significance has accompanied the workings.

Francis Poole named the island in 1862 after Robert Burnaby, a commission merchant in Victoria and one of the leading business men at that time. His firm, Henderson and Burnaby, was established in 1852 by Mr. Burnaby.

The Haidas called the island SKWA'IKUNGWA'I.

SMITHE POINT — is the southern extremity of Burnaby Island. Named in 1962 by the Hydrographic Service after William Smithe, Chief Commissioner of Lands, on whose behalf Newton Chittenden made his extensive exploration along the shores of the Charlottes in 1884. There are fossils in the cove northeast of Smithe Point.

SWAN BAY — dipping into the south shore of Burnaby Island, and

SWAN ISLANDS — which lie along the front of Swan Bay, were both named in 1962 by the Hydrographic Service after Judge J.G. Swan who also made a tour of the Charlottes. He was on the Islands from June 25 to September 21, 1883. The Smithsonian Institute commissioned Judge Swan to make collections and observations for the United States Fish Commission, the National Museum and the Bureau of Ethnology. Johnny Kit Elswa (Elswa Rock) was his guide and interpreter.

There are several fossil sites between Swan Bay and Kingfisher Cove.

KINGFISHER COVE — east of Swan Bay on the southeast shore of Burnaby Island. Named by Francis Poole and adopted to Dr. Dawson's map in 1878. When Poole worked at Pelican Cove, a group of Skidegate Haidas established a camp at Kingfisher Cove and were daily visitors to the mining site.

PELICAN POINT — a rocky point on the southeast end of Burnaby Island, and

PELICAN COVE — which lies inside Pelican Point, were both named in 1962 by the Hydrographic Service after Dr. C.F. Newcombe's 18-foot open sailboat *Pelican* in which he cruised the Charlotte waters in 1897. Pelican Point is one of the numerous fossil sites which abound in the area.

Francis Poole established his main camp in Pelican Cove in 1862 - 64.

ABOVE-THE-EDGES-FORT — at or near Pelican Point belonged to an Eagle tribe from Tanu.

BLUEJAY COVE — is the bay to the north of Pelican Cove and was named by Francis Poole in 1862 for a blue-jay he saw flying near the beach - the first bird of that species he had seen on the Charlottes. In March of 1863

188

on his return from a trip Poole, caught by a storm off this bay, was forced to spend the night in the open. "It will ever remind me of this benign climate," he wrote," that while the storm raged, I could take shelter under the outspread branches of a huge cedar tree and the next morning rise, unharmed and as refreshed as if I had been in bed."

*POOLE POINT** — extending from the tip of a pointed peninsula off the east side of Burnaby Island. First named GRANITE POINT by Dr. Dawson in 1878 who said of it, "Granite Point is a rather remarkable whitish crag, separated by a narrow neck of low land from the main shore." The Hydrographic Service renamed the point in 1945 because of duplications.

Francis Poole, for whom it is now named, had an unhappy time with his miners, but fell in love with the Charlottes and later dictated a book about his stay. "As far as the eye can see either way this land is a picture of loveliness. The very atmosphere seems laden with the perfume of its vegetation," he said. "it is a land of enchantment."

*FRANCIS BAY** — west of Poole Point. Named after Francis Poole by the Hydrographic Service in 1962.

*REBECCA POINT** — the northern tip of the peninsula which separates Francis Bay from Poole Inlet. Named in 1962 by the Hydrographic Service after the vessel *Rebecca* which, under Captain E.H. McAlmond, landed Francis Poole and his party on Skincuttle Island, August 11, 1862 - exactly 100 years earlier.

*POOLE INLET** — curves in a southwesterly direction into the lower part of Burnaby Island. The old timber-cruisers' map showed this inlet as KEATE INLET. In 1935 Mr. H.D. Parizeau suggested Poole Inlet, because of duplications of the other name. The suggestion was adopted. There are several fossil sites in Poole Inlet.

*THE TWINS** — between Poole Inlet and Burnaby Strait, are 2 conspicuous mountains which rise to over 1,800 feet. Similar in appearance they were called THE TWINS in 1878 by Dr.G.M. Dawson.

*HOWAY ISLAND** — lies off the entrance to Poole Inlet. A wooded island about 1 mile long and rising to 300 feet, it was the CHA'ODJSKE'LA of the Haidas. In 1962 the Hydrographic Service named it after Judge Frederic William Howay, an eminent jurist, historian and prolific writer. Many of the happenings of the fur trade connected with the Charlottes are known today because of his books and articles.

*SCUDDER POINT** — the northeast tip of Burnaby Island. First called KANSKEENI'S POINT by Joseph Ingraham in 1791. Ingraham must have known the chief well for he called the general region of the present Juan Perez Sound, Kanskeeni's Sound. He later divided this into two parts, the northern section being Kanskeeni's Sound and the southern section, immediately north of Burnaby Island, was shown as Port Geyer, after Frederick Geyer who had an interest in Ingraham's ship, *Hope.*

Kan'nskina was the Town Chief of a Raven Crest tribe which had its origin on House Island. As his tribe migrated along the east coast of the Charlottes, he and his successors were town chiefs of several sites, including villages at Benjamin Point and Harriet Harbour. (Site of Jedway townsite of the 1960s.)

In 1878 Dr. Dawson renamed Kanskeeni Point, calling it SCUDDER POINT after the Haida name for the point, SKWA-IKUN. "A considerable width of low land stretches back from Scudder Point," he wrote, "covered with an open growth of large, but gnarled spruces, the trunks of which are not simple, but fork upwards - as they are often wont to do in exposed situations. Little beaches of coarse, clean-washed gravel fill the spaces between the low shattered rock masses, which spread widely between high and low water marks, with evidence of the action of a heavy surf."

SKWA-I VILLAGE — when Dr. Dawson examined the place in 1878 a strongly built, but abandoned Indian lodge still stood on this ancient site located in the cove a little north of Scudder Point. The burial site lay in a cove on the south side of Scudder, and since the Haida name for Burnaby Island was Skwa-i kungwa-i, it would seem that the village may have taken its name from the island.

*SAW REEF — about 2 miles west of Scudder Point. Named in 1878 by Dr. Dawson for its jagged appearance. The reef is a large rocky patch which dries with several above-water heads. Kelp hugs the reef.

*ALDER ISLAND — midway along the north coast of Burnaby Island and named in 1878 by Dr. Dawson. Geologists say this flat wooded island is a geological stew containing almost every rock formation to be found on the Charlottes.

*NAKONS ISLET — west of Alder Island and off the southeast tip of Huxley Island. It forms the northeastern breakwater of Section Cove, Nakons is a small rocky islet with rocky shores. Named in 1962 by the Hydrographic Service for Nikons, Haida Great-House-People, a subdivision of the Yadus family of the Eagle Crest tribe. The most famous chief of this tribe, Nestecanna of Skidegate, was a slave on the mainland in his youth, but being freed by ransom managed to acquire enough wealth to remove all stigma by his lavish potlotches.

*SECTION COVE — on the northwestern corner of Burnaby Island. Named by Dr. Dawson in 1878 who noted with much interest the abundance of Triassic fossils in this region. There is a good beach at the head of Section Cove and two streams flow into the bay. It drew prospecting interest at various times and in 1963 the *Johnson Nickel* claim on the west side of the cove attracted the attention of Jedway Iron Ore Limited. They conducted an extensive survey of the claim's potential but concluded the mineralization was localized.

*SECTION ISLAND — forms the west outside portion of Section Cove. Named in this association by the Hydrographic Service in 1962.

190

Dolomite Narrows, also known as Burnaby Narrows, are the narrowest section of Burnaby Strait.

Photo - Anne Clemence

*BURNABY STRAIT — lies along the west shore of Burnaby Island and separates it from Moresby Island. Named in 1862 by Francis Poole, in association with his naming of Burnaby Island.

*DOLOMITE NARROWS — are the narrowest portion of Burnaby Strait and were named in 1878 by Dr. Dawson. Dolomite, after the Franch geologist Dolomieu, is vitreous, brittle and has no valuable mineral content. The Dolomite Narrows are frequently called BURNABY NARROWS and dry completely near the south end. Containing some fine butter clam beds, the shoreline on the east side of the Narrows appears to be composed of nothing but crushed clam-shells. Although there are hazardous rocks, the channel is used constantly and markers have been erected to give guidance. However, it is close navigation and requires much common sense and "reading" of the currents.

At the mouth of the stream at the north end of Dolomite Narrows, on the Burnaby Island side, are ruins of an old building, and pilings still stand at the edge of the grass line.

KET VILLAGE, Narrow-strait-village — stood on the west shore of Dolomite Narrows. The Haidas occupying it were relatives of the Bolkus Island Raven Crest people. The name of the chief at Ket meant the-resounding-of-a-copper-when-struck.

LANADANGUNA VILLAGE, bad-talking-village — an Eagle crest site which Dr. C.F. Newcombe said lay in the bay at the south end of Dolomite Narrows and placed it very definitely on Burnaby Island. James White in his *Indians of Canada,* however, described the village as being "south of Tangle Cove." Perhaps villagers moved from one site to the other taking the name with them, as was commonly done in ancient years. At any rate the village came by its name of Bad-talking-village because its occupants were reported to say unkind things about the people of the Bolkus Island village of Hagi.

*TANGLE COVE — on Moresby Island, at the south entrance to Burnaby Strait. This is one of Dr. Dawson's 1878 place names. The bay when he visited it was a tangle of kelp so great it filled the entire bight.

*BAG HARBOUR — named for its shape by Dr. Dawson in 1878, is on the west side of Dolomite Narrows. Shortly after the turn of the present century a clam cannery was built on the north shore of Bag Harbour. Known to have operated in 1908 then closed down for a period. When it reopened for processing in 1910 it had fallen into disrepair and men from the plant at Pacofi, at the head of Selwyn Inlet, were sent to rebuild it for that season's operation. The old boiler from this cannery is still lying on the shore at the site - long abandoned.

LANAHAWA, Swampy-Village — is reported to have been located at Bag Harbour. The Raven Crest tribe who owned this site may very easily have been attracted to the place by the excellent cohoe stream which enters the southwest corner of the bay. It is a favorite place for black bears and visitors anchored in Bag Harbour seldom fail to see at least one or two ambling along the shoreline.

*DOLOMITE POINT — the northwest entrance point to Dolomite Narrows. Not named until 1962 when the Hydrographic Service applied the name in association with the narrows.

*ISLAND BAY — entered to the west of Dolomite Point. Named in 1878 by Dr. Dawson who estimated it contained at least 17 islands and islets. "And 47 rocks," say old-timers.

There was a Haida settlement in ancient years at the head of this bay - probably true of most places with a good salmon stream and an abundance of shellfish. Clam-shells brighten several of the beaches on the islands of the bay, as well as along the shoreline of Island Bay.

*KAT ISLAND — north of Island Bay on the west side of Burnaby Strait. Named in 1962 by the Hydrographic Service after a former Haida village which their information showed to be on the west side of this island. Kat is a modification of the Haida word for deer.

*LIMESTONE ROCK — near the north end of Burnaby Strait, was named in 1878 by Dr. Dawson who said, "It is a dangerous reef, bare only at low water, but not extensive . . . though a second rock, dry at low water lies only a short distance southeast of it." Considering the maze of reefs and rocks they had already negotiated, it sounds as though the Dawson party must have come upon Limestone Rock unexpectedly, which caused him to label it as dangerous more so than the previous ones.

CENTRE ISLAND — named by Dr. Dawson for its position at the north end of Burnaby Strait.

WANDERER ISLAND — which Dr. Dawson named in 1878 for the 20-ton British trading schooner which took him and his party to the Charlottes.

They sailed from Victoria on May 27, 1878, and returned in the fall on October 17. In addition to Dr. Dawson and his assistant Rankine Dawson there were three crewmen. During the cruise natives with specific local knowledge were engaged for short periods. Wanderer Island is west of Centre Island and forms the east entrance of Skaat Harbour.

NOMAD ISLET — named in 1962 by the Hydrographic Service is the islet lying between Wanderer Island and Wanderer Point. It is connected to Wanderer Point by a drying bank.

WANDERER POINT — is the northern extremity of the penisula separating Skaat Harbour from Burnaby Strait and was named in 1962 by the Hydrographic Service in association with Wanderer Island.

SKAAT HARBOUR — is Dr. Dawson's modification of a Haida phrase which meant good-hunting-place, when he named the inlet in 1878. It is also the Haida word for *falcon*.

HAIDA ROCK — west of Wanderer Island is awash. Named by the Hydrographic Service in 1962 for the Indian people of the Charlottes.

SELS ISLET — west of Wanderer Island is 160 feet high and has a shoreline of ledges and rocks all round. Named in 1962 by the Hydrographic Service for the Raven Crest tribe, the Sels or Slaves, of the Kunghit Haidas.[1]

[1]See Nagas Point.

PARK ISLAND — about 175 feet high and wooded, it lies northwest of Wanderer Island. Named in 1962 by the Hydrographic Service after Mr. C.H. Park who invested considerable money in mining claims in the Harriet Harbour and Huston Inlet area during the mining boom of 1906 to 1909. The *Eagle Tree* property about 1 mile south of Harriet Harbour was his especial interest. In 1908 he had four men working continuously and spoke of putting in a tramway. That same year he bought the *Surprise* claim from Frank Watson in Huston Inlet. Mr. Park's name was frequently mentioned in mining reports of that era.

KOGA ISLET — lies off the west entrance to Section Cove and is southeast of Park Island. This small islet was named in 1962 by the Hydrographic Service for one of the Raven Crest tribes who owned a village in what is now McCoy

Cove, Cumshewa Inlet. They were a branch of the tribe originally from Lawn Hill, some of whom later owned Skedans and were extremely influential people. The Kogas, however, were not held in any esteem. Their gambling luck was even more dismal, so much so that in a game with the Skedans gamblers the entire inhabitants of this village - after losing everything else - finally put themselves up as the stake. And lost again, thereby becoming the property of the Skedans.

*HUXLEY ISLAND — bold and rising steeply from the beach on its east side to a height of over 1400 feet, has a conspicuous hump on its south end, with a smaller one at the north end. Evidence remains of early day logging and several log slides (not skid roads) down its hillsides.

Dr. G.M. Dawson named the island in 1878 for Thomas Henry Huxley the celebrated biologist, whose particular interest was the study of marine animals. Huxley wrote many scientific works, the most noted of which, *Man's Place in Nature,* overcame both scientific objections and religious alarm to the Darwinian theory.

Huxley Island shared in the prospecting boom of 1906 to 1913. "Ross and Abriel are the discoverers of a good showing of copper, with some free gold," read headlines in a report sent from the Jedway correspondent in 1907. The following year a Victoria syndicate hired Mr. J.M. Carlyle and a crew of two men to develop 13 claims of their *Rambler* group. Surface work, trails and cabins were put in - only to join the rest of the mining dreams in abandonment a few years later.

There are several fossil sites on and around Huxley Island.

Monument Rock in Juan Perez Sound, lies off the north end of Huxley Island. Bare and about 75 feet high, it appears to rise sheer from the water as if marking the site of some precious remembrance.

Photo - Anne Clemence

*MONUMENT ROCK — off the northeast shore of Huxley Island presents an interesting silhouette - similar to a piece of modern sculpture in its simplicity. Bare and about 75 feet high, it appears to rise sheer from the water as if marking the site of some precious remembrance. Named by Dr. Dawson in 1878.

*ARICHIKA ISLAND — east of Monument Rock and northeast of Huxley Island is wooded and there are fossil sites on the east side of it. Named in 1962 by the Hydrographic Service after the Cinderella of Ikeda Mines, Arichika Ikeda.

*ARICHIKA SHOAL — named by the Hydrographic Service in 1962 in association with the island and is to the northwest of it. There is a least depth of 14 feet over the shoal. It was the waters off this area of the Charlottes which Joseph Ingraham named PORT GEYER for Frederick W. Geyer who, with others, had a financial interest in the *Hope,* Ingraham's ship for this trading venture.

*ALL ALONE STONE — a dome-shaped wooded islet about 120 feet high, with a small islet close off. Named by Dr. Dawson in 1878, who felt that it, and Monument Rock, were good markers for vessels to use in entering Burnaby Strait.

*JUAN PEREZ SOUND — extends along the east side of Moresby Island from Burnaby Island's north shore to the southwest part of Lyell Island, at the entrance to Darwin Sound. The south part of it is believed to be the ETCHES SOUND of Captain James Colnett of the *Prince of Wales,* and Charles Duncan of the *Princess Royal,* who traded along these waters in 1787 and 1788. The principal owners of their ships at that time were Richard Cadman Etches, John and William Etches of the King George Sound Company, who also owned the *Queen Charlotte* and *King George* captained by Dixon and Portlock. Etches and Company later joined Meares in forming the Associated Merchants trading to the North West Coast of America.
In 1791-92 Joseph Ingraham named this body of water KANSKEENI'S SOUND with the south part being PORT GEYER.
It was Dr. G.M. Dawson who felt the original discoverer of the Charlottes should have at least one place in the Island's nomenclature, with the result that he, in 1878, applied the name of Juan Perez to this section of the Charlottes. "Juan Perez Sound has been so named," wrote Dawson, "in honour of the reputed discoverer of the Q.C. Islands, who - though he appears rather to have had that honour thrust upon him than earned it by courage in his exploration - probably deserves some recognition."

*NEWBERRY POINT — on Moresby Island, the south entrance to Werner Bay and

*NEWBERRY COVE — which is to the west of the point, were both named in 1962 by the Hydrographic Service after Major Newberry, who had mining claims under bond in several parts of the Charlottes - Harriet Harbour, Lockeport, Tasu and Mitchell Inlet. His name appeared frequently in reports in 1908 and he seemed very much on the scene as he moved from one project to another - not in any way satisfied merely to belong to a company and listen to reports.

WERNER BAY — on the east shore of Moresby Island, takes in the waters between Newberry Point and Werner Point. Named by Dr. Dawson in 1878 after Abraham Gottlob Werner, a German geologist and minerologist, who was born in 1749 and died in 1817. Considered to be the founder of scientific geology, the Mining Academy at Freiburg where he was an instructor for more than 40 years, attracted students from all parts of the world because of the high calibre of instruction.

There were several claims in the Werner Bay region, owned by the Queen Charlotte Pioneer Development Company in 1911 and 1912, which also owned the *Bird* and *Bismark* claims at Lockeport. The two arms extending west and southwest out of Werner Bay were known in early years as NORTH and SOUTH WERNER. (Now renamed as Matheson and Marshall Inlets.)

ABRAHAM POINT — separates Newberry Cove from Matheson Inlet at the head of Werner Bay. Named by the Hydrographic Service in 1962 for Abraham Werner in association with the bay.

MATHESON INLET — which fishermen call SOUTH WERNER BAY - and probably will for many years - despite the newer name of Matheson Inlet having been applied in 1962 by the Hydrographic Service. Named after Mr. J. Matheson, who with his partner, Mr. D. Bowser, owned copper claims near Lockeport in 1908. Their property lay adjacent to the well-known *Last Chance* group of Wintermute, Jones and McEacheran.

GOTTLOB POINT — is the northeast tip of the peninsula which divides Matheson from Marshall Inlet at the head of Werner Bay. The point was named in 1962 by the Hydrographic Service after Abraham Gottlob Werner, and in association with Werner Bay.

MARSHALL INLET — is the NORTH WERNER BAY of the fishermen. The Hydrographic Service named it in 1962 after Dr. T. Rhymer Marshall who came to the Charlottes in 1902 to examine the coal deposits for the British Columbia Mining Bureau.

W.A. Robertson, the original discoverer of coal in the Yakoun Valley, was his able guide for most of the inspection trip. Dr. Marshall was impressed with the quality of the coal at Wilson Creek, but felt the Robertson Mine seams had been overestimated as to amount.

On December 21, 1936, the region from Werner Bay to Hutton Inlet was the epicentre of an earthquake measuring 6 on the Richter scale.

GADO VILLAGE — according to Dr. C.F. Newcombe, this village stood between Werner Point and the mouth of Marshall Inlet. (Another village by this same name stood on the east side of Lyell Island, as well as one in De

La Beche Inlet.)

*MARCO ISLAND — off the southeast entrance to Hutton Inlet, and

*MARCO ROCK — off the east side of Marco Island, 26 feet high with a ragged reef extending for 2 cables off its northwest side, were both named in 1962 by the Hydrographic Service after Mr. J. Marco, superintendent at Ikeda Mines, killed in an accident on May, 20, 1909.

The 29-year-old Marco was an extraordinarily competent man and much tribute had been paid to his methods of developing the Ikeda Mines in all the 1908 news accounts.

In February of 1909 the mine suffered its first casualty when Ikeda yu Rimo, one of the miners, was killed in an explosion. This was said to have been caused by his picking at some powder with his candlestick. Nevertheless it was upsetting to Marco that the accident had occurred. On May 20 there had been considerable blasting done - at least 23 shots fired. Believing that some had not gone off, Mr. Marco felt it his responsibility to investigate. He entered the mine at 7:30 p.m. Alarmed by his failure to return in a few minutes, a party of men went in after him at 8:15 and found him dead in a small ditch - apparently overcome by fumes.

*HUTTON INLET — extends southwesterly for about 3 miles and was named in 1878 by Dr. G.M. Dawson after a Scot, Dr. James Hutton, geologist and philosopher. Born in Edinburgh in 1726 he became a doctor of medicine, but by 1768 had become so fascinated by geology he abandoned medicine to devote his whole time to his new interest, and wrote several scientific works, *Theory of the Earth* being one of the most important. As so often happens, not until after Dr. Hutton's death in 1797 did the value of his contributions to the science of geology become fully appreciated.

When Chittenden visited Hutton Inlet in 1884 he was particularly interested in a stone dam built across the stream at the head of the inlet. His Haida guides told him it had been used as a salmon trap. They also told him of the portage used by their forbears from the head of this inlet to the west coast. Chittenden, shown the route, found it led through a pasture-like terrain past a beautiful lake and eventually emerged at the head of Gowgaia Bay.

The abundance of large mussels in Hutton Inlet, some of which measured 10 inches in length, surprised Chittenden.

*HUTTON POINT — the northwest point to Hutton Inlet, and

*HUTTON ISLAND — in the middle of the entrance to Hutton Inlet, were both named in 1962 by the Hydrographic Service in association with the inlet.

PORTAGE CREEK — runs into the head of Hutton Inlet. Named by Newton Chittenden in 1884 when his Haida guides showed him the portage route which led along it, then turned southward to emerge in the northeast bight in Gowgaia Bay. Chittenden's name for the creek apparently never in use.

*HOSKINS ISLETS — two in number lie about ¾ of a mile to the north of Hutton Point and were named in association with Hoskins Point in 1962 by the Hydrographic Service.

*HOSKINS POINT — at the entrance to Haswell Bay. Named in 1948 by the Hydrographic Service after John Hoskins, supercargo on the second voyage of the *Columbia,* which left Boston in 1790.

John Box Hoskins, born in Boston December 14, 1768, the son of William Hoskins, a senior member of a large firm of builders, owners and operators of ships, was only 18 when his father died. Joseph Barrell, an old family friend, took the young Hoskins into his home and counting office.

When the first voyage of the *Columbia* was not a financial success, Barrell suspected incompetency on the part of the two captains, John Kendrick and Robert Gray. He put Hoskins aboard the *Columbia* as ship's clerk, supercargo and his special representative for the second trip.

Robert Gray, captain of the *Columbia* for the second voyage, deeply resented this action. The fact that Barrell had given Gray specific orders to treat Hoskins "with much amicability" resulted in the usual reaction - he grew even more resentful. Hoskins, for his part, realized that Kendrick, the former captain of the *Columbia,* had been less than efficient - nevertheless he liked the older man, and was not convinced of Gray's superiority over Kendrick. He thought Gray overdid the courageous, self-reliant role to the point of foolhardiness at times, and his reports were full of criticisms of Gray.

After he returned from the voyage aboard the *Columbia,* Hoskins went into partnership with Barrell's son and they carried on a successful business at Cadman's wharf in Boston. He died in 1824 at the age of 56. The log kept during the memorable voyage to the North West Coast provides today's readers with some fine descriptions of the journey, especially of the *Columbia's* cruises around the waters of the Charlottes - or WASHINGTON'S ISLE as he called it.

*HASWELL BAY — southwest of Hoskins Point. Named in 1948 by the Hydrographic Service after Robert Haswell who, like Hoskins, left accounts of the historic trips of the *Columbia.* Haswell, born November 24, 1786, in Massachusetts, was 3 weeks older than Hoskins. Unlike Hoskins, though, Robert Haswell greatly admired Captain Gray and had no use at all for Kendrick. Haswell sailed on both voyages of the *Columbia,* 1787 to 1790 and 1790 to 1793.

His father, William Haswell, served as a lieutenant in the British Navy and the family, loyal to the Crown, were interned during the Revolutionary War, until 1778, when they were sent to Halifax. They later moved to England.

Young Haswell returned to Massachusetts and at 19 years of age joined the *Columbia* as third mate under Captain Kendrick. When First Mate Simon Woodruff left the ship at Cape Verdes, Haswell was promoted to second mate. By the time the ship had reached the Falklands and prepared to round the Horn, relations between Haswell and Kendrick had become so intolerable, Haswell asked for, and received, permission to transfer to the smaller vessel *Washington,* captained by Robert Gray.

When Gray took command of the *Columbia* the following year, Haswell returned to the larger ship and became first mate. He held this position when the *Columbia* left for her second voyage in 1790 and at this time supercargo John Hoskins came aboard.

During the winter 1791-92 the crew of the *Columbia* built the *Adventure*, a 45-ton sloop, at Clayoquot Sound, Vancouver Island. Robert Haswell was put in charge of her and his log contains the story of his trip trading along the coast - most particularly of the Charlottes. The *Adventure* was sold that fall to the Spanish and Haswell resumed his old position of first mate on the *Columbia*.

He subsequently served on numerous ships, the final one as master of the *Louisa*. This ship cleared from Boston, August 1801, for Haswell's third voyage to the North West Pacific coast. She was never heard from again. Haswell, 33 years old, left a wife whom he had married only 3 years before, and two infant daughters.

He also left his valuable notes and observations in logs written on the voyages of the *Columbia* and his log from the *Adventure*.

There are two streams running into the head of Haswell Bay, both of which drain fair-sized lakes.

LAKE TWO FIFTY-FIVE — also known as REG YOUNG LAKE. This is the more northerly of the two lakes which drain into Haswell Bay and contains a small islet. During the mineral explorations by Texas Gulf Sulphur in 1971 a supply base was established on the shore of the lake and Reg Young of Skidegate piloted the plane which flew in the first supplies. The crew doing the mineral explorations called all the unnamed lakes on Moresby Island by their elevation height, such as Lake Forty-seven, Lake Five Eighteen and so on. Several of the names continue in local usage.

*SIVART ROCK — which dries at 10 feet, and

*SIVART ISLAND — northeast of the rock; both lie at the entrance to Haswell Bay and were named in 1962 by the Hydrographic Service after Mr. A. Sivart, pioneer storekeeper at Jedway in the early mining days. Mr. Sivart opened his store in 1907, carrying a little of everything in his amazing stock. Mrs. Sivart came with him to take part in the venture. Their son-in-law, C.A. Bourne, ran the sawmill. The first baby to be born at Jedway was the Sivart's grandson when, in July 1908, a 12-pound son arrived at the Bourne home. In 1912 the boom was over. Mr. Sivart closed the little store which had served the community so well under his amiable guidance.

*PEREZ SHOAL — about 1 mile to the northeast of Sivart Island, has a least depth of 15 feet and is usually marked by kelp. Named in 1962 by the Hydrographic Service in association with Juan Perez Sound.

*DE LA BECHE ISLAND — the outermost of the large islands off the entrance to De la Beche Inlet and named in this association in 1962 by the Hydrographic Service.

*DE LA BECHE INLET — received its name from Dr. Dawson in 1878 when he named it after Sir Henry Thomas De la Beche, an English geologist, born in 1796 and died 1855. De la Beche conceived the idea of a geological map of the British Isles and this became the basis for the organizing of a geological survey of Britain, with Sir Henry as its director in 1835.

He knew William Logan in Wales, when Logan prepared a detailed map of a Glamorganshire coal field for a copper-smelting firm there, and used Logan's maps for the government survey later. When Logan returned to Canada, De la Beche was among those who recommended that he be appointed director of the newly-established Geological Survey of Canada in 1842.

There were several former Haida villages and camping sites in the region of De la Beche Inlet. One of the Gado villages lay on the south side and one of the Kaidjudal sites of the Raven Crest Sels tribe also stood in this general region.

*SAC BAY — leads off the south shore of De la Beche Inlet, about 1½ miles from the head. Two creeks run into the head of Sac Bay, both draining small lakes. The bay was named in 1962 by the Hydrographic Service for the shape of the feature.

*SKITTAGETAN LAGOON — on the northwestern side of the approach to De la Beche Inlet. The Hydrographic Service named the lagoon in 1962 in reference to the name of the linguistic group composed of those Indians speaking Haida.

*DARWIN POINT — on the west side of Darwin Sound, at the south entrance. The point, named in association with the sound, has a light about 6½ cables to the northwest of it.

*DARWIN SOUND — is 13 miles long and extends from the north end of Juan Perez Sound to Logan Inlet,[1] and was named in 1878 by Dr. G.M. Dawson after Charles Robert Darwin, the greatest naturalist of the 19th century. Born February 12, 1809, at Shrewsbury, his father was Dr. Robert Darwin, F.R.S., and his mother the daughter of Josiah Wedgwood, famous manufacturer of pottery and china. Charles Darwin's theory of evolution was explained in his famous book *Origin of Species*.

[1]Darwin Sound shown in more detail on the map with Chapter 10.

EAST SIDE OF MORESBY ISLAND: RAMSAY ISLAND
TO CRESCENT INLET, INCLUDES LYELL ISLAND,
SHUTTLE ISLAND AND LOCKEPORT AREA.

CHAPTER TEN

*RAMSAY ISLAND — in the northeast part of Juan Perez Sound, is a densely wooded island with two bold hills on its eastern side. It is the XE'NA of Dr. Newcombe's map. In 1878 Dr. G.M. Dawson named it after Sir Andrew Crombie Ramsay, a natural choice for Dawson's list of esteemed men whose names he would apply to Queen Charlotte Islands' features.

From an early age Andrew Ramsay was fascinated by every aspect of geology. Only 27 when he received an appointment to the Geological Survey of Britain in 1841, he rose to become Director General in 1871 and was knighted 10 years laters.

A Haida legend concerning a large white stone on Ramsay Island is contained in the Lyell Bay information in this book.

*CROMBIE POINT — is at the extremity of a peninsula extending from the southwest shore of Ramsay Island. Named by the Hydrographic Service in 1962 for Sir Andrew Crombie Ramsay. A rock which dries at 6 feet lies 600 feet off Crombie Point. Dr. C.F. Newcombe's map indicates that there was a Haida fort in the vicinity of Crombie Point.

*TATSUNG ROCK — off the southeast part of Ramsay Island is 42 feet high and bare with another rock - still unnamed - 21 feet high lying to the west of Tatsung. Tatsung is a modification of the Haida word for hat, and was applied by the Hydrographic Service in 1962.

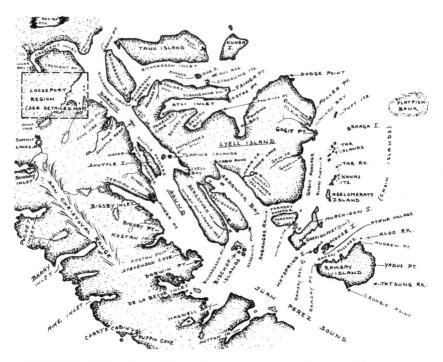

*YADUS POINT — lies mid-way along the east side of Ramsay Island. Named in 1962 by the Hydrographic Service for the Yadus tribe, a sub-division of the famed Stustas of the Eagle Crest. (Chief Edenso belonged to another branch of the Stustas.) The Yadus people lived in Alaska and were of the Kaigani Haidas. Their chief had a musical sounding name which meant *of-the-east-wind*.

*KLOO ROCK — which the charts show to be 5 cables offshore at the northeast of Ramsay Island and drying at 4 feet, is not, however, the Kloo Rock of the B.C. Pilot which describes the rock as 36 feet high and lying 1½ cables offshore. The name, a modification of the Haida word for canoe, was applied in 1962 by the Hydrographic Service.

*ANDREW POINT — the northeast point of Ramsay Island. Named in association with the island by the Hydrographic Service in 1962, after Sir Andrew C. Ramsay. This was the XE'NA KUN of Dr. Newcombe, who called Ramsay Island XE'NA. The ending "kun" means point.

*RAMSAY POINT — on the northwest corner of the island. Named in association with Ramsay Island by the Hydrographic Service in 1962. Midway between Ramsay and Andrew Points is a cove with rocks and islets straggling from it. A small stream enters the head of the cove and it is a favorite camping place and anchorage for small craft.

*RAMSAY ROCKS — lying 9 cables to the west of Ramsay Point, received their name from the Hydrographic Service in 1962. It applies to the entire group from the grass-covered 21-foot-high rock to others which are barely awash, some completely submerged.

*RAMSAY PASSAGE — also named by the Hydrographic Service in 1962, separates Ramsay Island from Hotspring and House Islands.

*HOTSPRING ISLAND — takes its name from a spring on the southwest side of the island where water issuing from the rocks has a temperature of 162⁰ Fahrenheit at one point. Noticing steam hovering about when he sailed into the region in 1791, Joseph Ingraham called this area SMOKE BAY.

Francis Poole made a side-trip to the island in 1862, when on a visit to Cumshewa Inlet from Burnaby Island, and named it VOLCANIC ISLAND. Accompanied by two of Chief Klue's men when he returned for a longer visit the following year, he found these Haidas extremely uneasy about landing on THE-ISLAND-OF-FIRE. Old tribal legends had given rise to some awesome superstitions. Klue, apparently, did not share the forebodings for he was high in his praise of the "miracle waters" and assured Poole that soaking in them would cure every ailment.

Dr. Dawson applied the name HOTSPRING ISLAND when he went ashore in 1878. "The location of the spring is easily found," he wrote, "for a patch of green mossy sward near it can be seen from a considerable distance."

The island became a popular holiday spot in early mining years, and Archie Ikeda of Ikeda Bay Mines sent men to build a comfortable log cabin on the island for visitors. Everyone was welcome to use it, and did. Men from nearby places flocked there to soak out bruises and lumps from prospecting and mining - and to laze for a few days. With pleasant beaches to visit around Hotspring, as well as neighbouring islands, and the abundance and variety of easily obtained sea-food, it was a veritable oasis.

It still is. In recent years people who bathe there frequently have erected a driftwood cabin over a roll-top bathtub. Water from the springs has been piped via two hoses which run constantly into the tub or into the stream beneath - depending on how the hoses are elevated.

One has hot water - the other is scalding. During fishing season there is almost always a line-up of people waiting for the bath. Despite this the place is immaculately clean, reminiscent of earlier years when it was an accepted fact that visitors left a place as they had found it.

The Jones family of Skidegate have built a cabin near the spring with rough but comfortable furnishings. They, too, leave the door unlocked as did Ikeda in years gone by. An interesting guest book on the table in the cabin contains the names and comments of visitors from many places, including one from Hawaii, another favorite holiday spot.

It was an earlier Jones who planned to make the island his home and livelihood. This was Jiggeroo (Fred B.) Jones - a great strapping man with a head of flaming red hair and beard to match. In 1909 Jiggeroo and his son Morton moved to the island to live and to work the mineral claim they had there in 1907. But a year's work produced nothing to warrant continuing the exploration and reluctantly the site was abandoned in 1910[1]

[1]Mr. Jones's story is in Q.C. Islands, Volume 1, pages 123 to 125.

*HOUSE ISLAND — east of Hotspring Island is the ATA'NA ISLAND of the Haidas. All the Sand-Town-People of the Raven Crest trace their ancestry back to Ata'na. The old village site in the cove on the west side is one of the prettiest locations on the Charlottes. A drying bank connects the curving beach with a small islet to the west - and everywhere is the mystic stamp of Haida. The name Ata'na meant a special type of house and it was from this that Dr. Dawson applied the name of HOUSE ISLAND to the legendary island in 1878.

ATA'NA VILLAGE — stood on the west side of House Island (see above). The remains of old hollows marking the lodge sites are easily seen and indicate that Ata'na was a village of some size.

*MURCHISON ISLAND — irregularly shaped, with a shoreline containing numerous intersting coves, straggles in an untidy line north of Hotspring and House Islands. There were several Haida village sites on this island. And prior to 1913, although the exact date is not known, there was a small abalone cannery on Murchison operated by some Japanese. Since they could not obtain licences they did not advertise what they were doing. The Fisheries Officers only learned of it afterwards when they came across the abandoned buildings.

The Haidas called this island DA'A according to Dr. C.F. Newcombe, but in 1878 Dr. Dawson honoured another geologist in the application of Sir Roderick Impey Murchison's name to the island. Murchison, born at Tarradale, Scotland, in 1792, began his career in the British Army at the age of 15, entering into the life with a vigor. Eight years later he changed his mind, became absorbed in the study of geology and published several works which contributed significantly to the science, and in 1855 became Director General of the Geological Survey of Britain.

The cove on the north shore of Murchison Island is a popular anchorage for small boats today and several mooring buoys have been placed there by the government to facilitate anchorage.

From this cove to Faraday Island, northward, a line of rocky ledges extend which contain a lush sea life. Abalones, rock scallops, sea-urchins, huge mussels, clams and seaweed of every variety, to mention only some of the easily obtained delights.

*FARADAY ISLAND — is almost connected to Murchison by the rocks and ledges which extend across the passage between the two islands. At the north end of this line of rocks on Faraday Island, and fronting a sandy cove, the remains of several old house pits and some of the timbers from an ancient Haida settlement may still be seen. What a gourmet's table these villagers must have enjoyed; not only in shoreline food, but also in the excellent fishing grounds all around which abound in many varieties of fish.

Faraday Island was named in 1878 by Dr. Dawson after the distinguished chemist and physicist, Michael Faraday. The son of the village blacksmith, Faraday was sent to learn bookbinding. His longing to leave bookbindery for the world of science was realized when he was 22, and an influential friend paved the way for him to enter the laboratory of the British Royal Institution. Faraday built the first dynamo which led to the power plants producing electricity. The electrical unit *farad* is named after him.

*FARADAY PASSAGE** — separating Faraday Island from Lyell Island was named in 1962 by the Hydrographic Service in association with the island.

*KOGANGAS ROCK** — which dries at 4 feet, is at the west entrance to Faraday Passage. Named in 1962 by the Hydrographic Service. The Kogangas were the Sea Otter tribe of the Raven Crest phratry. Their main village lay near Skidegate, but they formerly also had villages at Lawn Hill and Tlell. The great Qoona'tik was a Kogangas chief. A giant of a man known as One-who-touches-the-sky-with-his-head-as-he-moves. When he died his spirit dwelt under a reef off Lawn Hill.

*BISCHOF ISLANDS** — consisting of 1 large and 6 smaller islands, with numerous rocks and reefs, are a compact group southwest of Sedgwick Point. Named in 1878 by G.M. Dawson after Karl Gustav Bischoff, a well-known German chemist and geologist born in 1792 and died 1870. Islands formerly spelled with two "f's", but this was later changed by the Permanent Names Committee to the present one "f" ending.

*LYELL ISLAND** — lies at the north end of Juan Perez Sound and Dawson named it in the summer of 1878 after Sir Charles Lyell, a contemporary of Murchison's. Lyell, born in Scotland in 1797, met Murchison through the Geological Society and the two men travelled together through Europe in 1828. Later Lyell became a professor at King's College, London, and published several works, the best known of which were *Travels in North America* and *The Antiquity of Man*.
Lyell Island is a densely wooded, hilly island, rising abruptly from the shore and attaining heights of over 2,000 feet on its eastern part. It was an important logging headquarters for three logging camps in earlier years, Whalen Pulp and Paper, Kelley's, and Morgan's logging camps. And even earlier, much favored by the Haidas who had village and camping sites all round its shores.
Some of these will be included in the following place names which begin from the southwest tip and continue counter-clockwise around Lyell.

*RICHARDSON POINT** — the southwest extremity of Lyell Island, named prior to 1927 in association with Richardson Inlet, at the opposite end of Lyell Island.

*BERESFORD INLET** — which until 1949 was called BERESFORD ARM, is a slim inlet running in a northwesterly direction for about 3 miles between Richardson Point and Sedgewick Point at the south end of Lyell Island.
Named after Henry Lawry "Charlie" Beresford, pioneer prospector of Lockeport from 1908 to 1914. Mr. Beresford was appointed sub-Mining Recorder in 1908 and held the post until 1912 when the office was abolished. "He was

a tall man," recalls Charlie Hartie of Queen Charlotte City, "and even when on a drunk was always very much a gentleman. I often heard him called "The Admiral" as he was supposed to be some relation to the British Admiral Beresford. He went back to England when the 1914 war broke out."

In 1923 the Whalen Pulp and Paper Company had a camp on the east shore of Beresford Inlet. Joe Pollard, now of Vancouver, only 19 at that time and who worked in this camp, remembers a storm sweeping down the narrow waterway with such fury it tore the camp loose from its moorings, sending it sailing at a great pace down the arm. "Caused a real panic for a few hours," he says. The camp had just moved to the location from Marie Lake at Sedgwick Bay."

*SEDGWICK POINT — the west entrance point to Sedgwick Bay, named in 1962 by the Hydrographic Service in association with the bay.

*SEDGWICK BAY — the large inlet which extends for about 4 miles inland from the south shore of Lyell Island. Named by Dr. Dawson in 1878 after Reverend Adam Sedgwick, born in 1785 at Dent, Yorkshire. The son of a parson, he expected to follow his father's profession, but theology came out second-best in a growing fascination with geology. Appointed Professor of Geology at Cambridge University in 1818, he took a leading role in promoting the study of natural science in the university. In 1834 became Canon of Norwich and later offered a deanery.

A creek runs into the head of Sedgwick Bay and for years the remains of an old log cabin stood at its mouth - ownership still uncertain as is the date of occupation. Whalen Pulp and Paper had a camp on the east side of the bay in 1922; they took over an Imperial Munitions Board operation of World War I. During the 1930s the J.R. Morgan Logging Company made its headquarters for several years in a cove on the west side of Sedgwick Bay.

*A-frame logging, 1935.
Morgan's Logging Camp in
Sedgwick Bay,
Lyell Island.*

Photo - Mrs. Elmer Palmer.

GAESIGUSKET VILLAGE, the-strait-town-where-no-waves-comes-ashore
— is shown on Dr. C.F. Newcombe's map to be on the west side of Sedgwick
Bay, in a cove near the head. James White, F.R.G.S., another eminent
anthropologist, tells of a village of this name being on Murchison Island, opposite
Hotspring Island. Owned by the Raven Crest people whose ancestors, Striped-
Town-People, came from Bolkus Island it had for its chief, "He-of-
Ravens'-bones."

MARIE CREEK — which drains Marie Lake, and

MARIE LAKE — are on the east side of Sedgwick Bay. The lake is about
1/2 mile in from the salt water and is a round lake perhaps a 1/4 of a mile
across. It appeared on 1927 maps and is well-known locally. "The lake is
at the 400-foot level," said Joe Pollard. "I was 18 years old when I went to
work for Whalen Pulp and Paper there in 1922, and they had the camp on
the east side of the lake . . . on a sort of table-land. I understood that the
camp superintendent named the lake and creek after his wife. It had been
an Imperial Munitions Board operation during the First World War and many
of the logs still had the I.M.B. stamp on them. Beautiful timber.
"It was all skid-road logging. First into the lake then, via a chute into the
salt water down a 45⁰ slope. Quite a sight to see the big ones hit the water."

*FLATFISH BANK — off the east coast of Lyell Island at the edge of Hecate
Strait - some 4 to 6 miles east of Fuller Point. Formerly called HALIBUT
BANK, and as such appeared on charts dating back to 1868. Renamed
FLATFISH BANK in 1957 owing to duplications of its former name in other
coastal waters.

CHAIN ISLANDS — is an old name for the string of islands and islets which
lie off the east coast of Lyell Island. In 1878 Dr. Dawson used the term TAR
ISLANDS to indicate the major portion of the group, with the additional names
of TUFT ISLAND for the most northerly of the group and AGGLOMERATE
for the most southerly. Since that time several of the other islands have been
named, and the old name of Chain Islands has fallen into disuse.

*AGGLOMERATE ISLAND — as mentioned above, is the most southerly of
a chain of islands lying off the east coast of Lyell Island, and it is also the
largest. When Dr. Dawson named it in 1878 he wrote, "The island has apparently
been burnt over, and is covered with standing dead trees."

*KAWAS ISLETS — lie immediately north of Agglomerate Island and contain
5 main islets, surrounded by numerous rocks and reefs. Named in 1962 by
the Hydrographic Service after a subdivision of the Eagle Crest Stustas family,
who lived along the north part of the Charlottes - Chief Edenso being the
most famous of this tribe. A story is told of one of the chiefs of this family,
Chief Ildi'ni, being blown across to the Stikine country where he afterwards
became a chief among the Stikine people. Kawas is a modification of the Haida
word for sea-eggs.

*The Tar Islands, which lie off the east coast of Lyell Island.
This photo taken in 1901 by Dr. C.F. Newcombe.*

Photo - Provincial Museum, Victoria.

*TAR ROCK — lies between the Kawas Islets and the present Tar Islands.
B.C. Pilot describes the Tar Rock as being 10 feet high and bare.

*TAR ISLANDS — of current charts are the group of rocks, reefs and islets
which lie midway along the chain. This name originally applied to most of
the chain by Dr. G.M. Dawson in 1878 when the Indians with him told of
seeing, ". . . bituminous matter oozing out among the stones on the beach."
Several geologists have looked at the region since that time and have suggested a
variety of reasons for the presence of the tarlike matter, but so far all seem to
think it is not commercially significant.

In 1901 the Department of Mines sent Provincial Assayer Herbert Carmichael
to evaluate the tar reports on the islands off the east coast of Lyell. He reported
that not only did he find the substance on the outlying Tar Islands, but also
on the north and eastern shore of Ramsay, House and Agglomerate Islands.
Mr. Carmichael thought it would require extensive testing to give an accurate
estimate of the significance of the oozings.

*SKAGA ISLAND — lies off by itself to the northeast of the Tar Islands
and was named in 1957 by the Hydrographic Service for the word skaga, meaning
shaman or medicine man.

It was Skaga Island that Dr. Dawson named TUFT ISLAND in 1878, saying
"Outside of these islands (Tar Islands) lies a single low island with a few trees
which may be called Tuft Island." He had shown it this way on his map. Why

the island was renamed in 1957 is not known, because the name was not discarded, but reapplied by the Hydrographic Service to the group of islets northwest of this that same year.

*TUFT ISLETS — to which the name was applied by the Hydrographic Service in 1957 are a compact group of 3 islets connected to one another by drying reefs. The southernmost and highest islet has a few trees and some scrub on its summit; the remainder are bare.

GATE CREEK — is the local name for a stream south of Gogit Point on the east side of Lyell Island. In 1910 the Moresby Island Lumber Company, who ran a mill at Queen Charlotte City, secured a timber claim in this region and T.S. Gore surveyed it for them. About 1924 T.A. Kelley in logging this claim put a "gate" or log dam across the mouth of the creek to facilitate getting the logs out by sluicing them down the stream and, by opening the log gate, could take them into the salt water whenever he wished. With the gate closed he had a relatively protected booming ground.

When the Fisheries Department heard of the operation they were horrified, for this was an excellent salmon stream. They put pressure on him to remove the "gate" and to abandon using the stream for a log chute. But it was too late. By the time the operation came to a halt, the fish run had been completely wiped out. It never returned.

GADO VILLAGE — at the mouth of Gate Creek, belonged to an Eagle Crest tribe who were related to the Eagles at Tanu, Skedans and Cumshewa.

BLOODY FORT — was the graphic name for an islet off Gado village. This place of battle belonged to Chief Klue and his tribe and is shown on Dr. Newcombe's map.

*GOGIT PASSAGE — is the waterway separating Lyell Island from the chain of islands to the east, which includes the Tar Island, Kawas and Agglomerate. Named in 1957 by the Hydrographic Service for a legendary Haida creature. The "gogit" is a goblin possessing an evil spirit and is usually intent on doing harm. The Haidas also applied the term to a mentally unbalanced or demented person.

*GOGIT POINT — midway along the east shore of Lyell Island. Named in association with the passage by the Hydrographic Service in 1957.

HLKIA, Chicken-Hawk-Town — lay on the north side of the stream which enters Gogit Passage on the north side of Gogit Point. An Eagle Crest village, it was occupied by the people who later moved to Tanu and built a town on the east end of Tanu Island.

Chicken-Hawk-Town was notable for the size of the chief's lodge, an enormous house, the remains of which may still be seen. It belonged to Chief Klue. His house pole must have been a thing of beauty for it was covered from top to bottom with delicately iridescent abalone shells.

The village burial site now carefully preserved by the enfolding spruce and mosses, lay seaward of the village.

Alfred Moody of Skidegate, whose ancestors knew this coast intimately, remembers his people referring to an island off here as KUN KODDLE, and was told it meant a whale's blow-hole.

WINDY BAY — a local name still in current use, for the bay off the old Chicken-Hawk-Town site.

*FULLER POINT — about a mile to the west of Tuft Islets. Named in 1948 by the Hydrographic Service for Jonathan Fuller, a seaman on the first voyage of the *Columbia*, 1787 to 1790.

It was the KLIEW'S POINT of Joseph Ingraham in 1791. He must have known one of these hereditary chiefs by name during his trading along these shores, since it was the habit of traders to name a region for the head chief at that time. Kliew had many spellings in its modified English form, Kloo being the most common. It meant *southeast*.

Fuller Point was the LGAKUN of the Haida, after the name they gave to Lyell Island, LGA-KUNGWA-I, according to Dr. C.F. Newcombe.

*DODGE POINT — the northeastern point of Lyell Island. Named in 1948 by the Hydrographic Service after Josiah Dodge, a shipmate of Jonathan Fuller on the first voyage of the *Columbia*.

*ATLI INLET — named by Dr. G.M. Dawson in 1878 after a modification of the Haida name for the large inlet on the north end of Lyell. This was headquarters for Kelley's Logging operation for many years, and the names for the various parts of Atli Inlet reflect this. Takelley Cove, Powrivco Point and Bay, Beljay Point and Bay, were all associated with Thomas A. Kelley's operation.

*POWRIVCO BAY — extends 1 mile south along the shore following the east side of Atli Inlet. Several streams drain into Powrivco Bay and there is a beach at the head of the bay. Powrivco was the telegraph code name for Powell River Company, who purchased Kelley Logging Camp logs. It appeared first on the 1927 map.

*POWRIVCO POINT — separates Powrivco Bay from Beljay Bay and was named in 1957 by the Hydrographic Service in association with Powrivco Bay.

*BELJAY BAY — the arm of Atli Inlet to the west of Powrivco Bay, extends over 1 mile southwesterly, and has several streams entering near its head. The code name for B.L. Johnson and Walton Company Limited, general shipping agents for Kelley Logging. Beljay Bay appears on a 1927 map, but was not officially adopted until 1949.

*BELJAY POINT — at the western entrance to Beljay Bay and named in association with the bay. Confirmed in 1949.

210

Dr. C.F. Newcombe, light suit, stands with Mr. Lawler and Thomas A. Kelley (on right). Photo taken in Skidegate, June 1923.

Photo - Provincial Museum, Victoria.

*TAKELLEY COVE — the southwestern end of Atli Inlet. The code name for the T.A.Kelley Logging Camp. It is most fitting that Mr. Kelley's name should appear on a map of the Queen Charlottes, for he was one of its early pioneers, known to have been on the Islands at least as early as 1908. A tall good-looking man, Thomas A. Kelley graduated as a civil engineer in the United States. An excellent timber cruiser, but not a registered B.C. Land Surveyor, therefore he could not register any of the surveys he made. However, it was a simple matter to engage a properly qualified man to take over the technicalities, and Kelley obtained many of the early timber surveys using this method.

"He was an excellent business man," recalls Charlie Hartie of Queen Charlotte City, "and knew how to pick good men - men who could make things pay. He was a friendly man, and good to his employees. Kept many loggers on his payroll long after they could no longer work, under the pretense that he needed them for some of the jobs on his farm down in Washington."

It is as a logging operator that Tom Kelley is best remembered. When the demand for timber cruising slackened, he began logging on the Charlottes for the Whalen Brothers, who had started a pulp mill at Swanson Bay, about 120 miles south of Prince Rupert. In later years he became associated with the Powell River Company and his logging operation grew to be one of the largest on the Islands.

*USTAS POINT — on the west side of Atli Inlet near the entrance. Ustas point has a hook-shaped appendage and attached to this is an islet, 153 feet high, shaped like an artist's pallette. Named in 1957 by the Hydrographic

Service for a creature of Haida mythology. Ustas was the last remaining creature after the Flood had destroyed life on earth. This creature had the form of a raven, and legends say he is the source of all life on earth today and, consequently, is an ancestor of the Haida. He was given a prominent place in family totems. A variation of his name is NE-KIL-STLAS.

*TSINGA POINT— the northwest entrance point to Atli Inlet, it has a toothlike appearance when delineated on the chart. Because of this, it was named *tsinga,* a modification of the Haida word for tooth, by the Hydrographic Service in 1957.

TLGUNGHUNG VILLAGE, Face-of-the-ground — lay in the vicinity of Tsinga Point. An Eagle Crest site, it belonged to Chief Kloo's tribe.

*KUL ROCKS — northwest of Tsinga Point, consist of 2 large rocks - one 61 feet high and the other 31 feet, as well as a few drying rocks. They are about ½ a mile offshore. The largest rock has a few stunted trees and scrub on its summit. Named in 1957 by the Hydrographic Service after the Haida word for mussel.

*STANSUNG ISLETS — to the southwest of Kul Rocks, were named by the Hydrographic Service at the same time as the Kuls. Stansung is a modification of the Haida word for four. There are 4 islets in the group.

*DOG ISLAND — northwest of the Stansungs, is a wooded island about 45 feet high and named in 1878 by Dr. G.M. Dawson.

KUNGGA VILLAGE, Help-received-unexpectedly-town — an Eagle Crest site on Dog Island belonging to Chief Kloo's tribe. The head man in Kungga had a name which meant The Protector.

*SKUDAS POINT — on the north shore of Lyell Island and about 3¼ miles west of Dog Island. Named in 1957 by the Hydrographic Service after the Haida village formerly in the cove to the east of this point.

SKUDAS VILLAGE, The-too-late-town — located near the mouth of the stream which enters' the unnamed cove to the east of what is now Skudas Point. An Eagle Crest site belonging to Chief Kloo's tribe, the chief of Skudas was a brother of Kloo's. The village site was occupied at the same time as Chicken-Hawk-Town, on the east side of Lyell Island. When Dr. Dawson visited this cove in 1878 he found the ruins of one of the houses of Skudas village.

*RICHARDSON INLET — flows along the north side of Lyell Island and separates it from Tanu Island. Named in 1878 by Dr. Dawson for another geologist, James Richardson, who differs from other eminent men whose names were selected by Dawson for Queen Charlotte Islands features in that Richardson actually visited the Charlottes.

In 1872, using the sloop *Triumph,* James Richardson spent several days in

Skidegate Inlet assessing the Cowgitz Coal Mine prospects. Cowgitz had run into grave financial difficulties and the Geological Survey was requested to make an investigation by men interested in the mine.

Born in Scotland in March 1810, Mr. Richardson came to Canada as a youth to farm at Beauharnois - which soon took a second place to his growing interest in geology. Through this he met Sir William Logan (Logan Inlet) who persuaded him to join the Geological Survey. Logan was impressed with Richardson's practical approach, and in his writings, Logan makes several references to Richardson's service. A number of fossils were named after him.

*RICHARDSON ISLAND— at the west end of Richardson Inlet. Formerly called LITTLE LYELL ISLAND, a name from the mining maps of 1908 to 1912. Later renamed in association with Richardson Inlet, and appeared on the 1927 maps under its newer name.

*KWUN POINT— the northwest tip of Richardson Island. Named in 1957 by the Hydrographic Service after a modification of the Haida word for nose.

*RICHARDSON PASSAGE—separates Richardson Island from Lyell Island and was named in association with the Island and Inlet in 1962 by the Hydrographic Service.

RICHARDSON NARROWS — is the local name given to the west end of Richardson Passage, where the navigable width is reduced to about 500 feet because of an 18-foot rock and small islet on the south side. There is a fair current through this narrow portion, but mariners use this passage frequently, keeping north of the centre.

*LYELL POINT — on the northwest tip of Lyell Island. Named in association with the island by the Hydrographic Service in 1957.

*DARWIN SOUND — flows along the western side of Lyell Island. Named in 1878 by Dr. G.M. Dawson after the renowned naturalist, Charles Darwin.

*SHUTTLE REEF— lies mid-channel in Darwin Sound, to the southwest of Lyell Point. It is mentioned in Dawson's Report of 1878, but he did not name it although he named the island at that time. In 1922 the Hydrographic Service decided it should have a formal designation and named the reef in association with Shuttle Island.

*SHUTTLE ISLAND — lies midway along Darwin Sound. Dr. Dawson in delineating the island on his map was reminded of a shuttle being passed along Darwin Sound and named the 2½ mile long island in this context in 1878. There have been several mining claims staked on Shuttle Island, and quite a few attempts to recover gold from them. It is also thought to be the possible location of some "Lost Mines."

In earlier years when the story of Mulkley's Lost Mine circulated it was speculated that Shuttle Island might be the site of his "find". Cyrenus Mulkley and two partners, Andy Burge and Abraham Way, aboard Mulkley's brig *Eagle* were among those who flocked to Mitchell Inlet's GOLD HARBOUR during the 1852-53 excitement. Finding themselves out of luck Mulkley is said to have stayed to prospect along the eastern shore of Moresby.

Making camp on a beach one night, he picked up several pieces of rock which led him to investigate more thoroughly and he found what appeared to be the location of a good ledge. Taking several samples he hurriedly broke camp, sailed to Skidegate, thence to Victoria where he had his ore assayed. "$16,000 to the ton," came the report. As soon as he possibly could, Mulkley outfitted and returned to Skidegate with a party and proceeded to his bonanza. Sure that he had marked the site so clearly he would have no difficulty in locating it, he discovered that the maze of inlets and arms of Moresby Island were utterly confusing. The men searched for weeks and were unsuccessful in locating anything in the way of a marker. Mulkley could not identify any landmark or familiar beach anywhere.

The following year his nephew came up with another party and resumed the search - with no luck. A second trip the next year proved just as fruitless. Their only directions as to distance were that the gold lay "about a day's sail from Skidegate," which, as one old timer pointed out, could be anywhere from 30 to 60 miles depending on wind and tides.

During the First World War a logging camp began taking aeroplane spruce from the northeast part of Shuttle Island. There had been a slide at one part of the bay near the camp. The cook poked around one evening near the slide and found samples of rock. "He showed it to Slim Edwards, handy-man at the camp" says Charlie Hartie of Queen Charlotte City. "Slim had been an old mining man, but had had to give it up because of a back injury. One look at the cook's samples and Slim nearly fell over he was so excited. "Them's pure nuggets," he gasped. "He evidently convinced the cook," says Mr. Hartie, "and together they staked out a claim."

During the war aeroplane spruce took top priority and nothing else was permitted in that area during the logging. As soon as the war ended, the two men were hard at work and recovered at least $4,000. "Slim loved to be the big shot," remembers Mr. Hartie. "It was his joy when travelling on the *John* to haul out his poke and show his nuggets to the rest of the passengers . . . along with a good story about his mine. Some of the nuggets were thumb-nail size, but apparently the gold turned out to be only surface ore."

Several attempts to mine the region later included one plan which used a scraper. "You can still see the odd colour on Shuttle," says Mr. Hartie, "but no commercial possibilities."

*SHUTTLE PASSAGE— on the east side of Shuttle Island, separates it from Lyell Island. Named in association with the island in 1957 by the Hydrographic Service.

*TOPPING ISLANDS — the two islands on the east side of Shuttle Passage and north of the entrance to Lyell Bay. Named in 1962 by the Hydrographic Service after Colonel E.S. Topping, a well-known name of early day mining promotion at Rossland and Trail in southern British Columbia.

214

Colonel Topping was also an early speculator in mining on the Charlottes. His name would have been more properly applied to an island in Cumshewa Inlet — since that was the region of his specific interest.

Accompanied by James Johnstone, Colonel Topping made his first trip to the Islands in October 1906. Engaging Job Moody of Skidegate to skipper his boat and guide him, Topping was looking for another "Lost Mine." This had been reportedly found by a man named Lynch in Cumshewa. Like Mulkley of Shuttle Island, Lynch could never find the site of his discovery again.

Topping and Johnstone believed they found the Lynch "mine" in a bay east of McLellan Island at Cumshewa Inlet. They staked and subsequently promoted their find which lay about ½ mile inland.[1]

[1]See McLellan Island.

HOTKJIHOAS VILLAGE, Hair-seals-at-low-tide — lay to the east of the Topping Islands, in a cove on Lyell Island. It received its name from the abundance of hair seals along the shoreline at low tide. The villagers could easily creep down and club them - almost at will. It was a Raven Crest village, with ancestors from the Bolkus Island village, the Striped-Town-People.

*LYELL BAY— is southeast of the Topping Islands and about midway along the west shore of Lyell Island. Formerly called FALSE BAY, the name given in 1878 by Dr. G.M. Dawson. Renamed in 1952 because of the numerous duplications of that name, the name of Lyell adopted in association with the island.

In ancient years when the village near this bay was populated, a whale drifted ashore in Lyell Bay. It struck terror into the heart of the village shaman, for it was an ill omen - and he had foretold of it.

Almost immediately strange and unexplained things began to occur. Canoes would be seen by some - yet people standing beside them at that same time could not see them. An enormous bear out of all proportion, appeared on the beach at Hotspring Island, and a man sighted walking in an impossibly steep place on Ramsay Island - head down. Then one day a large white stone appeared on Ramsay Island. No one knew how it could have come there, but it was known to have been on the mainland shortly before. Immediately after this the people in the Lyell Bay region began to die, even people from Lyell Bay who had moved to other areas died. Finally only one boy and one girl were left and the boy became chief of the new town which sprang up.

Whales being washed ashore always were an ill-omen — usually meaning a death.

The *Lobstalk* mining property is at the north end of Lyell Bay, a group of 10 registered claims in connection with iron deposits. Two short packsack holes were drilled on the property in 1956 by Falconbridge.

*STEVENSON COVE— is near the south entrance of Darwin Sound, and is on Moresby Island above Darwin Point. Named in 1962 by the Hydrographic Service after one of two partners, Stevenson and Sullivan, prospectors who owned and operated an open-cut mine near Lockeport in 1907 and 1908. Their claim *Tiger* lay west of the *Swede* group off Anna Inlet.

*KOSTAN POINT— northwest of Stevenson Cove, is near the south entrance of Kostan Inlet and named by the Hydrographic Service at the same time. A small cove lies to the west of Kostan Point with an unnamed stream coming into its head.

*KOSTAN INLET — west of Kostan Point, opens off the west side of Darwin Sound, and was named in 1962 by the Hydrographic Service after the Haida word for crab. The inlet extends about 1¼ miles in a southwesterly direction and has a tricky entrance. About half-way along the inlet narrows to a width of about 100 feet, and with a least depth of 4 feet, a miniature reversing falls is caused at this section by the tidal currents at certain stages, where the current attains speeds of from 2 to 4 knots.

*BIGSBY POINT— is the north entrance point to Kostan Inlet. Named in 1962 by the Hydrographic Service in association with the inlet to the north of the point - Bigsby Inlet. North of Bigsby Point and almost at the entrance to the inlet, is an unnamed cove. The stream flowing into this cove drains 4 lakes, the lowest of the lakes is very close to the beach.

*BIGSBY INLET — named on July 2, 1878 by Dr. Dawon who spent more time in there than he had planned. In exploring its shoreline the party left it too late to get back to their ship. "We were overtaken by evening in this inlet and could scarcely find a strip of beach wide enough to spread our blankets on for the night," he wrote. "It is a gloomy chasm, barely half a mile wide and surrounded by mountains higher than any yet seen...and in places almost perpendicular. But they are generally well wooded . . . the trees clinging to crevices of the rocks. Farther back, especially to the south and west, massive summits of bare granite rise to great heights, their upper gorges and shady hollows still filled with snow."

Dr. John Jeremiah Bigsby, for whom Dawson named the inlet, was born at Nottingham in 1792. The son of a doctor, Bigsby adopted medicine as his life's work. Sent to Canada in 1818 his interest in geology developed and when he returned to Britain contributed more than 27 works on the subject of geology and associated fields. One of his most popular writings, however, was *The Shoe and the Canoe,* a narrative of travel in Canada, published in 1850.

A network of lakes drain into the 2½ mile long inlet, some via a stream at the head and others from creeks along the south shore of the inlet.

KINGGI MOUNTAIN, Always-looking-into-the-sea — the Haida name for a mountain on the north side of Bigsby Inlet. The mountain hangs precipitously over the water and Haida lore held a legend concerning the Flood aftermath which was connected with Kinggi. After the deluge had abated, Raven was adopted by Kinggi and, in order to receive his new father properly, he summoned four different tribes of men out of the ground - Tsimshian, Haida, Kwakiutl and Tlingit - and this was how the various races of men came into being.

*JEREMIAH POINT — the north entrance point to Bigsby Inlet. Named in 1962 by the Hydrographic Service in association with the inlet, after Dr.

John Jeremiah Bigsby.

*FINGER POINT — northeast of Jeremiah Point, from which it is separated by a small cove. The cove is almost blocked by rock ledges which extend from each side near its head. Finger point was named by the Hydrographic Service in 1962 for the shape of the feature.

*HOYA PASSAGE — separates Shuttle Island and Moresby Island and extends along the west side of Shuttle Island. Named by the Hydrographic Service in 1957. It is a modification of the Haida word for raven, which represents one of the principal divisions of the Haida phratry.

SHUTTLE ISLAND "WATERING" SITE — not on Shuttle Island, but in an unnamed cove on Moresby Island. The Fisheries Protection Branch have put in a hose from a good stream at the head of a cove near the north end of Hoya Passage to enable boats to obtain fresh water. (In 1971 boomsticks near the entrance of the unnamed cove served as identification).

*AMUR POINT — is the east entrance point of Echo Harbour, and lies on the west side of Darwin Sound - almost opposite the entrance to Richardson Passage. The name appeared on 1927 maps and honours one of the best-known vessels to ply Island waters in the early years of mining and prospecting. Named after the C.P.R.'s *Amur,* whose captain, Louis P. Locke, took an active and keen interest in all aspects of development possibilities - particularly along Moresby Island's east coast. He speculated along with others, did a bit of staking, sold a few claims, performed weddings and gave practical help to a family having a slim time financially. He lost his life a few years later on another ship, the *Sophia,* which sank in northern waters, October 25, 1918, *en route* from Skagway with a full load of passengers going south for Christmas.

*ECHO HARBOUR — on the west side of Darwin Sound, almost opposite the entrance to Richardson Passage. Named July 4, 1878 by Dr. G.M. Dawson who said, "We entered what seemed to be a shallow basin, in search of a place to anchor, and were surprised to find passage into a snug harbour, where we spent the night." It has been a favorite anchorage for countless small boats ever since. A beautiful little harbour.

*ECHO POINT — on the north side of the "shallow basin" mentioned above. Named by the Hydrographic Service in 1957 in association with the snug harbour which had entranced Dr. Dawson in 1878.

*GIL ISLET — lying between Echo Point and Klunkwoi Bay. Shown as ROUND ISLAND on mining maps of 1908 to 1912. By 1927 it had been renamed, probably owing to numerous duplications of its former name. Fossils are found in the region of Gil Island, which is connected to Moresby Island by a drying bank. Although the spelling has been changed, it is after James Gill, a broker whose name appears on an application for a large timber licence covering the region from Logan Inlet to Burnaby Island in October of 1907.

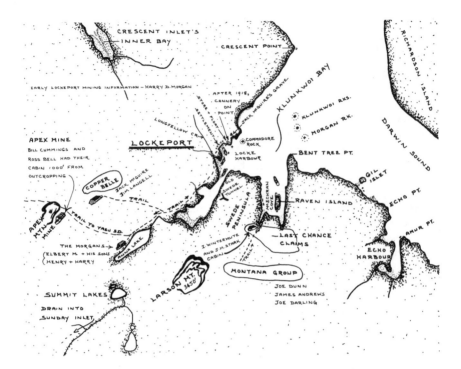

In 1910 the Queen Charlotte Pioneer Development Company owned claims near there, the *Bird* and *Bismark,* and had 5 or 6 men constantly employed. Trails, cabins and a 65-foot tunnel had been put in, "good copper ore all the way," read the Mining Report on that property in 1911. This same company also owned claims at Werner Bay.

*KLUNKWOI BAY — is Dr. Dawson's adaptation of the Haida name for the bay which lay at the head of Darwin Sound on the west side. "The desolate grandeur of the scenery here is almost oppressive," he wrote in 1878. "Several arms extend among the bases of rugged snow-clad mountains which rise very steeply from the shores. The axial mountains of Moresby appear to culminate here, forming a high and partly snow-covered sierra."

Thirty years after Dawson's visit the mountains around Klunkwoi resounded with the ring of axes biting deeply into virgin timber as cabins were built, hammerings, blastings and drillings, as claims were staked and even a few tunnels driven. Like Jedway, it was the lure of a possible copper strike which drew the hopefuls, and the peak of activity there paralleled that of Jedway's, 1907 to 1913.

*LOCKEPORT — on the west shore of Klunkwoi Bay a small settlement began to grow in Topsy-fashion, as the "boys" built cabins for their headquarters, to use when they came down from the hills. In 1908 W.H. Thompson and J.M. Stark opened a store at the north end of the row of homes which fringed the bay. With so many people in the area wanting to register claims, H.L. "Charlie"

Beresford (also known as The Admiral) was by popular consent appointed Deputy Mining Recorder, and a letter sent to the officials to advise them of the fact. It was Beresford who drew one of the first maps indicating where the claims were - an invaluable aid.

The C.P.R.'s *Amur* began making regular calls to Klunkwoi by 1908 and Captain Locke urged the miners to choose a name for the embryo townsite. The miners agreed. Although they could come up with some wonderful names for their claims, naming their "town" was something else. When the wealthy Johan Wulffsohn of Vancouver bonded the first claims - the *Swede* group - in 1908, some wag suggested WULFFSOHN CITY.

Elbert M. Morgan and his two sons, Henry and Harry, had come to Jedway from Nelson in September 1907. After prospecting briefly around Jedway they gradually moved north along the coast to Klunkwoi Bay, and in the hills to the west of the bay found some promising copper signs. They decided to stay. The boys' married sister, Noralee, and her husband, Ernie Marshall, joined them late in 1908. The store opened earlier that year by Thompson and Stark ran for only 6 months then closed as the two men went back to their first love, prospecting. The Morgans and the Marshalls bought the store, the plan being for the Marshalls to run it and the three Morgans to handle the mining end of things.

By this time Captain Locke, tired of waiting for the miners to find an appropriate name, took a more direct approach. Extolling the wonders of his hometown, Lockeport, on the other side of the continent, he suggested a duplication of the name on the Pacific coast - at this place. "The idea was an instant success," said Harry Morgan. "Adopted and carried. So we named our store in this connection, THE LOCKEPORT TRADING COMPANY."

The waters fronting the settlement were frequently called LOCKE HARBOUR and in the C.P.R. advertisements in 1909 Locke Harbour was listed as a regular port of call.

The Morgan family remained at Lockeport until 1912 and their names were associated with most of the major claims in the region, beginning with their own initial discovery at Anna Lake, and also with *Apex, Montana* and *McGuire* Group (*Copper Belle*). When they left Mr. Beresford bought their store and afterwards sold it to another Morgan, the well-known William Morgan - no relation.

"Jim Langell and Jack McGuire had the *Copper Belle*," remembers Harry Morgan. "Jim sold out his interest to do what he always talked about, buy a homestead in the wilderness on Graham Island.[1] Jack McGuire stayed to work the property, but suffered a fatal heart attack. We buried him at Lockeport by his own wish." wish."

The industrious Elbert M. Morgan took over McGuire's property and sent young Harry to be cook for the gang. "Don't know if that was the reason or not," says Harry today, "but the blacksmith quit soon after. Anyhow my Dad took me out of the cookshack and let me do the blacksmithing and promoted me to foreman . . . which suited me better.

"The *Apex* claim belonged to Ross Bell and Bill Cummings when we took

[1]Mr. Langell's story is contained in Q.C. Island, Volume 1.

Harry Morgan who, in 1907, came with his father and brother to prospect and mine in the hills around Lockeport. Photo taken in 1908 shows him in doorway of cookhouse of the Copper Belle.

Photo - Harry D. Morgan.

Lockeport in the 1920s after it became a cannery town. This photo taken by Alec Reid, engineer at the cannery from 1925 to 1927, shows the C.N. Steamer Prince John *at the cannery dock.*

Photo - Mrs. Betty Robertson.

it over in 1911. Dad was doing the development work for a Winnipeg company. We had closed the *McGuire* by this time and I was sent to do the blacksmithing for Henry, who was put in charge of the *Apex*."

Elbert Morgan, in spite of his ever-increasing mining operations, still found time to build a two-story house in Lockeport to which he brought a bride in a few years. "We had been batching there," remembers Harry, "so Dad got Ike Thompson's wife from Jedway to come and help us fix up the house for Dad's bride."

In addition to Elbert, Mrs. Morgan, Harry, Henry and the two Marshalls, there were two more Morgans during these years at Lockeport. When Harry ran the *Copper Belle* mine he had two Morgans working for him - both called Edward but no relation.

The William Morgan to whom the Lockeport Store was eventually sold has so many tales told of him that it is difficult to separate truth from imagination. His storekeeping was as casual as he - price of items pure guess or whim. But since it usually balanced in the long run he had few complaints.

Lockeport's mining days were drawing to an end in 1918 when a new industry became the focal interest. Captain E.H. Simpson who, for the previous two seasons had operated a fish-buying camp at Sedgwick Bay, put up a cannery at Lockeport. He had connections with an American firm, and they acquired the use of the ice-making and freezing plant at Pacofi, north of Lockeport, to run in conjunction with the cannery. They put up a huge pack of salmon. With the end of the war, however, the American firm backing the operation was caught by an embargo placed on all sales to the States and the operation went "belly-up." In the years 1925 to 1928 the Canadian Fishing Company took over Lockeport, but abandoned it to concentrate activities at their Lagoon Inlet plant. The post office remained open in Lockeport until July 27, 1938. Then the little pioneer settlement became one of the Charlottes' ghost towns.

In 1971 only the modern trailer and workshop of the Ana Lake Mining Company sits on the shoreline at Lockeport. The little cabins are gone and so is the cannery. But this cove, like many a Haida site, retains an atmosphere of the past, and one can sense the excitement of former years when young men with dreams and strong hearts were drawn to a life in the hills.

*LONGFELLOW CREEK — enters Klunkwoi Bay a little to the south of the former Lockeport settlement. When water rights were needed for the cannery, as it was planned to divert the stream for this purpose, the name of Longfellow was chosen because the creek flowed through the old *Longfellow* mineral claim which had been Crown Granted to Henry Lowry Beresford in 1913.

*BENT TREE POINT— a name applied during early prospecting days to the east entrance point of McEchran Cove on the south side of Klunkwoi Bay. In 1957 the Hydrographic Service attempted to have this point renamed WINTERMUTE POINT to give recognition to a man who very greatly merited it for the part he had played in the area's early history. However, the old name of Bent Tree Point had been in existence for too long. The Geographic Board ruled that it should be retained.

Captain Irving Wintermute, with Hugh McEchran and James Jones, discovered the *Last Chance* claims in 1907 near the head of McEchran Cove. "When McEchran and Wintermute first came to Lockeport," recalled Harry Morgan, "they were both so crippled they could hardly get out of bed. But within a few months, what a change! They could run and jump all over the place . . . hard to believe the difference."

Wintermute built a cabin at the head of McEchran Cove. After Stark sold the Lockeport store to the Morgans, he went to live with Wintermute and work on the *Last Chance*. Captain Wintermute operated his launch *Maple Leaf* transporting prospectors and supplies. He was there, too, for emergencies - be it a boat in distress or an accident to a miner and never failed to respond without hesitation.

*McECHRAN COVE — extends to the south off Klunkwoi Bay. Two streams run into its head, both of which drain small lakes. Named in 1957 by the Hydrographic Service after Hugh McEchran, partner with Wintermute and James Jones in the *Last Chance* group of claims which lay at the head of the bay there. McEchran seems to have left the development of this claim chiefly to his partners, for he was extremely active in the Huston Inlet region. It was McEchran who, with Frank Watson, was grub-staked by J.S. McMillan in the locating of 3 claims on the slopes of Thunder Mountain, off Huston Inlet. Watson left to operate another of the McMillan properties, leaving McEchran to supervise development work. His name was still associated with the Thunder Mountain claims in 1914. However, Lockeport was home for Hugh McEchran whenever he could spare time to come up and see the "boys".

*RAVEN ISLAND — is the larger and more southerly of the 2 islands in McEchran Cove. This is an old name, dating back to early prospecting days. Joe Dunn, Jim Andrews and Joe Darling would come by boat from Lockeport to take the trail which led past Wintermute's cabin and inland to their *Montana* claim. Whenever they passed this island, it seemed to have an overabundance of ravens in the trees.

SWEDE PENINSULA — not a gazetted name, but used in geological reports, including the recently published *Geology of the Q.C. Islands* written by A. Sutherland Brown. Frequently seen in news items of early years, it takes its name from the *Swede* group of mineral claims which were located on the peninsula separating McEchran Cove from Anna Inlet. This was the first important mineral find in the Lockeport area and Nels Larson, Nels Pearson and Alex Rogers located it early in 1907. Johan Wulffsohn sent his engineer E.R. Brobeck up to examine the find and, early in 1908, bonded the property. Under that bond 150 feet of tunnel was driven. Over the next few years more work was done - more adits, cross-cuts. Eventually like all other mining ventures of that day it was abandoned for the most part. Pearson, Larson and Rogers stayed for many years hoping the boom would start again, and enjoyed life in the little hamlet. Finally Pearson went to work as bullcook for Kelley's Logging Camp, later going to live out his days on Kelley's farm in Washington.

Alex Rogers's sister came to see him in June 1923 and persuaded him to go back east with her. Larsen became ill and was sent to a mainland hospital where he died. "Which left only Benny Benson, who had also joined the Swede Group," says Charlie Hartie who called at Lockeport regularly when on Fishery Patrol duties at that time. "Even when everyone else left, no one could persuade Benny to go. He stayed on until it was time to set his stakes in a Higher Claim."

LARSON MOUNTAIN — a 3,450-foot peak overlooking Swede Peninsula from the south. Owing to a typographical error this appears on some early maps as "Layson Mountain". It is considered definitely to have been named in early prospecting days after Nels Larson of the *Swede Group*. Mr. Larson had his own ideas about the best way to expose ore - and these were usually right, born of long experience. He had no patience with "dudes."

"I remember when Burns, Walkem and Gerle bought the *Tiger* claims which lay to the west of the *Swede*," says Mr. Morgan, now of Bellingham, Washington. "It was considered to be part of the same vein as the *Swede*. Gerle was sent up to take charge of both operations for some reason. It was a constant battle all the time between Gerle and Nels Larson. In fact the last time I ever saw Gerle, he and Larson were having a battle royal with their fists and poor Gerle was getting the worst of it."

*ANNA INLET— named in association with Anna Lake. First appeared on maps of the 1920s. The stream draining Anna Lake runs into the head of this inlet which is entered through a narrow neck at the southwest part of Klunkwoi Bay. Passing through this neck in the summer one can see the most unbelievable array of beautiful rock plants clinging to the rock face on the east side. Farther along as one enters the inlet the entrances to 3 shafts are clearly seen from the water and a rough tractor road leads to them. By 1971 all activity in this area came to a standstill.

The trail from Lockeport in the first mining activity 1907 to 1913 ran along the west side of Anna Inlet, a branch line leading off at the head of the inlet to go to the *Copper Belle* workings. The main trail continued to Anna Lake, thence to Apex Mountain, and over the hill to emerge at Botany Bay, Tasu side. At one time the branch line to the *Copper Belle* continued in a northerly direction to the head of Crescent Inlet, and from there it, too, went to the Tasu side.

*ANNA LAKE — at the 520-foot level, is drained by a stream running into Anna Inlet. Originally called LAKE ANNE by Elbert Morgan in 1907, it has became Anna Lake over the years. "I think," says Harry Morgan, "that Dad named it after an old girl friend. When we asked the boys down on the beach what the name of it was . . . none of them even knew about the lake. We located quite a few claims around it. The copper prospects looked pretty good."

SUMMIT LAKES — not gazetted, but they appear on 1908 to 1912 mining maps and have been placed on record in the Geographic Branch. The name is applied to 2 lakes south of the west end of Anna Lake. They drain into Sunday Inlet on the west coast of Moresby.

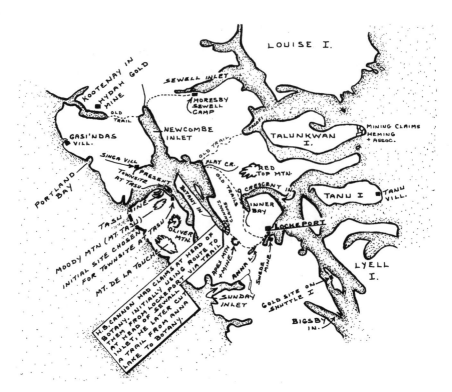

Map labels (as drawn): LOUISE I., KOOTENAY IN, MYDAM GOLD MINE, SEWELL INLET, MORESBY SEWELL CAMP, OLD TRAIL, NEWCOMBE INLET, GASI'NDAS VILL., SINGA VILL., TALUNKWAN I., MINING CLAIMS HEMING + ASSOC., PORTLAND BAY, PRESENT TOWNSITE AT TASU, OLD TRAIL, FLAT CR., RED TOP MTN., CRESCENT IN., INNER BAY, TANU I, TANU VILL., TASU MINE, BURNABY IN, OLD TRAILS, LOCKEPORT, MOODY MTN (MT. TASU), INITIAL SITE CHOSEN AT TASU FOR TOWNSITE AT TASU, OLIVER MTN., MT. DE LA TOUCHE, APEX MTN + MINE, ANNA L., SWEDE MINE, LYELL I., SUNDAY INLET, GOLD SITE ON SHUTTLE I, BIGSBY IN.

(H.B.CANNON HAD CLAIMS AT HEAD OF BOTANY. INITIALLY USING ROUTE TO THEM FROM LOCKEPORT VIA TRAIL AT HEAD OF SEWALL INLET. HE LATER CUT A TRAIL FROM ANNA LAKE TO BOTANY).

APEX MOUNTAIN — rises to nearly 3,000 feet and lies between the head of Botany Inlet and Anna Inlet. It received the name from the mining claim located there in 1908 by Joe Davis, Ross Bell and Bill Harris. Later on the names of Alex Patterson and Bill Cummings were connected with this mine.

Bell and Cummings were working the property in 1911 when Elbert Morgan took it over to develop the mine for a Winnipeg company. He put one son, Henry, in charge of the work, with a second son, Harry, to do all the vital "blacksmithing." "The camp buildings were about 1,000 feet from the outcropping," recalls Harry Morgan, "and it was at the *Apex* we had our worst accident. Joe Dunn from the *Montana* and Rand McDonald, hired to do the blasting, were in the tunnel when McDonald drilled into a shot which had missed fire the night before. The explosion was awesome. Miraculously the men survived. Dunn had a badly fractured leg and was in great pain, but poor McDonald was literally peppered with thousands of fragments of rock.

"Word was rushed down the mountain to the settlement to get a doctor quick. The nearest one was at Prince Rupert. It was then supper time but Beresford set off immediately for Ikeda Bay . . . a 45 mile trip . . . to wire for help. There was a revenue cutter tied at Rupert and she said she would bring the doctor over *if* the miners would guarantee to replace every bit of coal used for the trip . . . both ways."

It was a shock to Beresford to be asked to bargain in such an emergency after being used to the unhesitating help given by everyone in pioneering situations. But he gave his word that compensation would indeed be paid, ". . . now for God's sake, hurry!" he added.

The men at the mine began the tortuous operation of moving the injured miners to the cabin. "It was only 1,000 feet away, but it took us three hours to move them," remembers Harry Morgan. "How we would ever get them down the mountain we could not imagine." At 5 a.m. the descent began. For 13 laborious hours, with the tenderest care humanly possible, the gravely injured men were inched down. At 6 p.m. the travail came to an end and their charges were still alive - thanks to the infinite patience and total absorption of the entire community.

The cutter with the doctor waited at the dock - the journey from Prince Rupert had been made in a record 10 hours.

"Joe Dunn's fractured leg healed well," said Mr. Morgan, "but poor Rand was in hospital for over a year."

It might be supposed that they would have had enough of Lockeport and mining, but they were back as soon as the doctor gave permission.

*COMMODORE ROCK — in Klunkwoi Bay, is north and east of the old settlement site and lies about 600 feet offshore. There is a depth of less than 6 feet over it. Named in 1922 by the Hydrographic Service.

*KLUNKWOI ROCKS— are at the entrance to Klunkwoi Bay and consist of 2 drying rocks. There is a beacon on the northern one (1971). Named in in association with the bay by the Hydrographic Service.

*MORGAN ROCK — with a depth of less than 6 feet over it is southeast of Klunkwoi Rocks, at the entrance to Klunkwoi Bay. The name was suggested in 1950 by the Chief Geographer for Private L.H. Morgan (M.I.D.) killed in action.

With so many Morgans playing parts in the early history of Lockeport it is fitting that at least one feature of the region should bear the name. Harry D. Morgan, whose memories have provided most of the information about early Lockeport for this book, was listed as killed in 1918.

He had joined up from High River, Alberta. When that town erected a memorial in the 1930s, Harry's name was on a plaque listing all the dead.

A few days before the unveiling a visitor from Bellingham arrived and was amazed to learn he had been officially dead for 18 years. It was a happy task for his friends to have Harry D. Morgan's name deleted from that plaque before the unveiling.

*CRESCENT POINT— is the south entrance point to Crescent Inlet. Formerly called ROCK POINT, but renamed in the 1920s by the Hydrographic Service because of duplications of that name in coastal points.

*CRESCENT INLET— entered north of Crescent Point and Klunkwoi Bay, was named by Dr. Dawson in 1878 for the shape of the inlet when delineated on the chart. Approximately 3/4 of a mile wide at the entrance it curves inland for about 4 miles.

INNER BAY — the name given on early mining maps to the basin at the head of Crescent Inlet. In 1908 a trail was put in which ran from Barrier Bay (Tasu Sound) following the present Flat Creek. This trail emerged at Inner Bay, about 1 mile from the head then, skirting the shoreline, continued southward to connect with the Anna Lake trail, and into Lockeport.

There were several mining claims near the top end of Crescent Inlet. Arichika Ikeda owned some in addition to his better-known ones at Ikeda Cove. Mat Oledo and his partners who actively worked their Crescent Inlet properties were said by the Mining Report to have secured "excellent specimens of copper ore" in 1908.

Crescent Inlet was the GA'OINA of Dr. C.F. Newcombe's Haida map.

GAXITAGA'DSGO VILLAGE —lay at the head of Crescent Inlet where three streams enter.

***TRIUMPH POINT** — the northeast entrance point of Crescent Inlet. Formerly called WHITE POINT by Dr. Dawson in 1878. Renamed by the Hydrographic Service because of duplications. *Triumph* was the sloop which took James Richardson to Skidegate Inlet in 1872 to make a careful examination of the Cowgitz coal mining possibilities. Triumph Point named in association with Richardson Island which lies to the east of it.

***RED TOP MOUNTAIN** — rises to 3,285 feet and has a sharp summit which from some points of view appears to be triple. Dominating the heights north of Crescent Inlet and seen also from Tasu Sound, it is one of the most conspicuous peaks in the vicinity. Named in 1878 by Dr. G.M. Dawson who first saw it shining crimson in the evening sun.

EAST SIDE OF MORESBY, FROM TANU TO
LOUISE ISLAND. INCLUDES PACOFI, SEWELL,
TANU AND SKEDANS.

CHAPTER ELEVEN

The same rich tapestry of Queen Charlotte Islands names continues in this chapter as Haida names are interwoven with the names of noted geologists, sea captains, mining men, pioneers and those associated with fishing.

*TANU PASSAGE — off the west side of Tanu Island, separates that island from its neighbour Richardson Island. It is in reality the north arm of Richardson Inlet. Tanu Passage named in 1957 by the Hydrographic Service.

*STALKUNGI POINT — the northeast entrance to Tanu Passage, is on Tanu Island, and is the northwest tip of the island.

*STALKUNGI COVE — lies inside and to the southeast of Stalkungi Point. Both were named in 1957 by the Hydrographic Service. Stalkungi is a modification of the Haidá word for moccasin.

*TANU POINT — the southeast entrance point of Tanu Passage. Named in 1957 by the Hydrographic Service in association with the island.

*TANU ISLAND — which lies north of Lyell Island, was named in 1878 by Dr. G.M. Dawson, for the Haida village on its eastern end. Dawson used the spelling *Tanoo*. About 6 miles long, it is wooded and rises steeply to over 2,000 feet.

Only part of the village of Tanu shows in this photo taken by Dr. G.M. Dawson when he visited the site in 1878.

Photo - Provincial Museum, Victoria.

HLGAEDLIN VILLAGE — on the south shore of Tanu Island, is said to have belonged to the Sus-haidagai, the-lake-people, who owned the lake back of Skedans Bay. Eagle Crest people, they were related to the tribes at Tanu village and the name of their chief meant He-Who-Protects. Hlgaedlin means "where-they-wash-the-frames-which-salal-berries-are-dried-on."

*KLUE POINT — the southeast point of Tanu Island, at the south entrance to Klue Island. Named by the Hydrographic Service in 1957.

*KLUE PASSAGE — separating Tanu Island from Kunga Island, also named by the Hydrographic Service in 1957. Both are after Chief Kloo of Tanu, whose name has a variety of spellings when adapted to English—Kloo, Clew, Klue, Clough, Kliew and others. A Raven Crest chief, he is mentioned frequently in Francis Poole's writings of his mining venture on Burnaby Island 1862-64. A chief of this name was known also to Joseph Ingraham in 1791. The name means southeast in Haida.

*TANU VILLAGE, Sea-grass-town — the hauntingly beautiful Eagle Crest site on the east shore of Tanu Island. The Tsimpsheans called it Laskeek, Village-of-the-Eagles. The name has also been written TANOO and TAHNOO.

It lay on the north side of a rock ledge, along a curving beach to another rocky point, and extended even beyond. Some say that Tanu was really two villages, separated by only a few yards. The house pits which remain to mark the sites are large and lie in two rows facing the shoreline. The forests have grown protectively around, the moss has enfolded the ruins, but the dignity and romance of old Tanu touches a present day visitor almost before a foot is placed on shore. The people of Chicken-Hawk-Town, on the east coast of

Lyell, were the first to "slash the bushes at Tanu" according to legend and, as was the case in all large villages, people of both crests had homes there.

"In July (1878) when we visited this village, we found it to be the most flourishing of any on the Charlottes," wrote Dr. Dawson. "Sixteen well-built lodges ring the shoreline and thirty finely carved poles proclaim the artistry of its residents. The village, extending round a little rocky point, faces two ways and cannot easily be seen from any one point of view. This causes it to look less important than Skedans - although it possesses a greater population."

There was a lively potlatch celebration under way at the time of Dr. Dawson's visit. Numerous visitors had come to take part in the erection of another carved pole and to put the final beams and timbers in the chief's new house. It was such a large house it took longer than usual to complete. Named House-of-the-Long-Potlatch, it had necessitated a lavish potlatch to reward those who had helped in the building.

Dawson greatly enjoyed the zest with which the villagers joined in the affair - the shouting and heave-ho chants as the great hewn planks and beams were dragged into place. The nights of dancing, gambling and all manner of entertainment, after a strenuous day of work, left him marvelling at the fine physiques of these colourful people.

Chittenden visiting this same village only 6 years after Dawson, found 20 houses, but a population which had dwindled from over 500 to less than 150. Three years later there were only 80 people left in Tanu. Most of these were sick and dying. It was at this time some of the older ones approached Reverend Thomas Crosby and begged him to help.

After careful talks and assessment, he advised the abandonment of the village to change the pattern and improve the morale with a fresh start. It was decided to move to a creek on the north end of Louise Island, the new village to be called NEW KLOO. Old Kloo, or Tanu, was left to join the growing list of ghost towns.

Archaeologists in recent years found mute evidence of the desperate conditions which caused the decision - mass graves at one end of the village; people of all ages dying so fast there had been no way to give any type of ceremony to their passing.

During their inspection of the burial place of those dreadful years, the archaeologists were interrupted in their diggings by descendents of the villagers of Tanu. The Haidas, irate at this disturbance of their dead - permission or no - made it absolutely clear that this was a violation pure and simple. It must cease immediately. It did. Haida anger is still to be reckoned with. The knowledge that morally they *were* trespassing made the archaeologists leave the dead of Tanu to rest in peace.

*TANU ROCK — which dries at 3 feet, lies in Klue Passage, east of the old Tanu village site. Named in this association in 1949 by the Hydrographic Service.

*KUNGA ISLAND — lies east of Tanu Island and is about 1,500 feet high, wooded and with shorelines fringed by low rocky reefs and detached rocks. Named in 1878 by Dr. Dawson after the Haida name for the island.

There are several fossil sites along the east and north shores.

*KELO ROCKS — extend for about 1,500 feet from the southeast point of Kunga Island. Named by the Hydrographic Service in 1957 after the Haida word for shag or cormorant.

*TITUL ISLAND — a slim island off the northwest tip of Kunga Island. Named by Dr. Dawson in 1878 after the Haida word for loon. It is a wooded island with low limestone cliffs.

*NOB ROCK — named for its shape by the Hydrographic Service in 1957, lies about a mile off the northeast corner of Kunga Rock. It could as appropriately have been named "Submarine Rock" say fishermen. Bare and steep-to, this 17-foot rock looks remarkably like a "sub" from some directions.

*LOST ISLANDS — are about 3 miles to the northeast of Kunga Island. Consisting of 3 islands, 2 of which are wooded - all are joined by ledges. Several small islets and rocks lie close off. Named in 1923 by Mr. H.D. Parizeau, ". . . because up to the time of our survey of Atli Inlet (that year) this group of islands had never been shown on any chart." On a later map of 1927 they were shown as SEAL ISLANDS, but subsequent maps and charts all use Mr. Parizeau's name of LOST ISLANDS.

*REEF ISLAND — looks like an untidy jellyfish humping its way into Laskeek Bay, as it trails rocks and reefs from its underbelly like ragged streamers.

Named in 1878 by Dr. Dawson who noted that "a reef runs about a half mile southward from it." It is a wooded island with cliffs in places along its south shore and fossils along the north part. The people of Kloo (Tanu) had a fort on Reef Island - THIN FORT.

*LASKEEK BAY — is the area of water lying in the indentation between Dodge Point (on Lyell Island) and Vertical Point (on Louise Island). The bay was named by Dr. Dawson in 1878. Laskeek is an adaption of an old Tsimpshian name which meant "of the Eagle." The name was frequently applied in reference to the village of Tanu. Francis Poole, among others, described his friend Chief Klue as being of the village of Laskeek in 1852.

*LOGAN INLET — on the west side of Laskeek Bay and flowing along the north shore of Tanu Island. Named by Dr. Dawson in 1878 for William Edmund Logan, the first director of the Geological Survey of Canada when it was instituted in 1842. Born in Montreal in 1798, Logan was knighted in 1865 in recognition of his many contributions to the science of geology. He knew James Richardson (Richardson Inlet) and it was through Sir William Logan that Richardson later joined the Geological Survey.

*FLOWER POT ISLAND — at the east entrance of Logan Inlet. Named in 1878 by Dr. Dawson who described it as ". . . a small bold rock, covered with trees," It is actually about 225 feet high and was the site of a Haida fort called DOGFISH-FORT by the people of Kloo, to whom it belonged.

*TANGIL PENINSULA — separates Logan Inlet from Dana Inlet. Named in 1957 for its shape by the Hydrographic Service who used a modification of the Haida word for tongue - *tangil.*

*PORTER HEAD — is the eastern extremity of Tangil Peninsula. The name appeared on 1927 maps, but origin is not confirmed.

*HELMET ISLAND — named in 1878 by Dr. G.M. Dawson who said "In the mouth of Dana Inlet is a small, high rocky island, of rounded form which may be called HELMET ISLAND. A second small island is near it, and from most points of view, the channel between the two is not seen. Care must be taken to avoid mistaking this island for Flower Pot Island, which is to the south at the mouth of Logan Inlet."

*DWIGHT ROCK — also at the east entrance to Dana Inlet, but on the north side of the fairway, opposite Helmet Island. Named in 1957 by the Hydrographic Service after James Dwight Dana, in association with Dana Inlet.

*DANA INLET — flows along the north side of the Tangil Peninsula, and south of Talunkwan Island. Named in 1878 by Dr. Dawson after an American geologist, James Dwight Dana, who had been a member of the Wilkes Expedition sent by the U.S. Government to the Haro Archipelago in 1841. He was professor of Natural History at Yale College following this and was

Helmet Island at the east entrance to Dana Inlet taken in late evening.

Photo - Anne Clemence

editor and frequent contributor to the *American Journal of Science* for over fifty years. His outstanding contributions to geology and minerology resulted in his decoration by the Royal Geological Society.

*DANA PASSAGE — at the west end of Talunkwan Island, runs from the northwest end of Dana Inlet. Named by the Hydrographic Service in the 1920s in association with the inlet. The passage narrows at one point to a distance of about 300 feet, but is easily navigated by small vessels at, or near, high water. The hills all around Dana Inlet have been extensively logged - as has most of Moresby's east shore.

*BEATRICE SHOAL — at the north end of Dana Passage, almost in mid-channel, has a least depth over it of 13 feet. The name which was confirmed in 1947, is after the C.P.R. *Princess Beatrice*. She plied these waters from 1907 to 1912, when the C.P.R. withdrew their vessels from the Queen Charlotte Islands run.

The best known skipper of the *Beatrice* at that time was Captain Hughes, of whom Reverend Will Collison wrote, "Nothing gave him a more impish sense of fun than to toot the whistle at some ungodly hour of the night . . . until a few lights came on and the towsled heads came down to take his ropes. Haul on that lanyard he would. We all knew which ship it was and, most of all, we all surely knew what skipper it was. There he would be grinning from ear to ear," Collison had travelled with Hughes to the Charlottes in 1906, when Hughes was then the skipper of the *Tees*.

*TALUNKWAN ISLAND — about 7 miles in length, lies between Dana Inlet and Selwyn Inlet. Named in 1878 by Dr G.M. Dawson after the modification of the Haida word for phosphorus, which is particularly noticeable in the waters off this area. During the early mining years it was referred to in some reports as KLUM-WAI-UM- ISLAND. Several Vancouver men were interested in mineral claims on the east end of the island, Heming, Harbridge and McGee - all of whom have their names applied to features on Talunkwan island.

In recent years pilots flying the small float planes which service Thurston Harbour, on the north side of the island, have referred to Talunkwan Island as HORSESHOE ISLAND because of its shape.

*HEMING HEAD — on the east end of Talunkwan Island. Named in 1910 by Captain Louis P. Locke of the *Amur,* after Herbert Payne Heming. Born in Guelph, Ontario in 1863, Mr. Heming came to Vancouver in 1905 then moved to Victoria two years later. He died in 1932. Heming had large timber and copper interests on Moresby Island and the nearby islands off the east side. His best remembered claim was the *Hawk's Nest* near Heming Head, which he spent considerable capital to develop. "It is reported that Mr. Heming will spend another $10,000 on the mine," ran a newspaper item in May 1909. His consulting engineer was Campbell Johnson and that August, Heming along with H.O. McGee, had a crew of 4 men working overtime on the property. The old shaft used in development work on the claim is seen clearly today, on the hill facing Laskeek Bay.

The Haidas called the point the equivalent of PHOSPHORUS POINT and Talunkwan Island took its name originally from this.

PEOPLE'S-FORT — the old Eagle Crest fort which stood near Heming Head. It belonged to the tribe of Chief Kloo and had been used twice, according to Dr. J.R. Swanton. The second time was after a Haida raid on a Bella Bella fort, which had been completely destroyed, and the Haidas prepared themselves for possible retribution.

*McGEE POINT — on the south side of Talunkwan Island. Named in 1957 by the Hydrographic Service for Mr. H.O. McGee, who had an interest in Talunkwan mining claims with Mr. Heming. McGee did the actual opening up of the property.

*HARBRIDGE POINT — on the north side of Talunkwan Island. Named in 1957 by the Hydrographic Service for Mr. Harbridge who was interested in mining claims on Talunkwan Island in 1908.

*PROCTOR ROCKS — consist of a 12-foot above-water rock and some drying and submerged rocks extending for about 1,500 feet east from Harbridge Point, on the northern extremity of Talunkwan Island. Thomas G. Proctor was a mining man from Nelson, as were so many of the early prospectors who came to seek their luck on the east side of Moresby Island. He apparently did not stay long.

*THOMPSON POINT — on the north shore at the entrance of Thurston Harbour. Called Thomson Point in earlier years, then changed to Thompson for the 1963 maps. There have been several origins advanced for this name, but to date none have been substantiated and the man it honours is still not known.

*THURSTON HARBOUR — on the north shore of Talunkwan Island, stretches inland to give Talunkwan Island its horseshoe resemblance. The name applied shortly after the turn of this century is after the *Nellie G. Thurston,* a 79-foot schooner of about 80 tons. This harbour was a favorite bad-weather anchorage when she was halibutting off this area.

Built in 1883 in Gloucester, Massachusetts, the *Thurston* fished on the banks out of her home port until 1897 when the Pacific Mining and Trading Company chartered her for a trip to the Klondike - via the Horn. Thirteen men and one woman boarded her early in October for a voyage beset by bad weather. At one point it was feared she had been lost after passing through the Straits of Magellan, she took so long to arrive in San Francisco.

By 1902 she again became a fishing schooner, owned by the Pacific Fish and Cold Storage of Nanaimo, under the management of Captain Bradford. Bradford sent her to the Charlottes under an ailing Captain Johnson to find the halibut reported to abound in waters off the Islands. Early in April Johnson became so ill he could not continue and, finding the *Tees* at Skidegate, took the opportunity to go home to Victoria. It was expected the *Thurston* would follow shortly. But she did not.

Much anxiety was felt. Finally in May the steamer *Danube* brought news that the *Thurston* had gone aground in Skidegate Channel and sustained damage while attempting to sail from Hecate Strait out to the West Coast. Repairs were made and she eventually limped into her home port at the end of June. Her cargo of 62 tons of salted halibut soon unloaded and she made ready for another trip.

"Now that Captain Bradford has learned where the fishing grounds are," ran an item in the Nanaimo paper on July 25, 1902, "the next trip of the *Thurston* will not be nearly so long."

But it was over 5 months before she returned from her second trip - that time under Captain Madden. And for her 5 months - only 10 to 12 tons of halibut. The crew were close-mouthed about the trip and Captain Madden did not add much except to say, "There is no truth about an earlier report of mutiny, nor was I forced to return. But under no circumstances would I again go in command."

Nevertheless, the *Thurston* became a regular visitor to the fishing grounds off the Charlottes until 1906 when she made her last trip before being sold to E.J.Fader and ignominiously towed to New Westminster by the tug *Clive,* to be used as a receiving boat. Her days of active fishing were over, 23 years after launching.

The harbour which bears her name was a busy headquarters during the latter years of the First World War, when the Imperial Munitions Board used it as a collection base for aeroplane spruce cut on Moresby. Camps were dotted everywhere and the gigantically proportioned clear spruce was taken

234

at will under a government priority order of "select logging."

Thurston Harbour became a miniature metropolis - no expense spared. Hospital, warehouses, offices, scores of small houses, recreational building operated by the Y.M.C.A., wireless station and store, as well as a complete rafting camp were built. Three fine sawmills were almost completed when the war ended in 1918 and everything was either abandoned or sold for a pittance.

A few years later Whalen Pulp and Paper used it for their logging headquarters. Joe Pollard, now of Vancouver, has nostalgic memories of a July 1st spent there in 1923. "They put on a dance in the cookhouse," he recalls, "and most of the girls came from Sandspit and Skidegate. I think I had more than my fair share of dances with one from Sandspit, Peggy Gillatt. The song *Three O'clock in the Morning* still takes me back to that evening. I was an old man of 19 and most of the girls probably about 16."

Over the years it has remained a logging centre for a succession of operations by private companies. In 1971 the Frank Beban Logging Company, under contract to Rayonier Limited, had a neat land-based operation situated west of the World War I site. Only ruins mark that once elaborate operation today - and the scarred hillsides around which produced the lush crop for that operation and for camps which came after.

Pacofi plant in February 1910 when it first went into operation.

Photo - Provincial Archives, Victoria.

*PACOFI BAY — lies off the west end of Talunkwan Island and received its name from a $300,000 cold storage and ice plant, and a reduction plant, built at its head in 1909 by the Pacific Coast Fisheries. Alvo von Alvensleben of Germany headed the Pacofi company which included prominent Vancouver and Victoria business investors as well.

The 254-ton steam trawler *Kingsway,* purchased in England, arrived on the

Pacific coast in the summer of 1909 to begin fishing for the plant. A summer of constant rain caused building schedules to fall over 3 months behind time. Winter arrived before they could get the plant ready for operation. The *Kingsway* remained tied to a dock in Vancouver until February 1910 when production began. By March the plant was processing about 2 tons an hour - half the fish being frozen for the market and the rest being converted to oil and fertilizer.

The little settlement took an active interest in Island politics, and Mr. Thompson Low became a spokesman, writing letters to editors pressing for a member of parliament for the Charlottes and the creating of a separate district for the Islands. It became a subject which gained much interest on Graham Island as well.[1]

More than weather difficulties plagued Pacofi, for financially the operation experienced severe problems. In 1911 a new manager, Mr. Alford, took charge. The company hoped that the completion of the Grand Trunk Pacific Railway into Prince Rupert would provide more marketing possibilities. But it proved not so, and the company folded soon after.

Attempts by others to reopen several times were unsuccessful - mainly because of financing problems. In 1927 a salmon saltery began operation there, utilizing the old buildings, and ran until 1936. Two years later B.C. Packers bought the entire property and put in a new 2-line cannery and 10-ton reduction plant - only to see the whole thing wiped out by fire in 1943. It was rebuilt and ran until 1949 when it closed for the last time. Most of the buildings were either sold or razed. For many years one large structure remained and was utilized briefly by a logging camp, then eventually by campers and hunters. The ravages of weather and age have gradually made it uninhabitable. Pacofi has joined the other ghost towns.

A regularly used Haida encampment lay near the mouth of the stream entering the head of Pacofi Bay, close by the old plant.

[1]Q.C. Islands, Volume 1, page 271.

*LOCKE SHOAL — near the edge of the drying flat at the head of Pacofi Bay, is off the site of the old plant. The shoal has one rock which dries at 1 foot and two other rocks which are awash. The name applied in 1947 by the Hydrographic Service is after Captain Louis P. Locke who skippered the *Beatrice* for awhile before taking over the *Amur* during the years of C.P.R. service to the Charlottes which lasted until 1912.

Captain Locke lost his life in Lynne Canal on October 25 1918 when the *Princess Sophia* slid off Vanderbilt Reef taking everyone to the bottom. The vessel left Skagway with a full load of passengers. In a blinding snowstorm she got off course and, because of the snow, was unable to get an echo with the whistle. The ship struck at 3 a.m. In the violent storm rescue ships couldn't get near. The *Sophia* appeared steady and safe but in the huge waves began to take a mortal beating and the following evening slid off the reef. Only a dog survived.

In the inquiry which followed information showed the ship carried many experienced mariners in her passenger list and these men had backed Locke in deciding against launching lifeboats in such awesome weather.

Ironically it had originally been intended to put the *Princess Sophia* on the Charlotte run, but when the C.P.R. withdrew from servicing that route, she was placed on the northern run to Skagway.

*AMUR ROCK — with a depth of less than 6 feet over it, is a little to the northeast of Locke Shoal. An appropriate position. For it is difficult to think of *Amur's* days on the Charlotte run without being reminded of her skipper Louis P. Locke, who took such an interest in all the happenings of this region. The *Amur* was put on the Charlotte run in 1909 to assist the *Beatrice* in providing service.

*McCONNACHIE SHOAL — is almost in the centre of Pacofi Bay. It, too, is a name appropriate to the locality as Mr. McConnachie managed the Pacofi plant in 1910 during the difficult days of trying to keep the operation viable. There is a least depth of 17 feet over the shoal, named in 1947 by the Hydrographic Service.

*SWINBURNE ISLET — on the north shore of Pacofi Bay is connected by a drying bank to the shore. The islet is 74 feet high. Date of naming not known, nor for whom it is named. Pacofi Bay was surveyed in 1912 by Mr. L.R. Davies, whose name appears on charts of that era more than any other hydrographer connected with mapping Queen Charlotte Islands waters.

*ALFORD POINT — the north entrance point of Pacofi Bay, and

*ALFORD ROCK — a 2-foot-high rock, which lies on the rocky ledge extending from Alford Point. Both were named in 1947 by the Hydrographic Service after Mr. Alford, manager at Pacofi in September 1912.

*CECIL COVE — northwest of Pacofi Bay, is an arm off Selwyn Inlet and has a mud flat at its head. Commonly called BIG GOOSE BAY by many people, with Trotter Bay, to the north, being called Little Goose Bay.

The name of CECIL COVE was applied to BIG GOOSE BAY in 1957 at the suggestion of the Hydrographic Service, in association with Selwyn Inlet after Alfred Richard Cecil Selwyn.

*SELWYN INLET — named by Dr. Dawson in 1878 after the English geologist Dr. A.R.C. Selwyn, who became the second Director of the Geological Survey of Canada when he succeeded Sir William Logan in 1869. He was Dr. Dawson's superior at the time of the Q.C. Islands survey in 1878.

Selwyn Inlet separates Talunkwan Island from Louise Island and flows along the west side of Louise Island as far as Louise Narrows. Pacofi Bay is considered to be an arm of Selwyn Inlet, as are both Sewell and Lagoon Inlets.

*SELWYN POINT — at the west end of Selwyn Inlet, may be said to separate the two arms of Selwyn, one arm going south to Pacofi Bay and the other running north along the west side of Louise Island. Named in 1957 by the Hydrographic Service in association with the inlet.

There is a navigational marker on Selwyn Point, and from this it has received the local name of LIGHTHOUSE POINT. It is a popular cohoe fishing spot with the loggers from Sewell Inlet camp.

*TROTTER BAY — is the LITTLE GOOSE BAY of many people. (Cecil Cove is Big Goose Bay) It lies northwest of Selwyn Point (Lighthouse Point), and was named by the Hydrographic Service after Mr. W.W. Trotter, manager of the Lagoon Bay Cannery during its latter years of operation. "Mr. Trotter reported some dangerous rocks in this vicinity," is the notation on the card in the Hydrographic Office card. Trotter Bay has a drying bank at its head, making it more of a cove than a bay.

*SEWELL INLET — extending in a westerly direction from Selwyn Inlet, is entered north of Trotter Bay. The origin of this name is still a mystery. First shown on an Admiralty chart dated 1906, but in early newspapers of that time it was referred to as JEWELL INLET. Harry Morgan, who came to Lockeport in 1907, says it was called by a Haida name when he first arrived. When the Government put in the trail and cabin at the head of the inlet in 1908 it began to be called SEWELL INLET, at least locally.

During early mining boom years Sewell experienced its share of hopeful young prospectors and several cabins were built along its hillsides. The well-known Walter Dass built one, as did Pete Nelson. Nelson was in partnership with Captain Johnstone, owner of the sloop *Pride of the Islands*, who first came to the Charlottes in 1906 with E.S. Topping to look at a find in Cumshewa Inlet. In 1908 Nelson began to build a fine new cabin and in the building of it lost his life when a huge limb broke off a tree he was falling and struck him.

It is the trees of Sewell Inlet which today create the interest. The modern logging camp of Moresby-Sewell, owned by Rayonier Limited, nestled on the south shore near the head of the inlet, has many years of work in prospect as they harvest the fine timber of this area. This camp was recently moved from its former location at the head of Cumshewa Inlet, where the imagination and ingenuity of the residents had created one of the prettiest logging camps on the Charlottes.

In 1971 the newly-arrived Moresby-Sewell manager, Fred Mantic, directed the placing of the homes and camp buildings in the new site in a most attractive lay-out around a large central grass area. The buildings are modern, yet of an appropriately serviceable design for the isolated location of the community. There is a vitality about this camp and in summer the place looks like a small resort with speed-boats and water skiers zipping along inlet waters, picnic sites being laid out along the stream at the head and, further up-stream, anglers taking advantage of the opportunity to try their luck.

But a look at the side-hills around the inlet, with great logging trucks lumbering along laden with logs and the sound of all the machines connected with the removal of trees, makes a visitor aware that this is a place of much industry.

THLCAGGINS CASS — is the name James Deans gave to the portage route and trail from the head of Sewell Inlet to the head of Newcombe Inlet used regularly by the Haidas in the late 1880s. Robert Brown in his report of 1866 also mentions, "The Indians haul canoes over the neck of land from east to west (to Tasu.)"

In 1908 the Government detailed a foreman and 4 men to cut a trail along this old route, corduroying the way the following year. Cabins were built at either end of the path to shelter freight whilst portions were being carried from one side to the other. Over $1100 was allotted from public funds for the purpose - an indication of the lucrativeness the Provincial Treasury expected from mineral finds.

When the big mine at Tasu was brought into production in the 1960s, this old route again came into use when a gravel road was put in to enable supplies to be brought to the mine when weather prohibited travel along the west coast to Tasu. The freight is trucked across via the road, then placed on barges or similar conveyances, and taken by water along Newcombe Inlet and Tasu Sound to the mine site.

With the establishment of the Moresby-Sewell camp at the head of Sewell Inlet, the road receives much use today in the visiting back and forth of the people from Sewell to Tasu. It is a private road, however, and may not be used without permission.

*SEWELL POINT — the north entrance point of Sewell Inlet, named in association by the Hydrographic Service in 1957.

*LAGOON INLET — north of Sewell Inlet, received its name from the tidal lagoon at its head. About 1½ miles from the entrance the inlet contracts to a narrow obstructed passage, in which there are tidal rapids leading to a lagoon with an extensive drying flat at its head.

Lagoon Bay Cannery in 1926.

Photo - Mr. D.H. Lloyd.

239

In 1918 Colonel MacMillan of Vancouver built a cannery in the bay on the south shore of Lagoon Inlet near the entrance to the rapids, and named the plant Lagoon Bay Cannery. Following this the inlet itself was frequently called LAGOON BAY (instead of Inlet).

The Canadian Fishing Company bought the Lagoon Bay Cannery in 1922 and ran it until the plant was destroyed by fire in 1941.

*DASS CREEK — flows into Lagoon Inlet at the old Lagoon Bay Cannery site. Named after Walter Leach Dass who first came to the Charlottes in 1906. He prospected in the Jedway area until Marsh English engaged him to build and manage the first Jedway Hotel (which was later sold to Ben Metcalf.) Mr. Dass is best remembered today as the skipper of a number of boats which plied Charlotte's waters. Now in his nineties and living in Toronto, he says he believes the creek was named after him by William Morgan of Lockeport in the pre-cannery days.

Walter L. Dass in 1912. Dass Creek, Dass Point and Dass Lake were all named after him.

Photo - Mr. Charlie Hartie.

*CARMICHAEL PASSAGE — extends for about 5½ miles along the west side of Louise Island and is entered north of Lagoon Inlet, and also from Cumshewa Inlet. Called SOUTH ARM (of Cumshewa Inlet) by Dr. Dawson in 1878, it was renamed in 1926 by the Hydrographic Service because of numerous duplications of that name. It then became CARMICHAEL ARM after Provincial Assayer Herbert Carmichael who came to the Charlottes in 1901 in an open sail-boat to evaluate a reported discovery of asphaltum on the Tar Islands for the Department of Mines.

Arriving at Skidegate on October 1, he engaged a canoe and some Haida paddlers to take him along the east coast of Moresby as far as Ramsay Island.

Making a brief examination of Cumshewa Inlet, he travelled then through the passage which bears his name today. In 1948 the name was changed from Carmichael Arm to CARMICHAEL PASSAGE.

SOOK-I-TILLICUM — the name given by Mr. Carmichael's Haida guides to the lake-like expansion midway along Carmichael Passage. Carmichael also felt that the expansion was really a tidal lake, filled by the flood tide from each end. The Haidas called the narrow passages leading to the lake, the KAATSUS.

*LOUISE NARROWS — lies near the south end of Carmichael Passage, below the tidal lake, mentioned above as Sook-i-tillicum. Louise Narrows are the narrowest part of Carmichael Passage and in early years dried. In 1967 a channel was dredged to facilitate travel between Sewell and Cumshewa Inlet for the logging camps. Even at low water there is now a depth of 2 feet. Louise Narrows were named about 1925 by the Hydrographic Service in association with Louise Island.

Louise Narrows in 1971. Looking north to Carmichael's tidal lake Sook-i-tillicum.

Photo - K.E. Dalzell.

*CHADSEY CREEK — flows onto a pleasant beach at the north end of Carmichael Passage on the west side. Confirmed in 1926. It is after a Mrs. Mary Jane Chadsey, born in Grafton, Ontario, in 1845. Migrated to B.C. in 1867 and located in the Chilliwack Valley where she remained from that time on. She was one of the old-timers of B.C. taking part in the big 1924 reunion celebration of pioneers held in Victoria.

This creek was formerly called by the same Haida name as that which was used for Newcombe Peak - a modification of which is Kyhita.

*NEDDEN ISLAND — at the north entrance of Carmichael Passage, is on the west side of the channel, and is north of the mouth of Chadsey Creek. Named in 1926 after Captain H.E. Nedden, a well-remembered skipper who commanded the C.N.'s *Prince John* for several years before transferring to the larger *Prince Rupert* which operated on the mainland side.

*MABBS ISLET — also at the north entrance of Carmichael Passage, is on the east side of the main channel. The application of his name to an Islands feature is most appropriate, for Captain Edward Mabbs skippered the *Prince John* for many years on its Islands' run. His cheerful weathered face was familiar to all as he looked down from the bridge and rasped out orders to ensure his vessel came safely into the small wharves and settlements along his route. Mabbs Islet named in 1926.

*LOUISE ISLAND — a chunky mountainous island approximately 12 miles wide and 12 miles long, is the third largest island in the Queen Charlotte group. Dr. Dawson named the island in 1878 after H.R.H. Princess Louise Caroline Alberta, the fifth daughter of Queen Victoria. Her husband, John Douglas Campbell, Marquis of Lorne, that year had been appointed Canada's Governor-General. In commemoration of the young couple's arrival in Canada, Dr. Dawson named this island for the Princess during his survey.

*MOUNT KERMODE — on the western part of Louise Island, is a bare steep pinnacle which rises to 3,550 feet and is the highest peak on this island. Named in 1925 after Francis Kermode, Director of the Provincial Museum in Victoria from 1904 to 1940.

In July 1895, the 21-year-old Kermode accompanied Dr. C.F. Newcombe on an extended trip to the little-known Queen Charlotte Islands, the first time either had been to the Islands, and they brought back to Victoria a wealth of specimens related to their special fields. The collection was made along both coasts of the Islands from a small boat.

When a creamy coloured bear skin was sent to the Zoological Park in New York in 1900 for identification, Dr. W.T. Hornaday, the director, was mystified. He had never seen the species before. Finding that it had come from British Columbia, he alerted Francis Kermode, who traced the region from which the skin had been obtained as Princess Royal Island off the mainland - about due east of Louise Island. Kermode was successful in obtaining specimens of this rare bear for the Provincial Museum and, in recognition of his services, Dr. Hornaday named the bear *Kermodei*.

In 1907 Mr. Kermode, then in charge of the Provincial Museum, became interested in acquiring another rare species of animal, a Queen Charlotte Islands caribou, which was rapidly becoming extinct, the *rangifer Dawsonii* - found nowhere else in Canada.[1]

[1]The story of that quest is told in Q.C. Islands, Volume 1, page 307.

*MOUNT CARL — on the southeast side of Louise Island, is a prominent landmark rising to 3,150 feet. Named in 1948 by the Hydrographic Service in association with Mount Kermode. When Francis Kermode retired in 1940, Dr. G. Clifford Carl served for 2 years as Acting Director of the Provincial

Museum, and in 1942 was appointed Director - a post he held until his death in 1970. Dr. Carl published several books and articles which contributed greatly to the study of natural history in British Columbia.

Between Mount Carl and Mount Kermode is another high peak, which has remained unnamed.

YAOGUS VILLAGE — a Raven Crest village on the west shore of Louise Island, belonging to relatives of the Skedans people. Dr. Newcombe's map shows Yaogus to be on the south side of the unnamed creek on Louise Island, opposite the entrance to Lagoon Inlet.

TLHINGUS VILLAGE, Flat-slope-town — also on the west shore of Louise Island, lay to the south of Yaogus. According to Dr. Newcombe's map it appears to have been at the mouth of what is now Traynor Creek. It was a Raven Crest site belonging to the same family as Yaogus.

*TRAYNOR CREEK — flows into a shallow bay about 4 miles south of Louise Narrows, and drains Dass Lake on the western part of Louise Island. Traynor Creek appeared on maps prepared in connection with a timber sale about 1927. The origin of the name is not confirmed.

*DASS LAKE — drained by Traynor Creek, is at the 1000-foot level. A very small lake named about 1927 after Walter Leach Dass, who first came to the Charlottes in 1906, and for whom Dass Creek and Dass Point are also named.

*SELWYN ROCKS — lie north of the mouth of Traynor Creek and are about 900 feet offshore from Louise Island, opposite the entrance to Sewell Inlet. They are a reef of drying and submerged rocks, the largest of which dries at 7 feet. Named in 1957 by the Hydrographic Service in association with Selwyn Inlet.

*KILMINGTON POINT — is the southwest extremity of Louise Island. Dr. Alfred R.C. Selwyn, for whom Dawson named Selwyn Inlet, was born at Kilmington in 1824. Kilmington Point appeared first on the 1927 maps.

*ALFRED POINT — a mile to the northeast of Kilmington Point, and at the entrance to Rockfish Harbour, also honours Dr. Selwyn. Named in 1947 by the Hydrographic Service after Dr. Alfred R.C. Selwyn.

*ROCKFISH HARBOUR — is formed by a boot-shaped projection of low land off the southwest portion of Louise Island. Named by Dr. Dawson in 1878. Since Dawson named features for a physical characteristic when he did not name them for an eminent geologist or scientist, one wonders if he or his party fished in this small bay and the resulting catch led to the name.

It is the XI'LTSI of Dr. Newcombe's map.

*DASS POINT — at the extremity of a peninsula extending into Selwyn Inlet from the southeast side of Louise Island, and is the southernmost point of the island. Named in 1957 by the Hydrographic Service after Walter Leach Dass in recognition of his ownership of early day mining claims in the Selwyn Inlet region.

*HASWELL ISLAND — lies off Dass Point and has a navigational light on its south side. Formerly called ENTRANCE ISLAND, the name given it by Dr. Dawson in 1878. Renamed in 1948 by the Hydrographic Service because of duplications of that name in coastal areas. Named after Robert Haswell, mate under Captain Gray on both the *Columbia* and *Washington*, when those vessels traded in Charlotte waters.[1]

[1]See also the introduction to Chapter seven, and Haswell Bay.

SI'NGI VILLAGE — a small village which stood on Haswell Island.

*KINGSWAY ROCK — bare and 32 feet high with a rock covered by less than 6 feet of water off its east side. Named after the 254-ton steam trawler *Kingsway* which was purchased by the Pacific Coast Fisheries and brought out from England in 1909 to fish for their Pacific operation.

The 135-foot-long vessel was built at Lytham, England, in 1906 largely from left-overs. Her twin steam engines had been built for the Chilean Navy, but cancelled before delivery. Material left over from several light cruisers built for the Royal Navy were utilized in her construction.

When the Pacific plant under Alvo von Alvensleben failed the *Kingsway* was sold to the Canadian Fishing Company for halibutting in northern waters.

*BREAKER BAY — off the southeast side of Louise Island between Dass and Nelson Points. Named by Dr. Dawson in 1878. There is an interesting fossil site at the head of Breaker Bay.

*NELSON POINT — which has a semi-detached islet off it, forms the northeast shore of Breaker Bay. Named in 1957 by the Hydrographic Service for Pete Nelson, the young prospector-miner who owned mining claims in Sewell Inlet in 1907-08. He was in partnership with Captain James Johnstone, owner of the sloop *Pride of the Islands*. Harry Morgan, who came to Lockeport in 1907, remembers Nelson as a very likeable chap who owned a large black dog which was his constant companion. When Nelson was killed in 1908 by a falling branch when building his new cabin, the dog sat immovable by Nelson's body and would allow no one to approach. "Hours of coaxing brought no change in the situation," remembers Mr. Morgan. "Finally someone managed to distract the animal long enough for Nelson to be removed. The big dog was soon back at his post, worried that Nelson had been taken, but determined to remain where he had last seen him. He wouldn't eat," says Mr. Morgan, "just sat mute. Eventually he got so weak a friend of Nelson's, who knew the dog well, was able to get him into a crate and down to Vancouver to a vet. But it was no use. He never got over his mourning." The incident made quite an impact on the neighbours and has been frequently mentioned in recollections of early years.

*VERTICAL POINT — on the east side of Louise Island, and to which it is connected by a narrow spit, was named in 1878 by Dr. G.M. Dawson, "POINT VERTICAL from the attitude of the limestone beds, some of which are over 300 feet high." A drying but protected bay lies on the south side of the spit which is grassy with trees dotted park-like along its length.

This spit area has been used by successive admirers. In ancient years it was the site of the XA'LANIT village and ample midden signs remain from that occupancy. During the Depression years several handloggers took refuge there and in the bays north and south of the spit. The people who chose the spit have left a legacy of apple trees, honeysuckle and rose trees - and the ruins of their home show that it was a frame house. The remains of log cabins lie nearby, and a fine well.

Today it is the homesite of Bonita Saunders, the young artist from New York who has been coming to the Charlottes for a number of years, paddling the waters of the Islands expertly in her kayak. "At first I came just for a month, but each year it grew successively longer," she says. "I would tent as I gathered my material. But the urge to put down roots grew irresistible." When she was granted a conditional permit to establish a homesite behind Vertical Point, Bonita did put down her roots. She acquired a small cabin, put in a garden and set up her artist's paraphernalia. 'I begrudge the time I have to take out to return to the East each year," she says "and can hardly wait to get back." Lonely? Quite the contrary. A growing number of artistic people have found in these Charlotte Islands the perfect environment for their creativity. Bonita's lagoon is seldom without a boat, the visitors ex-

Artist Bonita Sauders (striped blouse) of Vertical Point and her diminutive 6 x 8 foot cabin is rarely without visitors. This photo taken in July 1971 shows her with Albert Dalzell, left, (author's husband); Anne Clemence, who supplied some of the photos for this book; and Sam Lamont (right) who as he says, ". . . just runs the boat." Anne and Sam are frequent visitors to the Charlottes.

245

Part of the village of Skedans in a photo taken by Dr. G.M. Dawson in 1878.

Photo - Provincial Museum, Victoria.

changing news and ideas, and Bonita offering suggestions about a certain cove or island she thinks might be exactly what her visitors would like.

XA'LANIT VILLAGE — stood on the spit of land which connects Vertical Point to Louise Island. One of the houses from this site still stood in 1878 when Dr. Dawson visited the place.

*LIMESTONE ISLANDS — two in number are off the northeast portion of Vertical Point. They were named by Dr. Dawson in 1878. The larger, outer Limestone Island is the GI'DJATS of Dr. Newcombe. There are several caves on one of the islands, one of which is reported to have been an ancient burial cave.

*LOW ISLAND — which has a navigational light on it, lies east of the Limestone Islands and is 215 feet high. The light is set at an elevation of 56 feet on an islet off the northwest point of Low Island. A drying rocky ledge connects the two.

*SOUTH LOW ISLAND — southwest of Low Island and only 125 feet high, has several rocks and reefs close by. Both these islands were named by Dr. Dawson in 1878 who designated them under the one title of the LOW ISLANDS. They were later differentiated for purposes of identification, the larger more northerly retaining the single name of LOW ISLAND and the more southerly, about 1 mile away, being shown as SOUTH LOW ISLAND.

*SKEDANS BAY — is the large bight between the Limestone Islands and the old Skedans village site. Dr. Dawson applied the name to the charts in 1878. There were at least two village sites in Skedans Bay at different times. Hlgaedlin stood at the head of the bay, and at some other time another settlement, Hlgai, lay a little to the north. Both were Eagle Crest sites.

HLGAI VILLAGE — shown on Dr. Newcombe's map on the north side of the mouth of Skedans Creek.

HLGAEDLIN VILLAGE — also in the general region of the mouth of the creek. Another village by this name on the south side of Tanu Island belonged to the same people. Hlgaedlin was the name of the lake at the head of the Skedans Creek, which these villagers owned and they took their name from it. The name referred to a frame for drying salal berries.

*SKEDANS CREEK — flows into the head of Skedans Bay and has a waterfall near its mouth which is visible for some distance. The creek drains several unnamed lakes, one of which was called by the Haidas, Hlgaedlin.

*SKEDANS VILLAGE — lay on the narrow neck of land which connects the high bluff of Skedans Point to Louise Island, and extended around the curve of the bay west of the point. Skedans is a corruption of the head chief's name, Gida'nsta. The village itself was known as Qoona or Kona, Grizzly-Bear-Town. Considered to be leaders in the setting of new fashions in the arts, the Skedans were seldom involved in wars although the Tanus and Skidegates on either side of them constantly battled.

The chief of Skedans, the Raven Crest Gida'nsta, was a friend of the Kitkatla chief, Tse'basa (on the mainland side), and their relationship led to the introduction of many new crests and stories. It is said that the ancestors of these chiefs had originally come from the Naas together and halfway to Skedans they separated, one family going to Skedans and the other to Kitkatla.

Traditionally a Raven Crest site, Skedans, like the other larger villages, had lodges belonging to both crests and they all had names. A family chief of the Eagles called his house, Black-Whale-House. The Raven Town Chief owned the largest home in the village. Said to have 5 steps under it, they called it Clouds-sound-against-it-as-they-pass-over. The chief who owned it was reported to have given 10 potlatches, an extraordinary feat, equalled only by two other chiefs, Edenso of Kung and Ninstints of Red-Cod-Island. (Anthony Island)

In his research at the turn of this century Dr. J.R. Swanton learned of 27 houses at Skedans, some of which were in ruins. When Dr. Dawson visited the village in 1878 he estimated that there were 16 habitable homes, and he considered the village to be long past its prime. Chittenden visited in 1884 and found only 12 people still living there. Between 1888 and 1890 Skedans was abandoned, except for seasonal use, when the villagers moved to Haina on the east end of Maude Island. In 1893 all moved to Skidegate. The region around the old Skedans village has been designated a protected reserve containing 169 acres. It belongs to the Skidegate band.

Many-Ledges, a Raven killer-whale spirit dwells under a rock behind the old village and guards those at rest. Many-Ledges figured prominently in the stories the old ones told around the fires at Skedans.

*SKEDANS POINT — extends outward and east from the main village. Known to the villagers as THE PENINSULA and the Raven Crest people who built homes there were called The Peninsula People. They had their own separate chiefs.

Skedans Point is the SUMMER POINT of Joseph Ingraham's 1791 map.

*SKEDANS ISLANDS — which were first shown on a H.B.C. map of 1852 as SKEDANCE ISLANDS, are a group of widely separated islands lying off the old village.

*GIRARD POINT — on the northeast portion of Louise Island, near the entrance to Cumshewa Inlet. Named by the Hydrographic Service and confirmed in 1926, it is after a pioneer of Queen Charlotte City, Mr. Emmanuel Girard.

Originally from Quebec, Mr. Girard brought his wife and four daughters, Azeline, Bertha, Juliette and Theoline, to live in the little hamlet, soon to be known as Queen Charlotte City. In 1908 he had been appointed manager of the Moresby Island Mill, under superintendent J.E. Corlett. Mr. Girard was such a competent mill man, Corlett was able to spend most of his time in the Tasu area taking part in the mining claim fever.

Mr. Girard's fifth daughter, Mrs. Dagneault, whose husband was a millwright, came to live in Queen Charlotte City near her parents; and her husband worked for Girard in the mill.

GOOSE BEACH — the name given to the shoreline west of Girard Point by Joseph Ingraham in 1791. Name does not appear on any other chart. On his sketch map, Ingraham notes that the stream on the west side of the present Girard Point is a "good place to obtain fresh water."

WASTE CREEK — about 2½ miles west of Girard Point, although not gazetted, is mentioned frequently in mining reports.

Between the mouth of Waste Creek and Girard Point a rough trail ran inland to the mining claim now known as the *Iron Duke*, which lay above the 1,000 foot level on the north slope of Waste Creek. The *Iron Duke* was first mentioned in mining reports of 1911 when it was noted that the property had been bonded through J.W.Sword to Western Steel Company of Irondale. By 1918 an 80-foot adit had been put in and a small amount of test pitting done. In 1961 Mr. Campbell-Robertson had a geological examination made of the showings and began to build a road into the property from the shore near Mathers Creek. Magnum Consolidated optioned the claims and did some test drilling. Later Silver Standard took out an option and did considerable testing in 1962.

*MATHERS CREEK — is the longest creek on Louise Island, with its headwaters well down into the southwest portion of the island, below Dass Lake. It flows in a northerly direction, emptying into the largest lake on Louise Island - named Mathers Lake in connection with the creek. From the lake

248

Hewn Log road used by the Kelley Logging Company trucks during World War 2 at Mathers Creek.

Photo - British Columbia Forest Service.

it begins again its inexorable search for sea level, sending out great branches at intervals as it turns and flows northeast and, emerging on the north shore of Louise Island, puts out a great sandbank heaped with boulders and gravel where it flows into Cumshewa Inlet.

Mathers Creek has been known by two other names, FALLS CREEK and, during World War II, CHURCH CREEK. The latter name given it by loggers who found remains of an old church nearby - the New Kloo church.

Named Mathers Creek by the Hydrographic Service, and this name confirmed by the Geographic Board in 1926, after John Mathers who came to the Charlottes in 1900 to look into the possibility of reopening the Cowgitz Coal Mine. When that did not appear feasible, young John Mathers went into partnership with the tempestuous Captain William Oliver. Oliver had been associated with the organization of an oilery in the Haida village of Skidegate. Sharp words between Oliver and the others one day made Oliver impulsively quit the operation on the spot, and he promptly bought out Bob Tennant's oilery project in the other Skidegate (now known as Skidegate Landing.) Oliver needed a partner to take over the active operation so he could concentrate on his main interest of evangelizing for the Methodist Church.

Johnny Mathers's connection with Oliver was to be even closer than partner, for he married Oliver's neice, Elizabeth Hall. The newly-wed Mathers lived at Skidegate for a few years, running the oilery, store, post office, sub-Mining Recorders's office and various other jobs in the small community, until 1907 when Mr. Mathers sold his interest in the oilery and moved with his family to Sandspit. The house he built at Sandspit in 1907 is still in use by members of his family today.

*MATHERS LAKE — at the 110-foot-level, lies northeast of Mount Kermode, and is about 2½ miles long. Mathers Creek runs into its south end and out of its north end. The lake was named in association with the creek.

NEW CLEW — also known as NEW KLUE, NEW KLOO, is the site chosen by the people of Tanu in 1887 for their new village when it was decided to abandon the site on the east end of Tanu Island. The houses for the new village were built near the mouth of Mathers Creek, a Raven Crest site owned by the people of Tanu.

A small church, store and oilery were added to the community under the guidance of Captain William Oliver who worked with Amos Russ and Thomas Crosby to aid the resettlement of the Tanu people. Oliver, however, lived in the community for the most part and took the active interest. Agnes Calder came from Tanu with her people, and worked for Oliver. In this calm girl, the stormy Oliver found the perfect counterpart to his impulsive nature. Her presence made his life more stable. The 23 years difference in their ages was an anguish to him, but after 2 years he mustered enough courage to ask her to marry him. They were married in 1896 and began life together in New Kloo. The next year the people of that village joined in the move of all outlying villages to Skidegate and the site on the north shore of Louise Island joined the roster of ghost towns.

The tombstones in the graveyard by Mathers Creek are poignant evidence that the sorrows of old Tanu had followed these villagers to the new location at New Kloo.

It was a pretty site for the village, with an attractive curving beach. Today it is being rapidly hidden in the lush second-growth which also encroaches on the clearing left by the logging operation conducted during the Second World War. In the middle of that clearing stands a tree with green lower limbs and a golden crown. It is thought to be one of the rare "golden spruces."

The beach at New Kloo has exquisite driftwood specimens. Small and beautifully shaped in an infinite variety, they are perfect for collectors who have a limited space.

Agnes Calder, of Tanu, and Captain William Oliver were married April 1896 and began their married life in New Clew.

Photo - Agnes Mathers.

*KITSON POINT — the northwest point of the bight into which Mathers Creek flows. Named after Jonathan Kitson who came to the Charlottes in 1905 and remained to take part in all aspects of pioneering. When the settlement of Queen Charlotte City was being established, Mr. Kitson built one of the first homes there. His eldest son, John went to the first school and the family took part in all community events. In 1910 Mr. Kitson, attracted to the possibility of farming at Sandspit, acquired land at Cape Chroustcheff where he built a comfortable frame home and cleared land for his ranch. It is appropriate that Kitson Point should be near Mathers Creek, for the Kitsons and Mathers were neighbours at Sandspit. Kitson Point was named in 1926.

*RENNER POINT — west of Kitson Point, on the north end of Louise Island, named in 1926 after Joe Renner by the Hydrographic Service.

Joe, born in Switzerland, had established a pre-emption at Lawn Hill by 1909. Like many homesteaders, he left his land to work elsewhere to earn a living. He was among those who worked at Tasu in 1913 and were unable to collect their pay when it shut down. In later years he married Mrs. Hubley, widow of a former Lawn Hill neighbour, Captain Hubley, and moved to the west end of Maude Island.

"They were very hospitable people," recalls Charlie Hartie of Queen Charlotte City, "and always had a batch of their 'sociable' ready for guests. It was desperate stuff. But if you didn't drink it they would be insulted." One day when she was busily boiling up a batch of the concoction Mrs. Renner upset the pot of scalding liquid over herself. Despite all that could be done she died of her burns. It was the finish of Joe - he never got over it. "That darn 'sociable' cost us two fine neighbours," says Mr. Hartie.

There are fossil sites at Renner Point and in the bay to the south of it.

*BEATTIE ANCHORAGE — southwest of Renner Point, 1¼ miles away, was named in 1926 by the Hydrographic Service after George D. Beattie, a pioneer of Queen Charlotte City.

Attracted by Windy Young's glowing advertisements in 1908, Mr. Beattie came to Queen Charlotte City to open the Islands' first drug store. His first small store stood next to the big Lauder Hotel. Later he engaged Mr. Barge and Jonathan Kitson to build his second and permanent store on the corner of Beach Road and Second Street. It is still in use - although not as a drug store.

Mr. Beattie became the first postmaster for the new townsite and married Emmanuel Girard's pretty daughter, Azeline. He found life on the Charlottes so much to his liking he remained to live out his life in the town he pioneered. despite the slim times which followed in later years - and which caused many other pioneers to join the migration south.

Beattie Anchorage was used extensively as a rafting ground during the days of Davis Raft construction.

North entrance to Carmichael Passage, off Cumshewa Inlet. Photo taken in October, 1944 shows a Davis Raft under construction at Beattie Anchorage. Bare Peak at top of photo on right is Newcombe Peak, formerly known as Kyhita.

Photo - B.C. Forest Service.

252

CHAPTER TWELVE

*CUMSHEWA INLET — north of Louise Island, received its name from the white fur traders, whose custom was to name a region after the most important chief of the area. In the early years it had the usual variety of spellings all Haida words received. Robert Haswell writing in the log of the *Columbia* called it TOOSCONDOLTH SOUND. Ingraham thought CUMMASHAWAAS was nearer when he drew his sketch map in 1791. Herbert Carmichael in making his mining report in 1902 said GUMSHEWA. The 1878 spelling of CUMSHEWA used by G.M. Dawson was officially adopted.

Fur traders made the inlet a regular port of call and many a rich harvest of pelts was taken aboard after a vigorous bargaining led by Eagle Crest Chief Go'mshewah. Like the Haidas of Skedans, the Cumshewa people did not engage to any extent in tribal wars with other Haidas. However, when Koyah from the Houston Stewart Channel engaged in his vendetta against the whites, he received some help from the Cumshewas.

The first white blood ran in Cumshewa in a gory massacre in July 1794 when the Haidas overpowered and killed Captain Burlington and all but one of the 11-man crew of the schooner *Resolution*. A sailor named Beyers escaped the slaughter by hiding in the rigging. He was later discovered and made a slave, to be ransomed the next year. Koyah initiated and led this attack, but he had willing assistance from some of the Cumshewas.

After the attack they plundered, then burned, the ship. When Francis Poole visited Cumshewa village in 1862 he saw the flag of the *Resolution* prominently displayed in one of the lodges, as well as yellowing linen said to have come

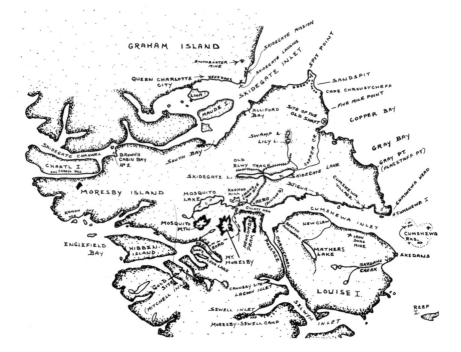

off that ship.

Koyah was killed in 1795, but now that the Cumshewas had tasted wealth by battle instead of laborious trading - they would try again. They made an attempt on the *Phoenix*, but were driven off. One sailor was killed, however, and the captain moved nearer shore to open fire, only to be met with cannon fire himself - booty from the *Resolution*. The *Phoenix* was forced to withdraw.

When in 1796 the *Sea Otter* put in to trade at Cumshewa she, too, fell victim. Captain Stephen Hill and the purser and steward, Elliott and Daggett, were killed. Mate William Bowles had to take command.

Two years later Captain Asa Dodge brought the *Alexander* into the big inlet to trade and got into a fight with the Cumshewas. Three of his men were killed, but he retaliated in killing 10 Haidas and managed to take several prisoners. The ransom price offered for the prisoners was 3 white scalps - a grisly reminder of the fate of the officers from the *Sea Otter*.

But Cumshewa, rich-at-the-mouth-inlet, has other more pleasant contributions to make to the pattern of Queen Charlotte Islands heritage. Her waters abound with fish, her hillsides support lush timber - or did. Great logging scars testify to how highly it is prized for the insatiable mills of the south. Her shores have seen innumerable wildlife and fowl. Ancient midden signs show many of her coves were chosen as favorite camping and village sites for her Haidas.

The last chapter traced the bays and points of this great inlet along the north shore of Louise Island, and ended at Beattie Anchorage. This chapter continues from there.

254

OLIVER ISLET — wooded and about 115 feet high, is northwest of Beattie Anchorage. Named in 1926 by the Hydrographic Service after William Oliver. Born in March 1848 in Bishopston, Scotland, Mr. Oliver was only 11 when the family moved to Dumbarton on the Clyde. Between jobs as a rivet boy in the shipyards, he managed to pick up a smattering of education in school.

His hard-working parents enjoyed a "wee tot" frequently and saw no harm in the boy joining in. When he was 16, Oliver became apprenticed to the trade of ship's carpenter. He loved the work and, to enable him to understand more fully, took night classes at the end of the long days work. He also retained his fondness for the "wee tot".

Working on the ships, the lad felt he could never he happy until he sailed on one - could feel the lift of a bow, the sting of salt spray. As soon as his apprenticeship finished he left the land and shipped to sea. Hard-working and ingenious, he became a valued member of the crew. But his time ashore was a wild spree of drinking and carousing. Several times his ships left without him. When this happened during a trip to Victoria he decided to stay ashore. It did not solve his problem. His skilled hands easily found work in southern mainland shipyards, but he rarely drew a sober breath.

During one especially bad session he met Reverend Ebenezer Robson of Mary Street Methodist Church in New Westminster. Robson, a sympathetic and practical listener helped Oliver out of the morass, and at last he broke free of his demon. He decided to dedicate his life to helping the church to which Robson belonged.

Always a practical man, Oliver began by offering to donate his skill. He would build the boat so badly-needed by Thomas Crosby for his missionary work on the north coast. The *Glad Tidings* built in New Westminster in 1884 remained in service along the B.C. coast for more than 20 years. Crosby was skipper and Oliver served as engineer. Later when Crosby went to another mission, Oliver took over as skipper. Every missionary who ever sailed with Captain Oliver noted his urge to arise early in the morning, Said one, "I can't understand how it is that the tide is always right for Captain Oliver at 4 a.m."

The *Glad Tidings* was wrecked in 1903 during a gale in Queen Charlotte Sound when being towed south by the *Boscowitch* for engine repairs. She drifted ashore on a rocky beach and for years the whitened timbers of the little "Come to Jesus ship", as the Indians called her, could be seen by passing vessels.

Oliver was offered a job as first officer on the *Boscowitch*, but his heart lay in mission work. He had been connected with the oileries at New Klue, and in the Haida village of Skidegate, then later at what is now Skidegate Landing, when he joined partnership with John Mathers. Finally he moved to Sandspit and, to engage more fully in his missionary work, built another boat, the *Udal*, using his own funds entirely. It was wrecked in Portland Inlet in 1908. The Church, impressed with Oliver's sincerity, bought another ship for him to use, the *Homespun*. Over the years other boats were to follow, The Thomas Crosby I, II, and III, the latter being built at Sandspit by Oliver.

In 1929 the Captain was 81 years old and it seemed best for him to retire from the arduous work of running a boat in all weathers in north coast waters. Old as he was, Oliver never did really retire, but began to build another mission boat at Sandspit, this time for the west coast of Vancouver Island. When finished she was named the *Melvin Swartout* and sent to Bamfield. Captain Oliver died in 1937.

*BARGE POINT — west of Oliver Islet, is the south entrance point to Gillatt Arm. Named in 1926 by the Hydrographic Service after John L. Barge who had been a carpenter in Victoria when he read D.R. "Windy" Young's advertisements in 1908 about possibilities on the Charlottes. He chose his homesite near the beach to the west of the mill, built a cabin and sent for his family For the next 20 years Mr. Barge made an active contribution to the town with his carpentry shop and served at various times as Government Agent, Mining Recorder, Road Superintendent and, during emergencies, accepted the duties of undertaker. His children attended the first school in the newly-formed townsite of Queen Charlotte City.

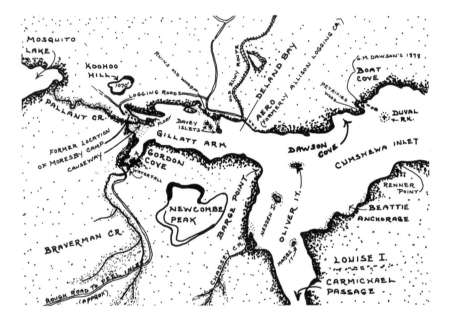

*NEWCOMBE PEAK — the majestic 3,445-foot mountain lying to the southwest of Barge Point formerly had a lilting Haida name - a modification of which is Kyhita. (What is now Chadsey Creek at the entrance to Carmichael Passage was known to the Haidas by the same name as the mountain). In 1926 Kyhita was renamed for Dr. C.F. Newcombe, the anthropologist who made many valuable contributions to the history of the Charlottes. The reason for renaming this mountain is unclear - there are numerous unnamed peaks in this region which would have served equally well to honour Dr. Newcombe.

Dr. Newcombe, born in 1851 at Newcastle-on-Tyne and married in 1878, had been married only twelve years when his wife died, leaving him with six children - one an infant. At that time he lived in Victoria, having moved there from Oregon where he had gone shortly after his marriage to practice medicine. The large country area covered during his rounds made him aware of the interesting flora and fauna. When he found Indian arrowheads his casual interest became much more. By the time he came to Victoria, medicine was quickly losing to his new ambition - to make an anthropological collection. He had become alarmed that the decay of culture and handicrafts among native people would result in complete loss.

Newcombe contributions are now the most impressive objects in great anthropological collections. One of his sons, William, accompanied his father and, absorbing the elder Newcombe's knowledge became, in later years, almost as well-known as the doctor. Both Newcombes knew Island waters well. In 1924 while travelling in the area, Dr. Newcombe became seriously ill, but could not get immediate transportation home. By the time he finally did arrive in Victoria, it was too late. He died October 19, 1924, at 73 years of age.

*GILLATT ARM — at the west end of Cumshewa Inlet. Formerly called WEST ARM, a name given it by Dr. G.M. Dawson in 1878. With many duplications of that term, the Hydrographic Service renamed it in 1926 for a pioneer of Sandspit. Captain Gillatt had been living in Port Simpson with his wife and two daughters, Belle and Peggy, when he met Captain Oliver. Hearing William Oliver's glowing description of Sandspit, Captain Gillatt packed up his family and moved to Sandspit in September 1911.

He built a large home where the Islander Hotel now stands, laid out a ranch complete with chickens, cattle, riding ponies and prepared to enjoy life to the full. They were an active family and there were always picnics and parties at the least excuse when the Gillatts lived at the Spit. He assisted the Hydrographic Service for a time by undertaking the tide-watching project in early years.

*GORDON COVE — at the head of Gillatt arm, off the south side. Named in 1926 after Mr. A.J. Gordon. When Gordon first came to the Charlottes is not known, but he was a resident of Skidegate Landing in 1908. Elected first president of the Graham Island Settlers' Association which was formed that November, active politically and socially, his name appears regularly in early Queen Charlotte newspapers. For some years he ran the store at the oilery in Skidegate Landing, taking over from William leary when Leary moved to Miller Creek.

Among his other interests he was bitten by the mining bug. In 1910 he and John McLellan bought the site of the Southeaster Mine from the Haidas and established a camp about 1 mile inland from the beach. Later, in 1932-33 he was listed as one of the directors of the company hoping to reactivate the mine at Gold Harbour.

"Only ill-health in his later years would have ever induced 'A.J.' to move away," say those who remember him, "but he had to have medical treatment he couldn't get here. He was a staunch Conservative and liked nothing better than a vigorous argument with an equally staunch Liberal."

There are fossils at a site near the east entrance point to the cove.

*BRAVERMAN CREEK — flows into the head of Gordon Cove. This creek has falls near its mouth and is a fine place to obtain drinking water from a small boat at the right stage of the tide. The pool above the first falls is a good place for campers to do laundry.

Named in 1926 after a B.C. pioneer who, like Mrs. Chadsey (Chadsey Creek) took part in the big 1924 reunion of pioneers in Victoria. Isidor Braverman was born in Pleschen Poland, in September 1829. He migrated to Victoria in 1858 and was 95 years old when he took part in the reunion. A man who certainly must have made a contribution to the growth and history of the young Province of British Columbia.

A rough road which goes out to the west coast from Cumshewa Inlet, runs along the valley of Braverman Creek for several miles before turning west to emerge at Peel Inlet. The road is only suitable for properly equipped vehicles.

*MOUNT MORESBY — is the highest mountain on Moresby Island. Its summit rises to a little over 3,800 feet to the west of Braverman Creek and south of Mosquito Lake. Named after Admiral Fairfax Moresby, for whom Moresby Island is also named. Name of the mountain confirmed in 1964.

*MOSQUITO MOUNTAIN — lies due west of Mount Moresby and the name was applied to the maps in the early 1960s. It towers over the southwest part of Mosquito Lake and received its name in this association.

*MOSQUITO LAKE — about 4 miles long and in places about a mile across, contains several islets. Located in a parklike setting, except that the hillsides have been ruthlessly logged and left in the usual mess. The name has been on maps since 1909, although frequently shown by a modification of its Haida name, KALLAHIN. (The Ga'oquns of Dr. Newcombe.)

*PALLANT CREEK — drains Mosquito Lake into the head of Gillatt Arm. Haida legends say that this was the home of the greatest of all Creek-Women, Djila'qons, a grandmother of the Eagle Crest people. (In Haida legends Ocean-Spirits were usually male. Their female counterparts were the Creek-Women. All important fish streams had a Creek-Woman living at the head. It is to see her that the salmon and other fish run up, but all die before reaching her dwelling place - except steelhead and mountain trout.)

Djila'qons was not native to the Charlottes, her mate brought her from a mainland inlet. One story says she came from the Naas region and another from Bella Bella. She was placed in Ga'oquns Creek, at the head of Cumshewa Inlet. Ga'oquns meant "of the great inlet." Ten children were born to them, one of which became Greatest-Mountain, ancestress of the Eagles of Ninstints.

Early maps refer to Pallant Creek as KALLAHIN, the same name as was applied to Mosquito Lake, this is a modification of Haida name which Dr. Newcombe shows as GA'OQUNS.

In 1926 the Hydrographic Service named the creek after Mr. A.C. Pallant who came to the Charlottes in 1907. Working on a Humphries, Tupper and Rice survey enabled him to see a great deal of Graham Island. He found it challenging and satisfying. Deciding to become a homesteader he chose a site at Tlell, carefully pacing out the desired land. When the Government

Mr. A.C. Pallant stands at back of group beside well-known Haida Joe Grey,
his mother, and wife of Dr. Pallant, stands in front beside Captain John Haan.
The Pallant's Chinese cook, standing on left, was delighted when Mrs. Pallant showed
him how to make brandy sauce - so much so that for the first while the family had brandy in almost
everything they ate, cakes, puddings, vegetables and so on, until the novelty wore off.

Photo - Agnes Mathers.

"Cap" Davey on right, wearing bowler hat, talks with Jimmy Campbell, left,
who printed Windy Young's paper, and Dr. Winters on verandah of the Queen Charlotte
hospital in 1912. For years the scarlet-beaked oyster-catchers
known locally as "Cap Daveys"
in remembrance of the beetroot coloured nose which was Cap Davey's distinguishing feature.

Photo - Mrs. Benny Cromp.

survey lines were put through, he learned he had chosen land already taken for the most part, and the rest, according to his description, lay out in Hecate Strait. His father, a dentist from London, England, had bought the big Cood house at Sandspit. Knowing he couldn't run the big place himself, he urged his son to "come on down." When Dr. Pallant died, Cecil Pallant fell heir to the entire place. [1]

There are extensive mud flats off the mouth of Pallant Creek which entirely fill the small cove into which it empties. The Rayonier Camp, now at the head of Sewell Inlet, formerly stood on a spit on the north side of the mouth of Pallant Creek. A causeway has been built to connect the spit with a rock ledge at the edge of deep water, to provide adequate moorage facilities for the camp. facilities for the camp.

During the 1940s this was the site of the J.R. Morgan Logging Company camp. The Morgan logging operation necessitated the installation of a sawmill to cut lumber for the plank road they built to Mosquito Lake. The plank road followed Pallant Creek for the most part and was used in connection with the logging from the lake to the inlet.

[1] Mr. Pallant's story is contained more fully in Q.C. Islands, Vol. 1.

MORESBY CAMP — formerly at the head of Cumshewa Inlet, now moved to Sewell Inlet, and commonly called Moresby-Sewell camp today.

*KOOHOO HILL** — northwest of the old Moresby Camp site, is 1,070 feet high. Named by the Hydrographic Service in 1964, Koohoo is a modification of the Haida name for marten, frequently observed near the hill.

*DAVEY ISLETS** — off the north shore of Gillatt Arm, consist of 2 treed islets, with a drying rock close off. The larger islet, 52 feet high, is connected to the shore by a drying bank and there are fossil sites in the vicinity, along the shoreline at the head of the drying bank.

The islets were named after "Cap" Davey, a Cornishman with a beetroot coloured nose. As well as running the Land Office in Queen Charlotte City in early years, he was a Notary Public and ranched on Maude Island. For years the scarlet-beaked oyster-catchers have been known locally as "Cap Daveys" in remembrance of his scarlet nose.

*DELAND BAY** — named in 1962 by the Hydrographic Service is the bay the old Aero Camp faced. Origin of the name is not confirmed. The logging railroad had its base at the head of Deland Bay and the camp connected with the operation lay on the east part of the shoreline fringing the bay.

*AERO** — now abandoned. The name given to the settlement formerly on the east shore of Deland Bay near the entrance to Gillatt Arm. Originally the site of the A.P. Allison Logging Camp which had the distinction of operating the only railway on the Queen Charlotte Islands. A locomotive and flat cars for transporting logs ran along tracks laid from salt water to Skidegate Lake, with spurs from that point leading east, west and north.

During World War II the Crown Corporation of Aero purchased Allison's

*Logging train hauling timber for Allison's Camp
at Cumshewa Inlet.*

Photo - British Columbia Forest Service.

camp to log aeroplane spruce. But by the time a post office opened under
the name of Aero on October 23, 1948, the camp was no longer a Crown
Corporation operation, having been bought by Powell River Company at cessation
of hostilities. They got a bargain. For $90,000 Powell River Company not
only acquired the entire assets of this camp, but also the other Crown camp,
Aero of Juskatla, which had even greater potential.

By 1967 the Cumshewa Aero camp was completely abandoned - only a few
derelict buildings, twisted track and the inevitable logging debris remained.
Vandals and weather soon made short work of anything that had been habitable.

*DAWSON COVE — to the east of the old Aero camp by about 2 miles.
Named in 1948 by the Hydrographic Service after George M. Dawson. It is
commonly supposed that this is the BOAT COVE shown on Dawson's map
of 1878, but a close examination of Dawson's small sketch map shows this to
be an error. The Boat Cove of Dawson's map has rocks and islets in it and
is, therefore, the bay to the northeast of what is now Dawson Cove.

BOAT COVE — this is Dr. Dawson's name for the cove lying northeast

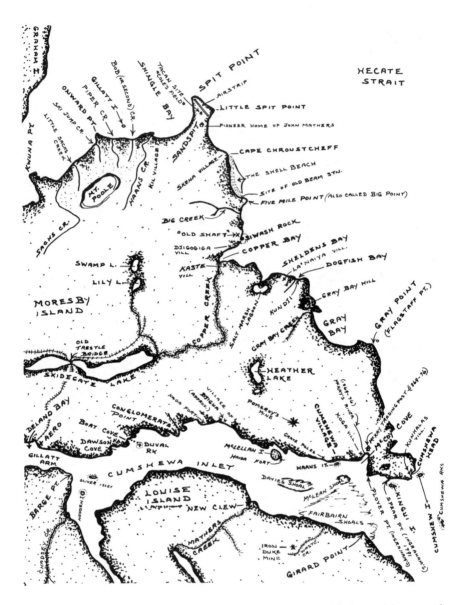

of what is now Dawson Cove. There are fossils and petrified wood in several places on the peninsula separating the two coves. One of the distinguishing features of Boat Cove is the string of islets and bare rocks which stretch from the shoreline, like a finger, pointing to Duval Rock.

*DUVAL ROCK — off the north shore of Cumshewa Inlet, at the end of a string of islets and bare rocks as mentioned above. Duval Rock has a depth of less than 6 feet over it and received its name in April 1926 from the Hydrographic Service. Named after Mr. Archie Duval.

Mr. Duval, born in Ontario in 1878, spend his early years in Revelstoke, Nelson and Vernon, working as a carpenter. He came to the Charlottes in 1908 to work for a group doing considerable opening up of mining claims in Mitchell Inlet (Gold Harbour), which were owned by John McLellan. He left the Charlottes that fall, but came back the following year to live on the Islands for the rest of his life. His wife, Lottie, was a nurse in the Queen Charlotte hospital when they were married in 1910. The Duvals built their home in Charlotte City and took part in all aspects of pioneering and community life.

* **CONGLOMERATE POINT** — is the middle point of 3 similar peninsulas which jut from the north shore of Cumshewa Inlet, midway between Aero and McLellan Island. Conglomerate Point is steep and rises abruptly to a summit of 320 feet. It is a fossil locality. A stream flows into the bay on the east side of Conglomerate Point, and at low tide that bay is completely filled by a drying flat. Midden signs indicate Haida occupancy in ancient years.

Conglomerate Point was named in 1878 by Dr. Dawson for its physical characteristic. About 1925 the name of GIFFORD POINT was suggested after Mr. Gifford G. Gray, wireless operator at Dead Tree Point for 7 years, but the name was not adopted.

DJIGUA VILLAGE — lay between Conglomerate Point and McLellan Island, with a fort site located a little to the west of it. Djigua was the ancient Eagle Crest village destroyed by fire under mysterious circumstances, according to legend.

One day the sons of the Town Chief of Djigua went to Ga'oguns (Pallant Creek) to fish. There were five boys in the canoe and all were successful, catching a fine string of trout. Lighting a fire they roasted a few before turning in for the night at a camping site along the edge of the creek. They were eating their fish when one boy noticed a large frog near the fire and on an impulse threw it into the flames. As it burned, it exploded with a large bang. The flames parted and lo! there was the frog - unharmed. Again coals were heaped on it and again it exploded - then appeared later, unharmed.

They built a huge fire all round it and over and over tried to destroy this "thing." But always with the same result. Eventually they gave up and went to sleep.

When they walked to the mouth of the creek in the morning and climbed into the canoe to go home, someone called to them from the point nearby saying, "Wait. I have a message." They stopped in surprise for they realized they could see right through the stranger's body. "One by one you will die," said the stranger, "at each point you pass on your way home. Only the boy in the stern will be saved - but he too will die as soon as he reaches home and tells the story."

"Foolish old man," muttered the boys, "what nonsense he talks." But they were uneasy. And during the dreadful trip home - it happened as he predicted. The people of Djigua were apprehensive. This was indeed bad. But the children were sent to play at the fort west of the town as was the custom. They came home saying they had seen a supernatural woman. At another playing place other strange beings were seen. The men out fishing could catch nothing. Steam rose from the surface of the inlet and burning coals dropped from the sky. Finally the town of Djigua began to burn and all save one woman were destroyed in the fire. It is said that people of Djigua visiting elsewhere also died mysteriously at this time.

The woman who survived fled around the coastline to Sandspit, where she met a man and went with him to live on the mainland. Years later she returned to the Charlottes, bringing with her seven of her children, three boys and four girls. From these women a subsequent branch of the Eagle Crest tribes stemmed. People of this branch could be found at Scotsgai Beach, near Skidegate, Kaisun, Skedans, Tanu, McKay's Harbour as well as in the village of Cumshewa.

The town of Djigua lay in ruins never to be reoccupied, for it was believed that its annihilation had been caused by the wrath of Djila'qons the Creek-Woman (at Pallant Creek), as she sought retribution for the actions of the young fishermen bent on destroying, wantonly, a creature under her charge.

Mr. and Mrs. John McLellan.

Photo - Mr. A.C. Pallant..

*McLELLAN ISLAND — connected to Moresby Island by a drying bank, is 305 feet high and on early maps was shown as a peninsula - not an island. It lies east of Conglomerate Point and almost directly north of the New Klue village site on Louise Island. The Haidas had a fort on McLellan Island in ancient years.

Named in 1926 by the Hydrographic Service after John McLellan, a former B.C. assayer who, in 1906, staked the property covering the old H.B.C. gold site at Mitchell Inlet (Gold Harbour). Originally from London, Ontario, Mr. McLellan and another mining engineer, F.J. Bourne of Cobalt, acquired the property and began developing it in 1907. They found no gold in the old H.B.C. workings, but did locate a small rich vein in nearby quartz.

Naming it the *Early Bird*, they soon had a crew of men employed (among them, Archie Duval - Duval Rock) and by 1910 had a three-stamp mill in operation. McLellan did well in the operation of the mine and that same year joined with A.J. Gordon of Skidegate to develop the Southeaster Mine, north of Skidegate. This proved an unsuccessful venture. When he married pretty Leslie Baraclough who taught in the small school at Queen Charlotte City, Mr. McLellan built a house on the east end of Lina Island, Skidegate Inlet, which drew much admiration.

In the cove east of McLellan Island, a wagon road, built in 1913, led to another gold mining prospect about 1½ miles from the shore.

The story of this find goes back to about 1896-97, when a man named Lynch called in to see Sam Pierce who worked at the New Klue oilery. Lynch showed Pierce a lump of ore which he said assayed to a fabulous value. Sam knew little about minerals, but Lynch seemed to be an honest man. Lynch said he had found the ore "across the bay" and pointed to the present McLellan Island. When he returned to stake his find though, he could never locate the site of his ledge again and it became, like Mulkley's (of Shuttle Island) one of the "lost mines" of the Charlottes.

James Johnstone and E.S. Topping came from the southern interior to see what created all the interest in mining circles on the Islands and in 1907 announced that they had found Lynch's Ledge. Topping, a great promotor, had no difficulty in finding speculators. In 1908 half of the property called the *Go East* was bonded to a Victoria group and the other section, *Homestake* given serious consideration. In 1910 Topping looked for greener fields and persuaded an English syndicate to buy them out. The Queen Charlotte Mining and Prospecting Company came into being and two tunnels begun. By 1911 ten men were employed, buildings erected and Charles E. Pomeroy appointed superintendent, with J.W. Austin as assayer.

By 1913 the wagon road was put in, 12 men were on the payroll, 600 feet of tunnels in and ore being "sacked" with - of course - high values reported. By 1914 only five men were working and things were off peak. Prospects did not look at all promising. It came to be known locally as "Pomeroy's Mine." The Stevens family were also connected with its early days.

*CUMSHEWA VILLAGE — lay about 2 miles east of McLellan Island. Known as HLKENUL, this was the home of Chief Go'mshewah, the leading chief of the inlet. An Eagle Crest town, it contained a complement of Raven Crest lodges as well - customary in all larger Haida villages. There were two rows of houses, estimated to have totalled about 21 by Dr. J.R. Swanton. The Sky-House of the town chief stood about the centre of the back row and had a magnificent view of the inlet.

A creek flows through the village site which had a name meaning to-stand-in-water-and-dip-oneself-entirely-under.

When Dawson visited the village in 1878 there were still a few people living

Cumshewa Gold Mine in 1910. Known locally as Pomeroy's Mine, the tunnels connected with the venture were about 1 1/2 miles in from the shoreline.

Photo - Provincial Archives, Victoria.

Photo taken 1970 from the graveyard of Cumshewa Village. Haans Islet lies left centre, with the islands off Skedans in the distance.

Photo - Cliff Armstrong.

there, but Cumshewa was long past its prime. Dawson estimated from 12 to 14 houses remained, many showing advanced decay. In the 1890s these villagers joined with the Skedans and New Klue people in the final move to Skidegate. The old Cumshewa village was used only as a seasonal fishing camp. Today it is part of a Haida Reserve containing 56 acres. The vigorous second growth spruce strives to enfold the ruins of the house timbers and few remaining poles - now almost obliterated by weather and normal decay. But the same aura of dignity exists in Cumshewa as is felt in other abandoned Haida villages.

*HAANS ISLET — connected to the shoreline in front of Cumshewa Village by a drying spit. Named VILLAGE ISLAND by Dr. Dawson in 1878, it was renamed in 1926 by the Hydrographic Service owing to numerous duplications of that name. Named after Captain John Haan, pioneer of the Islands.

Captain Haan had skippered schooners sailing out of Victoria as far as the Bering Sea in the early 1900s when employed by a fur sealing company. *Umbrina* and *Jessie* were two he served on. When fur sealing ended, he joined the C.P.R., taking charge of the *Lorne* towing sail-boats from Cape Flattery to Victoria. Then in 1907 he and Simon Leiser bought the oilery at Skidegate Landing and Captain Haan brought his 85 foot steam tug *Ranger*, with Billy Rhineheart aboard, to fish dogfish for the oilery.

When the oilery failed after a few years Captain Haan bought a smaller boat, the *Wee Jeannie*, which was soon in much demand for charter trips. The Olivers and Mathers, relatives of Mrs. Haan, were living in Sandspit - which looked to Captain Haan like a fine place to raise his large family. About 1911-12 they moved to a homesite near the creek in Sandspit which now bears their name. In later years they moved to Queen Charlotte City, when Captain Haan went to work for Pacific Mills running their launch *Dot*. He died suddenly in 1940. His three sons, Jack, Peter and Charlie, all followed the sea - well-known captains in northern waters.

*DAVIES SHOAL — lies about the centre of Cumshewa Inlet near the mouth, and is southeast of McLellan Island. There is a least depth over the shoal of 18 feet and thick kelp is often present over it, especially during summer months. Joseph Ingraham in 1791 showed it on his sketch map, and noted he had found 'fine sand' at that place in his soundings.

Named in 1926 by the Hydrographic Service after Captain A.M. Davies who commanded the *Prince John* for a time, and who later became Examiner for Masters and Mates at Victoria.

*FAIRBAIRN SHOALS — due south of Cumshewa Village, cover an extensive area. From Girard Point they spread westward for about 1½ miles, then outward and northward to within a 1/2 mile of the shore off Haans Islet. A rock drying at 8 feet is near the centre of the shoals which are usually covered with thick kelp in the summer months. They were first shown on Ingraham's 1791 chart of Cummashawaas Harbour.

The shoals were named in 1926 after Howard Fairbairn, another well remembered pioneer of early days. Mr. Fairbairn came to the Islands with Clarence Johnston in 1911 to hand-log. Soon afterwards the two men purchased the tugs *Aimee* and *Edwin* and had more business than they knew how to handle. Mr. Johnston married Mrs. Fairbairn's sister and the two friends became brothers-in-law.

Few people knew the coastline of the Charlottes better than Mr. Fairbairn. During his many years as Fishery Protection Officer he spent much time on the west coast and named, so appropriately, several features on that coast such as PIPE ORGAN ROCK, CATHEDRAL BAY, HIPPA FANGS, CHIEF SKELU and, at Langara Island, the MOTHER-OF-THE-FLEET rock.

*McLEAN SHOAL — a gravel shoal with a least depth of 11 feet, it is at the northern extremity of Fairbairn Shoal and is about opposite the east end of the old village of Cumshewa: Named in 1926 by the Hydrographic Service after Captain Neil McLean, who skippered the *Prince John* for a time, but is much better remembered on Island runs as master of the *Prince Charles*, pride of the C.N. boats on the Charlotte route.

*McCOY COVE — lies east of the old Cumshewa site and has a stream flowing into the northwest portion of its head. Shown as BERRY COVE in 1791 by Joseph Ingraham. The following year Robert Haswell, commanding the *Adventure,* named the bay HOPE COVE and wrote of having anchored off it and noting that, "it is the first cove on the north side of Tooscondolth (Cumshewa) Sound, after passing the barren island."

It is probably best known, historically, as McKAY'S HARBOUR, after Captain Hugh McKay. McKay, associated with William Spring of Sooke, on Vancouver Island, bought the trading schooner *Favourite* in 1868 and entered the sealing industry - rounding out his many other interests. The *Byzantium* under Captain Calhoun also fished the coastal waters. The two men thought it would be an excellent idea to establish a shore base in the Charlotte Islands to facilitate supplies and possibly engage in some trading with the Indians.

Under McKay's direction Calhoun took a party of men to build a small post in the cove east of Cumshewa village. Laying in a good supply of trade goods, McKay engaged Mr. Hargreaves to run the base for him. It remained in operation until about 1874 or 76, but when Dawson visited the bay in 1878 it had closed down. The store building appeared to be still in good repair. Dawson referred to the bay as McKAY'S COVE.

Renamed McCOY COVE by the Hydrographic Service in 1921 after a fireman on board the *Lillooet* which made a survey of this area.

The remains of the old store may be found on the east side of the stream, in the grassy clearing.

KOGA VILLAGE (Qa'gal) — a Raven Crest site on one side of the stream entering the head of McCoy Cove. These villagers were inveterate gamblers and not too successful. In one gambling spree with a Raven family from Skedans, they gambled and lost, time after time, until all they had left for the "pot" was themselves. They lost that game, too, and became the property of the Skedans family.

STAWAS VILLAGE — the Eagle Crest village on the opposite side of the stream at McCoy Cove. These people had formerly lived at Cumshewa Village before going to Tasu for a time, when one of their women married a chief there. It was at the potlatch connected with this wedding that tattooing was first initiated. When the relatives of the woman returned to Cumshewa Inlet they chose a location across the creek from the Raven family. It happened to be a favorite haunt of screech-owls. The owls set up such a racket one of the Raven Crest boys declared that their neighbours ought to be called the Witch-People, witch being also the word used for screech-owl. The name stuck and, when they moved back to live in the old village of Cumshewa, was applied not only to them, but to all Eagle families in Cumshewa village as well.

PLOVER POINT — at the east entrance to McCoy Cove is unnamed on maps of today, which seems strange since the Hydrographic Service have an important range light on it, plus a red spar buoy off it, to aid in the difficult navigation of this part of Cumshewa Inlet. The name PLOVER POINT was applied in 1791-92 by Joseph Ingraham, but the name did not appear on any other navigator's maps. There was no village at McCoy Cove at that time, according to Ingraham's map.

*KINGUI ISLAND — with a navigational light on its west end, lies near the mouth of Cumshewa Inlet, and is connected to the shore by a drying ridge. Named in 1878 by Dr. Dawson who wrote, "It bristles with dead trees." Joseph Ingraham in 1791-92 called the island WORNOUT ISLAND.

SPEAR POINT — appears to be the name Ingraham gave to the point from which the drying ridge extends from Moresby to Kingui Island. The name applies to the Moresby Island side of the ridge and is only shown on Ingraham's maps.

*CUMSHEWA HEAD — is the north entrance point of Cumshewa Inlet. Named about 1860. Some geological maps show it as CUMSHEWA POINT.

KUNHALAS VILLAGE — an Eagle Crest site which lay inside the point at Cumshewa Head, opposite Cumshewa Island. Long abandoned, the lodges were in ruins when Dawson visited it in 1878. He felt it had not been an important village.

*CUMSHEWA ISLAND — lying off Cumshewa Head and first shown on the 1852 sketch map made by Captain T. Sinclair for the Hudson's Bay Company. About 50 feet high and quite conspicuous from the north, the island is described by Dawson in his report as "a barren rock."

*CUMSHEWA ROCKS — are a widely scattered group lying between 1/2 to 1½ miles southeast of Cumshewa Island. They dry anywhere from 3 to 22 feet. Named by Dr. G.M. Dawson in 1878.

*GRAY POINT — five miles northwest of Cumshewa Head, was named by the Hydrographic Service about 1925 in association with Gray Bay to the north. Locally this is known as FLAGSTAFF POINT, acquiring the name from a Hydrographic survey marker placed there some years ago. Strong tides swirl off Gray Point at certain stages, making it an uncomfortable place for small boats to pass sometimes.

In 1970 tenders were called for construction of a Loran Station at Gray Point. When fully operational it will be one of the master stations in the Long Range Navigation system of the Telecommunications Branch of the Department of Transport.

*GRAY BAY — curving west and north from Gray Point has a beautiful stretch of sand beach for picnics, but all this part of the coast is a mariner's headache as shallow water extends well offshore. Not known when it was named but shown by this name on Dawson's 1878 map.

GRAY BAY HILL — a local name for the steep hill on the peninsula which juts out at the north end of Gray Bay. During logging operations in this area, loggers frequently referred to it as BURMA HILL, and the name still occasionally is heard. A climb to the top of this hill is well worth the effort, for the view is superlative.

GRAY BAY CREEK — enters Gray Bay at the foot of Gray Bay Hill.

GEORGE LEARY MEMORIAL BRIDGE — this item is being included because of numerous queries as to its origin, not because it is a place name in the usual sense. The bridge crosses Gray Bay Creek near the foot of Gray Bay Hill, and is at the entrance to the road leading to the Gray Bay Loran site. Sandspit residents say the sign was placed on the bridge by a Ministry of Transport employee who named the structure for himself. Mr. Leary, who makes his home in Burnaby, was employed during the survey of the road to the Loran site.

*HEATHER LAKE — lies about 3 miles to the southwest of Gray Bay Hill. It is about a mile long and has a smaller, unnamed lake lying to the south. Named between 1927 and 1954, the origin of the name is unknown.

*DOGFISH BAY — is a bight at the southeast end of Sheldens Bay. It is about 3½ miles northwest of Gray Point. Dogfish Bay goes dry and there is a large boulder bank close offshore.

As far as is known the name began in the pioneering days just after the turn of the century and is of local origin. One of the earliest settlers was George Shabot who, with Eddie Stevens, fell heir to the big Cood house and ranch at Sandspit. [1] Shabot, suspicious of the whole thing, took his share of the cattle and moved to Dogfish Bay about 1907, or possibly earlier. He was joined in later years by several other settlers and for years the remains of a dam and cabins could be seen encircling the shoreline of this bay. A creek runs into the head of Dogfish Bay.

[1] This story is in Q.C. Islands, Volume 1, pages 239, 240.

KUNDJI VILLAGE — stood on the east side of the creek coming into the head of Dogfish Bay. A Raven Crest site, the tribe was known as people-of-the-town-where-they-always-give-away-food. They occupied sites all along this coast from Gray Bay to Alliford Bay.

*SHELDENS BAY — between Dogfish Bay and Copper Bay is where Captain and Mrs. Shelden built their cabin and homesteaded.

LA'NAIYA VILLAGE — according to Dr. Newcombe's map, was on the shore of Sheldens Bay, and lay between Dogfish Bay and Salt Marsh Lagoon.

SALT MARSH LAGOON — towards the west part of Sheldens Bay is a triangular bight which dries at low water. At the head of this bight a short stream flows onto the beach from a tidal lagoon close inland. About 1909 Mr. and Mrs. Norman Fraser (Ma and Pa Fraser) settled on the shoreline of the lagoon from which the stream originated. Their hospitality made it a natural gathering place for settlers along this part of Moresby, and the tidal lagoon became known as FRASER'S LAGOON, a name it held for many years.

However, with a young family of school age, the Frasers had to leave their homesite and move to a settlement with a school. Moving first to Queen Charlotte City, Norman worked in the mill and Mrs. Fraser ran the mill boarding house. During the Doughty boom of 1912, they bought de Pape's hotel at Skidegate Landing and expanded it to a 20-room hotel cum boarding-house. When the Frasers, after some years, moved to Prince Rupert, they again went into the business their hospitable natures made such a success of, and named their Prince Rupert enterprise, Queen Charlotte Rooms, in memory of happy years on the Islands.

The pioneering homesite at Fraser's Lagoon was reclaimed by Nature, the old name fell into disuse and a newer one replaced it. Today the lagoon is called locally, SALT MARSH LAGOON.

In 1884, Chittenden visiting this place wrote that he felt it was suitable for "settlers wanting to enter agriculture or dairying."

*COPPER BAY — west of Sheldons Bay, is midway along the coast between Sandspit and Gray Point. Named in 1878 by Dr. Dawson, who said he did so " . . . from the fact that work was done here at one time in examining a deposit of ore." (See Old Shaft.) The head of Copper Bay dries extensively.

Copper Bay attracted early homesteaders - even as it had Haidas - who established several sites in this part. Probably the first white homesteader to arrive was Walter Rudge, who brought his wife and twin daughters from Port Essington in 1907. Joe Molitor came with his family, and later a baby was born to them at this homesite. But young families required schools. The Molitors left to live on Graham Island and the Rudges went to Sandspit. The batchelor settlers were freer and many of them stayed there for years, leaving only to work for a short period to obtain the necessary cash to live but, as one of them said, "It took very little cash to live adequately in that land of plentiful wildlife."

*COPPER CREEK — flows into the head of Copper Bay and is named in this association. Formerly known as SKIDEGATE CHUCK, SKIDEGATE CREEK, and also as KASTE RIVER. Locally it is usually called either THE COPPER, or COPPER RIVER - and is never referred to merely as a "creek." It is one of the top fishing places for sportsmen on the Charlottes.

A 38-acre Haida Reserve lies at its mouth and in 1884 when Chittenden arrived for a visit he found Chief Skidegate and 20 of his people there busily engaged in catching and drying salmon. It is still very much a part of Skidegate life and when the run is on several Skidegate Haidas will be there, much as their ancestors were over the centuries, processing the fish. Today an occasional modern innovation is used to ease work.

*Homesteaders Scotty and Duncan Fraser, with neighbour Walter Rudge (right),
net fishing at the Copper River in early years.*

Photo - Mrs. Belle Brandon.

KASTE VILLAGE — at the mouth of the Copper River on its east bank.
A Raven Crest site formerly occupied by the tribe known as the Food-giving-people. This village site is now part of the 38-acre Kaste Reserve.

DJIGOGIGA VILLAGE — on the north shore of Copper Bay, lay a little
west of the north entrance point of the bay. It, too, was a Raven Crest site
owned by the Food-giving-people.

* SKIDEGATE LAKE — a slim lake about 8 miles long, lying inland, is drained
by the Copper River. It has a narrow neck towards the centre of the lake
which in earlier years was bridged by a trestle to permit the logging train to
cross. Later the trestle was reconstructed to permit trucks to cross at this point,
but it is in disrepair today.

For many years a sawmill stood on the south side of Skidegate Lake near
the trestle. Built by the Allison Logging Company primarily to cut ties for
the railroad, it also cut other lumber in small quantities from time to time.

When the lake was named is not definite, but it undoubtedly received its
name from the creek draining it - formerly called Skidegate Creek. (Now is
the Copper.) Extensive logging around this lake plus a devastating fire left
Nature with a king-sized reclamation job. But gradually a lush second growth
is developing and the view from the road following the north shore of the
lake is once again pleasant.

OLD SHAFT (historic site) — although known locally, is unmarked by any
sign or plaque. It is near the north entrance point of Copper Bay in the vicinity
of a 62-foot rock pillar on the shoreline. The shaft site is on the west side

of the road near there. It is because of this shaft Copper Bay received its name.

Twenty-five year old Edmund Cosworth Waddington arrived in Victoria from Australia about 1862, lured to B.C. by stories of gold in the Cariboo. However, reports of a possible copper strike on the Charlottes made him impulsively decide to go north instead of east.

He found copper signs at this part of what is now Copper Bay and that same year hired a crew and began sinking his first shaft. Visitors to the scene wondered greatly at the expense of such an undertaking on such a slim showing of ore, but Waddington said confidently, "I will very soon be striking a large body." By the end of 1863 he abandoned the project, returned to Victoria, then left for Australia and was never heard from again.

The "Old Shaft" as it had now become known, lay untouched until about 1907 when promotor Daniel R. "Windy" Young became interested in the idea. He made a deal with Shabot and Sheldens concerning it and employed three men to "unwater" it. By 1908 they found that the shaftwent down to 190 feet and had two cross-cuts made at the 90 foot level - which extended east and west for about 25 feet. The unwatering process was a laborious one, but at the bottom they said they found good showings of copper. Although he did get several people to look over the property, even the excellent promotional abilities of Windy Young were unequal to the task of selling it. By 1909 the project was once again abandoned and, as far as is known, nothing more ever done. Several years ago a logging company filled in the deep shaft as a safety measure.

SIWASH ROCK — the local name for the 62-foot-high rock on the edge of the shoreline in the vicinity of the Old Shaft.

FIVE MILE POINT — lies about half-way between Copper Bay and Cape Chroustcheff. "It has had that name, locally, for as long as I can remember," says Agnes Mathers who has lived in Sandspit since 1907. "We never knew what it was 5 miles from - Sandspit or Copper Bay - but it was always our resting point in early years when we walked between the two places. In 1942 the men from Crown Zellerbach cleared the area on the point for a Radio Beam Station which was built there soon afterwards by the Department of Transport."

The Beam Station is a valuable aid to pilots of aircraft during foggy or cloudy weather. Skippers of vessels receive guidance from it also.

Another name for this point by local people was BIG POINT.

BIG CREEK — slightly south of Big Point (or Five Mile Point), was named locally in association with the point.

THE SHELL BEACH — local name for the beach between Five Mile Point and Cape Chroustcheff. Only a few steps along that shoreline show it to be well named. The shells along that stretch of beach are exquisite and plentiful.

*SWAMP LAKE — on Lot 928 is 3½ miles west of Copper Bay and is a recently applied name in connection with a timber survey. A stream runs out of the south end of this lake into

LILY LAKE — which is on the east border of Lot 914. Lily Lake had not been gazetted when the 1966 gazetteer was published, but is on file in the Geographic Branch in Victoria. It is believed that both Lily and Swamp Lakes were named for their physical traits. A creek leaves the south end of Lily Lake and runs southward to join the Copper near the east end of Skidegate Lake. The old Allison Logging Railway had a spur line part way up this creek's valley.

* CAPE CHROUSTCHEFF — a name left on the map from the old Russian charts made during the first part of the 1880s when the Russian ships, often with Aleut hunters, came down to reap a harvest from the waters off the Charlottes. In 1810 one such ship, under Commander Kuckoff, using Aleut hunters took 1400 sea otters. A bloody battle took place in Dixon Entrance and eight of the Aleuts were killed in the skirmish when the Haidas tried to drive them off. The Hudson's Bay vessel *Otter* came by and played no small part in assisting the Haidas - not for their sakes, but to discourage the Russians from trespassing on H.B.C. preserves.

The first Admiralty chart on which the name of Cape Chroustcheff appeared was issued in 1856 and it included information from Russian charts of 1849. Further Russian charts were prepared in 1864 by Lieutenant Zazoskin which included the Queen Charlotte Islands. Chroustcheff has also been shown as KHRUSHCHOFF and as CHROUSTEHEFF. It is the first point southeast of Sandspit.

SKENA VILLAGE (Sqe'na) — stood at Cape Chroustcheff. Many legends have the story of Skena woven into them. The stories are varied. In general it is considered to have been a Raven Crest town, although some say Eagle Crest people from Cumshewa and Skidegate also lived in this village. Its size is reported to have been from a 5-row town in one version to one of only a few families in another.

A story of its abandonment says that some boys in the village had made themselves new bows and arrows. To test them they went through the town shooting at dogfish eggs strung up inside the houses - aiming the arrows to go through homes at the corners of the houses. When they shot into the chief's house, trouble followed hard and quickly.

A bitter quarrel ensued which grew out of all proportion, turning family against family and causing such enmity they all quit the village, separating as they did so and moving to different areas on the Charlottes. Only the hereditary Raven owners of the site remained. They, too, moved later, occupying several sites in Copper Bay and at Shingle Bay. These were the Food-giving-people. Eventually, like all other Haidas of Moresby Island they moved to Skidegate.

*SANDSPIT — the community at the northeast extremity of Moresby Island, has grown from the leisurely pioneering pace of the early 1900s to that of a busy centre today. Scheduled jet planes call there daily from the mainland; smaller aircraft, with headquarters in Prince Rupert, maintain regular runs to

Pioneer home of John Mathers in Sandspit. Still owned and lived in by two of his daughters.

Photo - Agnes Mathers.

Sandspit and from Sandspit to other Island points - both by charter and scheduled trips. From Sandspit a daily bus service takes passengers to Alliford Bay and thence by ferry to Graham Island where, continuing by bus, one can journey to all communities serviced by the main road from Queen Charlotte City to Masset. The Northland Navigation Company includes Sandspit among its other Island ports of call and heavy freight items are brought in by steamer weekly.

The main economic base is the Crown Zellerbach division which began operations there in 1940 as a small camp, gradually developing into one of the larger logging headquarters on the Islands. A fair proportion of Sandspit residents are connected with the Department of Transport which operates an important communications centre in the community, along with the airport.

It is a neat little settlement and the row of houses along the curve of Shingle Bay have an appearance of being located on the shoreline of a tropical island - a similarity frequently commented on by visitors.

For all its progressiveness - swimming pool, service clubs, modern hotel and airport - it retains a sense of fun which often develops when people have to make their own amusement. There, for instance, is held the annual earwig race. Sandspit people also retain an awareness of the contribution pioneer families have made. On October 18, 1970, in an unanimous decision, the new Sandspit school was named after Agnes L. Mathers, eldest daughter of pioneer Islander, Johnny Mathers. Agnes, who taught school for more years than she cares to add up, was born at Skidegate Landing in 1903. The greater part of her teaching career has been in the small schools on the Charlottes. Having received her own education in them, she knew exactly what was needed and

275

used her own good sense about the application of rules laid down by some far-off Board of Education office. It is not all happiness at Sandspit, for busy airport that it has become, it is perhaps inevitable that one of the worst tragedies to occur there was associated with aircraft.

On January 18, 1952, a Northwest Airlines, Douglas DC4, left Anchorage Alaska, for Tacoma with 40 passengers, Pilot J. J. Pfaffinger, Co-pilot K. H. Kuhn and Stewardess Jane Cheadle. The plane took off at 9:11 p.m. Three hours later the pilot radioed to say his number one engine had been feathered and he was proceeding to Sandspit. Moments later the oil cooler in that engine broke. The aircraft made a 3-engine approach at Sandspit and touched down at 1:38 a.m. A third of the way down the runway the pilot decided to make another landing and applied power to become airborne near the end of the runway, but the port wing struck the water causing the plane to crash into the sea about 3/4 of a mile offshore.

All survived, but radio contact had been lost. It was pitch dark with a heavy snowstorm. Sandspit assumed that the pilot had decided against landing and gone to another base. Not until 3:30 a.m. - two bone-chilling hours later - did they learn the aircraft's true position. Only seven survivors were found. During that endless wait - the waves, snow and terrible cold - 36 people lost their hold and slipped off the plane which had settled in 10 feet of water. Their calls for help went unheard by those on land as the wind tore the sound out to sea and darkness hid everything.[1]

[1]Information from Mr. L.A. Trapp, Accident Division, Department of Transport, Ottawa.

LITTLE SPIT POINT — is the local name given to the heel of the boot-shaped peninsula which extends off the northeast extremity of Moresby Island.

*SPIT POINT — is the extreme northeast point of Moresby Island and is the toe of the boot-shaped peninsula mentioned above. The name SPIT POINT appears on charts dating to 1866.

The Haidas called it KIL'KUN.

There are tremendous seas and cross-currents off Spit Point during storms, but it is not reckoned to be as dangerous as its counterpart on the northeast extremity of Graham Island, the notorious Rose Spit.

TACAN ROAD — is the name given by the Department of Highways to the short road south of Spit Point which leads inland from the main highway to the TACAN site. (Tactical Air Navigation, for short range air navigation.) The area containing the navigational aid was for years known to Sandspit residents as "Cole's Field."

Sandspit roads with names such as CAMP ROAD, SPUR ROAD and COPPER BAY ROAD are a legacy from its logging industry, with the others:- SCHOOL ROAD, PARK ROAD and NORTH and SOUTH BEACH ROADS having been added also when it was deemed necessary to have identifications in case of fire.

* SHINGLE BAY — between Spit Point and Onward Point. Applied to the charts during Pender's survey of Skidegate Inlet in 1866. The shores of the bay are fringed with the sweeping shingle beach which gives the bay its name.

KIL VILLAGE, Sand-Spit-Point-Town — lay east of, but near, Haans Creek. Formerly owned by the Eagle Crest Lanachaadus family who shared it for a time with the poor Gitingidjats. The people of Kloo had enslaved so many of the Gitingidjats, they gradually gave up hope of having a town of their own, even on a shared basis, and eventually entered the homes of other Eagle tribes, the Gituns, as servants. Their name meant "servants-of-the-Gituns."

* HAANS CREEK — at the west end of Sandspit settlement. Named by Captain P.C. Musgrave of the survey ship *Lillooet* 1911-16. The Haans family lived near the creek. [1] The Department of Highways sign on the bridge over the creek showed the name as HANS CREEK as of 1972 - and is an error in spelling.

[1] See Haans Islet.

BOB CREEK — is the name given by the Department of Highways to the small creek west of Haans Creek. In early years Sandspit people called this creek SECOND CREEK. Between Haans and Bob Creek is a fossil site, located on the shoreline.

PIPER CREEK — flows into Shingle Bay in the vicinity of Gillatt Island and received its name from the Department of Highways.

DAIYU VILLAGE — on the east side of Piper Creek belonged to the Raven Crest tribe known as Giving-Food-to -Others, a hospitable people who also occupied several sites along the coast as far south as Gray Bay.

* GILLATT ISLAND — at the west side of Shingle Bay. Formerly called GRASSY ISLAND, a name given it in 1866 by Captain Dan Pender during his survey of Skidegate Inlet. Owing to duplications of the name the Hydrographic Service suggested renaming it Gillatt in 1946, after Captain Gillatt of Sandspit in recognition of his tide-watching services for them. (See also Gillatt Arm). Gillatt Island is only 11 feet high and is covered with low vegetation.

*ONWARD POINT — lies about 3¾ miles southwest of Spit Point. First named WELCOME POINT by Captain Pender in 1866, it later was known for a short period as MISSION POINT. The name "Onward" suggested by the Hydrographic Service in 1946 is after the schooner *Onward,* chartered in 1865 by the Cowgitz Coal Mining Company to take supplies from Victoria to miners at Cowgitz. Onward Point has a fossil site.

SKI JUMP CREEK — on the west side of Onward Point was given its name by loggers living at Sandspit several years ago. When first constructed the bridge across the creek was level with the road on one side, but on the opposite side the road was noticeably lower. Truck drivers passing from the level to the lower side said they felt as though their vehicles almost "took off" as if on skiis.

More than one privately owned car is reported to have taken off in reality and ended up ignominiously in the creek when the approach to this bridge was misjudged.

LITTLE SACHS CREEK — with a fossil site at its mouth, lies to the east of Sachs creek and received its name in this association. The Department of Highways sign on this bridge reads LITTLE SACS CREEK.

* **SACHS CREEK** — between Little Sachs and Kwuna Point is after John Sachs, a pioneer storekeeper of Queen Charlotte City. Named by Captain P.C. Musgrave of the survey vessel *Lillooet* 1911-16.

Mr. and Mrs. John Sachs and their son arrived in the new townsite on June 12, 1909, accompanying Robert Scharfee. Attracted by enticing advertisements in Windy Young's newspaper the two men came from New Westminster and Vancouver to open stores. Scharfee got into business immediately. Sending for Mrs. Scharfee, he opened a small general store beside George Beattie's first drug store. In 1910 he sold out to Sachs and moved to Lawn Hill. Sachs ran the store in "Charlotte" until 1924.

"John was a real old warrior," recalls Charlie Hartie, " and liable to break your head if you complained about anything in his store."

* **MOUNT POOLE** — rising to 1,600 feet, lies between Onward Point and Kwuna Point. Named TABLE MOUNTAIN in 1866 by Captain D. Pender, it was renamed by the Hydrographic Service in 1945 owing to duplication of that name. Named after Francis Poole, the mining engineer who was associated with the Skincuttle venture of 1862 to 1864.

CHAPTER THIRTEEN

*SKIDEGATE INLET and SKIDEGATE CHANNEL — separate Moresby Island from Graham Island. The east basin is shown as Skidegate Inlet. After the waterway passes Sandilands Island and continues west to the Pacifc Ocean, it becomes Skidegate Channel. The narrowest parts of Skidegate Channel are known as East Narrows and West Narrows, respectively - the entrance to Trounce Inlet dividing the two narrow sections.

Like other inlets on the Charlottes it has had several names. The early visitors did not realize it was a connecting link between east and west coasts, so they named each end separately. The east entrance was given its first European name in 1788 when Charles Duncan, master of the sloop *Princess Royal*, named it TROLLOPE'S RIVER. This name subsequently appeared on British Admiralty charts.

In 1791 Captain Robert Gray on the *Columbia* named it HATCHES SOUND, after Captain Crowell Hatch, one of the owners of the *Columbia*. The next year another American skipper, Joseph Ingraham on the *Hope*, following the customary method of naming regions for the leading chief, named it after Chief "Skit-i-kiss", and showed it as SKIT-I-KISS BAY on his map. The west entrance to Skidegate Channel received the name THE GREAT SOUND from Ingraham.

When gold was discovered at Mitchell Inlet on the west coast, it did not take long for the water short-cut through the centre of the Charlottes to come into its own - with Haida guides to take the newcomers along the intricate channel. On charts issued at this time the centre portion of the channel was called SWANSON LABYRINTH. When Captain Daniel Pender was engaged to survey

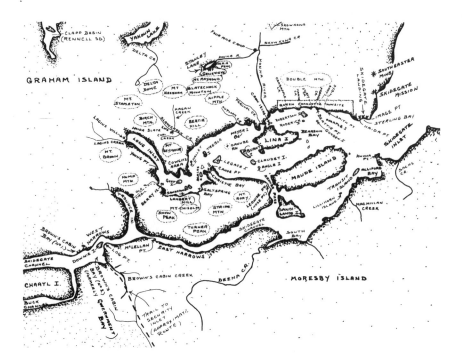

the waterway in 1866 he standardized the name of SKIDEGATE for the inlet and channel and, in 1878, Dr. Dawson added the East and West Narrows to indicate the tortuous section of the fairway.

The name Skidegate is commonly thought to be a modification of a Haida word for the "red-paint-stone" - a type of rock found on the shores of the inlet which, after being calcined by heat, was ground into powder to be used by the Haidas as paint. But there is another much more romantic story associated with the name.

Skidegate is said to be a greatly corrupted Haida word for a type of sea-flower, exceedingly difficult to obtain. One of the young Haidas, very much in love with a girl, was not making much progress in his suit. When he learned that the maiden greatly desired the rare sea-flower, the man determined to present her with one hoping thereby to win favour. So diligent and constant was his search, and so lengthy, the other Haidas dubbed him by the name of the flower.

Eventually he did find the rare bloom and won the girl. He also became chief and, in memory of the episode, took for his name that of the flower. It became a hereditary name from that time on, to be handed down to his successors as they came into the chieftainship.

The Skidegate Inlet region has contained numerous village and camp sites as well as forts, and midden signs from this ancient Haida occupancy are everywhere.

Some of the early white traders lost their lives in Skidegate Inlet skirmishes, but there was no comparison in this respect with the battles at Houston Stewart Channel or, for that matter, even with Cumshewa. Captain Bernard Magee of

280

the *Globe* was killed off Skidegate in 1801 when on a trading trip and there are reports of others having had near escapes after that.

The shores of Skidegate Inlet and its islands are considered by geologists to be one of the finest collecting grounds for Jurassic and Cretaceous marine fossils in North America. Several geological field parties have made detailed examinations of its shorelines - often arriving at conflicting assessments.

This chapter will list the place names of Skidegate Inlet, beginning with Kwuna Point and continuing in a westerly direction to just beyond Downie Island along the south shore, then will return in an easterly direction to complete the list of inlet names as far as Image Point. (The west end of Skidegate Channel was covered in Chapter 4, and the section between Sandspit and Kwuna Point included in Chapter 12).

AGGLOMERATE PENINSULA — is the name given by Dr. F.H. McLearn in 1921 to the peninsula forming the east side of Alliford Bay. Dr. McLearn was engaged in a field trip researching stratigraphy of the Mesozoic formations of Skidegate Inlet. He named numerous fossil sites on Maude Island and in the Alliford Bay region to assist in identification. Subsequent geological parties use the names in their reference to these bays and points. They are, therefore, included in this book, although they are not local nor gazetted names.

*KWUNA POINT — is the extremity of Agglomerate Peninsula. It has had two other names in former years. In 1853 Captain T.S. Sinclair of the H.B.C. named it POINT JAMES on his sketch map of Skidegate Bay. Between 1911 and 1916, Captain Musgrave applied the name of ALLIFORD POINT. This name passed and confirmed by the Geographic Board. His successor Mr. H.D. Parizeau felt confusion might arise with that name, since it is similar to Alfred and Alford Points. The name KWUNA suggested and confirmed in 1946. Dr. Newcombe on his map called it KU'NT'ALAS.

A chain of islets and bare rocks leads off Kwuna Point in a northwesterly direction.

*FLOWERY ISLET — which has a navigational light on it, is at the end of the islets leading off Kwuna Point. Captain Pender applied the name in 1866.

*BUSH ISLAND — also named by Captain Pender in 1866, is only 7 feet high. It lies south of Flowery Islet and is slightly larger.

*BARE ROCKS — a little to the south of Bush Island, appeared on Captain Pender's chart following his 1866 survey. They dry at from 4 to 24 feet and are an extension of the Bush Island shoal.

*ALLIFORD BAY — lies west and south of Kwuna Point. Captain Pender appointed William Alliford A.B., to be coxswain of the boat sent to do the soundings in this bay in 1866, then named the bay after him. The H.B.C.'s valiant *Beaver* had been especially chartered to help in the massive hydrographic surveys needed on the coast. Skidegate Inlet received detailed attention because

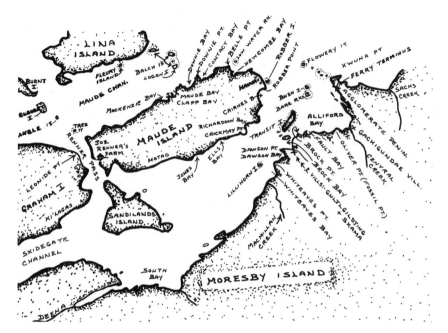

of the coal interest at Cowgitz - and pressure was brought by the merchants of Victoria on its priority.

Fish, not coal, caused the first land survey of Alliford Bay about 1879. Torrens Island, Skidegate (Landing) and Alliford Bay were all part of the land application connected with the pioneer oil works at Skidegate (Landing), Alliford Bay became Lot No. 4 on the Queen Charlotte Islands list of lots. But little was done with it then.

In 1911 the bay really came into the news when it was selected as the site for Sir George Doughty's "model cannery town," and the grandiose schemes that ensued put Alliford Bay into the headlines for some time. But the plans were a little too marvellous for the capabilities and, in 1913, the whole operation went into receivership. [1]

During World War II it again came into focus when selected as the location for a seaplane base. At the peak of operation 700 men were stationed at this base.

Today it is best known as the Moresby Island terminus of the inter-island ferry which plies several times a day between Alliford Bay and Skidegate Landing.

[1]Q.C. Islands, Volume 1, Chapter 40.

*CENTRAL CREEK — flows into the head of Alliford Bay. This was one of the streams Captain Pender favoured for replenishing his fresh water aboard the *Beaver* during the 1866 survey.

GACHIGUNDAE, Village-moving-to-and-fro-all-the-time — lay on the east side of the mouth of Central Creek. These Raven Crest Haidas were a branch of the Skidegate Sqoa'ladas, who had separated from the main branch after a feud. They were not held in much esteem and the village considered rather a miserable one. Chief Lu'got was the head man.

*OLIVER POINT — west of central Creek on the south shore of Alliford Bay. Named by Captain Musgrave 1911-16 after William Oliver, the well-known Methodist missionary and enterprising pioneer who first came to the Charlottes in the 1880s. (See also Oliver Islet, Rock and Mountain). When the point was named, Captain and Mrs. Oliver were living at Sandspit and Musgrave knew them well.

In 1921 geologist Dr. F.H. McLearn named the point FOSSIL POINT, and even geological books of recent issue show the point under that name. However in 1946 the Geographic Board adopted the older name OLIVER POINT.

FAULT BAY — on the west side of Alliford Bay about 1/2 a mile northwest of Oliver Point. Named by Dr. McLearn in 1921. His map shows a fault running parallel to the shoreline on the west side of the small cove.

BROCK POINT — a rocky point connected by ledges to the shoreline west of Fault Bay. Named in 1921 by Dr. F.H. McLearn after Dean Reginald Brock, Director of the Geological Survey 1908 to 1914, and Dean of the Faculty of Applied Science at the University of British Columbia for many years.

BROCK BAY — southwest of Brock Point and approximately south of the southern extremity of Transit Island, has a creek running into its head. Named in conjunction with Brock Point by Dr. McLearn in 1921. (See also Brock Islands).

GULJLGILDJING Mussel-chewing-town — stood in Brock Bay. It belonged to the same Raven family as Gachigundae, at Central Creek. The head man of Mussel-chewing-town was known as The-Young-Chief. It was only a small place and not highly rated by other Haidas.

SKAMA, Needle-case-village — near Mussel-chewing-town, or may even have been another name for the same site, according to Dr. J.R. Swanton who did an extensive examination of these old villages about 1905.

DAWSON POINT — is the west point of Brock Bay, a sharp rocky point. Named in 1921 by Dr. G.H. McLearn after geologist Dr. G.M. Dawson.

DAWSON BAY — also named by McLearn in 1921, is immediately south of Dawson Point. This fossil site has been of much interest to geologists who appreciate particularly that the specimens are fairly well exposed. With the addition of these two names there are a total of seven Queen Charlotte Islands' features named after the little geological surveyor, Dr. G.M. Dawson, who visited these shores in 1878.

WHITEAVES POINT — a good fossil site, this is the point between Dawson Bay and Whiteaves Bay, in the vicinity of Lillihorn Island. Named by Dr. McLearn in 1921.

WHITEAVES BAY — south of the point was named at the same time. Both are after Mr. J.F. Whiteaves of the Geological Survey, whose identification of fossils brought back from many field trips, played a significant role in the expeditions. He made three valuable contributions to lists and data concerning the Mesozoic Fossils of Skidegate Inlet: the first in 1876 contained information about invertebrates from the coal-bearing rocks of the inlet; the second in 1884 concerned fossils brought back by the George M. Dawson expedition; and in 1900 he identified additional fossils from the Cretaceous rocks and did a revised list of species from these rocks.

His one error in interpreting a fauna species caused some confusion in early studies of Q.C. Islands geology, when he thought all the fauna belonged to one era - Cretaceous. Later studies showed it to be a mixture of both Cretaceous and Juriassic, an estimated 50 million years apart. It was from Whiteaves Bay that Dr. G.M. Dawson gathered some of his specimens in 1878.

*MACMILLAN CREEK — flows into the cove west of Whiteaves Bay. Named by the Hydrographic Service after Mr. S. MacMillan, owner of Lot 836, at the mouth of the creek, since 1910. Named confirmed in 1954.

*TRANSIT ISLAND — forms the west side of Alliford Bay. This wooded island is about 325 feet high and from the northeast side has a dome-shaped outline. It is joined to the shore by a drying bank and connecting islets. Named LEADING ISLAND by Captain Daniel Pender when he conducted the 1866 survey of this part of Skidegate Inlet and was a key factor in his instructions for safe entry into the inlet. "The west side of LEADING ISLAND must be kept in a line with the east side of Bare Island (now Torrens Island)" advised Captain Pender. "When this is achieved a ship can safely enter knowing it will clear Bar Rocks off Dead Tree Point and will also clear the end of the Spit shallows."

In 1946 the Hydrographic Service renamed the island, using the designation of "transit" in association with the context of a leading line.

*LILLIHORN ISLAND — southwest of Transit Island, and to the west of Whiteaves Bay is small, steep-sided and has a rock off its northeast point which dries at 9 feet. Lillihorn Island was named by Captain Musgrave 1911-16. Not known who it is after.

*SOUTH BAY — midway along the north end of Moresby Island, has Deena Creek flowing into its west side. When Dr. Dawson applied the name in 1878 he meant it to include a larger area than is identified with the name today. Dawson's South Bay included Sandilands Island (which he called South Island in this association).

B.C. Packers built and operated a small cannery at South Bay, which ran during the 1920s then was abandoned about 1928 or 1931.

*SANDILANDS ISLAND — due north of South Bay. It is connected at low water at its extreme north tip to its neighbour, Maude Island. A wooded island showing logging scars today, this was the SOUTH ISLAND of Dr. G.M.

Dawson's 1878 map. Renamed about 1925 by the Hydrographic Service because of duplications of that name.

Named after E.M. Sandilands, Gold Commissioner on the Charlottes. His first office was in Jedway, when he received his appointment in April 1908, and was also made Stipendary Magistrate for that region. When the mining boom died down in the Jedway area, the Gold Commissioner's Office moved to Queen Charlotte City, opening there in May 1912.

The job did not prove very taxing, and additional governmental duties were given him, for he became Government Agent and Superintendent of Roads for the Charlottes. And he got married.

"He married an old flame," recalls Mr. Hartie of Queen Charlotte City, "but Mrs. Sandilands did not care for the Islands at all, and didn't hesitate to let him know. Sandilands didn't stay too long after this."

There are several fossil sites on the southeast part of the Sandilands Island.

*DEENA CREEK — like many names taken from Haida words, Deena has a variety of spellings, Dina, Dena, De'nah and so on. Formerly shown as DEENA RIVER, changed to CREEK on maps in 1961. Locally it is usually called simply THE DEENA. The headwaters of this stream rise within a few miles of Security Inlet, 8 to 10 miles away, and the mouth of the river contains an extensive flat. A Haida Reserve of 119 acres surrounds a camp site near the mouth of the Deena, a camp which has been used by Haidas since ancient times.

*SKIDEGATE CHANNEL — is regarded as being that portion of waterway extending westward from Sandilands Island to the Pacific Ocean - a distance of about 17 miles.

*EAST NARROWS — the name given to that portion of Skidegate Channel beginning about 3 miles west of Sandilands Island which grows progressively narrower until at McLellan Point there is only about 200 feet between the high water marks on either shore. It gradually widens to an open basin opposite Trounce Inlet. Named in 1878 by Dr. Dawson.

* MCLELLAN POINT — the narrowest section of Skidegate Channel. Named after John McLellan, owner of Gold Harbour Gold Mine in the early 1900s (See McLellan Island). Named by the Hydrographic Service about 1925.

*WEST NARROWS — is the portion of Skidegate Channel which narrows as it curves around the north and west sides of Downie Island. Some sections are constricted to about 900 feet in the passage. West Narrows named by Dr. G.M. Dawson in 1878. EAST and WEST NARROWS of Skidegate Inlet present an extremely hazardous waterway, and should not be attempted without careful attention to the charts or knowledgeable local guidance. Several ships have come to grief along there.

A proposal to dredge and straighten the channel received strenuous arguments from some quarters, the contention being that straightening and dredging (similar to that done in Louise Narrows) would make Skidegate Narrows almost unnavigable - the tide would rush through with such force. The greatest tidal range on the Pacific Coast occurs at the east end in Skidegate Inlet, a difference of level between high and low tides of 26 feet on the larger tides. Vessels passing along the Narrows at certain stages of the tide encounter a physical slope of water. The tidal streams from Skidegate Inlet and Skidegate Channel meet about 2 miles west of Sandilands Island.

*DOWNIE ISLAND — which is responsible for the West Narrows of Skidegate Channel, was considered by Dr. Dawson to be part of Moresby Island. He named the west side of the island LOG POINT. Later surveys revealed it to be an island attached to Moresby by a drying bank and it became known as LOG ISLAND for several years. In 1948 the Hydrographic Service felt a more distinctive name would ensure clarification in navigational instructions. They suggested DOWNIE ISLAND after William Downie an old California miner and explorer who stayed a short time in Skidegate Inlet in 1859.

Mr. Downie had been commissioned in July of 1859 to go to the H.B.C. gold site at Mitchell Inlet. Taking 27 men and provisions for 3 months Downie conducted a diligent search of the old gold find then, exploring farther, prospected the shorelines of both Douglas and Skidegate Inlets. The search for gold proved unrewarding. All he could find, he said, was some coal measures in Skidegate Inlet.

His discovery of the coal was near the headwaters of what would later be named Hooper Creek. In 1865 a company was formed in Victoria to exploit the deposit and the Cowgitz Coal Mine came into existence. Because of this the survey of Skidegate Inlet was ordered in 1866. Captain Pender brought the *Beaver* into the inlet to do the job, leaving as a result a great many place names for this region.

LOG POINT — is considered to be the northwest tip of Moresby where the drying flat extends to Downie Island. There is a 3-foot high islet on the flat off Log Point. (Information from the Hydrographic Office, Victoria, 1969.)

BROWN'S CABIN BAY — is the name applied in earlier years to an indentation on the north shore of Skidegate Channel, about 3/4 of a mile west of Downie Island. There were two cabins in the bay, one of which belonged to Mr. Brown, a much respected Haida of Skidegate. He and his family used the place regularly. It is a good bay for crabs and the Haidas caught some particularly large and succulent specimens which they generously shared with anyone passing. A small stream entered the head of the bay making it a delightful camping place.

In later years logging operations destroyed the site. In the bay south of Downie Island, on the opposite shore, another was established. Today this is called BROWN'S CABIN BAY and the creek entering the head of this second camp site in knows as

BROWN'S CABIN BAY CREEK — the creek which flows from the south to enter the bay. In earlier years this stream was known as GOVERNMENT CREEK, say old timers. It acquired its name when the government put through a trail in 1908 from there to the head of Security Inlet and built a cabin at each end for trappers and others who might need shelter. The trail allowed access to the Gold Harbour region when west coast seas were too stormy for boat travel. The bay, too, was frequently called GOVERNMENT BAY.

*TROUNCE INLET — lies midway between the two narrowest sections of Skidegate Channel, about a mile west of McLellan Point. Extending northward into Graham Island for about 2 miles, this inlet was named NORTH ARM by Dawson in 1878 Renamed in 1945 by the Hydrographic Service because of duplications. Shown as TA'NU on Dr. Newcombe's map.

Named after Thomas Trounce, chairman of the Queen Charlotte Coal Company which operated the Cowgitz Mine. Mr. Trounce was born in 1813 in Cornwall and studied architecture. Lured by beckoning seas he shipped aboard several vessels before settling in Tasmania and joining in the Australian gold rush. When news came of the 1848 San Francisco gold find, he was soon aboard a ship to engage in that mad scramble for wealth. It petered out at about the same time as the Cariboo rush came into the news. Trounce again could not resist. He did well in this one.

Settling in Victoria afterwards, he opened a business and designed a number of Victoria buildings. With money and mining experience Thomas Trounce was a natural choice for the chairmanship of the coal mining venture on the far-off Charlottes.

Near the head of Trounce Inlet a trail ran from the east side through a valley and came out on the shore of Long Inlet by the Berry Islands. A well-used trail by the Haidas at the time of the 1866 survey.

The foot-shaped peninsula extending off the south end of Graham Island between Trounce Inlet and Long Inlet has numerous mountain peaks along it, many of which were named during the 1866 survey by Captain Pender.

*MOUNT BROWN — at the top of the peninsula, is about 2,340 feet high. Thomas Brown R.N. was master on the *Beaver* during Pender's survey. Robert Brown was a mining engineer who made a report in 1866. The mountain is believed named for one of these two men. There is a small lake near the top of Mount Brown.

*HUMP MOUNTAIN — south of Mount Brown is a hump-shaped mountain of 2,205 feet. It was in the valley south of Hump Mountain that Pender noted the trail leading from Long Inlet to Trounce Inlet.

*SNOW PEAK — Pender's descriptive name for the 2535-foot mountain on the instep of the footlike peninsula. This is the highest mountain in the group.

*MOUNT CHISOLM — east and north of Snow Peak rises to only a little over 1,000 feet. Named by Pender in 1866.

* LAMBERT HILL — named by Pender, is only 685 feet high and lies below Mount Chisolm to face Saltspring Bay.

*TURNER PEAK — is a later addition to the name list, appearing first on the 1954 land map. A conspicuous mountain, 2,420 feet high, it is south of Mount Chisolm. A creek with its headwaters near Turner Peak flows north to enter Saltspring Bay, creating a large flat off its mouth.

*STRIPE MOUNTAIN — the name Captain Pender gave to the 1,770-foot mountain lying northeast of Turner Peak.

*MOUNT RORY — almost 2,100 feet high is the most easterly of the named peaks and is about the centre of the toe part of the peninsula. It too, received its name during the 1866 survey by Captain Daniel Pender.

KI'LAGAS VILLAGE — shown on Dr. Newcombe's map, lay on the south side of the peninsula, near Sandilands Island.

*LEONIDE POINT — on the north part of the toe. Named NOSE POINT by Captain Pender in 1866. Renamed in 1945 by the Hydrographic Service because of duplications. *Leonide* is after the name of the sloop which Francis Poole chartered to bring him back to Burnaby Island following a trip to Victoria in 1863 to make a report to the Victoria stockholders. (See Poole Inlet).

RENNER PASS — a local name for the waterway separating Maude Island from the peninsula (of whichLeonide is the northeast tip.) The pass received its name because the hospitable Joe and Mrs. Renner had their homesite in a cove on this pass, on the west end of Maude Island. The Renner home, first a series of lean-tos, was finally rebuilt by Joe into quite a sizeable place. Now privately owned, a large clearing still marks the location of "Renner's Place."[1]

[1]See also Renner Point.

*MAUDE ISLAND — the largest island in Skidegate Inlet, its wooded hillsides bearing the scars of successive logging operations, was named by Captain Pender during the 1866 survey. That same year an island in Nanoose Bay off the east coast of Vancouver Island also received the name of Maude, resulting in some confusion over the years. In 1945 the Hydrographic Service suggested the Maude Island of Skidegate Inlet be renamed RECOVERY ISLAND after the H.B.C. brig of that name. Surprisingly the request was denied. Maude Island of Skidegate Inlet remained unchanged.

The old Haida name for the island was HA'INA. There are several midden sites on this island, but only the names of two villages, Haina and Hotao, are commonly known today and will be described later.

During the pioneering days several homesites were established on Maude, with cabins and clearings and hopeful young dreams.

In 1921 it became the recipient of a dozen names when Dr. F.H. McLearn identified some particularly interesting fossil sites, at the same time as this was done in the Alliford Bay region. Since these names are still in use in geological reports, they will be listed here as well.

HOTAO VILLAGE (Xo'tao) — a Raven Crest site on the southwest side of Maude Island. A story is told that the daughter of a chief of this village brought such disgrace to her father she was ostracized by the entire village. (Her offence, however, is not remembered.) Taken to a bay on Graham Island she was told, "Go!"

The terrified girl started walking north, stumbling and falling in her wretchedness. Darkness began to fall as she came to a rocky part of the shore near what is now Dead Tree Point. Sitting on a log to collect her wits, she was surprised to see two young braves come out of the forest. One of them took pity on the girl and married her. From this union came a new tribe who later moved to live in Skidegate.

JONES BAY — east of the old village of Hotao, is a fossil site named in 1921 by Dr. F.H. McLearn after Mr. R.H.B. Jones, a student at U.B.C. at that time, who gave valuable assistance to McLearn in the field trip to Skidegate Inlet researching Mesozoic formations.

ELLS BAY — northeast of Jones Bay, named by Dr. McLearn after Dr. R.W. Ells.[1]

[1]See Ells Rocks and Point for more information about Dr. Ells.

CRICKMAY POINT — is the tip of the peninsula east of Ells Bay on Maude Island. Named by Dr. McLearn after Mr. C.H. Crickmay, another U.B.C. student who gave valuable assistance during the 1921 field trip.

RICHARDSON BAY — is immediately east of Crickmay Point and is after James Richardson of the Geological Survey of Canada, who came to Skidegate Inlet in 1872 to report on coal measures of Cowgitz. Richardson Bay named in 1921 by Dr. F.H. McLearn.

CAIRNES BAY — at the east end of Maude Island, southwest of Robber Island. Named by Dr. McLearn after D.D. Cairnes, well-known geologist who worked with J.D. Mackenzie on a survey. He was a brother of Clive Cairnes, one of Mackenzie's assistants during the 1913-14 geological survey of Graham Island (and for whom Cairnes Creek was named.)

ROBBER POINT— is the north point of Cairnes Bay, and is the more southerly of the two small points which extend from Maude Island in the direction of Robber Island. Named by Dr. McLearn in 1921.

*ROBBER ISLAND — named during Pender's 1866 hydrographic survey of Skidegate Inlet. Connected to the east end of Maude Island by a drying bank, it is a rocky little island noted today for the historic grave it contains. Captain John, chief of Haina, who died in 1882, before the move of his villagers to Skidegate, was not put in the burial position accorded his ancestors, high and free in a tree-slung coffin. He was part of the change from old to new and his remains were interred. A neat iron fence marked and protected the site.

HAINA VILLAGE, Sunshine-Town — on the east end of Maude Island.

Originally a Raven Crest town belonging to some of the Sqoa'ladas, the successful-fishermen. For a time presided over by a chieftainess. With passing years it became abandoned. Then, about 1870, when the agonizing decline of the Haidas wreaked such havoc with their way of life, west coast families, both Eagle and Raven Crest, began to move back to Skidegate Inlet, most of whom settled on Maude Island.

The first families to go were the Eagles from Kaisun - Gold Harbour - and their chief became the town chief of Haina. The village became known after this as NEW GOLD HARBOUR. Most of the houses built in New Gold Harbour were named after houses previously occupied by the owners in villages on the west coast. The chief, evidently a very sociable man, named his lodge, "The-house-that-is-always-looking-for-visitors."

It became a village which combined the old and new, mixing totem poles and ancient rites with those of a Methodist Church. The money to build the church came from the sale of the old articles of ritual, as times gradually changed and these things diminished in importance. In 1893 the New Gold Harbour village itself was abandoned when these Haidas joined with others to establish one main village at Skidegate.

Haina is now part of the 210 acre Haida KRHANA RESERVE.

NEWCOMBE BAY — lies northwest of Haina, and has a stream entering its head. Named in 1921 by Dr. McLearn after Dr. C.F. Newcombe who made a large collection of fossils from Skidegate Inlet in 1895 and 1897.

*BELLE POINT — formerly called GEORGE POINT following the Pender survey of 1866, it is the west entrance point of Newcombe Bay. Renamed in 1945 after Belle Gillatt, daughter of Captain Gillatt of Sandspit. When Captain Gillatt was hospitalized in Prince Rupert, she took over his duties of tide-watching for the Hydrographic Service.

LOW WATER ROCK — about 2¼ cables northeast of Belle Point, it dries at 4 feet. Shown by this name on Pender and Dawson maps.

CONTACT POINT — another fossil site named by Dr. McLearn in 1921. It is on the north side of Maude Island about 3/4 of a mile west of Belle Point. Named for a geological formation.

DOWNIE POINT — separates Contact Bay from Downie Bay.

DOWNIE BAY — on the north side of Maude Island about a third of the way from the east end. Both Downie Bay and Point were named by Dr. McLearn in 1921 after William Downie, the California miner commissioned by James Douglas to look for gold on the Charlottes and who found instead the coal measures which precipitated opening of the Cowgitz Mine.

MAUDE BAY — the name given by Dr. McLearn in 1921 to the bay west of Downie Bay, and named in association with the island.

290

CLAPP BAY — separated from Maude Bay by a small rocky point, could almost be considered to be the same bay. Named by Dr. McLearn after Dr. Charles H. Clapp whose 1912 geological reconnaissance of part of Graham Island made the fuller study of that area apparent, thus J.D. MacKenzie was delegated to undertake the 1913-14 survey.

MACKENZIE BAY — lying almost midway along the north shore of Maude Island is after James D. MacKenzie who made the 1913-1914 survey mentioned above.

*BALCH ISLANDS — three islands which stretch across Maude Channel between Maude Island and the east end of Lina Island. The two outer islands were named CHANNEL ISLANDS during the Pender hydrographic charting in 1866. Locally they still go by this name to a large extent.

The most southerly of the group was named LOGAN ISLAND in 1921 by Dr. McLearn, after Sir William Logan (See also Logan Inlet).

In 1945 the Hydrographic Service requested a change of name owing to numerous duplications of Channel Islands in coastal waters. Balch is in memory of Captain Lafayette Balch of the schooner *Demaris Cove*. It was Balch who agreed to rendezvous with the *Georgianna* off Mitchell Inlet in the fall of 1851. Later Balch went to the rescue of the men of the *Georgianna* following the vessel's loss and subsequent enslavement of the men by the Skidegates.[1] The name Balch Islands adopted by the Geographic Board in 1946.
1946.

Dr. C.F. Newcombe's map shows an ancient Haida fort site on one of the Balch Islands.

[1]Story of the Georgianna on pages 89 to 92.

*MAUDE CHANNEL — the waterway separating Maude Island from Lina Island. Named in association with the larger island and confirmed in 1933.

*FLEURY ISLAND — on the north side of Maude Channel, and connected to Lina Island by a drying bank. Named TUFT ISLAND during the 1866 survey by Pender. Geographic records show that it has also been called DRIFT ISLAND. In 1945 the Hydrographic Service with an overabundance of Tuft Islands, suggested FLEURY, the maiden name of Mrs. Francis G. Claudet, whose husband assayed the samples of coal found at Cowgitz by William Downie in 1859.

In the early days of homesiting, Jim Werst chose this small island for his pioneer homestead.

*LINA ISLAND — named during Captain Pender's 1866 survey and is a modification of the Haida name for the fort island off its east end. During the long years of Haida occupancy it is likely several parts of the shoreline may have held settlements. Only three are known about today, two on the south shore and one on the east end. All had streams which did not go dry, and sheltered coves with sand beaches.

GASINS VILLAGE, Gambling-Sticks — a Raven Crest village which lay in the cove on the south shore of Lina Island, to the east of Withered Point. The chief of this village was known as He-who-mends. The people of Gasins village were former residents of Skidegate. When a war broke out between the Massets and the Skidegates, several families moved farther up the inlet hoping to get out of the endless fracas. One tribe established Gasins.

LINA ISLAND PETROGLYPHS — These rock carvings were found close to the old village site near Withered Point, the Gasins Village. They lie in the barnacle zone on large boulders and consist of four petroglyphs in all. To date they are the first to have been located on the Charlottes, although found frequently elsewhere along the British Columbia coast. Discovered by Betty Unsworth of Port Clements during a field trip with the Queen Charlotte Islands Museum Society in the spring of 1972.

GAODJAOS VILLAGE, Drum-Village — also on the south shore of Lina Island, stood in a cove west of Fleury Island. Established by another of the Raven Crest families who took part in the same exodus from Skidegate as those of Gasins. Drum Town featured in a legend told by the old ones. Once when there was a severe famine in the inlet, the chief of Drum-Town, known as The Possessor, still had food. He decided to share everything he had and spread the word, "Everyone is to come to a potlatch!"

When the people came they were in the last stages of starvation and their hunger was awful, said the old ones. But he allayed their suffering and when they went home, all were recovered and made well.

LINA VILLAGE — at the east end of Lina Island, still had a few totem poles left when it was purchased for a homesite by Mr. and Mrs. John McLellan in the early 1900s. Nothing has been recorded about this village, but it appears to have been of more recent occupancy than Gasins and Gaodjaos. The McLellans were very conscious of their trust when occupying this place and took particular care of the poles. The old lodge ruins were not disturbed.

Eight families lived on Lina Island in the pioneering days. They hoped a road would be built from Queen Charlotte City to Lina Narrows, a bridge built across the Narrows, then the road continued around the south shore which had a good grade for road building.

McLellans lived on the east end of the island. Fred and Ivor Mattock's property adjoined McLellans. Mattocks were the green thumb gardeners who grew unbelievably excellent produce and walked off with most of the first prizes in any fair with a vegetable competition, not only on the Charlottes but in some of the big mainland events.

Donald Cochrane had the lot next to Mattocks. The remains of some of the huge slabs of the houses of Drum-Town were on his land. Ben Harmer was on the west side of Cochrane, with George Freeman's homestead to the west of Harmer again. A small portion was surveyed out of Freeman's land to become the minute homesite of Percy Wiggs.

On the north shore of Lina Island Charlie Beck took out a pre-emption. The tales told about Mr. Beck are legion. "A stoop-shouldered man, his particular delight was to put on his "mean" look and torment people," says Charlie Hartie.

The McLellan home on the east end of Lina Island.
John McLellan bought the mine at Gold Harbour (Mitchell Inlet) in 1907
and successfully operated it for a number of years.

Photo - Agnes Mathers.

View from the verandah of the McLellan home on Lina Island.
The Haida house pole (left side of photo) had begun to deteriorate when
this photo was taken a few years after the McLellan's left.

Photo - Agnes Mathers.

293

"Nothing gave him greater joy than to be able to raise the hackles on someone and, once he found a mark, he would push the poor victim almost beyond endurance." Beck was a hardworking, industrious man, his place on Lina still has the fruit trees, shrubs, holly trees and remnants of a large garden patch, indicating its former beauty when under his crusty care.

*DYER POINT — the most westerly tip of Lina Island. Named during the Pender survey in 1866.

*WEED ROCK — off Dyer Point. The name was applied during Pender's survey to a rock midway between Meyer Island and Dyer Point.

*LINA NARROWS — the narrow section of the waterway separating Lina Island from Graham. It dries. Lina Island homesteaders hoped a bridge might be built there linking a proposed road from Queen Charlotte City with another to the south shore of Lina Island.

CROW ISLANDS — a local name for the two islands which lie on the drying flat to the east of Lina Narrows.

COCHRANE'S BAY — local name for the bay on the south side of Lina Island, off Lot No. 1305, formerly owned by Donald Cochrane. This was the site of Drum-Village, Gaodjaos.

FREEMAN'S BAY — local name for the bay on the south side of Lina Island, off Lot No. 1304, formerly owned by George Freeman. Gambling-Sticks-Village, Gasins, lay a little to the west of this.

*WITHERED POINT — a promontory 280 feet high which is connected to Lina Island at the southwest part of the island. The connection is only a narrow neck, causing the descriptive Withered Point to be applied by Captain Daniel Pender in 1866 during the survey.

*TREE ISLET — off the northwest end of Maude Island, is the south tip of a chain of islets and rocks, running in a northwesterly direction, which includes Angle, Claudet and Burnt Islands. Named during Pender,s survey in 1866.

*ANGLE ISLAND — named during the 1866 survey by Pender, lies about 1/2 mile northwest of Tree Islet, and close by Claudet Island.

*CLAUDET ISLAND — lying between Angle and Burnt Island is connected to them by drying spits and islets off either end. Named WEDGE ISLAND by Captain Pender in 1866, after its shape when delineated on the chart. Renamed in 1945 by the Hydrographic Service because of duplication of that name. It is after Mr. Francis George Claudet, superintendent of the Assay Office at New Westminster. Claudet assayed the samples of coal from the Cowgitz that were left with him by Thomas Trounce (Trounce Inlet) in August

1865. And on this assay the decision was made to mine coal at Cowgtiz.

*BURNT ISLAND — north of Claudet Island and the largest in the chain. Named in 1866 by Captain Daniel Pender. At one time it became the scene of a bloody episode when a Raven Crest family satisfied a grudge occasioned by a deliberate insult to one of their woman by an Eagle Crest man.

The Raven family had been camping on a fort island near Anchor Cove, to the west. One day they were visited by a family of Eagle Crest people, one of whom was named Shaman's Batons. Batons made a big palaver about wanting to marry one of the Raven women. The marriage was agreed to, but when the woman went to get into Batons's canoe, he quickly pushed out from shore and in the most insulting manner left her standing - intimating that the *last* thing on earth he would do would be to marry with *her*.

The Raven family were astounded at his derisive action. But the old ones said, "Good riddance. Let him go. It would be no bargain with that one."

Batons apparently could not leave well enough alone. Soon afterwards a message was sent to the Ravens that he had reconsidered and was now truly coming for the woman. No more pranks. The Raven family moved to the fort on Burnt Island to await the visit.

In a few days the canoe arrived. Possibly a little unsure of his welcome, Batons did not immediately go the camp himself, but sent his nephews. The Ravens made a fuss over the nephews, talking very loudly so Batons in the canoe would not miss a word. Since Batons was not in evidence, said the Ravens, they would give the woman to the eldest of the nephews. Batons was horrified.

Jumping out of the canoe he ran up to where the discussion was being held. The nephews and some of the Ravens sat in a circle inside the house. Batons entered. Hardly was he inside when the chief gave a signal. Like lightning Raven knives were drawn from concealment and the entire Eagle party killed except for three who escaped from the house. They were quickly hunted down and finished off and all the bodies thrown over a steep cliff. Only miserable Batons survived to become the slave of the people he had insulted.

The Ravens left Burnt Island after the episode, moving to live on Torrens Island - another fort island. Retribution worked both ways. There was no water on Torrens. This meant crossing to Skidegate to fetch some each day - a hazardous operation since the family of Batons lived among the people of Skidegate. The Ravens were in great fear and made their trips furtively at night. On one trip the chief of the Raven tribe at Torrens was betrayed by another Raven family, and the relatives of Batons trapped him when he came for water.

They surrounded him and drove him out into the sea. A bright moon burst through the night clouds at that time. Batons family closed on the fleeing chief and killed him before the eyes of his watching people, then cut off his head - holding it up for all to see. In retaliation the Torrens Island people took a cross-cut saw and sawed the enslaved Batons in two.

The grisly affair happened in the fall. In the spring the Torrens Island Ravens moved to Lawn Hill. The Ravens who had betrayed them came up shortly after to do battle, landing at high-tide. A fierce fight followed and the attackers were forced to retreat with heavy losses. Some attempted to flee up Tlell way but were followed and killed. Only a few managed to escape by getting far into the woods. Their canoes were promptly smashed by the Torrens Island Ravens. The wretched escapees, whose home was at Chaatl, at the west end of Skidegate Channel, faced a grim ordeal making their way back to their home. At one point to cross some water they had to use grave boxes to float on. It did nothing to enhance their already shattered reputation.

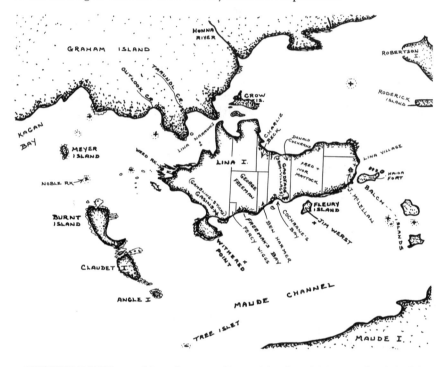

*NOBLE ROCK — midway between Burnt island and Meyer Island, it dries at 19 feet. Named during Pender's 1866 survey.

*MEYER ISLAND — only one foot high, is north of Burnt Island. Formerly called REEF ISLAND, a name applied during Pender's survey. Because of duplications the Hydrographic Service requested a change in 1945. MEYER is after Captain William Meyer, master of the *Danube* when she struck a rock near here in 1891.

William Meyer, born in Germany in 1850, arrived in Victoria after seafaring in most parts of the world. He commanded the barque *Estells* then, and delivered a cargo of water pipe, the first to be received in Victoria. The *Estells* sustained severe damage in a gale at Esquimalt and, while awaiting repairs, Meyer met and married Henrietta Moore, daughter of the well-known steamboat man. Later he went into business with his father-in-law. When Moore retired, Meyer joined the Canadian Pacific Navigation Company. His main charge was the steamer *Danube*, usually on northern routes, with occasional trips to the Columbia

River. In 1884 he commanded the *Princess Louise* and won Newton Chittenden's gratitude by making a special trip to Masset - Skidegate was the usual port of call - to unload the men and supplies for Chittenden to begin his exploration.

*DANUBE ROCK — southwest of Meyer Island, dries at 5 feet and discovered the hard way when the steamer *Danube* struck it in April 1891. An iron vessel, she had been built near Glasgow in 1869 for the Scottish Oriental Company and put on the London to China run. In 1890 the Canadian Pacific Navigation Company bought her to add to their growing list of ships. Her name appeared frequently in connection with transportation in northern waters in early newspaper items. It was the *Danube* which brought news of the overdue *Nellie G. Thurston's* grounding in 1902. (Mentioned under Thurston Harbour).

*KAGAN BAY — which lies to the west of Lina Island, is a modification of the Haida name for the summit of the Slatechuck Range which dominates the skyline of the bay. It has also been called KAHGAN BAY, COWGITZ BAY and WATERFOWL BAY.

*LEGACE ISLAND— one mile west of Burnt Island and triangular in shape. Formerly called TRIANGLE ISLAND, a name given it following Pender's 1866 survey. Its Haida name is HOW'KU'YNDA. The name of LEGACE was suggested by the Hydrographic Service in 1945 after Peter Legace, who accompanied John Work in 1850 from Port Simpson to investigate reports that gold had been found by some Haidas in Mitchell Inlet. Mrs. Work's maiden name was Legace.

*TREBLE ISLAND — is 1/2 a mile northwest of Legace Island, and appeared on the chart following Pender's 1866 survey of Skidegate Inlet.

*CANOE POINT — there are varying opinions as to the exact location of this point. Both the Pender chart and the B.C. Pilot say it is the northern extremity of the most easterly unnamed island off Christie Bay. However Dr. Dawson and the Hydrographic Service in Victoria say it is not on the unnamed island, but is the point on Graham Island off which the unnamed islets lie - on the east side of Christie Bay.

*CHRISTIE BAY — south of Treble Island in the Anchor Cove area. Named by Pender in 1866. Thought to be after George Christie, master of The *Sparrowhawk* . Pender named two other places after Christie that same year - Christie Islands and Christie Pass. (Not on the Q.C.I.)

*SCALUS ISLAND — west of Christie Bay and near the entrance to Long Inlet. Appeared on the chart following Pender's 1866 survey. It is a modification of the Haida name.

*LONG INLET — which is entered between Anthracite Point and Scalus Island, arches in a westerly, then northwesterly direction, to form the top part of the outline of the boot-shaped peninsula extending off Graham Island at this point. Formerly called LONG ARM by both Pended and Dawson, it was renamed during the 1945-46 period of reassessment by the Hydrographic Service. Several islands lie in the first half of the inlet and a good fishing stream runs into its head.

*SALTSPRING BAY — southwest of Christie Bay, on the south shore of Long Inlet near the entrance. Shown on both Pender's 1866 maps and Dawson's 1878 map. At the east side of the mouth of the stream entering the bay, the bay, Dawson indicated a coal measure which he felt to be a possible mine site.

*SANDSTONE ISLANDS — a somewhat scattered group of rocks and islands north and west of Saltspring Bay. Pender called them Sand Stone Islands. Dawson adapted this to SANDSTONE.

*GUST ISLAND — north and west of the Sandstones, a modification of a Haida name; applied by Pender in 1866. In ancient times it was used as a grave island by the Haidas, but has been completely vandalized by souvenir hunters in recent years.

*BERRY ISLANDS — west of Gust Island, are 2 in number and connected to the shore of Graham Island by a drying bank. They lie off the mouth of an unnamed stream which has its headwaters on part of Hump Mountain. One tributary of this stream drains a small lake. Along a valley near the stream the Haidas had a well-used trail from Long Inlet to Trounce Inlet, first noted by Captain D. Pender in 1866.

*YOUNG POINT — northwest of the Berry Islands, is a hook-nosed point which is one of the many fossil sites abounding in Skidegate Inlet.
W.A.G. Young was Colonial Secretary of the Colony of British Columbia 1863-68. Pender made his report to Young following the 1866 survey of Skidegate Inlet. Young Point named in connection with the survey.

*LAGINS CREEK — flows into the head of Long Inlet and is an adaption of the Haida word for the creek. Fossils are located at its mouth.

LAGINS VILLAGE — lay on the north side of the mouth of the creek. The name meant "a good place." The village site is now part of the Haida LAGINS RESERVE containing 40 acres.

*BIRCH MOUNTAIN — east of the head of Long Inlet, is 2,845 feet high. At the time of Pender's survey in 1866, the Honourable A.N. Birch was Administrator of Government for the Colony of British Columbia. Prior to being appointed to that post, Birch had been Colonial Secretary and during earlier surveys of other regions, Pender had made reports to him. Birch Mountain named in connection with the 1866 survey.

*MOUNT SEYMOUR — lying between Kagan Bay and Long Inlet is 2,190 feet high. Named in 1865 by George Robinson, superintendent for the Cowgitz Mining operation. When Mr. Robinson made his report to the directors of the company on August 4, 1865, he added, "In compliment to his Excellency, Governor Seymour, I have named MOUNT SEYMOUR."

Frederick Seymour succeeded Sir James Douglas as governor of the mainland Crown Colony of B.C. In 1864. Vancouver Island was a separate colony at that time with Arthur Kennedy as its governor. When the colonies joined in 1866, Kennedy left and Seymour was sworn in as Governor of the United Colonies. Seymour wanted New Westminster to be capital, thus infuriating the Victorians. When, after a terrific row, Victoria was decided upon as capital Seymour was not forgiven for his stand.

The Seymours moved to the capital city and met with an icy reception. They ignored it and went about their duties in a normal manner. Seymour further antagonized the politicians by not being keen about confederation, partly because he could not bring himself to become involved in all the problems which would have to be resolved to bring this about. Some historians say that had Seymour lived it is possible British Columbia would have become part of the United States - along with that country's acquisition of Alaska.

In June 1869 word came to Victoria of trouble with the Indians at Bella Coola and on the Charlottes. Seymour, who had been very ill with dysentry when the news arrived, nevertheless felt he must personally investigate the report. Taking Joseph Trutch with him he left for northern waters on the *Sparrowhawk* under Captain Mist. It soon became obvious that Seymour was far from recovered. He grew worse daily. The ship's surgeon, Dr. Comrie, insisted they go directly from the Charlottes to Victoria. But for once Seymour became strangely insistent, in contrast to his usual distaste for making decisions. They must go first to Bella Coola. He would settle the fuss with the Indians. Barely had they arrived at Bella Coola when on June 10, 1869, Frederick Seymour died aboard the ship. He was 49.

Events in B.C. as a result of his death took quite a different tack. His successor Musgrave moved quickly and in 1871, 2 years after Seymour's death, British Columbia became a province of Canada.

*JOSETTE POINT — north of Gust Island, near the entrance to Long Inlet. Named STEEP POINT in 1866 by Captain Pender, and renamed by the Hydrographic Service in 1945. JOSETTE Work, was the wife of the H.B.C. factor, John Work, who went from Port Simpson in 1850 to investigate reports of gold at Mitchell Inlet. (Mrs. Work's name has also been shown as Suzette in some histories.)

*GOSSET BAY — lies between Josette Point on its west and Anthracite Point on its east. It has had other names. Pender and Dawson show it as SHOAL BAY. James Richardson (Richardson Inlet) in his 1873 report to Alfred Selwyn called it SHALLOW BAY. It has also been called GOSSET SHOAL.

In 1945 the name of GOSSET was suggested by the Hydrographic Service after Mr. W.D. Gosset, treasurer and postmaster of the Colony of British Columbia in 1859 and under whom Francis Claudet worked as Assayer.

Hooper Creek runs into the head of Gosset Bay.

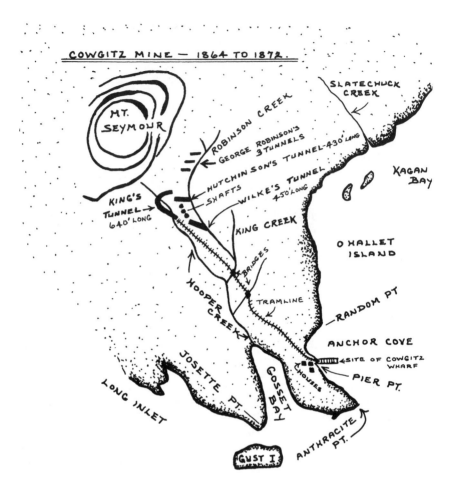

COWGITZ MINE — 1864 TO 1872.

HOOPER CREEK — not a gazetted name, but surely should be, for it was on this creek the first discovery of coal was made - and coal was *the* big speculation on the Charlottes for many years. In 1971 coal was still in the news when several extensive areas were under application by two companies.

William Downie found coal near the headwaters of this creek in 1859. The site was called Cowgitz, but the creek not named. When the work party came up to open the claim, Hooper was among the first party arriving in 1864.

In 1867 a Mr. King working in this area found a coal vein; the subsequent tunnel into it enabled over 800 tons of coal to be extracted, a portion of which was shipped to Victoria. This was on the west bank of Hooper Creek, at the point where the creek descends steeply from the base of Mount Seymour. The tunnel was called variously, Hooper Creek Tunnel, King's Tunnel and also Nicholson's Tunnel.

300

ROBINSON CREEK — a tributary of Hooper Creek, it flows from a general northeast direction to join Hooper Creek about 1/3 of a mile from the mouth. There were several tunnels in the proximity of Robinson Creek - Wilkes Tunnel, 450 feet long, entered from the west bank of the creek; Hutchinson's Tunnel, 430 feet long, north of Wilkes; and above both of these George Robinson had three smaller tunnels driven in.

The first party of miners sent to open up Cowgitz left Victoria on August 1, 1864, arriving at Skidegate (Landing) on September 15. The lengthy trip almost exhausted their supplies so they accomplished little except to obtain proof that anthracite coal was there.

In June of the following year, a second party went up on the vessel *Random,* with George Robinson, Mining Superintendent for the Cowgitz operation in charge. He secured enough information to give a report to the stockholders, had Captain Hallet of the *Random* make a sketch survey of Anchor Cove, and established a good relationship with the Haidas, ". . . who are very friendly," he said, "and seem anxious for whites to come and settle among them."

KING CREEK — is a tributary of Robinson Creek. It joins Robinson Creek a short distance north of the bridge built over Robinson for the tramline. Named after Mr. King mentioned under Hooper Creek.

COWGITZ — the name given to the coal site at Hooper Creek and surrounding area. On the strength of samples obtained by William Downie in 1859, some Victoria businessmen decided to open a mine. Called the Queen Charlotte Coal Mining Company, with Thomas Trounce as chairman, the company obtained a government reserve of 20,000 acres, 5,000 of which they paid for at a lease fee of $100 a year. The rest was to be purchased as required at $1 per acre. The 1864 work party arrived and on the strength of their find, a more extensive operation was begun under George Robinson in 1865. To obtain legal title an official survey of the property was ordered, and Cowgitz area became Lot No. 1 when surveyed in 1867, with the Crown Grant being given to the company in 1868.

They were beset by continual problems - not the least of which was lack of coal in commercial quality and quantity. Operations ceased in 1872.

The property subsequently changed hands several times, but very little real mining was ever done. Charlie Hartie of Queen Charlotte City recalls being hired to work there in 1923. "I was to open up the old workings," he says, "so a mining engineer could make an examination of them. . .there was a wild scheme to use the Cowgitz coal for power at a *pulp mill* to be built at Slatechuck. The boss, McMorris, found a plan of the old workings in Victoria, so we were able to locate all the old tunnels and shafts. Thank goodness nothing ever came of it."

*ANTHRACITE POINT — at the entrance to Long Inlet, is also the east entrance point of Gosset Bay. Formerly called SOUTH POINT, a name it received back in the days of Pender and Dawson's mapping of the region. The change of name, because of duplication, requested by the Hydrographic Service in 1945. ANTHRACITE suggested in association with the coal found in this vicinity.

*ANCHOR COVE — north of Anthracite Point. First referred to as INNER BAY,it was soon given the name by which it is now known, when boats began to anchor offshore there to unload supplies for Cowgitz Mine.

*PIER POINT — is in Anchor Cove. A small point juts into the cove and the wharf was built at the end of this point. The tramline came down to the wharf. There were several buildings located near the 700-foot dock in connection with the mine - bunk houses, mess house and offices.

*RANDOM POINT — the north entrance point of Anchor Cove. Formerly called NORTH POINT. (Anthracite Point was South Point) RANDOM was suggested by the Hydrographic Service in 1945 after the sloop of that name which cleared from New Westminster on June 5th, 1865, ". . . to sail to the North West Coast." She had on board George Robinson and a party of coal miners bound for the newly proposed mining venture at Cowgitz.

*HALLET ISLAND — north of Anchor Cove and about 2 cables off the west shore of Kagan Bay. On the charts of Pender and Dawson in 1866 and 1878 three small islets are shown in this vicinity. They were named SHIP ISLETS. The Hallet Island of today appears to be the most southerly of the former Ship Islets.

Hallet was suggested in 1945 by the Hydrographic Service after the master of the sloop *Random.* (see above) Captain Hallet at George Robinson's request made the first hydrographic map of the immediate region when he sounded and sketched the INNER HARBOUR in 1865.

*SLATECHUCK CREEK — flows into Kagan Bay about a mile northeast of Anchor Cove. Newton Chittenden in 1884 called this creek KLICK-A-DOON. James Richardson, assisted by James Dean in 1873. made an investigation of the Cowgitz coal measures and reported that he had asked Dean to cut a trail into SLATY CREEK. Dawson gave it the present SLATE CHUCK, now modified to SLATECHUCK.

A mile and a half from Kagan Bay the Haidas have a Crown Granted mineral claim centered on the site of a small quarry near the Slatechuck Creek. Containing over 43 acres, it is called the *Black Slate.* This is the source of the slate used in the carving done by the Haidas and is under the strict control of the Skidegate Band.

In 1923 W.G. McMorris promoted a scheme to put in a pulp mill at the Slatechuck. Mercifully that was one hot air plan which evaporated.

COAL CREEK — is a small stream coming into the Slatechuck from the west. Coal is exposed in the stream bed about 1/2 a mile above the junction of the creeks. In 1912-13 a 757-foot adit was driven in across the measures by the British Pacific Coal Company. A number of specimens were collected by J.D. MacKenzie in 1914, but all had to be taken from the dump outside. The adit was in a dangerously gassy condition.

*KAGAN CREEK — is a tributary of the Slatechuck, coming into it from the northeast and joining the Slatechuck north of Coal Creek's intersection.

BERTIE HILL — rising to 800 feet, is east of the Slatechuck valley and first appeared under this name on Pender's map after the 1866 survey.

*OUTLOOK CREEK — flows into a small cove north of Meyer Island in Kagan Bay. Named in connection with coal claims, it first appeared on J.D. MacKenzie's geological map of 1914.

* TARUNDL CREEK — flows south to enter Lina Narrows. A modification of a Haida name, it first appeared on MacKenzie's 1914 geological map.

* HONNA RIVER — a corruption of the old Haida name XAH'NA in use when Captain Musgrave adopted it as HONNA to the charts in 1911-16. It drains from Stanley Lake, flowing to the east as it leaves the lake, then about 4 miles from the mouth it makes a right-angled turn and flows south to empty opposite Lina Island. The main trail into the Yakoun Valley in early years followed along the Honna as far as the right-angled turn. Four Mile Camp lay a little to the west of this. From this camp the trail had two branches, one leading out to Camp Robertson and the other going northward along the Yakoun Valley to Camp Wilson, thence to Masset Inlet.

Today a logging road runs along the main valley of the Honna, enabling the huge MacMillan and Bloedel logging trucks to transport the timber from the lush interior region of Graham Island to their log dump near the mouth of the Honna.

FOUR MILE CAMP — a well known stopping place in early trail travel. It was about 4 -miles from the mouth of the Honna where the Honna makes its right-angled turn.

*SKOWKONA CREEK — flowing from the east, joins the Honna via an unnamed stream a little north of the right-angled turn of the Honna. An adaption of the Haida word for knife-edge according to some, but others say it was also the work for blue grouse. At any rate it was applied during the land survey of this region in the early 1900s, in connection with the coal interest.

*SKOWKONA MOUNTAIN — formerly shown as SKOWKONA RIDGE, is north of Skowkona creek. An unnamed creek from its slopes intersects with the Honna River, at which point it becomes one and the same as the Honna. The Skowkona creek is a tributary of this unnamed creek.

MOUNTAIN RANGE - LONG INLET TO THE HONNA

The location of the various mountains on maps of this region is as inconsistent as their given heights and it depends on which map one consults as to a particular identification. So as not to add to the confusion, this book takes as its guide the charts and maps of 1963 as they seem to agree more than those of any other year.

*MOUNT STAPLETON — about 3,675 feet high is north of the head of Long Inlet. Named during the Pender survey.

*DELTA DOME — a little to the northeast of Mount Stapleton. Originally called DOME MOUNTAIN on the chart following Pender's 1866 survey. Rises to 2,720 feet.

*DELTA CREEK — has its headwaters on the slopes of Delta Dome. This creek empties into Yakoun Lake to the north and will be covered more fully in the next chapter, which takes in this region.

*MOUNT NEEDHAM — rises to 4,000 feet and is southeast of Delta Dome. Named during the Pender survey or shortly after. Mr. Justice Needham was a highly esteemed judge of that day. A man who could not be sidetracked by red tape, but would cut right through to the essence and apply good common-sense - even if it meant making new rules of application to effect a fair settlement.

*SLATECHUCK MOUNTAIN — with its twin peaks, 3,310 feet and 3,265 feet is one of the most conspicuous heights in the range.

*MOUNT RAYMOND — another peak named following or during the Pender survey. Slightly northeast of Slatechuck Mountain, it is 2400 feet.

*MOUNT GENEVIEVE — north and east of both Mount Raymond and Slatechuck Mountain is estimated to be about 2,370 feet high. The name dates back to the Pender chart.

*MARIE PEAK — close by and east of Mount Genevieve and much the same height. It first appeared on J.D. MacKenzie's 1914 geological map.

*NIPPLE MOUNTAIN — named for its silhouette. Shown on Pender's chart. It rises to a little over 2,300 feet.

*BEARSKIN BAY — the northeast part of Skidegate Inlet, fronting Queen Charlotte City. First shown as a hyphenated word BEAR-SKIN on Pender's chart. Origin of the name not confirmed.

*MAPLE ISLAND — in Bearskin Bay off Smith Point. On an old 1852 chart made of Skidegate Inlet it was called OBSERVATION ISLAND. Following the 1866 Pender survey renamed MAPLE ISLAND. A pretty island it became a favourite picnic place, especially for the Smith family who lived on the point opposite. "We really regarded it as our own special island," says Bessie Smith today, "and at every opportunity would be out there."

*GOODEN ISLAND — west of Maple Island, is opposite Beattie Point. About 90 feet high, it was named during the 1866 Pender survey.

*RODERICK ISLAND — west of Gooden Island and close south of Robertson Island. Named during the Pender survey and believed to be after Roderick Finlayson, Chief Factor for the H.B.C. owners of the vessel *Beaver* engaged in the survey. That same year Pender also surveyed waters on the mainland side, naming as he did so Finlayson Channel and another Roderick Island for Roderick Finlayson.

*ROBERTSON ISLAND — lies off the west portion of Queen Charlotte City. Named for and by William A. Robertson who once owned it. Mr. Robertson with the ex-sealer, Jimmy Shields, staked coal areas in the Yakoun Valley in 1885. Robertson Island, now privately owned, contains numerous middens.

KOAGAOGIT VILLAGE Wide-waters-flowing-down-rapidly-town — one of the many former Haida village sites in this area, lay east of the mouth of the Honna on the north shore of Bearskin Bay. An Eagle Crest town, its chief was Qa'gon, one-who-travels-about. This tribe was a division of the Gitins of Skidegate, known as the Seaward Eagles.

DADJINGITS VILLAGE, Common-hat-village — another Eagle Crest site, stood east of Kaogaogit. These villagers, also a division of the Skidegate Gitins, were known as the Rotten-House-People. Their chief was called The-one-they-become-jealous-of.

*QUEEN CHARLOTTE (CITY) — lies along the north shore of Bearskin Bay and covers most of Lots 15,15A, 16 and 16A. In 1889 this entire 703-acre strip of choice waterfront property belonged to three men. James R. McKenzie and James Shields purchased the eastern portion, Lots 15 and 15A. Mr. R. Sturdy put a down payment on 16 and 16A. Purchase price: one dollar per acre.

Mr. Sturdy, however, changed his mind. His options on Lots 16 and 16A were promptly picked up by T.S. Gore and in 1891 Gore, McKenzie and Shields received their Crown Grants.

Jimmy Shields first came to the Charlottes in 1885 with W.A. Robertson to prospect for coal, making several return trips later to help Robertson prove up on the coal claims. The oilery at Skidegate (Landing) was the headquarters of the expected business growth of the Charlottes, it seemed logical to assume that any community springing up as a result would be in this vicinity, thus Shields chose the land immediately adjacent.

T.S.Gore had another idea. He persuaded his partners to enter into a townsite company. An American syndicate had secured a 30-year lease on 90 square miles of virgin timber around Skidegate Inlet, but to hold the lease, they had to put in a mill. Gore's company provided the site. The town would develop around it.

The first survey for streets and lots was made on Gore's property. As the town grew, portions of 15 and 15A were acquired and additional streets and lots laid out on them.

Naming was something the townsite owners had little time for. Gore's property

Queen Charlotte City. Picnic Held May 24, 1912.
Copy Photo - Provincial Archives, Victoria.
Identifications by Dorothy Barge, who owns the original of this photo.

1. Miss Barge
2. John Murdoch, Presbyterian minister
3. Sam Scowcroft
4. James E. Corlett, managing-director of the mill at Q.C. City. (Corlett Peninsula, Tasu Sound named after him.)
5. Mr. Scowcroft, ran a boarding house in Q.C. City
6. Mrs. Scowcroft
7. Jimmy Hickey (Hickey Lake)
8. Clarence Johnston came to the Charlottes in 1911 and went into partnership with Howard Fairbairn, owning and running tugboats
9. Mrs. Clarence Johnston, sister of Mrs. Fairbairn
10. Emmanuel Girard, ran the mill in Q.C. City. (Girard Point)
11. Mrs. James Campbell

12. *James Campbell, printer for Windy Young; later set up his own newspaper in opposition to Windy*

13. *Miss Cameron*

14. *B. Russell, student Methodist preacher*

15. *Miss Atkins, teacher*

16. *John L. Barge, carpenter (Barge Point)*

17. *Mrs. John Barge, who came with her husband to Q.C. City in 1908.*

18. *Howard Fairbairn, partner in the tugboat business with Clarence Johnston (8). (Fairbairn Shoals)*

19. *Donald Cochrane, storekeeper in Q.C. City. (Cochrane Bay, Lina I.)*

20. *Mrs. Emmanuel Girard*

21. *Jack Cochrane (baby)*

22. *Mrs. Donald Cochrane, sister of Charlie Hartie (Hartie Creek)*

23. *Morna Phair*

24. *George D. Beattie, druggist in Q.C. City (Beattie Anchorage and Beattie Point)*

25. *Azeline Girard, who later married George Beattie*

26. *Mrs. Howard Fairbairn*

27. *Fosey Fraser, daughter of Ma and Pa Fraser, (Fraser's Lagoon, Sheldens Bay)*

28. *Lillian Scowcroft*

29. *Bob Scowcroft*

30. *Edwin Fairbairn, drowned in July of this same year*

31. *Bertha Girard*

32. *Theoline Girard*

33. *Dorothy Barge, who provided the identifications for this photo and who says that when the picture was taken she was trying to keep the wad of gum in her mouth from showing.*

34. *Juliette Girard*

35. *Freddie Scowcroft*

Queen Charlotte City 1910 or 1911. Left to right the buildings were:-
Lauder's Hotel, dimly seen through the trees; George Beattie's first drug store;
John Sachs' store (with verandah); Windy Young's newspaper office;
Moore's Pool Hall. John Barge had an undertaking parlour on the first floor for a time.
The second floor was used as a hall and a school in early years.

Photo - Mrs. Roy Field

307

never advanced beyond numbers, 1st,2nd,3rd and so on for streets and avenues. With the opening of the eastern part they did provide a few extras in the names of trees. But the best they could do for the town itself was merely The Townsite. Then they hired a man to promote the sale of lots, who more than made up for their lack of imagination - Daniel R. "Windy" Young.

He immediately relegated the pallid "Townsite" name to the wastebasket where it properly belonged. A new name was installed. QUEEN CHARLOTTE CITY. What matter if there were only a few tents?

Windy knew the value of publicity. He started a newspaper - the first of his many activities. He promoted everything and anything from oil to coal to fish - and the vigour of his sales pitch put life-blood into his first love - "the townsite."

It spelled the end of the capital status enjoyed up to then by Skidegate. Windy's "city" took that distinction for her own as though it had been predestined from the time the first volcanic upheaval had thrust the Islands into being. And kept it. It is not the largest settlement today, nor does it have official village status, but it is still Windy's Queen Charlotte City which is the unofficial capital of the Charlottes.

Because of water rights, all the creeks of any size flowing through the townsite are named, some of which are gazetted.

CRABAPPLE CREEK — which enters Bearskin Bay on the east side of the MacMillan and Bloedel log dump, is best remembered for the old gentleman who made his home at its mouth. Sam Larsen had a shack and kept his boat there for so many years they almost seemed part of the landscape. This picturesqueness was captured by a photographer for *Beautiful British Columbia* when Crabapple Creek appeared in colour.

*HARTIE CREEK — named by and after Mr. Charlie Hartie when he secured the water rights to the creek. Charlie came to Queen Charlotte City in the summer of 1911 to work for his brother-in-law, Donald Cochrane. "Cochrane had the store," he says, "and I just came up for the summer holidays to run a boat for him delivering supplies up the coast. Well, I suppose I'm still on those holidays." An active member of the Rod and Gun Club, he is an authority on most matters to do with the outdoors - be it timber cruising, prospecting, fishing or general local knowledge. He has been an invaluable aid in the preparation of both my Queen Charlotte Islands books. In addition to a fantastic memory, his keen interest in ensuring that pioneering history is preserved has led to a comprehensive file of maps and memos.

ISOBEL CREEK — east of Hartie Creek, acquired its name through a water rights application.

*STURDY CREEK — much better known locally by its former name of HOSPITAL CREEK, because it served the first Queen Charlotte hospital. In changing the name of this creek, the Geographic Board noted that the creek flowed through Lot 16A. The first application to purchase that lot came from Mr. R. Sturdy on November 11, 1889. The creek is named for him. Sturdy never acquired title to the lot, however, for after making a down payment he let it lapse. In February of 1891 T.S. Gore took it over, paid the balance and immediately secured a Crown Grant.

*PREMIER CREEK — also named in conjunction with water rights. The Premier Hotel stood on the left bank of the stream. Built in 1910 by W.J. "Hotel" Smith, it boasted a liquor licence in addition to the usual rooms and meals. Also a barber shop, run by Fred Mattock, the able gardener of Lina Island. In later years the hotel was renamed Haida Hotel.

*ANDY'S CREEK — runs into Bearskin Bay near Beattie Point. Named when Andy Christenson took out water rights. Before moving to live in Queen Charlotte, Mr. Christenson pioneered at Lawn Hill, working his land in 1909 along the Inside Road.

*BEATTIE POINT — named after George DeWitt Beattie, one of Queen Charlotte's earliest residents. Born in Ontario, Mr. Beattie spent most of his youth in Victoria, where he was well-known as an active lacrosse player. On the Charlottes he was not only a druggist - he was the only one. In conjunction with his store he also became Queen Charlotte City's first postmaster.

The Government wharf extends from Beattie Point and to the west of it are the floats for smaller craft.

*SMITH POINT — lies east of Beattie Point and is named after Captain Thomas N. Smith. "My mother and dad were married in Wrangell, Alaska," says Bessie Smith, now with the Registrar General's Office in Ottawa. "Dad had been sent out from eastern Canada to help in the Salvation Army's work amongst the gold miners north of Skagway."

It was a rough country for a bride, but little Jessie Randall didn't hesitate when Tom Smith asked her to meet him there. Two sons, Alex and Ted, were born to them in this northern outpost. Then Captain and Mrs. Smith were asked to take charge of the Salvation Army Corps at Port Simpson. Visitors from the Queen Charlotte Islands were frequent in Port Simpson. Their description of opportunities on those far-off islands intrigued Tom Smith. It sounded like a fine place to bring up a family. So their move to the Charlottes in 1910 was not a church posting - it was one of the heart.

"They settled at Sandspit first," says Bessie, "and became firm friends with William Oliver, missionary for the Methodist Church. The Olivers and my parents seemed to have a lot in common in their practical approach to things."

However, with more job opportunities in the embryo Queen Charlotte City, Mr. Smith moved his family to Windy's town. He worked in the mill and Mrs. Smith took the job of cooking for the mill crew. At every opportunity the little family went on picnics and fishing trips. Hunting to supply the family larder had to be undertaken occasionally, and one day Tom's gun discharged unexpectedly - killing young Teddy - an incident still too painful to be discussed.

Tom bought some land about 1½ miles from the settlement and the hard work of creating a home and garden in the wilds helped ease their grief. In 1913 a baby girl, Elizabeth, was born - "our Bessie" as she soon became known. Shortly afterwards a son, Tommy, made his entry. Alex, Bessie and Tommy all went to school at Charlotte, walking the rough trail each day from their isolated home.

Concerned that the children were not having Sunday School training, Mrs. Smith and Mrs. Howard Fairbairn started one. People didn't worry too much about denominationalism in those early days, so the little Salvationist taught the children, and Mrs. Fairbairn, who was not of that faith, helped her. Children from all around came with eagerness, and enthusiastic assistance was given by their parents. "They represented just about every church going," says Bessie.

Tom Smith earned a living by working in Beattie's Drug Store, then Cochrane's Groceries, did a stint at Pacofi and even found employment on the survey vessel *Lillooet* as an oiler for some months - which is no doubt why his name was applied to an Island feature at that time.

By 1924 the older Smith children were ready for high school, and reluctantly the family decided to leave for a larger centre. Like so many pioneers the Smiths left a little bit of their hearts behind, taking with them a great many happy memories of the years spent at SMITH'S POINT.

SYBIL CREEK — flows down Cedar Street in Queen Charlotte City. Named in connection with a water rights application by Mrs. Sybil de Bucy in 1946. A long time resident of the Charlottes, she came first to be with her family at Tlell on the Richardson Ranch. It was Mrs. de Bucy who, with her friend Mary Sinclair (later Mrs. Bert Roberts), ran The Bakery at Nesto Inlet in the 1920s.

JARVIS CREEK — named in connection with water rights for Harold Jarvis who bought Tom Smith's house at Smith Point.

VALLEY CREEK — after Charlie Valley, long time resident of Queen Charlotte City, who had water rights on the creek.

MUNCORD CREEK — water rights were taken out on this stream by the Munro and Secord families, who used a combination of their names in the application.

*DOUBLE MOUNTAIN — which lies at the back of Queen Charlotte City, received its name for the shape of the outline. Rising to about 1,430 at both summits, the name was applied to the charts following the Pender survey of 1866.

*HAIDA POINT — the sharp point at the west entrance of Skidegate Landing bay. Named by Captain P.C. Musgrave 1911-16 when making a hydrographic survey of the region on the *Lillooet*.

GUHLGA VILLAGE — an ancient Haida town on the shoreline between Haida and Image Points. The oilery was later built on the site, now part of Skidegate Landing. Nothing has been recorded about the village of Guhlga.

310

*IMAGE POINT — east of Haida Point. Named during the 1866 survey by Captain Pender on the *Beaver*. Legends say it is the location of a shaman's grave. Originally from the Rose Point village, when he went into his trances he became the mouthpiece of a Tlingit spirit and, during the trance would speak this language fluently as though it were his mother tongue. Yet in his normal state he was totally ignorant of Tlingit and could understand nothing said to him. Out of respect to this extraordinary gift, people ceased calling him by his own name, calling him instead a Tlingit word which meant Mother-of-the-People.

SKIDEGATE HARBOUR — lies between Image and Haida Points. It came into use when the townsite plan was drawn up in 1910 for Graham City. (Now known as Skidegate Landing.) Prior to 1910 the bay was frequently referred to as STERLING BAY after William Sterling who, with J. McB. Smith, set up a pilot plant to extract oil from the livers of dogfish in 1876. Their operation stood on the site of the old Guhlga village on the shoreline of this bay.

W.A. Robertson (of Robertson Mine
and Captain John Haan (by mast)
on Captain Haan's **Wee Jeannie**
at Skidegate in 1908.

Photo - Provincial Archives, Victoria.

311

*SKIDEGATE — is the gazetted name for the settlement between Image Point and Haida Point. Locally it is known as SKIDEGATE LANDING. Its registered townsite plan still shows it to be GRAHAM CITY. Prior to 1910 it was known simply as THE OIL WORKS and, in fact, was usually known by the latter title as long as the oilery operated.

The townsite owners of Graham City took more effort and care in the lay-out and naming of their streets than T.S. Gore's company did in their embryo town. First for Graham City came provision for a park, KINGS PARK, in the centre of the town.

The streets beginning with GREY on the west, include LAURIER, SKIDEGATE, McBRIDE and GRAHAM. The avenues, BAY, TORONTO, CHARLOTTE, VANCOUVER, VICTORIA, KING, RUPERT, QUEEN, COLUMBIA and ONTARIO were chosen in the hope that the odious context of Oil Works would be banished forever. The townsite plan duly registered March 1910, Graham City was launched with lavish newspaper advertisements and write-ups.

However, the Post Office continued under the old name of Skidegate. No one wanted to risk losing this asset on any technicality. Especially when the other Skidegate (Haida village) still hoped for one. Dropping an established name could be tricky at that time.

But under Windy's promotion, Queen Charlotte City proved to be too much competition. Graham City (or Skidegate) did not die, as Windy hopefully predicted. It continued. The population fluctuated over the years from a handful to the growing residential area of today.

The home base for the inter-Islands ferry is there. This led to it being called locally Skidegate Landing. Situated overlooking the bay, its sloping terrain provides every home owner with a panoramic view. The main highway of the Islands passes through the village, enabling residents to be in Charlotte City in minutes for shopping, banks, schools and so on. With the ferry at their door they can as easily be in Sandspit to board the jet for the mainland cities whenever desired.

The old Oil Works which was the origin of the settlement has been gone for many years - only a few stubby pilings mark its site.

GRAHAM ISLAND. NORTH ALONG THE
YAKOUN VALLEY TO THE MOUTH OF THE
RIVER. INCLUDES THE MAMIN RIVER AND
JUSKATLA CAMP.

CHAPTER FOURTEEN

This chapter begins at the headwaters of the Honna River. It takes in the region from there, north along the Yakoun Valley to the mouth of the river and will include the Mamin River Area and Juskatla Camp.

*STANLEY LAKE — lying north of Mount Genevieve and Marie Peak, is the headwaters of the Honna River. A pretty lake of about 60 acres, surrounded by mountains on its north, west and south sides, it was named by James D. MacKenzie during his 1913-14 geological survey of Graham Island. Stanley E. Slipper, for whom it was named, served as Mackenzie's chief assistant for the first year of the survey.

*KATRINE CREEK — flows north into Stanley Lake, entering the lake midway along its south shore. Named by MacKenzie, but inspiration for naming not known.

The early maps show a trail along Katrine Creek which ran in a diagonal direction from the vicinity of Tarundl Creek to Yakoun Lake. As one oldster remarked, "They were good climbers in those days . . . followed valleys where possible, but it was up and over in most cases." The trail thus indicated would certainly have fallen into that category.

CAMP TRILBY — west of Stanley Lake, is about 2¼ miles from Yakoun Lake. A trail led into it from the mouth of Delta Creek, although the camp was close to a tributary of Baddeck Creek. Charlie Hartie of Queen Charlotte

City says that W.A. Robertson, who came to the Charlottes in 1885 with Jimmy Shields to prospect for coal, told him Jimmy named the camp. Trilby was a famous dancer whom Jimmy absolutely idolized. A cabin and shaft, about 40 feet deep, marked the location of Camp Trilby.

*MOUNT ETHELINE — northwest of Stanley Lake is estimated to be about 2,600 feet high. Named by W.A. Robertson after his second daughter, Etheline Matilda, born January 19, 1873. She later became Mrs. James Bell. After his wife died, Mr. Robertson leaned heavily on this daughter. When he eventually sold all his coal interests they took a long trip together, which included touring Europe.

*DELTA CREEK — which has its origin on, and takes its name from, Delta Dome. Delta Dome was formerly called Dome Mountain. Delta, the Greek name for the letter D, was used in the renaming of the mountain. The trail to Camp Trilby ran along Delta Creek for part of its length. MacKenzie, during his 1913 geological survey, located a 50-foot adit a prospective miner had driven in earlier near the mouth of Delta Creek. "Forty feet in from the entrance of the adit we found a 3-inch seam of anthracite coal. Outside the adit were some interesting impressions of small tree trunks in the black shale," he wrote.

TRAP HILL — a recent addition to land maps, is off the southeast of Yakoun Lake between Baddeck and Delta Creeks. Name confirmed in 1961. A geological term.

*YAKOUN LAKE — the headwaters of the Yakoun River, lies at the 350-foot level and is about 5 to 6 miles long. Yakoun is said to mean "in the middle," "on the east" and also "straight point." The latter refers to the prominent west entrance point at the river's mouth. Logging roads pass near the lake, providing access for those who do not mind walking a short distance. A bear trail from one of the spur roads is frequently used, not only to walk along, but also in some instances to drag in a small aluminum skiff. The trail emerges at Etheline Bay.

SANDSTONE CREEK — flows into the west side of Yakoun Lake. Formerly called CANYON CREEK and gazetted under that name, it was renamed in 1961 to avoid confusion with the better known Canyon Creek, 20 miles or more to the north. Sandstone Creek has also been shown on mining maps as CANNON CREEK, and men who knew this creek in early years call it by this last name. It is believed to have been named after Mr. H.B. Cannon, who actively engaged in early prospecting. He was in the Lockeport and Tasu regions in 1910.
A well-established trail followed Cannon (now Sandstone) Creek from Yakoun Lake and eventually came out at Shields Bay in Rennell Sound, at the mouth of Rockrun Creek. There are Cretacious fossils along this trail where it leaves Sandstone Creek to follow Rockrun Creek.

*BADDECK CREEK — enters Yakoun Lake on the east side. "It was named in 1913 by J.D. MacKenzie after his home town of Baddeck in Nova Scotia," says Mr. Brent Lea, who was with MacKenzie on the survey.

In Baddeck Creek are a number of bright brick-red beds. Taken in sections this rock has an almost opaque appearance and is a type of basalt. Some specimens are mottled and geologists say the bright and dark reds are caused by the presence of iron.

*ETHELINE BAY— on the east shore of Yakoun Lake, north of Baddeck Creek, and

*ETHELINE CREEK — which flows from the south to enter the head of Etheline Bay, were both named after Mr. W.A. Robertson's second daughter, for whom Mount Etheline was also named. The Yakoun River begins its journey to Masset Inlet from Etheline Bay.

*YAKOUN RIVER — which flows in a northerly direction from Yakoun Lake via Etheline Bay, emerges at the southeast corner of Masset Inlet and puts out flats at its mouth which dry for 1½ to 2 miles. It is the longest river on the Charlottes. Magnificent forests grow all through its valley and almost the entire region is under the tree farm licence of MacMillan, Bloedel and Powell River Company. One can drive from Masset Inlet to Queen Charlotte City along their logging roads. Spurs leading for miles in every direction from the main road have opened up areas formerly inaccessible.

Because of the endless log jambs, the river is unnavigable for more than a few miles at a stretch. In earlier years when the coal mine was mooted for Camp Wilson, an effort was made to keep the river open for canoes to freight supplies as far as Wilson Creek. The balance of the supplies went into the camps on the sturdy shoulders of the back-packers.

*BRENT CREEK — which has a veritable network of tributaries, joins the Yakoun River shortly after the Yakoun leaves Etheline Bay. Named in 1913 by J.D. MacKenzie after Mr. Brent T. Lea, a member of the geological survey party. In 1902 this creek was known as ROBERTSON CREEK to the Department of Mines, but the later application of Brent became the gazetted name.

After working with MacKenzie on the survey, Mr. Lea went to work with William Barton, running a drill at the Wilson Creek Mine. During the latter years of the first World War, he played an active role in the planning and construction of the big Buckley Bay mill, built to cut the superb Queen Charlotte Islands aeroplane spruce into cants for shipment to mainland mills for re-manufacture. Like all those who knew MacKenzie, Brent Lea held him in high esteem. "He was one in a million. Had a special way with the men who worked on the survey and made each fellow feel that his particular task was important to the survey."

*CAIRNES CREEK — flows off the south side of Brent Creek and is the first tributary after the site of the main bridge which today spans Brent. Named by J.D. MacKenzie in 1913-14 after Clive Cairnes, a brother of D.D. Cairnes, noted geologist. Stanley Slipper served as MacKenzie's chief assistant for the first year. Clive Cairnes was next in command to Slipper.

*SUE CREEK — enters Brent Creek from the north, and

*SUE LAKE — to the northeast, from which Sue Creek drains, were both named by J.D. MacKenzie after a friend from his home town of Baddeck. "She used to send him home-made socks when he was on the survey," remembers Mr. Lea. "However, the romance didn't lead to anything serious. MacKenzie was wounded by shrapnell during the first World War and married the head nurse of the hospital where he convalesced."

James D. MacKenzie, left, with Brent Lea and Clive Cairnes (right) at the camp near the mouth of the Honna in 1913. "We always flew two flags," recalls Mr. Lea, "a Canadian flag and the Federal Mining Division flag."

Photo - Brent Lea.

SLIPPER CREEK — is after Stanley E. Slipper, MacKenzie's assistant. Mr. Lea remembered MacKenzie naming this creek well. It is the small creek running into the east end of Sue Lake. There are two streams which do this, Slipper is the more northerly of the two.

"Slipper was a rather cantankerous chap," says Mr. Lea. "He seemed to put everyone's back up. MacKenzie figured I was the most easy-going of the crew so to keep peace in the party, he paired Slipper off with me. We had to overnight at Sue Lake at one point in the survey, so pitching our tents near one of the streams, we soon sacked out."

It began to rain heavily during the night. The water level in Sue Lake rose, backing up into the mouth of their small creek and Lea awoke suddenly to find water in the tent. Their blanket rolls in imminent danger of being soaked, he tried to rouse Slipper so they could move camp to higher ground. But Slipper when awakened would not budge. "He had gone to bed there and by crikey that was just where he would stay until morning . . . water or no water," said Mr. Lea. "There was nothing I could do to persuade him so I set about moving the tent, supplies and my own bedding. The water by this time had pretty well covered Slipper. But he still wouldn't move. I noticed it was so high on him that he was blowing it out as he exhaled, and I put a pot under his head so he wouldn't drown."

Fortunately at about this time the water stopped rising so Slipper's head remained out of the water - on top of the pot. But his stubbornness cost him dearly. Rheumatism set in so badly after his night of emersion in the cold stream, he became crippled. "MacKenzie just couldn't get over the man's foolishness," says Mr. Lea, "and declared that the stream was to be known as Slipper Creek . . . and that a few appropriate adjectives should really go along with the name because of the incident."

The second year of the survey Mr. Dolmage replaced Stanley Slipper as MacKenzie's chief assistant.

LAKE ROAD — is the name given by MacMillan and Bloedel to their logging road running alongside Sue Creek to Sue Lake and beyond it for a short distance. This road intersects the main road to Charlotte City, at the bridge over Brent Creek.

CAMP ROBERTSON — one of the main camps during the coal interest, lay in the west part of Section 20, Township 5, about 3 miles east of Yakoun Lake. Named after William A. Robertson who staked this area in 1887. (Mr. Robertson's story is carried in some detail in the Volume 1, of Queen Charlotte Islands.)

The first development work of value at this camp was done in the spring of 1893 and was still being carried on when the MacKenzie survey reached this region 1913-14. A trail went through to Yakoun Lake from Camp Robertson.

WAWA CREEK — which means "talking creek", begins in a muskeg a little to the west of Camp Robertson. The trail to Yakoun Lake followed it for a short way from the camp. About 1,000 feet from the camp along this trail the *Oliver Mine*, consisting of some thin seams of coaly shale, lay on the south bank of Wawa Creek. From *Oliver Mine* the creek flows toward the old Camp Robertson site then arcs gradually to the south and east to join Falls Creek. The trail from the Honna to Camp Robertson ran along the west side of Wawa. About 150 feet south of Camp Robertson, along Wawa, the first shaft of main coal interest of this region went in. South of this were other shafts, slopes and tunnels.

PROSPECT CREEK — flows from the west to intersect Wawa Creek about a ½ mile south of Camp Robertson. Near the intersection of the two creeks lay another working called the *Nutter Mine*. A trail led from it to Camp Robertson.

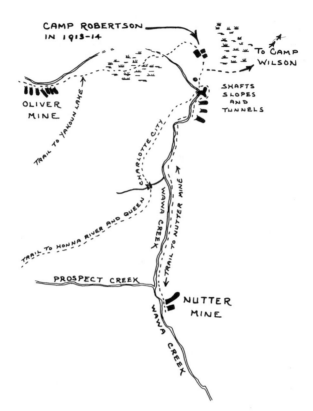

*FALLS CREEK — a tributary of Brent Creek. Wawa joins Falls Creek about a mile southeast of Camp Robertson. There is a 45-foot waterfall on the creek which gave it its name. In 1906 Dr. Ells referred to the stream as FALLS BROOK, but MacKenzie changed it to FALLS CREEK and it was so gazetted. A logging spur, Spur 333, goes a short way along Falls Creek today.

*ANTHRACITE CREEK — is a tributary of Falls Creek and joins Falls Creek about a ¼ of a mile above the intersection of Wawa and Falls.

CAMP ANTHRACITE — on Anthracite Creek about a ¼ of a mile from its junction with Falls Creek. First staked by W.A. Robertson in 1887, it received its name from him a little later on. When MacKenzie visited the camp in 1913 he found a 45-foot adit on the right bank of the creek. The coal seam appeared to be about 9 feet thick and faulted.

ELK ROAD — leads off to the northeast from the main MacMillan and Bloedel road through the Yakoun Valley and runs to the headwaters of Survey Creek, a tributary of the Tlell River. The road follows one of the Survey Creek streamlets for a short distance and has several short spurs *en route*. Engineers laying out the road had been searching for their customary brief road identifying name. They found their inspiration in a chance remark made by Ken Richardson of Port Clements, an employee of the logging company. "It looks as though this would be good elk country," he told them.

*PHANTOM CREEK — flows from the south and west to join the Yakoun River about 2½ miles north of Yakoun Lake. The old name for this creek was HIDDEN CREEK, the name by which it is shown on J.D. MacKenzie's 1913-14 geological map. A good trail went out to Rennell Sound along this creek to a point where it intersected another coming down Ghost Creek valley, thence crossing to follow Riley Creek to the west coast.

Several fossil sites lie along the Yakoun River north of its junction with Phantom Creek.

CAMP EMMONS — stood on the north bank of Phantom Creek about a mile from its junction with the Yakoun River. C.D. Emmons, veteran prospector of the Queen Charlotte Islands, made his headquarters there when he discovered oil shale in the region. Building a sturdy cabin, Mr. Emmons took in a condenser to test his find, then prepared to interest speculators.

*GHOST CREEK — flows from the west to enter the Yakoun River north of Phantom Creek. Today a logging road follows the north side of Ghost Creek for a few miles. A bridge crosses the Yakoun River close by the junction of Ghost and Yakoun and west of this bridge is a fossil site.

Ghost Creek came sharply into the news in the early years of this century with the announcement that its valley would have the mooted railway spur to carry coal from Camp Wilson to the proposed deep-sea port at the head of Rennell Sound. (Mentioned under Yakoun Pass and Riley Creek.) Three applications were filed by three separate companies to run railroads along the Yakoun Valley and south to Queen Charlotte City then north to Stewart Bay. One even expected to go all the way to Masset. The only concrete action taken was the survey through Yakoun Pass made by Mr. Riley.

WILSON CREEK LANDING — where Wilson Creek joins the Yakoun River. Still referred to by this name by people who were connected with any phase of the coal interest in the Yakoun - and is in local use to some extent even today.

The barges which took the drilling equipment for Wilson Mine were left at this junction. Canoes freighted additional supplies regularly from Masset Inlet along the Yakoun to the abandoned barges. From this point the back-packers took over, lugging everything in along a trail to Camp Wilson about ¾ of a mile from the Landing.

*WILSON CREEK — flows from the southeast to join the Yakoun River north of Ghost Creek. It took its name from the coal-mining operation on its **banks known as Camp Wilson. (See next page.)**

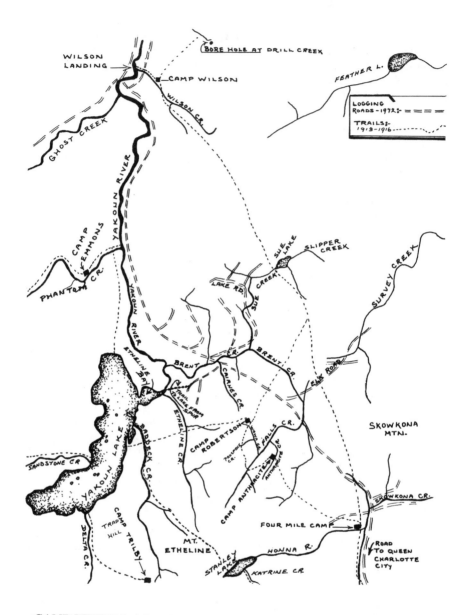

CAMP WILSON — lay ¾ of a mile from the mouth of Wilson Creek. The first coal site to be staked by W.A. Robertson when he and Jimmy Shields covered the region in 1885. Not named until about 1892 when the wealthy William Wilson took an active interest in financing Mr. Robertson.

It was Fred Nash, B.C.L.S., who located Camp Wilson's exact position on the map, and the rest of the land survey was tied in with this siting. Brent Lea recalls that it took Nash three nights, taking bearings on the stars to achieve the desired accuracy. Nash named most of the creeks in the Yakoun region

*Clearing the Yakoun River
of debris to enable
the canoes to
freight supplies to
Wilson Creek.
Ole Van Valkenberg
in bow.*

*Photo - Mrs. Frank
Van Valkenberg*

during his survey for the coal companies in the early 1900s.

In 1971 MacMillan and Bloedel applied for coal mining rights in this area.

*KING CREEK — flows from the west to enter the Yakoun River north of Wilson Creek. This stream was shown as WEST YAKOUN on a 1902 sketch map. Today a logging road follows the south side of King Creek for some distance and one can see several fossil sites along the creek. Believed to have been named during Fred Nash's initial survey.

*DRILL CREEK — flows from the southeast to enter the Yakoun River north of King Creek. It acquired its name in connection with the Wright and Green undertaking in 1911-12 when the Skid Road was built into the Yakoun Valley from Port Clements. (The term "road" is courtesy only. The Skid Road was merely a slashing to permit the sleds with drilling machinery to be dragged inland.) Wright and Green put down a bore hole to a depth of 860 feet at Drill Creek and it marked the end of the Skid Road in this direction. Following this test drilling they back-tracked along the Skid Road for some distance then turned east to the Pontoon region of the Tlell, where the final drill hole of the company was put down, west of the Pontoon Meadow.

THOMPSON MOUNTAIN — is north and west of the junction of the Yakoun River and Gold Creek. A number of timber claims were staked in this and other areas by the Graham Steamship, Coal and Lumber Company in 1907.

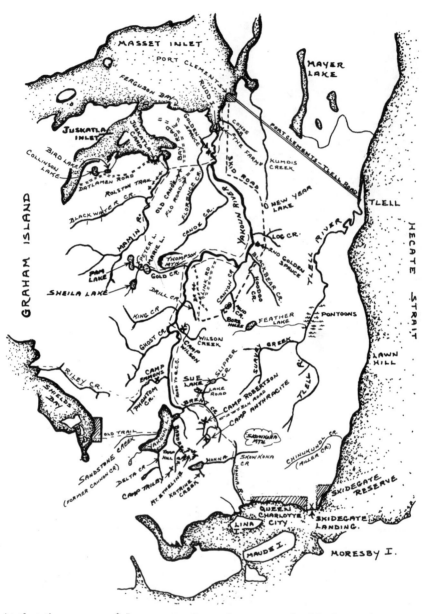

At that time many of the names of people connected with the project were applied, Shannon Bay, McClinton Bay and so on. Captain Thompson brought the Graham Steamship party around Masset Inlet in his vessel *Eurus*.

*GOLD CREEK — flows from the west to join the Yakoun River south of Thompson Mountain. It is a gazetted name applied about 1926. There is a deposit of perlite at the junction of Gold Creek and the Yakoun.

322

*MARIE LAKE — an attractive little lake with an islet in it. Drained by Gold Creek and named at the same time, along with Sheila, Pam and Peter Lakes nearby. A logging road runs along the north side of Gold Creek and passes close to Marie Lake.

PETER LAKE — not gazetted as of 1966, but is on record at the Geographic Branch. A minute lake about halfway between Marie and Pam Lakes and named at the same time, 1926.

*SHEILA LAKE — the most southerly of this group of lakes. Named after the daughter of Mr. R.D. Gillespie, the B.C.L.S. who took part in the 1914 survey of the northwest part of Graham Island as well as other Q.C. Islands' surveys. In 1926 during the survey of a section of the Yakoun Valley, the chief of the party invited members of his crew to name these lakes. "I chose Sheila, after you," Ernie Money told the 17-year-old Sheila Gillespie, now Mrs. J.W. Anderson of Victoria, "because it was such a pretty lake."

"I was thrilled and delighted with the compliment," says Mrs. Anderson. "In fact I still am, and would so very much like to have seen my lake." Ernie Money was a hard-working surveyor hoping to become a B.C.L.S. and doing well. Then a severe leg injury during a rugby game against the All Black team finished any such idea. He died some years ago.

*PAM LAKE — between the Mamin River and headwaters of Gold Creek, is the most westerly of the lake group. It is also the largest. Named in 1926 with the others.

*MAMIN RIVER — a modification of its Haida name, the adaption being applied in 1878 by Dr. G.M. Dawson. It flows in a general northerly direction and has its mouth in the eastern arm of Juskatla Inlet. Like the Yakoun, its valleys contain superb timber and it is in the MacMillan and Bloedel tree farm licence.

Logging roads follow the Mamin for most of its length and at the mouth is a 6-acre Indian Reserve, the former village site of the Eagle Crest Masset Gituns. Not only was the river a good fishing stream, it was also a favourite region for obtaining the big cedars which provided the canoes and versatile bark for weaving innumerable items in common use. Evidence of early Haida interest in the "Land of Big Cedars" may still be frequently seen; square openings cut into the lower trunks of large trees so that soundness could be determined; remains of partially hewn canoes, some merely felled and slightly shaped, others with more work done then abandoned for some reason. One such site easily accessible from the road is being preserved by the Queen Charlotte Islands Museum Society and is located on the south side of the road between Port Clements and Juskatla Camp, a little west of the Bay Road entrance.

*BLACKWATER CREEK — a tributary of the Mamin, for a time called CEDAR CREEK and shown under that name on 1927 maps. The old name of BLACK-WATER CREEK has been restored to subsequent maps. Logging roads from MacMillan and Bloedel's Juskatla operation run almost the full length

Colonel J.M. Rolston in 1945 (on right).
Photo - Frank Clapp

of Blackwater and there are several bridges to facilitate this. During road construction a quarry opened on seemingly solid rock proved to contain very poor road material. When sent to Victoria for analysis it turned out to be bentonite.

ROLSTON TRAIL — the local name given to a section of one of the survey lines laid out in the mid-1920s by Colonel John M. Rolston for Powell River Company. The part known as the Rolston Trail lies along the west side of the Mamin River, south of the bridge near Juskatla Camp. When Powell River acquired the large timber tracts in the Yakoun Valley area they believe a railroad offered the most feasible way to get the logs to salt water. Colonel Rolston was engaged to, among other things, lay out the railroad route from the heart of the big timber region to either Ferguson Bay or near the mouth of the Mamin.

His trim mustache and erect stature gave the sturdily built Rolston a military appearance when he arrived to assume his duties and the crisp efficiency with which he entered into the projects won the admiration of all who were associated with him. He came to the Charlottes several times, one of his last visits being in connection with the survey for the Tlell to Port Clements road.

Born in Devonshire in 1881, John Michell Rolston came to Manitoba as a boy. After graduating from Kingston Royal Military College with honours he began a lifetime career in civil engineering - most of which was spent in British Columbia. He died suddenly in 1950 while engaged in a survey at Creston.

To return now to the junction of Gold Creek and the Yakoun River and the

324

The "donkey-engine" winching
in the four sleds for
Wright & Green to Wilson Creek,
creating the famous
SKID ROAD.
Eighty-three tons of
equipment were hauled along
on a four-sled train affair.
Each sled consisted
of 2 logs,
four feet in diameter
and sixty feet long,
with necessary cross-pieces
and fastenings.
The donkey-engine
was on the first sled.

Photo - John Locker

Drilling for coal
in the Yakoun Valley.

Photo - Clarence Martin.

base of Thompson Mountain: it is at this section the main logging road divides into two branches, one branch leads to Juskatla Camp and thence to Port Clements, the other branch follows the Yakoun River which forms an S bend at this point, flowing in an easterly direction for about 5 miles before returning to its northerly path to Masset Inlet. Logging roads follow both sides of the river for a short distance. The road on the south side has several spurs.

LINK ROAD — the name given by MacMillan and Bloedel engineers to one of the spurs leading off the road mentioned in the previous paragraph. It links with another spur, Branch 44, which also leads off the same main road. Branch 44 has 2 old boreholes along its route. One in the southwest corner of Lot 18, Township 7, and a second at the headwaters of Drill Creek (which gave Drill Creek its name) at the northeast corner of Lot 36, Township 9. Some of the old drills and pieces of equipment connected with these 1912 test holes have been found recently by loggers from MacMillan and Bloedel's operation.

THE SKID ROAD — a mere slashing through the trees with skids placed at intervals to enable the big sleds with Wright and Green's drilling equipment, bunk-houses and cook shack to be laboriously dragged from Port Clements to the coal fields, 1911 through to 1912. It went as far as the drill hole at the headwaters of Drill Creek, mentioned in the previous paragraph.

(The story of the Skid Road is contained in some detail in Volume 1, Q.C. Islands on pages 186, 187, 221 to 222.)

CENTRE MERIDIAN TRAIL — followed the north part of one of the main survey lines running north and south and used in the laying out of the townships in the initial survey. It lay east of the Skid Road which ran parallel to it for some distance from Port Clements. Several early homesteaders took up land along the Centre Meridian Trail and this was their route to come into Port Clements for supplies and mail.

CANYON CREEK — about 4 or 5 miles from the intersection of the Yakoun River and Gold Creek, it runs into the Yakoun River from the south. It has a small canyon and received its name from Fred Nash B.C.L.S. for this reason when he made the first survey of the Yakoun Valley 1909-10. Owing to confusion or typographical error a stream named Cannon Creek in Township 10, 20 miles or more to the south, appeared on record as Canyon Creek and was subsequently gazetted. (It is now shown under its new name of Sandstone Creek.)

The original CANYON CREEK is the one Fred Nash located and named in Township 7. In earlier years a rough bridge spanned this creek and several trappers built cabins near the area.

MUD CREEK — a tributary of Fred Nash's Canyon Creek, leaves Canyon Creek between Lots 9 and 10, flows across the Skid Road into the northwest part of Lot 3. A well-known name in the days of coal drilling. A little beyond Mud Creek, Wright and Green, builders of the Skid Road, put down their first two test drills - one went to 400 feet and the other 390. They set up camp at Mud Creek while this went on. Supplies were brought to the camp on the burdened shoulders of the back-packers who lugged them from Port Clements over the crude Skid Road.

*BLACKBEAR CREEK — flows north to join the Yakoun River northeast of Canyon Creek. Named by Fred Nash 1909-10 during his survey. Bears are plentiful all along the Yakoun.

*HOODOO CREEK — a delightfully expressive name which came into use at the same time as the survey and Skid Road projects were under way. Hoodoo Creek is a tributary of Blackbear Creek and the Skid Road crossed it and one of its streamlets.

On the east bank of the Yakoun, midway between Blackbear and Log Creek stands a "golden spruce." A pale edition of the more famous tree nearer the mouth of the Yakoun, this inland spruce is about 100 feet high and only the top branches have the golden tinge. The sun's action on some deformity in the tree cells causes the golden reaction. Formerly surrounded by trees, it took the removal of enough of them by logging to permit the sun's action on the deficient cells to produce this golden spruce. It is a mutation not a species.

*LOG CREEK — joins the Yakoun River north of Blackbear Creek and named at the same time. The Skid Road crossed it. Today a logging road follows the north bank of the Yakoun River from Gold Creek to a little beyond Log Creek. Dr. Sutherland Brown reported the only known marine diatomaceous rocks of British Columbia lie along this section of the Yakoun.

*NEW YEAR LAKE — named by the Skid Road heroes as they struggled inland with their train of sleds to the drilling site, having left Port Clements November 4, 1911. New Year Lake lies in a muskeg with no visible stream leading from it. Kumdis Creek's headwaters are close and the general seepage is towards that creek. However, the lake is only 1½ miles from the Yakoun River.

*CANOE CREEK — which flows in a general northerly direction to enter the Yakoun River from the west. The junction of the two is easily seen today as the road from Port Clements to Juskatla is close to the river there. Canoe Creek was named by Fred Nash during his 1910 to 1911 survey according to old timers who took part in this era of Queen Charlotte Islands' history.

*FLORENCE CREEK — flows in a general northerly direction to enter Yakoun Bay a little to the west of the Yakoun River. Rudd Island lies off the mouth of Florence Creek.

RUDD ISLAND — in the estuary of the Yakoun River, a heart-shaped island which grew from the deposit of river silt over the centuries. It is difficult to understand how the name of this island has been omitted from the maps - it is so well-known locally. Bob Rudd pre-empted there in 1911 and the island has borne his name ever since. It was the site of a magnificent stand of trees.

A few years ago they were logged off and the unbelievable chaos left behind is an inexcusable desecration of a beauty spot. When one compares the relatively undisturbed appearance of a region after it has been harvested by pole cutters, with a similar area given into the hands of loggers, the contrast cannot help but raise some very big "whys." The supervision of those entrusted with the handling of our forests appears centred solely on stumpage and royalty payments - none of which are paid to the area of desecration.

It is not possible to circumnavigate Rudd Island, for during the spring run-offs the Yakoun River brought down a variety of debris, some of which hung up on the southeast tip of the island. Silt was trapped and seeds took root, until now the little island is joined to Graham Island via this log peninsula. Small boats can pass around the west side of Rudd Island to a little beyond the mouth of Florence Creek before encountering the jamb.

YAGUNKUN LNAGAI, straight-point-village — stood on the north end of Rudd Island at the mouth of the Yakoun River. It belonged to the Kuna-lanas, a great Raven clan family, the Point-Town People.

HLAKEGUNS VILLAGE, near-the-point-village — stood on Graham Island, opposite and west of Rudd Island. Owned by the Raven Kuna-lana Point-Town-People.

LANASLNAGAI, people's-town — immediately south of Hlakeguns, and belonged to the Raven Stleng-lanas, Rear-Town-People. Both Hlakeguns and Lanaslnagai are now part of the LANAS RESERVE which contains over 192 acres and is owned by the Masset Band. It is still used seasonally. Several houses occupy part of the old village site along the river bank, but a good portion of the reserve is now logged off, by permission of the Masset Band.

*COHOE CREEK — comes into Yakoun Bay from an easterly direction a little below the north end of Rudd Island. In early years it was a fair-sized stream, especially during spring runoffs. A log bridge spanned it a little to the south of Geordie McQuaker's pre-emption. Geordie had a large clearing which later developed into a magnificent alder patch. Upstream along the Cohoe, the Skid Road crossed, and in this area were 5 or 6 pre-emptions with comfortable cabins. All were abandoned when the First World War broke out.

UNDL-SKADJUNS-VILLAGE, Skadjuns-River-Camp — an Eagle Crest site belonging to the Gituns of Masset, it lay near the mouth of the Yakoun River on its east bank, not far from Cohoe Creek.

THE FARM — at high tide the channel on the east side of Rudd Island is navigable by small boat for a couple of miles. The farm that pioneer John Locker hacked out of the dense woods may be seen on the east bank of this channel - and also seen from the road to Juskatla. Commonly known as *The Farm*, it now belongs to MacMillan and Bloedel and is frequently used as a pasture for riding horses owned by some of their employees. Mr. Locker died in eastern Canada but at his wish his ashes were scattered on his old farm.

THE GOLDEN SPRUCE — grows on the west bank of the Yakoun River, about a mile south of John Locker's old farm. (See above.) Until very recently it was considered to be the only one of its kind in the world. But with the opening up of new forest areas on the Charlottes at least 5 other trees have been discovered which possess the same characteristics. Due to some quirk in their make-up, the chlorophyll in the needles of these mutated spruces breaks down under the influence of direct sunlight, and the green pigment takes on a golden hue. Tree growth is maintained by the needles not exposed to sunlight and which, therefore, remain green.

None of the recently discovered trees compare in size or number of golden needles to the first known and most famous of all "golden" spruces. Whenever a reference is made to *The Golden Spruce*, it is this tree on the west bank of the Yakoun which is referred to.

The tree is unusual in its outline as well as its colour, for it has the shape of a jack pine rather than that of a Sitka spruce. Foresters estimate it to be about 160 feet high and probably 300 years old. It can be seen from a trail leading off the Port Clements to Juskatla road. The entrance to the trail is 1 mile south of The Farm.

FLO ROAD — the name given by MacMillan and Bloedel to their branch road leading off the south side of the Port Clements to Juskatla road a little west of Florence Creek.

BAY ROAD — the MacMillan and Bloedel name for the branch road leading off the north side of the Port Clements to Juskatla road, and running towards Ferguson Bay. West of the entrance to Bay Road is the blazed trail to a partially hewn Haida canoe of ancient years.

*JUSKATLA (CAMP) — in Mamin Bay, west of the mouth of the Mamin River in the southeast portion of Juskatla Inlet. Today it is the headquarters for the MacMillan, Bloedel and Powell River Company logging operations on the Charlottes. The Juskatla logging camp began as a Pacific Mills, Crown Zellerbach project. Known as the B40 Camp, it had been built in 1940 in Queen Charlotte City on the old sawdust pile, site of the first Queen Charlotte City mill. (B40 signifies that it was the second such camp and was built in 1940. Another camp known as A35, had been built in 1935 in South Bentick Arm.)

When B40 opened in Charlotte City, George Blomgren was superintendent and logging was done in all areas adjacent to Charlotte City, such as the west end of Skidegate Inlet, Renner Pass, Maude Island and so on. Only aeroplane spruce could be taken and all trees to be cut had been previously marked under the direction of the B.C. Forest Service. This meant an extremely scattered operation, 6 to 8 trees at one place, then on to the next. Only the choicest timber.

After about a year's operation in Charlotte City, the camp split up. Jim Carstairs, who had been with A35, took over the running of the Charlotte City part which was shifted to another location then - on Moresby. Mr. Parker S. Bonney took charge of moving the balance of B40 to Juskatla Inlet. Bonney was well-known, having been District Forester in Prince Rupert before working for Pacific Mills, and in later years became a consultant in the Terrace region and also at Kitimat for Alcan.

"Bonney planned the move like a military operation," says Len Orr of Terrace. "According to his schedule a scow would leave Charlotte City at such and such time, arrive at Rose Spit and then Port Clements in exactly so many hours. If only the weather had co-operated! But at any rate the entire move was successfully completed in about 3 weeks and in only three stages . . . one of the tows being taken up via the west coast of Graham Island."

The move began in July of 1941 and by the time Len arrived at Juskatla in August of that year, the entire camp had arrived in Juskatla and was established near the mouth of the Mamin River.

Here, as had been at Charlotte City, only select logging was permitted, and all trees had been previously marked by the Forestry Service. Pacific Mills ran only for about a year when it was taken over by the Crown Corporation AERO. (See also Aero at Cumshewa Inlet.) There were many who felt that it was a squeeze - forcing Pacific Mills out. Aero had bought out the Allison Logging in Cumshewa at the onset of World War II and, under superintendent George Fife, then took over the Juskatla operation.

After the war the Powell River Company bought the entire Aero assets both at Cumshewa and Juskatla. Considering what the assets consisted of, the selling price fixed by the Crown Corporation was scandalously low and caused more than a few raised eyebrows.

DATLAMEN ROAD — goes from Juskatla Camp to the west arm of Juskatla Inlet, and is a logging road belonging to MacMillan and Bloedel's Juskatla operation. Along its route are 2 easily accessible lakes: -

*BIRD LAKE — named about 1911-13, and

*COLLINSON LAKE — west of Bird Lake and named at the same time in connection with a timber survey. They lie in the lee of Towustasin Hill.

EAST COAST GRAHAM ISLAND: FROM SKIDEGATE
TO MAYER RIVER. INCLUDES TLELL RIVER
VALLEY AND MAYER LAKE.

CHAPTER FIFTEEN ❧

*The village of Skidegate as Dr. G.M. Dawson found it in 1878 when
he took this photo.
Photo - Provincial Museum, Victoria.*

SKIDEGATE HAIDA RESERVE — on the southeast tip of Graham Island is the largest reserve on the Charlottes. Containing over 846 acres it belongs to the Skidegate Band and, like all Haida reserves, has a great deal of history attached to it. Four villages are known to have been located along its shoreline, one of which, Hlgaiu, formed the basis of Skidegate Village of today. It would require an entire volume to do justice to the development of Skidegate from ancient years to the present - a book which must be written by someone with his roots in that aspect of Queen Charlotte Islands history.

SCOTSGAI BEACH — at the south end of the reserve, is a picturesque curving beach frequently called SECOND BEACH locally. This is the mooted site for the proposed Queen Charlotte Islands museum - an ambitious undertaking in which people from every part of the Charlottes are joining, aware only too keenly that it is long overdue.

KAE VILLAGE, Sea-Lion-Town — the Eagle Crest village at Scotsgai Beach years ago. When difficulties arose with their former good neighbours in Pebble-Town, the Kae villagers moved to the west coast, living first at Chaatl then taking over Kaisun.

HLGAHET VILLAGE, Pebble-Town — a little north of Kae, belonged first to the Raven Crest Kogangas, Sea-Otter-Tribe, who sold it to another Raven tribe, the Yakulanas of Lawn Hill. Both these Eagle and Raven people lived at Pebble-Town in later years.

HLGAIU VILLAGE, Place-of-Stones — originally belonged to a Raven tribe from Dead Tree, who named it after their old village at Dead Tree. They were not to have their new village for long. One of their men married a woman of the Eagle Gitun tribe and had a daughter by her. One day the girl and a Raven lad went into the forest to get gum from the trees to chew. It was the practice to light a fire under the tree and let the pitch run down the hollows in kelp stems. The youngsters were doing this and the girl glanced upwards. As she did so some hot pitch fell into her eye, blinding her.

Legends say the boy's family offered three slaves to atone for the injury. It was considered inadequate. At last the boy seized his mother's digging stick and threw it out. This meant that his family gave up the town completely to the Gituns, who have owned it ever since. The Raven family (of the boy) moved to Drum Village on Lina Island.

Under the Gituns the village of Hlgaiu became known as SKIDEGATE, and from it came many famous chiefs one of whom, the great Nestacanna, overcame the stigma of having once been made a slave. Through successive potlatches he became one of the most important chiefs in the area, and during his heyday house-poles first came into being. As Skidegate grew in importance, like all big villages, it contained permanent homes of both Eagles and Ravens.

*SKIDEGATE MISSION — as the village of Skidegate is officially gazetted, grew out of old Hlgaiu, and is today regarded as one of the model Indian communities of Canada. Large well-designed homes have all amenities; electricity, water, sewers and, above all, a gorgeous ocean view. There are two excellent general stores, a community hall and a recreation hall that is unequalled anywhere on the Charlottes. The United Church is still the church of the village and maintains a resident minister.

SKIDEGATE CREEK — the more southerly of the two creeks running through Skidegate Village has been named by the Department of Highways for purposes of bridge identification. Named in association with the village.

*SLARKEDUS CREEK — runs through Skidegate at the north end of the village. Two meanings have been given for *slarkedus,* which is a modification of a Haida word. One version is that it means gravel or stoney. Another says that this creek was a funnel for debris of every sort coming from the height behind the village. Its name means "where the debris came to rest."

There are two opinions also as to which creek is Slarkedus. The Department of Highways found that some of the Skidegates felt the creek now tagged as Skidegate is really the one to be called Slarkedus. Since the majority of the villagers felt Slarkedus is the creek on the north, this is the way it has been entered on the maps.

KOSTAN VILLAGE, Crab-Town — lay on the north side of Skidegate. It belonged to the Kogangas, Sea-Otter-Tribe. One of their chiefs, Qoonatik, is supposed to have gone to live by a reef off Lawn Hill after death, and was called upon for aid during storms.

*STONY PEAK — behind Skidegate Village is a little over 1,000 feet high. The name appeared on the charts following Captain Daniel Pender's 1866 survey of the waters of Skidegate Inlet.

*JEWELL ISLAND — northeast of Image Point. Named TREE ISLAND during the 1866 Pender survey. Owing to duplications of this name the Hydrographic Service suggested Jewell in 1945 after Ambrose Jewell, one of the 22 passengers on the schooner *Georgianna* wrecked in a gale off Skidegate in 1851. (See story under Georgianna Point.) Known locally as INDIAN HEAD ISLAND for the shape of the rock cliff on the north end of the island as seen in silhouette from the adjacent shore.

*TORRENS ISLAND — north of Jewell Island. Named BARE ISLAND in 1866 by Captain Daniel Pender, it figured largely in his directions for entering Skidegate Inlet - together with Transit Island.

It came into the news in 1884 when Newton Chittenden reported that rabbits placed on the island by George Robinson, a Methodist missionary worker, had grown into a flourishing colony.

In 1945 the island was renamed by the Hydrographic Service after Captain Robert William Torrens. Torrens, an ex-army officer, had come to Victoria in 1859 and in July Governor James Douglas commissioned him to search for the elusive gold on the Charlottes which Douglas thought must be there if someone would look thoroughly. William Downie was sent at the same time.

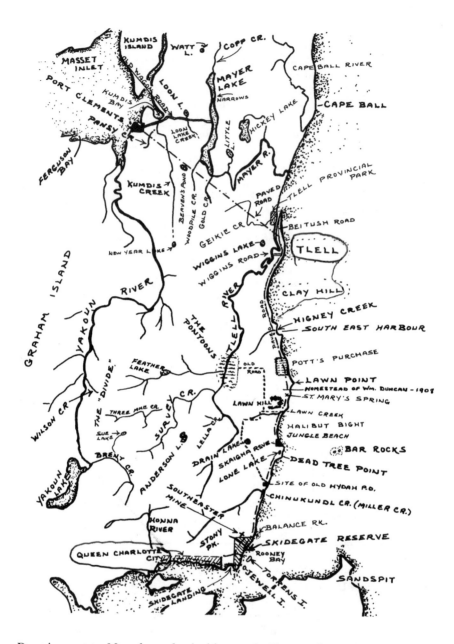

Downie went to Moresby to begin his search. Torrens began his exploration from Rose Spit at the northeast tip of Graham Island, then worked his way south along the east coast.

An aroused and highly suspicious group of Skidegates nearly murdered them when they visited that village to pay their respects to Nestacanna, and only his intervention saved them. They were obliged to flee whilst he tried to calm the hot-heads, and a few shots were fired at their departing heels in spite of Nestecanna.

Torrens returned a short time later at the invitation of the Haidas living near the Mitchell Inlet gold find, but his men's morale was so bad he had to leave before much prospecting could be undertaken. The party had split up, Torrens taking half the men to go to Mitchell Inlet whilst the rest went with Chief Edenshaw to Skincuttle Inlet, where they found encouraging samples of copper. It was these samples that brought Waddington up in 1862. He subsequently sank a shaft at Copper Bay, The Old Shaft.

The story of the bloody battle on Torrens Island may be found under Burnt Island, page 295 to 296.

*ROONEY BAY — fronts along Skidegate Village. Formerly called VILLAGE BAY. Renamed by the Hydrographic Service in 1945 after Captain Matthew Rooney, master of the schooner *Susan Sturgis*. It was at Skidegate that Rooney met Chief Edenshaw in 1851 and decided, after talking with the chief, to go to Edenshaw's village near Langara Island. Rooney had come from the gold site at Mitchell Inlet; not finding anything he had sailed around Moresby and was proceeding northward when he called in at Skidegate late in September.

Edenshaw agreed to pilot the *Susan Sturgis* from Skidegate to his own village. They were about 4 miles northwest of Masset when Weah and his tribe boarded the American ship to plunder her. During the ensuing fracas the vessel drifted off the village of Yan and was later burned by the Massets. The *Susan Sturgis* men were held hostage until ransomed by the H.B.C. from Port Simpson.

SOUTHEASTER MINE — at the north edge of Skidegate Reserve; a road ran inland for about 1 mile to this mine. In 1910 A.J. Gordon and John McLellan bought the land from Skidegate Haidas after gold-bearing quartz had been found at the site. Considerable cross-cutting was done and samples obtained which assayed well. Later results proved that the ore did not exist in any quantity. The *Southeaster* consisted of 3 claims, *Southeaster*, *Sunrise* and *Beaconsfield*. It had a succession of hopeful managers under many owners. One of the latter was W.G. McMorris who, at one time, had proposed a pulp mill for the mouth of the Slatechuck.

"Over $200,000 was put into the *Southeaster*," says Charlie Hartie of Queen Charlotte City, who knew it well, "only to prove there was little of value there." From 1919 to 1936 it is recorded that 41 ounces of gold, 27 ounces of silver, 259 pounds of copper and about 665 pounds of lead were recovered. The mine closed in 1936.

BALANCE ROCK — a large boulder lying close to the shoreline about 1/3 of a mile north of Skidegate Village. Geologists say that it was deposited there by a glacier with the probable source 16 miles away in the Alliford Bay region. The story is told of a farmer in earlier years who determined to dislodge this rock - for no good reason, just that it was there. It is said he tried everything, including pries and a team of horses, and was contemplating dynamite when neighbours persuaded him to let it be.

335

Balance Rock lies on the shoreline a little north of Skidegate Village.

Photo - K.E. Dalzell

What might have been a tragedy on April 1, 1920, was averted by a quick thinking skipper when the Prince John *and the* Prince Albert *collided in a blinding snow storm off Lawn Hill. Realizing that "John", under Captain W.S. Moorehouse, was in danger of sinking immediately, Captain H.L. Robertson of the "Albert" kept his bow in the gaping hole and, ordering full steam ahead, pushed the stricken "John" onto the shore near Miller Creek. Everyone was safely taken off and the damaged vessel later salvaged.*

Photo - Mrs. Roy Field.

*CHINUKUNDL CREEK — which is known locally as MILLER CREEK, flows into Hecate Strait from the southwest and has its headwaters a short distance from Queen Charlotte City. *Chinukundl*, now rarely used, is a modification of a Haida name. An early pre-emptor, Mr. Müller, had a homesite near the creek before 1908. First called Müller's Creek, it has gradually become the Miller Creek of today. (Müller is the man who, before he went south for treatment in a mental home, was sure he had found gold at the mouth of Mayer River. His excitement over that 'find' caused the Mayer River to be called Gold Creek - a name it still bears in local reference.)

Miller Creek is one of the places in which lignite is found, beds of about 1 foot thick lie near the mouth.

HYDAH (POST OFFICE) — a little to the north of the mouth of Miller Creek. When Mr. William Leary took his family to live on land near Miller Creek, he applied for a post office. The application was denied under Miller Creek, because of duplication elsewhere so the name HYDAH was submitted and subsequently accepted. The post office has been closed now for many years, the old Leary home succumbed to the ravages of weather and time, and all that remains to mark the site of Hydah today is a grassy clearing surrounded by a thicket of vigorous young spruce. The road which arched inland from there to emerge at Lawn Hill has become overgrown, but is still passable on foot. The entrance to the road is north of the Leary place and easily found.

*DEAD TREE POINT — about 7 miles north of Skidegate Village, shown on Joseph Ingraham's sketch map of 1792 under the notation, "White cliffs on which there are many dead trees." In 1853 Captain T. Sinclair of the H.B.C. officially applied the name, DEAD TREE POINT, to the feature.

There were two ancient Haida villages in the vicinity of the point, one belonged to the Ravens and the other to the Eagles. In 1910 the Dominion Government purchased two lots at Dead Tree to build a wireless station. The ruins of the old lodges and depressions of the house pits were clearly visible on the north side of the station, and during the excavations it was common to find human bones. The men who worked on the buildings carefully removed and reburied them. "We were very conscious all of a sudden that we had intruded on an ancient gravesite," said one man.

Improved communications in recent years have made the old wireless station unnecessary and it has been abandoned as such. The United Church purchased the site to convert to a camping place for youngsters - open to all creeds.

THE GOOSE FLATS — a local name in constant use in earlier years for the grassy area around Dead Tree Point.

LONE LAKE — a little north of Dead Tree Point, lies between the road and the ocean. Also known by old timers as THE POND, THE DUCKPOND, LONESOME LAKE, and MOLITOR'S LAKE - this latter name developed because in earlier years the Molitor homesite was close by. (Now abandoned.) Lone Lake is a favourite haunt of ducks.

*HALIBUT BIGHT — the indentation north of Dead Tree Point. Formerly called HALIBUT BAY. Along the south part of this bight in years past there were a group of cabins used seasonally by Haidas from Skidegate. Because of this the bay was referred to locally as *The Halibut Shacks.*

SKAIGHA RESERVE — containing 62 acres, belongs to the Skidegate Band, and fronts on the Halibut Bight at the location of the shacks mentioned in the preceeding paragraph. The shacks have been gone for many years. Skaigha was set aside as a reserve by Commissioner O'Reilly in 1882 and surveyed in 1887.

JUNGLE BEACH — a local name for a picnic site on the shores of Halibut Bight. During the 1930s, Roy Mackenzie, proprietor of the Premier Hotel in Queen Charlotte City and owner-operator of a taxi, chose this beach for a picnic site. He promoted picnics and expeditions to the place at every opportunity, undoubtedly hoping to drum up a little taxi business from the Charlotte end, but gave a friendly welcome to everyone regardless. It is said that each winter the seas cast up such a jungle of logs at the entrance to the beach, this inspired his choice of name.

*BAR ROCKS — lie about 2¾ miles offshore from Halibut Bight and were first shown on an 1853 map of Captain T. Sinclair's for the H.B.C. The west rock dries at 5 feet and the eastern rock at 1 foot. The sea does not always break over them. The channel for ships entering Skidegate Inlet lies between the shore and the rocks and is well marked with buoys. According to legend Bar Rocks are not ordinary rocks.

In ancient years a man went camping on the west coast and found two dogs who fished for him. So adept were they the man always had an abundance of fish. When he returned to his wife's people at Skidegate he learned of the terrible scarcity of food. His mother-in-law had food but would not share it, hiding it from others.

The man, disgusted with her, took his family to the west coast, but she went with them. He refused to give her any food except fat. At this his wife became angry and said she would punish him. When the dogs went out to fish, she created a potion of blue hellebore and urine which she poured into the sea, causing such a storm the dogs could not land. They swam through Skidegate Channel then north to Lawn Hill where they became two rocks - now called Bar Rocks.

DRAIN LAKE — due west of the Halibut Bight, was located on Lot 511, near the old INSIDE ROAD, the branch of the Lawn Hill road which curved inland to service settlers, then swung eastward to emerge at Hydah, near Miller Creek. Thomas J. Drain pre-empted a lot to the south of Lot 511 and liked it so well, he purchased Lot 511 which had a lake near the centre. It became known by all his neighbours as DRAIN'S LAKE, and from that came into general local use.

ANDERSON LAKE — west of Drain Lake, is about 6½ miles from the beach at the Halibut Bight. Part of Anderson Lake is on the northwest corner of Lot 1842 "It is named after Ed Anderson," recalls Charlie Hartie of Queen Charlotte City. "This lake was his favourite fishing spot in the years around 1911 or so. I think he learned about it on a survey. It was his story that there were so many fish in the lake he had to hide behind a tree to bait his hook."

*TLELL RIVER — a long meandering river with its headwaters reaching the region of Chinukundl Creek. It has numerous tributaries equally meandering, and flows in a northerly direction to empty into Hecate Strait well over 20 miles away. The upper region of the river, particularly near the mouth, is famed as a sport-fishing area.

The major portion of the Tlell system at one time held a stand of red cedar of superlative quality, according to Charles de Blois Green, B.C.L.S., who made an extensive study. About 1840 the grandfather of all Queen Charlotte Islands' forest fires began near Masset. Legends say a wax vesta match carelessly thrown aside after a pipe was lit started the blaze. A combination of excessive dryness[1] and the right wind, quickly fanned the small fire into an inferno.

From Masset it spread through the interior of the east part of Graham Island, raging southwards and along the valley of the Tlell. For over 50 miles the land lay charred and wasted. Haidas of the area fled in panic to the west coast to escape the holocaust.

Over the years all this region became thickly carpeted with moss. Gradually a new growth covered some of the desolation, the rest became an expanse of muskeg. Charred remains of the old trees can still be seen in the new forest. Some of the trees were not burned, but were killed - their craggy white outlines standing as a silent reminder. These fire-killed trees, almost indestructible, were greatly prized in earlier years as foundation posts for houses.

Mr. C. de B. Green wrote, "Eventually the burned trees blew down and where they fell across the Tlell River, a most effectual dam was formed backing water up over the Pontoon Plain to the north after every rainfall."

[1]See page 33 also for reference to this fire.

*LELLA CREEK — enters the Tlell River from the southwest, at a point west of Lawn Hill. Named during a survey preceeding 1913, and is thought to have some association with the Tlell in context of name.

*SURVEY CREEK — on the maps of today is the creek flowing into the Tlell from the Yakoun Valley to join the Tlell north of Lella Creek. Oldsters who were on the early surveys and who back-packed in this region are unanimous in saying this is not the Survey Creek they knew. Their Survey Creek was the tributary to the north, the one that drains Feather Lake.

The Survey Creek on the maps of today - and as far back as MacKenzie's 1913-14 geological map - has its headwaters not far from Brent Creek. A logging road called Elk Road extends from Brent Creek to Survey Creek's streamlets.

THREE MILE CREEK — is a tributary of Survey Creek. It flows from the west and is north of Sue Lake, whereas the main branch of Survey is to the south of Sue Lake. Three Mile Creek was named by Dr. R.W. Ells in 1905 and has still to be entered in the Gazetteer. For years this stream was shown as Survey Creek proper, and the name of Three Mile did not appear. It was included on the 1963 land map, with Survey Creek finally being established as a more southerly located creek.

*FEATHER LAKE — on Lot 35, Township 6, was named prior to MacKenzie's 1913 geological survey. An unnamed creek with its headwaters on the *Divide*, near Wilson Creek, runs into the west side of Feather Lake, then leaves via its east side to empty into the Tlell in the Pontoon area. This is the creek the men who back-packed into the drill camps and who also worked on early surveys, call Survey Creek.

THE PONTOONS — which have also been known as PONTOON MEADOW and PONTOON PLAIN, is the marshy area of the Tlell lying east of Lawn Point. Pontoon is a name given by Louisiana people to this type of terrain and during the coal interest, someone coined the expression for this region. The last Wright and Green bore-hole, put down in 1912 on the west side of the Pontoon Meadow, had one trail into it from Lawn Hill and a second trail in from Pott's Purchase (Lot 117.) Both trails converged on the Pontoons, with a single trail into the drill camp from that point.

Near the middle of the Pontoon Meadow, the men from the camp made a serviceable bridge, using materials from the log jamb lashed with a cable.

The DIVIDE (of the Yakoun) — a name given to the high region which lies between the Yakoun Valley and the Tlell in the vicinity of Camp Wilson. A name in common use during the back-packing days of the coal drillers, 1911 to 1914.

*LAWN HILL — which gives its name to both point and creek, was also the name of a former settlement close by. It is only 560 feet high. Located north of Dead Tree Point and the Halibut Bight, the hill has had other names in earlier years - LONE HILL and LONG HILL. Old-timers feel that Lawn is a modification of one of these, and not the original name.

*LAWN CREEK — flows from the west to empty into Hecate Strait on the south side of Lawn Hill.

*LAWN HILL (settlement) — was the name given to the small community which developed during the pioneering years in and about Lawn Hill. The post office and store, the focal point of the community, were on the south side of the creek, and faced the road which lay along the shoreline. From the store another road, known as the LAWN HILL ROAD, followed the survey line westward for several miles, with a branch road called the NORTH ROAD, leading off it to the north to the Experimental Farm, a showplace in its day. This North Road eventually turned west towards the Pontoons.

Another branch of the Lawn Hill Road went southward and east in a rough semi-circle, to emerge at Hydah, near Miller Creek. This road was called the INSIDE ROAD. These roads are overgrown for the most part today, but are passable on foot.

Once actively settled by pioneers, the Lawn Hill region has had many recent applications by a new group of young pioneers who, tired of world progress, want to return to the way of the old pioneers and a simpler life. They are having a difficult time to persuade the government that such a life holds the compensations they expect and their applications for land have met with little success to date.

ST. MARY'S SPRING — between Lawn Point and Lawn Hill has a legend of the Charlottes firmly attached. A drink from this spring, it is said, and one must ever return to the Islands. Strangely it is a comparatively recent legend.

In early years this watering place was called DUNCAN'S WELL, and travellers stopped to water their horses there. In the early 1920s Mrs. Annie Richardson of Tlell decided to name it after a spring she had known in her native England - St. Mary's Spring. Twenty years later someone said, "Drink and you must ever return." The idea caught on to become firmly entrenched in part of Island history.

Looking southward along the east coast of Graham Island. Islanders call the point with the large boulder lying off it, Lawn Point. (The official Lawn Point is to the north out of the photo.) St. Mary's Spring is on the south side of the Lawn Point shown here, and the grassy clearing on the north side (right) is part of William Duncan's pioneer homesite. Mr. Duncan had a sluice-box along the shoreline in front of his place and recovered enough gold for years to live in moderate comfort.

Photo - British Columbia Government.

*LAWN POINT — midway between Tlell and Skidegate Mission. The location of this point on maps and charts, as well as its description in the B.C. Pilot, puts the name on a different feature from that of resident Islanders. The official

Lawn Point is *north* of the navigational beacon and *north* of the old farm of William Duncan.

Islanders, however, regard that point as being unnamed. Their Lawn Point is the steep bluff on the *south* side of the old Duncan farm and a boulder with a white patch lies off this Lawn Point. For years there has been a navigational marker on its hillside.

A huge midden extends along the shoreline between the official Lawn Point and the local Lawn Point. Many artifacts have been recovered from the shoreline bank in the past, but severe erosion during winter storms has caused much of the bank to be washed out to sea in recent years.

On the hill north of the midden a dig was undertaken in 1970 by archaeologists from the University of Calgary. It is suspected that some of the artifacts recovered may date back to a pre-Haida occupancy of the Charlottes. Findings from this dig are still being assessed.

In 1908 William Duncan pioneered in this bay between the official Lawn Point on the north and the local Lawn Point on the south, and gradually established a small farm. To supplement his income he placer-mined the beach in front, recovering enough gold to give him a modest income for years. Subsequent attempts to put the gold on a more lucrative base by others met with disappointment.

DAHUA VILLAGE — the Raven Crest village at Lawn Hill. At one time a great battle took place there between the Skidegate Haidas and the people of the north coast of Graham Island, in which the latter were defeated.

A reef lies off Dahua Village and it is said that the spirit of the great Chief Qoona'tik dwells under it. Qoona'tik was a Kogangas chief of the Raven Sea-Otter tribe. A hugh man whose exploits on earth were legendary in his time, he was known as He-who-touches-the-sky-with-his-head-as-he-moves-about. When he died he chose the rocks off Lawn Hill for his resting place. Apparently as gigantic after death as he had been on earth, he became known as He-who-makes-it-thunder-by-his-voice and, during storms Haidas would call upon him for help. No one ever spat upon the ocean in the region.

POTT'S PURCHASE — the name given in early years to Lot 117 which lies a little north of Lawn Point. Old-timers were intrigued because Arthur Potts bought the land as opposed to the customary pre-empting. He bought it in June of 1909 for $1450 and sold it 3 months later for $1750 making a nice little profit for those days - and all on paper.

SOUTHEAST HARBOUR — is the name given to the bay off the old Gus Ross farm. A hook of land gives a measure of protection, but only for the small craft of earlier years which could be drawn up on shore. The name appears on earlier maps but never reached the Gazetteer. Local use of it is lessening, probably because the mode of travel along this shoreline has changed from small boats to cars.

John and Jennifer Davies, former teachers in Queen Charlotte Islands' schools, bought one of the old farms at Southeast Harbour and are busy setting up their *Bottle and Jug Works* pottery shop. John, an expert potter, creates much local interest as he turns out a variety of items. His craftsmanship is drawing off-Islands interest as well and he and his wife are receiving orders for their products from mainland shops.

HIGNEY CREEK — a local name from pioneering days. It flows into Hecate Strait north of the old Gus Ross farm, near the Government gravel pit. John Higney, a tall Britisher partly deaf from his years in the army as a gunner, and his Scots neighbour Jim Reid, ranched on this land until World War I, when they both enlisted for overseas service. It was their abandoned homesite which Gus Ross later acquired. The creek flowed through Higney's homesite, thus receiving its name.

CLAY HILL — a few miles south of Tlell, is a name which has been in continuous local use since early homesteading days. Named for its physical properties. When the first road was built along the edge of the coast it laboriously wound up to the brow of Clay Hill then, in a quick hairpin turn, just as laboriously descended. Always considered a major hurdle. Today the paved road swoops up in such a gentle grade one is hardly aware of "going over the Hill." The Doug Leach farm lies close by the south side of the hill. This is the headquarters for the only newspaper on the Charlottes - *the Q.C.I. Observer* - which commenced publication in May 1969. It is a family project, all members of the Leach family helping to get the paper out each Thursday.

***TLELL (settlement)** — stretching from Clay Hill to the mouth of the river is considered one of the choice residential sections of the Charlottes. Property in the area is almost unobtainable today. Land not privately owned is held in the uncompromising grip of the Crown, who seem as unwilling to make any common sense disposition here as they are in the several other areas for which there have been numerous applications by young couples.

The settlement takes its name from the proximity of the river and is of Haida origin. Said to mean place-of-big-surf and, alternately, land-of-berries. The post office is located on the big Richardson Ranch, which was the original dream ranch of the legendary Mexican Tom. (Tom's story is carried in some detail in Q.C. Island, Vol. 1.)

WIGGINS ROAD — south of the Richardson Ranch in Tlell, connects the coastal highway with the Tlell River to the west. Named after Ed Wiggins, pioneer homesteader of Tlell. A branch road from Wiggins Road leads to the former Wiggins property. Wiggins Road named by the Department of Highways.

RICHARDSON ROAD — is the name given by the Department of Highways to a branch road off Wiggins Road, leading to the property of Mr. C.K. Richardson, long-time resident of Tlell.

WIGGINS LAKE — is the local name for the small lake lying west of Tlell. The Wiggins property touched this lake. Ed Wiggins came to the Charlottes in 1908 on the same boat which brought the lively William Leary family and pioneer George McRae. He took part in all the activities of that early era with

*Robert Paul "Bob" Beitush
who pre-empted land
near the mouth of
the Tlell River
in 1912 and remained
to live out his life
on his chosen spot..*

Photo - Bob Beitush

the other young men and was proud of the fact he had built the foundations under the first Queen Charlotte hospital.

In 1912 Ed and his bride, Charlotte Laughlin, were married in a double wedding ceremony with Ed's buddy Benny Cromp, and his bride Chrissie Goodall. It was the Islands' first double wedding and an occasion for much celebration.

BEITUSH ROAD — branches off the main highway on the east side of the Tlell bridge. It is named after Robert Paul "Bob" Beitush who pre-empted land near the mouth of the Tlell River in 1912 and remained to live out his life on his chosen spot. Beitush Road follows the Tlell River's east bank, north to the Beitush property - now owned by Mr. Beitush's son, Bob.

*TLELL PROVINCIAL PARK (Class C) — occupies 312 acres on the west bank of the Tlell River near the mouth. Adequate road access to this park is badly needed to make it the useful property it should be. The fine all-weather two-lane road shown on current maps, supposedly running the full length of the park has still to materialize - as of 1972.

GEIKIE CREEK — which has its mouth in Tlell Provincial Park, empties into the west side of the Tlell River opposite the main entrance gate to the Beitush farm. Still an ungazetted name, it has been in local use since the building of the first Tlell to Port Clements road. A winding stream which has its origin in the muskegs east of Tlell, it crosses the Tlell to Port Clements road three times. At each crossing there is a bridge designating each as 1st, 2nd or 3rd Geikie, depending on the crossing. Owing to a typographical error (presumably) orders came for the highway signs on these bridges to be spelled GEIKLE.

344

An error totally ignored by Islanders who continue to call the creek as they always have - GEIKIE.

2nd Geikie originally known as WARD CREEK, was changed in 1928 to 2nd Geikie, according to Dept. of Highways in Victoria.

Pioneer homesteader Dave Crocker hiking across the Mexican Tom trail.

Photo - Mrs. Louise Ward

MEXICAN TOM TRAIL — initially little more than a succession of blazed trees leading from Masset Inlet to the Tlell River, first put there in 1904, became a "road" in 1928 when two narrow ribbons of planks spanned the 12 miles close on the old Tom Trail route. This was the famous Plank Road, a subject for several magazine and newspaper articles. In 1967 a modern blacktopped road replaced the hazardous planks. On the north side of the paved road the Mexican Tom Trail, now blocked by numerous windfalls, is followed today only by hunters who use its winding path for easier access to the quiet muskegs.

GOLD CREEK — an ungazetted name for the creek which crosses the Port Clements to Tlell road west of the Geikies. It flows from a muskeg on the south side of the road, crosses the road, then enters the south end of Mayer Lake at the point where the Mayer River leaves the lake. Gold Creek does not actually enter Mayer Lake, but forms its own bight to join the river. Its name is a carry-over from the days when the Mayer River was called Gold Creek. The Department of Highways have adopted the name for their bridge identification, a name in use since the days of the Mexican Tom Trail.

WOODPILE CREEK — west of Gold Creek (above) flows into the south portion of Mayer Lake from a pond in the muskeg at the south side of the Port Clements to Tlell road. In the early years when the Mexican Tom trail consisted of a succession of blazed trees, there was a sizeable log jamb on this

*Original plank road
between Tlell and
Port Clements.
Later six-inch
planks were added
to each side and
centre. Photo taken
from Dyson's Corner
in Port Clements.*

Photo - Mrs. E.M. Dyson

creek. The logs were piled high enough at one point to make it an excellent place to cross. Early hikers referred to the jamb as The Woodpile, thus the name became associated with this creek. Not a gazetted name, but the Department of Highways have put their sign on the bridge across the creek today identifying it as WOODPILE CREEK, giving the name a measure of official recognition.

BEAVEN'S POND — west of Woodpile Creek, about half-way between Woodpile and Kumdis Creek, is a man-created pond. Scooped out during the gravelling of the Port Clements to Tlell road after the planks were taken up. Lying on the south side of the road it is named in association with the Beaven Tie and Timber operation run by H.R. Beaven of Queen Charlotte City during the depression years. Mr. Beaven established a small camp near this site to get out fire-killed cedar from which he proposed to cut ties for the Canadian National Railway. He set up a mill in Port Clements on the site of the old Barton mill to manufacture the ties but ran into financial difficulties. They did, however, cut a small amount of ties and planks for the Plank Road between Port Clements and Tlell.

PANSY CREEK — a small muskeg creek about two miles from Port Clements. The origin of the name is not known, but this name has been in use for many years and pre-dates the Plank Road of 1928.

*MAYER LAKE — a slender lake about 8 miles long lying in a north and south direction, may be reached today by a short gravel road which leads off the north side of the Port Clements to Tlell highway, between Gold Creek and Woodpile Creek. When the Richfield Oil Company put down a 3,855-foot test hole near the lake in 1958 they built the first part of the access road.

In the summer of 1967 crews came in to lay the black-topped highway. The old Mexican Tom trail lies for the most part on the north side of this road. Photo taken from the Port Clements end, looking east.

Photo - K.E. Dalzell

In the 1960s Baxter Pole Company extended the road to the shoreline at the south end of Mayer Lake to enable trucks to haul poles cut at the lake to their booming grounds at Kumdis Bay. In recent years Rod and Gun Clubs have put in a small floating dock and boat launching ramp where the gravel road emerges at the lake.

Mayer Lake is named after George Hardy Mayer who came to Masset Inlet in 1907 and is credited with being the first white man to see and map this lake. It was named during a survey in 1908.

About this same time a Mr. Gray Donald, employed with the Humphries, Tupper and Rice survey party at Tlell, became lost in the woods for two days. When he made his way back to camp he told of finding, ". . . a lake in there, maybe 10 or 12 miles long. I have named it GRAY DONALD LAKE," he announced. Since Mayer Lake is the only lake fitting his description in that part, it seems certain he discovered and named Mr. Mayer's lake.

By 1909 the lake was rimmed with cabins and staked land. One land staker, George Yuill, divided his lot (number 474) into small building sites complete with provision for a lakeshore road. During World War II a young prairie boy, Jim McGarvey, was aboard one of the Navy ships patrolling Charlotte waters. Jim thought he would like to return to the Islands after the war. But busy earning a living for his family and having established his home in Alberta he never got around to it. Then in the 1960s he received queries about poles on land reported to be owned by him at Mayer Lake.

Gradually the pieces of the puzzle came together. His father had bought two of those building sites on George Yuill's divided lot and bequeathed them to Jim. In the summer of 1970 Jim decided it was time to take his long delayed trip to the Charlottes, using for an excuse he should take a look at his land.

347

And as Wes Singer had done many years earlier (see page 169, Vol. 1, Q.C. Islands), Jim McGarvey, too, fell instantly under the spell of this lovely lake and plans to make his home eventually at "McGarvey's Shangri-la" - the name he has given his property on the east shoreline of Mayer Lake.

In the late 1920s and early 1930s Baxter Pole Company set up pole camps at Ferguson Bay, Kumdis Island and Mayer Lake. A flanged-wheeled carrier took the poles from the cutting grounds to tide water over a road constructed with log rails, similar to a railroad. For the Mayer Lake operation this road ran from Mayer Lake to the head of Kumdis Bay.

In the mid-1960s the company returned to the lake to cut the poles which had been mere saplings during the first operation. In the second operation the poles were trucked out via the gravel road mentioned earlier, which leads off the Port Clements to Tlell highway. The method in which Baxter Pole Company conducted their harvesting deserves mention, for they have left the area relatively unspoiled. If it had been a logging operation the result would have been a chaotic mess - the whole lakeside scarred and waters fouled with debris.

*LOON LAKE — named during the survey of this region 1908-09, lies midway between Mayer Lake and Kumdis Bay. A small lake, it was completely circled with settler's cabins close by. The survey trail which went from Kumdis Bay to Mayer Lake was in constant use and Loon Lake became the place for Mayer Lake settlers to take the halfway rest and a visit. In later years a wagon road replaced the trail as means of access to the lake. Then came the 1914-18 war and the mass evacuation as the young men flocked to the enlisting offices.

The area returned to its haunting silence. The casualty list for those volunteers from the Charlottes was incredible.

LOON LAKE CREEK — at the south end of Loon Lake, crosses the old wagon road and may be used as a bearing to locate Loon Lake, on the north side of the road. The lake is not visible from the road.

MAYER LAKE ROAD — is the name still applied to the wagon road, now badly overgrown, which led from the west shore of Mayer Lake to near the head of Kumdis Bay, where it joined a road leading into Port Clements. When the pole road was built in later years it intersected the wagon road near Loon Lake. The first telephone line to the east coast followed the wagon road to Mayer Lake most of the way, then, spanning the lake, continued overland to the region slightly south of Cape Ball. When the telephone line was relocated to follow the Port Clements to Tlell road, the old wire along the Mayer Lake road was laboriously gathered up and hauled into Port Clements by wagon for use on future lines.

*COPP CREEK — runs into the north end of Mayer Lake. Named after Charles Copp, prospector turned land speculator. Copp first came to Masset Inlet in May 1908 with T.L. Williams (now of Port Clements) and another fellow prospector, Jack Davis. They found no mineral prospects but Williams became so attracted to the place he applied for a pre-emption on the east side of Masset Inlet. Davis left for good. Copp, however, thought he would capitalize on the growing land interest. He persuaded a Vancouver company to back him and, in the fall of 1908, took a survey party out to Mayer Lake to lay out the land. It took in most of the region surrounding the north end of the lake. Copp, himself, did not stay to live on it.

*WATT LAKE — lies in the same muskeg that Copp Creek drains from and is a little to the northwest of Mayer Lake. Named after James Watt who was with the Humphries, Tupper and Rice's survey of this area in 1908 to 1909. In September of 1909 Jimmy Watt took charge of the crew making a trail into Mayer Lake from the west. This area became solidly covered with pre-emptions and, strangely, it was to the edge of Watt Lake that a pre-emptor named Hugh Watt came in 1913. His neighbour William Bert had a portion of Watt Lake on his land and Hugh Watt's land adjoined Bill Bert's. Like nearly all the homesteaders the 1914-18 war took them, almost to the last man.

*LITTLE LAKE — to the east of Mayer Lake, has a creek flowing from it to enter the Mayer River. Named during the initial survey of this region around 1908-09.

*HICKEY LAKE — east of Mayer Lake and northeast of Little Lake. Named after Jimmy Hickey, a member of the survey crew. Jimmy is remembered especially as a man with a huge crown of unruly Irish hair. He was a prospector and made his headquarters in Charlotte or Skidegate when not out in the hills. "Sometimes he would take a job with a survey party for extra cash," says Charlie Hartie of Queen Charlotte City. "He was Ontario Irish and belonged to the Fenians. There was quite a crowd of young fellows in Charlotte, among them Walter Dass, who was almost bald and who took an endless ribbing about his lack of hair. When Tom Kelly's sister began on him, Dass decided to get some of his own back and told her, 'Well, at least I don't wear a wig like Hickey.' The surprised young lady didn't think Hicky did wear a wig, but Dass was pretty convincing. At any rate she became greatly intrigued with the possibility.

"One day when Jimmy was seated in the bar at Smith's Hotel in Charlotte," Mr. Hartie went on, "he tilted his chair back and put up a hand to scratch his thick mop . . . just as she passed the door. Well, the temptation to settle her doubts about the wig question was irresistible. She moved behind Jimmy and plunged both hands right to his scalp and pulled hard. Jim's howl of pain was the real McCoy and only the fact that she was an extremely attractive young lady saved her from his Irish fist."

Jimmy Hickey had a pre-emption north of Tlell for some time where he put in periodic appearances to "prove up."

*MAYER RIVER — flows in a roundabout fashion to eventually empty into Hecate Strait north of Tlell. Like all streams draining muskeg country, it is a rich coffee colour. Shown on old maps variously as NAHGUN, MEYER and GOLD CREEK, it is reported to have 5 waterfalls as it descends to the sea from the lake at the 74-foot level, which bears the same name. Mayer Lake lay in the path of the great fire of 1840 which swept from Masset to below the Pontoon area of the Tlell River. The dense scrub which grew up between

Mayer Lake and the coast after this fire made one telephone lineman describe the route of the Mayer River as "pure jungle country."

The river acquired the name GOLD CREEK in pioneering days when Mr. Müller (of Miller Creek south of Dead Tree Point) reported he had found gold-bearing black sand at its mouth. He built a sluice-box and was all set to become rich, but became unbalanced to such a degree he had to be sent south for treatment. The sluice-box fell into disuse, but the name of GOLD CREEK became firmly attached and is still used locally when reference is made to the mouth of this creek.

MAYER RIVER is the gazetted name.

NORTHEAST GRAHAM ISLAND. FROM THE
MOUTH OF THE TLELL RIVER TO ROSE SPIT,
THEN WEST TO SKONUN POINT. (INCLUDES
THE INTERIOR REGION.)

CHAPTER SIXTEEN 𝒪

The mouth of the TLELL RIVER is rarely without an angler along its banks, and the outer beaches of the region are the happy-hunting ground for strolling beachcombers looking for treasures cast up by the surf. The early Haida found the area equally interesting and the signs of their occupancy are everywhere at Tlell.

Near the mouth of the river, on its east bank, the remains of two wickiups are easily distinguished. This particular fishing station was in active use when Chittenden visited in 1884.

On the opposite side of the river, slightly north of the mouth, is the section of the bow of the *Pesuta* which has been a landmark for years. She was one of a number of barges built about 1919 by Sanderson and Porter Company of Raymond, Washington, many of which were purchased by the Pacific Coyle Navigation Company of Vancouver for use as log barges. (The *Black Wolfe* which came to grief on Robertson Island off Queen Charlotte City in April 1929 was another of that group.)

The *Pesuta*, 264 feet long, was under tow by the tug *Imbrecaria* in Hecate Strait on December 11, 1928, when a violent southeast gale developed. Desperately manoeuvering with her unwieldy tow in the storm, the tug ran too close to the shallows off this part of Graham Island. The *Pesuta* struck bottom and the tow line snapped. With the *Imbrecaria* in mortal danger herself in the raging seas, the captain had no choice but to leave the *Pesuta* and try to save his tug.

*Remains of one of the two
wickiups at the mouth
of the Tlell River.*

Photo - K.E. Dalzell

*Mouth of the Tlell River.
Bow of* Pesuta *in distance
on opposite shore.*

Photo - K.E. Dalzell

*Remains of an old
lodge at K'ahlenskun in 1971.*

Photo - K.E. Dalzell

The Pesuta *in 1929. She was driven ashore in a violent gale on December 11, 1928 and became so firmly bedded salvage was hopeless.*

Photo - Mrs. Sybil de Bucy

All that remained of the Pesuta in 1971.

Photo - K.E. Dalzell

The waves carried the *Pesuta* ashore and high tides put her well up on the beach. Drifting sands quickly piled around, bedding her so firmly all hope of future salvage was eliminated.

K'AHLENSKUN VILLAGE — at the mouth of the Mayer River (Gold Creek,)[1] on the south side. The people from this village moved to Skidegate. Only the remains of one old lodge may be seen at this Haida site of early years as drifting sands and weather take their toll. For many years the clam shells from a midden associated with K'ahlenskun extended down the steep bank towards the sea, but these are now covered by the encroaching sand. Artifacts, such as bowls and other stone utensils have been found along the sand dunes south of K'ahlenskun even as far away as the vicinity of the *Pesuta*.

[1]See page 353 for Gold Creek

*CAPE BALL CREEK — formerly called the CAPE BALL RIVER, changed to creek status by the Geographic Board in 1954. (But still appearing on 1963 maps as a river.) It has also been shown as BONEHEAD CREEK. The Cape Ball makes a large semicircle from its headwaters in the vast muskeg west and north of the mouth (about 4 miles north of the mouth of the Mayer River), with numerous streamlets joining it *en route* as it winds to the sea.

LITTLE CAPE BALL CREEK — is the local name given to the small stream on the south side of the Cape Ball River, which joins it near the river's mouth. The old Giegerich farm is at the junction of the two. Nick Giegerich pioneered this land about 1908, bringing a wife and small son from Missouri. He built up a fine ranch and was a staunch promoter of this way of life on the Charlottes, writing frequent and eloquent letters to the editors of several papers. Three children were born to Mr. and Mrs. Giegerich on the Charlottes. To enable them to go to school he lived for a time in various Island settlements, working as a telegraph operator. Later they left the Charlottes so that their children could continue their education.

In later years Mr. Giegerich returned - the love for this place too strong to resist. But ranching in the old Cape Ball homesite was for a young vigorous man. His advancing age made resumption of the life he had known there impossible.

*OTTER CREEK — a tributary of the Cape Ball River, has its beginnings in the muskeg north of Mayer Lake and flows in a northerly direction to merge with the Cape Ball. Before reaching the river, Otter Creek spreads its banks to encompass a small lake. Old-timers think the creek may have been named about 1909 by Jimmy White and his brother Bill. They trapped extensively in that area, running trails in from the Oeanda River where they lived.

*CAPE BALL — the headland north of the Cape Ball River. The old name for it was KUL-TOW-SIS. Geologists say that during glaciation fluctuations the sea level at Cape Ball was at least 25 feet higher than it is today and there are evidences of three former channels of the Cape Ball River between its present mouth and Cape Ball headland.

In 1961 the Richfield Oil Company put down a bore-hole at Cape Ball for nearly 8,000 feet. It was unrewarding, but the inland area of this part of Graham Island is criss-crossed by bombadier roads used in connection with the various oil explorations conducted in the 1950s and 1960s.

Haida legends say that Ball was the greatest of all the ocean spirits. Known by several names, the most frequently used being Great-Swashing-of-the-Waves, he was always invited to all the feasts made by the people living at the Cape - the food sent to him through the fire to ensure his pleasure.

His wife came from a reef near Kung, at the entrance of Naden Harbour. During a visit to her home, Ball made a jest about his wife which offended her and she complained to her father. Whereupon her father arranged it so that when Ball and other members of his family came out of the father-in-law's house, a crab bit a sizeable hunk out of each of them. It was a grave error against the powerful Ball.

Shortly afterwards when the father-in-law and his people, in the form of

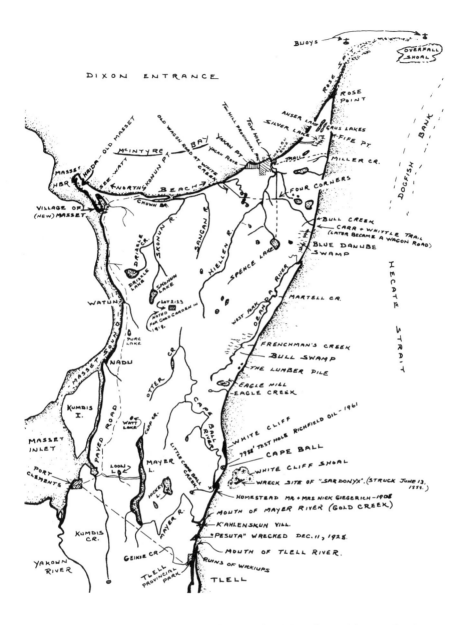

killer whales, were swimming past Cape Ball, old Ball got his own back. He ordered the waters to dry. The whales were stranded and transformed into rocks which may still be seen there.

Actually Ball's greatest forte lay in raising waters. He seemed to be able to raise floods at will and is credited with having caused the great Flood.

WHITE CLIFF SHOAL — about 1½ miles off Cape Ball, may be some of

355

those whales old Ball transformed into shoals. Several vessels were to curse them in later years. In 1878 when Dawson visited the Charlottes the Indians told him of a vessel going ashore on the shoals which managed to get off by throwing everything overboard to lighten her. Among the objects retrieved by the Cape Ball Haidas from this jettisoning was a fine brass cannon.

The photographer, Maynard, accompanying Chittenden in 1884 had a narrow escape when the canoe he rode in hit these rocks. A few years later the Canadian Pacific Navigation vessel *Sardonyx* struck the shoal at 4 a.m. on a June morning and was so badly holed she had to be abandoned.

The shoals were named in association with the conspicuous white cliffs to the north of Cape Ball.

BIG CLIFF — the local name for the high part of the Cape Ball headland.

WHITE CLIFF — local name for the 420-foot-high conspicuous white cliff on the north side of Cape Ball headland. (White Cliff Shoal lies to the southeast of WHITE CLIFF.)

LANAS VILLAGE, Peoples'-town — a Raven Crest village which lay a little south of Cape Ball.

GAHLINSKUN, High-up-on-a-point — also a Raven Crest site, said to have been a little north of the point of Cape Ball.

HUADOS VILLAGE, Standing-Water — an allusion to the swampy nature of the land back of these towns. It, too, belonged to the Ravens. Not necessarily occupied at the same time as the others, it is said to have been north of Gahlinskun.

HLGIHLA-ALA VILLAGE, Swamp-hollows or Place-of-ditches — the most northerly of the sites along the Cape Ball shoreline area, and also a Raven site. Dr. G.M. Dawson's map shows it to be in the bight on the north side of Cape Ball. Several of the houses were still standing when he was in the area in 1878. "It is said to have been populous, and is near some excellent halibut banks. It is doubtless the A-SE-GUANG in Mr. Work's list and said to have nine houses," wrote Dr. Dawson. Later historians believe that John Work may have been referring to more than one village when he arrived at a total of nine houses at the Cape Ball village.

*EAGLE CREEK — about 6 to 7 miles north of Cape Ball, a short creek flowing from a small lake and emptying into Hecate Strait south of Eagle Hill.

*EAGLE HILL — north of the creek above, is 422 feet high. There are steep cliffs all along the shore at this portion of the beach, rising to 250 feet.

The LUMBER PILE — an identification which dates back to the turn of this century and still in current local use. The Lumber Pile is on Lot 116 between two small ponds and is about 4 or 5 miles north of Eagle Creek. Said to have originated when a Hecate Strait storm swept a great quantity of lumber on

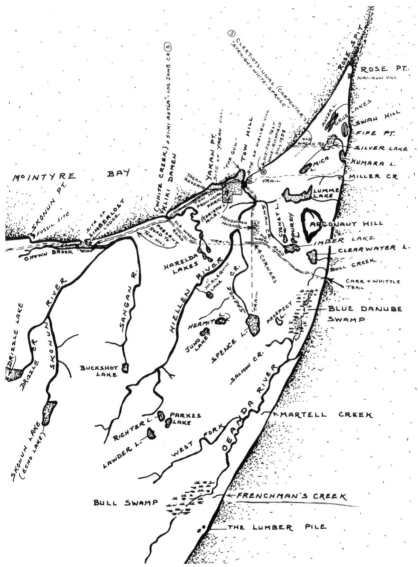

All names supplied by Mr. Charles A. Smith are shown on this map by Ⓢ

to this shoreline.

BULL SWAMP — a marshy region slightly inland and north of the Lumber Pile. Named by Mexican Tom Hodges about 1910-12, when he noticed the fondness the wild cattle had for the lush forage in this swamp.

FRENCHMAN'S CREEK — also frequently called THE FRENCHMAN'S.

The creek originally drained a small slough which was known as Little Lake and which is now pretty well washed into the ever encroaching sea. During Depression years Frank Gagnon built a cabin on the shore of Little Lake and eked out a living by washing gold dust from the black sands on the beaches nearby. When he died a few years later, he was buried close by. To mark his grave Jimmy White, his neighbour from the Oeanda, carefully gathered armloads of glass balls from the shoreline along this section of beach and circled the plot with them. When the souvenir hunters with the aid of modern 4-wheel-drive transportation made this once-quiet beach part of their itinerary the glass balls around Frank Gagnon's grave were soon taken.

MARTELL CREEK — named for a homesteader who lived north of Frenchman's Creek, and who had another cabin along the trail Jimmy White put in between the.Oeanda and Nadu, to the west. Martell is said to have had a machine with which he sifted the black sands for the elusive gold.

Seth Frederickson, early resident of Port Clements, (left) admires Jimmy White's fine garden. Jimmy, with pipe, is the best known of all Oeanda pioneers, staying on long after most had left.

Photo - Mrs. W.G. Campbell

*OEANDA RIVER — a rambling river about 12 miles north of Eagle Creek. The musical name is a modification of *Hoyagundla*, the Raven Creek of the Haidas. This area was thickly dotted with cabins in early years.

HOYAGUNDLA VILLAGE, Raven-Creek-Village — at the mouth of the Oeanda River was occupied at various times by people of the Raven Crest, then by the Eagles, both originally from the old Rose Point village. Under Raven ownership one of the chiefs was Taholdia-qona, Great-Foaming-of-the-Waves.

WEST FORK — is the name given to the tributary of the Oeanda which originates in the region of Lawder Lake, and joins the Oeanda to flow northward for a short distance before coming out on the beach. The name appears on all pre-emptor maps and blueprints of the 1913 issue. These maps are interesting in their graphic illustration of the great number of pre-emptions covering the entire area of northeast Graham Island, many of which had become Crown Granted by 1913. Almost all were vacated when the young pioneers joined up for the 1914-18 war. The deep ditches and wells remain to remind of interrupted dreams.

SALMON CREEK — shown on all early maps. The Oeanda has a swampy tributary leading northward from its mouth. From this north branch a tributary winds from the region of Spence Lake - this tributary is Salmon Creek. Named in surveys made in 1908 to 1913.

*LAWDER LAKE — on the borders of Lots 1786 and 1791. Shown in outline on all early maps, but not named until the 1927 land map was issued.

*PARKES LAKE — about a mile northeast of Lawder Lake. Named during the surveys of 1908 to 1913 for one of the pre-emptors who worked on a survey crew, according to old-timers.

*RICHTER LAKE — about ¼ of a mile northwest of Parkes Lake. Named at the same time for another pioneer who worked on one of the surveys.

*JUNO LAKE — on Lot 1048 west of Spence Lake, had pre-emptions all around it and the pack-trail from well inland into the muskeg swung by this lake *en route* to Tow Hill. This pack-trail was marked out on the maps and blueprints and was much in use. Juno Lake is a comparatively recent name, and did not appear on maps until the 1950s.

*HERMIT LAKE — northeast of Juno Lake is on Lot 1042 and named at the same time. Origin of the name not known.

*SPENCE LAKE — one of the largest of the many lakes in the northeast part of Graham Island, lies west of the Blue Danube Swamp. Spence Lake named during the initial survey 1907 to 1908, is after Charlie Spence, an early Graham Island pioneer who stayed to live out his life on the Islands. He took part in every aspect of early-day life, prospecting, surveying, homesteading, land staking, guiding (Dr. C.F. Newcombe was one he accompanied) and was road foreman in the Masset area for some years. His first homestead was at Kumara Lake, where he combined pre-empting with a little placer mining in the black sands in this region. Spence, with Victor Virgalias, was the first to recover gold in paying amounts from the sand.

There were several settlers in the Spence Lake region, with many of the pre-emptions advancing to Crown Grant status. A road came south from Tow Hill to Four Corners and a good trail continued to Spence Lake. One of the most valued settlers at the lake was Mrs. La Farge, a registered nurse, who helped her husband break the soil and build their home.

SPENCE CREEK — runs northwest from Spence Lake to join the Hiellen River at Lot 851. The Pre-emptor's Map referred to it as EAST BRANCH, but all former homesteaders from that area knew it as SPENCE CREEK.

*HARLEQUIN LAKE — near the east border of Lot 1032, lying northwest of Spence Lake. There are a cluster of lakes in this region. All are unnamed except the centre and largest one, Harlequin, which received its name with the issuance of maps in the 1950s.

*PROSPECT LAKE — named during the initial land survey 1907-12, is a crescent-shaped lake to the east of Spence Lake, and surrounded by hills rising to about 500 feet. Land all around it was solidly settled by 1913.

*BLUE DANUBE SWAMP — north of the mouth of the Oeanda River. Named by one of the Islands' most colourful pioneers, Mexican Tom Hodges, for a wild and bellowing bull about 1911 or 1912. Hodges, a Mexican-Texan cowpuncher, and 16-year-old Ridge Purdy were living out on the east coast and had made camp for a time near this swamp. There was one particularly huge bull among the wild cattle they called The King. That is, until one evening when Tom brought home a gramaphone to entertain himself and "the Kid" (Ridge.) "It had a big horn," says Ridge, "and among the roll-type records was the selection *Blue Danube Waltz*. Each time Tom would put that tune on, the big bull would come to the top of the hill above and bellow." After about the third or fourth time, Tom called to the lad "Listen to him bawl, Kid. . . that's sure an old Blue Danube bull!" From that time on the swamp region became known as Old Blue Danube's Swamp which, over the years has been modified to BLUE DANUBE SWAMP.[1]

[1]The story of Mexican Tom Hodges and Ridge is contained in Q.C. Islands, Volume 1.

CARR AND WHITTLE TRAIL — a local name for the east end of the trail, which later became a wagon road, leading from the beach north of the Blue Danube Swamp to Four Corners and thence to Tow Hill. Bill Carr and Ernest Whittle, residents of the Oeanda region, worked on this trail at its east end. They said that since Mexican Tom had his name applied to the Tlell to Port Clements trail, they might as well honour "their" trail and promptly nailed up a sign near the beach entrance to the trail. Oldsters still refer to it by this name.

BULL CREEK — the creek which flows into Hecate Strait north of the entrance to Carr and Whittle Trail. Bull Creek is south of the unnamed creek draining Clearwater Lake.

FOUR CORNERS — at the intersection of Lots 850, 851, 852 and 853. The road which began as the Carr and Whittle trail, north of the Oeanda, ran in a general northwesterly direction to this intersection, then turned north to follow the survey line for the most part, finally emerging behind Tow Hill. At the Four Corners, two branch trails led off, one went south to Spence Lake and the other led west past several pre-emptions, gradually curving north to the beach and emerging west of White Creek (now gazetted as Kliki Damen.) Charlie Smith, one of the former pre-emptors in this area told the writer, "It was little Jimmy White of the Oeanda who named FOUR CORNERS. Jimmy was from Arizona and had known a place by this name down there. The name really caught on and I don't think I ever heard it called anything else.."

MENDHAM'S MUSKEG — about 1½ miles north of Four Corners, lies along the west side of Lot 828. It was named by his neighbours after a Mr. Mendham who pre-empted on the swamp, built a cabin on the southwest quarter, then in the spring of 1910 went to the Skeena River to work for the Grand Trunk Pacific Railway. "Don't know what happened to him," says Luther Lundberg, pioneer of the area, "I came in 1912 and there had been no word of him, but the name was always used for that swamp." When the road was being built to accommodate wagons, the men dug a ditch to drain this swamp and 18 inches down encountered sand. "We dug it up and piled it on small logs over the muskeg," says Luther," and it packed down to make a pretty good trail. Funny thing, when I went back 50 years later on a visit, that ditch was still working . . . as good as the day we put it in."

*SWAN CREEK — a tributary of the Hiellen River, which runs through Mendham's Muskeg to join the Hiellen northwest of the swamp. Its headwaters are at Imber Lake.

SWAN CREEK ROAD — the name frequently given to the road leading from Tow Hill to Four Corners. It crossed Swan Creek near its intersection with the Hi-ellen.

CAPE FIFE ROAD — went in from the beach about 3 miles east of Tow Hill, going to Silver Lake, with a trail from there to Fife Point. However, the trail which went from Tow Hill to Kumara Lake is also commonly called the Cape Fife Road by old-timers. Department of Highways work sheets of 1910 applied the name to the first mentioned road, and from this it came into local usage.

*IMBER LAKE — the headwaters of Swan Creek, has apparently suffered from a typographical error. It was named TIMBER LAKE during the initial survey 1907-12, and appeared on the first maps under that name.

*CYGNET LAKE — a very small lake to the northwest of Imber Lake, on Lot 855. Named between 1927 and 1954, presumably in association with Swan Creek whose streamlets drain it.

*PURDY LAKE — a kidney-shaped lake straddling the border of Lots 855A and 858A, to the west of Cygnet Lake and named at the same time. It is after R.H. Purdy, "the Kid," who spent memorable early years on this east coast with the colourful cowboy Mexican Tom. (Mr. Purdy's story is contained in some detail in Q.C. Islands, Volume 1.)

*CLEARWATER LAKE — east of Imber Lake and a little larger. A stream drains from it to the east coast. All four lakes, Cygnet, Imber, Purdy and Clearwater, lie on the north side of the road leading from Four Corners to the east coast. Clearwater Lake named 1907-12.

*ARGONAUT HILL — a conspicuous mesa-shaped hill, 535 feet high and wooded to its summit, is about 6½ miles southward from Rose Point. Called KLIKI DAMEN by the Haidas. (C. Smith) Pre-emptions, several of which became Crown Granted, surrounded this hill.

Although Argonaut Hill was delineated on early maps, it was not shown under a name until the 1950 issue of maps. Origin of the name not confirmed.

*LUMME LAKE — at the foot of the north side of Argonaut Hill is one of the larger lakes in this part and, like the rest of the region, was solidly flanked by pre-emptors in the heyday of land interest in the years when the government permitted it to be used. Lumme Lake named during the initial survey 1907-12.

MILLER CREEK — has its headwaters between Lumme and Mica Lakes and flows east to the beach off Lot 1212. The original owner of Lot 1212 was Albert Morice Miller who obtained his Crown Grant in 1912. Miller and Joe Reid were two of the more than 20 men working the black sands along this portion of the beach in 1909. They had adapted a process for recovering the placer gold using blankets instead of the usual sluice-box method.

Miller Creek was well-known to Ridge Purdy when he and Mexican Tom lived on the east coast, as they had one of their main campsites by this creek. When the Miller homesite was abandoned it was, eventually, sold in a tax sale and now belongs to an absentee owner. With the current government land policy, owners like this have a seller's market.

All that land formerly dotted with homesites, the young owners of which for the most part died in the First World War, is now part of a huge park and blocked from homes of any type today - despite the urgent pleadings of young people. With a common sense approach there is no reason why such a huge area could not support both a park and a few homesites for people willing to accept pioneer conditions, and live on the land - not just own it.

*MICA LAKE — about 2 miles inland from the mouth of Miller Creek, received its name during the first survey of the area 1907-12. One of the families at Mica Lake was the Hansens from Denmark who built a homestead which included among its outbuildings one of the largest barns in the region. They were hard-working people who seemed to know exactly how to create a comfortable home from the wilds.

*KUMARA LAKE — a little to the south of Fife Point. (Cape Fife) It is the mouth of a creek which ran from Mica Lake to Silver Lake, then to Kumara. Over the years it has been eroding steadily and, although old maps show it to be a tidal lake with land between it and the ocean, today it is open to the seas and filled with a mass of debris. The homesite of Charlie Spence which

Charlie Spence sits outside his cabin at Kumara Lake. This photo was taken by Dr. C.F. Newcombe when Mr. Spence and Mr. Charles A. Smith accompanied Dr. Newcombe for one of his trips along this part of the Charlottes. Picture taken in 1911.

Photo - Mr. C.A. Smith.

lay between the coast and the lake has long since gone into the ocean. Chittenden in 1884 named this tidal lake LONG LAGOON.

CHAWAGIS, also known as DHIHUAGITS, Always-Low-Water-Town — lay in the vicinity of Kumara Lake. Occupied first by Raven Crest people from the Rose Point village who later moved to Cape Ball, then to Skidegate. Later it was owned by the Stastas, the great Eagle Crest family from which Chief Edenshaw became a hereditary chief of much renown.

*SILVER LAKE — lies a little to the northwest of Kumara Lake and was named during the first survey of the area about 1907-12. At one time a stream came from Mica Lake, entered Silver Lake, then flowed from Silver Lake to Kumara Lake to enter into Hecate Strait. Three settlers remained in this region long after everyone else had gone; Mr. Ronald Currie and his niece, Alice Harling, and their neighbour Charlie Smith. The three formed a partnership and created a 1500-acre ranch.

"We ran a pretty fair-sized herd of Jerseys and made butter with the label CH&S on our wrappers," said Mr. Smith. "Afterwards we went into white-faced Herefords with a pure-bred Shorthorn bull." The herd they built up was excellent. Their ranch took in Lots 867A, 1009, 1010 and 1216, completely surrounding Silver Lake and extending part way up Anser and the Grus Lakes, then south to Kumara. Part of the ranching venture involved digging a ditch which worked so well it has almost dried what used to be Silver Lake.

Charlie Smith left to do his stint in the navy during the 1914-18 war, then returned to join his partners - and married Miss Harling.

"Alice Harling was a remarkable woman," remember old-timers. "A former secretary in the Parliament Buildings, she first came to visit her uncle, but remained and took part in a life which must have contrasted unbelievably with what she had been used to. She held her own in every way with those two men, sharing in all aspects of the ranch."

*FIFE POINT — about 3 miles south of Rose Point. Formerly called CAPE FIFE and still known locally as this. It was shown and named on charts dating back to 1868. From the sea it can only be distinguished by the 230-foot-high Swan Hill rising behind it.

The big attraction of Cape Fife for many years was the gold-bearing black sands, which have been known since 1859 when Captain R.W. Torrens reported finding "colours" along the beach. After the turn of the present century several schemes were tried to recover the gold in commercial amounts. None was successful. Some individual efforts did return a small amount, but generally speaking the dust was so fine, and storms sweeping along this shoreline sifted and disturbed the sands so frequently, it was an elusive proposition.

Dr. C.F. Newcombe found more than gold to interest him. It was in the Cape Fife region that he uncovered relics which he believed came from the Tahltan Indians of the mainland. He also said that he was positive, from signs he found in this region, that there had been a big caribou drive there, the caribou having been driven into Hecate Strait. Newcombe considered the drive had been so extensive it could have been a contributing factor in the decline and subsequent elimination of the Queen Charlotte Islands' caribou.

Charlie Smith, who was with Dr. Newcombe during one particular visit, remembers hearing him muse about what may have happened. Did the Tahltans drive the animals off before fleeing from the Charlottes to live at Portland Inlet? Why were the Tahltans on the Charlottes? How long ago?

*SWAN HILL — is the 230-foot hill at the back of Cape Fife (Fife Point), which is thickly wooded. A portion of the ranch belonging to Charlie Smith, Alice Harling and Ronald Currie lay along the slope of Swan Hill. It is the last height of land between this point and Rose Point.

*ANSER LAKE and

*GRUS LAKES — lie northwest of Swan Hill, with Anser Lake the more westerly. Long narrow lakes, they look like enormous ditches from the air. All were named during the early surveys. At first they were shown as FRASER LAKE, the term used to include the group. By the 1920s the name Fraser had been dropped; Anser applied to the westerly lake and Grus Lakes used to indicate the other two.

Looking westward over the bottom end of Rose Point. The outline of Tow Hill stands in the distance.

Photo - Major George Nicholson

*ROSE POINT — on the northeast tip of Graham Island, and

*ROSE SPIT — the sand and gravel spit which extends off Rose Point for 7 miles. Parts of the spit dry and the rest is dangerously shallow. This is probably the best known region of the Charlottes both in legend and navigationally. It has been the nemesis of all too many ships.

A growing promontory - the prevailing southeast gales erode the east coast shoreline and drive the sands northward to build the spit farther into Dixon Entrance. The whole process is aided by the meeting of the waters of Dixon Entrance and Hecate Strait in a violent turbulence.

The Haidas called Rose Point, NAI. The spit was NAI-KUN, the-long-nose-of-Nai. (C. Smith)

In 1788 Captain William Douglas on the *Iphigenia* named them after George Rose, the same British M.P. for whom Rose Harbour on the south end of Moresby Island had been named. In 1791 Captain Robert Gray of the *Columbia* named Rose Point, CAPE LOOKOUT. In 1792 Joseph Ingraham, master of the *Hope* showed them on one map as SANDY POINT and on another as MASSET SPIT. That same year Jacinto Caamano in the *Aranzazu* named it PUNTA YMISIBLE, Invisible Point. It was William Douglas's names which were officially adopted.

NAI-KUN VILLAGE, Point-Town-Village — stood on the east side of Rose Point. Originally a Raven Crest village occupied by several tribes. Owing to internal troubles they separated, abandoning the town. Some years later it was

365

taken over by the Eagle Crest Stasta family and much later on, one of the original Raven families returned for a short period. John Work in 1836-40 said there were 5 of the great lodges remaining at the site and he estimated that about 122 people made their permanent home there. Shifting sands have obliterated the village now, but careful searching will still produce occasional evidence of it, providing the sands have been blown in an accommodating direction.

In 1970 the Provincial Government announced that the Rose Spit area had been set aside as part of the Ecological Reserve now applied to most of Northeast Graham Island. The Department of Transport took a step regarding the navigational hazards and placed an unmanned weather station on the inner part of the Spit. Designed primarily to give wind readings at the Spit, it was beset by mechanical problems for its initial period of operation, but is reported to be living up to expectations at the present time.

Inland from Rose Point lay the pioneer Tom Bradly homesite. Part of Tom's home still remains in the secluded shelter of the thick spruce which protect it from icy ocean blasts.

*OVERFALL SHOAL — at the outer end of Rose Spit, has a depth of 1½ fathoms. A light and whistle buoy has been placed there to give all mariners warning, and a light and bell buoy is moored near the drying portion of the Spit.

The meeting of the two waters, Dixon Entrance and Hecate Strait, at certain stages of the tide produce an awesome appearance in this region - and which gave rise to the name "overfall" - a seething mass of breakers and huge waves. Bert Tingley, pioneer of the Port Clements townsite, remembers the time he and his brother Eli, in their 26-foot *Little Johnny* sporting a 7-HP Fairbanks-Morse, came across from Prince Rupert in 1911. "We ran into a howling southeaster," said Bert, "and in the thick weather got too far south to clear Rose Spit, which meant we had a lee shore with heavy breakers when we sighted land. We had only the choice of running the long distance around Overfall Shoals . . . which were really boiling by that time . . . or take a chance and jump the Spit at its narrowest point where the seas were not all breaking.

"Eli chose the last. Running up close, he watched until we got an immense breaker coming up astern, then gave her full speed and in minutes we were safely across."

Eli's father-in-law, Mr. Woods, was not so lucky. The party he came with got caught in the Overfall maelstrom and were cast up onto the Spit, lucky to save their lives - everything else lost. Overfall Shoal has claimed many victims, small boats and large.

The Haidas called it NAI TAS CUDLAY, The-offshore-bank-of-Nai. (C.Smith)

*DOGFISH BANK — lies in a northeasterly direction, stretching from Kumara Lake region to beyond the drying portion of the Spit and is about 5 to 10 miles offshore in the Spit area.

NORTH BEACH — is the local name given to the great stretch of sand beach fringing the shoreline from Rose Point to Masset. It is the home of the famous razor clams.

CLEET-OTS-UNAS, straight-white-spruce — was the Haida name for the place along the North Beach now called, locally, CARPENTER'S, the former homestead of Howard Carpenter and his family. (C. Smith)

It is at Carpenter's one finds a rough road leading along the top of the dunes to the Spit.

Looking east from Tow Hill to Rose Spit and Rose Point. Remains of the clam cannery near the mouth of the Hiellen River still visible among the new growth of trees. The clearing near the bridge at the bottom of photo is where J.K. Anderson had his store.

Photo - British Columbia Forest Service

*HIELLEN RIVER — a modification of the old Haida THEE-ELL-EN or TOU-UNDL-AY meaning the RIVER-BY-TOW. (C. Smith) The mouth of the Hiellen emerges onto the North Beach on the east side of Tow Hill, the waters flowing around the base of the hill to reach the ocean. Branches of this river with the musical name, go deep inland to drain muskegs some 13 to 14 miles southeast and reach out in all directions as they gradually drain northward. Dr. G.M. Dawson first adopted the name to the maps in 1878. "It is a stream of some size, frequented by great numbers of salmon in autumn," he wrote.

On the west bank of the river, at the base of Tow Hill, J.K. Anderson built a store in pioneering days which later included a post office and telephone station. Opposite the store, Nellie and Jim Hammond had their overnight stopping place. Several entrepreneurs ran charter trips from Masset to Tow Hill, both by wagon and by boat. "Fare $1.50 one way and baggage extra," ran the advertisements. All this area was solidly settled well inland.

367

HIELLEN VILLAGE — lay on the east bank of the river and is said to have been a village of some size at one time. A Raven Crest site, like all large villages, it had lodges owned by both Eagle and Ravens.

The-house-so-big-it-can-hold-many-people belonged to the Eagle Crest Family Chief Edenshaw and was still habitable when Chittenden camped there in 1884. Cloud-House belonged to the Town Chief of the village, but it was in ruins in 1884. The old Hiellen village is now part of the 70.5 acre reserve belonging to the Masset Band.

Permission was obtained to build a clam cannery on this reserve. It operated for several seasons between 1923 and 1930.[1]

About a mile to the east of the old village site the Richfield Oil Company put down a drill hole in 1958 to a depth of 6,015 feet. It proved unfruitful. The large clearing at the site is easily seen from the beach and, except for driftwood cast up with every storm, formerly accessible from the beach for suitably equipped vehicles.

[1]See page 166, Vol. I., Q.C.I.

*TOW HILL — the 500-foot hill facing out to sea with a cliff composed of columnar basalt, is probably the most distinctive navigational landmark on the entire North Beach. It has as many legends about it as its more easterly neighbour Rose Spit. The name Tow, from a Haida word rhyming with "cow" - although pronounced today as "toe" - means place-of-food. (C. Smith) It was sometimes called LITTLE MOUNTAIN by the Haidas. One legend says Tow once stood with his brother Towustasin in Juskatla but left in a jealous rage when he imagined he had been unfairly treated in the disposition of fish.

Tow was a miserable neighbour when he came to live at the mouth of the Hiellen. Constantly making night raids on the Haida village, he stole everything he could lay his hands on to satisfy his gluttonous appetite - even children. One day he sent word that his next victim would be Beautiful Star, the chief's daughter.

Terrified though the Haidas were, they decided something had to be done and a meeting hurriedly got under way. It was decided they would hide at the foot of the path and kill Tow when he descended. Volunteers were called. No one responded. Then they would draw straws, said the elders. The panic became great. No one wanted to pick a straw lest the short one be his. Then the outcast crippled Hopi stepped forth, his homely face causing the others to shrink back. "If the chief will promise me Beautiful Star for my bride, I will kill Tow." The roar of scorn which greeted Hopi nearly bowled him over. The very idea of that old man even thinking he could match Tow - let alone the audacity to ask for Beautiful Star. He must be mad. But Hopi stood his ground.

Finally the elders said, "What have we got to lose? No one here will do anything. If Hopi can kill Tow before the monster gets his hands on the girl, then he should have her for his wife."

"There is one condition more," said Hopi. "Everyone must go into his lodge and stay until sundown. Even so much as a peek and I will let Tow take you all."

It was then late afternoon. Hopi got out his powerful whalebone whistle and a big rawhide drum and stood in front of the hill. He blew the whistle and beat the drum with all his might. Tow, just waking from his sleep was hungry and cranky. "Stop that infernal racket," he roared down at Hopi. But Hopi just made more noise. "If you don't cut that out, blast you, I'll send my eagle to tear you apart," screamed Tow. Still Hopi continued to beat the drum. The eagle was loosed - a great 20-foot bird - which swooped down on the little cripple. Hopi let forth a piercing whistle on the whalebone and the eagle became paralyzed, slammed against the face of the hill and turned to stone. Parts of him may still be seen there.

Tow was enraged. Calling his pet whale, he ordered it to swallow Hopi. The whale began to obey, but when he heard the beat of the drum, he overshot his mark and ran aground. He, too, turned to stone. There he lies to this day, his place marked by the blowhole - the only part of him which still continues to function.

When he saw what had happened to his whale, Tow's rage knew no limit. He began to heave down boulders on Hopi, which the little man dodged easily. Finally there were no more rocks to throw and Tow said, "Stop that noise damn you or I'll come down myself and eat you alive." At this Hopi drummed all the louder and blew his whistle to a screaming whine. Suddenly Tow ran to the edge of the cliff and jumped. But he had become so fat and lazy he could not control his jump and hurtled onto the beach head first to dash his brains out on the boulders he had thrown down shortly before. It is said that the rocks are still there and old Tow's big fingerhole marks may easily be seen.

Hopi, our little hero, not only got the girl, but became a very important man in his village from that moment on.

George Dawson applied the name Tow Hill to the charts in 1878. Prior to this it had been shown as NAGDON HILL and also as MACROON HILL on early charts.

THE GUN — a blow-hole in the rocks at the base of Tow Hill, through which the sea, at certain stages of the tide, shoots up through it with a resounding boom. A local name coined in pioneering days.

CHRISTIE'S MILE — adjoined the Hiellen Indian Reserve and surrounded Tow Hill, which was cut out of it. It had been the dream of A.S. Christie, the genial boot manufacturer from Vancouver, to own a cottage on the top of the hill, but the site was taken over by the Hydrographic Service for a navigational marker. Christie, although disappointed, proceeded with his acquisition of the balance of the 640 acres, planning to create a townsite at some future time. The lot was surveyed for him by Fred Nash in 1908, along with other properties near the Sangan River and at Delkatla which he also bought.

In 1912 following the death of the beloved "Father" Hogan in Masset, Mr. Christie announced that one of his first acts would be to donate a lot and build a church on his townsite, dedicated in the memory of Mr. Hogan. In October of that year he made a trip to Prince Rupert and gave extensive interviews to the newspapers telling of his plans. It never amounted to anything more than that "telling."

The name of Christie's Mile was used for years by local people in connection with this region. Today it is the Tow Hill Provincial Park.

The Haidas knew it as GUL-AH-YONUN, big-high-open-place. (C. Smith)

*TOW HILL PARK — a Class B park. On January 13, 1948, the Provincial Government announced they were setting up such a park at Tow Hill. On December 2, 1954 the park was confirmed. In 1972 under a Local Initiative Program two attractive picnic sites with tables and barbecue pits were set up - one on the west bank of the Hiellen not far from the old site of J.K. Anderson's store, the other on the ocean side of Tow Hill. A trail has been cut up and over the hill and along the beach.

*YAKAN POINT — west of Tow Hill is a modification of a Haida name.

YAGAN VILLAGE — formerly at Yakan Point, was first a camping site, then a town. The town, which took its name from the camp site, was well back from the present shoreline, for the ocean has receded along the North Beach. Where the old house ruins now lie was once a sandbank over which the sea broke. Dawson reported in 1878 there were six or more houses there as well as a few potato gardens, and the village was occupied at that time only during the dogfish and halibut fishery. It belonged to the Eagle Crest people.

The Yagan village site is now part of the 80-acre reserve owned by the Masset Band.

*KLIKI DAMEN — the creek west of Yakan Point. Known locally as WHITE CREEK, a name it received during the pioneering era. In early years transportation rates from Masset to White Creek were $1 in the service offered by Bert Swain. Today a road runs inside the treeline as far as Tow Hill (from Masset), but in Bert's day it was along the beach, or by boat, with tides and weather ruling all.

The Haidas called White Creek SI-KI ANTLA, Log-jamb-creek. (C. Smith)

*HARELDA LAKES — a small group of lakes about 2½ miles inland, which are drained by the Kliki Damen (White Creek.) Originally shown on an old blueprint as one lake, HER LAKE, subsequent maps showed it as HERALD LAKE. Recently the name of HARELDA LAKES has been applied to the group, and this is now the gazetted name.

*McINTYRE BAY — the waters off the North Beach. Named on June 19, 1789, by Captain William Douglas when on his second trip to the Charlottes in the *Iphigenia*. On his first trip, the previous year, he named Rose Point. John McIntyre, a shrewd merchant of Macoa, with influential connections in Canton, had a direct link with Douglas in some way. Joseph Ingraham, who knew McIntyre also, found him to be "all business" and as their acquaintanceship grew into a friendship, Ingraham realized McIntyre was merely edging for the most profitable way of buying and selling furs the traders brought from the northwest Pacific coast. "The pleasantries and friendliness shown to me were for ulterior purposes only," wrote Ingraham later.

370

*SANGAN RIVER — flows into McIntyre Bay at Chown Brook. The Skonun River, Sangan River and Chown Brook all enter McIntyre Bay through a common mouth. All names are modifications of early Haida names.

For some years there was a holiday resort in operation on the east side of the Sangan, near its mouth. But transportation difficulties to the Charlottes and an unexpectedly cool climate at this part of the North Beach made the venture financially unsuccessful.

In ancient years it was a Haida village site, being used as a fishing station by them when Chittenden visited in 1884.

*BUCKSHOT LAKE — about 7 miles inland, is drained by the Sangan River. Named during the early land survey about 1908.

*SKONUN RIVER — empties through the same mouth as the Sangan, which it joins about 2 miles from the mouth. The Skonun has its headwaters even farther south than those of the Sangan, for it comes from a lake east of Watun River. On early maps this river was shown as the CHONUN RIVER, and on a Pre-emptor's Map both it and the Sangan were called SANGAN.

*SKONUN LAKE — east of Watun River and drained by the Skonun River is 164 feet above sea level. Formerly called ECHO LAKE, this name changed to Skonun Lake in the 1920s. In the pioneering days a road ran east from the mouth of Watun River to the lake and there were many settlers in that area.

Lot 2123, about 1½ miles east of the south end of the lake made news in a Government bulletin published in 1919 when used as an illustration of what could be done with muskeg when it was properly handled. This lot in the heart of muskeg country produced a good garden the first year, when wood ashes were mixed into the soil to sweeten it. J.C.A. Long, the B.C.L.S. who became a land-owner himself across from Masset, verified this report and said he had found the muskeg soil was exceptionally fertile with similar treatment.

*DRIZZLE CREEK — a tributary of Skonun River. Named in association with the lake it drains.

*DRIZZLE LAKE — named during the initial land survey 1907-12, is located about 2 miles east of Griffith Point, off Masset Sound. The lake, 172 feet above sea level, was solidly surrounded by pre-emptions. Drizzle Lake is drained by Drizzle Creek into the Skonun River and empties into McIntyre Bay off the North Beach.

*CHOWN BROOK — flows from the west parallel to the North Beach and joins the Skonun and Sangan Rivers to enter the sea by a common mouth. The name is from an old Haida word CHOWN-KATHLI, the word *kathli* means open bay or slough and often indicates an inside location. (C. Smith)

*SKONUN POINT — west of the mouth of the Sangan River is frequently called CHOWN POINT locally, presumably because the Chown Brook flows from nearby.

The building by the Department of National Defence of a signals station in 1970 at Skonun Point, in the form of a circle, has resulted in a new name coming into local use for this area, THE CIRCLE. It is quite common to hear people refer to the road leading out to it as *The Circle Road*.

Skonun Point was the site of two bore-holes in 1912. One near the highwater mark behind a sand dune close to the point, and a second about 1½ miles west of the first, close to the border of Lot 10. Both holes went to over 1,000 feet and were under the direction of the American-Canadian Coal Company. McIntosh, the ex-Chief of Police from New Westminster had an active part in the operation. McIntosh had hoped to take over Charles Harrison's ranch on Delkatla Flats through a tax sale at the turn of this century. Harrison was able to raise enough money to redeem his property, but McIntosh, greatly intrigued by speculative possibilities on Graham Island, remained on the Charlottes for many years. His name was later associated with almost every venture of an entrepreneur nature - coal, oil and land. (See also McIntosh Point.)

Skonun Point has an interesting fossil site on its beach, a sandstone formation with fossilized clam-shells. Lignite coal may also be seen at low tide on the shoreline in this vicinity.

SEE-WATT — also known in later years as The Alexander Place, fronted along the North Beach, west of Skonun Point. It was the ranch established by J.M. Lindsay Alexander in partnership with two other men in the late 1880s. Mr. Alexander, an ex-H.B.C. man, was to do the actual ranching. The cattle left behind by Alexander formed the basis of the wild cattle of Graham Island written about during pioneering years.

"By the time we moved out to live at See-Watt, the name the Haidas had given our place, the cattle venture had been under way for several years," said Wiggs O'Neill, Alexander's step-son. "There was already quite a herd running on the range between Masset and Rose Spit. Three men were on the payroll looking after them while Dad had filled in for Dodd at the H.B.C. store in Masset. From my memories it seemed to be an ideal set-up. The cattle really looked after themselves.

"My brother, Will, and I ran barefoot the whole three years we spent on the Islands. We played with the Haida boys, one of whom, Yaquas, was my special hero. The area was alive with big blue grouse among all the small spruces beyond the beach. Yaquas would pick up a stone, stop and wait until the big cock grouse would swell up his neck, getting ready to drum, then let drive and put the stone right through the grouse's neck. He never missed."

Wiggs and Will were fair stone-throwers themselves and one day got into a battle against some of the Haida boys. Will's first rock clipped one of the Haidas and drew blood. Instantly adults came into the picture. "A big pow wow got under way with lots of shouting," recalled Wiggs. "Will and I took to our heels and beat it for home. When we told Dad what had happened, he got very serious and ordered us both upstairs and to silence.

"It was not long before the big crowd gathered at our door, everyone shouting and talking in Haida. They demanded Dad produce the two culprits. Haida blood had been spilled - they wanted White blood in return. The old man was on the spot. After a lot of bargaining and talk he managed to make a settlement with the injured boy's parents by giving them two Hudson's Bay blankets, a gallon of black-strap molasses and two boxes of M.R. Smith's famous hardtack 'Biskets' made in Victoria.

"Dad wasn't too happy about the incident, but felt he had been lucky to settle with worldly goods in place of blood, knowing the Haidas ideas of retribution. To impress us with the seriousness of the situation we had got him into, while he did not draw blood, he warmed our backsides good and plenty," Wiggs said, and added, "Perhaps the fact that the Haidas had been converted a few years before by Collison saved a few white scalps that day."

SEE-WAS-KWOON, White folks' cemetery (of New Masset.) — (C. Smith)

CHAPTER SEVENTEEN

*VENTURE BANKS — lie on the eastern side of the approach to Masset
Harbour. They are fairly steepto on their northern side and the sea frequently
breaks heavily on them. The shallowest spot, about 3½ miles northeast of Entry
Point, has about a fathom over it.

The banks were named in 1907 by Captain F.C. Learmonth of the *Egeria*
during the hydrographic survey of these waters. Named after the British steamer
Venture, which grounded on the banks in 1906.

*TROUP BANK — south and west of Venture Banks, extends for 1½ miles
northward from the vicinity of Entry Point, and dries in patches. Named in
1907 by Captain F.C. Learmonth after Lieutenant J.A.G. Troup, a member
of the survey party on the *Egeria* at that time.

The Haidas called Troup Bank, TAS'CUDLAY. (C. Smith)

*OUTER BAR — west of Venture Banks. Composed of sand and gravel,
it extends to Venture Banks and south to Inner Bar.

*INNER BAR — also composed of sand and gravel, runs in a northeasterly
direction for 2½ miles at the entrance to Masset Harbour.

*YAN VILLAGE — on the west side of the entrance to Masset Harbour.
Wiped out by a smallpox epidemic, it was once a village of importance, with

The village of Yan in 1911.
Photo - Jessie Bradley.

a forest of totem poles which stood for years. A hereditary Raven Crest site, it contained lodges belonging to both crests - customary in all large villages. When Chittenden visited Yan in 1884 it was an abandoned village with 20 lodges and about 25 carved poles.

The name means "to go in a straight line" to a rock below the town. Another name for the village was TOWN-OF-NO-BAY. (C. Smith)

The village of Yan is now part of the 264-acre reserve belonging to the Masset Band.

THE STONE PILE — the old Haida name for a reef off Yan, only seen at extreme low tide. (C. Smith)

ASTOWA VILLAGE, also known as OLD YAN — lay immediately north of Yan. The name meant Big-Rock-Town. (C. Smith)

KATLANKWOON, Waves-Point — the rocky point on the north side of Yan. (C. Smith)

SKOOS-OO, Shag-Rock — the 14-foot-high rock south of Yan. (C. Smith)

*STURGESS BAY — the shallow curving bay south of Yan. Named in 1907 by Captain F.C. Learmonth during the hydrographic survey, after the American schooner *Susan Sturgis* which was hi-jacked off Masset Harbour in September, 1852, by Chief Weah and some of his tribe from Masset. During the fighting the vessel drifted into this bay. The Americans were taken prisoner in anticipation of their being ransomed by the H.B.C. at Port Simpson. The *Susan Sturgis* was stripped of everything which appealed to her captors, then burned in the bay which bears her name. (See also Susan Sturgis Point.)

WHOT CUD LASKIN, Bottom-End — the Haida name given to the head of Sturgess Bay. A cabin formerly stood on the north side of the stream at

375

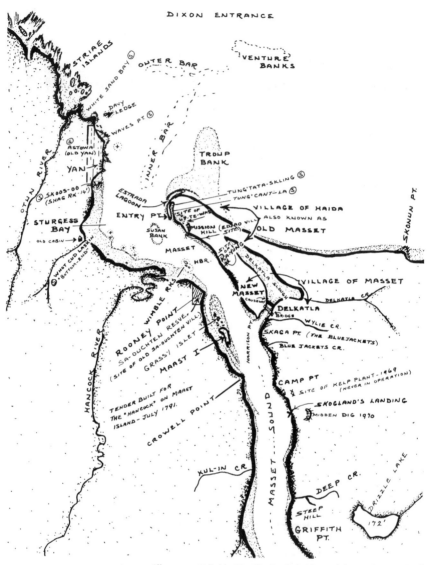

All names supplied by Mr. Charles A. Smith are shown on this map by Ⓢ

this place. (C. Smith)

*SUSAN BANK — lies off Sturgess Bay and was named by Captain Learmonth in 1907 at the same time as the bay. This bank almost dries.

*WIMBLE ROCKS — southeast of Susan Bank, dry at 9 feet. Lying off the vicinity of the mouth of the Hancock River, they were named in 1907 by Captain Learmonth after the artificer engineer, Mr. Wimble, aboard the *Egeria* at the time of the hydrographic survey of the area.

*MASSET HARBOUR — the basin-like approach to the north end of Masset Sound. Entered between Entry Point and Yan, skippers keep a careful line on the leading lights for safe entry. Named in 1853 when Mr. H.N. Knox, mate of the *Virago* under Captain James Prevost, made a detailed sketch of the harbour. (Prevost had been sent to make an investigation into the *Susan Sturgis* incident.) A detailed hydrographic survey of these waters was made in 1907 by Captain F.C. Learmonth during his commission to do the waters from Rose Spit to Frederick Island.

*HANCOCK RIVER — flows into the south end of Sturgess Bay. It drains a vast area of muskeg and has tributaries extending well inland for 15 miles or more. Formerly called the KA-WON RIVER and also KOWLING RIVER. Named HANCOCK RIVER in 1907 by Captain Learmonth, after the fact that in 1791 Captain Samuel Crowell had called what is now Masset Sound, Hancock's River, after his ship and after John Hancock, Governor of Massachusetts.

The *Hancock* was a 157-ton brig from Boston, owned by Captain Crowell and his partner, Creighton. She had left her home port in November 1790 and, after a boisterous trip around Cape Horn, put in to the Hawaiian Islands where she was almost captured by natives. Fortunately the plot was discovered in time. Arriving on the Pacific coast in July 1791, she proceeded directly to the Charlottes.

On the island now called Maast, a temporary ship-building site was established and between July 14 and August 20 of that year the crew of the *Hancock* built a sloop. (See story under Maast Island.) It was at this time Crowell named Masset Sound, Hancock's River.

*ROONEY POINT — at the south end of Sturgess Bay. Named in 1907 by Captain Learmonth after the master of the *Susan Sturgis*, Captain Matthew Rooney, and named in association with Sturgess Bay.

The Haida name for Rooney Point was SCHUL STUE KWOON. (C. Smith)

SA-OUCHTEN VILLAGE — the Raven Crest site at Rooney point. Ingraham found it occupied in 1792 and showed it on his map. Now part of the 28-acre Sa-ouchten Reserve belonging to the Masset Band. This reserve has been logged extensively in recent years.

*GRASSY ISLET — rising to only 6 feet is north of, and connected to -

*MAAST ISLAND — which is south of Rooney Point. They are really one island, although at high tides a section between them may be covered by water for short periods. This was called GOOSE ISLAND by both Captain Crowell and Joseph Ingraham in 1791 and 1792, and it was so named by Crowell in July 1791 when he selected it as the site for building a sloop to use as a tender for his brig *Hancock*.

The material for building the boat had been brought from Boston on the *Hancock*. It was the fourth ship built by Europeans on the Northwest Pacific coast. (First was *North West America* built by Meares in 1788 at Nootka; second was *Santa Saturnia* No. 1 by Martinez, 1789; and the third was the *Santa Saturnia* No. 2 built also by the Spanish at Nootka, 1791 - prior to July.

When the *Hancock's* new tender was ready for launching the natives from one of the nearby villages appeared in a body, presumably to interfere with the launching, and a battle ensued in which at least four Haidas were killed and several others wounded. There were more skirmishes after that, before the boat was finally readied to sail. Said to have been a longboat, rigged as a sloop, she immediately put out under the command of the *Hancock's* mate, John William Adamson, who sailed to the Naden Harbour area to begin the season's trading.

About this time another American ship, the *Columbia*, hove into Masset and Hoskins the clerk wrote, "Captain Crowell has named this fine waterway Hancock's River, but it is called by the natives MASHEET."

A story told in Haida Masset today of how the name *Masheet* came into existence, says that one of the first ships to come into Masset Harbour anchored off what is now New Masset. One of the officers, a man named Massetta, died and was buried on the little island off which the ship lay anchored. The Haidas called the island after him and finding it too difficult to pronounce, corrupted the word to Mah-sh-t. From this in 1878 G.M. Dawson named the island MAAST, saying as he did that he felt this island had been the origin of the name Masset.

In 1884 Chittenden called Maast Island MASSETT ISLAND. In pioneering days when goats were put there, it became known for awhile as GOAT ISLAND. The Geographic Board have adopted Dawson's name, MAAST ISLAND.

*ESTRADA LAGOON** — lies off the north end of Entry Point at the east side of the entrance to Masset Harbour. A crescent-shaped shingle spit forms a ridge on the seaward side. This spit is building.

In 1866 Robert Brown in his report referred to the ridge as MASSET SPIT and noted that he had also heard it called MASSET BAR.

On July 25, 1792, Captain Jacinto Caamano of the Spanish ship Aranzazu named the entrance to Masset Harbour, PUERTO ESTRADO, after one of his officers, Nicolas Estrado. That name was adopted by Vancouver on his map for the present Entry Point. In recent years the Hydrographic Service reapplied the name, transferring it to the lagoon formed behind the gravel ridge off the north end of Entry Point.

*ENTRY POINT** — the east entrance point to Masset Harbour. There are two leading lights located on the west side of the point. They are about 700 feet apart and no skipper of a large ship enters without lining up these strategically placed aids to navigation.

Shown as ESTRADO POINT on Captain Vancouver's map, it was renamed ENTRY POINT by Captain F.C. Learmonth of the *Egeria* in 1907. The Haida name for it was KOW KEGAS, North-Beach (of the peninsula.) (C. Smith)The Haida cemetery is at the south end of Entry Point with the much beloved Father Hogan's grave "resting beside my Haida braves," close to the rear leading light. During the early missionary days this picturesque cemetery became known as "God's Acre."

TUNG'CANT-LA — the name given by the Haidas to the slough which runs in from Masset Harbour to almost create an island out of Entry Point. (C. Smith.)

TUNG'TATA-SKLING — the Haida name for the head of this slough. (C. Smith) In early summer this region is covered by a wide variety of wildflowers to the edge of the shoreline.

This photo taken about 1875 shows the big lodge of Chief Weah
in right centre, in the section of Old Masset
formerly known as Ut-te-was, "White-slope-village".

Photo - Provincial Museum, Victoria.

*OLD MASSET — now commonly called HAIDA, is the prettily situated

379

village of the Masset Haidas lying southeast of Entry Point on the east shore of Masset Harbour. The largest Haida village on the Charlottes, over 1,000 people are listed on its Band record.

Originally a Raven Crest site called UT-TE-WAS, White-slope-village, from the prominent 60-foot-high hill in the village, a good landmark for canoes in early years. As its people became known as the Massets in later years, the village itself became called this. Another change was the transferring by a Raven Chief of the ownership of the site to his son, the Eagle Chief Weah. (Normally the ownership would have gone to the chief's nephew. Haida social structure is described in Q.C. Islands, Volume 1, Chapter 10, in more detail.)

The name MASSET was adopted by the villagers and used exclusively until it was pirated by townsite promoters of the White settlement to the north, Graham City, in an endeavour to more easily obtain rights to a post office. For years the two villages, both named Masset then, were differentiated by calling the Haida settlement OLD MASSET and the White settlement NEW MASSET. In recent years, wishing to have their individual identity, some of the younger Haidas renamed their village HAIDA. At first the older Haidas deeply resented the change. After all it was their Masset first. Why should they change? But the new name is gradually gaining favour with everyone.

*MISSION HILL — the 60-foot-high hill in the village of Old Masset. Name applied in 1907 during the survey by the *Egeria* hydrographers.

EDJAO VILLAGE — lay around what is now Mission Hill. Owned by a Raven Crest tribe who had formerly lived to the south in Masset Inlet, there were 6 lodges and about 100 people. It was usually identified as being part of the Masset village.

*KA-YUNG VILLAGE — south of both Ut-te-was and Edjao was traditionally an Eagle Crest site and, like Ut-te-was, occupied by people of both crests. For many years Ka-Yung had the only remaining totem pole in the Masset area. Finally it fell. Nature reclaiming her own. Signifying, perhaps in a graphic way, that the era which produced the pole is forever a part of history.

In 1969 Bob Davidson carved and erected a new totem pole which he gave to his village of Haida Masset. The times and motivation were of a new generation, the pride of heritage and culture, however, spanned the gap to complete a circle strong and sure. In 1971 Lawrence Bell, also of Haida Masset, was commissioned by the British Columbia Government to carve two more poles, replicas of the *Raven Pole* and the *Eagle Pole* of Yan. In a change of custom, the Government directed that the poles remain in Masset. They were erected with full twin-pole raising ceremonies on September 18, 1971, across the field from Bob Davidson's pole.

Ut-te-was, Edjao and Ka-Yung are now all part of the 729-acre Masset Reserve laid out between Entry Point and the neighbouring Village of Masset.

*MASSET SOUND — is the river-like tidal inlet which connects Masset Inlet, 15 miles or more away, to the ocean. The current runs about 5½ knots during spring tides. This was the HANCOCK'S RIVER of Crowell in 1791. Named MASSET SOUND by G.M. Dawson in 1878.

Alan Jessup, Sam Ives and Charlie Spence on main street in New Masset 1914-15.

Photo - Charlie Ives.

*MASSET — the only incorporated village on the Charlottes, includes today the townsites formerly known as New Masset and its neighbour, Delkatla.

In 1907 the Anchor Investment Company, townsite promoters and developers for the Graham Steamship, Coal and Lumber Company, proceeded to set up a townsite about two miles south of Haida Masset. Named GRAHAM CITY after the president of the parent company, Benjamin Graham, all streets had been surveyed and lots laid out by April 1909.

When the townsite plan was registered on July 30th of that same year it was deposited under the new name of MASSET. During the intervening months an opportunity had arisen to acquire a post office in the new townsite. The postmaster of the Haida village of Masset left. Adopting the name, Masset, Graham City promotors applied for the office. Far-off government officials unaware of the subterfuge, accepted and the transfer made. On June 7, 1909, the old name for Graham City was dropped and the new one of Masset adopted. (The next year Skidegate (Landing) took the name Graham City for its townsite development.)

In 1961 New Masset and nearby Delkatla agreed to pool their assets and become one incorporated village under the name MASSET. The first municipal election after the merger was held November 7, 1961, and resulted in Sam Simpson being elected Chairman (mayor), with four commissioners (aldermen) to assist him - Alex Taylor, Robert Wylie, William Hilton and Kurt Lindner. First village clerk, Mrs. Isobel Minaker.

The decision of the Department of National Defence to build an important signals station at Skonun Point, a few miles out of Masset, resulted in an influx of Armed Services personnel to the little hamlet a few years later. A sub-division of spanking new look-alike houses to accommodate the military and their families was created and crisp military efficiency soon in evidence. The announced intention of becoming part and parcel of the community sounded all right. But the transition period produced difficulties. The rush and bustle which accompanied the new entrants - modern young people demanding city-type housing, shopping facilities and so on - seem gradually to be succumbing to an appreciation of a slower pace, complete with all its *do-it-tomorrow* attributes which so infuriated them when they first arrived.

As the military sub-division was created, streets connected with it were named mainly for trees. In the older part of Masset the street names were applied in 1909 -

Edenshaw - after the well-known Haida chief and his descendants.

Fraser - for Dr. A. Ross Fraser, Masset's first medical doctor.

Francis - "Cap" Francis, who owned a portion of Delkatla.

Hogan - Reverend "Father" William Hogan.

Rupert - with an eye to Prince Rupert and the Grand Trunk Pacific Railway prosperity which would bring about development of feeder resources on the Charlottes.

Langside

McBride - Premier of British Columbia at that time.

McDonald - after George McDonald who, in 1909 with his partner Bill McLeod, not only worked on the townsite clearing, but also built a smoke-house near the wharf where they processed some excellent smoked fish.

McLeod - after Bill McLeod who, in addition to the above mentioned, married Masset's first schoolteacher, the pretty Jessie Peck, who began teaching in Masset October 1909.

Orr - after Allan Orr who worked on the townsite clearing, then set up the first blacksmith shop in Masset. His family, with some personable and comely daughters were as much of an asset to the community as his blacksmithing.

Main Street - scheduled to become the business section.

Cook - after two brothers, Jack and Bill Cook, the Anchor Investment Company representatives, who organized the townsite clearing.

Millard - honours two other well-known pioneer brothers, Frank and Bert Millard. They came with their families in 1908.

Wallace - Bill Wallace cooked for the townsite clearing gang.

Delkatla - the name of the slough and flats bordering the south and east shores of the townsite.

*Charles Harrison's farm on Delkatla Flats, established in the 1880s,
it was the first farm on the Charlottes.*

Photo - Mabel Nelson.

Harrison - after Charles Harrison, from whom the land for the townsite had
been purchased by the Anchor Investment Company, and who was to Masset
what Windy Young was to Queen Charlotte City. Harrison, a real Graham Island
booster, arrived at Haida Masset in 1883 to take charge of the Anglican Church.
He and Mrs. Harrison left about 1919 to return to England.

*The fine vegetable garden nurtured by Charles M. Wilson at the outskirts of his
newly developing Delkatla. Photo taken about 1915.*

Photo - Mrs. Cecil Baker.

Collison - for the two Collisons, Archdeacon W. Collison, first white man to bring his family to live on the Charlottes and to establish a church, and for his son, Will, who later came back to officiate in the mission his father had founded at Haida Masset.

Hodges - after the colourful cowboy, William Thomas Hodges, "Mexican Tom", who came to Masset to round up the cattle left by J.M. Lindsay Alexander, and remained to live out his life.

Alden

Larmour

Delcartlet

DELKATLA — now part of the Village of Masset, was the dream town of Charles Wilson in 1911 when he listed it in advertisements in local and mainland newspapers. It was registered in April 1913 with streets at that time being

Christie - after A.S. Christie, owner of the adjoining parcel of land and an avid promotor of the Charlottes.

William - for William Burgess, owner of the back part of the townsite.

Wilson - after himself, Charles M. Wilson.

Charles - as above.

Daisy

McBride - Premier of British Columbia, all townsites of that era had a McBride Street.

Marguerite Street

Rosalie

Maud

Burgess - after William Burgess, owner of the back portion of the town.

Clements - for Herbert S. Clements, M.P., in the hopes it might spur action on the badly needed bridge connection between Delkatla and Masset.

Harrison - after Charles Harrison of Masset.

It was Mr. Wilson's hope that pre-emptors would make Delkatla the place for their "town" homes, as they proved up on their isolated acreages under rules laid out by the Government for the acquisition of land by pre-emption.

At one time it must have been a large Haida settlement. Early townspeople of Delkatla in preparing their gardens unearthed stone utensils and other artifacts constantly. "Nearly everyone had several boxes of them," said one old-timer, "there are midden signs all over the area, but nothing recorded about these ancient sites."

*DELKATLA INLET — the gazetted name for the big slough which has its mouth on the south side of Harrison Point, and extends inland behind the old village of Ka-Yung and New Masset.

DELKATLA FLATS — the local name given to the grassland at the head of the slough. Before he moved to live in New Masset, Charles Harrison had established his farm on the east side of the flat. The See-Watt ranch of the Alexander family lay to the east, nearer the beach.

The name Delkatla is from an old Haida description meaning, water-drifting-in-to-the-inside. The slough and flats are a waterfowl haven.

*HARRISON POINT — is the north entrance point to Delkatla Inlet. Named in 1907 by Captain F.C. Learmonth after Rev. Charles Harrison, who came with his wife in 1883 to take charge of the Old Masset church. When he resigned from the ministry in 1890 he went to live on the large tract of land he had acquired around Delkatla Slough and established the first farm in the area.

When the Anchor Investment bought part of his holdings, one of the conditions of the sale was the erection of a house for the Harrisons on the edge of the proposed townsite of Graham City. It was the first frame residence in Masset and is still in use today, the Church of England vicarage.

There is a large drying flat off Harrison Point and, with the strong tides in the inlet, tying to the Masset dock has always involved good seamanship, plus a measure of good luck. If the skipper misjudged, the current would carry his vessel onto the drying bank off Harrison Point to sit in embarrassment until the next tide.

WYLIE CREEK — is the name given by the Department of Highways to the creek which flows into the mouth of Delkatla Inlet, on the south side. Their spokesman believed the creek to have been named for long-time Delkatla resident, Alex Wylie, who lives nearby. Mr. Wylie is well-known as a boat designer and builder of exceptional ability.

*SKAGA POINT — a little south of the entrance to Delkatla Inlet. *Skaga* is a modification of the Haida word for shaman or medicine man. Behind Skaga Point a hill rises to 350 feet. There are old midden signs all along this area. In pioneering days a road went inland from the point for about 4 miles to assist settlers located in there.

THE BLUE JACKETS — is a name used locally for the region of Skaga Point. It came into use about 1907 during the survey of these waters by the *Egeria,* a Royal Navy vessel. Some of the naval ratings built a cabin there during the survey, which became known as the Blue Jackets' cabin. Only a rude shelter,

*Pete Keay, right foreground, and his placer mining operation at
the Blue Jackets (Skaga Point).*

Photo - Mrs. Fred Nash

but frequently used in early days by travellers caught in a storm.

BLUE JACKETS CREEK — flows onto the beach on the south side of Skaga
Point and even current geological books refer to it by this name. In early years
Pete Keay set up his placer mining equipment close to the mouth of the creek.
Only a small amount of gold was recovered. In 1970 there were two cabins
by the creek and they were referred to as "the Blue Jackets cabins" - proving
that old names tend to die hard, if ever, on the Charlottes.

*Kelp plant on the south
side of Camp Point.
Built in 1969
by Canada Kelp Company,
it went into receivership
before going into operation.
This photo taken in 1970,
facing north.*

Photo - K.E. Dalzell.

*CAMP POINT — south of Skaga Point, on the east side of Masset Sound. Early maps show 'shacks' near this point, and it is thought surveyors used it for their camp, naming the point in this association.

In 1969 a large kelp processing plant was built a little to the south of Camp Point by Canada Kelp Company Limited. It never came into operation, the company going into receivership before construction was completed - placed in bankruptcy by the Dillingham Corporation which built the plant.

SKOGLAND'S LANDING — slightly south of the kelp plant mentioned in the preceding paragraph, is about 4 miles south of Masset. It acquired its name several years ago when Skogland Logging utilized the site for log storage and barge loading to ship logs from the Masset area to mainland markets. Other logging operations subsequently utilized the landing similarly from time to time, but it has become better known recently as the established barge landing for the weekly freight service between Prince Rupert and the north end of Graham Island.

On the hill overlooking the loading ramp a dig was undertaken in 1970 by archaeologists from the University of Calgary. Findings from this project are still under study, but many of the artifacts appear to pre-date Haida occupancy of the Charlottes.

*CROWELL POINT — on the west side of Masset Inlet, looks across to Camp Point. Named in 1907 by Captain Learmonth after Captain Samuel Crowell, master of the American brig, *Hancock,* which anchored in this vicinity in July and August 1791 to build a sloop on Maast Island. During her stay there she was visited by another American ship, *Columbia*. Hoskins, the clerk on the *Columbia*, wrote that on August 18, 1791, the *Hancock* had sailed about 12 miles south along Hancock's River (now Masset Sound) then went aground. By the time the crew managed to break her free, the tide had begun to ebb and it was decided not to try to proceed any further. This is probably the first documented trip of a vessel sailing south along Masset Sound.

KUL-IN CREEK — which appeared on early maps, including G.M. Dawson's 1878 map, flows from the west to enter Masset Sound south of Crowell Point. The mouth of the creek is at the southeast corner of Lot 2195.

KITZ-HAWN CREEK — on the Dawson and other early maps, flows from a small unnamed lake on Lot 2044. The mouth of the Kitz-hawn is at the southeast corner of Lot 1746, flowing into the bay opposite Griffith Point. Two well-used pack-trails led in from the mouth of this creek, one of which went west as far as the Hancock River. Crown Grants and Applications to Purchase covered most of the land in here to a depth of more than 8 miles.

KUK CREEK — shown on the Dawson Map of 1878 and several subsequent maps of earlier years. It flows from the south to enter Masset Sound at Lot 2037. (Kul-in, Kitz-hawn and Kuk are all on the west side of Masset Sound.)

*ALLAN POINT — also on the west side of Masset Sound, is about 2 miles north of the north end of Kumdis Island. It is generally believed that the point

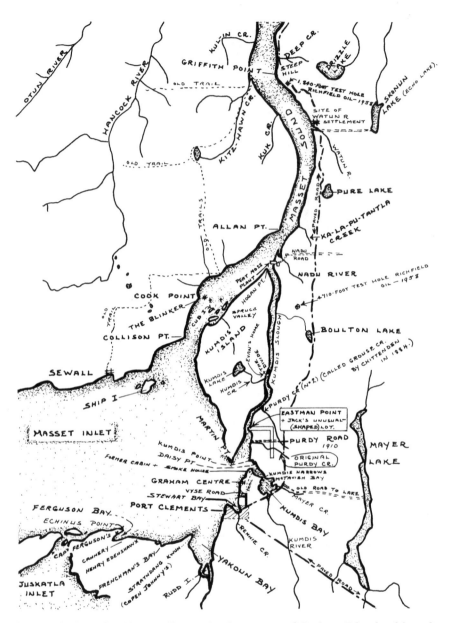

is named after Alan Jessup, pioneer land surveyor of Graham Island - although Mr. Jessup spelled his name with one "l". But it is also suggested that it may have been named for Allan Reid, manager of the Anchor Investment Company. who committed suicide in July 1908. This was the company promoting the townsite of Masset. (Graham City at that time.)

*COOK POINT — southwest of Allen Point, is the narrowest navigational section of Masset Sound. Named after the Anchor Investment Company's townsite managers, Jack and Bill Cook, who supervised the clearing and laying out of Graham City and agreed to having the name expediently changed to Masset in 1909.

THE BLINKER — the flashing light which is located at the extremity of the drying bank off Cook Point. Known by this name locally ever since it was installed.

*COLLISON POINT — on the west side of Masset Sound, south of Cook Point. The common impression is that the point is named after Will Collison, son of the Archdeacon. Will Collison was in Masset at the time of the surveys and very active in land dealing and timber staking along Masset Sound.

At this time it is proposed to leave the west side of Masset Sound and return to the Camp Point area on the east side, near the north entrance, and move in a general southerly direction along the east side.

DEEP CREEK — between Camp Point and Griffith Point is a local name. Lawrence Rennie, with the Department of Highways for years, and a local man from birth, says he understood the name - which is in widespread local use - came from the fact that there are very steep banks on each side, making the creek deep down from road level, not from a sense that the water in the creek is deep.

STEEP HILL — lies on the south side of Deep Creek. The view north to the Massets from the brow of this hill is superb. Some misguided souls began dumping garbage at this view site to such an extent it became one of the most obnoxious places on the entire road. Steps were recently taken by the Village of Masset to correct the situation - although they deny that it is only their residents which created the offence, they are striving to change the practice in the hope that Steep Hill will once again become the view point to be enjoyed.

*GRIFFITH POINT — is due west of Drizzle Lake, and a name which appeared on land maps of the 1950s for the first time. Origin not confirmed. In 1958 the Richfield Oil company put down a drill hole to a depth of 1,840 feet, a little to the south of Griffith Point.

*WATUN RIVER — flowing into the bight south of Griffith Point, has also been shown as WA-TOON and WODEN, the latter name being heard locally even today to a large extent. All are modifications of a Haida name. In pioneering days it was sometime referred to as The HOLY CITY, because so many of its leading citizens were "of the cloth."

Reverend J.B. McDonald, the Roman Catholic priest who operated the post office and store, built a small church and started a school, then persuaded Mrs. A.R. Mallory, a staunch Presbyterian to be its first teacher - which meant she had to leave her own home at Port Clements. Tom Watson, Seventh Day Adventist pastor, brought his flock from Sewall to settle at the Woden. Two of the men who accompanied him, Roy and Don Hazelton, built a boat-shop from which several Island boats were launched. Then, also, there was the giant parson from Masset, the beloved Anglican "Father" Hogan who at 80 years of age took up a pre-emption on the south bank of the Watun River, built a cabin and looked forward to the day when he would *retire* and make a real ranch out of it. His missionary duties proved to be full-time and he was unable to live on his pre-emption enough to hold it, so his application was cancelled.

In the 1920s a cannery was moved from Naden Harbour to the Woden by Wallace Fisheries (later taken over by B.C. Packers) and wharves and living accommodation built. It closed in 1930 and marked the end of Woden River settlement, as the remaining families gradually moved away and it was abandoned. In the 1960s ten acres were purchased by a young couple from Masset who built a comfortable home from which they commuted by car to work in Masset each day.

Watun River was a much-used fishing site by early Haidas. They had an established camp there in regular occupancy during season.

*PURE LAKE — along the Masset to Port Clements road, is halfway between Watun and Nadu Rivers. A popular picnic site, the benches, tables and barbecue pits installed by the Forest Service are put into constant use. Recently the Masset Lions Club, under the Local Initiative program, erected an impressive gateway which holds aloft a replica of a Haida canoe. More picnic tables, fire-pits, and a place to change clothes for swimming were added to make this lakeside retreat more enjoyable.

Named WHITE LAKE during the initial survey 1908-10, it was renamed PURE LAKE about 1913. Surrounded by pre-emptions, one of which, Crown Granted, straddled its north end. It has a white sand beach with small freshwater agates in some profusion.

KA-LA-PU-TANTLA — was the name given to Newton Chittenden in 1884 by his Haida guides to indicate the small stream entering Masset Sound south of the mouth of Watun River.

Pioneer home of Edward Evans, built in 1911 near mouth of the Nadu River by the two master axemen of the Nadu, Ole Anderson and Alec Johnson.

Photo - Mrs. Brent Lea.

*NADU CREEK (RIVER) — flows from the southeast to enter Masset Sound near the north end of Kumdis Island. The word *Nai* is from the Haida "nose". This river has a sharp point at its entrance. Shown on early maps as NEDO and NEDOO. A seasonally used Haida camp-site lay at its mouth.

The pioneers flocked to the Nadu area to take up every available niche in

Peat moss plant at the mouth of Nadu Creek, photo taken facing north shortly after plant came into operation in 1967. Moss and water were siphoned from the muskeg through pipe "x" into tank, extreme right. From there it went into plant on lower level. Cement road, left, led to loading dock.

Photo - K.E. Dalzell

the early years of this century. A landing float, store, post office and wagon road, which climbed the steep hill from the mouth of the river and ran inland for several miles, served them. This road was rebuilt in 1967 when a peat processing plant came into brief operation at the mouth of the river. Speculations as to the reason for its premature closing are rife. Rumours persist that the plant may reopen again under new owners, but to date the only employee is a watchman.

The reopening of the Nadu River road made the old homesites along it more accessible and two of them have been reoccupied. These new pioneers soon had comfortable log cabins erected on the old cabin sites and report that all the ditches dug by the former owners work as well today as they did in earlier years. Wells, so laboriously dug by early pioneers, needed little to put them in shape and the land, which held such promise and hope for those first residents, is in good hands with the second crop of pioneers.

A little to the south of the mouth of the Nadu River the first coal drilling on the north end of Graham Island was done in the fall of 1909. The results were disappointing and this venture had a short life.

NADU WHIRLPOOL — caused by the back-eddy off the mouth of the Nadu at certain stages of the tide. The whirlpool moves up and down off the Nadu with the change of tide. Sometimes there are two sizeable eddies with a narrow channel in between, 16 to 20 feet apart.

*KUMDIS ISLAND — the large island at the south entrance to Masset Sound. Half the island lies in the south entrance of the Sound with the rest extending well into Masset Inlet to form a large portion of the Inlet's east shoreline. Kumdis is a modification of its Haida name which meant island-with-long-points-lying-at-the-mouth-of-the-channel. Early maps showed it variously as CUNDIS, KUNDIS, and CUMDIS. Chittenden in 1884 applied the name CUB to it believing, erroneously, that this was what his Haida guides called it. The island they called Cub is a small one lying off the west side of Kum-

View from the Edward Evans home. Looking south. This is the north entrance to Kumdis Slough, with Kumdis Island on the right.

Photo - Mrs. Frank Van Valkenberg.

dis Island.

*CUB ISLAND — is the outermost and smallest of 4 small islands on a drying bank off the west side of Kumdis Island - opposite the blinker at Cook Point. It was a favourite Haida camping spot. Even in pioneering days a cabin belonging to them was in regular use on the northeast side of the island. They had a potato patch nearby which flourished in the rich silt along the flats.

In 1878 Dawson showed it by this name on his map - although he did not show any name for the much larger Kumdis Island. Chittenden applied the word CUB to Kumdis Island in 1884 and the 1913 Pre-emptor's Map also designated Kumdis as being Cub Island. It would appear they misunderstood which island was meant.

*HOGAN POINT — the north point of Kumdis Island and once the site of the powder house, containing the settlers' stumping powder. The point was named after William "Father" Hogan, the much-loved Anglican parson who was in charge of the Masset churches from 1909 until his death in February 1914.

*KUMDIS SLOUGH — the narrow passage which separates Kumdis Island on its east side from Graham Island. It has also been called CANOE PASSAGE.

The centre portion dries at low tide, but it is navigable for small boats at high tide.

About a mile from the north entrance to Kumdis Slough a pioneer from Pitt Meadows, Freeman Tingley, established his "Pioneer Ranch" on the east side of Kumdis Island in June 1906. In later years the place had several successive owners, but was always known as TINGLEY'S PLACE. Mr. Tingley was a crony of another early pioneer, Mexican Tom Hodges, and it was Tom who gave him the nickname "Stud" Tingley to avoid confusing him with his son, also called Freeman Tingley.

SPRUCE VALLEY — running in a east-west direction, near Tingley's Place on Kumdis Island.

THE DIVIDE — is the portion of Kumdis Slough which dries, and was in front of Francis Evans's home. Many a traveller has had to "drag her over the Divide" when he arrived at this spot a little late. Our own last visit here in the fall, brought us from the north end on a flood tide. The crimson crabapple leaves were brilliant against the yellowing of the wild hay along the shoreline. As we neared the Divide, our boat touched bottom. Too early on the tide. But it provided a fine excuse to stay and look about the abandoned Evans place. (Now the property of MacMillan & Bloedel.) It brought back memories too, of earlier years when, much younger, a group of us would row to Masset for the dances and, coming home singing most of the way, would misjudge and be late on the tide. The frantic pulling and dragging to get our boat across seemed all part of the venture.

A family of beavers have taken up residence beside the Evans home, a fitting successor to the hardworking Francis and his wife, Daisy, the original owners.

*KUMDIS LAKE — in the centre of Kumdis Island, has a tributary stream running out to the vicinity of Cub Island and another draining east to the Divide. During the Baxter Pole Company operation in the early 1930s their pole road ran in to the lake from the Slough. The Jugaway tractor used to haul poles was left near the entrance to the road.

KUMDIS CREEK — the local name given to the streamlet which drains from Kumdis Lake into the Slough at the south end of the Divide. (The Kumdis Creek of the maps runs into Kumdis Bay several miles away.)

*BOULTON LAKE — on Lot 430, is east of Kumdis Slough, with a streamlet running from it into the Slough. The lake is accessible from the Masset to Port Clements road, and is about 4 miles south of where that road intersects the Nadu Road. Named after Mr. G. Boulton, surveyor with Humphries, Tupper and Rice. Mr. Boulton took charge of the survey of this region in 1908, finishing up at Kumdis Island in December of that year. Boulton was connected with surveys in other areas of the Charlottes, including coal claims and the laying out of a portion of the Queen Charlotte City townsite in 1909 known as Keith's Addition.

Boulton Lake received particular attention in 1970 and '71 when two fish researchers arrived to study and count the sticklebacks in the lake. The conditions in the lake provide a unique environment which made their investigation of much value.

GROUSE CREEK — is the name Newton Chittenden gave in 1884 to the large creek which enters the east side of Kumdis Slough at Lot 340. This creek is also called Purdy Creek, but it is not the original Purdy Creek which has its mouth at Lot 339.

On the Kumdis Island side, opposite Lot 340, several people made their homes during the 1930s. One of these, Tom Pelton, put in a huge garden and was amazed to uncover numerous stone utensils, bowls, chisels and so on. His daughter, Mrs. Jack Hewison, has since donated several of the items to a museum.

EASTMAN POINT — lies between Lot 339 and 340, and is the minute waterfront portion of a narrow ribbon of a lot homesteaded in 1911 by Jack Eastman. "Jack was a fisherman," recalls Sid Wormald of Victoria, one of the many former pre-emptors east of Kumdis Slough. "He built his cabin on the point and I visited him often when going in to my own place. His lot was the exact shape of a carpenter's steel square and was the result of a surveyor's miscalculation."

PURDY CREEK — "Purdy Creek flowed out through Lot 339," says Sid Wormald. "The Purdys cut out a road allowance alongside this creek to give them access to their pre-emption behind 339 . . . which was covered by a Timber Licence. When I took up my pre-emption east of Purdys, I packed my stuff up along this road usually. They had built a rough log cabin at the mouth of Purdy Creek, with a couple of bunks in for emergency use.

The creek was given an official recognition in 1910 when foreman George Mayer was granted $400 in government funds to "grub out and grade an 8-foot-wide road at Purdy Creek." $150 of his grant was expended on stumping powder.

*MARTIN POINT — is the south tip of Kumdis Island. Named after James Martin, pioneer merchant of Graham Island who at one time had four stores in operation. The headquarters of his enterprise was in the big, well-stocked Masset store, with branches at Nadu, Sewall and Port Clements. Arriving in 1908, Jim Martin was one of the pioneers who remained to live out his life on the Charlottes.

There is a long drying point extending from Martin Point with numerous boulders. On the east side of the point in ancient times there was a village of some size according to the extensive midden signs found on the hillside recently.

KUMDIS POINT — the north entrance point of the channel leading off the east side of Masset Inlet into Kumdis Bay. Opposite, on the south entrance point, stood an Indian cabin used seasonally by Masset Haidas and, also, often by pioneers caught in a storm when travelling. When Charlie Adam pre-empted this land he burned the cabin down.

DAISY POINT — close by and east of Kumdis Point. When Bert Millard and his wife left their homestead on the triangular lot at the entrance to Kumdis Bay, the grassy place which had formerly been their garden became a profusion of daisies, the flowers spreading from Mrs. Millard's borders. The roaming cattle kept the grass down, but did not care for the daisies. It was a favorite picnic spot in the pre-road days for people from Port Clements.

KUMDIS NARROWS— the narrowest portion of the entrance leading into Kumdis Bay and a good fishing place at the right stage of the tide. Charlie Adam had his first cabin on the south side of the Narrows and Gus Lundquist built on the opposite side. Adam's has reverted for non-payment of taxes, but the Lundquist place is owned by two Masset people who hope to develop it into a homesite.

*KUMDIS BAY — the shallow bay lying east of the Narrows, off the east side of Masset Inlet. In early years all this region was ringed with cabins.

McTAVISH BAY — the bight at the northeast corner of Kumdis Bay. Alex McTavish had his homesite at the head of the bay. "Not that he spent much time on it, he was far too busy out socializing and promoting," say those who remember the huge New Zealander. "Oh, he was a great lad. Any party he attended was bound to be a success. Every so often he would leave the Island with some wild scheme, for which he always seemed to find a backer . . . then he would return to the Charlottes with a flourish and plenty of money to tide him over until he could think up another idea."

MAYER'S CREEK — flows into the east side of Kumdis Bay, near the head. A small creek, it flows past pioneer George Mayer's cabin which was at its mouth. Their farm, purchased by MacMillan and Bloedel many years ago, has never been used since they left, but the trees and shrubs planted by this pioneer family have thrived and grown to become a colourful reminder of the industrious homesteaders who found many years of satisfying living in this wilderness homesite.

*KUMDIS CREEK (RIVER) — flows into the head of Kumdis Bay from a muskeg 10 to 12 miles south in the Yakoun Valley. Gazetted as a creek, but given river status locally.

GRAHAM CENTRE— lay on the west side of the peninsula separating Kumdis Bay from Masset Inlet. In 1907-08 when Charles M. Adam worked on the surveys in this region he discovered that this peninsula was free of the noxious Timber Claims which ringed so much of Masset Inlet. He pre-empted and subsequently received a Crown Grant for the site covering the north end of the peninsula. His land adjoined that of T.L. Williams, who was south of him.

Eli Tingley's dream of a town at what is now Port Clements had received a disastrous blow. In the survey of the region he learned that the Timber Licence covered the greater part of his land - contrary to what had been shown on earlier blueprints. He was given the Crown Grant to the property, but the timber interests made it clear they would vigorously protest any clearing. Charlie Adam decided to capitalize on this and the growing demand for land. In 1912 he announced the creating of a full townsite on the western portion of his sizeable lot, 1½ miles to the north of Eli.

From the vantage point of hindsight it seems incredible that his venture failed. He was ideally located. All existing trails passed through his property, or close enough that a diversion would be easily effected. The Kumdis Bay area provided shelter for small boats - in contrast to Eli's cruely exposed location. Larger vessels could obtain protection in the lee of Kumdis Island, and deep water for an anticipated dock was only 400 feet offshore on his southwest boundary. It lay over 700 feet off Eli Tingley's townsite. Best of all, Adam had a completely clear title to all his land.

He and his hard-working friend, Geordie McQuaker, soon had a store, post office and properly surveyed lots, streets and acreages laid out, with a large clearing made in the trees for the "business section."

His main rival in the townsiting business was Eli, but he also faced competition from the other embryo town promotors - the Star Realty in Sewall; the blandishments of Wilson in Delkatla; Harrison for New Masset; and last but not by any means least, the fast-talking Windy Young at Queen Charlotte City. But Adam with no townsite company to answer to, no financial problems - since he had obtained his land via the economical method of pre-empting - was in a singularly favourable situation. Instead of taking advantage of this and getting the project off the ground by putting his first lots on sale at prices which would have attracted the essential nucleus immediately, Adam short-sightedly put his Graham Centre lots out on such stiff terms only a few people desperate for land became his customers.

Like Adam, Eli Tingley was a free agent also in that he owned his land and did not have to work with profit-hungry companies. His burden was that, aside from a few outlying acreages, he could not sell any of his lots, because the timber company would not allow any clearing of the trees. Nevertheless, he set about soliciting the interest of families, the crux of any town, by giving them the land he could sell at reduced prices, and organizing work-bees to assist them to build homes. Families mean schools. As quickly as possible he arranged for a school, and this in turn soon brought other families.

When Tingley eventually bought out the timber claim on the rest of his property, Charlie Adam could never catch up. The hoped-for government wharf went in at Tingley's townsite; the bridge - badly needed across the Kumdis and which should have gone in at the north end of Adam's townsite - was placed in such a position it could only lead to a road favouring Tingley's town. These two bonanzas were the result of political manoeuvres, but they were as open to Adam as they were to the interests in Tingley's town. The war of 1914-18 finished what little hope he had. "The-town-that-never-was" is an apt description of a project which had so much in its favour it seems unbelievable it did not succeed. The Tingley townsite, which in the beginning was so stymied by obstacles it appeared hopeless, is now the townsite of Masset Inlet, Port Clements.

Only a grassy clearing marks the site of Graham Centre today. A few piles of squared rotting timbers indicate the location of Adam's old store and post office.

The now abandoned townsite received its name in January 1912, when an application was made for the post office. T.L. Williams, Adam's neighbour suggested GRAHAM CENTRE, ". . . because it lay almost in the centre of Graham Island," says Mr. Williams, who today lives on the outskirts of Eli's townsite. His home faces out to Yakoun Bay and Masset Inlet - the inlet he fell in love with in 1908 and could never bear to leave. "When I came back from the war

*Mrs. T.L. Williams beside the cabin her husband built near Graham Centre
in 1910, and to which she came in April of that year as a bride,
straight from Swansea, Wales.
Photo taken in 1910 by T.L. Williams.*

*Trevor L. Williams.
It was a bitter blow to him to
learn that Graham Centre was no
more when he returned from
overseas following the
First World War.*

*Still living in Port Clements
in 1972, fully active at 92,
and as much in love with the
Masset Inlet area
as he was when he first
saw it in 1908.*

and found Adam's town was no more, it was a bitter blow," says Mr. Williams.
"Our cabin was so conveniently close to the Centre. . . With a young family
we had no choice then but to move into Eli's town so they could go to school.
I held on to my pre-emption for years . . . expecting to go back sometime.

But money grew too scarce in Depression years to continue paying taxes on land I wasn't living on."

*MASSET INLET — the large tidal basin almost mid-centre in Graham Island. Also shown on early maps as MASSET LAKE and is frequently referred to by local people as "The Lake." About 16 to 17 miles across at its widest, it has several arms and inlets extending off its south and west sides, and a large shoal area in parts of the north and east regions. Like all lakes it is tricky and can change from mirror calm to white-capped violence in a deceptively short period.

The name of Masset Inlet appears on G.M. Dawson's 1878 chart.

*STEWART BAY — the drying bay between Graham Centre and Port Clements. Named in 1907 by Eli Tingley after his friend Allan Stewart. Eli, Stewart and another man, Emerson Calhoun, had hiked across the Mexican Tom trail to seek a townsite location. Making camp near a creek (now called Rennie Creek) at the west end of the trail, Stewart's axe slipped, cutting his foot badly. The other two made him comfortable in the tent, then set out on foot for the north end of Kumdis Island and "Stud" Tingley's Pioneer Ranch. Borrowing a boat from Mr. Tingley (no relation to Eli), they took Stewart to the Tingley ranch to recuperate while they continued their exploration of the region. As they left, Eli declared that from that time on, the bay where they had made their first camp would be named STEWART BAY.

RENNIE CREEK — is the name given by the Department of Highways to the creek flowing into the head of Stewart Bay. Beside this creek Tingley, Stewart and Calhoun made their camp in 1907. (See above.) Beside this creek, also, Tingley later built his first log cabin which subsequently became Port Clements's first school. This little stream had been named much earlier. In 1884 Newton Chittenden wrote in his report that he had named it CEDAR CREEK because he found a large cedar tree growing on its bank.

The name of Rennie is appropriate for its present name. Mr. and Mrs. William J. Rennie, pioneers, first at Mayer Lake then at Graham Centre, moved when Graham Centre was depopulated, to live by this creek, on its east bank. Bill Rennie had the townsite's first Ford garage and both he and his wife were vigorous supporters of all community activities and remained to live out their lives here. Their children, all born on the Charlottes, went to school in Port Clements and a son now owns the land his parents lived on. Today great-grandchildren of the pioneering Rennies are growing up in this same town.

VYSE ROAD — running north for 1 mile from the northeast corner of the Port Clements townsite is named after William Vyse. The road followed the survey line to the former homesite of Mr. Vyse, a gentle, hard-working man with a ready sense of humour. When he first came to the Islands Bill Vyse pre-empted at the Nadu in the heart of the muskeg. After the 1914-18 war he moved to the Port Clements area, buying his lot from T.L. Williams who had acquired this property in addition to his original pre-emption beside Charlie Adam's Graham Centre.

William Vyse, who first pre-empted at the Nadu. After World 1, he bought land from T.L. Williams on the outskirts of Port Clements, where he remained to live out his days.

Photo - Lawrence Rennie.

The cemetery Mr. Vyse cleared and donated to the community, and placed in the care of the Anglican Church, lies at the intersection of Vyse Road and the Masset to Port Clements road.

Port Clements in 1915. Bert Tingley's hotel extreme left.

Photo - Mrs. Agnes Lea

*PORT CLEMENTS — on the peninsula between Stewart Bay and Yakoun Bay. Named in 1913 by the townsite owner, Elias J. Tingley, for Herbert S. Clements, M.P. The village was originally called QUEENSTOWN, a name applied by Mr. Tingley in December 1908, at the suggestion of James Martin who built his first store there. Queenstown, Ireland, had been Mr. Martin's home town.

When the application for a post office was denied under that name, Eli later changed the name of his townsite and in March of 1914 when the townsite plan was registered, the name of PORT CLEMENTS came into official use. Herb Clements, for whom it was named, did not let·Eli down and a short time later announced that the long-awaited government wharf would be built at Eli's town.

For some reason Eli did not name the streets in his town. Not until recently was this lack of street designations rectified. The local committee appointed by the Improvement District worked with the Department of Highways in supplying names for the streets. Few towns have the rare opportunity of naming all their streets 50 years after they have come into existence. With all the history of the region to draw from the committee chose tree names, Bay View drives and so on.

Fortunately the names of Rennie Creek and Dyson Corner had been in use for too long for the committee to change, and the name of Tingley Street had been adopted by the Highways Department in 1964 - to give the town some measure of historical appreciation.

Dyson Street - evolved from Dyson Corner, which is at the south end of this street and is named after Mr. and Mrs. L. "Bob" Dyson, who owned a home at the corner. Their garden became one of the beauty spots of the town. When he first came to the Charlottes Mr. Dyson took up a pre-emption on Kumdis Island. His homestead occupied ¼ section in the region of the Divide and lay about ½ mile inland along the survey line running north and south marking the timber limits boundary. He enlisted for the 1914-18 war. When he returned from overseas he was accompanied by his bride and decided to abandon the isolated pre-emption and move to Eli's town.

Tingley Street — named for Eli Tingley, founder of the town. This name suggested by the writer and adopted by the Department of Highways in 1964, the 50th year of the village as a registered townsite. It was also the year Mr. Tingley died.

At the top of Tingley Street, overlooking the broad expanse of Masset Inlet, is the site chosen in 1971 by book publisher J. Michael Yates to establish his Sono Nis Publishing Company. By 1972 this enterprising young publisher had upwards of forty titles in his catalogue.

YAKOUN BAY — the broad drying bay at the mouth of the Yakoun River, a haven for waterfowl. Named in 1910 by Captain P.C. Musgrave during the hydrographic survey. Musgrave named it in association with the river.

*STRATHDANG KWUN, — the west entrance point of Yakoun Bay was named in 1878 by Dr. G.M. Dawson for the Haida village, Sahldungkun, located on the point. The point is thought to have been the Yah-koon, "straight-point" of the Haidas of early years - and from which the river subsequently took its name. When the first settlers came they knew it as COOPER JOHNNY POINT, *cooper* being a corruption of a Haida word for strong or outstanding in some special way. Today this word has been corrupted even more and the point is now called, locally, COPEN JOHNNY POINT. Masset Haidas say they know it now as simply JOHNNY POINT.

There was still one Indian house in seasonal use when pioneers came to the region in 1908, and a good-sized clearing with the ruins of several other lodges easily seen. On the west side of the point rocks had been cleared from the beach to make a broad canoe approach.

Copen Johnny's Point is covered in spring with a profusion of wild columbine and has a park-like atmosphere so attractive that even the crude logging slashing behind did not spoil it.

SAHLDUNGKUN VILLAGE — extended across the point mentioned above. Occupied by an Eagle Crest tribe of the same family as those who had originally occupied the Rose Spit village. They had separated from the main branch owing to some internal differences and, gradually moving along the shoreline, had chosen this site. Later they moved to the village of Ka-Yung, a little south of Old Masset.

The site of old Sahldungkun is now part of an Indian reserve containing 9 acres, the SATUNQUIN RESERVE, and is owned by the Masset Band.

FRENCHMAN'S BAY or HOLE-IN-THE-WALL — is about a mile or so to the west of Strathdang Kwun. These are local names for a little bight which at high tide fills with water. Andre Quirielle had a pole camp there in the 1960s, and for a time the bay was named after this friendly man of French origin. A good neighbour, Quirielle ran a commendable camp leaving the location relatively unspoiled by his operation. During the time his men were there, they put in trails and created a small park beside a stream near the camp, complete with benches and tables made from logs.

*FERGUSON BAY — 3 miles west of Strathdangkwun. Named after Captain S. Ferguson, the original owner of the property which lay along the west part of the bay. Ferguson, who ran B.C.L.S. Fred Nash's big survey boat *Polaris,* discovered while on a survey with Nash that this piece of waterfront was, amazingly, free of the all-too-prevalent Timber Claims. It had been shown as covered on old maps issued to early settlers. Ferguson put up a log cabin about 1912 and lived there until 1920 when he was drowned going from Port Clements to his cabin in his small boat. The fruit trees "Cap" Ferguson planted around his cabin still bear some fruit each season.

In later years the Bill Hastie family of Port Clements bought the place and used it as a summer home. It has been abandoned for many years and only traces of the cabin remain today.

Henry Edenshaw of Old Masset owned the land on the east shore of Ferguson Bay and built a comfortable house near a creek about a half mile from Ferguson's cabin.

Francis Millerd operated a cannery at Ferguson Bay for a few years in the 1920s. Buying an old sailing hulk, *Laurel Whalen,* he had it fitted up as a floating cannery and anchored her in the bay. Later he drove pilings for a wharf, built a shore cannery across the bay from "Cap" Ferguson's old cabin, and lashed the *Laurel Whalen* to the wharf to serve as an auxiliary cannery. When forbidden by the Fisheries Protection Officers to use her thusly, Millerd converted the ship to a storehouse as well as installing sleeping quarters for the cannery workers under her decks. Then he ran the shore cannery on a double shift.

In the late 1920s the Baxter Pole Company operated in the Ferguson Bay area for a short time. They built their camp close to Henry Edenshaw's house and, in fact, utilized the Edenshaw home for living accommodation for awhile. Portions of the old pole road connected with the Baxter operation may still be seen in the forest. (From Ferguson Bay, the Baxter Company moved their operations to Mayer Lake and then to Kumdis Island.)

*ECHINUS POINT — the west entrance point of Ferguson Bay. This rocky point extends under the water for a considerable length and more than one boat has struck bottom when misjudging the distance. *Echinus* is the generic name for sea-urchins, which are plentiful in this part of the inlet.

The point was named in 1878 by Dr. G.M. Dawson.

CHAPTER EIGHTEEN

CANOE PASS — a local name for the "back door" entrance to Juskatla Inlet, and entered on the east side of Fraser Island. As the name suggests, it is a shallow channel. On a fine day this is an interesting route in a small boat, for in the clear waters one can see a lush marine garden all along the bottom. The sea-urchins form a solid carpet at one point, as do mussels in another section.

*****FRASER ISLAND** — the largest of the islands at the entrance to Juskatla Inlet was named during the 1910 hydrographic survey of Masset Inlet by Captain P.C. Musgrave in the *Lillooet*. G.M. Dawson, visiting in 1878, called the island SLIP-A-TI-A. Newton Chittenden in 1884 called it ENTRANCE ISLAND.

The Haidas knew it as DJUS, at-the-entrance-island. The inner waters were Djus-kathli. A village stood on its northwest corner and a second one lay on the small islet off its southeast shore. This islet is connected to Djus at low tide.

Until logged in 1970, Djus was a picturesque and beautiful island. The chaos resulting from the 1970 operation is desecration. Upturned roots, grossly mangled trees lying at all angles, wasted and dead - victims of a project which could only have netted a pittance. The contrast in removing this timber to that of Andre Quirielle's handling of his pole removal a few miles to the east in Frenchman's Bay, makes one wonder why the Forest Service permits such an unnecessary pillage.

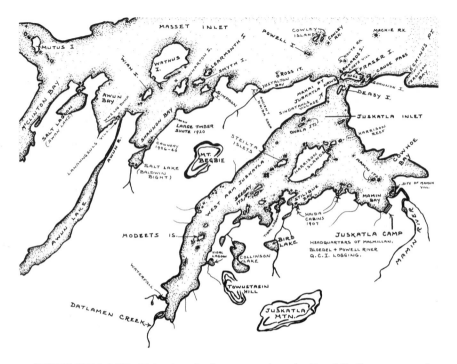

CHETS VILLAGE (Tc'ets) — is the name given by Dr. J.R. Swanton to the Haida village which lay on the northwest end of Fraser (Djus) Island. It was an Eagle Crest site with the Djus-People and the Chets-Gituns in occupancy.

SHANNON ISLAND — is the local name for the small islet off the southeast side of Fraser Island to which it is joined by a drying bank. G.M. Dawson called this islet CHITZ. A favourite camping site and in use for many years after the village of Chets was abandoned on the northwest corner of Fraser Island. People called Shannon owned a cabin and garden there. Mrs. Shannon was Gertie Brown, sister of the well-known Haida, Captain Andrew Brown of Old Masset. When she and Ed Shannon left the islet the strawberries they planted in their garden continued to flourish in the rich midden soil for years.

"After they left, a fellow named Blanchard set up a still there and did quite a roaring trade. As well as making booze, he also made his own brand of machine oil. You could smell it for miles," recall local people. "God only knows what he used . . . old rotten fish or something."

There is an unnamed island off the northeast end of Shannon Island and Fraser Island. All are connected at low tide.

*RICHARDS ISLAND — is off the northwest part of Fraser Island. A drying bank extending from Richards to the old village of Chets connects the two islands. Named during the 1910 hydrographic survey of Masset Inlet by Captain P.C. Musgrave who, at that time, had a tidal gauge installed on the north side of Richards. For months T.L. Williams had the onerous task of rowing the nearly 8 miles, each way, from his pre-emption to make the necessary readings and readjustments of the clock, insert fresh rolls and so on. "There was no one else available to take on the job," he says. "And undoubtedly the records would be of inestimable value to everyone in the region."

Richards Island fell victim to a party of inept campers a few years ago. Their carelessly attended fire ravaged the islet.

*KOUTZ ROCK — is 3 cables northeast of Richards Island, off the entrance to Juskatla and has a depth of less than 6 feet over it. There is a black can buoy off its north side.

Named in 1953 by the Hydrographic Service after Koutz, a slave of Eagle Chief Edenshaw. Archdeacon Collison is said to have cured Koutz of a serious illness after the medicine man in the village had been unable to do so. Koutz's recovery did much to enhance Collison's reputation and help lessen the power of the medicine man who was striving to discredit Collison.

*MAKAI POINT — the west entrance point to Juskatla Narrows. Named in 1953 by the Hydrographic Service after a Tlinget man adopted into the Masset tribe. Makai was a violent man, to the point of being dangerous, especially during his periods of drinking and gambling. When converted to Christianity by Collison the change in him was so great the Masset Haidas were enormously impressed.

There is a boulder bank off Makai Point which dries right to the shore. The bank extends west and north from Makai Point.

*JUSKATLA NARROWS — along the west shore of Fraser Island, is the main entrance to Juskatla Inlet. Officially named by the Hydrographic Service in 1953, but known locally by that name for many years before.

The Haidas called this narrow neck "belly-of-the-rapids" and also "place-of-strong-tide-to-the-inside." Tidal streams in the narrows attain speeds of 6 to 9 knots on the ebb, and more than this when the rivers and creeks are in flood.

SINDATAHLS, Gambling-place-village — belonging to the Raven Crest Djus-hade, People-living-near-Djus, lay in the vicinity of Juskatla Narrows. Some people say it was in the bight inside the Narrows, while others claim it lay on the outer shore, west of Makai Point.

*DEASY ISLAND — at the south end of Juskatla Narrows. Named in 1953 by the Hydrographic Service after Thomas Deasy, Indian Agent at Masset. Deasy became the second resident administrator of Indian Affairs on the Charlottes and took up his duties in Masset in 1910. The first Agent, Charles Perry served in Masset from December 1909 until May 1910. In April of 1910 the Liberal Association recommended Deasy for the job and in June he and Mrs. Deasy arrived in Old Masset. Although resident in Masset, his duties included the entire Queen Charlotte Islands.

In 1878 Dr. G.M. Dawson referred to the present Deasy Island as HLOUT.

KE-NI-A (Q!e'na) — shown on Dr. Newcombe's map in the vicinity of Deasy Island, was an Eagle Crest site.

*JUSKATLA INLET — the largest of the inlets to open off the south side of Masset Inlet was the TSOO-SKATLI of Dr. Dawson in 1878. It is a modification of the Haida name meaning "inlet on the inside of Djus Island." Juskatla is divided by Harrison Island into two arms, the west and larger arm is about eight miles long. There were numerous early Haida camping sites in the inlet, both for fishing and for canoe-builders getting out the big cedars. There were also a number of logging camps along its shores during World War I, all getting out the high grade spruce for the Imperial Munitions Board.

The headquarters of the big MacMillan and Bloedel logging operations on the Charlottes is located at the head of the east arm of Juskatla Inlet and is called in this connection, JUSKATLA. The camp is described in Chapter 14, page 330. See also Mamin Bay, page 407.

*HARRISON ISLANDS — consist of one large wooded island and several smaller islets, also wooded. They separate the eastern and western arms of Juskatla Inlet. In 1878 Dr. G.M. Dawson called the largest island HAS-KEIOUS after the Haida name for it.

Renamed in 1907 by the official of the Graham Steamship, Coal and Lumber Company after Charles Harrison the ex-Anglican parson of Masset. (See also Harrison Point.) It was the timber claims laid out by surveyors and timber cruisers for this company which, when granted by the Provincial Government in return for substantial lease fees for Victoria coffers, created such undue hardship for settlers - and which were never used by the company at any time, making the injustice even harder to bear. The name of Harrison for the large island in the group eventually extended to include the nearby islets off its north end.

*HARRISON REEF — extends from the easternmost of the Harrison Islands (see above) to the east shore of Juskatla Inlet. The reef consists of large boulders and gravel which dry at 2 feet. Named by the Hydrographic Service in association with Harrison Islands.

*COWHOE BAY — at the east side of Juskatla Inlet, and northeast of Mamin Bay, has a pleasant beach at its head. The hillsides all around the bay have been heavily logged and "cat" roads may be seen criss-crossing the hills. Named by the Hydrographic Service in 1953 after Cowhoe, the eldest son of Chief Edenshaw. Cowhoe was the first Masset Haida to be converted to Christianity, and also the first teacher in the little church school. It was to Cowhoe that Admiral Prevost in 1853 gave a bible, saying as he did he hoped he was "casting bread upon the waters." This bible is still in the possession of his relations.

After his baptism Cowhoe took the name of George Edenshaw. Following his example, his brother Henry also took the name of Edenshaw, an act contrary to Haida tradition. Edenshaw being a hereditary Eagle name should not have been used by Edenshaw's sons who, according to Haida custom, were of the same crest as their mother - Raven.

Haida canoes; photo taken in 1896. Sails could be set up quickly.
Mother, in centre, uses her waiting time to get on with some sewing.

Photo - Provincial Museum, Victoria.

Haida boats in 1909.
Indian schooners at Old Masset.

Photo - Mrs. Frank
Van Valkenberg.

Plane landing off the Nadu River, September 14, 1924. One of the first planes to ever land on Masset Sound. The houses in background were Alec Johnson's at the mouth of the river.

Photo - Mrs. Frank Van Valkenberg.

C.G.S. Lillooet *anchored at Sandspit during survey, 1913.*

Photo - Mrs. Belle Brandon

*MAMIN RIVER — flows into Juskatla Inlet between Cowhoe and Mamin Bays and has an extensive delta off its mouth. G.M. Dawson first applied this modification of the Haida name to the river in 1878. When Dawson visited the river he wrote, "It is navigable by small canoes for several miles, but is very much obstructed by logs." Today logging roads more or less follow the full length of the river as the lush valley is probed for its magnificent timber.

MAMUN VILLAGE — the Eagle Crest village at the mouth of the Mamin River, occupied by a branch of one of the most important of Eagle families, the Gituns of Masset. This branch took its name from the river and were known as the Mamun-Gitunai. The old village site is now part of the 6.30-acre MAMMIN RESERVE owned by the Masset Band.

*MAMIN ISLETS — two in number, are off the broad delta of the Mamin River and were named in 1953 by the Hydrographic Service in association with the river.

*MAMIN BAY — in the southeast part of Juskatla. Named in 1953 by the Hydrographic Service in association with the river. A large part of the bay is used by MacMillan and Bloedel as a booming ground. Their headquarters are in the Juskatla settlement, a company town, at the head of Mamin Bay. This settlement has its own store, post office and community club, but there is a close liaison with the Port Clements community. Children from Juskatla go to elementary school in Port Clements and the seniors go with others from Port Clements and Tlell by bus each day to the secondary school at Masset.

*STILIQUE BAY — west of Mamin Bay and south of the largest of the Harrison Islands. Named in 1953 by the Hydrographic Service after a modification of a Haida word for land otter. In 1906 and 1907 when surveyors and timber cruisers for the Graham Steamship, Coal and Lumber Company were staking out this area, there were Indian cabins both in this bay and between here and Mamin Bay, which were used by the canoe cutters.

The stream from Bird Lake drains into Stilique Bay, passing through a small unnamed lake before it comes out to the beach.

*TOWUSTASIN HILL — south of Collinson Lake, rises to about 1,350 feet, with a steep cliff on one side. This is the legendary "Brother-of-Tow" (Tow Hill) and the name of Towustasin was applied to the charts by Dr. Dawson in 1878. Towustasin was the good-natured brother who one day grew so weary of Tow's incessant and unfounded grumbling that the Chief of the Sea gave more fish to Towustasin than to him that Towustasin decided to give old Tow something to really complain about. That afternoon when Tow was napping, Towustasin set to and ate up every scrap of food he could find, not leaving as much as a scale for Tow.

In a towering rage Tow took off in a northerly direction to the sea, eventually following the North Beach to the mouth of the Hiellen River where he made his home. Towustasin remained in Juskatla, grateful for the peace.

*JUSKATLA MOUNTAIN — named in 1953 by the Hydrographic Service in association with the Inlet, is 2,370 feet high. It lies between Towustasin Hill and Blackwater Creek, south of Collinson Lake.

*DATLAMEN CREEK — flows into the head of the west arm of Juskatla Inlet. Called TA-TLIM-IN by Dr. Dawson in 1878 and TATLAMEN by Dr. Ells in 1906, all names are modifications of the Haida name for the mythological Creek Woman who had charge of that creek.

"I ascended the Tat-lim-in to the rapids in a canoe," wrote Newton Chittenden when he arrived in 1884," then walked several miles further, finding as I went a succession of rapids, shoals and log jams." It has changed little since he made his excursion, except for some logging in the forests of its valley.

North of the mouth of the Datlamen, and on the west side of the west Juskatla arm, is another creek, as yet unnamed, which has a spectacular waterfall. This waterfall curves around in an S bend as it descends from a creek draining a small lake only a short distance inland.

*MODEETS ISLANDS — consisting of 4 islands with a scattering of rocks in and around them, lie in the west arm of Juskatla about 3 miles from the head. Named in 1953 by the Hydrographic Service after Modeets, the last of the Haida medicine-men. Chittenden interviewed Modeets in 1884 at the Maude Island village of New Gold Harbour, and was told that Modeets never once cut his hair after taking his vow. Modeets performed a dance for Chittenden, then dressed Chittenden in his wildest costume and invited the good-humoured visitor to imitate him. "It brought down the house," observed Chittenden.

On the east shore of this arm of Juskatla, a little south of the Modeets Islands, is a tidal lagoon. Near the mouth of the stream entering the lagoon is a good fishing spot.

*SEEGAY ISLETS — three in number, wooded and with the highest summit rising to about 190 feet, lie off an unnamed bay to the southwest of the largest of the Harrison Islands. Numerous unnamed islands and islets lie between the Seegays and the unnamed bay. At the northeast corner of this bay, on the peninsula separating it from Stilique Bay, is a tidal lagoon which has a small rapids at certain stages of the tide.

Seegay Islets were named by the Hydrographic Service in 1953 after Chief Seegay, the Raven Crest chief, with whom Collison first had contact, and at whose request Collison first went to Masset.

*STEILTA ISLETS — are west of the largest of the Harrison Islands. Named in 1953 by the Hydrographic Office after the Eagle Chief Steilta of Masset, a tall, well-built man, who blamed his premature death on "too much hootchum." He was the first husband of Mrs. Agnes Russ. Converted to Christianity shortly before he died, he was the first Haida chief to be interred - at his own request. There is a stained glass window in the Old Masset church to his memory.

*OHALA ISLETS — in Juskatla Inlet, are northwest of the largest of the Harrison Islands. Named in 1953 by the Hydrographic Service after Ohala, a slave girl belonging to Chief Steilta before his conversion. According to a report made in 1878 by Rev. Collison, Ohala had figured largely in the heated property dispute between Steilta and Chief Blakow-Connehaw.

*MACKIE ROCK — is in Masset Inlet, northeast of the entrance to Juskatla Inlet. Named by Captain P.C. Musgrave of the *Lillooet* during the 1910 hydrographic survey of the inlet. Mackie Rock dries at 8 feet and has a white beacon on it, not a light.

*COWLEY ISLANDS — two islands to the west of Mackie Rock. The westernmost and larger of the two, rises sheer out of the water to 182 feet and has practically no walkable shoreline. It is heavily timbered. The eastern island has a flat shelf on its east side, which has been the recipient of much driftwood. It is a favourite oyster-catcher haunt.

The Cowley Islands were named after Mr. F.V.P. Cowley who assisted in the 1910 hydrographic survey (with Davies, Ross and Powell) of this area.

*COWLEY ROCK — about 1,200 feet east of the easternmost Cowley Island, has a depth of less than 6 feet over it. Named in association with the islands.

*POWELL ISLAND — south and a little west of the Cowley Island, is really a glorified rock rising to about 26 feet. No timber or even stunted trees grow on it, but the islet has a profusion of every variety of grasses, rock plants, wild roses and strawberries. A favourite nesting place for sea-gulls, who protest vigorously any intrusion by humans. Named during the 1910 hydrographic survey and is after Mr. W.H. Powell, one of the surveyors taking part.

*ROSS ISLET — southwest of Powell Island, Ross Islet is off Yestalton Bay. Named during the 1910 hydrographic survey, and is after Mr. C.C. Ross, who with Cowley, Davies and Powell, assisted in the survey. Ross Islet's rocky shoreline is not so steep it cannot be walked for the most part. It has some scrubby trees, salal bushes and a profusion of grasses and moss which appeal to the oyster-catchers and sea-gulls who favour this islet for nesting.

*YESTALTON BAY — lies midway between Shannon Bay and Juskatla Narrows. A creek runs into the head of the bay which has a rocky, but walkable shoreline for the most part. The spit on the west bank of the stream, at its mouth, is said to have been a Haida camping site. The name of the bay is believed to be a modification of the name of the camp site.

The red, yellow and green jaspar found along this part of the shoreline is of much interest to rockhounds.

*LEARMONTH ISLAND — at the entrance to Shannon Bay, has a navigational light on its northwest side. The light has been erected on a group of rocks close offshore. This island is named after Captain F. C. Learmonth who, in 1907, made a survey of the waters from Rose Spit to Frederick Island in the *Egeria*.

S.S. Princess Beatrice *at Ikeda Bay, 1907.*

Provincial Archives photo.

The beloved Amur, *whose skippers took a personal interest in all Island developments.*

Photo - Puget Sound Maritime Historical Society.

Union Steamship vessel approaching wharf at Skidegate Landing in 1949. They had three converted corvettes, Camosun, Chilcotin and Coquitlam.

Photo - Mrs. Isobel Moore

Northland Navigation Company's vessel, Skeena Prince at the dock in Sandspit, 1966. Photo taken by Reverend J.C. Kay.

413

*SMYTH ISLAND — named during the 1910 survey, is in the centre of the 4 islands grouped off the entrance to Shannon Bay. It lies south of Learmonth Island and is about 220 feet high with an islet close off its southwest tip.

*SIMPSON ISLAND — also named during the 1910 survey conducted under Captain P.C. Musgrave. Simpson Island lies to the east of Smyth and has a rock close off its south end which dries at 4 feet.

*WHARTON ISLAND — shaped like an inverted comma, is the largest of this group of 4 and was named at the same time. The channel between Wharton and Wathus, its large neighbour to the west, is much encumbered by ledges and rocks.

*WATHUS ISLAND — is the largest of the islands on the west side of Masset Inlet. Lying midway between Awun and Shannon Bay it was first shown on the charts in 1878 by Dr. Dawson as WAT-HOO-US.

In 1907 it was renamed YOUNG ISLAND by the Graham Steamship, Coal and Lumber Company after John Young who spent 8 months timber cruising for the company in 1906 to 1907 prior to their extensive timber claims application which played such havoc with the settlement of the area. For some years it was called variously Wathus or Young, blueprints issued in 1920 still having the name of Young for the island. The gazetted name is now WATHUS, and this name is used on all current maps.

There are curious crystal formations in the rocks on Wathus, particularly on the east side in the region of the lagoon formed by a rock ledge.

*MOUNT BEGBIE — the name given in 1948 to a 2,165-foot mountain lying in the centre of the peninsula separating Juskatla Inlet's west arm from Shannon Bay.

*SHANNON BAY — the large bay to the west of Juskatla. Named in 1907 after Charles M. Shannon, vice-president of the Graham Steamship, Coal and Lumber Company, by the company officials in connection with a map drawn at that time to illustrate the extent of their holdings along Masset Inlet.

Its first name was ZOOS INLET, bestowed in 1884 by Newton Chittenden because of the tremendous number of jelly-fish in the bay when he visited that summer.

Charles Shannon, whose name the bay now bears, was born in Lexington, U.S.A. in 1853 and had a varied career which included prospecting, news reporting and owner of several papers. Largely through his newspaper career, he served as a Senator in the Territorial Legislature in New Mexico for three terms. During President Cleveland's second term, Shannon became Collector of Internal Revenue and a member of the Democratic National Committee. With the election of McKinley, he dropped out of politics and devoted himself to mining. He was the original owner of the big Shannon Copper Mining Company of Clifton, Arizona and had a large interest in the Greene-Cananea Copper Mining Company.

Shannon was 53 years old when Benjamin Graham interested him in the promotional scheme behind the formation of the Graham Steamship, Coal and Lumber Company for the Queen Charlotte Islands. He accompanied the party who came to the area in 1907 to look over prospects.

On the east slopes of Shannon Bay for years there could be seen a huge logging shute. It was on a timber claim worked by Jameston and Israel just after the close of the 1914-18 war. "They had a skid road at the head of the shute," recalls T.L. Williams who was with the Forestry Service at the time, "and used 3 donkey-engines to bring the logs along the various lengths of the skid road leading to the shute. Once on the shute, whoo-oof . . .! Down they would go at a terrific pace. Watching, you would wonder when some of the big hemlocks would surface they seemed to go down so far when they hit the water. Rafting was done at the head of Shannon Bay."

A fine modern 6-line cannery was built on the small island at head of Shannon Bay. First water rights to the stream on the east of the cannery were taken out in this connection by Gosse and Millard in 1925. The cannery came into operation in 1926 and later became a B.C. Packers plant following the amalgamation of several companies under this name. After the 1940 season it was demolished.

Today the bay is the booming grounds for MacMillan and Bloedel.

SALT LAKE — is shown on current marine charts as the southerly extension of Shannon Bay. MacMillan and Bloedel's recent brochure show this lagoon as BALDWIN BIGHT. Chittenden in 1884 called it RAPIDS INLET saying, "At low tide it discharges its waters with a loud noise down a steep rock-bound passage lying between it and Zoos Inlet."

COMBE'S POINT — the name given to the southeast entrance point of the above, by Chittenden in 1884. It is unnamed today.

*WIAH ISLAND — lies off the south end of Wathus Island and was named in 1910 after Chief Henry Weah of Masset. Weah (or Wiah) is the hereditary name of the Eagle chief to whom a Raven Crest father gave the village of Old Masset. According to the Haida tradition, sons did not normally inherit from their fathers so for his son to take over the village, the Raven Crest ownership had to be transferred to the Eagles. Wiah became the hereditary chief of Masset from that time on.

The Wiah who pillaged the *Susan Sturgis* in 1852 was a forebear of Henry. Henry became Town Chief of Masset in 1882 and was an immensely popular man. When he died in 1932 he was succeeded by his nephew, William Mathews who, in turn, has become a respected and much-revered chief.

*AWUN BAY — west of Shannon Bay, officially named about 1910 in association with the river of that name which runs into the east side of the bay. This bay and river mouth figured largely in the plans of the Graham Steamship, Coal and Lumber Company in 1907, when they tentatively considered a mill site there. It was this plan which forced the early survey of Masset Inlet, much against Captain Musgrave's will, but pressure brought on the Government caused Musgrave to be over-ruled.

*AWUN RIVER — which has been spelled AUAN on some early maps, is an adaption of the Haida name. Applied to the charts in 1878 by Dr. Dawson. It drains the Awun Lake, a slim lake, 6 miles in length and a favourite with anglers. At the south end of the lake a stream runs in from the southwest. It, too, is considered as Awun River and is shown as this on current maps.

*AWUN LAKE — from which the river drains, is about 1½ miles from the salt water at its north end. Although shown on 1907 maps as Awun, for some reason Captain Musgrave renamed it LONG LAKE. But the old name of AWUN subsequently restored. The mountains beyond this region are said to be most beautiful by those who have climbed them. Rolling grassland and alpine flowers, with small trees dotted about give an appearance of a park.

LANAUNGSULS VILLAGE, the-town-that-hides-itself — the Raven Crest site at the mouth of the Awun River which in its heyday was under Chief Ni'djins. Latterly used seasonally for the salmon run and as a garden site; potatoes did especially well in the fertile soil. It is now part of the 7.5-acre OWUN RESERVE owned by the Masset Band. During World War II Aero logging operation had a camp and log dump at the old village site. A planked road, still passable, led from the water's edge to the shores of Awun Lake to facilitate removal of logs.

SALT LAGOON — the name given on current charts for the tidal lagoon between Awun Bay and McClinton Bay. It has also been shown on earlier charts as SALT LAKE. Locally it is called SWAN LAKE, a name which dates back at least to 1908. Received its name because swans are frequently seen there. The outer bay, protected by islets at its mouth, was used in earlier years as a storage for floating logging camps.

*McCLINTON BAY — west of Awun and Shannon Bays. First called TIN-IN-OW-A by Dr. Dawson in 1878. Chittenden also called it by that name in 1884 and spoke of the two streams which enter the head of the bay, one of which he and his party ascended until they came to a log jamb.
In 1907 when the area was mapped by the Graham Steamship, Coal and Lumber Company, it was renamed after Mr. S.R. MacClinton, a civil engineer from Vancouver who had assisted in the location of the timber claims for the company around Masset Inlet. MacClinton and John Young, the timber cruiser, preceded the main party to Masset Inlet then in April 1907 returned with the officials when they made a tour of all properties staked for the company.
By 1909 MacClinton had become associated with the Moresby Island Development and Prospecting Company, holding the post of managing director. They owned timber rights on the northern part of Moresby Island, around Mosquito Lake, as well as mineral claims farther south, in Carpenter Bay and Huston Inlet. The timber claims interested MacClinton chiefly, according to a report he filed that year.
In the late 1920s and early 1930s a fish hatchery operated on the stream running into the southwest corner of McClinton Bay. Fingerlings were taken from the Tlell River and released from the McClinton stream after tagging,

416

to see if a run of "pinks" could be made to come into Masset Inlet every year (instead of the natural cycle of every second year). Thought to have been unsuccessful when the plan was abandoned. Then, amazingly, a few years ago someone spotted fish schooling up in an odd-numbered year. This return of fish, still very small, is gradually increasing.

MacClinton Bay has apparently, through a typographical error, been gazetted as McClinton.

*TAN MOUNTAIN — northwest of the head of McClinton Bay. Named in 1962 by the Hydrographic Service after the Haida word for black bear.

*DAVIE PEAK — on the west side of McClinton Bay is 2,175 feet high. It apparently suffered a typographical error, the original name being DAVIL PEAK.

*MOUNT DRAKE — rises to about 1,830 feet and lies north and west of Davie Peak on the peninsula separating McClinton and Dinan Bays. Shown on land maps of 1954 for the first time.

*MUTUS ISLAND — at the entrance to Dinan Bay, first appeared on the 1878 Dawson map as MUT-OOS. Known to old-timers as "Musgrave's excuse" in a lighter vein of story-telling. Captain Musgrave conducted the hydrographic survey of Masset Inlet in 1910 much against his will, feeling that more important work remained to be done in outside waters and only political pressures stemming from the interests of the Graham Steamship, Coal and Lumber Company caused his being ordered to survey Masset Inlet at that particular time.

Encountering Mutus Island and the surrounding islets at the entrance to Dinan Bay, he declared the waters of that region to be unnavigable and used this as his excuse for not proceeding any farther with the survey. He felt, also, that the group of islets extended far enough for him to exclude the survey of McClinton Bay. To this day (1972) there are still no official hydrographic charts for Dinan and McLinton waters.

*DINAN BAY — the most westerly of the arms running off Masset Inlet. The first recorded naming of this inlet was in 1884 when Newton Chittenden wrote, "As it has no name on the chart I have called it NEWTON INLET." Like most of Chittenden's place names, it never reached the maps. On the chart made in 1910 during Musgrave's survey, it was indicated as DEENAN, a modification of the Haida name. J.D. Mackenzie in 1913-14. used the spelling DINAN and it has been shown as this ever since.

An old trail led from the head of Dinan Bay to Seal Inlet. Little is known of who made it or why. Although Haida legends tell of a route such as this their stories do not pin-point the location. It is always just "from the west side of Masset Inlet." When Mackenzie undertook his geological survey of this region he asked Mr. Dolmage, his assistant, to make a traverse line to the west coast along this old trail. Reported to be overgrown today.

In the fall of 1972 active preparations were in progress under the direction of MacMillan and Bloedel for a sizeable logging operation in Dinan Bay. Over

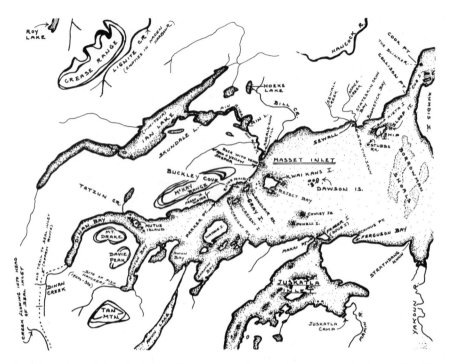

8 miles of road is scheduled for construction and the camp to be built will have a capacity of 80 men. The operation, geared to be long term, is expected to produce at least 50,000 cunits annually.

Rockhounds greeted the news with glee, hoping the project will bring to light some of the fabulous crystal reported to lie along the hills of Dinnan Bay. Ecologists hope that the forestry and fishery officials will do a better job of their duties when this lovely inlet is sacrificed to the pulp and lumber mills of the lower mainland.

*DINAN CREEK — flows into the head of Dinan Bay. This creek rises in the same area as the creek flowing into Seal Inlet. The old trail mentioned above (under Dinan Bay) followed the valley of these two creeks, a distance of from 8 to 10 miles.

*TATZUN CREEK — flows from a lake at the 305-foot level into the north side of Dinan Bay. First put on the map by Dawson in 1878, who called it TA-TZUN-IN, from the name given him by his Haida guides. Chittenden, visiting six years later, gave the same name when he and his guide ascended it by wading with considerable difficulty and reported that he found its bed to be chiefly of limestone rock.

*McKAY RANGE — on the west side of Masset Inlet in the Buckley Cove region. Named after John W. McKay, a timber cruiser from Seattle, who accompanied the Graham Steamship, Coal and Lumber Company party to Masset

Inlet in April 1907. He had been asked by the publication *American Lumberman* to assess the claims of the company as to the value of the timber, most especially in the region of southwest Masset Inlet. Named in 1907.

*PARKER POINT — on the west side of Masset Inlet, southwest of Buckley Cove. Named after Mr. O.R. Parker, a surveyor with the *Lillooet* during the 1910 charting of Masset Inlet. Mr. Parker also assisted in the Port Louis survey in 1913 and completed it in 1914-15.

There is a good fresh water stream at the head of the bight on the west side of Parker Point. Deep water right to the shore makes it convenient for small boats to replenish their water supply.

Buckley Bay Mill during its peak in the early 1920's.
A Los Angeles Lumber Company vessel loads lumber cants in the left foreground,
whilst at the mill wharf a four-masted schooner takes on lumber
and to the right of the schooner the C.N.S.S. Prince John busily
discharges freight and passengers.

Photo - Mrs. Brent Lea.

*BUCKLEY COVE — formerly called BUCKLEY BAY and still referred to by this name locally. It lies midway between Parker Point and the mouth of the Ain River, and became the site of the big mill built in 1918 to saw aeroplane spruce. Named after Frank L. Buckley, managing director of the Masset Timber Company.

Buckley had been interested in this timber asset for several years. An item in the *Prince Rupert Optimist* dated Feburary 22, 1911, noted,

"Newly organized British-Canadian Lumber Company, capitalized at 25 million dollars will have Frank L. Buckley as its managing director. The firm owns an immense timber area on Masset Inlet containing a large spruce tract. The company plans to erect a large sawmill and pulp mill in the Inlet."

Buckley later became involved in a scheme regarding the old Harrison farm on Delkatla Flats, raising produce and beef for sale to all the logging companies streaming into the area to get-rich-quick on the spruce bonanza in the latter years of the First World War.

As someone remarked, "He was always great on Buckleyism. Short on fact."

The mill had barely come into production when the war ceased and the demand for lumber fell off. In 1922 the Los Angeles Lumber Company bought the mill and ran it until 1924. For years afterwards only a watchman remained as the houses, mill machinery and all items connected with the operation were sold piecemeal at give-away prices.

Today all that is left of the big mill are the bits and pieces of saws, tools, bricks, engines and cement forms, with part of a slab pile to indicate that this was once indeed the site of a saw-mill. Nature has claimed her own. Typical are the two old wooden frames from boat windows, piled one on top of the other. From the exact centre grows a tree, now completely filling the frames.

*McCREIGHT ISLAND — offshore and south of Buckley Cove, is 177 feet high and wooded. Named during Musgrave's 1910 hydrographic survey.

*McCREIGHT ROCK — covered less than 6 feet lies about 1¼ cables off the northwestern side of McCreight Island. Named in 1910 by Musgrave.

*GRAY ISLAND — named in 1910 by Captain P.C. Musgrave, lies in front of Buckley Cove. On the pre-emptor's map issued in 1913, this island is shown as BARBARA ISLAND. During the operation of the mill at Buckley Cove, it became known as HOG ISLAND and PIG ISLAND, because pigs were kept on it to provide fresh meat for the dining tables in the mill mess hall.

Gray Island has some attractive sand beaches on its shorelines.

*SINCLAIR ROCK — named by Captain P.C. Musgrave during the 1910 hydrographic survey, lies midway between Gray Island and the group of islets off the west side of Kwaikans, and is only one of the many rocks in this region. Sinclair Rock dries at 10 feet.

*KWAIKANS ISLAND — the largest island in this group off Buckley Cove, lies east of Gray Island. Dr. Dawson applied the name in 1878, a modification of the Haida's descriptive name which meant big, rocky island. Chittenden in 1884 referred to it as EDWARD KWA-KANS.

From 1913 to 1919 it was shown on blueprints and the pre-emptor's map as WATSON ISLAND. During the Buckley Bay Mill operation it became known as REJECT ISLAND, a name commonly used for it still, locally. All the reject logs were stored in the lagoon on the southeast side of the island, this in turn was known as Reject Bay. (Only No. 1 spruce was used in the mill, everything else classed as "rejects.")

420

REJECT BAY — the lagoon on the southeast side of Kwaikans Island. (See preceding item reason for naming.) One attraction of Reject Bay is the seams of jaspar. A particularly large seam was the object of much admiration until recently when some idiot, to secure a few chunks, set a blast in the surrounding rock to facilitate removal. There is a fair amount of petrified wood on Kwaikans, some of which has become opalized. In ancient times the vicinity of Reject Bay was used as a burial ground by Haidas. Kwaikans Island is privately owned today.

Lion's Head Rock on the north end of the largest of the Dawson Islands.

Photo - K.E. Dalzell.

*DAWSON ISLANDS — a little to the west of the centre of Masset Inlet. Named during the 1910 hydrographic survey after Dr. G.M. Dawson, who supplied many names for Queen Charlotte Islands features when he made a geological study in 1878. There are 5 main islands in the group, ranging from 9 feet to 94 feet high. A navigational light is exhibited on the 17-foot-high rock at the southeast extremity of the Dawsons. An interesting group, each island quite different from its neighbour, some rugged, some with fine sandy coves and the largest with a unique lion's head silhouette at its north end. This island is a favorite sea-gull nesting place. It also has a fine patch of wild strawberries.

*AIN RIVER — the modification Dr. Dawson used in applying this name to the map in 1878. It is from the Haida *Qua'nun*. A long sandy point extends off the east side of the mouth, and the peninsula which has built up behind this over the years has created a region full of wild flowers, various mosses, grasses and so on. A small lake lies sheltered among the shrubs and trees and the area is thick with bear and deer tracks. The Ain River drains 3 lakes, Ain, Skundale and Ian, the latter the largest lake on the Charlottes. It is a stream which rewards even the most inept fisherman with a good catch.

In 1911 there were several applications for permits to set up power plants, dams and flumes. The Ain River Development Company with Orlan Merrill, who had drilled for coal at the Nadu, and George Mayer among its officers had an elaborate plan. Another application which also involved an ambitious scheme came from two Masset Haidas, George Young and Henry Edenshaw. Since the Ain is such an important salmon stream the applications did not receive the needed approval.

The shoreline between the mouth of Ain River and Buckley Cove has numerous showings of jaspar in a wide range of hues. One rock formation not far from the river has two large veins of jaspar in red and yellow, as well as numerous small ones, many of them marbled.

KOGALS-KUN VILLAGE, Sand-Spit-Point-Village— a Raven Crest site at the mouth of the Ain River, on its north bank, which has been used for centuries during the salmon run. It is a clean encampment, no garbage or litter. Cabins and smokehouses in various stages of repair today are sited along the bank inside the protecting curve of the spit. Moss-covered remains of many other houses used over the centuries lie close by. This is all part of the 164-acre AIN RESERVE owned by the Masset Band.

*AIN LAKE — named in 1910 in association with the river, which Dawson had named in 1878, is the first lake above the mouth of the river. A scenic place with wild violets everywhere in the lush grass, it also is a good fishing spot. An old canoe is said to lie in the vicinity of this lake. Ranging in length from 50 to 90 feet, depending on the narrator, quite finished it was left covered with shakes awaiting help with launching. It is said that the builders succumbed to small-pox before this could be effected.

*SKUNDALE LAKE — is the next lake above Ain Lake. It has been shown as TSUSKUNDALE on early maps. Believed to have been named during the 1910 Musgrave survey.

*IAN LAKE — at the 116-foot-level, is the largest lake on the Charlottes, and is about 14 miles long. The Haida name for the lake is I-IN-TSUA. This has been shortened to I-IN and, to make it more confusing pronounced the same as Ain, and subsequently spelled IAN.

In 1884 Chittenden thought the lake was called SOO-O-UNS, but added that he had renamed it CLIFFORD LAKE. In 1907 the Graham Steamship, Coal and Lumber Company showed it on their map as the original I-in-tsua, and it seems probable that the shortening of this name took place after 1907.

*CREASE RANGE — overlooking Ian Lake from the northwest, first appeared on maps about 1910. It is believed to be named after Mr. Justice Crease of Victoria.

BILL CREEK — flows into Masset Inlet between Ain River and Sewall. The name has been in constant local use since 1910 or earlier. It has also been occasionally called JIMMY CREEK, but how it acquired either of these names is not known. In ancient years a small Haida fishing camp lay at the mouth of the creek, with cabins which were in seasonal use. The beach between Ain and Bill Creek is, for the most part, sand. Good walking, it has an assortment of driftwood and a variety of rocks which attract rockhounds.

HOEKS LAKE — the headwaters of Bill Creek. This lake was named by settlers after Mr. Adrian Hoeks who homesteaded near there with his friend Bert Goedkoop about 1912. Hoeks Lake is on Lot 1644.

STATESKINSKUN BAY — the name given by the Department of Indian Affairs in 1913 to the bay off Sewall, on the north shore of Masset Inlet.

STA-TIN-SKUN— the name given by the Department of Indian Affairs in 1913 to the point on the east side of Sewall Bay (See above.)

Julius Grewe who actively farmed his land at Sewall until felled by a stroke in 1966, in his 90th year.

Photo - Mrs. Frieda Unsworth.

Mr. and Mrs. Paul Bastian at their home in Sewall shortly before they retired and moved to Masset to live.

Photo - Mrs. Frieda Unsworth.

Paul's daughter, Frieda, with her husband, Stanley Unsworth, and their three children, David, Betty and Elaine (right) Photo taken in 1964. Today the Unsworth family make their home in Port Clements.

Photo - Mrs. Frieda Unsworth.

423

*SEWALL — on the southwest portion of Lot 1577, nestles in the cove west of Ship Island. At one time the site was a promising real estate venture. Tentatively begun as STAR CITY, it was eventually decided to name it after Samuel Dart Sewall, one of the officials in the Star Realty Company who were promoting the townsite. The venture got off to a good start, but with no possibility of a road connection and a waterfront which is a horror for boats, it had little chance of real success, especially with the tough townsiting competition going on at that time. After the First World War as the families moved away, Paul Bastian, one of the original homesteaders, bought most of the land and remained to raise his family there. Only Julius Grewe and his family stayed on with the Bastians.

In later years Paul's daughter Frieda and her husband, Stanley Unsworth, bought a lot and joined the original homesteaders to raise their own three children.

1969 saw the beginning of a new era for Sewall. Bruce and Kit Gifford of Seattle, tired of the pace of city life, bought the holdings of the Bastians and moved to Sewall with their young daughter, Janet. The Bastians who retired to live at Masset were not to enjoy many years after leaving their beloved farm. Paul, the bull-of-the-woods for so many years at Sewall, died a few years later, and his wife passed away early in 1972. The Unsworths, who still retain their home at Sewall, have moved to Port Clements to enable their youngest daughter to complete her education more easily. With them moved Mrs. Grewe, now a widow. The pioneers of Sewall are no longer there and a new family will shape the destiny of this lovely site.

SEWALL CREEK — runs in at the west side of the bay near the old Bastian home. On this stream the first saw-mill was built by the Seventh Day Adventist colony in 1912. They later moved to Watun River and Eli Tingley bought the mill and moved it to his Port Clements townsite to go into the saw-mill business.

OFFICE CREEK — flows into the bay at the northeast corner of Sewall Bay. "It came by its name during the first World War," remembers Mrs. Unsworth. "The office for the second Sewall saw-mill was near this creek. I know the name was well-established when I was a little girl and was always used by us and people who visited." The second Sewall saw-mill was built on the point of land extending into the east side of the bay, the Statin-skun of the Department of Indian Affairs. Bricks from this old operation are still strewn along parts of the beach.

GITINKA-LANA VILLAGE — the Raven Crest site formerly on what later became part of Sewall's townsite. Mrs. Bastian said they dug up great quantities of artifacts when clearing for their garden, and a huge clam-shell midden was found on the hill behind, where the Gifford home now stands. Bones and burnt rocks were frequently uncovered. All seemed indisputable evidence of a former village. Julius Grewe, some distance from the Bastian home, also uncovered artifacts and bones when putting in his garden patch. One curious place on the Grewe land baffled everyone. "It was a circular place," said Mrs. Bastian, "and had an awful smell. It wasn't a swamp though. Julius used to fuss with this place, cultivating and draining and so on. But oats planted there would only come up a few inches, although all around it they grew strong and tall."

BOOMSTICK BAY — is the name coined by loggers in later years for the bay across from Ship Island, and which is east of Sewall. There has been extensive logging around Sewall over the years and this bay, which has a natural rock breakwater extending from the outer point of its west side, was used as a temporary holding ground. "It was the loggers from the camp by Collison Point who first used it," says Mrs. Unsworth. "Through their constant reference to Boomstick Bay. . . it just seemed to come into general use." When the Unsworth's initiated their own log salvage business they, too, used this little bay for their log-holding ground for a few years.

*STUBBS ROCK — named during the 1910 hydrographic survey under Captain P.C. Musgrave, lies off the southwest end of Ship Island about 5 cables from the Island. A red spar buoy is moored near it. The rock dries at 6 feet and there is foul ground between it and Ship Island.

*SHIP ISLAND — at the entrance to Masset Sound is 275 feet high and has a natural spring. Most of the small islands in the inlet do not have water on them. It may have acquired its name through a typographical error, for Dawson showed the island on his map in 1878 as SUPF, a modification of the Haida name. Other maps showed it as SURF ISLAND, but during the hydrographic survey, it became established as SHIP ISLAND.

It has been the nemisis of boats from Port Clements during the violent winter southeast gales when they break loose from their moorings and are swept out by tide and wind to smash up against Ship Island. "Aye, a good reason for its name if you ask me," said one boat owner ruefully contemplating the wreckage of his own boat.

There is an attractive sandy beach on the inside of Ship Island and it is said that shrimp fishing in the passage on its northwest side is usually rewarding.

During the early pioneering days Jim and Andy McCrea cleared some land and built a few cabins near the spring on the northwest portion.

*SHIP KIETA ISLAND — is the small island off the west side of Ship Island, to which it is joined by a drying spit. It has also been shown as LITTLE SHIP ISLAND and as WEST SHIP ISLAND. During the 1910 Musgrave survey, the name of SHIP KIETA was applied and adopted by the Permanent Names Committee.

J.D. MacKenzie, in his examination of this island during his geological survey in 1913-14, said that one of the big vents during the volcanic period had probably been in this vicinity. Tachylyte, a rare type of glassy basalt, was found in the agglomerate on the west side of Ship Kieta, and from this his conclusions were drawn.

*SLOOP ISLET — only 6 feet high, lies off the northeast end of Ship Island. Named in 1910 by Captain P.C. Musgrave during the hydrographic survey. There is a navigational light on Sloop Islet.

*BORROWMAN SHOALS — which occupy nearly the whole of the eastern part of Masset Inlet waters, consist of two extensive shallow areas, with a deep channel in between. At one place on the north shoal the water is only 3 feet deep.

Borrowman Shoals were named by Captain P.C. Musgrave in 1910 after Andrew W. Borrowman, second engineer on the *Lillooet* at the time of the survey. He was second engineer from 1908 to 1911, then became Chief Engineer, a position he held until 1932 when he retired at the age of 67.

NORTH END OF GRAHAM ISLAND. FROM
WESTACOTT POINT TO MAZARREDO ISLANDS.
FEATURING HAIDA NAMES FROM THE STUDY
MADE BY MR. CHARLES A. SMITH.

CHAPTER NINETEEN

*WESTACOTT POINT — northwest of Yan at the entrance to Masset Harbour. Shown on maps issued in 1913 and believed to have been named during the 1907 hydrographic survey conducted by Captain F.C. Learmonth. Some of the early maps showed it as WESTCOTT. It is a rocky point with kelp lying offshore.

*DAVY LEDGE — close off Westacott Point, dries at 5 feet, with kelp growing around it. Named in 1907 by Captain Learmonth of the *Egeria,* after Lieutenant B.O.M. Davy, R.N., who, assisted by Lieutenants Troup and Harvey, surveyed Masset Harbour in 1907.
The Haidas called the reef KATL'AGUE-CLA (rocks). (C.Smith)

WHITE-SAND-BAY, *Katlans-klung* — the Haida name for the bay immediately north of Westacott Point. (C.Smith)

*OTUN RIVER — empties into a drying bight northwest of Westacott Point and White-Sand-Bay. Formerly called the ADAM RIVER, it has presumably been given its present name after a modification of the Haida name for the river, UDDEN. (C.Smith)
Designated as a small stream by navigational standards, the branches of this river go inland for 12 miles or more to help drain the large marshy region west of Masset Sound.

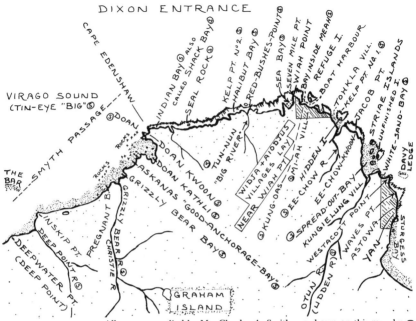

All names supplied by Mr. Charles A. Smith are shown on this map by ⑤ .

SPREAD-OUT-BAY, *Ant Kwock-oas* — the Haida name for the drying bay off the mouth of the Otun River; this bay dries out to include the Striae Islands. (C. Smith)

KUNGIELUNG VILLAGE — the Raven Crest village which, according to Dr. C.F. Newcombe, lay near the mouth of the Otun River.

*STRIAE ISLANDS — northwest of Westacott Point at the entrance to Masset Harbour. Named by Dr. G.M. Dawson in 1878 for their physical aspect. The most easterly of the Striae Islands has a navigational light on it, The Blinker.

UNFINISHED ISLAND, *Gway-tu-wuns* — the name given by the Haidas to the outer Striae Island, this name sometimes used to include the group. (C.Smith). There is a legend attached to one of the rock formations in the Striae group. Called Wind-Rock, it harboured a supernatural being. If a man desired a certain wind, he tapped a small hole in it with a stone, upon the side from which he wished the wind to blow.

*JACOB POINT — between the Striae Islands and Hidden Island. First shown on maps issued in the 1920s.
This was the EE-CHOW-KWOON of the Haidas, and so named in association with the small river to the northwest of the point. (C.Smith)

EE-CHOW (RIVER) — a small stream flowing from the southwest with its mouth a little south of Hidden Island. (C.Smith)

428

Grand Trunk Pacific's
Prince Albert, *former*
Bruno.
*In later years she was
purchased by J.R. Morgan
and renamed for him.
This photo taken off
Masset about 1911.*

*Photo - Mrs. Frank
Van Valkenberg.*

G.T.P.'s **Prince John,** *formerly the* **Amethyst.** *This photo taken August 31, 1911
when she was under the command of Captain Cecil Wearmouth.
Sold in 1941 to Union Steamship Company and renamed* **Cassiar.**

Photo - Mrs. Frank Van Valkenberg.

Canadian National Steamship vessel, Prince Charles *as she looked in 1926,
the year after she was put on the Charlotte run. Built in 1907 in Scotland
she was first called* Chieftain, *then the St. Margaret, before being purchased by
the Grand Trunk Pacific in 1925. Sold to Union Steamship Company in 1940 and
renamed Camosun, and in 1945 sold to a Greek firm who renamed her* Cairo.

Photo - Lawrence Rennie

Delkatla Floats

Photo - B.C. Government

*HIDDEN ISLAND — about 1½ miles to the southeast of Wiah Point. (Seven Mile Point.) A wooded island with an extensive drying rocky ledge stretching off its northeast side. It is joined to Graham Island by a drying bank.

The Haidas called this island KLICK-DEA. (C.Smith).

KELP POINT, *Th'cama Kwoon* — the name given to the north side of the ledge off Hidden Island. (C.Smith).

TOHLKA VILLAGE — the Eagle Crest village which Dr. C.F. Newcombe noted in the vicinity of Hidden Island.

*REFUGE ISLAND — to the northwest of Hidden Island, lies close by Wiah (or Seven Mile) Point. As boats flee for protection from storms on this outer coast and find sanctuary in the shelter behind Refuge Island, its name becomes singularly appropriate. A small island with a large rocky ledge on its outer side, during fishing season it becomes a headquarters when a fish camp is anchored inside the island to service the fleet. Commonly called the Seven Mile Camp.

MI-AH VILLAGE — lay on Graham Island, in the shelter of Refuge Island. (C.Smith)

KUNG-OAS, Where-The-Trail-Ends-At-Grass-Flats — the site beside the Mi-ah village. (C. Smith)

*MIA KWUN — the present name for the old village site of Mi-ah, and a surrounding 49-acre parcel of land, the MEAGWAN RESERVE, which belongs to the Masset Band.

BOAT HARBOUR — the descriptive name given to the anchorage behind Refuge Island.

The Haidas called it WEE-CHOW, bay-inside-Mi-ah. (C.Smith).

WIDJA VILLAGE — an Eagle Crest village, shown by Dr. C.F. Newcombe to be in the vicinity of Refuge Island.

AIODJUS VILLAGE, All-Fat-Meat-Village — a Raven Crest site occupied by Haidas who later moved to Alaska. Dr. Newcombe shows this to be located in the vicinity of Refuge Island also.

*WIAH POINT — named by Captain F.C. Learmonth in 1907 after the hereditary Masset Chief, Henry Wiah (or Weah), uncle of the present Chief Wiah, the much respected patriarch William Matthews. Wiah Point is known locally as SEVEN MILE POINT (7 miles from Masset.) There are several navigational lights in this region.

It is generally assumed that PUERTO DE PANTO JA which Caamano named after his chief pilot in July 1792, was the present Wiah Point.

Mr. C. Smith said that this point, now called Wiah, was the Mi-ah Kwun

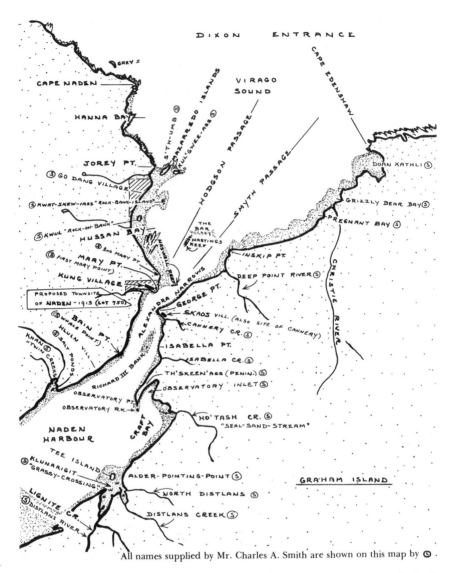

All names supplied by Mr. Charles A. Smith are shown on this map by Ⓢ .

of the Haidas and so named because of its proximity to the village of Mi-ah which lay inside, beside Kung-oas.

SEA BAY, *Ses-un-kathli* — the bay on the west side of Wiah Point. (C. Smith)

RED BUSHES, *Set-kul-cho-ose* — off the northeast corner of Lot 2250. It was the landmark for locating the entrance to the Tun-nun River. (See next page) (C. Smith)

BIG RIVER, *Tun-nun* — entered the bay of Lot 2250. There is a detached, drying rock off the mouth of this river. (C.Smith)

HALIBUT BAY, *Chisley-sun* — a small bight west of Tun-nun (or Big River). (C.Smith)

KELP POINT *(second one)* *Th'cama Kwoon* — a rocky point off a small stream to the west of Halibut Bay. (C. Smith)

SEAL ROCK, *Lal-un* — the 12-foot-high rock approximately midway between Kelp Point and Cape Edenshaw. A creek runs into Dixon Entrance on the west side of this rock. (C.Smith)

INDIAN BAY, also called Shack-Bay-with-rock — is an indentation on the north shore, immediately east of Cape Edenshaw. (C.Smith)

CAPE EDENSHAW — the east entrance point to Virago Sound. Named in 1853 by Captain G.H. Inskip, in charge of the hydrographic survey of the area with the *Virago*. Named after the wealthy and influential Eagle Crest chief, who became Albert Edward Edenshaw many years later when baptised following his conversion to Christianity.
The Haida name for the point was DOAN KWOON. (C.Smith)

DOAN — the Haida name for the small indentation at Cape Edenshaw. Doan Kwoon referred to the point. (C.Smith)

DOAN KATHLI, Inside-Doan — the large drying bay on the south side of Cape Edenshaw. (C. Smith)

ASKANAS, The-good-anchorage-bay — the name given to the bay south of Doan Kathli. Numerous rocks front this little bay, providing a hazard to any but the knowledgeable Haida who used it. (C.Smith)

GRIZZLY BEAR BAY — lay south of Askanas, and named in conjunction with Christie River, which the Haidas called Grizzly (Bear) River. (C.Smith)

CHRISTIE RIVER — flows from the south to enter Virago Sound on the east side. It appeared on 1913 maps but was not officially confirmed by the Permanent Names Committee until 1933.
The Haidas called this river WHOOTSUN, Grizzly Bear River. (C.Smith)

PREGNANT BAY, *Antskiskias* — the Haida name for the small bay immediately south of the mouth of the Christie River. It is fronted by numerous rocks. (C. Smith) A small lake on Lot 2484 lies near the shore to the southwest of Pregnant Bay.

INSKIP POINT — near the entrance to Naden Harbour, on the east shore of Virago Sound. Named after George Hastings Inskip by Commander James

Paddle sloop Virago *in 1853, the year she was engaged in surveying waters from Cape Knox to Naden Harbour, along the north end of the Charlottes, and Houston Stewart Channel at the south end of the Islands. During these surveys her officers applied many of the place names we know today for features in these areas.*

Photo - B.C. Archives.

Prevost in 1853. Inskip was in charge of the survey. He also made hydrographic surveys at Inskip Channel and Houston Stewart Channel on the Charlottes, as well as at Port Simpson on the mainland, that same year.

Inskip Point was the SCHLOOT-KWOON of the Haida (C.Smith)

*VIRAGO SOUND — the waters off Naden Harbour. Named by Commander James C. Prevost during the 1853 survey, after his ship engaged in the charting. They had been sent to investigate the *Susan Sturgis* hijacking of September 1852 and also to establish British sovereignty by their presence in surveying strategic waters off the Charlottes. An ownership gesture made mandatory by the pressures of the H.B.C. to ward off foreign encroachment into their trading preserves. Although they had acted to help the stricken crew of the *Susan Sturgis*, the fact that she had been another American ship in this area was alarming to the H.B.C. (Houston Stewart Channel was also surveyed by the *Virago* in 1853.)

In 1792, before any British Admiralty ship appeared to make Queen Charlotte Islands surveys, American Joseph Ingraham of the brig *Hope* had been engaged in drawing maps and naming various features of the Islands. He named this sound PORT CRAFT after the mate on his ship John Craft. (Also spelled

Cruft, Cruff and Craff in early logs.) Mr. Craft died shortly after they left the Charlottes following the *Hope's* initial voyage in 1791, dying while the vessel was *en route* to Hawaii to winter.

The Haida name for Virago Sound was TIN-EYE, "Big". (C.Smith)

DEEP POINT RIVER — the stream which enters the south part of Virago Sound, south of Inskip Point. The mouth of the stream is in the bight off Lot 2478 (C.Smith) "What is now Deepwater Point was known to us at Naden as Deep Point, and the stream was always called in this association the Deep Point River," said Mr. Smith, who spent years at Naden Harbour.

*DEEPWATER POINT — southwest of Inskip Point, is the east entrance point to Alexandra Narrows. The name for the point suggested by the Hydrographic Service in 1947 and adopted by the Geographic Board in 1948. Local name was DEEP POINT. The two leading lights on this point are placed to guide vessels into the Narrows via the west side of Hastings Reef.

*SMYTH PASSAGE — the eastern channel to be followed in Virago Sound by vessels entering Naden Harbour. In following this course the lights of George Point and Bain Point are used to keep on course and clear Hastings Reef. Captain F.C. Learmonth named the passage in 1907, during a resurvey of the Virago Sound area, after Lieutenant Sydney Keith Smyth of the *Egeria,* who assisted in the resurvey. Lieut. Smyth was the son of Captain Smyth, the first commander of the *Egeria* when she entered survey work on the British Columbia coast.

*HODGSON PASSAGE—the western channel which may be used to enter Naden Harbour, to ensure safe clearance of Hastings Reef. Bain Point and Mary Point are involved in the navigational instructions for this entry course. Hodgson Passage was named in 1907 by Captain Learmonth after another of the lieutenants on board the *Egeria* during the 1907 survey, Lieutenant Oswald Tyson Hodgson, R.N.

*THE BAR — off the entrance to Naden Harbour, long known locally by this name and given official status in 1947. Composed of stones and gravel and covered for the most part by kelp in summer and fall, it extends from Inskip Point to the outer edge of Hussan Bay. A red conical buoy with a radar reflector has been moored on it.

*HASTINGS REEF — situated near the middle of The Bar, off Naden Harbour, is almost awash during lowest tides, especially near its northwest extremity. Kelp does not lie over it. Named in 1907 by Captain F.C. Learmonth of the *Egeria* for the original British Admiralty surveyor of these waters, George Hastings Inskip, and in association with the nearby Inskip Point.

It is believed that the RICHARD ROCKS referred to by Walbran in his description of the wrecking of the hulk *Richard III* is actually Hastings Reef. (See Richard III Bank.)

The Haidas called Hastings Reef TAS'KOO-WASS CUDLAY. (C.Smith)

*ALEXANDRA NARROWS — connects Virago Sound with Naden Harbour. It appeared on maps issued in 1913, but origin of name not confirmed. The tidal stream through the Narrows is between 2 and 2½ knots and here are no eddies.

On a chart published in 1868 the south portion of the Narrows was shown as MAZERREDO HARBOUR, a name long associated with this region.

*HASWELL REEF — at the north entrance to Alexandra Narrows, is the end of a drying flat which extends eastward from Mary Point. Named in 1947 by the Hydrographic Service after Robert Haswell, mate of the American vessel *Columbia* and, for a short time, master of the *Adventure* (See Haswell Bay).

The Haida name for the reef was TAS'KOO-WASS. (C.Smith)

*GEORGE POINT — which has a navigational light, juts into Alexandra Narrows from the east shore. Named in 1853 after George Hastings Inskip, shown at that time as POINT GEORGE. In the logs of the whaling ships, this point was frequently referred to as CANNERY POINT.

The Haida name for the point was DA'HL KWOON. (C.Smith)

SKAOS VILLAGE — an ancient Eagle Crest site which lay in the bight south of George Point. The name is a modification of the Haida phrase "town-above-the-sandbank-near-the-point", the sandbank being the Richard III Bank.

During the building of the salmon and crab canneries, it was common to unearth artifacts at this location. Wallace Fisheries built a cannery there and operated it from 1910 to 1919, when they moved to Watun River. Captain E.H. Simpson and his partner, Captain Hume Babbington, took over the vacated site and built a crab cannery which they operated until about 1924 when they decided to can razor clams and move their operation to New Masset. In 1933 Captain Simpson's son, Sam, and his wife Jessie, reopened and rebuilt the plant at old Skaos, canning crabs during season until about 1940 when the little cannery was abandoned.

The original crab cannery at Naden Harbour. Built on the site of the old Skaos village. This photo taken in 1920 shows the well-remembered Simpson boat Crab *on the grid.*

Photo - Sam Simpson.

CANNERY CREEK — the local name for the creek on the south side of the crab cannery.

*NADEN HARBOUR — is the water inside Alexandra Narrows. The first reference to this name is in Robert Haswell's log when as master of the newly-built *Adventure* he took the vessel from Vancouver Island to the Charlottes on her maiden voyage. He referred to being "Off Neden" in April 1792, and again in July of the same year.

When Inskip conducted the survey of the area in 1853, he named it TRINCOMALEE HARBOUR. The *Trincomalee* under Captain Houstoun, and the *Virago* under Captain Prevost, had been sent that year to investigate the *Susan Sturgis* hi-jacking.

In 1878 Dr. G.M. Dawson in the course of his geological exploration of part of the Charlottes, applied the name of NADEN after the Raven Crest family living near the mouth of the river, the Ne dan hadai, the Naden-River-People. The words *ne dan* refer to the fact that there were numerous settlements in the harbour. (Information from Mrs. Alfred Adams, formerly of Old Masset.)

The Haida name for the harbour waters was OW'WAY, "many-sandbanks." (C. Smith)

*RICHARD III BANK — which dries at 4 feet near its central part, is south of George Point and fronts the eastern shore of Isabella Point for 1¼ miles. Named by Captain Learmonth during the 1907 survey because an old ship of that name, which was being used as a coal and ore hulk in the Alaska trade, drifted onto rocks in Virago Sound during a storm in the winter of 1906. She was salvaged and towed into Naden Harbour by some Haidas, but became stranded on this bank. She was still lying there when the 1907 survey was in progress.

Walbran in his excellent place names history, wrote that the vessel drifted onto Richard Rocks and gave the location as Virago Sound. But he later identified the place where Inskip and party saw the hulk as being off Bain Point, which would put it on Richard III Bank. It is very likely the hulk fetched up on Hastings Reef or The Bar, from which point it would have been salvaged by the Haidas.

The Haida name for Richard III Bank was OW'WAY-STAH, in association with Ow'way. (Naden Harbour) (C.Smith)

*ISABELLA POINT — east of Richard III Bank, and south of George Point, at the entrance to Naden Harbour. Named by George Inskip in 1853 after the wife of Archibald Bain, chief engineer aboard the *Virago* at that time. (Bain Point is opposite.)

ISABELLA CREEK — the local name for the creek south of Isabella Point, which has its mouth in the bight on the west side of Lot 2468. (C.Smith)

*OBSERVATORY ROCK — off the tip of the peninsula which shelters the north portion of Craft Bay. On older maps it was shown as OBSERVATORY ISLET, but this later changed to Rock, since it is only 2 feet high.

TH'SKEEN'ASS — the Haida name for the peninsula which has Observatory Rock off its tip. The name refers to the fact that there is water in the bay behind this peninsula in contrast to the other bays of Naden Harbour which are filled by drying flats. (C.Smith)

OBSERVATORY POINT — the local name for the tip of the above peninsula. Observatory Rock is on the drying bank off this point. The Haidas called the point TH'SKEENA'ASS KWOON. (C.Smith)

OBSERVATORY INLET — the local name for the bay inside Th'skeen'ass Point. (C.Smith)

*CRAFT BAY — a bay filled for the most part by drying flats on the east side of Naden Harbour. It was the name Joseph Ingraham gave to Virago Sound in 1792 and the Hydrographic Service named Craft Bay in recognition of this. In 1884 Newton Chittenden named the bay TIDE BAY, but his name was not adopted.
The Haidas called the bay HO'TASH, "seal-sands." (C.Smith)
Shown on all charts as an anchorage. But recent logging and booming operations have left so many "dead heads" and "sinkers" the bay is a hazard and cursed by mariners who enter it today.

HO'TASH CREEK, Seal-sand-stream — the Haida name for the creek flowing into the east side of Craft Bay. Also called NORTH CRAFT CREEK locally. (C. Smith)

SOUTH CRAFT BAY VILLAGE — an old Haida site in the south part of Craft Bay. (C.Smith)

*TEE ISLAND — on the east side of Naden Harbour, on a drying bank off the mouth of Lignite Creek. The name is from a Haida work and means Death Island. (C.Smith)

ALDER-POINTING-POINT, *Kul'kwinan'uns* — directly east of Tee Island. (C.Smith)

GRASSY-CROSSING, *Klunakigit* — the grassy place at the head of the bight into which flow 3 streams, one of which is Lignite Creek. This all dries out past Tee Island. (C.Smith)

*LIGNITE CREEK — the gazetted name for the most southerly of the 3 streams which enter a common bight off the south end of Tee Island. Named LIGNITE BROOK in 1878 by Dr. G.M. Dawson. This creek goes inland for 15 to 16 miles and has its headwaters at the back of Ian Lake.
The Haida name for this was DIS-TLANS RIVER. Local name was Lignite River; with Lignite Creek being the middle stream and North Lignite the name given to the third stream entering this common bight. (C. Smith)

DISTLANS CREEK — the Haida name for the middle of the 3 streams. Unnamed today, it was the LIGNITE CREEK of earlier years, locally. (C.Smith)

NORTH DISTLANS — the most northerly of the 3 streams at this place. Also called NORTH LIGNITE. (C.Smith)

*MIDDLE HILL — about 1,450 feet high, is north of Crease Range and east of Marian Lake. Named about 1910.
Called DISTLAN HILL by the Haidas. (C.Smith)

SPRING-WATER-POINT, *Kwadoos kwoon* — the Haida name for the hooked point between Chittenden Point and the mouth of lignite Creek. (C.Smith)

*CHITTENDEN POINT — on the east side at the mouth of the Naden River, and south of Spring-Water-Point. It lies on the same drying flat as Spring-Water-Point. Name appeared on maps of the 1920s but not confirmed until 1948. It is after Newton Chittenden, who made an extensive exploratory trip for the British Columbia Government in 1884. An injury to his right hand at the onset of the trip made it more awkward for him to manage, but in spite of this he visited every inlet and river, following many of these to the lakes at their heads, and climbed many of the mountains. He wrote a vivid account of his trip. His mileage estimates were often inaccurate but his descriptions of the features are immediately recognized. As far as can be learned the report was simply filed away.
Chittenden Point was the KE AS KWOON, Sunlight-Point, of the Haida. (C.Smith)

*NADEN RIVER — flows into the head of Naden Harbour and named by Dr. G.M. Dawson in 1878. This river drains a lush valley and 3 lakes, Eden, Roy and Marian. There is an area of drying flats off the mouth which extend for 2 miles. A logging road follows the river inland for some distance today, and is expected to go from Eden Lake to Otard Bay eventually. At present the headquarters for the logging camp are near the south end of Eden Lake. (1972)
The Haida name for Naden River was DUCK RIVER, *Ha-andless.* (C.Smith)

*EDEN LAKE — the largest of the 3 lakes in the Naden River system, is about 4 miles long. Although Dr. Dawson did not give the lake a name in 1878, he knew of its existence. Chittenden in 1884 was aware of its name. Eden is believed to be a corruption of Naden.

KOSE RESERVE — about 3 miles from the mouth of Naden River, contains 9 acres and belongs to the Masset Band.

FLOATING VILLAGE, *Klock-Ghee-ahgans* — the Raven Crest village at the mouth of the Naden River (C.Smith) Now part of the NADEN RESERVE containing 27 acres and is owned by the Masset Band.

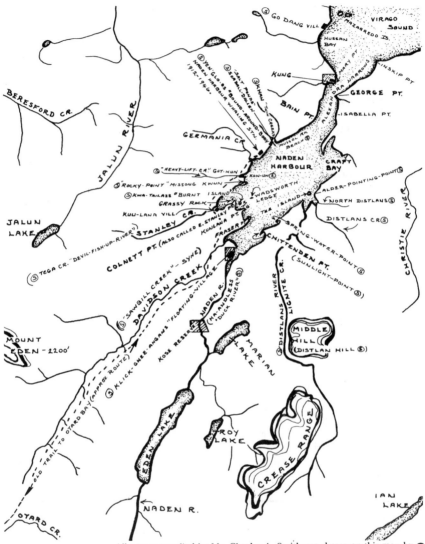

All names supplied by Mr. Charles A. Smith are shown on this map by ⊗

*ROY LAKE — east of Eden Lake and the smallest of the 3 lakes drained by the Naden system. First appeared on maps in 1913 and believed to have been named during a timber survey.

*MARIAN LAKE — lies at the 115-foot level and is the most northerly of 3 lakes on the Naden River system. First appeared on 1913 maps.

MOUNT EDEN — rises to 2,200 feet and lies northwest of Eden Lake. Two streamlets from Davidson Creek flow from its slopes. Said to have been named when the trail was cut through from Naden Harbour to Otard Bay about 1911, and which followed the valley of Davidson Creek.

*DAVIDSON CREEK — enters the head of Naden Harbour to the west of Naden River, its tributaries extending almost to Otard Creek. In 1911 a trail was cut through from Otard Bay and followed the valley of the Davidson Creek for most of its length. This trail, originating at the Tian Bay drill site went first to Otard Creek then turned northeast to cross to Naden Harbour via the valley of Davidson Creek. Near the mouth of this creek the trail turned north eventually emerging at the Whaling Station on the west shore of Naden Harbour.

The Haida name for Davidson Creek was SAWBILL CREEK, *Syne*. (C. Smith)

*FRASER POINT — is the west entrance point of the bay into which both the Davidson and Naden Rivers empty, causing an extensive drying flat which surrounds Fraser Point. First appeared on maps of the 1920s.

*KUNLANA POINT, Marten-Point — is on the same drying flat as Fraser Point, and lies between Fraser and Colnett Points. There is a semi-detached islet, 74 feet high, off Kunlana Point.

*COLNETT POINT — on the same drying flat as Fraser and Kunlana Points, which lie southeast of it. Colnett Point forms the east entrance point to Stanley Creek.

The KWILUNT SLUE-ASS of the Haidas, and also called EAST STANLEY POINT locally. (C.Smith)

KUU-LANA VILLAGE, also shown as KUNLA'NA — shown by Dr. C.F. Newcombe to have stood on the east side of Stanley Creek, at its mouth. A Raven Crest site.

*GRASSY ROCK — is the gazetted name for the 8-foot-high-rock close off the north tip of Colnett Point. Formerly called GRASSY ISLET, later changed to Rock.

BURNT ISLAND, *Kwa tailass* — the Haida name for the 66-foot-high islet off the east side of Colnett Point and on the same drying bank. (C.Smith)

*WADSWORTH LEDGE — in the shallow waters off Colnett Point, beyond Burnt Island. Origin and date of naming not confirmed. It dries at 12 feet.

The Haida name for the reef was SEAL ROCKS, *Kwiltl-kwunce*. (C.Smith)

*STANLEY CREEK — flows into the southwest corner at the head of Naden Harbour. Named by George Inskip in 1853 after a close friend, Captain Owen Stanley, whom he first met in 1846 when engaged in a survey of Australian waters. Stanley commanded the *Rattlesnake* engaged in the operation. The survey was not completed when Captain Stanley died in 1850, and Inskip wrote that he had indeed "lost a most true and influential friend." The following year, 1851, Inskip joined the *Virago*.

There is a 6.5-acre Haida Reserve at the mouth of Stanley Creek and a drying flat fills up the entire bay into which the creek flows.

The Haidas called the creek TEGA, devil-fish-up-river. (C.Smith)

ROCKY POINT, *Missong Kwoon* — the Haida name for the first point north of the mouth of Stanley Creek on the west side of Naden Harbour. *Missong* is descriptive of the rocky point. (C. Smith) A creek flowed into the small bight north of this point.

HEAVY-LIFT-CREEK, *Gut-kun* — the Haida name for the stream entering the bay between Stanley Creek and Germania Creek. (C. Smith)

KON-UN — the Haida name for the bight off the mouth of Heavy-Lift-Creek. (C. Smith)

*GERMANIA CREEK — flows into the west side of Naden Harbour near the site of the old Whaling Station. Named after the whaler *Germania* which operated out of both Naden and Rose Harbours during the early days of whaling. The creek was named in conjunction with the building of the Naden Harbour Whaling Station, about a ¼ of a mile north, in 1911-12.

NADEN HARBOUR WHALING STATION — built on Lot 55, about ¼ of a mile north of the mouth of Germania Creek on the west side of Naden Harbour. Construction was begun in 1911 by the Canadian North Pacific Fisheries and operation commenced in 1912. In October 1912 a post office opened under the official address, Naden Harbour. About that time ownership of the plant passed into the hands of British Empire Trust Company, who sold it in 1915 to the Victoria Whaling Company. By 1918 the Consolidated Whaling Incorporated of Toronto bought both Rose and Naden Harbour Whaling stations and operated them continuously until 1943 when they encountered the financial problems which forced them into bankruptcy in 1946. The profitable days of whaling were over.

The following year Western Whaling Corporation Limited bought both properties for $7,000 and everything not obsolete was moved to Coal Harbour Whaling Station on Vancouver Island. B.C. Packers own all three locations today.

Only a few old pilings and pieces of rusting equipment mark the site of Naden Harbour Whaling Station. "That and wonderfully fresh air." remarked a fisheries officer who remembered all too well the stench associated with the processing of whales.

The Haida name for the whaling station was BOUND-AROUND-BODY, *Yen'glo-os.* (C.Smith)

In 1972 deep concern was being expressed by local environmentalists about the installation by Goodwin Johnson Limited of a sawmill on the old whaling station site. Extensive logging along the Naden River has already caused apprehension for the safety of salmon spawn. It is felt that this area requires careful and informed guidance in the harvest and subsequent handling of its timber if it is not to suffer the fate of the once mighty Yakoun whose fish runs were so enormous they were almost legendary.

Goodwin Johnson Limited proposed to refit the ex-Canadian National Railway ferry *Canora* into a floating sawmill. At Naden Harbour the vessel will be dredged into the bank, backfilled and left in place for 4 or 5 years, then refloated and moved to a site at Otard Bay.

TWIN CREEK, *Khan* — on the west side of Naden Harbour, flow into the bight to the northeast of the old whaling station (C.Smith)

SALT PONDS, *Soa Dal-dallen* — off the mouth of Twin Creeks. (C. Smith)

HLULN VILLAGE — on the north side of Twin Creek. Little seems to have been recorded about this village site (Shown as No. 109 on Dr. Newcombe's map.) Mr. C. Smith knew this site as KWIL-OW-N, North-Mussel-Rock.

MUSSEL-ROCK-BEACH, *Khow-tutch-kus* — between Twin Creeks and Bain Point. (C.Smith)

*BAIN POINT — which has a navigational light, is at the west side of the south entrance to Alexandra Narrows. Named by Commander Prevost in 1853 after Archibald Bain, R.N., Chief Engineer on the *Virago* at that time. Mr. Bain accompanied George Inskip in the boat when Inskip made his initial examination of Virago Sound and Naden Harbour in August 1853. Bain became chief engineer in 1849 and retired in 1874.
The Haida name for the point was WHALE POINT, *Kit kwoon*. (C.Smith)

Proposed TOWNSITE of NADEN — on Lot 750 which is between Bain Point and Kung Indian village. In June 1913 Reverend Will Collison, son of the Archdeacon, sold this lot to a Winnipeg firm who planned to use part of it for a townsite. Much talk was being bandied as to the promising lignite and coal finds in the Naden region as well as the established whaling and fishing of these waters. Typical get-rich-quick promotion which apparently did not entice many customers. The townsite never got past the dreaming stage.

*KUNG — an abandoned Eagle Crest village which lay on the north shore of the bight inside Mary Point. An unnamed stream has its mouth on the south side of the village. The name *Kung* means "dream town" in that it was the dream village of the great Chief Edenshaw. Established about 1853, eventually 15 lodges and nearly 300 people occupied the village.
Edenshaw, a Family Chief, and the most important of the chiefs in the district - by virtue of his wealth - made Kung his head village and owned by far the largest home there. He was not Town Chief of Kung. This position was held by Chief Gu'las "abalone", an Eagle Crest chief of another family closely related to Edenshaw. Edenshaw being a wealthy Family Chief maintained homes in several villages, but Kung was always dearest to his heart.
In 1875 as times became slim he decided to establish another village on the outer coast near Klashwun Point, hoping the new site would attract trade from Alaska. He called the new village Yatza.
There were still some inhabited lodges at Kung when Dawson visited in 1878,

but when Chittenden arrived six years later in 1884 he wrote, "Deserted Kung, pleasantly situated. . . its fifteen houses pretty well in ruins, except for two or three, one of which our party occupied."

The old village is now part of KUNG RESERVE containing 71 acres.

*MARY POINT — forms the north point of the bay in which Kung stood. Named in 1853 by George Inskip after his fiancee Mary Liscumbe Jorey. Mary Point is a hook-shaped feature. A trail ran across at the back of the point from Kung village to the outer beach north of the point. Mr. C. Smith said it was common to refer to Mary Point as FIRST MARY POINT, and the point north was SECOND MARY POINT. The Haidas called this second Mary Point *Kate'ass kwoon.*

*HUSSAN BAY — named in 1878 by Dr. G.M. Dawson after a modification of the Haida name for the bay. There is considerable kelp in Hussan Bay, which lies at the southwest side of Virago Sound. Boulders are scattered throughout the kelp.

GO DANG VILLAGE — at the north end of Hussan Bay, near Jorey Point. It is now part of the 21-acre DANINGAY RESERVE of the Masset Band. One of the Haida miracle legends occured at Go Dang.

Two couples were said to have been starving at Go Dang. One of the men prepared to go sealing the next morning at daylight and high tide. He drew his canoe down to where it would float at daylight, fastened his harpoon upon its shaft securely then turned in for the night.

Upon waking in the morning he was horrified to find he had overslept and the tide fallen too far. What would they do? Their hunger was acute.

He went dejectedly down to the canoe. To his surprise he found that his harpoon was detached from its shaft and now lay imbedded in a seal; the seal lying alongside the canoe. He could not believe his eyes, and woke the others. "It is a miracle," cried his wife. "The Great Spirit knew we starved. Another day might have been too late." (C. Smith)

KWUL, rock-on-bank — the 13-foot-high rock on the beach a little south of Go Dang village. (C. Smith)

KWAT-SKEW-IASS, Rock-bank-island — the Haida name for the summit of a boulder reef north of Kwul. A wedge-shaped boulder reef lies close offshore at Go Dang and is joined by a drying reef to the shore. The summit, which is named, dries at 15 feet. (C.Smith)

*JOREY POINT — named in 1853 by a romantic young hydrographer for the girl he hoped to marry. George Inskip named this point, and Mary Point, after his sweetheart Mary Liscumbe Jorey who waited patiently for him in England. The wedding finally took place two years later, in 1855.

It was Jorey Point that Captain Vancouver earlier named MASAREDO POINT, apparently believing this to be what Jacinto Caamano intended. However, historians of a later date say that Caamano wrote *Puerto* (not Punta) de Mazarredo for Virago Sound, applying the name on July 25, 1792 for Jose Maria de Mazarredo y Salazar, a noted Spanish naval commander of that day.

There are 2 islands on a drying bank off the point which Vancouver indicated to be "Masaredo Point." Today it is these islands which bear the name intended to honour Jose de Mazarredo.

*MAZARREDO ISLANDS — on the west side of Virago Sound, are connected to Jorey Point by a drying bank. The Mazarredo group consist of 2 islands, 160 and 100 feet high, with a rock 8 feet high off to one side. They were officially named by Captain Learmonth in 1907.

S'TH-UMB — the Haida name for the larger, inside Mazarredo Island. (C.Smith)

KUL'GWEE-ASS — the smaller, outside Mazarredo Island. (C.Smith)

CHAPTER TWENTY

*HANNA BAY — between Jorey Point and Cape Naden at the west side of Virago Sound. The Haida name for Cape Naden was Kan-nah kwoon and this bay was called in association, "the-bay-below-Kan-nah" occasionally. Hanna is a modification of the old Kan-nah. The common Haida name for the bay, however, was AHK-GWANS. (C. Smith) The bay has numerous rocks, some of which dry. *Gwans* or *gans* means rocky.

*CAPE NADEN — the north entrance point to Hanna Bay on the west shore of Virago Sound. Named CAPE NADON in 1853 by Commander Prevost and George Inskip during the hydrographic survey, and is a modification of the name of the Raven Crest family who owned river rights in Naden Harbour, the Ne dan hadai. In subsequent years Inskip's spelling was changed to Naden.
The Haidas called Cape Naden KAN-NAH KWOON. (C.Smith)

KAN-NAH KWOON CUDLAY — the offshore reef on Kan-nah kwoon (Cape Naden.) (C.Smith)

KID-JHEW-SHIN — the 13-foot-high rock immediately off Cape Naden. (C.Smith)

GREY ISLAND — a local name for the small crescent-shaped islet, 28 feet high lying northwest of Cape Naden. It was the JUTT ISLAND of the Haida. (C.Smith)

STAH-KUL, place-of-shack-used-as-camp — about 1½ miles along the rocky shoreline northwest of Cape Naden. (C.Smith)

HEEL-UM, Rock-Island — a descriptive Haida name for a rock peninsula, 2 miles northwest of Cape Naden. (C. Smith)

YATAH BAY (campsite) — on the west side of Heel-um. (C. Smith)

ANTS-KLAWK-AWAS (creek) — flows into the sea through what is now Lot 2740 and a smaller creek comes in through this same lot, north of Ants-klawk-awas. The name connotes a spreading. (C.Smith)

LITTLE POINT, *Kats-ca jouse* — about ½ mile northwest of Heel-um point. (C. Smith)

YATS BAY — to the southeast of Klashwun Point, is the bay off Yatza Village. (C. Smith)

YATZA VILLAGE, Knife-village — lay to the southeast of what is now Klashwun Point and was an Eagle Crest site established about 1875 by Chief Edenshaw. (See also Kung.) He chose Yats Bay in the hope that his people would more easily attract trade from Alaska in this location. It is only about 40 miles from the southern tip of Alaska to this point and the conspicuous hill behind Yats Bay enabled canoers to more easily direct their course.

When Dawson visited the village in 1878 he found 10 houses and a few poles, all roughly built. With his customary flourish Edenshaw was making preparations to hold a potlatch to officially launch the project of a new village.

Six years later, in 1884, when Chittenden went there he found Edenshaw, bowing to the inevitable, had moved to Masset the year before. Yatza had been abandoned as a main village, but served for years as an occasional stopping place for Indians *en route* to and from the west coast. For many summers the Haidas planted small vegetable gardens both at Yatza and at Go Dang, in Hussan Bay

Yatza in now part of the 45-acre YATZE RESERVE owned by the Masset Band.

LITTLE MOUNTAIN, *Klashwun* — the name given by the Haidas to the hill which rises behind the village of Yatza. The promontory with a height of 340 feet on its west side is visible for a considerable distance and provides a most useful landmark. (C.Smith)

*KLASHWUN POINT — the point lying north of Little Mountain. Named KLAS-KWUN by Dr. Dawson in 1878, using a modification of the Haidas' POINT-OF-LITTLE-MOUNTAIN. Over the years the middle K has been changed to an H. On July 25, 1792, eighty-six years before Dawson arrived off this coast, Jacinto Caamano had named the point in honour of his chief pilot, Juan Pantoja, PUNTA DE PANTOJA.

All names supplied by Mr. Charles A. Smith are shown on this map by ⓢ .

YATS-KWOON, the-point-of-Yats-Bay — the Haida name for the north entrance point to Yats Bay. (C. Smith)

*SHAG ROCK — about 4 cables to the northeast of Klashwun Point, this rock which dries at 13 feet and is steepto, was named in 1878 by Dr. G.M. Dawson.

The Haida name for the rock was Y'AH. (C.Smith)

The *Shag Rock* mineral claim, containing manganese veins, is at Yats-Kwoon and extends for a short distance offshore as well as on land. Originally staked in 1955 by Mr. J. Pauloski, it now consists of 17 recorded claims held by the Naden Harbour Manganese Limited. In 1965 Falconbridge Nickel Mines took out 150 to 200 tons of bulk samples and drilled two packsack diamond-drill holes.

THUNDER ROCK — is a 15-foot-high rock on the shoreline at Klashwun Point. According to legend it was never covered by waves and a stone lay on top which was called Thunder's Drum. When the Ocean Spirit there was going to give the people a whale or similar present, the people said they heard his drum sound. (A legend told to Dr. J.R. Swanton.)

SMALL-TEETH-BAY, *Chootsum* — descriptive of the rocks along this beach to the west of Klashwun Point. (C. Smith) A stream runs into this bay.

448

HALIBUT CAMP, *Kwintlass* — lay on the west side of the point which forms the west side of Small-Teeth-Bay. The camp lay about 2 miles west of Klashwun Point. (C.Smith)

UTTKISS BAY — lay between the Halibut Camp (Lot 680) and Whootan Kwoon (Lot 217). It was an abreviation of a Haida description meaning tide bay whose waters or shores could be dangerous. (C.Smith)

LONG-ROCKY-BEACH, *Kate·utsun'ice* — a descriptive name for the beach along the shoreline of Uttkiss Bay. (C.Smith)

WHOOTAN KWOON — the point of Lot 217. (C.Smith)

LONG-SAND-BEACH — lay between Whootan Kwoon (Point) and Nankivell Point. (C.Smith)

*NANKIVELL POINT — on the east side of the Jalun River. Named by Captain F.C. Learmonth after Lieutenant John Howard Nankivell of the *Egeria*, in 1907. Shown on some maps as Nankiwell.

DAHKUT-TEN — a Haida name for the reef off Nankivell Point. (C.Smith)

*JALUN RIVER — with its headwaters some 12 to 14 miles inland, drains a huge marshy region between Naden Harbour and the west coast. The mouth of the Jalun, about 6 miles west of Klashwun Point, has a small boat harbour close inside the entrance which was a favorite canoe harbour and camp site of Haidas in earlier years. The name Jalun is an adaption of the Haida name and was applied to the charts in 1878 by Dr. G.M. Dawson.

The Jalun River is a favourite angling stream today for those fishermen who like to be away from the usual throng on the more accessible rivers. To get to the Jalun and upstream to the best places for fishing requires so much planning and ambition only the dedicated will consider it worth the effort. But for those who do it is a fisherman's paradise on the broad gravel bars of this river.

The camp site at the mouth of the river so enjoyed in earlier years by Haidas is now part of the 17-acre JALUN RESERVE owned by the Masset Band.

*JALUN LAKE— is at the 315-foot level and lies about 11 to 12 miles south of the mouth of the Jalun River.

CRAB-BEACH, *Kwoos'stan* — lies to the west of the Jalun River. (C. Smith)

GHLA-AH — the descriptive Haida name for the rocky shoreline between Crab-Beach (Kwoos'stan) and Seath Point. (C.Smith)

*SEATH POINT — at the east entrance to Pillar Bay. Named in 1907 by Captain F.C. Larmonth, after Paymaster Seath of the *Egeria* engaged in the hydrographic survey from Rose Spit to Frederick Island that year. The rocky point has been shown on some maps as SNEATH, but is gazetted as SEATH

POINT.

*PILLAR BAY — the bight between Seath Point and Gunia Point, takes its name from the Pillar (rock) which stands in the eastern part of the bay. (See below.) Ancient burial caves have been found along the shoreline of this bay.

*PILLAR ROCK — a 95-foot-high column of sandstone and conglomerate rock, crowned with bushes and small trees. It is near the edge of a rocky ledge which is connected to the shore at low water. The Pillar is about 25 feet in diameter and was named by Dr. Dawson in 1878. Dawson put its Haida name as "Hla-tad-zo-woh." Mr. C. Smith wrote it as "Ghla'kedj-oas" and said "The Haidas will probably write it as something else again, and with as many varieties as we have."

*GUNIA POINT — to the west of Pillar Bay, lying between Coneehaw Rock and Douglas Rock. Old Chief Blakow-Coneehaw (or Gunia - both are corruptions) was the head chief at Kiusta when the white traders first arrived, and it was he who exchanged names with William Douglas (As described in Q.C. Islands, Volume I.) He was so well-known by all traders that Parry Passage was commonly called "Cunneyah's Straits" in the first years of trading. Gunia moved to Alaska during the migration of his tribe and was buried there. The Edenshaw who succeeded him was of a different family, but somehow related. He took over the Kiusta chieftainship and, in some way, also got claim to the name of Douglas. But he did not take the name of Gunia. That name continued in another tribe. The famous Chief Albert Edward Edenshaw, who became so well-known through his lavish potlatches and ever-increasing wealth was a descendent of the Edenshaw who succeeded Gunia.

The Haida name for Gunia Point was OTUS KWOON. (C.Smith)

*CONEEHAW ROCK — off Gunia Point to the northeast, is also named after the old chief of Kiusta. (See preceding item.) A low rock about 2 feet high with a shoal off its south and west sides.

The Haidas knew it as OTUS KWOON CUDLAY. *Cudley* means bank or reef. (C.Smith)

*DOUGLAS ROCK — on the west side of Gunia Point. Named by the Hydrographic Service in honour of the historic meeting between William Douglas and Chief Blakow-Conneehaw on June 20, 1789, and the symbolic exchange of names. Douglas made two trips to the Parry Sound region in the vessel *Iphigenia Nubiana*, owned by John Meares and Company of Nootka. The first trip in 1788 and the second in 1789.

By 1790 he owned 2 ships himself, the *Fairy* and *Grace*. Appointing William Rogers as master of the *Fairy*, Douglas took command of the 85-ton *Grace* and the vessels came to trade in Queen Charlotte Islands waters. The *Grace* was returning to China following a season of trading in 1791, when Douglas became ill and died *en route*.

STOAS (Haida camp site) — southwest of Douglas Rock in a cove at the west side of the bight on the west side of Gunia Point. (C.Smith)

*BRUIN BAY — west of Gunia Point and Douglas Rock, and south of Lucy Island. Named in May 1853. The *Virago* anchored there during the hydrographic survey of these waters. One evening a large bear came down on the beach to feed, almost abreast of the ship as she rode at anchor. An attempt was made by some of the men on the *Virago* to shoot the animal, but they were unsuccessful. In memory of the event George Inskip named the bay BRUIN BAY.

AHKWANS (Haida camp site) — at the head of Bruin Bay a stream comes into the bay on the western part. The Ahkwans camp lay on the west side of the stream in a small cove. Rock ledges protrude from each side of the cove. The name refers to this. (C.Smith)

On the shore of this cove in July 1792 Jacinto Caamano had a marker erected to signify Spanish claim of ownership of the Queen Charlotte.Islands.[1]

"At 10 o'clock in the forenoon of the 22nd (July) I landed with my seamen and marines in the pinnace," he reported. "Mass was celebrated under an awning formed of the ship's flags. This service was attended by the Chief and several other Indians, all of whom showed great attention and respect. I then went through the ceremonies of taking possession of the country with all the prescribed formalities and set up a Cross, over twenty-eight feet in height, charging the natives not to over-set it, which they failed to observe.

When all this was finished I returned on board (the *Aranzazu*) accompanied by the Chief and one of his sons, who is also chief of another village. I kept them to dinner with me and during the meal explained I must weigh and get under sail directly."

The Spaniards had received a warm welcome from all the Haidas, but had been especially well-treated by Chief Conneehaw of Kiusta who tried hard to persuade Caamano to stay longer, however the ship weighed anchor and left the area about 4 p.m.

[1] See also page 19 and 20. On the plan prepared by the Spaniards the site of the cross is shown to be at the west side of Ahkwans bay near the head.

*ASTROLABE ROCK — at the eastern extremity of Marchand Reef, off Kiusta. It has a depth of less than 6 feet over it. Believed to have been named by the Hydrographic Service about 1912.

In 1875 the French Government sent out a scientific expedition consisting of 2 ships, the *Boussole* under Captain Jean Francois Laperouse, and the *Astrolabe* under Captain de Langle. During their round-the-world voyage they arrived off the Queen Charlottes in the summer of 1786 and, in passing down the west coast, Laperouse applied several names to features of that coast.

The vessels reached the Samoan Islands in December of 1878 where Captain de Langle and 11 of his crewmen were murdered by the natives. Laperouse and the remaining crew continued to press on. It proved an ill-fated venture. Both ships were lost the following year, the wreckage later found washed up on a reef north of the New Hebrides.

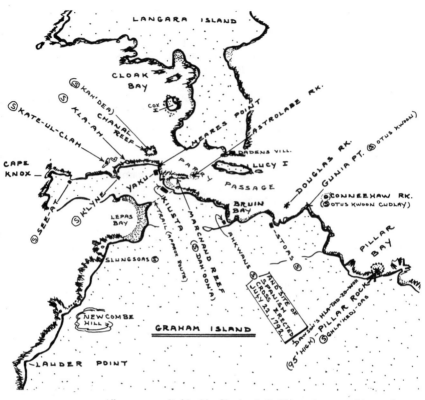

All names supplied by Mr. Charles A. Smith are shown on this map by Ⓢ .

*MARCHAND REEF — a rocky ledge which dries as it extends eastward from the shoreline between the deserted village sites of Yaku and Kiusta on the south shore of Parry Passage. Named by the Hydrographic Service after Captain Etienne Marchand, master of the French ship *La Solide* which came to this region in 1791, five years after Laperouse. Marchand spent much time exploring and taking careful notes, in addition to sending his officers in the longboats to make surveys and soundings of this area. He was destined never to see his work in print, for he died in 1792 and all his carefully documented papers were lost. Fleurieu, who recounted the voyage, did so from the entries in the log of the *Solide*, plus a diary of second-in-command Captain Prosper Chanal.

The Haida name for this reef was DAH'OON'A. (C.Smith)

*KIUSTA (Kewsta) VILLAGE — lay east and south of Marchand Reef. One interpretation of the name is "at the end of the trail" while another is "place of plentiful clams."

When William Douglas first saw the place in 1788 it was a thriving village under the chieftainship of the colourful and vibrant Eagle Chief Blakow-Coneehaw. Coneehaw joined with his tribe in the migration to Alaska not long afterwards, apparently with some reluctance. A chief with the hereditary name of Edenshaw took over as head chief of Kiusta which he made his main place of residence, although he also maintained a home at the Tow Hill village of Hiellen. When he died about 1850 his nephew Gwai-gu-unlthin, of Cape Ball succeeded him and became one of the most famous of all Haida chiefs, Edenshaw of Kung.

About 3 years later the new Chief Edenshaw, an anglicized form of the Haida name, moved his family to the entrance of Naden Harbour and established the village of Kung. He became immensely wealthy and exerted much influence among his people.

When Dr. Dawson visited Kiusta in 1878 he wrote, "It is difficult to imagine on what account this village has been abandoned, unless from sheer lack of inhabitants, as it seems admirably suited for the purposes of the Haidas. Many of the larger articles of property such as boxes, troughs and other wooden utensils as well as stone mortars and such, have not been removed from the houses."

It had been abandoned about ten years when Dawson saw it, and was used only as a temporary camp in bad weather by travellers. The estimated number of houses range from 9 to 15 and the main village lay on the west side of the trail which goes from this point across the narrow neck of land to Lepas Bay on the west coast. The cemetery lay on the east side of the trail.

Dr. Dawson applied the modified village name to the maps in 1878, showing it as KIOO-STA.

One of the finest of all totem poles at Kiusta is the triple totem, an Edenshaw mortuary pole. It still stands guard with infinite dignity.

*YAKU VILLAGE — northwest of Kiusta. Yaku has had a haunting effect on visitors from the days of Chittenden, who wrote in 1884 of the mesmerism he felt as he pondered the mystery of the long deserted lodges and carved poles. "We found large beds of strawberries," added Chittenden in some surprise, "with vines of most luxurious growth. Nearby were fine carvings of male figures, complete in every detail."

In 1971 a Victoria visitor, Bill Holbroek, wrote of his feelings as he entered the ancient site at dusk. "There is not much in the way of ruins left to see, but what there is, is magnificent. A few old houseposts, uncarved. Three fallen totems with really beautiful carvings on them, but all now weathered and rotted, also a short double mortuary pole with a flat slab still across the top showing where the body had been placed.

"But the best thing about Yaku is the stupendous setting that it faces. Here one can see the edge of the open Pacific itself. Huge rollers break on the reefs across at Cloak Bay, on the outside of Langara Island. It is utterly lonely and utterly beautiful. One of the most isolated and impressive spots I have ever encountered."

It is an old site which was first occupied by an Eagle tribe who owned most of the northwest coast of Graham Island before their migration to Alaska. No one really knows when the migration actually began, but Haidas were in residence in Alaska in 1741, as it was Tlingit Haidas who massacred men from Chirikof's ship. (Chirikof had set off with Vitus Behring for his voyage of discovery.)

453

With the abandonment of the Graham Island territory by the Eagles, it was gradually taken over by a group of Raven Crest Haidas, the Rear-Towns from the west coast. Another branch of this family owned Dadens, across the way. Members of these tribes joined in the migration also in later years as it gained momentum. Yaku is from a Raven family name.

Kiusta and Yaku are part of the 101-acre KIOOSTA RESERVE belonging to the Masset Band.

*MEARES POINT** — north of old Yaku and about 5 miles east of Cape Knox. Named by the Hydrographic Service after John Meares, one of the owners of the *Iphigenia Nubiana,* which Douglas sailed to this area in 1788 and 1789.

Meares Point, low and partly clear, has a conspicuous solitary tree growing on it and an attached islet close off. The prevailing ocean swell is felt here.

*CHANAL REEF** — dries at 12 feet and on which the sea always breaks, is about 3 cables north of Meares Point. There is a 5-foot rock on its northeast corner. Foul ground off the west side is marked by huge kelp beds. Named by the Hydrographic Service after second-in-command Captain Prosper Chanal, a retired French naval officer and hydrographic surveyor when he joined the voyage of the *Solide* under Captain Etienne Marchand. The vessel dropped anchor in Cloak Bay on August 25, 1791.

Captain Chanal's diaries contained interesting accounts of the officers landing at some of the Parry Passage villages and of their reception by the Haidas. For 3 weeks Chanal, accompanied by Louis Marchand, brother of the Captain, made the first real survey of Cloak Bay, Parry Passage and the west coast of Graham Island, going as far south as Hippa Island in a long boat. They gave names to several features at that time, such as Otard Bay, Port Louis and Port Chanal.

The Haida name for Chanal Reef was KAH'DEA. (C.Smith)

KLA-AH — a rock about 2/3 of a mile west from Meares Point. The Haida name is descriptive of the rock, but in an abreviated form. Kla-ah is at the edge of the shoreline and lies on a drying ledge. (C.Smith)

K'LYNE — a bay used by hunters for emergency camping. It is about a mile west of Meares Point. (C.Smith)

KATE-UL-CLAH — this 10-foot rock lay on the outer edge of a reef a little west of K'Lyne Bay. There is a canoe passage along the shore from this bay in calm weather. The reefs are on the outside of the passage. Skirting the rocky shoreline and paddling to the west canoers passed a bay with cliffs rising from 50 to 100 feet.

SEE-AT — at the west end of the bay mentioned in the preceding paragraph, a small beach faces east. This is See-at, campsite of Haida hunters. (C.Smith)

To the west of See-at camp is the rugged point of the most westerly feature of Graham Island, GWAIN-TAS-KWOON or, as we know it, CAPE KNOX. (Described on page 36.)

EPILOGUE

It was at the western entrance of Parry Passage that the listing of Queen Charlotte Islands places and names began in this book and, with the return to Cape Knox, has now come full circle. A list which is undoubtedly far from complete, since so much of the history of the Islands has not been recorded. But it is a start.

On these islands of enchantment, cultures have evolved, developed, fulfilled their destiny, then passed, to be replaced by others.

How long human beings have lived on the Charlottes remains obscure. Anthropologists believe that parts of the Islands may have been habitable for man and animals for 13,5000 years. A 75-foot drop in sea level would have connected the Charlottes to the mainland and presents an intriguing possibility that initial human occupation may have occured during the lowered sea level associated with one period. Recent findings indicate continuous human occupancy stretching back at least eight or ten thousand years. From artifacts uncovered, archaeologists believe the first known occupants possessed an extremely simple culture which in no way compared with that of the resourceful and imaginative Haida. Their fate is still a mystery.

The Haidas have known these Islands as home for several thousands of years. Believed to have been originally of one crest, the Raven, they were later joined by people from the north - an Eagle tribe. Through marriages they gradually became intermingled with others from the mainland and, through trade, with peoples across the Pacific - from whence it is suspected they have their own basic roots.

Today both Haida and non-Haida people these Islands. The lands themselves survive us all and, as Nature repairs our ravages, will for untold centuries provide their own especial charm to generations still to come. . . who will wonder. As we do.

*Little is known about this unique mortuary pole at Kiusta, but
anthropologists believe it may have been erected sometime between 1830 to 1850.
Since it is typical of the elaborate and lavish ceremonials
the wealthy Chief A.E. Edenshaw is associated with,
there is a tendency to believe that when he succeeded to the Edenshaw name
he may have erected this pole with much pomp and flourish to his predecessor.
Rear view of the Edenshaw Mortuary taken in 1964 by Mr. G. Gray Hill.*

*On symbolically carved poles, the mortal remains of an Edenshaw chief
were borne aloft so that his spirit might remain free.
Front view of the Edenshaw mortuary pole at Kiusta.*

Photo - G. Gray Hill.

INDEX

Gazetted names have an asterisk

460

465

M

466

470

471